To my brothers and sisters,
their children and grandchildren

A History of Russia

Medieval, Modern, Contemporary
c. 882–1996

Third edition

Paul Dukes

DUKE UNIVERSITY PRESS
DURHAM 1998

First published in the United States in 1998 by
Duke University Press
Durham, NC 27708-0660
and in the United Kingdom in 1997 by
Macmillan Press Ltd
Houndmills, Basingstoke, Hampshire, RG21 6XS

Library of Congress Cataloging-in-Publication Data
Dukes, Paul.
A history of Russia : medieval, modern, contemporary, c. 882–1996
/ Paul Dukes. — 3rd ed.
p. cm.
Includes bibliographical references and index.
ISBN 0–8223–2082–7 (cloth : alk. paper). — ISBN 0–8223–2096–7
(pbk. : alk. paper)
1. Russia—History. 2. Soviet Union—History. 3. Russia
(Federation)—History. I. Title.
DK40.D84 1997
947—dc21   97–15047
                                                  CIP

Typeset by EXPO Holdings, Malaysia
Printed in China

Acknowledgements

Arthur Ransome, *Six Weeks in Russia in 1919*, reprinted by permission of Mrs. Arthur
Ransome.

Contents

Maps

Chronology of Key Events

RUSSIA		THE WEST		THE EAST	
882	Oleg conquers Kiev	800	Charlemagne becomes Holy Roman Emperor	*c.* 800	Uighur Empire
c. 988	Vladimir adopts Christianity	1066	Norman Conquest of England	*c.* 1000	Steppe peoples convert to Islam
1240	Mongols seize Kiev; Teutonic Knights defeated	1215	Magna Carta	1206–27	Rule of Genghis Khan
1380	Mongols defeated at Kulikovo	1348–50	Black Death	1360–1404	Tamerlane
1550	Code of Laws issued by Ivan IV, the Terrible	1588	The Spanish Armada	1520–66	Rule of Suleiman the Lawgiver
1655	Patriarch Nikon's church reform	1649	Execution of Charles I	1644	Manchus take Beijing
1704	Peter I, the Great founds St. Petersburg	1648–1715	Reign of Louis XIV	1689	Treaty of Nerchinsk
1767	Catherine II, the Great issues her *Instruction*	1776	Declaration of Independence	*c.* 1750	Chinese take control of Tibet, Mongolia, Turkestan

RUSSIA		THE WEST		THE EAST	
1825	The Decembrist Revolt	1815	Napoleon at Waterloo	1839–42	Opium War
1861	Alexander II emancipates the serfs	1863	Lincoln proclaims Emancipation of the Slaves	1860	Treaty of Beijing
1917	Russian Revolution under Lenin	1914–18	First World War	1911	Sun Yat-sen begins Guomingtang Revolution
1929	The Stalin Revolution	1929	Wall Street Crash begins Depression	1927	Communist Rising in China
1941–5	The Great Fatherland War	1939–45	Second World War	1949	Communist Revolution in China
1962	Khrushchev provokes the Cuba Crisis	1964	U.S.A. enters Vietnam War	1965	Great Cultural Revolution in China
1991	Yeltsin elected Russian President; collapse of the Soviet Union	1989	Reunification of Germany and collapse of Soviet power in Eastern Europe	1989	Tiananmen Square

Preface to the First Edition

While this History of Russia does not claim to be any better than its many predecessors, it does aim at providing a distinctive interpretation, even if through change of emphasis rather than complete novelty. Its basic purposes may be placed in two main groups:

(1) Since the Revolution of 1917, and particularly since the death of Stalin, Soviet historians have produced an impressive amount of useful information and interpretation, which has still to receive the recognition it deserves in works produced primarily for those who do not read Russian. While all too obviously suffering from an imperfect acquaintance with Soviet historiography, I have tried to take coverage of it at least a little further. At the same time, with similar handicaps, I have attempted to make use of pre-revolutionary Russian historical writing and of the publications of Western scholars, old and new.

(2) Economic and cultural developments are sometimes considered as appendices to the mainstream of political analysis; this book aspires to inclusion in the number of those which have achieved thematic integration. Similarly, its division into three distinct sections – medieval, modern, contemporary – has been implemented as an expression of agreement with those who hold that history has a fundamental pattern rather than constituting a disconnected series of essentially unique events. Moreover, it attempts to reveal the limitations of an exclusively national approach to Russian history and to contribute to its analysis in a comparative framework. To put it briefly, my intention has been to adhere to the view of history put forward by E. H. Carr.

The errors and misunderstandings in the book are all my own work. For the rest, I have depended heavily on the published work of others, the principal debts being acknowledged in the Select Bibliography and References. Of those who have helped directly in the writing of the book, I owe most to Barry Hollingsworth of the University of Manchester. He has made penetrating comments on the entire manuscript, and his comprehensive erudition tempered by a profound charity has been invaluable. Next I am pleased to record my gratitude to Rosie Mackay for her patient and careful reading of successive drafts; to Ron Grant for his incisive appraisal of most of the contemporary section; and to David Longley for giving me the benefit of his specialist understanding of the Russian Revolution. I have received generous advice from the History Department, King's College Library staff and others at the University of Aberdeen. These include Roy Bridges, John Hiden, Jean Houbert, Leslie Macfarlane, George Molland and Bill Scott, and all the members of the Russian Department – Jim Forsyth, Richard Hallet, John Murray, Jo Newcombe and Cor Schwenke. Maureen Carr, Lily Findlay, Ann Gordon, Christine Macleod and Ann Murray all helped prepare the typescript.

A more general debt is to the hundreds of students at the University of Aberdeen who have contributed to the unfinished process of my historical education. I consider myself more than lucky to have studied the subject under consideration with them in a locale which has many connections with it. Not many miles from here, an embassy from Ivan the Terrible was wrecked on the north-east coast of Scotland. Patrick Gordon and many other Russian mercenaries set sail from the local harbour. Aberdeen was a port en route from and to Petrograd during the momentous years of the Russian Revolution. There are Soviet fishing boats and timber ships at its docks today. A few technical matters need to be touched on. The system of transliteration used is a variation of that adopted by the *Slavic Review*. Final -ii is rendered thus rather than -y, and all hard and soft signs have been omitted. Russian names are strictly transliterated on their first major appearance, but are normally given in their most usual form, particularly when they are well known. The names of Western scholars of Russian descent are given as they themselves spell them, and the authors of books and articles given as on the title page. Measurements have been made metric: those used most frequently are the hectare – just under 2 1/2 acres; the kilometre – just over 3/5 mile; and the metric ton – a little less (36 lb) than the avoirdupois ton. Billions are American rather than British, that is a thousand million rather than a million million. The maps drawn by Lawrence Maclean are intended to give no more than location. For further geographical reference, the items listed in the Selected Bibliography should be consulted.

Dates from Chapter 5 to Chapter 10 inclusive are given Old Style: eleven days behind New Style in the eighteenth century, twelve in the nineteenth and thirteen in the twentieth.

King's College, Old Aberdeen   PAUL DUKES
December 1973

Preface to the Second Edition

The mostly positive response to *A History of Russia* on its first appearance and since have encouraged me to produce this Second Edition, adding two new chapters on the Brezhnev years and a fuller conclusion which takes in some of the developments since 1985, as well as revising the whole of the original text. As to the book's special features:

(1) As far as possible, I have attempted to illustrate recent developments in Soviet and Western historiography. *Glasnost* and *perestroika* have made a huge impact on the Soviet treatment of some periods, especially the 1930s, but have left others comparatively untouched: I have attempted to indicate differences between 'traditional' and 'new' thinking wherever they exist. In the past fifteen years or so, there has also been a vast flood of relevant publications in the U.K., U.S.A. and Canada, the Antipodes, everywhere in the English-speaking world. As much of this as possible has been noted either in the Notes or Select Bibliography. Certainly, as before, it would have seemed inappropriate to present a work, even of this general nature, without giving a clear indication of the sources of information and ideas.

(2) Equally, economic and cultural developments have appeared even more worthy of integration with the political narrative and analysis for each period, rather than being added without full regard for chronological sequence. I am also more convinced than before that the medieval, modern and contemporary division of Russian history has an intrinsic validity as well as making for a greater degree of clarity. In general, although his reputation has been under severe attack since his death, I continue to hold to the view that E. H. Carr made a greater contribution than any other Western academic analyst towards the establishment of the study of the Soviet Union on a sound, scholarly basis while giving as good an answer as any to the question *What Is History?*

I acknowledge with deep gratitude the comments and advice readily given by colleagues here and elsewhere: Lindsey Hughes, Roger Bartlett and Bob Service, all of the School of Slavonic and East European Studies, London – the medieval, modern and contemporary sections respectively; Simon Franklin, Clare College, Cambridge – Chapter 1; David Saunders, Newcastle – Chapters 7 and 8; Peter Gatrell, Manchester – the economic sections of Chapters 8 and 9; Ray Pearson, Coleraine – Chapters 9 and 10; Bob Davies, of the Centre for Russian and East European Studies, Birmingham – Chapters 11 and 12; John Keep, formerly of Toronto – Chapters 15 to 17. Here in Aberdeen, David Longley rendered a similar service on Chapter 2, while Jim Forsyth made a number of useful observations on the text in general and on the maps. The errors and misunderstandings are again all my own work. Ann Gordon and Moira Buchan of the History Department and associates of the Arts Faculty Office all made indispensable contributions to the completion of the project. A succession of editors at Macmillan, most recently Vanessa Graham, must be saluted for their polite patience.

Back again at Aberdeen, I remain fortunate enough to attempt to teach and certainly to learn Russian history at an institution founded when Ivan III was tsar. In 1496, the year after Pope Alexander VI issued the Bull incorporating what became known later as the University of Aberdeen, a herald originating from this city if sent from Denmark, was received by Tsar Ivan in Moscow. Thus, in a somewhat indirect manner, began a chain of connections between Russia and north-east Scotland virtually unbroken from the sixteenth century onwards. If Soviet fishing boats and timber ships appear more rarely than in the early 1970s at the local docks, representatives of the Soviet oil and gas industry are often to be found here, while an academic exchange has been set up between the University of Aberdeen and the Institute of History of the U.S.S.R. of the Academy of Sciences of the U.S.S.R. in Moscow.

The technical apparatus remains the same as in the First Edition, as does the dedication.

King's College,
Old Aberdeen   PAUL DUKES
February 1990

Preface to the Third Edition

Developments since the Second Edition have been so uncertain that I find it necessary not only to append a question mark to my additional chapter on the Gorbachev and Yeltsin years 'Reform or Ruin?' but also to revise my aims in general:

(1) Although I believe it more than ever necessary to recognise the achievements of Soviet historiography, since – to put it mildly – they are out of fashion, I attempt also to attain a measure of justice for publications since 1991 as well as before 1917. Already, however, I detect new continuities as well as discontinuities, a line of development transcending both the arrival of 'Marxist–Leninist' dogma and its departure. I have attempted to support such a view through an extensive revision of the text along with the Notes and Select Bibliography. Moreover, in the attempt to show what is new and what is not, especially for medieval and modern Russia, I have also made even more use than before of the 'classical' interpretation of V. O. Kliuchevskii, making it indeed the yardstick against which other interpretations, pre-Soviet, Soviet and post-Soviet, may be measured. At the same time, I have attempted to take note of new Western writing without forgetting the old.

(2) Is today's Russia capable of democracy, the free market and a pluralist ideology? Since these questions are closely interconnected, and the answers depend on Russia's similarities and differences with the West and other parts of the world, the case is strengthened for the consideration of political, economic and cultural history in parallel, as well as for the comparative approach as a whole. As ever, I continue to draw stimulation from E. H. Carr's *What Is History?*, although increasingly as a book to argue with rather than to accept uncritically. That response appears to be in line with the author's own reasoning.

In the preparation of this Third Edition, I have received indispensable help on sections of the Select Bibliography from Ray Scrivens at Cambridge University Library and Denis Shaw of Birmingham

University, and on parts of the text from Bob Davies, Sarah Davies (no relation), John Erickson and Stephen White of the Universities of Birmingham, Durham, Edinburgh and Glasgow respectively. Russian colleagues in Moscow and St Petersburg, and elsewhere from Archangel to Vladivostok, have also provided useful updates. Locally, a number of friends have given assistance and advice, especially Cathryn Brennan. While recording my thanks to all of the above, as confidently as ever I recognise the errors and misunderstandings that remain as all my own work.

My present location continues to provide inspiration. The University of Aberdeen's celebration of its quincentenary in 1995 has provided a boost to the contemplation of the past in general. The presence in Aberdeen harbour of *Neftigaz* (Oilandgas) and other supply ships is just one reminder of how priorities have changed, although Klondykers and other Russian fishing boats off the coast recall older connections.

While the technical apparatus remains unchanged, a new generation has been added to the dedication.

King's College   PAUL DUKES
Old Aberdeen
28 February 1997

General Introduction

Everybody knows that the Russian land is vast, cold and mostly flat, with mighty rivers but little access to the sea. Like most common knowledge, this particular example is in an important sense correct, but it also requires some modification. Even now, after the collapse of the Soviet Union, the Russian Federation remains a huge state, still stretching half-way around the globe – anybody who does not appreciate this basic fact should spend a week or so on the Trans-Siberian Railway. In winter, the coldest spot in the world is to be found in Siberia, while warmth is to be found near the Black Sea only. In summer, heat is more widespread, but much of the land remains too cold for agriculture of any kind to be carried on, while some is too dry for it to be attempted without irrigation. The exploitation of Russia's natural resources has been hampered by difficult problems of distance and climate.

These problems combine with a uniform geological structure and relief involving a widespread unvarying landscape to produce, in the view of many observers from at least as far back as the eighteenth century, a strongly centralised political arrangement. After each extension of the area of settlement, the government soon attempted to impose its control. The huge Eurasian plain, with no clearly demarcated frontiers except for the rivers and part of the Urals, has been the wide stage for the continuous process of colonisation which the great pre-revolutionary historian Kliuchevskii singled out as the major theme of Russian history.[1] Towards the end of this process, it is true, the frontiersmen came up against the Arctic and Pacific Oceans to the north and east and high mountains to the south, but before the nineteenth century they were essentially plainsmen.

The flat monotony is to some extent broken up by the variation in soil and vegetation from north to south. First, there is the *tundra*, where little grows naturally except for shrubs and mosses. Then comes the *taiga*, coniferous forest for the most part, and the source of great wealth in the shape of timber and furs. Next there is the mixed forest in which deciduous trees join with the conifers. This area, which is wide in the west but tapers towards the Urals, has been the centre of Russian civilisation from early days onwards, even though it provides by no means ideal conditions for agriculture. Finally, we come to the steppe, wooded to the north and desert to the south, with the grassland in between. Here is the best farmland, the Black Earth, at least to the west of the Volga.

Cutting through these zones are the mighty rivers, most of which flow north to south, like the Volga, Don and Dnepr, or south to north, like the Dvinas west of the Urals and the Siberian rivers east of them. But the tributaries often flow laterally, as it were, thus enabling people and goods to move across the country without insuperable difficulty before the coming of the railroad.

The 'urge to the sea'[2] that many analysts have seen as another of the great themes of Russian history is too strong to be denied. The struggle for outlets to the Black Sea and the Baltic, then to the Pacific Ocean, occupied the attention of successive governments for many centuries. And yet the sea has not been so absolutely vital to the prosperity of Russia as it has to that of smaller states. With a whole continent to explore and develop, and then to control, governments have been obliged to look inwards at least as much as outwards. Even today, the Russian leaders are deeply concerned with such problems as the improvement of the economy and the maintenance of order, at the same time as attending to the various aspects of international relations, both near and far. Theirs is an inheritance which comes not only from 1917 and 1991 but from thousands of years before them.

In the early days of human history, the warmer regions to the south first encouraged the growth of organised tribal communities. Neither the Black nor the Caspian Sea is far from the valleys of the rivers Tigris and Euphrates, which have often been called the birth place of civilisation, and archaeological discoveries have revealed the connection between the ancient cities of the Middle East and the peoples to the north of them. Greece and Rome then colonised the Black Sea in particular; Byzantium followed in their wake, sending expeditions up the Dnepr and other rivers. As a result of such contacts as well as migration and internal evolution, tribal organisations gave way to that of an embryonic Slavonic state from the seventh to the ninth centuries. During this period, towns such as Novgorod and Kiev came into existence. In their hinterlands, settled agriculture came to be practised as the steppe and the forest receded before the plough. Foreign contacts were established not only with Byzantium but with other peoples to the east and west. Intercourse with the Islamic and

Christian cultures of Central Asia and Transcaucasia was mutually beneficial, as was that with fellow Slavs, Germans and Norsemen.[3]

Of all these contacts, it is the last, with the Norsemen, Normans, Vikings or, Varangians, that has been the most famous or notorious in Russian history.[4] These restless itinerants came down the rivers from the Baltic to the Black Sea not only to seek slaves (the word itself derives from Slavs), silver and furs, to trade and to fight, but also to settle. As well as making good use of the commercial route to Byzantium, they hired themselves out as mercenaries to one Russian city in its struggle with another. In this manner, they probably came to furnish Novgorod and Kiev with their first well-known dynasty. But they were not complete conquerors or cultural innovators; rather they worked hand in glove with the native ruling class and became assimilated by it, leaving little trace of their language or customs. If the Rus, as many of their contemporaries called them, gave Russia its name, that was almost the full extent of their abiding legacy.

Part One

Medieval Russia: Kiev to Moscow

Introduction

The myth persists that Russia was cut off from Western civilisation until the reign of Peter the Great. In fact, ties were often close with West as well as East during the early medieval period in the political, economic and cultural spheres of life. Nevertheless, the Western contacts that were established during the prosperous days of Kiev were severely curtailed during the worst days of the so-called 'Mongol yoke'. They grew again by fits and starts with the rise of Moscow.

The first chapter commences with a brief analysis of another myth – that Kievan Rus was the creation of immigrant princes rather than the culmination of a process unfolding itself during the course of several centuries. Most attention, however, is given to Kievan Rus from its construction and development in the ninth, tenth and eleventh centuries, to its collapse in the twelfth century. At its peak, Kievan Rus was not only a powerful state carrying on diplomatic and economic relations with a large number of its fellows throughout Europe and the Middle East, but also the centre of a remarkable culture. Some of its princes deserve inclusion among the ranks of the great rulers of medieval times. Nor should it be forgotten that, during the same period, a high level of civilisation was reached in the regions of some of the future neighbouring republics in Transcaucasia and Central Asia.

1   Medieval Russia, 882–1645

The two centuries or so which followed the disintegration of Kiev were among the least helpful for the development of Russia. For the major part of that time, the Mongols dominated the fragments into which the state had broken, and their general influence was for the most part negative. German, Polish, Lithuanian and Swedish incursions from the West added to the problems faced by Novgorod and the other principalities. While many of the figures who passed across the national stage in the thirteenth and fourteenth centuries remain shadowy to the point of anonymity, there are individuals such as Alexander Nevsky who have come to occupy a prominent place in the pantheon of national heroes. Moreover, processes were at work leading the way towards the emergence of a new centre of political unity, Moscow, and it would also be wrong to look upon this period as one of undiluted economic depression and cultural inactivity. Some scholars have argued that even the Mongol influence had its positive, constructive side. Such views are discussed in Chapter 2.

Chapter 3 is devoted to the consolidation of the Russian state under Moscow. It is there argued that this was a process in broad conformity with a European pattern. The chronological termination of the chapter and of Part One comes after Moscow's collapse at the end of the sixteenth century in the Time of Troubles, with its resurgence at the beginning of the seventeenth century under a new dynasty, the Romanovs.

Throughout the medieval section, the principal underlying theme is feudalism. Some historians emphasise the political, others the economic or even the cultural aspect of this term, while at least a few are unhappy with its use at all. But there is no other single word that can serve in such a comprehensive manner.[1]

1 The Construction and Collapse of Kiev, 882–1240

'Let us seek a prince who may rule over us, and judge us according to the Law', said the warring tribes of ancient Russia to each other in 862 according to the *Primary Chronicle*. And so: 'They accordingly went overseas to the Varangian Russes: these particular Varangians were known as Russes, just as some are called Swedes, and others Normans, English and Gottlanders … ' As the old story continues, the tribes then said to Varangian Russes: 'Our whole land is great and rich, but there is no order in it. Come to rule and reign over us.'[1] Three brothers in particular were chosen, and the eldest of them, Riurik, settled in Novgorod and began the princely dynasty that was to rule over Kiev from 882 onwards.

The old story is colourful and persistent, but essentially Russian history no more began in 862 than British history in 1066. Rather, both dates mark signal moments in the Norman 'aristocratic diaspora'. The difference between them is that we know far less about the first than the second. If Kliuchevskii notes that 'Later generations remembered Kievan Rus as the cradle of Russian nationality',[2] we must recognise that their memory was supplemented by patriotic imagination. After all, the Kievans themselves could not have been aware that they were living in a kind of Camelot. Henceforth, we shall refer to the writings of pre-revolutionary historians such as Kliuchevskii, to those of their Soviet and post-Soviet colleagues as well as to those of historians working in the West. We shall also attempt to make some reference to the principal sources for the history of Kiev, or 'Kievan Rus' as Kliuchevskii and others have called it. These include the *Primary Chronicle* and other early indigenous documents, supported by evidence of foreign origin, particularly Byzantine and Arabic, and of domestic oral tradition, epics, songs and tales. Other disciplines, notably archaeology, which have also made additions to our knowledge and understanding of Kiev, will receive at least some mention.

While both the nature of the sources and our aspiration for objectivity will persuade us not to neglect the contributions of individuals to the construction and collapse of Kiev, we must recognise that they often stand as the embodiments or reflections of more general political, social, economic or cultural processes. Moreover, we shall see that these processes are often inter-related. For example, discussion of the basis of the Kievan economy as agriculture or commerce has important implications for the typification of its society. At the same time, the international setting of Kiev will have to be sketched in, to the east as well as to the west. Readers who start with the assumption that Kiev was backward in comparison with the rest of the European continent will have to be reminded that more than almost any other early medieval state, Kiev had contact with the greatest of contemporary Western civilisations – Byzantium, and close contact with the Arabic and Turkic cultures of the Middle East and Central Asia.

Having commenced with the argument that the part played by the rulers of the Kievan state should not be exaggerated, this introduction should properly end by escaping the opposite danger of complete anonymity. While Riurik possibly did not exist, such princes as Vladimir I (980–1015), Iaroslav the Wise (1036–54) and Vladimir Monomakh (1113–25) undoubtedly made a significant personal impact on the course of the events which will be unfolded in the following pages.

Political

While the *Chronicle* tells us that Riurik's successor, Prince Oleg, came down from Novgorod with an army of Varangians and Slavs to capture Kiev in or about 882, the fact of the connection between the two great cities should be underlined, irrespective of its exact manner and timing. The emergence of the Kievan state as the centre of ancient Rus was primarily the result of its proximity to Byzantium and to other communities adjacent to the Black and Azov seas.

Having established himself in Kiev, Oleg set about the fulfilment of three principal tasks. The first was the subjugation of those tribes which constituted centrifugal forces in the nascent feudal state. The second was the prosecution of wars against rivals for dominance to the east and west. The third was the commencement of a series of campaigns against Byzantium which constituted a kind of struggle for recognition. Oleg led Kiev a considerable way towards the realisation of these three aims; the culmination of his reign was probably the expedition against Byzantium in 907, which produced treaties giving the Russians privileges and guarantees.[3]

Oleg died soon after this triumph and was succeeded as Grand Prince by Igor, whom Soviet historians looked upon as 'the true beginner of the Russian princely line'. Late in his reign, Igor led two further attacks on Constantinople (or Tsargrad, as the Russians called it), which ended by 944 in the elaboration of earlier treaties. Igor maintained his predecessor's policy of wars against rivals from the Caspian Sea to Eastern Europe, invading Muslim Azerbaidzhan, for example. He necessarily continued the struggle against neighbouring tribes, too. On his way back to Kiev in 945, Igor decided to stop off to gather tribute from one of these tribes, the Drevliane. Mal, their prince, agreed with his followers that: 'If the wolf makes a habit of coming to the fold he will carry away the whole flock, unless he is killed. So will Prince Igor, too, destroy us all, unless we kill him.'[4] And so, as Igor and his small bodyguard revealed an insatiable appetite for tribute, the Drevliane attacked and killed them.

Mal made overtures to Igor's widow Olga for a marriage alliance, but Olga used her cunning to extort a cruel and ingenious revenge for her husband's death. Over 5000 Drevliane fell in a campaign which constituted the final reduction of the tribe's independence as well as a widow's vengeance. For nearly twenty years, Olga remained in power during the minority of the son she had borne Igor, Sviatoslav. A formidable ruler, Olga managed not only to hold Kievan Russia together but even to strengthen it, particularly through her substitution of a system of regular taxes on surrounding tribes in place of their regular collection of tribute that had brought about her husband's death. She also maintained contact with Byzantium, which brought about the event for which she was best remembered later and canonised by the Orthodox Church, her conversion to Christianity. But Sviatoslav remained true to the pagan faith of his fathers, and the official state acceptance of Christianity did not occur until after the accession of his son Vladimir.

The consolidation of Kievan Russia was completed during the reigns of Sviatoslav and Vladimir. Sviatoslav (962–72) himself expressed the nature of his policy in a proposal to transfer his capital from the banks of the Dnepr to those of the Danube, saying: 'Here is the core of my lands, since the good things of different countries converge here: silk cloth, golden utensils, wine and fruit of various sorts from Byzantium; silver articles and fast horses from Bohemia and Hungary; and valuable furs, beeswax, honey and captive slaves from Rus.'[5] To foster such interests, Sviatoslav had carved his way in campaigns of the years 963–8 from the Volga to the Caspian Sea, then along the north of the Caucasus, the Azov and Black Seas to Bulgaria. And now established on the Danube after the defeat of many enemies, Sviatoslav turned his attention to his previous ally,

Byzantium. Under a new and vigorous Emperor, John Tsimiskes, and with the help of the Bulgars, the Byzantine forces were able to defeat the Kievan Russians and to force their Grand Prince to sign a treaty in 971, renouncing all claims to Bulgaria and the Crimea.[6] On the way back to Kiev, Sviatoslav met an end similar to that of his father. Attacked by a hostile Turkish tribe of the southern steppe, the Pechenegs, Sviatoslav was overcome and killed, his skull being made by them into a drinking cup.

Before setting off on campaign in 970, Sviatoslav had divided the trust of Kievan Russia among his three sons. After a period of fraternal strife in which two of the brothers were killed, Vladimir emerged as sole ruler by 980 and remained in power until his death in 1015. Perhaps the principal concern of Vladimir's reign was the struggle against his father's murderers, the Pechenegs, although reasons of state were at least as important a part of the motive as personal retribution. To defend Kievan Russia from the incursions of this and other tribes, he caused to be constructed along the northern banks of the rivers of the steppe five series of forts. Vladimir thus provided 'a model for generations of Russian rulers to come, and "fortified lines" as a protection against the nomads were still built by the Russians in south and east Russia as late as the eighteenth century and in Turkestan even in the nineteenth century.'[7] To man the forts, Vladimir brought down northerners to join the local people, and heroic tales were later being told at celebratory banquets and in epic ballads of the deeds accomplished among them by individuals such as the brave knight Ilia Muromets.

In an attempt to stabilise the state further, Vladimir followed his father's example by sending his sons to rule the cities in his name. But precedent was followed in the negative as well as in the positive sense, for family quarrels broke out during the last years of his reign, notably with Iaroslav in Novgorod.

Like Sviatoslav, Vladimir also carried on a vigorous foreign policy throughout Asia and Europe, relations with Byzantium remaining the central concern and continuing their earlier variable course. Under a new Emperor, Basil II, Byzantium found itself under threat from both the nearby Bulgars and internal dissidents based in Asia Minor. In desperation, Basil turned to Vladimir for assistance, apparently going so far as to hand over his sister Anna in marriage as one of the reciprocal concessions, a gesture which would be made to 'barbarians' only in the most extreme circumstances. When Vladimir moved his forces to bring relief to Basil, however, the Emperor defaulted on his agreement, and did not attempt to keep to it until Vladimir laid siege to an important Byzantine fortress in the Crimea. The story goes that Anna herself refused to marry Vladimir before he was baptised.

Vladimir's baptism, in or around the year 988, meant for him allegedly the abandonment of six wives and 600 concubines, and for Kievan Russia certainly the adoption of Christianity as the state religion. The importance of this step for the medieval and modern history of Russia is incalculable, from both spiritual and secular points of view.[8] In a materialist conception, the adoption of Christianity meant that society had reached a new level of complexity for which pagan cults were no longer sufficient. (More of this below.)

After the death of St Vladimir, as the Orthodox Christians know him, in 1015, it immediately became apparent that the internal Christian values had not been assimilated along with the external observances of the new religion. The fratricidal conflict which preceded the reign now followed it in a more virulent form, and the separatist forces that were to play such a large part in the dissolution of Kievan Russia were already in clear view before the process of formation was completed. Such ebb and flow was possibly a common feature of the early history of feudal states, although we must not superimpose anachronistic order or too clear a pattern.[9]

Following the death of Vladimir, from 1015 to 1036 his twelve sons (albeit by different mothers) struggled among themselves for the succession, finding allies wherever they could to strengthen the power bases which they had established in various cities throughout the land. Iaroslav in Novgorod emerged the ultimate victor. Married to a daughter of the King of Sweden, he had invited Varangians in to help him fight his father, but the mercenaries were slaughtered in August 1015 by the Novgorodians. In retaliation, Iaroslav killed a thousand Novgorodian warriors. With the news of the death of Vladimir reaching him immediately after these reprisals, he quickly tried to conciliate the two sides, part of the terms of reconciliation being made concrete in the first section of the *Russkaia Pravda*, or Russian Law, which will be generally examined later. As a consequence, the warriors of Novgorod fought in uneasy alliance with the Varangians to take Kiev. The struggle was by no means over, however, for the brother ousted from Kiev gained support from both the Pechenegs and the Poles, and took up the counter-attack. This particular fight was not finished until 1019, and other fraternal squabbles kept Iaroslav busy for a further fifteen years. Most of Vladimir's sons died tragically, two of them, Boris and Gleb, becoming the first martyr-saints in the Russian Orthodox calendar.

In his years as Grand Prince from 1036 to 1054, Iaroslav the Wise, as he came to be called, helped to make Kiev a great cultural and ecclesiastical centre, and extended its contacts with the outside world, not only with Poland and Hungary but also with Germany and France. Among the Grand

Prince's Viking associates was Harald Hardrada, who lived at the Russian court and married a daughter of Iaroslav before going off to fight for fame and fortune in Sicily and Italy, then to become King of Norway before losing his life at the battle of Stamford Bridge in 1066.[10]

Nearer home, Iaroslav continued the vacillating relations with Byzantium, fighting against the Emperor's forces in 1043 on the one hand, but probably cementing ecclesiastical and commercial relations with a dynastic marriage in 1052 on the other. Before he died, Iaroslav divided the Russian lands among his sons, giving Kiev to the eldest Iziaslav and other cities to the other four, urging them: 'Heed him as ye have heeded me, that he may take my place among you.'[11] Although Iziaslav was assigned to be senior prince, in fact a triumvirate emerged and managed to exercise an uneasy control until 1073. Then two of its members conspired against the third, Iziaslav, who fled to Poland and sought the help of both the Holy Roman Emperor and Pope Gregory VII. The death of one member of the old triumvirate, Sviatoslav, brought Iziaslav back in 1076 to ally with the other, Vsevolod, only to be killed fighting for his patrimony in 1078. From 1078 to 1093, Vsevolod ruled Kiev, surrounded by younger feuding princes. From 1093 to 1113, the son of Iziaslav, Sviatopolk, managed to retain power in Kiev while his cousin, the son of Vsevolod, Vladimir Monomakh, ruled in Chernigov, one of the cities which were increasingly emerging as rivals to Kiev.

In the second half of the eleventh century, Kiev was being weakened by internal social conflict and fratricidal princely disputes as well as by external threats. All three of these elements combined in 1068 to produce probably the largest civic disturbances that Kievan Russia experienced. With the growth of the political influence of the cities, their assemblies, known as *veche*, became more important. The Kievan *veche* was assembled in 1068 by the army which had just been defeated in the first full-scale invasion by the successors to the Pechenegs as southern steppe Turkish tribesmen, the Polovtsy or Cumans. The *veche* decided to raise a new army from among the common people, but Iziaslav attempted to overrule the decision. In an ensuing popular riot, Iziaslav took flight and the crowd released his imprisoned cousin, Vseslav, to be their prince. Vseslav the Sorcerer, as he was widely known, was the subject of folk epics, and was described as a grey wolf or a lynx as well as a magician. Little is known of his brief rule in Kiev, but he almost certainly encouraged a popular reversion to paganism. There was a disturbance in Novgorod too, during the year 1068, but with Polish help, Iziaslav soon managed to restore an uneasy control.[12]

His son, Sviatopolk, could hardly be said to have enjoyed a more secure reign from 1093 to 1113. This Grand Prince made himself personally unpopular, particularly through his assumption of a monopoly on salt. Various and devious interprincely feuding continued, although a general conference at Liubech near Chernigov in 1097 attempted to quell it. According to the *Chronicle*, the princes said to one another: 'Why do we ruin the land of Rus by our continued strife against one another? The Polovtsy harass our country in divers fashions, and rejoice that war is waged among us. Let us rather hereafter be united in spirit and watch over the land of Rus, and let each of us guard his own domain ... . '[13] While the principle of Kievan seniority was not formally rejected at Liubech and succeeding conferences, emphasis was put on the autonomous rights of each princely branch to its inheritance. In order to preserve his own rule, Sviatopolk was not above making peace with the Polovtsy by marrying the daughter of their khan or removing a rival by blinding him, a Byzantine practice held to be unprecedented in Russia.

At the death of Sviatopolk in 1113, social disturbances and princely squabbles flared up at a time when the threat from outside was still great. There was another revolt in Kiev, put to an end by the *veche*'s hurried election of Vladimir Monomakh, who had made a considerable reputation for himself by leading Russian resistance to the Polovtsy and through his comparatively honourable conduct in family feuds. Vladimir Monomakh, 1113–25, enjoys the reputation of a true knight, stern yet just, a devout Christian while keen on the manly arts of hunting and fighting. He was first married to the daughter of Harold of England, Gytha, who had escaped to Denmark after her father's defeat at Hastings in 1066. For the sons that she bore him and possibly for his followers in general, Vladimir composed a *Testament*, in which he told of his own life and of his views on life in general.

Vladimir Monomakh's reputation at large was clearly demonstrated at his death by the unopposed succession of his eldest son Mstislav, who had previously been Prince of Novgorod. His mother was English and his wife was Swedish, and he worked to keep his Baltic connections secure, while successfully struggling to maintain order among his princely relations. His reign, from 1125 to 1132, largely achieved its aims, since Mstislav, like his father, managed to keep the support of Kiev and a sufficient number of other towns. From about the end of the first third of the twelfth century, however, the various centrifugal forces which had been in existence from the beginning now assumed strength enough to threaten Kievan Russia with complete disintegration.

Moreover, the Polovtsy and other tribesmen continued to harry the beleaguered Russians and to hamper their communications with the outside world. Changes in this outside world were also to the detriment of Kiev, notably the creation of trade routes from Byzantium to Western Europe via Venice by sea or by way of Bohemia overland. The Crusades encouraged the growth of Italian and French cities on the Mediterranean and German cities along the Rhine to the detriment of Byzantium. The fourth Crusade in particular consisted of little more than the sack of Constantinople in 1204.

As Kiev declined, so three other important centres arose within the loose framework of the Russian state. The first of them was Novgorod, the eclipse of which had never been total, and which was now benefiting from the revival of trade in the Baltic. With a huge hinterland providing furs, wax and other items to supply and supplement its handicrafts industry, Novgorod gained the resources to establish an independent republic at the end of the first third of the twelfth century. The *veche* assembly possessed the supreme power, elected its own civil and military governors and managed relations with the princes. However, Novgorod was an oligarchy rather than a democracy, for, although the *veche* consisted of all free citizens, a smaller group of boyars, as the leading nobles were called, was actually in control. Much the same might be said of Pskov, the city to the south-west of Novgorod at the foot of Lake Peipus.

A second focus of political organisation was to the north-east, with Vladimir the most important of a number of principalities. Rostov and Suzdal were more important cities earlier on, particularly during the reign of Iurii Dolgorukii, a son of Vladimir Monomakh, although he is best remembered as the founder of Moscow, first mentioned as a fortified settlement in 1147. It was during the reign of Iurii's son, Andrei Bogoliubskii, that Vladimir gained its political predominance. Andrei managed to get sufficient support from new men and new towns to establish something like control in the north-east and to conduct a successful campaign against Kiev in 1169, capturing the old capital and sacking it. But his attempt to conquer Novgorod in 1170 ended in failure, and in 1174 Andrei was assassinated by his boyar opponents. After a confused interregnum, Andrei's younger brother, Vsevolod Bolshoe Gnezdo (Big Nest – because of his fertility) took Vladimir to greater heights in a long reign lasting to 1212.

A third area to gain importance as Kiev lost it was composed of Galicia, Volynia and other principalities to the south-west. The area received a great boost from the passage through it of the new land trade route from the East, and possessed considerable strategic value because of its situation bordering on Poland and Hungary as well as Russia. A notable ruler was Roman Mstislavich of Volynia who united his own principality with Galicia at the end of the twelfth century. On the eve of the Mongol invasions then, the unstable federation of Kievan Russia was already passing the point of disintegration.

The process of disintegration could be said to have been under way already before the federation was properly set up; nevertheless, the Kievan state was, at its peak, much more than an anarchic conglomeration.[14] If political relations between the princes often appeared to consist of nothing more than unrestrained fratricide, there were other times at which a father's testament or a brother's seniority could not be ignored. Similarly, while the day-to-day behaviour of the citizens of Kiev and the other cities was governed largely by force or custom, there were also attempts to put it on a more regular basis. The most notable example of such an endeavour was the *Russkaia Pravda*, which Kliuchevskii deemed 'a good but broken mirror of Russian law in the eleventh and twelfth centuries'. From this and other imperfect sources, at least some kind of composite picture of Kievan society can be assembled.

At the apex, of course, stood the princes, supported by their *druzhina* which came to be composed mainly of boyars. The *druzhina* comprised the commanders of the armed forces, the chief administrators and the greatest landlords, and, in the words of Kliuchevskii, 'became the governing class'. The merchant class was important in the towns, its most important members allying with the boyars to dominate the *veche*. Capital was for Kliuchevskii the most important element in the *Russkaia Pravda*.[15] Most of the peasants and townsmen were legally free, the slaves proper constituting a comparatively small class. But the degree of freedom enjoyed by the Kievan people has sometimes been exaggerated in talk of 'good old days' which in fact never existed. Payment of extortionate taxes and recruitment to military and other severe forms of service often pushed the people towards actual if not legal servitude. Even when the legal freedom was strictly observed, there could be no guarantee of complete security for the threats of famine and epidemic, fire and war were never far away. A conflagration in Kiev in 1124, for example, was said to have destroyed 600 churches, and another in Novgorod, in 1211, 15 churches and 43,000 houses.

A final word must be added here about the contemporaneous situation in Central Asia and Transcaucasia. Waves of Muslim-Turkic invaders into Central Asia merged with the older settlers there to create a number of states in the eleventh and twelfth centuries. With the reception of the Arabic language and Muslim culture, the region enjoyed a high level of civilisation, creating fine works of art and literature and making important contributions to philosophy, mathematics and the sciences. Transcaucasia, Christian Georgia, Armenia and Muslim Azerbaidzhan had already acquired a distinctive personality by the twelfth century; again, the arts and sciences were at an advanced level of development. Thus, even the most superficial acquaintance with the early medieval history of Central Asia and Transcaucasia obliges the investigator to realise that we should not look exclusively westwards for feudal societies to compare with Kievan Russia. This realisation is thrust on his attention much more forcefully as we turn to consider the impact of the Mongol invasions.

Economic

Within the wide and loose boundaries of Kievan Russia, there were ample natural resources from which its people could extract a living – forests, arable lands, lakes, rivers and mineral deposits. However, historians have not been able to agree on how these resources were put to use.

In his 'classic' description of the early Russian economy, Kliuchevskii wrote:

> The history of our society would have been substantially different, if our economy had not been for eight or nine centuries in historical contradiction to the nature of the country. In the eleventh century, the bulk of the Russian population was concentrated in the Middle Dnepr black-earth region, and by the mid-fifteenth it moved to the Upper Volga area. It would seem that in the former area, agriculture should have become the basis of the economy while in the latter, foreign trade, forestry and other activities should have come to predominate. But external circumstances were such that while Rus remained in the Dnepr black-earth territory she engaged predominantly in the sale of forest products and so on and began vigorously to plough only on the loamy Upper Volga soils. As a result, both leading economic forces, land-ownership by servicemen and urban trade took an artificial turn and failed to develop where natural conditions were most propitious, but where they developed with success, their achievements were artificial and were accompanied by a delay in national successes in other directions.[16]

A categorical antithesis to Kliuchevskii's formulation was given by Grekov, who declared: 'Agriculture became the main occupation of the Eastern, as well as of the other Slavs long before the formation of the Ancient Rus state. It continued to develop in Kiev Rus, assuming new forms with the growth of the productive forces ... . Feudal land tenure and peasant economies remained the basis of Rus life for several centuries.'[17] Grekov's argument (although modified) has been substantiated by the research of his successors to such an extent that it can no longer be rejected by appeal to the authority of Kliuchevskii. They would not deny the importance of trade to the Kievan economy, but they insist on the primacy of agriculture.

The total number of people engaged in economic pursuits of all kinds is impossible to estimate. Vernadsky tentatively suggested about 7,500,000 for the late twelfth century, with not less than a million, or about 13 per cent, living in cities, but this method of compilation was necessarily so primitive that no firm reliance can be placed on it.[18] Therefore, we cannot exactly tell how many unsung peasants were involved in farming or how many anonymous townsmen pursued commerce or industry, but can only record their activities in a proportionately representative manner.

The evidence for the argument that agriculture was from early times the way of life for the majority of Kievan Russians has been partly documentary but more archaeological; it is above all the spade that has revealed the predominance of the plough. Many remains of implements, animals and grains have been unearthed. Moreover, their disposition strongly suggests that there was an expansion of agriculture up to the twelfth century, new fields being opened up with the slash-and-burn method (*podseka*) in forested regions, with the more wasteful extensive approach (*perelog*) being adopted in the grassy steppe. By this time, perhaps, the two-field and even three-field crop rotation system had come to be partly adopted in the more settled regions. The basic unit of production was the peasant commune, which was increasingly based on territory rather than on blood, according to Blum, while Vernadsky prefers to talk of the 'greater family' (smaller than the clan but larger than the nuclear family) as the norm.[19]

Superimposed upon many communes by the eleventh century were the estates of the princes, the nobility or the Church. Although they probably occupied less land than did the unattached communes, these estates are more fully described in written sources, for the obvious enough reason that nearly all such evidence was produced by or for the people who owned them. The organisation and activities of these estates, which would not be unrecognisable to anybody familiar with the Western European manor, are recorded adequately enough. However, as Grekov rightly pointed out, 'the chroniclers pay very little attention to the rural population. It continued to plough. With its corn it fed itself and those who either could not or would not plough. It paid state taxes punctually and went to war, but the better service it rendered, the less mention it got ... '[20]

Since hunting was at least as popular with Kievan princes and boyars as it was with their Western European counterparts, we learn more about their performance at the chase than about the workaday activities of their social inferiors. Even the devout Vladimir Monomakh was proud to enumerate his active and passive experiences in his *Testament*, writing:

> At Chernigov, I even bound wild horses with my bare hands or captured ten or twenty live horses with the lasso, and besides that, while riding along the Ros, I caught these same wild horses bare-handed. Two bisons tossed me and my horse on their horns, a stag once gored me, one elk stamped upon me, while another gored me, a boar once tore my sword from my thigh, a bear on one occasion bit my kneecap, and another wild beast jumped on my flank and threw my horse with me. But God preserved me unharmed.[21]

Hunting was subject to strict regulations, since it was often part of even a nobleman's livelihood as well as his pastime. For the rank and file, particularly those to the north, hunting was a basic necessity as a source of food and clothing and, especially in the case of furs and hides, a provider of the means of paying taxes or engaging in commerce. Forest dwellers would often go in for bee-keeping, from which the honey and even more the wax could be exchanged or sold for internal or external trade. A further companion or alternative to hunting, as in later days, was fishing.

Hunting or fishing, bee-keeping or farming, Kievan Russians in the countryside often lived in a near-subsistence manner, salt and metal artefacts being among the few items of daily use that had to be purchased. Nevertheless, few rural inhabitants could be completely unconscious of the possibilities of selling surpluses for urban consumption and industry or for export, and most of them would be liable for taxes.

As for the urban population, the majority consisted of craftsmen, making use of the produce of their provincial brethren, including flax and hemp, as well as of domestic iron and foreign raw materials, notably non-ferrous and precious metals, to process and fashion goods for sale at home and abroad.[22]

Domestic trade – between forest and steppe, town and country – preceded foreign in time and probably always surpassed it in volume. Nevertheless, the foreign branch of trade is the more fully described, indeed the most widely recorded of all Kievan Russia's economic activities. This partiality is easily explained by the fact that foreign observers were usually most interested in commercial possibilities, and should not persuade us to over-emphasis in our description. But we cannot talk of humble dealings in local market places, their very frequency making them unremarkable to contemporary commentators.

So more space will be devoted here to Kiev's participation in international trade, the degree of which by early medieval standards certainly encourages special mention. The importance of Kiev's place on main routes converging on Byzantium – from the Baltic to the Black Seas and from the Orient to the West – has already been noted, as has its reduction from the end of the eleventh century with the interference of the Polovtsy, by the rise of Venice and the start of the Crusades. In the twelfth century, Kiev retained some of its commercial importance as overland trade grew through central Europe, while Novgorod prospered from trade with the Baltic. In her heyday, Kiev exported furs, honey and wax to Byzantium, with slaves in addition in earlier times and grain later. Luxury items, such as wines, silks and jewels, predominated among the imports from Byzantium. The same exports – furs, honey and wax – together with woollen fabrics were sent to the Orient to be exchanged for silks, spices, jewels, luxury metal goods and horses. In the earlier period, Kiev supplanted Novgorod as the main intermediary between the Orient and the West, but by the twelfth century, Novgorod was regaining her predominance. From Novgorod, as well as from other cities in the north-west such as Pskov and Smolensk, went not only furs, honey and wax, but vegetable and animal raw materials and semi-manufactures such as flax and hemp, tallow and hides. Such a volume of international trade took Russians abroad and brought foreigners in. This interchange had a great political and social importance, as we have seen, and a great cultural influence, as we are about to see.

In conclusion, the attempt must be made to typify the economy of Kievan Russia as a whole. Following Kliuchevskii, Vernadsky uses the term 'commercial capitalism'[23] pointing out that the furs and cattle used in earlier times as media of exchange were replaced by gold and silver, and that credit transactions were in wide use, particularly in foreign trade. For Soviet historians and many of their successors, on the other hand, landlord and peasant agriculture predominated.[24] The implication of the foregoing description is to express agreement with the second of these two views.

Cultural

'If, before you inspect Kiev's Sophia Cathedral', the 'classic' Soviet historian Grekov advised his fellow citizens, 'you are inclined to be condescending regarding the ability of our ancestors to express the great and the beautiful, then you will be extremely astonished.' He continued:

You no sooner cross the threshold than you come under the spell of its grandeur and magnificence: its imposing interior, its austere proportions, its ornate mosaics and frescoes captivate you by their perfection even before you have had an opportunity to examine the details and to comprehend what it was the creators of this outstanding work of architecture and painting had in mind.[25]

Foreign visitors, too, might well find themselves echoing Grekov's words, not only in Kiev but also in Novgorod, Suzdal and Vladimir. Interpretations will vary as to the exact significance of the culture of Kievan Russia, but nobody could doubt the worthiness of its inclusion at a high level of achievement in early medieval Europe as a whole.

However, in Russia as elsewhere, before the reception of Christianity, paganism flourished for several centuries, and, even after it, persisted for several more. For the common people, Christianity was as difficult to accept in the Kievan period as was materialism in Soviet times. And while paganism produced nothing on the scale of the early medieval cathedrals, it can in no way be equated with barbarism; some of the idols, jewels and decorations which have survived possess their own power and subtlety.

To an atheistic historian such as B. A. Rybakov, paganism and Christianity are not to be neatly separated, they rather merge into each other. But even he can distinguish the two enough to make the following appraisal of the sequel to the conversion of Vladimir in 988:

The Russians church played a complex and many-sided role in the history of Rus during the 11th–13th centuries. On the one hand there was the undoubtedly progressive role of the church as an organisation that helped to consolidate the young Rus statehood in the epoch of the vigorous development of feudalism. It also undoubtedly helped in the development of Russian culture, bringing it closer to the cultural treasures of Byzantium, in the spread of education, and the creation of literary and artistic works of great value.

But it must be remembered that the Russian people paid dearly for that positive contribution of the church: the poison of religious ideology penetrated (deeper than in pagan times) into all the pores of the people's life, it dulled the class struggle, revived primitive notions in a new form, and for centuries fastened in the consciousness of the people the ideas of a world beyond, of the divine origin of rulers, and providentialism, i.e., the concept that the fates of people are always governed by God's will.

The Russian people were not as religious as the church historians try to make out, but religious ideology was nonetheless a hindrance on the road to a free understanding of the world.[26]

From the other side, G. P. Fedotov concludes that:

Kievan Russia, like the golden days of childhood, was never dimmed in the memory of the Russian nation. In the pure fountain of her literary works anyone who wills can quench his religious thirst: in her venerable authors he can find his guide through the complexities of the modern world. Kievan Christianity has the same value for the Russian religious mind as Pushkin for the Russian artistic sense: that of a standard, a golden measure, a royal way.[27]

As for medieval Russian literature in general, Franklin and Shepard urge us not to exaggerate the originality of medieval Russian literature for 'the book culture of the Rus was almost entirely a culture of translations'. But they also tell us that 'the signs and products of native book-learning became steadily more numerous and diverse' from the mid-eleventh century.[28] In particular, Fedotov recommends for our attention the *Confession of Faith* and the sermon entitled *On Law and Grace* by Ilarion, the only Metropolitan of Kiev of Russian origin for over a century and 'unanimously acknowledged the best theologian and preacher of all ancient Russia, the Muscovite period included'. He considers that in Boris and Gleb are to be found the prototypes of a peculiarly Russian kind of martyr-saint. He reminds us that the first European scholar to study the Russian *Chronicles* in the eighteenth century thought that 'Nestor, the supposed author of the ancient *Chronicles* had no rivals in the West'. And he finds in the *Testament* of Vladimir Monomakh 'Russian lay religion at its best'.[29] All these examples are taken from Kievan Russia in the period of its greatest cohesion and influence. If the list of the most outstanding works alone were extended to include the following century and the other principalities, those who share Fedotov's outlook on life would find ample evidence to accept his conclusions with enthusiasm.

Moreover, the list would not have to be restricted to works of religious authorship or emphasis. For example, a prominent place would have to be given to the famous *Slovo o Polku Igoreve* or *Tale of Igor's Campaign*, provided, that is, that its authenticity is taken for granted.[30] Concerned with the vicissitudes and failure of the campaign against the Polovtsy undertaken in the late twelfth century by Prince Igor of Novgorod

Severskii, it is a Russian equivalent to the later Viking sagas, to the French *Song of Roland* or the German *Saga of the Nibelungen*.

So far, however, we have been talking for the most part of the higher levels of activity; we must now attempt to say more about the middle and lower levels, about literacy and education, and about folk culture. With some justification, Soviet historians asserted that literacy was widespread; some evidence for this was found in the birch-bark documents dug out of the soil of Novgorod.[31] The written language used in Kievan Russia was based on the *kirillitsa* or Cyrillic alphabet, one of the two uniform systems introduced at the time of Christianity and replacing more primitive and disparate systems. While the reception of the Cyrillic alphabet was obviously a progressive step, Fedotov would not be alone in regretting the limited scale of the move forward when he writes: 'Russian cultural aspirations, however open and sincere, found a drawback in their Slavonic language, narrowly limiting the circle of available translated literature. This fact, be it by contingency or destiny, explains a tragic lack in ancient Russian culture, a complete absence of rational scientific thought, even in the theological field.'[32] In so far as they agreed about such absence, Soviet historians blamed neither contingency nor destiny, but the obscurantism of the Orthodox Church.

The folk culture, as has already been pointed out, would often escape the influence of the Church by remaining resolutely pre-Christian in nature. Such persistence was encouraged by the liveliness of oral tradition, at the centre of which stands the songs. As Seaman says of the ancient Slavs: 'Their whole life seems to have centred round the seasonal year, and their music took the form of songs to alleviate the task of manual labour.'[33] Echoes of pagan sun worship are intermixed with Christian themes in celebrations of the sowing, harvesting and other stages in the farming cycle. Love, marriage and death also receive appropriate musical attention. And the great epic songs tell of the exploits of such peasant heroes as Ilia Muromets.

To the illiterate, the wonders of Christianity could best be conveyed by imposing buildings and powerful icons and frescoes. We have already indicated that the impact is still strong on twentieth-century atheists; its strength in the early medieval period for the religious is immeasurable. But such creations are better seen to be believed. We will therefore not attempt here to describe them in words or talk about their comparability with the contemporary creations of the West, even though there have been very interesting stylistic suggestions, such as the architecture of Vladimir and Suzdal as 'reminiscent of the Romanesque'.[34] Let us make the simple assertion that there is less in Kievan culture to stimulate the mind than to delight the ear and to excite the outer and inner eye. And let us remember in conclusion that the Byzantium influence that brought Kiev the icon and many other features of her Christian culture did not set her apart from the rest of the Western world. Discussing this point, Dimitri Obolensky writes:

> Russia was … closely linked with central and western Europe, by trade, culture, and diplomacy, above all by the consciousness of belonging to one world of Christendom, where, for the most part, there was still no Hellene nor Latin, but a common culture and a common faith. It is highly significant that Russia entered the European family of nations through her conversion to Christianity, for which she is indebted to Byzantium. The heritage of East Rome was not, as it is sometimes suggested, Russia's 'mark of the beast' that isolated her from medieval Europe: it was, in fact, the main channel through which she became a European nation. Byzantium was not a wall, erected between Russia and the West: she was Russia's gateway to Europe.[35]

Accepting much of what Obolensky says, some scholars would feel that his enthusiasm carries him too far. For his part, B. A. Rybakov declared: 'The depth of the popular culture allowed Rus to survive the onerous times of the Tatar–Mongol yoke, and to conserve an inexhaustible strength for the overcoming of the consequences of foreign domination.' Yet other historians would argue that Rybakov could be carried away by *his* enthusiasm. Even more has such a fault been attributed to Grekov, whose implication that Russian architects and artists, rather than Byzantine, created St Sophia Cathedral in Kiev, is just one example of the patriot overtaking the scholar.[36]

The debate about the culture of Kiev has not ceased with the collapse of the Soviet Union. Indeed, a new dimension has been added as Russian historians argue with Ukrainian and Belarussian colleagues about their share of a common inheritance. Perhaps they should give their attention to scholarly outsiders: 'The story of the land of the Rus could continue in one direction towards modern Russia, or in other directions towards eventually, Ukraine or Belarus. The land of the Rus is none of these, or else it is a shared predecessor of all three.'[37] In the short run, however, only one of the three, still bearing the name Rus and coming to be centred on Moscow, carries the process into consolidation as a medieval state.

2 Invasion and Disunity, 1240–1462

At the beginning of the thirteenth century, the Mongols under Chingis (or Genghis) Khan began the great conquests that brought upon the Russian principalities the much-lamented Mongol or Tatar 'yoke'. (Although strictly different, the two terms have often been used interchangeably and will be here.) According to Grekov, who on this occasion speaks for many historians before 1917 and after 1991 as well as for his Soviet colleagues, Rus in the heyday of Kiev 'was ahead of many European countries which only later outstripped her when she bore the impact of the Mongolian hordes and acted as a shield to Western Europe'.[1] To Mongol historians, on the other hand, Chingis Khan is an Alexander the Great, and the empire set up by him constitutes a high point of history rather than a low. Chinese historians have also stressed the positive side of the Mongol impact, one of them, Han Ju-Lin, writing of Chingis Khan that 'his war horses broke through the iron walls of forty large and small states in which the people had become locked. As a result their peoples came to see a broader world in which they could act and become familiar with a higher culture from which they could learn.'[2] And for the 'Eurasian' school of historians, G. V. Vernadsky was an eloquent spokesman, who saw in the Mongol expansion of the thirteenth century 'one of those crucial and fateful eruptions in the history of mankind which from time to time change the destinies of the world'.[3] The views of Vernadsky and his followers will be pitted against those of their opponents below.

At the same time as the 'Mongol yoke' was being imposed, other invaders – Swedes, Teutonic Knights and Lithuanians – were attacking the Russian principalities from the western side. Such an additional challenge together with a great problem of internal disunity called for heroic leaders to arise from among the Russian people. Some, such as Alexander Nevsky and Dmitrii Donskoi, did appear at critical moments. But the period as a whole is probably the most colourless of the medieval era, and the remarks of John Fennell concerning the silence of the sources on the first half of the fourteenth century tellingly echo the complaints by Kliuchevskii and other predecessors about the years preceding and following:

> No references are made to physical characteristics; there are no attempts to describe any recreational activities as hunting or drinking which might throw even a glimmer of light on personality ... . The meagre obituaries or eulogies dutifully supplied by the chroniclers are little more than a concoction of clichés which tell us nothing of the men whose piety or goodness they extol.[4]

Thus, little can be said about the rulers or their administrations.

The central figure in the political story of Russian development at this time is not so much an individual or an institution as a principality – Moscow (as Moskva is generally called in English). Denied the opportunity to exercise his great talent for characterisation on one of its princes, Kliuchevskii turned to Moscow itself for the subject of one of his clear and convincing portraits. But here as well as elsewhere, the 'classical' picture presented by the great master has been under heavy criticism from his successors, and it can no longer be completely accepted.

Moreover, in the comparative setting to which historians are increasingly turning, analysis of Russia's disunity and subsequent unification reveals that it was by no means a completely unique experience, even though it possesses special features of which the Mongol yoke is perhaps the most important.

Political

After their conquest of Northern China and Central Asia, the Mongols fanned out to establish their control over a vast area of Western Eurasia, including Transcaucasia and the Russian principalities. An early scouting raid led to the first encounter with Russian forces in the south-east at the river Kalka in 1223, the Mongols enjoying an overwhelming victory. The death of Chingis Khan in 1227 brought a lull, but ten years later a large army under his grandson Batu Khan embarked on a more thorough campaign. Contemporary descriptions of the fall of the Russian cities were horrific in the extreme, one of them stating that:

> The prince, with his mother, wife, sons, the boyars and inhabitants, without regard to age or sex, were slaughtered with the savage cruelty of Mongol revenge; some were impaled, or had nails or splinters of

wood driven under their finger-nails. Priests were roasted alive, and nuns and maidens ravished in the churches before their relatives. No eye remained open to weep for the dead.[5]

The northern principalities fell one by one, with the exception of Novgorod; Kiev was sacked in 1240. The Mongols swept into Central Europe, collecting nine large bags of the ears of their victims after a battle in Silesia in 1241. Terror spread as far as France and the Low Countries, according to the chronicler Matthew Paris.[6] Neither the Holy Roman Emperor nor the Pope could unite Christendom against the invaders, and if Batu had not turned back at the news of the death of the Great Khan in 1242, Mongol destruction might have penetrated as far as the news of it.

Meanwhile, far from coming to the aid of their fellow Christians, the Catholic Swedes and Livonian Knights viewed the predicament of the Orthodox Russians as a perfect opportunity for their own hostile invasion. In the summer of 1240, a strong force led by the son-in-law of the King of Sweden, Earl Birger, blocked Novgorod's access route to the Baltic Sea, the river Neva, and threatened the great city itself. A determined counter-attack drove back Birger and the Swedes, and gained for the leader of the Novgorod forces, Prince Aleksandr, a title taken from the river Neva to commemorate the success – Nevskii (Alexander Nevsky). Meanwhile, the Livonian Knights, who had been called away from their attack on Pskov to help their brethren resist the Mongols, were able to return and take Pskov in 1241. Advancing on Novgorod in 1242, they were met by Alexander Nevsky's army and decisively crushed on 5 April in the battle on the ice of Lake Peipus, which was later celebrated by Eisenstein in his famous film named after the great leader. In a Soviet evaluation which would be shared by patriots of other persuasions, the victory 'saved the Russian people from sharing the fate of the Baltic tribes and the Slavs of the Elbe who were enslaved by the Germans'. Even if this was so, pressure from the West continued to be an important feature of Russian history through the years of the more notorious infiltration from the East. And as for Alexander Nevsky himself, John Fennell has emphasised that the Prince did nothing to defend the integrity of the Orthodox Church (even though it later made him a saint) or to assist the spirit of resistance to the Mongols (even though he also later became a great national hero).[7]

On his return to Mongolia, Batu did not manage to get himself made Great Khan or even to exert much influence at the centre of Mongol power. However, he gained some consolation from founding what came to be known later as the Golden Horde with its capital at Sarai on the Lower Volga. Batu inaugurated the custom that was to last for 200 years of the

Russian princes coming to Sarai to pledge their allegiance and to pay their tribute. Emissaries from as far away as Western Europe also came to Sarai or passed through it on their way to the Great Khan, the most famous of them being Marco Polo in the late thirteenth century. To keep the Russians in subjection, the khans of the Golden Horde did not hesitate to form alliances with European princes, notably the Lithuanian, or to encourage internecine rivalry among the Russian princes themselves. Such is the broad framework in which the rise of Moscow must be examined.

But before embarking on such an examination, let us consider the nature of the Mongol impact on Russian development. While Kliuchevskii attributed little significance to the Mongols, and other historians have emphasised only the negative aspects of the 'Tatar yoke'. Vernadsky was a skilled and moderate advocate of the 'Eurasian' view that the Muscovite state contained a considerable admixture of Mongol elements in its political, social, economic and cultural aspects. Concentrating for the moment on government and society, let us take a brief look at Vernadsky's exposition.

He asserted that if the mixed (partly monarchic, aristocratic and democratic) system of Kiev is contrasted with the absolutism of Moscow, then obviously and necessarily 'the process of the transformation of the free society into a service-bound society started during the Mongol period although it was not completed until as late as the mid-seventeenth century'.[8] The destruction of the cities which had been the main bastions of democracy and the discouragement of the boyars from forming themselves into an aristocracy meant that the way was clear for the Grand Prince of Moscow to become an autocrat.

During the period of the emergence of the Muscovite autocracy, moreover, its administration was being formed under the tutelage of the Mongols. Of the three major spheres – judicial, military and financial – the first was least affected, although capital and corporal punishment and torture became more widespread in Muscovite than in Kievan law. Western practices as well as Mongol could be important here, it is true. Much clearer and less equivocal was the Mongol contribution to Moscow's tax arrangements and army organisation. The mere fact that the Russian word *kazna* or treasury is of Asian origin is powerful evidence of the significance of the Grand Prince's role as collector of tribute for the Golden Horde. Both the five-part division of the late medieval Muscovite army and its tactics of encirclement, as well as its universal conscription and emphasis on mobility, can all be said to possess Mongol roots. Moreover, both the service obligations of the upper class and the enserfment of the lower stemmed partly from the centuries of the 'Tatar yoke'. A significant phenomenon at the higher social level was the infiltration

into the Muscovite service class of Mongol elements, which is said to have
contributed later to a lower level of racial consciousness in Russia than in
other expanding empires. Finally, some of the ritual of the Muscovite
court and diplomatic procedures had Asian as well as Byzantine origins.

Vernadsky concluded his work on the Mongols with the assertion that
'Autocracy and serfdom were the price the Russian people had to pay for
national survival'. Here, he would find himself more in general agreement
with Soviet historians than in some of his other assertions concerning the
Mongol impact. On the other hand, many Western historians would now
agree that the rise of autocracy and serfdom had little to do with the
Mongols, and that while Mongol influence was 'significant but not wholesale' on politics, it was limited on society and small on culture. This
would not be to deny that during the years of the Mongol rule, the Russian
princes needed to consider the Mongol position on every question for their
very survival.[9] Let us now turn to consider the manner in which the survival was effected, particularly through the agency of Moscow.

We have already observed that the first documentary mention of
Moscow is in the year 1147, and that the founder has traditionally been
named as Iurii Dolgorukii, Prince of Suzdal, who built a castle by the
Moscow River, the beginning of the famous Kremlin. While the town was
destroyed by the Mongols in 1238, it had recovered sufficiently by the end
of the thirteenth century to be in a position to struggle for supremacy with
other principalities. With Vladimir–Suzdal in decline, Moscow's chief
rival was Tver, situated about a hundred miles to the north on the river
Volga.

In 1304, Prince Mikhail of Tver and Prince Iurii of Moscow were rivals
for the succession to the Grand Principality of Vladimir. They both presented their claims before the Golden Horde, which decided to give its
authorisation or *iarlyk* to Mikhail in 1305. Initially supported by the
Church and by many boyars, Mikhail was the first to adopt the title 'Grand
Prince of All Russia', and he attempted to make the title into more of a
reality by asserting his authority over Novgorod and other cities in particular. But Iurii continued to oppose Mikhail's rule, and won the Tatars
over to his side, marrying the khan's sister. Mikhail was executed in 1318
for resisting the decision of the Golden Horde to replace him as Grand
Prince by Iurii. The reign of Iurii was troubled in turn until 1324, when he
was assassinated by the son of Mikhail.

Out of the confusion, Iurii's brother Ivan emerged as Prince of Moscow,
and by 1331 he had become Grand Prince of Vladimir, too. Ivan I, known
as *Kalita*, or Moneybag, has often been looked upon as the real founder of
Moscow's power, although the case for the maintenance of such a view

rests not so much upon Ivan's parsimony and skilful land purchase as upon his remunerative subservience to the Tatars. Ivan Kalita succeeded in gaining for himself their approval not only to rule as Grand Prince but also to collect tribute on their behalf from all the principalities. As a further addition to his income, he carried on campaigns in the north to strengthen Moscow's grasp on the fur trade. To counter the growth of Moscow's control, Tver and other principalities attempted to gain the support of the Lithuanians. But they were not able to muster sufficient strength to over-throw Ivan, who gained the support of the Church and the boyars as well as of the Tatars. At his death in 1340, the tomb of Ivan Kalita in Moscow became an object of veneration, the chronicle celebrating his reign as the time from which 'there was a great peace in all the land'.[10]

During the reigns through the 1340s and 1350s of Ivan I's immediate successors, his sons Semen the Proud and Ivan II, Moscow's policies remained broadly the same, as did those of Tver and other rival principal-ities. The threat was fairly constant of Tatar intervention on the one side and of Lithuanian intervention on the other, while the princely families quarrelled among themselves about seniority and rights of succession. At the death of Ivan II in 1359, Moscow lost the ascendancy for a few years at the beginning of the reign of his son Dmitrii.

Dmitrii Ivanovich (1359–89) was to see Moscow through a further important phase of its rise to supremacy. During his early years, he was assisted, even replaced by the Metropolitan Aleksei, who came near to equating the interests of the Moscow principality with those of the Church, for which he gained canonisation in return. The struggle with Moscow was carried on by the principalities, including old rivals such as Tver and new such as Nizhnii Novgorod. Conflict with Lithuania arose while that with the Golden Horde continued as before, the most celebrated event of Dmitrii's reign being the victory over the Tatars at Kulikovo on the banks of the river Don in 1380.

For some years the power of the Golden horde had been weakening, with various groups attempting to break away and numerous candidates putting themselves forward for the office of Khan. Irritated by a decline in the acquiescence of the Russians, the Horde decided to re-establish its firm control over them by inflicting complete defeat on Moscow. Although Lithuania in alliance with the Tatars and the other principalities refused to help him, Dmitrii nevertheless managed to muster a large army. After a fierce battle in which the blood was said to flow like rain, he put the Tatars to rout, winning for himself the honorific title of Donskoi. True, after further internecine conflict, the Golden Horde was able to revenge its defeat and to reimpose a harsh tribute, while patriotic historians have exaggerated the significance of Moscow's victory. Of course, there was some way to go before the drive towards unification was completed.

After the death of Dmitrii Donskoi, Vasilii I (1389–1425) managed to retain the Golden Horde's licence to rule. He also effected at least a fluctuating *rapprochement* with Lithuania, marrying the daughter of the Grand Duke Vitovt in 1391. Vitovt attempted to lead a crusade against the Tatars, but was defeated by them in 1399. He was nevertheless strong enough to assert his influence over Novgorod, to annex Smolensk and in 1410 to defeat the Teutonic Knights at the famous battle of Grünwald or Tannenberg. Before this time, Vasilii had broken with Vitovt and sought the support of the Tatars, themselves experiencing a great resurgence under the leadership of Timur, or Tamburlaine as he is often known. But by the time of Vasilii's death, with the centrifugal forces of the principalities, particularly Tver, constituting a severe threat, he had turned again towards Lithuania, asking Vitovt to protect his wife and his son and heir.

The first years of the reign of Vasilii II, also known as the Blind (1425–62) were disturbed by another succession struggle, the principal rival being his uncle Iurii, who could claim seniority. Supported by other disaffected princes, Iurii was able to take Moscow in 1433, but he could not hold it, and had to yield his seniority to Vasilii. The sons of Iurii were not prepared to give up the struggle immediately, however, and Tver and Novgorod showed signs of disaffection from Moscow. Moreover, after the Council of Florence in 1439, there were elements in the Church who wished to acknowledge papal supremacy. The Tatars caused great concern, too, a khan who had defected from the Golden Horde making Vasilii his prisoner in 1445. Meanwhile, one of Iurii's sons, Dmitrii Shemiaka, took advantage of the situation. By the time that Vasilii had secured his release from capture through a large ransom, Dmitrii had mustered sufficient support from princes and merchants to take Moscow, to seize his cousin and to have him blinded. Like his father, however, Dmitrii Shemiaka found it impossible to retain Moscow and was forced to free Vasilii who re-entered Moscow at the beginning of 1447, supported by the Tatars. In the last twelve years of his reign Vasilii strove to achieve a more certain legacy for his successors.

After this bare narrative of the early stages of the unification of Russia under Moscow, some analysis must be attempted. Let us as elsewhere start with the 'classical' account of Kliuchevskii and then note the criticisms of it made by other historians. Essentially, Kliuchevskii argued that the principalities of the north-east had much less solid social structure and cohesion than had Kiev. Their very weakness therefore made them comparatively easy prey for the one among them that was best placed to merge them into a national unit. Moscow was the successful candidate for reasons both geographical and historical. In the first place, the Moscow river, on which it stood, was connected to the Volga with its outlet on the Caspian Sea and led towards the rivers of the north-west flowing into the Baltic Sea. It was well placed to receive immigrants coming in from the south-west. Secondly, the Moscow princes did not have legal seniority and could therefore pursue their expansionist aims in a manner unrestrained by legal considerations. For example, they could ardently court the Golden Horde for the licence to rule and to gather tribute on behalf of the Tatars. When they had gained sufficient strength, however, they were able to gain further prestige by biting the hand that had fed them, so to speak, and defeating the Tatars at Kulikovo under Dmitrii Donskoi. The princes of Moscow were also assisted by the support of the Church. They made their own distinctive individual contribution by siring progeny sturdy enough to allow an unbroken line for more than a century.[11]

Some historians, finding Kliuchevskii's analysis too neat and too Moscow-centred, look for a more reliable interpretation of Moscow's rise in the work of A. E. Presniakov, who died in 1929.[12] Presniakov pointed out that while unification reflected a natural tendency and a human aspiration, it was also a dual dynastic process, with both the weakening and strengthening of principalities going on at the same time. The fierce civil war that produced Moscow's autocracy involved many fluctuating fortunes for the princely families rather than a smooth and relentless gathering together of the Russian lands. Moreover, the 'Mongol yoke' that Kliuchevskii sees as a peripheral factor is put by Presniakov at the very centre of his explanation, giving strong emphasis to Moscow's use of the Golden Horde to gain sufficient strength to defeat it in collaboration with the Church.

Agreeing with Presniakov for the most part, John Fennell emphasised that the geographical argument falls down in face of the fact that Tver was in a better position for the task of unification than was Moscow. For him, too, the emergence of Moscow in the first half of the fourteenth century is explained by 'the will of the khan and, though still in a relatively embryonic stage, the support of the Church'.[13]

The most elaborate Soviet interpretation came from L. V. Cherepnin, who, not surprisingly, stressed the economic aspects of the argument.[14] The development of agriculture, the growth of towns and the increase of commodity circulation constituted the key to his understanding of the process of unification. We will examine this argument more closely below.

Concentrating for the moment on the political and social aspects of the problem, let us take a wider comparative view, first recalling that, with the decline of Kiev, two other centres rose along with the northeast. One of them was Novgorod, which bore under Alexander Nevsky the brunt of invasion from the west, but was also able for several centuries to make good diplomatic and commercial use of its situation near the Baltic Sea and the frontier. Although its economic hinterland was vast, and although its government was by the standards of the time efficient and progressive, it remained fundamentally a city state and was not therefore in a position to lead a nation. A second centre was Galicia–Volynia to the south-west, much of which by the fourteenth century became incorporated in Lithuania. A threat for the most part to the unification under Moscow, as we have seen, Lithuania has also been seen as an alternative candidate for the leadership of that process. Some analysts, such as M. K. Liubavskii, have looked upon Lithuania as a state more worthy than Moscow of being considered feudal, and the inference has therefore sometimes been drawn that a Russia led by Lithuania would have been less autocratic. Such speculation is idle, since, as Liubavskii himself pointed out, population movement was centred on Moscow.[15] Moreover, Lithuania lacked the government and the society to withstand the pressures exerted upon it during the late medieval period, when it became absorbed by Poland. Meanwhile, the Baltic peoples to the north and the Ukrainians to the south were under foreign domination, either Teutonic, Tatar or Polish, although the Cossacks were able to achieve a measure of independence in the broad southern steppe.

To the east and south of Moscow, the states of Central Asia and Transcaucasia were able to achieve something like their former status as the Mongols withdrew, but this process had not gone very far before the middle of the fifteenth century. In the case of Central Asia, it is true, the 'Mongol yoke' had more constructive features than elsewhere. During the empire of Timur in the late fourteenth century, Samarkand was transformed into a magnificent capital; in the early fifteenth century, it enjoyed a remarkable artistic and scientific flowering.[16]

To return in conclusion to Moscow, and to assert that its polity and society may still best be typified as frontier European rather than as Asian. This assertion will be supported by the ensuing examination of its economy and culture.

Economic

The population of Russia towards the end of the thirteenth century has been roughly calculated by Vernadsky at ten millions; possibly the town population was about half a million.[17] But the sources are no more helpful on this than those from the Kievan period, and lack of evidence is a general problem for the economic aspects of the later period as a whole.

As far as agriculture, which remained the basic activity, is concerned, the characteristic feature of the period is the spread of arable farming in the forested non-black-earth region. The *podseka*, or slash-and-burn and *perelog* or long fallow methods were gradually giving way in places to some kind of three-field system.[18] For this transformation to take place, a somewhat improved set of farming practices had to be employed, an essential item of which was a better plough. Another necessity was manure to intensify production, and so cattle numbers had to be increased. Although progress was slow, and although the Mongol incursions delayed it, by about the end of the fourteenth century it had gone far enough in the lands of Novgorod and Pskov as well as those of the north-eastern principalities for the very terms 'village' (*derevnia*) and 'peasant' (*krestianin*) to assume more certain meaning. The villages of the period were not large, many of them consisting of no more than one or two households, but their organisation was nevertheless communal rather than individualistic, with the arable strips often subject to periodic redistribution and perquisites such as forests and meadows usually being held in common. The basic peasant social unit remained not the nuclear family but the extended family, or even the clan based on territory as well as or even instead of blood.

Increasingly, the communes were obliged either to give their labour (*barshchina*) or their rent, usually in kind, (*obrok*) to landed proprietors, both secular and religious. Because of the large scale of their operations, secular lords and the monastic communities could go in for such activities as breeding, vegetable cultivation, beekeeping and handicrafts more readily than those peasants who were unattached. In the fifteenth century, particularly its later decades, the landlords appear to have intensified their interest in agriculture and therefore their demands on the peasants. Both labour and rent rates were raised, and restrictions on peasant movement were tightened. Domestic manufacture increased as well as arable and cattle farming. The village was becoming involved in at least the local market, and some rents began to be paid in money rather than in kind, in the Novgorod lands, for example. A further consequence was the build-up of economic links within the principalities, and between them. The foundations were laid for the unification of the principalities in one state. Far from seeing the period as one of general decline, the Soviet historian G. E. Kochin concluded by saying:

The second half of the thirteenth, fourteenth and fifteenth centuries were taken up by a great and powerful feat of the working people of old

Russia, as a result of which huge areas of northern forest were brought into arable farming; tens of thousands of new settlements were created, villages built permanently and surely for centuries, lasting down to our own times; hundreds of thousands of well organised and by the standards of the time highly productive units of agricultural economy were created or structurally renewed.[19]

Not only Kochin, but other less economically specialist colleagues such as L. V. Cherepnin based their interpretations of the unification of Russia on economic developments. For Cherepnin, these included not only the centrally important agricultural expansion but also urban growth. Of this, he wrote that throughout the fourteenth and fifteenth centuries several settlements became towns and several old towns took on new life as centres of trade and manufacture. The princes became conscious of the need to encourage these activities by freeing commercial routes, partly under the pressure of the leading merchants. However, like agriculture, manufacture and trade were subject to restrictions characteristic of feudal society elsewhere.[20]

Novgorod and its 'little brother' Pskov were the major commercial cities at the beginning of the period. Novgorod was one of the major European cities, with its own well-developed political system and cultural life as well as an energetic economic activity; exciting archaeological discoveries have revealed a considerable amount about all these aspects. Its principal contact was with Germans and Central Europeans and with the Hanseatic League, the representatives of which carried on their business under strict controls. The trade consisted mainly of the export of furs and wax, leather and hemp, and the import of woollen and other textile materials, metal goods, wines and spices. The fur trade was of prime importance and the acquisition by Moscow of a monopoly was one of the key reasons for the ascendancy of that principality.[21]

Newer towns such as Nizhnii Novgorod on the Volga began to develop their economic importance round about this time. Trade with the east down the Volga and through the Tatar capital of Sarai started to grow as the Mongols stopped their interference. The Don was also an important commercial artery, with the Genoese capital of Tana at its mouth. Sarai and Tana were both bustling, cosmopolitan centres for the exchange of oriental silks, spices, precious stones and other luxury goods with Russian furs, wax, honey and caviar. The Genoese also had another colony called Sudak, or Surozh in Russian, in the Crimea. A special group of Muscovite merchants dealt with the Genoese.

We must be careful not to exaggerate the intensity of economic activity throughout the period of invasion and division. But a greater danger is to look upon it as a period of complete ruin and stagnation. Of course, feudal society was not conducive to rapid growth. Undoubtedly, the devastation brought about by the invasions of the Mongols and others, as well as the squabbling between the principalities, acted as braking forces. It would be premature in the extreme to talk of national markets or budgets. And yet, to divorce the economic aspects of Russian life from the others and not to note the part played by the extension of agriculture and the expansion of commerce in the process of unification is to omit from consideration a vital part of the explanation of that process.

Cultural

During the period of Mongol invasion and feudal division, at least the 'official' Russian culture remained in the care of the Orthodox Church. This was recognised by the princes and even by the Mongols. While churches and clergymen were at first as much the object of Mongol attack as anything and anybody else, the Church was soon exempted from tax assessment. After 1266 it was given further immunities, ostensibly under the authority of Chingis, in return for which it was expected to pray for the Great Khan's successors. As a powerful economic force and as a political intermediary between the princes, the Metropolitan and his associates by no means confined their activities to the spiritual life. With new churches and monasteries being built and the administration being extended into rural areas as well as the towns, Russian Orthodoxy was basically well prepared to take on the succession after the failure of the union of the Greek and Roman Churches concluded at the Council of Florence in 1439 and the fall of Byzantium in 1453. It continued to produce great works of art and architecture, of which more below. With such individuals as St Sergius of Radonezh, founder of the Trinity Monastery to the north-east of Moscow and adviser to Prince Dmitrii before the battle of Kulikovo, it produced outstanding figures deemed capable of deep piety and national leadership.

However, the Church by no means completely succeeded in carrying its message to the people. Its comparative failure was inevitable if Florinsky's assertion is correct that 'the indifference of the masses towards religion is one of the characteristics of Russia's history'.[22] Soviet historians would certainly have agreed officially with him on this point, if not on many others. But it is also the case that the rank and file of the priesthood

were often incapable of their pastoral duties. Genadius, Archbishop of
Novgorod in the fifteenth century, complained:

> They bring me a peasant to be ordained as a priest or deacon. I bid him
> read the Epistles, and he does not know how to begin. I bid him read the
> Psalter, he cannot take the first step …. I order him to be taught at least
> the liturgical prayers, but he is unable even to repeat the words one
> gives him. When told to read from the alphabet, after a short lesson he
> begs to leave, does not want to learn. And if I refuse to ordain him, I am
> told such is the world, your Holiness, we cannot find anyone versed in
> knowledge.[23]

The ignorance and the poverty of the ordinary or 'white' clergy were to
remain problems for many centuries. So were the luxury and corruption of
many church leaders and others in the 'black' monastic orders. In order to
retain or regain their purity, many hermits removed themselves ever
further from the great ecclesiastical centres, several of them seeking the
simple, direct approach to God of hesychasm. As a more positive response
to the situation, various heretical sects arose. Among these were the
strigolniki, who appeared in Novgorod and Pskov in the late fourteenth
century and early fifteenth century respectively. Rejecting the Church hierarchy and appealing for a return to the ideals of the early apostolic church,
the *strigolniki* were persecuted with severity. Their ideas would obviously
bear comparison with those of Wyclif in England and Hus in Bohemia.
For Soviet historians, their significance lay less in their religious than in
their social protest.[24]

While the Orthodox Church might often have failed in its humanitarian
and spiritual duties, it certainly continued to play an outstanding part in
the preservation and development of education, literature and the arts.
Commerce and, to a lesser extent, government would also play their part
in the maintenance and expansion of literacy, numeracy and learning, but
such schools and libraries as there were would almost exclusively be
found attached to the monasteries and churches. Orthodoxy also produced
not only works of spiritual uplift and admonition but more records of the
past as well, including the *Trinity Chronicle* destroyed by fire in 1812 but
skilfully reconstructed by Soviet scholars. Universal history as well as
national (both in a medieval sense) retained the interest of Russian clerics.

The outstanding artists of the period were Theophanes the Greek and
Andrei Rublev. Theophanes came from Byzantium to Novgorod in the
late fourteenth century, both teaching the style he brought with him and
assimilating that which he now encountered. He worked in Moscow and

Nizhnii Novgorod as well as in Novgorod. Among his collaborators was Andrei Rublev, who at the beginning of the fifteenth century, brought the art of icon-painting to a new level. His masterpiece is generally agreed to be the Old Testament *Trinity*, dedicated to St Sergius of Radonezh and now kept in the Tretiakov Gallery in Moscow. This charms Vernadsky with 'the serene quiet of the composition and the symphony of delicate colours'[25]; and an outstanding Soviet critic V. V. Lazarev writes: 'The wonderful compositional rhythm of the icon is enhanced by the colouring, which is musical beyond all words. Amity – such would be the most appropriate terms for the colour scheme of the icon, so clear, so lucid, so transparent; for it expresses with remarkable force the amity, the harmony among the three angels.'[26] Facing such a work, one can hardly doubt that inspirations to the eye and to the mind's eye continue to be the major achievement of early Moscow as of Kiev.

This is so even though stone building was interrupted for several years by the Mongol invasions. By the middle of the fifteenth century, however, both Novgorod and Moscow were adorned with great churches as well as with their Kremlins. Moscow, it is true, had to wait for its real architectural flowering until the reign of Ivan III. And as far as European parallels are concerned, while it is possible to talk of a Russian Romanesque and a Russian Renaissance style, the great Gothic achievement finds almost no expression except perhaps in the Novgorod Kremlin, where there was at least some help from 'Germans across the sea'.

A considerable amount of the cultural activity of the period under discussion was secular rather than religious in its emphasis. This remained the case with much of the folk culture, including the songs of the peasants, even though the Church attempted to adapt some of its music to the folk style. Outstanding among the creations of the time are the great epics or 'military tales' lamenting the calamities wrought by the Mongols or celebrating the great deeds of Alexander Nevsky or Dmitrii Donskoi. At the same time, a certain amount of artistic as well as technical improvement in the manufacture of the materials of war and peace can also be detected – for example, in the casting of cannon and the minting of money.[27]

Russia's culture, like her political, social and economic activity, was open, from 1240 to 1462, to influences from both Asia and Europe. Vernadsky and others have rendered great service in reminding us of the Mongol impact; and yet there can be little doubt that a white race with a Slavonic language and folklore, and a considerable involvement in the Orthodox variation of the Christian world-view, must be considered fundamentally as an outpost of the West even in the severest days of the 'Mongol yoke'. To an extent still much to be debated, the pace of Russia's development from about 1240 to 1462 was conditioned by her situation on the frontier of Europe.[28] Was her backwardness as much the responsibility of the Teutonic knights and the Hanseatic League as that of the successors of Chingis Khan?[29]

3 Consolidation under Moscow, 1462–1645

The period from the middle of the fifteenth century to the middle of the seventeenth century is known in the Western world as that of the formation of nation-states, of great geographical discoveries, of the Renaissance, Reformation and Counter-Reformation. Parallel developments occurring at the eastern extremities of the Western world clearly demonstrated that remoteness by no means constituted complete separation in this period any more than in its predecessors.

Under such powerful tsars as Ivan III or Great (1462–1505) and Ivan IV or Terrible (1533–84), the hold of Moscow was strengthened over much of Great Russia if by no means over the whole of the future Empire and Soviet Union. The government became somewhat better organised, and the armed forces acquitted themselves well enough against enemies to the east and west at times, although suffering painful reverses at others. Social stratification from the highest to the lowest level was more clearly demarcated, with both the service nobility and the enserfed peasantry taking on recognisable if still embryonic shape. As well as arousing the hostility of foreign powers, particularly its neighbours, of which Poland–Lithuania was the most formidable, Moscow also became the centre of diplomatic blandishments proferred by European states, from England to Venice, not to mention the contacts reinforced in Asia. In order to support such rising status, the economic resources of the state had to be exploited to the full, and even beyond. Activity both internal and external was directed whenever possible towards increasing the government's wealth, to the distress and even ruin of many of its subjects. Under the appalling strain, which was compounded by a dynastic crisis at the end of the sixteenth century, Moscow fell apart during the Time of Troubles. Boris Godunov (tsar from 1598 to 1605) was the most notable of a rapid series of rulers, several of whom were no more than puppets in the hands of the Poles and other invaders. Recovery only partly occurred by the end of the reign of the first Romanov, Mikhail or Michael (1613–45).

Meanwhile, landlocked as they were for the most part, Muscovites could not hope to make much of a contribution to the exciting sea voyages of discovery during the period, but found their nearest counterparts to Columbus and Drake in such freebooters as the Cossack Ermak.[1] His passage eastwards through Siberia was assisted by Ivan the Terrible's conquest of the Kazan Tatars, and the weakness of the remnants of the Golden Horde elsewhere. But Muscovites were not the only people to cast their aggressive eyes on areas vacated by the Mongols. Persia and Turkey between them managed to subjugate most of Central Asia and Transcaucasia, and increased their importance as rival claimants for the steppe. Diplomatic and other forms of contact in the vast, amorphous frontier areas continued to necessitate the crossing of cultural as well as political barriers.

Similarly, Russia could hardly fail to become more caught up in the cultural changes occurring in the Christian West as involvement in that direction grew more intense. Michael Cherniavsky has drawn an interesting portrait of Ivan the Terrible as Renaissance prince, and Soviet and post-Soviet historians have amplified the assertion of predecessors such as S. F. Platonov that neither the Reformation nor the Counter-Reformation left Russia untouched. Moreover, if the fall of Constantinople did not initiate the Western Renaissance, it soon served to strengthen Muscovite self-consciousness as the Orthodox Church claimed for itself the true Roman inheritance and the princes declared themselves to be Caesars or tsars. Ivan the Terrible addressed himself to Elizabeth of England in terms of by no means distant formality, while the first Romanovs set up amicable relations with the Stuarts in a similar manner. The majority of their subjects shared the tsars' view that Russian culture was more than the equal of its European counterparts, even if few of them actually looked outward.

Equally, the condescension of Western travellers to Muscovy (as the contemporary British called it) was often the result of a reciprocal insularity of viewpoint rather than of an objective estimation. For example, if Muscovy presented itself to an English visitor as a 'rude and barbarous kingdom',[2] the first ambassador to England from Ivan the Terrible could hardly have formed a more flattering picture after his shipwreck on the north-east coast of Scotland and his subsequent despoliation by, to use Hakluyt's words, 'the rude and ravenous people of the country thereunto adjoining'.[3] The problems of cultural relativity that always confront the historian using travellers' accounts as sources are compounded in the

Muscovite instance by the circumstance that they are often of outstanding importance owing to the scarcity of sources in general, largely the consequence of fires destroying vast amounts of documents.[4] Uncritical use of the travellers' accounts by historians of Russia has led to some fanciful hypotheses. From *critical* use of them and other extant sources, however, historians have been able to extract convincing interpretations of governmental policies and interesting portraits of the tsars themselves.

Ivan III stands in relation to Ivan IV rather as Henry VII of England stands in relation to Henry VIII, at least as far as popular conceptions are concerned. Ivan the Great comes over as a somewhat colourless but determined figure, while Ivan the Terrible exhibits not only a peculiar kind of flamboyance but also a taste for multiple matrimony. In fact, not a great amount is known about Ivan the Great, although some anecdotes about him from a near contemporary Habsburg emissary, Von Herberstein, indicate the sardonic bonhomie usually associated with Ivan the Terrible or Peter the Great. For example, Von Herberstein reports that 'he generally drank so excessively at dinner as to fall asleep, and while his guests were all struck with terror and sitting in silence, he would awake, rub his eyes and then first begin to joke and make merry with them'.[5] Ivan the Great's harsh treatment of all those who stood in the path of final unification would more than adequately explain the terror of his dinner guests. And yet, as Michael Cherniavsky argues in his discussion of Ivan the Terrible, tsarist cruelty in the sixteenth century was by no means wholly gratuitous and was usually tempered by at least a crude sense of justice. Referring to a wide range of sources including Machiavelli on this point, Cherniavsky cites the argument of a Soviet historian concerning Tsepesh of Wallachia, the original Dracula, to the effect that 'the ambivalent image of cruelty and justice was in response to men's hopes that in an age of many small feudal dragons, one great dragon would provide justice and peace'.[6]

Kliuchevskii considered Ivan the Terrible to be 'a remarkable writer, even perhaps a bold political thinker, but he was not a statesman'. He was more 'like a blind knight of old who, to kill his enemy, brought down upon himself the house on the roof of which they were sitting'.[7] On the other hand, the normal translation of his byname is unfortunate, since *groznyi* means less horrible than awe-inspiring. Many of the English and other visitors who described him made frequent reference to his warmth and charm, while Soviet pathologists who have examined his exhumed skeleton have argued that his apparent insane sadism might well have been less the result of an unhinged mind than of a diseased spine. Boris Godunov has also suffered somewhat from the image projected abroad, Mussorgsky's operatic adaptation of Pushkin's verse drama being far from completely fair. In Kliuchevskii's estimation, 'On the throne Boris proved as wise and cautious an administrator as he had shown himself to be when standing beside it.' As for Michael Romanov, Florinsky describes him as 'an ailing, self-effacing and docile young man ... only too anxious to let others govern in his name'.[8] While Boris has sometimes received too bad a press from historians, Michael has often been given by them one that is too good.

The principal subject of this chapter, the process of consolidation, is inextricably connected with the tsars just described and with others lesser known, and with the all-conquering principality of Moscow. Yet we must also recall that the period from the middle of the fifteenth to the middle of the seventeenth centuries, during which the term 'Russia' as well as 'Russian land' and 'Russian state' come to be used, is of comparable significance for other European nations too.

Political

The history of the period from 1462 to 1645 falls into four main sections comparable in significance if not in chronological length: the reign of Ivan III; the reign of Ivan IV; the Time of Troubles; and the reign of Michael Romanov.

By the accession of Ivan III in 1462, Moscow had become the political as well as the religious centre of the Russian lands. A considerable amount of ingathering remained to be accomplished, however, before the process of the consolidation of the Muscovite state became complete. Ivan III's reign marks 'an important stage' in this process, according to Soviet historians who on this point are in agreement with Kliuchevskii that 'The great Russia in process of formation gave birth to the idea of a national state, but did not place limits on it'.[9]

To take the political foundations of that state first, the Boyar Duma was transformed from an advisory organisation into a more formal supreme council attended by the greatest princes and aristocrats. Arguably, this 'oligarchic cast of the duma membership intimates that the Grand Prince succumbed to pressures benefiting a number of select families. The price was minimal, for he derived inestimable gain from long years of loyal service by the many members of these families who vied for appointments and competed for promotion.'[10] The price was not raised by the circumstance that Ivan was obliged to pursue policies broadly acceptable to the boyars and the nobility as a whole, if not to dissident or centrifugal individuals among them, since the interests of the Grand Prince and of his chief servants basically converged. While most important problems were considered by Ivan presiding over the Duma, a larger body was summoned for such supreme matters of state as his own testament or war and peace. Consisting of the Boyar Duma and the Holy Conclave of the Church, and sometimes of lower-ranking members of the nobility, too, this occasional assembly was the forerunner of the *Zemskii Sobor*, or Assembly of the Whole Land, which was to be convened in the sixteenth century. The executive functions of the central government began to be carried on by departments known as *prikazy*, while local government was continued on the basis of the *kormlenie* or 'feeding' system, by which lucrative offices were farmed out to favourites. An attempt at a uniform judicial system for central and local government was made by the *Sudebnik* of 1497, a code of laws applying for the first time to the whole of Muscovy.

These organisational and procedural changes both reflected and initiated notable socio-political adjustments. The Muscovite aristocracy and nobility, along with the leading members of the commercial class, for the most part gave their support to the Grand Prince, but some princes and boyars from the centre as well as the periphery were disaffected as their old liberties and privileges yielded before the process of centralisation. In order to regulate clashes between the various families and clans, the system of appointment to places known as *mestnichestvo* received something like its final form during the reign of Ivan III. At the same time, *mestnichestvo* received further encouragement from the tendency for more than half of the personnel of the Boyar Duma to become 'more deeply involved in ceremonial and administrative affairs'. In other words, the bureaucratisation of the nobility discerned by historians of contemporaneous Western European states was a phenomenon of late medieval Russia, too.[11]

For this to be so, the Russian monarch, like his brethren elsewhere, had to demonstrate a new confidence in the authority of his own government. As Ferdinand and Isabella were putting together Spain, Charles VIII was consolidating France, Henry VII asserting control over England, and Maximilian I extending, possibly over-extending, the control of the Habsburgs over much of central Europe in the Holy Roman Empire, Ivan III was celebrating his own comparable performance by assuming the title of Tsar (or Caesar). This title was derived from the first Rome by way of the second, Byzantium, the niece of the last emperor of which became Ivan's second wife in 1472. Furthermore, Ivan adapted Byzantine ritual for his own court, and took the double-headed eagle of the Palaeologoi to accompany the Kievan St George as a royal coat-of-arms.[12] The Church assisted the formation of tsarist self-confidence through the following years with its development of formal coronation, elaboration of saintly contributions to Russian history and promulgation of Moscow as the Third Rome. These innovations by no means met with universal acceptance, but it was a measure of the tsars' power that they could not be long withstood.

The principal physical extension of Ivan III's power in particular was through his continuation of the process of the ingathering of the Russian lands, a prerequisite for the more final subjugation of the Tatars. Unification still involved questions of foreign as well as of domestic policy, since the state remained somewhat amorphous. For example, in a bid to preserve the optimum measure of independence, Novgorod attempted in 1470 to exchange vassalage to Moscow for that to Poland and Lithuania. In the following year Ivan III conducted a successful campaign against Novgorod which compelled the great city to reaffirm its former oath and to sever all foreign political connections. Further factional fighting in Novgorod brought about another campaign against it in 1478, and within a year Ivan fulfilled his threat to silence the *veche* bell forever, even if its echoes were to linger on. The fall of Novgorod made the position of other principalities more precarious, and several of them, notably Tver, succumbed in the following years, those which retained any measure of independence doing so only on the sufferance of Moscow. Tension with Poland and Lithuania, heightened by the defection to Moscow of a considerable number of members of the Polish – Lithuanian nobility, led to the outbreak of a series of wars. At the peace arranged in 1503, the successes of Russian arms were marked by the recognition of Russian control over large areas to the west and south. In the same years, a treaty with the Livonian order marked the acceptance of Muscovy's right to conduct trade with the West.

Lands acquired during the ingathering process, especially from Novgorod, were distributed among the adherents of the tsar on the basis of conditional service tenure. In such a manner, both the loyalty of the new regions and the maintenance of the army were to be guaranteed.

The victories of the army during the reign of Ivan III indicated that Moscow was not particularly backward at this time from the military point of view: for example, Russia adopted the bronze cannon and the iron cannon ball almost as soon as other European states. Foreign craftsmen, including Germans, Italians and Scots, assisted in this adoption, and some of them contributed towards the necessary modification of fortresses, including the Moscow Kremlin. But artillery was still of secondary importance, for siege and pitched warfare had yet to reach the eastern extremity of Europe, where the peculiar qualities of the steppe made mobility a primary consideration.[13]

Under Ivan III, the Russians demonstrated that they had mastered the art of fighting on the steppe. With Ivan's position strengthened by the reduction of the principalities and the Golden Horde disintegrating into mutually hostile khanates, the time was ripe for the final removal of the 'Tatar yoke'. When Khan Akhmed attempted to reunite the Golden Horde and reimpose its yoke in 1480 with the encouragement of the Poles and Lithuanians, Ivan allied with the Crimean Tatars who kept the Poles and Lithuanians busy while he himself concentrated on turning back Akhmed from Moscow. The khan was killed during his retreat in the internecine conflict, and the Golden Horde soon fell apart completely. Meanwhile, Ivan was able to force Kazan to make obeisance to Moscow, and to continue his drive into Siberia, incorporating into his state a number of tribes as far over as the Ob River and the Northern Sea. Expansion to the south could not be taken to the Black Sea, since the Crimean Tatars became disillusioned by Ivan's exploitation of them and turned to Turkey for protection.

The unification and expansion of Russia were sufficient by the end of the reign to have brought her to the closer attention of other European states. Contact with Venice, Genoa, Naples and the Papacy was increased, as well as with governments nearer home in central Europe. Relations were also developed with the Orient, both the easily accessible and the remote.

During the reign of Vasilii III (1505–33), existing foreign and domestic policies were continued, the Holy Roman Empire and India being added to the number of diplomatic contacts. The fundamental ingathering of the Great Russian lands was brought to a successful conclusion after the principalities of Pskov and Riazan had been incorporated in 1510 and 1521 respectively, and a war with Lithuania from 1512 to 1522 had resulted in the acquisition of Smolensk. Expansion to the east was less to be embarked upon, for in 1521 the khan of the Crimean Tatars engineered the downfall of the pro-Muscovite khan of Kazan, and then, with the support of Lithuania, brought both hordes into an attack on Moscow, devastating large areas as he did so. Disaster threatened as several princes conspired with the enemy to attempt the separation of their lands from Muscovy. Vasilii stifled the conspiracy, but discontent lingered on in the higher circles of the aristocracy, particularly after the tsar divorced his first wife, a daughter of an old boyar family, in 1525, on the grounds that she was incapable of bearing him children. Before the discontent was stilled, Vasilii died suddenly in 1533, instructing his second wife Elena to institute her regency along with the Boyar Duma until their son Ivan attained his majority.

In 1534 Elena assumed power for herself, aided and abetted first by her uncle and then by her lover. Elena and her associates soon found themselves assailed from all quarters, by the Tatars and Lithuanians from without, by dissident boyars and hard-pressed peasants from within. A revolt in 1537 by the inhabitants of Moscow on behalf of the claims to the throne of a younger brother of Vasilii III was crushed, but then in 1538 Elena died as suddenly as had her husband, probably poisoned by the boyars. Three groups of them, the Shuiskiis, Glinskiis and the Belskiis, now struggled for power in a ding-dong manner, each in turn sharing out the spoils among their followers and making some attempt to secure the support of other social strata such as the service nobles. The attempt was in vain for by 1547 a sufficient number of service nobles had joined with a quorum of boyars to promote the cause of the Grand Prince. Ivan's coronation as tsar in January of that year, followed by his marriage to his first wife Anastasia in February, is usually said to mark the beginning of the independent reign of Ivan the Terrible, although he had already demonstrated a precocious independence, notably in his instigation of the assassination of one of the Shuiskii princes in 1543.

The reign continued according to a pattern already well established, in violence. The summer of 1547 brought the greatest town revolt of the sixteenth century as a resurgence of popular dissatisfaction was intensified by a severe drought followed by a 'Great Fire'. Ivan fled from the capital as his mother's kinsmen, who were his own advisers, were blamed for the 'Great Fire' and made the chief object of the crowd's attack. Flames both real and metaphorical arose throughout Moscow.

Regaining a grasp on the situation after one of his many bouts of religious melancholia and a public confession of his sins, Ivan moved towards reform with the advice and support of a different entourage, the 'chosen council'. This was a confidential circle of advisers including Metropolitan Makarii, the tsar's tutor, Father Silvestr, the tsar's confessor, and Aleksei Adashev, one of his boyhood friends, along with his wife's relations, the Zakharin family.[14]

At the beginning of 1549, new policies were announced by Ivan himself, first to the Boyar Duma and Holy Conclave in joint session, and then to officials and nobles summoned to Moscow for what appears to have been the first *Zemskii Sobor*, or Assembly of the Whole Land. In his declaration, Ivan preached and promised social peace and the restoration of law. Practical steps towards such an end were taken later in the same year with decrees regulating relations between the various strata of the ruling class and the commencement of preparation of a new code of laws or *Sudebnik* to replace that of 1497. Promulgated in 1550 and approved by a *Zemskii*

Sobor, the *Sudebnik* attempted to bring further stability into relations not only between the individuals and groups who composed the ruling class, but also between the class as a whole and the peasantry, whose legal freedoms became restricted. At the same time, the *Sudebnik* gave heavier emphasis to the power of the *prikazy* of the central administration and reduced the power and influence of the leading officials in local government. The former steps were carried out in conjunction with a further extension and bureaucratisation of the Boyar Duma, while the latter move may generally be seen not only as part of the completion of the unification process, but also as a reflection of the government's awareness of the wastefulness of the *kormlenie* or 'feeding' system by which officials lived off the provincial population, at a time when the meagre resources of the country had yet again to be exploited for the purpose of making war.

The national resolve strengthened by a reform in the Church, which we will examine later, the government soon moved towards more down-to-earth military preparation with a sweeping army reform. The Service Regulations of 1556 encouraged the merger of hereditary and service land tenure and thus furthered the tendency for all members of the upper class to serve in return for estate ownership. The contribution in men, horses and material was more precisely fixed according to estate size. At about the same time, Ivan organised a new standing force of *streltsy* (musketeers) to carry out police duties as well as to supplement the irregular levies. As the structure of the army was remoulded, its strategy was adapted too, with more emphasis being given to the fortified line and to the artillery, which was now supported by an arms industry not greatly inferior to that of many European states. Although by no means invincible, the Russian army enjoyed a number of considerable successes during the 1550s.[15]

The most important and permanent of these were to the east, and included the final reduction of the khanates of Kazan and Astrakhan, as well as the extension of Russian control over the Middle and Lower Volga regions. Despite a flank attack from the Crimean Tatars urged on by the Turks, the Russian forces were able to lay a carefully prepared siege to the town of Kazan in 1552, bombarding and starving the citadel into submission. Soon afterwards, the fertile lands of the Volga and its many peoples – including the Chuvashes and Bashkirs as well as Tatars – were obliged to pledge their loyalty to the tsar, and the town of Astrakhan at the mouth of the Volga fell in 1556. Although the Tatars had now been neutralised on the eastern flank from Kazan to the Caspian Sea, their brethren in the Crimea Khanate remained an irritating thorn in Moscow's southern side.

War to the west broke out in 1558. The ostensible reason was Livonia's non-fulfilment of the obligations of its treaty with Ivan III and the underlying cause was the problem of Moscow's access to the Baltic Sea. Initial Russian success meant a setback for both the Livonian Order and its Polish and Lithuanian allies. However, Russian acquisitions of the important port of Narva and other footholds on the Baltic provoked the alarm of Western European states as well as of those near the littoral. Poland and Lithuania, formally brought together by the Union of Liublin in 1569, worked with Sweden and Denmark throughout the 1560s at pushing the Muscovite forces back in the Baltic region. The English, while solidifying their access to Moscow via the Northern Cape route (first accidentally discovered by Richard Chancellor in 1553 while searching for the North-East Passage to the Indies), held back from full alliance.

With some, if by no means total, justification, Ivan the Terrible blamed the reverses of the 1560s on the opposition to the war of many boyars and the defection of Prince Andrei Kurbskii, who had been prominent in the siege of Kazan and then commander of the Baltic army. The tsar decided that the moment had come for a new internal policy involving a break with the boyars and even with his erstwhile close advisers. Suspecting Silvestr and Adashev of implication in a plot to poison his first wife Anastasia Zakharina, who died suddenly in 1560 never to be adequately replaced by her six successors, he banished them. Metropolitan Makarii died in 1564, by which time the Zakharin family was losing its favour and Ivan therefore losing the last of his nearest entourage. After striking out, not for the first time, at suspected boyar opposition, Ivan decided at the end of 1564 to go into a seclusion that threatened to become monastic. Having in such a dramatic manner blackmailed people of all classes to petition for his return – an episode most graphically if not accurately represented in Eisenstein's famous film, *Ivan the Terrible* – he then persuaded them to confirm his introduction of the *oprichnina* (or lands apart).

According to the traditional interpretation, this notorious institution divided the whole country into two halves – the *oprichnina* and the *zemshchina* (or national lands) – even the town of Moscow itself being split in this manner. Some of the boyars and service nobles were incorporated into the administration of the *oprichnina*: the rest were put into the *zemshchina* supposedly administered under the tsar by the *Zemskii Sobor*, which was convened in 1566 to give its support to the prosecution of the Livonian War. Opposition expressed there and elsewhere to the *oprichnina* decided Ivan in favour of an intensification of his peculiar institution and the introduction of terror. From 1566 to 1572, the black-cloaked *oprichniki* rode amok throughout the land, their 'gnawing' and 'sweeping' symbolised by the dog's head and broom fixed to the saddles of their black horses. Ivan himself participated in the tortures and executions, the rapes and orgies, alternating such bouts of sadism with contrite hangovers of sackcloth and ashes. Yet for all its horrific drama, the body count of the *oprichnina* must not be exaggerated. The leading authority on the subject, R. G. Skrynnikov, has calculated that one of the most notorious incidents, the sack of Novgorod, accounted for 2700–2800 lives and that the *oprichnina* as a whole for no more than double that number. On the other hand, quantity is not everything, and Skrynnikov also considers that the demoralization accompanying Ivan's terror could be compared with that of the 'Mongol yoke'.[16]

With most of the opposition – aristocratic, ecclesiastical and commoner – both real and imagined, having been purged by the beginning of the 1570s, and with the whole country threatened by Crimean Tatar incursions culminating in the ravage of Moscow itself, and by the renewal of the Livonian War, not to mention harvest failure, famine and plague, Ivan decided in late 1572 to bring the *oprichnina* to an end, strictly prohibiting any future mention of the term itself. A united army had by this time pushed back the Tatars from Moscow, but the Livonian War proved to be a much stiffer proposition. Although the Russian army met with some successes in the 1570s and early 1580s, these were more than outweighed by the reverses suffered, particularly when the forces of Poland – Lithuania and Sweden engaged them on two fronts. Treaties of the early 1580s resulted in a net loss of territory for Russia. A high price, both economic and social, had been paid for small returns. Nevertheless, Soviet historians argued that the Livonian War was by no means completely negative in its effect from the Russian point of view: the Livonian Order had been crushed; and the way ahead was cleared for Ivan's successors, culminating in Peter the Great.[17]

Although the *oprichnina* was over, Ivan's behaviour in the last decade or so of his reign did not lose its apparent eccentricities. In 1575, he not only resumed executions, but put on the throne for a short time a converted Tatar prince, Simeon Bekbulatovich. And then in 1581, either accidentally or on purpose, he killed his son Ivan during a quarrel. According to some interpretations, this last incident, added to the bloody experiences of his youth and adulthood and the death of his first and favourite wife Anastasia, took him over the brink into a painful madness from which he had not recovered by his death in 1584.

Both the personality of Ivan the Terrible and the significance of his reign continue to arouse a lively debate. Possibly, the one is best seen as the reflection of the other. Thus, the 'madness' of Ivan is to be looked upon as an indicator of the great difficulty of putting Muscovite absolutism upon a certain foundation at a time when the symptoms of dissolution which were to show themselves clearly in the Time of Troubles were already more than dimly apparent. He himself appears to have been often convinced of the insuperability of the obstacles in his path, revealing his despair, either in suggestions to Elizabeth of England for mutual asylum or in his bouts of religious melancholia and bloody sadism. However, as has already been pointed out, at least part of Ivan's passive and active frenzy might have been caused by a painful disease of the spine. Moreover, as Cherniavsky has argued, there may have been more than a little Machiavellian method in Ivan's madness. An extreme and influential version of such an interpretation was put by J. V. Stalin to the actor N. K. Cherkasov (who took the part of Ivan in Eisenstein's film). Cherkasov reported the Soviet leader as saying not only that the *oprichnina* played a 'progressive role', but also that Ivan's greatest error was not to have taken his purges far enough, an omission which led to the Time of Troubles.[18]

Subsequent discussion has at least demonstrated the limitations of any too clear-cut distinction between the interests of the boyars and other upper-ranking nobles on the one hand and those of the service nobility at large on the other. At the same time, the confluence of noble interests as opposed to those of the peasants has been vigorously propounded. Examining the reign in a wider focus, some historians have attempted to compare the Russian type of absolutism with that of other European states. While much work remains to be done in this very difficult area, and while it is already apparent that there are significant specific differences as well as similarities between, say the *Zemskii Sobor* and its European counterparts, there can nevertheless be little doubt that the process of the formation of states throughout the continent conforms to a basic general pattern.[19]

Fedor Ivanovich, or Theodore (1584–98), was not very strong either physically or mentally and left most of the business of government to his advisers, particularly to his brother-in-law, the boyar Boris Godunov. Apart from some important economic and ecclesiastical developments, which will be considered below, the reign was primarily significant for its wars and for its expansion of the national territories.

Peace was maintained with Poland so that the Russian army in the west could be directed principally against Sweden. Between 1590 and 1595, the foothold on the Baltic was regained, although Narva was not. As Russia's international prestige was raised by the establishment of a Russian Patriarchate in 1589, diplomatic contacts were being broadened with western and central European countries. To the south, the Crimean Tatars were pushed back and Russian control was extended as far as the Caucasus, a protective alliance being arranged with Transcaucasian Georgia in 1587.

Even greater penetration was achieved to the east. A Cossack party under the patronage of the commercial Stroganov family and the swashbuckling leadership of Ermak had already succeeded by 1582 in reducing the Tatars of Western Siberia through a combination of bravado and firearms. Although Ermak himself was killed in 1585, both the Stroganovs and the government continued to send expeditions to the region, confirming the Russian hold on it. Yet Western Siberia was looked upon as an outpost of the nation rather than as a constituent part of it; by the end of the sixteenth century, Moscow was composed essentially of five parts, two inner and three outer. At the centre were the regions surrounding the towns of Moscow and Novgorod. To the north, there was the seaboard and its hinterland, to the south-east the Middle and Lower Volga, while to the south there was the steppe. This basic structure was still in a condition too new and incomplete to be firmly established when it was struck by the catastrophe of the Time of Troubles.

In his *Of the Russe Commonwealth*, published in London in 1591, Giles Fletcher had predicted that the 'wicked and tyrannous practice' of the *oprichnina* had filled the country 'so full of grudge and mortal hatred ever since, that it will not be quenched (as it seemeth now) till it burn into a civil flame', and that the military despotism of the tsar and his entourage 'maketh the people for the most part to wish for some foreign invasion, which they suppose to be the only means to rid them of the heavy yoke of this tyrannous government'.[20] Both the 'civil flame' and the 'foreign invasion' were to strike Moscow more severely than anybody could have predicted or feared in the fifteen years following the death of Fedor Ivanovich in 1598. Not that the *oprichnina* and tsarist tyranny were wholly to blame; the reasons for the Time of Troubles can clearly and comprehensively be seen in the nature of the three stages into which the great historian Platonov divided it.[21] Firstly, from 1598 to 1606, there was dynastic confusion, as the Godunovs, Shuiskiis and Romanovs bickered among themselves for the succession along with the first 'False Dmitrii'. Secondly, from 1606 to 1610, there was social struggle, as the Cossacks became the focus of the discontent of the lower classes against a background of further impersonation of the Tsarevich Dmitrii. And thirdly, from 1611 to 1613, there was the fight for nationhood, as foreign intervention, notably from Sweden and Poland-Lithuania, brought about a suppression of personal and collective rivalries in a flush of nationalism concentrated to drive the alien from the Russian soil. Such nationalism was far from ignored by

Soviet historians, who nevertheless gave more emphasis than did Platonov to the social struggle.

After a *Zemskii Sobor* had elected him tsar in 1598, Boris Godunov found it more difficult to rule in his own right than to rule in fact behind the legal façade of the tsardom of Fedor Ivanovich, the last of the line. Although Boris almost certainly had not instigated the murder of Fedor's step-brother, Dmitrii Ivanovich, the ghost of the tsarevich rose up to torment him metaphorically if not literally. For at the beginning of the seventeenth century, the news spread that the young son of Ivan the Terrible had been spared, and had appealed to the Polish nobility and King Sigismund himself for support in gaining his rightful inheritance. With the connivance if not the active assistance of Sigismund and the fervent encouragement of the Jesuits, groups among the Polish nobility canvassed the candidacy of the first 'False Dmitrii' and prepared for invasion as the rumour became disseminated among the ranks of the Cossacks and the peasantry. In the spring of 1605, Boris Godunov died unexpectedly, perhaps through self-administered poison, and the boyars took the army over to the side of the pretender and his sponsors. In June, after Godunov's wife and son had been murdered by the boyars, the invading forces entered Moscow in triumphant procession. In order to secure his position, however, 'False Dmitrii' had to make concessions to the desire of his protectors for the acquisition of land and the spread of their faith. The xenophobia of the Russians was inflamed to fever pitch during the pre-parations in Spring 1606 for the pretender's marriage to the daughter of a Polish landowner, thousands of Poles coming to Moscow and beginning a round of celebrations which arrogantly flouted local custom and prejudice. And so without great difficulty, Vasilii Shuiskii was able to rise above Romanov and other rivals to lead both boyars and people against the heathen. 'False Dmitrii' was killed, the Poles were driven out, and Shuiskii had himself declared tsar by a 'popular acclamation' specially arranged in Red Square.

The Cossacks and other provincial dwellers who had been excited by their ideal vision of the Tsarevich Dmitrii and had not seen the sordid reality of the Polish occupation of Moscow were alarmed by the news of the accession of Shuiskii, whom they rightly suspected of promoting poli-cies to the principal benefit of his fellow boyars. It was not long before a new and more powerful wave of discontent was swollen into a revolt great enough for Soviet historians to have deemed it the first in a series of 'peasant wars'. Led by Ivan Bolotnikov, a courageous shrewd and well-travelled Cossack, the insurgents were joined by several members of the nobility, and a formidable force moved from the Ukraine towards Moscow, gathering supporters en route. However, as the capital was laid to siege and the peasant war spread throughout the whole country, the ideological weaknesses of the movement became apparent, particularly its 'naive monarchism'. Many nobles defected to Shuiskii, who also gathered support from the west and north, and the 'boyar tsar' was able to inflict a cruel and crushing defeat on Bolotnikov and his forces by the autumn of 1607. At his surrender, a promise was given to Bolotnikov that his life would be spared, but, after he had been exiled to the north, he was first blinded and then drowned. Meanwhile, a section of the Polish nobility had finally succeeded in finding a second 'False Dmitrii', and laid siege to Moscow from the summer of 1608 onwards, gaining support from various sections of the Russian community. In desperation, Shuiskii appealed to the Swedes to intervene on his behalf. The raising of the siege and the death of the second 'False Dmitrii' angered Sigismund of Poland, who sent his own troops to assist those of the Polish nobility. As the Poles threatened Moscow again, the boyars ousted Shuiskii as a sop to the lower orders and concluded an agreement to put the Polish king's son on the throne in his place. And so the second phase of the Time of Troubles came to an end with the Poles in occupation of Moscow and several others towns, while the Swedish presence was also being fully felt.

Although several attempts were being made to drive out the invaders, the national fortunes had fallen to their lowest ebb by the summer of 1611. But then a new popular force was formed at Nizhnii Novgorod at the instigation of a town elder, Kuzma Minin, and under the leadership of Prince Dmitrii Pozharskii. A renewed attack on Moscow, succeeded by the autumn of 1612 in partly fighting, partly starving the Polish invaders into submission. And then at the beginning of 1613, in a turbulent atmosphere full of factional squabbling and the threat of more pretenders, a *Zemskii Sobor* elected as tsar a young member of an old boyar family, Mikhail Fedorovich Romanov. With their unity still sufficiently intact, the national forces were able to pursue the task of driving the foreigners from the Russian land. By 1617, the Stolbovo Treaty brought peace with the Swedes who gave up Novgorod, but maintained their control of the coastal regions and thus cut Moscow off from the Baltic. In 1618 the armistice of Deulino with the Poles, which was to last for fourteen years, involved their more complete withdrawal. In other words, the principal aim of the national resurgence had been imperfectly achieved to the north-west and west, but the new dynasty could now turn its attention to the maintenance of domestic stability in a difficult but no longer desperate situation.

In 1613 Tsar Michael was sixteen years old, in poor health and of by no means strong character. These very inadequacies assisted his election, according to Platonov, who saw him as 'the single figure around whom both sides of the still not finally reconciled segments of Muscovite society – the service class of the countryside and the Cossacks – could unite'.[22] The early years were by no means easy for 'Romanov the Cossack Tsar' as disgruntled opponents called him, but centrifugal social forces had been weakened by the Time of Troubles and the spirit of united nationalism continued to reveal itself in the buttress of Michael's power constituted by the *Zemskii Sobor*. Great personal strength accrued to Michael in 1619 with the return from Polish exile of his father: a former aspirant to the throne now monasticised, the Patriarch Filaret became virtual ruler of Moscow until his death in 1633, while sharing the title of 'Great Sovereign'.

Filaret exercised strong control over all parts of the administration and worked against what he saw as dangerous innovations. In the words of John Keep, 'Filaret was a medieval figure, for whom stability was the *summum bonum*. He idealised the past and saw himself not as a reformer but as a restorer.'[23] And so the *prikaz* apparatus of the central government was maintained as much as possible, although in local government, a new leading representative of the tsar's power, the *voevoda*, had to be introduced. At the same time, Filaret made minimal use of the Boyar Duma and the *Zemskii Sobor*, depending for his social support on the leaders of the army, who came mostly from the service nobility.

As the national resources were put into strengthening and modernising the army, with the restoration of Moscow's armaments and munitions industry and increased use of foreign mercenaries, attention could now be given to the major tasks of foreign policy. Filaret's main aim was to revive the struggle against Poland for Smolensk and other western lands; significant secondary purposes were to make secure the southern steppe frontier and to extend Russian interests elsewhere in Europe and Asia. In 1632 the fourteen-year armistice of Deulino came to an end, and war broke out with Poland, Smolensk being the main bone of contention. Peace was arranged in 1634 (after the death of Filaret) through the Treaty of Polianovka, by which Poland retained Smolensk. Meanwhile, much effort was being expended on the construction of the Belgorod fortified line to keep out the Tatars and to keep in peasants tempted to run away to join the Cossacks. In 1637 the Don Cossacks took the Turkish fortress on the sea of Azov, but the government had no desire to become embroiled in a war with Turkey and so encouraged the Cossacks to withdraw. At the same time as preparing for war with Poland, Filaret had attempted to weaken her through support of Sweden. Encouragement and subsidies were given to the Swedish King Gustavus Adolphus to consolidate his move into the German lands and thus to arouse Polish fears of a partial Swedish encirclement. The Soviet historian Boris Porshnev forcefully argued that relations between East and West Europe were more active then has often been assumed in the period of the Thirty Years' War (1618–1648). As he pointed out, Russian diplomats entered into negotiations for a Pan-Christian anti-Turkish crusade, and maintained a close interest in developments throughout Europe and Asia. For example, at the death of Michael in 1645, the government was watching as closely as possible the intensification of the English Revolution.[24]

Economic

By the mid-seventeenth century, the Russian population numbered about ten million people, with the urban population totalling just over half a million. In other words, the demographic situation had not radically changed since the end of the thirteenth century, even though the Russian lands had increased enormously in size. Such an assertion, however, must be strongly qualified. In the first place, the figures remain the broadest of approximations calculated on the basis of inadequate data. Secondly, natural disasters such as famine and epidemics and man-made reductions such as wars often meant a decline in population for which there would have to be a compensating rise. Thirdly, on no account should these figures be taken to suggest that the economic picture as a whole was unchanging.[25] In fact, as well as witnessing important political and social adjustments, the two centuries before the mid-seventeenth century also saw significant developments in agriculture and commerce; indeed, to Soviet historians especially, these developments were an indispensable accompaniment to the whole process of consolidation under Moscow.

Agriculture was still the predominant way of life for the vast majority of the Russian people. While the technical level of farming does not appear to have risen significantly, its organisation went through a considerable alteration as many of the large estates of the old boyar aristocracy were broken up and given to the embryonic new service nobility, the *dvorianstvo*. Students of English history will be familiar with the problems associated with the investigation of 'the rise of the gentry', however, and will therefore be reluctant to accept without good evidence the assertion of such a transformation of the pattern of noble, and of peasant, landholding.

These processes are inextricably connected with the process of the enserfment of the peasantry which was taking place throughout the period of Muscovite consolidation. Not only the peasants attached to the noble landlords, but also those dependent on the Church or the court, found their right of transfer restricted more and more. For example, the *Sudebnik* or code of laws of 1497 finalised a tendency that had been spreading for some time in its general restriction of peasant movement to the week before and after St George's Day. At the same time, and continuing later, the two basic systems of the exploitation of the peasantry, the labour *barschchina* and the rent *obrok*, were being intensified, with payments in money rather than in kind becoming a more widespread form of *obrok*.

The adoption by the *dvorianstvo* of the newly acquired lands of Novgorod and elsewhere coincided with the spread of a new form of tenure, the service *pomeste*, in place of the former hereditary *votchina*. In such a manner the socio-political and economic aims of the consolidating government could be more fully realised, as well as those of the *dvorianstvo*. Meanwhile, at the old centre of Moscow, at least some of the great estates, both secular and ecclesiastical, remained relatively unscathed. With the defeat of Kazan and the penetration into Siberia, the state acquired a vast amount of largely unpopulated territory, into only a small part of which, notably along the Volga, new noble landlords had introduced their system of farming by the middle of the seventeenth century. Many peasants in the North also remained unattached.

During the two centuries under discussion, the commercial life of Moscow took on a different shape, both internally and internationally. From the sixteenth century onwards, industry began clearly to separate from agriculture. The extraction and processing of metals, particularly iron, and the manufacture of pottery, textiles, wooden and leather goods, all became more subject to specialisation, even though many peasants at the same time still aimed at subsistence. Separate areas in the towns were set aside for craftsmen and for traders. The latter found themselves not only dealing in the wares of their neighbours, but also travelling to other towns to buy and sell there as well. Regions as well as individuals became involved in specialisation, for example, flax and hemp becoming a prime concern for the north-west towns of Novgorod, Pskov and Smolensk, while grain occupied much of the attention of the towns along the Volga. Tula was an early centre for the iron industry. Moscow itself was the focal point of the internal trade, although it is still too early to talk of a national unified market.

It is certainly not too early to talk of an extended international trade, both to west and east. While access to the Black Sea was interrupted after the fall of Constantinople in 1453 and to the Baltic with the rise of Sweden at the end of the sixteenth century, the curtailment of Russia's trade with the rest of Europe was neither severe nor permanent. Regular trade with England was established after Richard Chancellor, in an attempt to find the North-East Passage to India with the encouragement and advice of Sebastian Cabot, came to the White Sea and then to Moscow in 1553. The Russia Company was chartered in the following year to follow up and exploit the contacts made by Chancellor. The Dutch as well as the English were keen to develop commercial relations with Moscow during the next hundred years, and in the seventeenth century surpassed their rivals. Russia's principal exports to the West continued to be such items as furs and leather, wax, tallow, flax and hemp, increasingly supplemented by naval stores, with weapons and luxury goods prominent among the imports.

Luxury goods – silks, spices and jewels – were still among the important imports from the East, with Russian exports in that direction following the pattern of those westwards to some extent but including a higher proportion of manufactured goods. Sometimes, the Tatars interfered with the oriental trade, but they could mediate sometimes, too. Russian merchants penetrated deep into Asia and Asia Minor, one of them, Afanasii Nikitin, making a journey to India more than twenty years before the more celebrated voyage there from Portugal of Vasco da Gama.

Involved as it was both through trade and war with powerful neighbours such as Turkey, Poland and Sweden, Muscovite Russia found it necessary to devote a large amount of its energy to building up the strength to be able to coexist with them. At the end of the sixteenth century and beginning of the seventeenth, as we have seen, the attempt became almost too demanding, and the nascent state came near to falling apart in the Time of Troubles. Even at more settled times, there could be little relaxation or lowering of the guard, and before the official introduction of serfdom in its complete form, the peasants who constituted the vast majority of its scanty population were very conscious of the taxation and service demands made upon them by their immediate landlords and by the more remote government. Their task was made all the harder by Russia's involvement in European monetary and other economic fluctuations of the sixteenth and seventeenth centuries.[26]

Cultural

As Moscow was completing the unification of Russia, regional divergences from the national norm were already under threat. So were some of the bequests from the past. For example, the Orthodox faith which was superimposed upon pagan belief now found itself challenged by the spirit of the Renaissance, Reformation and Counter-Reformation. But all these movements were weaker at the eastern extremity of the continent than in many other areas of Europe; indeed, some historians would deny their presence in Moscow. And so the old was more powerful than the new, and the first two components of Russian culture, mixed together in the heathen–Christian 'double faith', had barely begun to lose their dominance by the middle of the seventeenth century.

This would very much be the case with the mass of the people, particularly rural inhabitants. Their songs and stories, proverbs and superstitions, handed down from generation to generation, carried around and improvised upon by strolling players and sometimes inscribed in woodcuts, vigorously resisted the discouragements and prohibitions of the Church. Nevertheless, even at the popular level, the persistence of tradition did not mean complete absence of change. Some Soviet historians maintained that at the end of the fifteenth and beginning of the sixteenth century considerable progress occurred. Russian peasants deepened the recognition of themselves, not as the slaves of God, but as real people living on earth. Epic tales began to comment more on the conditions of the people and to acquire a new popular estimate of the strength of Russia. And so old subjects took on new details: for example, the legendary hero Ilia Muromets, while liberating Tsargrad or Constantinople, now saves the Emperor Constantine.

Even members of the upper classes were neither able nor wished to remain completely aloof from the culture of their Slavonic ancestors, but publicly at least they acknowledged the supremacy of the 'official' culture. By the middle of the fifteenth century, Orthodox Christianity was of sufficiently long standing in Russia for it to have evolved into maturity, and to be able to stand on its own feet after the Council of Florence of 1439 and the fall of Byzantium in 1453. The Council of Florence appeared to be reconciling East and West, but in fact officialised the schism between them. As for the fall of Byzantium, it was first understood as a prelude to the end of the world, which was calculated to occur in 1492, the year believed to mark 7000 years from the creation. In 1492, as everybody knows, a new world was discovered rather than an old world lost. The leaders of Russian Orthodoxy were by now more confidently seeing themselves as the leaders of the Eastern Church in general, and could concentrate on the legitimisation of their assumption of the Byzantine inheritance. They came to accept the view expressed by a Pskovian monk Filofei or Philotheus in a famous letter to Vasilii III written in about 1523:

The Church of old Rome fell for its heresy; the gates of the second Rome, Constantinople, were hewn down by the axes of the infidel Turks; but the Church of Moscow, the new Rome, shines brighter than the sun over the whole universe. Thou art the ecumenical sovereign, thou shouldst hold the reins of government in awe of God; fear Him who has committed them to thee. Two Romes have fallen, but the third stands fast; a fourth there cannot be. Thy Christian Kingdom shall not be given to any other ruler.'[27]

For an Eastern Orthodox historian, the first Rome gave Christendom 'law, order and discipline' and the concept of universality, while the second Rome offered 'intellectual leadership', doing much 'to formulate creeds and combat heresies'. Moscow – the Third Rome – 'expressed the conviction that the entire corporate life of a nation should be inspired by the Holy Spirit'.[28] For Soviet Marxist and some other secular historians, on the other hand, the adoption of the new ideology was an integral part of the contribution of the Church to the unification of Russia, for which the Church in return received protection against its opponents.

Whichever point of view we adopt, we cannot help observing that there was no shortage of opponents, both from within and without. The central internal dispute was between the 'possessors' and 'non-possessors', led respectively by Joseph of Volokolamsk and Nil Sorskii. As their name probably suggests, the 'possessors' believed in the secular as well as the spiritual power of the Church, making no real distinction between them. They supported the authority of the Grand Prince, accepting that it should extend as far as the administration of the Church. They advocated strict ritual and ruthless eradication of dissent. For their part, the 'non-possessors' argued for more complete absorption in the world of God and less in that of Caesar. The clergy, particularly the 'black' clergy of the monastic orders, should not own great lands or other wealth, but concentrate on simple labour and spirituality. The World of God rather than ritual should be sacrosanct, and dissent overcome by dissuasion rather than persecution. While both Joseph of Volokolamsk and Nil Sorskii were canonised after their deaths, their beliefs could not be held in equal reverence or even for long coexist. While there was some hint of secular support for an early 'dissolution of the monasteries', the state gave its support to decisions taken in favour of the 'possessors' by Church councils throughout the sixteenth century. The Church responded, as it were, by creating a considerable number of Russian saints and accepting a genealogy which also connected the princes with the Roman inheritance. At the

Stoglav or Hundred Chapter Council of 1551 and others, the Church attempted to keep its organisation efficient and its doctrines pure, tackling such problems as the profound ignorance of many of the rank-and-file members of the 'white' clergy or parish priests, and the corruption of many of their superiors.

Although the Russian Church did not escape the blows of Ivan the Terrible's *oprichnina*, he and other tsars in general gave it their support. Moreover, the establishment of the Moscow Patriachate in 1589 meant that it had been sufficiently successful in the eyes of its Eastern Orthodox peers for it to be acknowledged by them as worthy of entrance into the highest rank.

Meanwhile, however, the Russian Church was under external threat as well as internal, particularly after the Liublin Union of Poland and Lithuania in 1569. This strengthened Roman Catholicism, with the Jesuits and other orders moving eastwards in increased numbers, reaching as far as Moscow itself during the Time of Troubles. A considerable number of Lithuanians and Ukrainians became Uniates, that is Orthodox acknowledging the supremacy of the first Rome rather than the third, the Pope rather than the Patriarch. Moreover, Protestantism encroached as far as the Russian borders, too, especially as a consequence of the extension of Swedish power in the Baltic. The Russian Church was able to withstand the onslaught for the most part, the attitude of most of those who heard of the Reformation being well expressed in the reported words of Ivan the Terrible to a visiting pastor, 'Go to the devil with your Luther'.[29] And yet Soviet Marxist historians were able to devote considerable attention to what they call the 'reformation movements' of the period.[30] They took as their point of departure the assertion of Engels that such movements and the struggle connected with them were no more than the repeated attempts of the bourgeoisie, the urban plebeians and the peasants – becoming revolutionary with them – to adapt the old theoretical outlook to the changing economic conditions and the position of the new class. They went on to examine such heretical movements as the Judaisers in the late fifteenth century and such individuals as Feodosii Kosoi and Matvei Bashkin in the mid-sixteenth century, and Ivan Khvorostinin in the early seventeenth century, and to look for evidence of the desire to bring into the liturgy words in ordinary usage and to introduce a new humanity. While the bourgeoisie was not yet strong enough in Moscow for 'reformation movements' to make such an impact as elsewhere, there is a sufficient basis for the authoritative D. S. Likhachev to talk broadly of 'a crisis of the medieval manner of the representation of man occurring at the beginning of the seventeenth century'.[31]

This crisis would express itself in learning, literature and the arts as well as religion, although it is an indication of the distance that the secular spirit had to travel that religion was still a powerful influence on all other branches of cultural activity. The career of the cosmopolitan scholar, Maxim the Greek, in Moscow after 1516 is an illustrative example, giving Russians 'a unique opportunity of enlarging their mental and spiritual horizon by linking their cultural life with the Renaissance in Italy'.[32] Maxim soon ran into difficulties and finished up with twenty years in prison. On the other hand, Michael Cherniavsky's plausible attempt to portray Ivan the Terrible as Renaissance prince includes a comparison of the writings of Ivan Peresvetov with those of Machiavelli. Educated Russians knew Latin and Greek, and read the ancient authors. From the fifteenth century onwards, Russians went more often abroad and foreigners more often visited Russia. Ideas were exchanged, albeit in a tightly restricted manner.

The general degree of literacy and intellectual awareness during the period has been placed by Soviet historians at a somewhat higher level than many of their Western colleagues would be prepared to accept. The first recorded printed book was the *Apostle* in 1564, and it was followed by about twenty others mainly of a liturgical nature in the rest of the sixteenth century. There were other works on such subjects as arithmetic, history and geography, although these remained in manuscript, and the *Domostroi* or *Household Management*, which gave authoritarian instructions for the arrangement of the lives of upper-class families.[33] At least the beginnings of a lay literature can be detected by the mid-seventeenth century. Even for those who could not read, experiences such as the invasion by foreigners during the Time of Troubles could not help but be educational.

As in earlier periods, it is in painting and even more in architecture that the cultural achievement of Moscow makes its most striking impact on us. Its seclusion from the Roman Catholic world meant that the spirit of Byzantine tradition would be stronger than that of the Renaissance, but a number of Italian masters invited in by Ivan III – Fioravanti, Ruffo, Solari and Alevisio – were able to adapt their styles to local taste in the cathedrals, palaces and walls of the Moscow Kremlin. A more exclusively Russian hand was at work in the construction of the church outside Moscow at Kolomenskoe about 1532 and in Moscow of the famous, fantastic Cathedral of St Basil in Red Square from 1555 to 1560. The icon-painting tradition was carried on at a high level and somewhat adapted by the artist Dionisii and his sons. By the middle of the seventeenth century, Moscow had been transformed into one of the more celebrated of

European cities, thus standing as a symbol of the development generally achieved within the course of some two centuries. While her basically Orthodox 'official' culture and Slavonic 'unofficial' culture set her as apart figuratively as did her frontier situation literally, Russia had nevertheless undergone a process of national consolidation in many ways comparable to that of many of the other states in Europe.

Part Two

Modern Russia: The Tsarist Empire

Introduction

Pre-revolutionary historians placed the commencement of modern Russian history at the end of the Time of Troubles soon after the beginning of the seventeenth century. Kliuchevskii gave four reasons for such a choice: the arrival on the throne of a new dynasty, the Romanovs; the extension and consolidation of the boundaries of the state, a process continued during the following two centuries or so; the emergence of a new nobility, the *dvorianstvo*; and new economic developments, particularly the enserfment of the peasantry and the appearance of industry.[1] Soviet historians did not disagree completely with such an argument, although they virtually dismissed the first of Kliuchevskii's reasons and placed heavy emphasis on the fourth. For them, above all, the story of modern Russia consists of the rise and fall of capitalism and of the absolutist State which accompanied it. As a convenient point of departure, they have chosen the middle of the seventeenth century. Here, with some concession to the traditional view of the matter, but also with misleading exactitude, 1645 (the date of the accession of Aleksei Mikhailovich, or Alexis) has been selected.

For the modern section of this book, and making adjustments to retain the chronological divisions by the reigns of the Romanovs and to accommodate the views of successive generations of Russian and Western scholars, I have adopted the following broadly accepted six phases of development: 1645–98, 1698–1762, 1762–1801, 1801–55, 1855–94 and

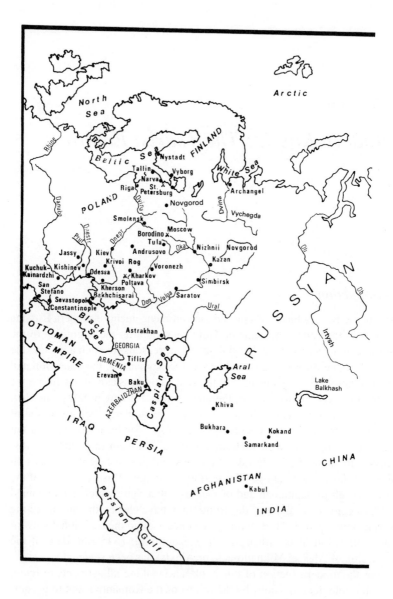

2 Modern Russia, 1645–1917

2 Modern Russia, 1645–1917

1894–1917. The first phase contains the birth of absolutism and the foundation of the Empire. The second is dominated by Peter the Great's vigorous attempt to consolidate and enlarge upon the work started under his predecessors, and the third, the period of 'enlightened absolutism', sees a continuation and variation of his work by Catherine the Great. Up until now in some ways progressive, absolutism takes a more clearly reactionary turn in its fourth phase under Alexander I and Nicholas I as it strives to retain the increasingly outmoded serf order within a nationalist framework. But, by the fifth, the pressure is too strong and a step is reluctantly and incompletely taken by Alexander II towards a transformation of absolutism into constitutional monarchy, with the emancipation of the serfs and other measures, although Alexander III tries to move in the opposite direction. In the sixth and final phase capitalism reaches a level sufficient for it to make at least a partial entry into what Lenin saw as its highest stage, that of imperialism. Tsarism is forced to take further steps towards constitutional monarchy, but cannot adapt itself sufficiently under Nicholas II to avert revolution. Accompanying these economic and political trends throughout the six phases is the less perceptible but equally significant gradual assertion of a secular culture. Moreover, far from taking place in its own remote enclosure, Russian modernisation is intimately connected with the same phenomenon taking place at different speeds in other societies. Indeed, the key to an understanding of Russian modernisation may be found in its relative tempo.

Baldly presented as above, our schema is crude in the extreme, for all historical periodisation entails inconsistency and distortion. In the present case, there were elements of 'enlightened absolutism' in the policy of Alexander I, while that of his father Paul before 1801 was in part reactionary. Crudest of all is the proposition that modern Russian history begins and medieval Russian history ends in 1645. There are strong feudal elements (particularly in the economic and cultural senses) in the Russia that succumbed to revolution in 1917; some of the characteristics of capitalism and absolutism may be detected in the reign of Ivan the Terrible, or even earlier. The choice of 1645 for the dawn of the modern age approximates also to widespread Western convention, although some Western historians would be reluctant to include Moscow in that dawn. Our reasons for doing so are elaborated during the course of Chapter 4.

Meanwhile, as we move into a phase that is better documented and more accessible than its predecessor, we should not forget the medieval legacy in general. For example, Richard Hellie and Edward Keenan both argued in different ways that the nature of the later Soviet Union was already predetermined to a remarkable extent by the end of the fifteenth century. Both impressed by the pronounced insecurity of existence in the early Muscovite period, Hellie stressed the formation of a 'garrison state' with emphasis on service, while Keenan focused on the collectivist nature of society from village to court.[2] To a debatable extent, the medieval legacy is still with us today.

4 The Foundation of the Russian Empire, 1645–1698

Arguments concerning the beginning of modern European history, like arguments concerning the origin of the universe, fall into two broad categories, the initial 'big bang' and subsequent evolution. The 'big bang' consists of the 'general crisis' thesis, which maintains that in the years around 1650 the continent of Europe was subject to a series of political, economic and cultural shocks which gave birth to absolutism, capitalism and the secular outlook. Moscow was both the taker and giver of such blows, as we shall see. The core of the evolutionary process is described by E. N. Williams in the following manner: '… absolute monarchy arose out of the need for internal and external security which made a standing army as a royal monopoly essential. This army required higher revenues; the revenues required economic growth; they all required the formation of a royal bureaucracy to eliminate, or push aside, the manifestations of the corporate state'.[1] Generally speaking, Moscow conforms to such a pattern, although it also possesses peculiar features. Among these is the enserfment of the peasantry, a phenomenon occurring throughout much of central and eastern Europe at a time when the western part of the continent was developing a freer form of society.

In its formative days, then, the Russian Empire exhibited two principal features, absolutism and serfdom. Both these institutions took on something like a definite shape during the last half of the seventeenth century. The period also saw a great expansion with the takeover of a large part of the Ukraine and the infiltration of most of Siberia. This enlarged area was loosely interlocked by trade, kept in rough order by the army and subject to the administration of a somewhat improved central bureaucracy. Orthodoxy provided a cohesive influence, and the first glimmerings of a secular rationale for empire are discernible. By the end of the century, Russia had reached a sufficiently advanced stage for Peter the Great to build the imperial superstructure on a fairly firm foundation.

Peter's predecessors on the throne were not as forceful as he himself and the laying of the foundation was therefore an exercise which transcended royal personality. Nevertheless, their proclivities and distinguishing characteristics gave a special flavour to society at the top level, and even in the passive mode, their lives distilled the spirit of the times even if they did not infuse it.

Aleksei Mikhailovich, or Alexis (1645–76) was sixteen years old at the time of his accession. In a welter of threats from pretenders and rumours about his own authenticity, the young tsar was more than ready to turn for support to his tutor, the boyar B. I. Morozov, who became the ruler of the country in fact. According to a foreign contemporary, Morozov was driven by a thirst for gold as great as other Muscovites' thirst for drink. He was also a master of court intrigue, consolidating his power by marrying the tsar's sister-in-law, a member of the Miloslavskii family. Alexis combined the business of government with strict observance of the rituals of church and court. While Kliuchevskii finds him a most excellent fellow but somewhat passive, helping the reform movement but unable to direct it, his most recent biographer Philip Longworth considers him to have been 'intelligent as well as cunning, obstinate and persevering', that 'it is primarily as a manager of men that he stands out as a monarch above the ordinary.' Alexis had some literary aspirations, and allowed foreign music and theatricals, as well as furniture, into the tsar's palace for the first time. In this he may well have been partly under the influence of his second wife, who had been brought up in the Westernised household of another favourite, Artamon Matveev, whose own wife was from the Scottish Hamilton family. In a more traditional manner, Alexis kept around him a bunch of beggars and idiots, venerated by the Orthodox as holy fools. The favour of Alexis was bestowed on A. L. Ordin-Nashchokin and the Patriarch Nikon, as well as on Morozov and Matveev. But favour could also be withdrawn, as we shall see.

Alexis died suddenly in 1676 and was succeeded by his ailing fourteen-year-old son, Fedor Alekseevich, or Theodore (1676–82). The great families struggled for power, the Miloslavskiis related to the late tsar's first wife squabbling with the Naryshkins related to his second wife and with the Matveevs. As the favourites disposed of each other, outsiders managed to grasp the best positions, while Theodore married twice, but without lasting issue, thus leaving behind him a tricky situation at his death in 1682.

The temporary victress in the bloody crisis which followed the death of Theodore was his elder sister Sofia Alekseevna, or Sophia, who was installed as Regent (1682–9) in the name of her younger brother Ivan and half-brother Petr or Peter, who were declared joint tsars. Her biographer Lindsey Hughes quotes with approval the later judgement of Catherine the Great that the Regent was capable of governing', before going on to observe that apart from Catherine, 'Sophia has claims to being the most determined and capable woman ever to rule Russia'. Although she fell from power in 1689 after a coup in favour of Peter, Peter did not become sole ruler in law until 1696 and was not secure in power in fact until two years later.[2]

Political

During the first two years of the reign of Alexis, the boyar Morozov built up a network of power in the central bureaucracy, at the time alienating the functionaries of the *prikazy* and the *streltsy* musketeers. To these two dissatisfied groups were added the nobility of the capital and of the provinces, who protested about unjust judges and inadequate arrangements for the recapture of runaway peasants. Readjustment of the taxation system led to a more general malaise which soon broke out into positive action.

After some minor disturbances to the north and south and in Siberia, a revolt broke out in Moscow in June 1648. Townspeople annoyed by exactions and encroachments upon their privileges joined with provincial nobles to petition the tsar, and the loyalty of the *streltsy* was soon in question. Alexis himself, icon in hand, made an appeal to the insurgents and then delivered up to them as a sop to their unabated anger some of his chief advisers, although he successfully pleaded for the life of Morozov. Land and higher payments were given to the nobles, money was handed out to the *streltsy*, presents distributed to the people at large, and negotiations carried on between the government and the town leaders, while the dignitaries of the Church preached peace and Morozov was sent to a monastic exile.

A wave of revolts with similar origins broke out in 1648 throughout European Russia. A *Zemskii Sobor* was summoned to satisfy some of the demands being made everywhere, and after some stormy elections it met in Moscow from September 1648 to January 1649. The representation heavily favoured the nobility and to a lesser extent the burghers; the people as a whole had no voice at all. Petitions from the two dominant groups strongly influenced the formulation of the Code of 1649: the landed and other privileges of the Church and nobility were guaranteed, while serfdom received fuller definition; exemptions from urban taxation were reduced, and a fairer division of such burdens was therefore achieved. However, the burghers were not given the control over trade and industry that they had been hoping for. As for the poor townsfolk and the peasants, they gained nothing from the Code, which was to remain in legal force until the nineteenth century.[3] However, serfdom was imposed upon the communal structure raiher than destroying it.

Meanwhile Morozov returned to a lesser position of influence until his death in 1661, only for the government to be confronted with another wave of town revolts in 1650. This time the largest outbreaks, which were compounded by poor harvests and regional as well as class conflict, were in Pskov and Novgorod. Moscow did not escape entirely, but in the capital a much larger disturbance took place in 1662. The long war with Poland concerning the Ukraine had physically weakened the inhabitants of the capital, and they had suffered from an epidemic of smallpox in the mid-1650s. Its financial difficulties if anything greater than usual, the government went beyond harsh taxation to debasement of the silver coinage by copper. The corruption of officials at all levels was a further aggravation. In July 1662 a mob of about 5000 confronted Alexis at his home in the suburb of Kolomenskoe, and demanded that those guilty of fraud – including the tsar's father-in-law – be brought to justice. As Kliuchevskii described the further actions of the insurgents and the response of the government:

> Some of them held the tsar by the buttons of his kaftan, while he was made to take an oath that he would deal with the matter himself, and he was forced to shake hands on it. However, the first mob was joined by a second from Moscow, and both boisterously began to demand that the tsar hand over the traitors to them; if he did not they would be taken by force. Tsar Alexis called on the *streltsy* and his courtiers for assistance, and an indiscriminate slaughter ensued, followed by tortures and executions. Hundreds were drowned in the River Moskva, and whole families were exiled permanently to Siberia.[4]

The government was shaken enough to bring back silver in 1663, but was now generally more confident than before of the support of the service nobility, which was coalescing into a distinct class and becoming the chief bastion of absolutism, at the same time as the boyar aristocracy was in decline.

The policies of the government at the time clearly revealed that it knew where its main support was to be found. The concessions given to the nobility in the Code of 1649 were extended in subsequent legislation. The nobles banded together to make sure that the residual rights of their peasants were much reduced and persuaded the government that it had the duty to catch runaways. The government also conducted a generous land policy towards the nobility, particularly in the aftermath of successful wars which both encouraged the tsar to reward his servants and acquired for him the land to use as a reward. The burghers also received state encouragement in the years following 1649. The administration of the towns was reorganised in the years 1649–52, internal customs were regularised in 1653 and again in 1667, and the New Commercial Regulations of 1667, as we shall see, boosted the position of Russian merchants in relation to their foreign counterparts. At the same time, we must remember that neither the nobility nor the bourgeoisie were as yet completely formed as classes in the socio-economic sense, even less in the juridical, and so the relations between them and the government were not as clearly consistent as this summary account makes them appear.

However, as with the two top classes so with tsarism itself, a relatively more articulated structure was evolving during the middle years of the seventeenth century. Although the relations between the tsar and his subjects could sometimes be informally direct, as they were during the town revolts, the ceremonies and processions in which the tsar normally took part were attended with great pomp and elaborate ritual, which made a deep impression on both reverential populace and visiting foreigners. Samuel Collins, the tsar's physician, believed of Alexis that 'As for his Treasure of Jewels, I think no Prince does exceed him', and the secretary of an English embassy to him in 1664 wrote that 'The Tsar, like a sparkling sun...darted forth most sumptuous rays, being most magnificently placed upon his throne'. Behind this splendid façade, which had not changed significantly for some time, the real strength of the tsarist apparatus was achieving a new degree of consolidation: central and local government were both made somewhat less inefficient. The *Zemskii Sobor* continued to meet after the middle of the century, but by then had lost any independence it had ever possessed. Something similar might be said about the Boyar Duma; although the Duma was not yet a cipher, the *prikaz* of Secret Affairs replaced it as the tsar's privy council during the latter part of the reign of Alexis. The *prikaz* of Accounts was created in the attempt to bring order into financial affairs, and there was a more general attempt to rationalise the *prikazy*, both as to sphere of competence and to geographical area of jurisdiction. The key figure in local government was the *voevoda*, who ruled his province in a manner as absolute as the tsar ruled the state. Local peasant officials were powerless before the *voevoda* and the army detachments which supported him.[5]

Neither the control of the central government nor that of the local government was complete enough to avert passive and active resistance, of which the most common symptoms were peasant flight and banditry. Occasionally, there were large-scale outbreaks of violence in the provinces, as there were in Moscow and other towns. The biggest of these was the second of the peasant wars, as Soviet historians knew it, or the Razin Revolt as it is more traditionally called. Having gained a wide reputation through bold piratic adventures along the Caspian Sea, Stenka Razin moved against Moscow in 1670. Having achieved great success in the Volga region, where he attracted a large following from the peasantry, Razin was crushed by regular army units near Simbirsk and fell back to the Don, where the Cossack leaders handed him over to the authorities. He was executed in Red Square, Moscow, in June 1671. The reasons for the failure of the Razin Revolt are isolated by a Soviet historian, V. I. Buganov, as: 'spontaneity, localism, disorganisation of the movement, the absence of a clear political programme, poor armaments. The heterogeneity of the composition of the insurgents led to disagreements in their midst.' Nevertheless, he asserts that 'The Second Peasant War was distinguished by a clear polarisation of the class forces'.[6] Razin had been executed, but his name lived on in song and legend. The descendants of his followers were to move in support of Bulavin and Pugachev in the peasant wars of the eighteenth century, still exhibiting the naïve monarchism that could see no wrong in the tsar and believing that peace and justice would come to the Russian land after the eradication of its lesser lords, the nobility.

After the death of Alexis in 1676, there was no radical change in governmental policy, rather a move several stages further forward for the policy already inaugurated. Thus, in the reign of Theodore (1676–82), serfdom was further entrenched and more land distributed to the nobility. The solidity of the ruling class was at the same time encouraged by the convergence between different types of landholding, and by the continued reduction of the boyars. The process was brought an important stage forward by the abolition in 1682 of the system of *mestnichestvo* by which upper-class families had been awarded places in the government hierarchy according to their birth. This last measure contributed to the further improvement in the structure of the central government, which was also encouraged by more rearrangement of the central *prikazy*. The administration of the provinces was improved by the introduction of the household as a new tax unit.[7]

The period between the death of Alexis and the consolidation of the power of Peter the Great showed continuity not only in the tsarist policies but also in the opposition to them. The acquisition of the Regency by Sophia in 1682 was attended by civil disturbance demonstrating the dissatisfaction of several groups, particularly the *streltsy*, and the same might be said about her loss of it in 1689. A third and more violent outbreak by the *streltsy* occurred in 1698 while Peter was away on his first visit to Western Europe. Loyal troops under the leadership of the Scottish General, Patrick Gordon, suppressed the *streltsy* for the final time, and Peter came back hastily not only with ideas for progressive reform but also with the burning desire for torture and execution of a more traditional Muscovite nature.

The reduction of the *streltsy* was a significant step in a late Muscovite development of enormous importance not only for internal stability but also for imperial expansion and foreign wars – the regularisation of the army. Peter the Great, who has often been given the credit for this measure, himself accorded the honour to his father, pointing out that in 1647 Alexis began to use regular forces on the basis of the military manual published in that year. In fact, the process was more gradual, having been inaugurated in the reign of Michael, but a tremendous growth in the proportion of the new order occurred by the 1680s, when the army was not only more numerous but also largely composed of 'foreign' units – cavalry and infantry of the 'new model' kind making up more than half of a total now exceeding 200,000 men. German, Scottish and other mercenaries trained and to some extent led these units. Russia was by this time nearly self-sufficient in the production of cannon and gunpowder, if not of handguns. These developments, which were in rough parallel with military changes elsewhere in Europe, had important social consequences in Moscow as well as in foreign states. During the transitional period they included the decline and fall not only of the *streltsy* but also of what Richard Hellie calls the 'middle service class' composed of cavalry archers.[8] By the end of the century, the consolidation of the service nobility, or *dvorianstvo*, as the modern officer caste was nearer to completion, although mercenaries still made an important contribution, and the rank and file was largely recruited on a regimental rather than a militia basis.

The army was improved in response to the challenge facing Moscow as it became consolidated as the Russian Empire. First of all, there was the task of maintaining order in the more settled central regions. Then, the frontiers and fortified lines had to be protected against Tatar and other incursions, a problem which increased in complexity as the frontiers expanded. During the later seventeenth century, infiltration of Siberia went as far as the Kamchatka peninsula and the Amur river valley, where a clash with China forced Russia to make the concessions of the Treaty of

Nerchinsk of 1689. The Church lent the weight of its authority to the Cossack and other units, which were carrying out the penetration for the exploitation of fur and other resources. For their part, the natives did not always appreciate the privileges of paying tribute, undergoing conversion and being subjected to imperial control, and such tribes as the Kalmyks and the Bashkirs resisted their assimilation as forcibly as they could.

The most demanding task imposed upon the reformed army was the engagement of the state's external foes, principally the Poles, the Turks and the Swedes. The war of 1654–67 against the Poles succeeded in achieving aims similar to those which had been frustrated in the 1630s, the acquisition of Smolensk and Left-Bank Ukraine including Kiev. The new success was due partly to the increased relative strength of the Muscovite forces, but mainly to the alliance between them and the Ukrainian Cossacks, who rose up in 1648 in a great war of liberation under the leadership of Bogdan Khmelnitskii. Having inflicted considerable defeats on the Poles, which won for him the recognition of Oliver Cromwell and other Western Europeans, Khmelnitskii led the Ukrainians into union with Russia in 1654. War with Poland inevitably broke out again, and continued with intervals until the Treaty of Andrusovo in 1667.

At several points, the war took on a more complicated international character as the Turks and the Swedes joined in. For example, Russia fought against Sweden from 1656 to 1658 to protect the gains which had been made and to seek the long-desired outlet to the Baltic. And then, in the aftermath of the war, the Turks with their allies forced the Muscovite government to promise to resume an annual tribute to the khan of the Crimean Tatars at the armistice of Bakhchisarai (1681). Vasilii Golitsyn, the favourite of the Regent Sophia, conducted two unsuccessful campaigns against the Crimea in the late 1680s, partly as a contribution to a Pan-Christian campaign inaugurated by King Jan Sobieski of Poland against the Turkic Muslims after their siege of Vienna in 1683. In 1686, the Treaty of Moscow confirmed the terms of Andrusovo nearly twenty years earlier, conclusively bringing Kiev and the Left-Bank Ukraine into the Russian orbit. While Soviet historians criticised Golitsyn's priorities and gave their approval rather to such statesmen as A. S. Matveev who usually placed the complete defeat of Poland at the top of their list of aims, even Peter the Great began his military career in the 1690s with campaigns against the Black Sea fortress of Azov.

At the beginning of the seventeenth century, Moscow had shrunk to the size of a principality; by the century's end, it grew into the largest state in Europe, with encroachments not only into the Polish sphere of influence but also deep into Asia. Closer diplomatic relations had been established with a whole range of states from France to China (though the Treaty of Nerchinsk of 1689 made a temporary halt to Russian expansion into the Amur valley). Not only was the nascent Empire more of a force to be reckoned with in the international relations of all these states, but its expansion had exerted an effect throughout Eurasia. For example, the assimilation of the Ukraine, leading to the weakening of Poland, had in turn made less secure the eastern flank of the Habsburg Empire, and thus the rise of Moscow generally received a warm welcome from the enemies of the Habsburgs throughout Europe. Already playing an important part in the denouement of the Thirty Years' War and the continental crisis which followed it, the Russian Empire was poised by the dawn of the eighteenth century for an even greater appearance on the international stage. Of course, the impact was mutual, and many analysts would argue that the changes undergone by Moscow as a result of her widened contact with other states were far more profound than those she inflicted on them. To take again the example of the Ukraine, Russian political strength, economic growth and cultural progress all received a considerable and lasting boost from the reunion of Moscow with Kiev.[9]

Economic

It is still virtually impossible to say anything definite about the size of the population in the late seventeenth century, although it is probable that earlier losses had been made up and that the total was now approaching fifteen millions. Certain tendencies may be more positively observed in the various branches of the economy, even though here too it is difficult to talk with any confidence in a quantified manner. In agriculture, the various groups comprising the nobility retained a preponderant share of the populated land, making good use of the enserfment of the peasantry. According to the assessment of 1678–9 which roughly covered the European part of the state, the tsar possessed about 9 per cent of a total of 812,000 households; townspeople and state peasants, something more than 10 per cent; the Church, just over 13 per cent; and the feudal lords, around 67 per cent. Towards the end of the 1640s, the top boyar B. I. Morozov owned more than 30,000 serfs living in more than 300 different places. Noble landlords moved into the southern Oka and Volga regions, cultivated new fields in the centre and occasionally raised the technical level of farming, although the spread of agriculture was more normally extensive than intensive. While the spread of the area under cultivation was to some degree a political and social phenomenon, it also reflected increasing possibilities for marketing produce, themselves partly the result and partly the cause of the incorporation into the state of the Ukraine, Volga and Ural territories. The growth in commercial agricultural activity was also revealed in the increased specialisation of, for example, the southern black-earth region, where labour on the land was the usual kind of peasant service, and the central non-black-earth region, where the serfs often spent some of their time in manufacturing enterprises. The same process was at work in the sharper distinction becoming apparent between town and country, although even in Moscow itself townspeople sometimes still farmed.

Specialisation may also be seen in manufacturing and industry. Textiles were made in several districts to the north-east of Moscow, and iron was produced to the south of the capital at Tula, where the Dutchman A. Vinius had set up a works in 1632. By the 1660s, there were 119 people, nearly half of them foreigners, employed at seven works in the Tula region. By the end of the century metallurgical activity was also started in the north-west and in the Urals, where enterprises included at least a dozen large armaments works. Although the transfer from domestic production of the blast furnaces meant more quantity and higher quality, wind and water remained the sources of power and ore was usually mined on or near the spot. Raw materials were not always so locally acquired for industrial enterprises, however. For example, the hides for the tanneries of Kazan were brought from many different places, including the distant Urals. As far as the necessary entrepreneurial initiative for these various industrial activities was concerned, it came largely from the state, but also from nobles, monks, merchants and peasants. Such families as the Stroganovs were already prominent. Various groups were involved in producing not only textiles, metals and leather, but other items such as salt, potash and pitch too.

The beginnings of the all-Russian market could be seen mostly in the grain rather than the industrial goods trade. State needs for distillation purposes, for the supply of some districts in Siberia and for the export market were a major stimulus. Sometimes large contracts were given for the supply of grain, and the middleman flourished. Peasants were important suppliers, but Morozov and other landlords were also interested in the business. The unification of markets could be seen as local centres merged into a larger system of regions formed on the basis of the grain trade. Smolensk was a focal point in the west, Voronezh another in the south. Flax was grown commercially in the north-western territories with Pskov as an *entrepôt*, and animal products, particularly leather and lard, were bought and sold in Archangel. The fur trade was on a huge scale in Siberia and elsewhere.[10]

Goods were usually transported by routes which coincided with the great river networks, most of them converging on the Sukhona–Northern Dvina route which led to Archangel, Moscow's only sea port. In 1653, goods to a value of just over one million roubles were exported from Archangel, including furs, potash, leather, lard and cloth and more than a million bushels of grain. Imported through Archangel in 1671 were a wide range of items including diamonds, gold and silver goods, paper, hats, pins and needles, wine, ginger, pepper, herring, apothecary materials and arms. The principal foreign intermediaries for most of the century were the Dutch, followed by the British.

Northern markets were linked with the Volga region, where the most important commercial centres were Nizhnii Novgorod, Kazan and Astrakhan, and with Siberia. The Oka River and its upper tributaries served as a link with the Ukraine, and in the south and south-west, the Dnepr and Western Dvina systems were much used, with Smolensk at the cross-roads. Through Smolensk, as well as through the declining towns of Pskov and Novgorod, commercial land routes made their way to the rest of Europe, and a not insignificant trade was carried on through the Baltic by Swedish and other intermediaries, who dealt especially in naval stores.

The centre of the growing all-Russian market was, of course, the town of Moscow, with nearly all the trade routes leading to it and contacts established with more than 150 other towns. Here were to be found Ukrainians, Tatars, Mordvinians and representatives of many of the other peoples of the nascent Empire. All sorts of foreign intermediaries lived in Moscow, too, confined from 1652 onwards in their so-called German settlement. (All foreigners were Germans as far as the masses were concerned, the word *nemets* meaning German or foreigner coming from *nemoi* meaning dumb; that is, unable to speak Russian.) A wide variety of goods from all parts of Eurasia were to be bought in the capital and at the great fairs such as that of St Macarius near Nizhnii Novgorod.

Large mercantile fortunes were being made in the late seventeenth century. Huge profits accrued from import, export and some internal trade. The state patronised the rich merchants, particularly the so-called 'guests', favoured in return for special services with this title, leases and contracts. There were not many 'guests', about thirty only in Moscow, for example, but they possessed great influence as well as riches. The most outstanding of them was G. L. Nikitinov, who dealt in wool cloth, salt and fish, plied a fleet of ships down the Volga as far as Astrakhan, and owned the equivalent of one quarter of the total capital of all the other Moscow 'guests', many of whom were worth up to 100,000 roubles themselves. Another 'guest', M. Gurev, claimed to have spent 200,000 roubles on the construction of a town at the mouth of the river Iaik which bore his name and protected his fishing interests. The size of state contracts can be seen from the example of one Fedor Silin living near Moscow, who sold more than 60,000 metres of cloth to one of the government departments in 1676, as well as being a supplier of salt and iron.[11] At a lower level than the 'guests' were a growing number of middlemen or *skupshchiki*, travelling far and wide to buy and sell. Although a lot of manufacture and trade was still local, there were few Russians, from the tsar and the boyars down to the meanest peasants, who were not affected in a direct or indirect manner by the commercial network.

A preponderant part in late Muscovite economic change was played by the state. Its taxation policies, stemming from a constant extreme need for money, were severe enough to produce serious revolts. Its commercial policies could either restrict or aggrandise Russian merchants. For example, the latter tendency was encouraged by the New Commercial Regulations of 1667, which forbade foreign merchants to involve themselves in retail trade and imposed high tariffs on foreign goods. Moreover, the tsar and his entourage formed by far the largest commercial concern, retaining several monopolies for themselves. Samuel Collins called Alexis 'The chief Merchant in all the Empire'.[12] Some observers have selected this circumstance as the major reason for the weak development of Russian capitalism, although the part played by the state elsewhere in Europe may have been as great. Others have wondered if this backwardness might not have some connection with the absence from Russia of Protestantism and the failure of comparable Russian religious movements to provide an adequate alternative.

Undoubtedly, Moscow was in some measure economically backward in the late seventeenth century. Her remoteness from the major trade routes of burgeoning Western capitalism made this so, although the importance of the Muscovite trade to this process was by no means negligible. The institution of serfdom was in part the response of a less advanced region to a region that was beginning to move quickly forward, although we must not forget that the commercial revolution of the Western European world could not have taken place without the institution of Negro slavery.[13]

The degree of Moscow's backwardness in the seventeenth century might well never be exactly calculated because of the paucity and unreliability of statistics. What can certainly be said is that it was not always apparent to contemporary visitors to Moscow. One of the outstanding foreign descriptions, that by Olearius in the 1630s, notes the bustle of Russian markets and says that the people's 'cleverness and shrewdness are manifested in their commerce, among other activities'. Olearius considers that the merchants 'are shrewd and eager for profit' and that the artisans have learned foreign techniques quickly, and 'with technological improvement, they sell their manufactured goods at higher prices than before'.[14] Beyond this, it appears reasonably certain that about three-tenths of the manufacturing enterprises of the eighteenth century were founded in the seventeenth century. And so, there is a strong if not incontrovertible case for concluding that the great leap forward in the economy associated with Peter the Great was in fact the culmination of a more gradual process and that Lenin was broadly correct in dating the growth of Russian capitalism 'approximately from the seventeenth century'.[15]

Cultural

During the seventeenth century, the process of secularisation gradually infiltrated Europe as churches lost influence to encroaching state authority and a humanistic element firmly forced its way into a still predominantly religious culture. The struggle between the old outlook and the new in Moscow was fought against the background of the Schism in Orthodoxy.

In the city of Moscow in the 1640s there was formed a revivalist group called the Zealots of Piety, aimed at the purging from the Church of impurities and deviations. The leader of the group was the tsar's confessor, and its members included the two future protagonists of the Schism, Nikon and Avvakum. Both born near Nizhnii Novgorod – Nikon the son of a peasant, Avvakum the son of a priest – they were both men of great intellect, powerful character and tremendous self-righteousness. Each was a firm believer in the power of miracles, and each was a strict ritualist. Fierce fanatics, they had no mercy for their opponents, who came to include each other. And both of them came to a disastrous end.

Nikon became Patriarch in 1652, after a career which took him from priest to monk to archimandrite to Metropolitan of Novgorod. His elevation to the highest power was attended with much ceremony, which entailed Alexis prostrating himself on behalf of the people before Nikon, who asked for and received full authority to purify the Church and to reform it. Such a policy involved changes in the number of alleluias and genuflections made at certain moments of the service and in the number of fingers used in making the sign of the cross, as well as emendations in the holy texts on the basis of Greek models. Such alterations were certainly important for a Church which believed very much in ceremony and ritual, but their implications went considerably further. To put it bluntly, Nikon was making an attempt at the establishment of his complete authority over the 'Third Rome' and even hoping that he might lead it to a predominant position throughout the whole Orthodox world. With such aims Nikon drew on the historic Byzantine tradition and the more recent example of Filaret.

For both religious and political reasons, if the two can be separated in seventeenth-century Moscow, Nikon soon ran into opposition. He alienated most of his friends among the Zealots of Piety, who began to look upon him as a wolf in sheep's clothing. At first trying to conciliate the two parties in the dispute, Alexis broke with Nikon in 1658. By this time, the tsar had grown tired of the Patriarch's overweening manner, and he took advantage of Nikon's resignation in a fit of pique to accept him at his word. A long period of jockeying for position ensued, at the end of which in 1666 a Church Council was summoned with the Patriarchs of Alexandria and Antioch in attendance to put Nikon to trial. After some stormy sessions, the Council condemned a defiant Nikon to be reduced to the clerical ranks and exiled to a remote monastery. Nikon was disgraced, but his policy was continued in most aspects except the most important – the reduction of the Patriarch was a significant step towards the final subjection of the Church to the state.

Meanwhile, Avvakum, whom Nikon had sent into exile, was emerging as the leader of those who would not accept the Church reform. These, the Old Believers, were condemned by the same Council that broke Nikon. From *The Life of Archpriest Avvakum by Himself*, we learn much of the trials and tribulations of the schismatics: the unspeakable hardships of exile in Siberia and in the Arctic North; and the circumstances which brought it about, the religious and to a lesser extent the secular. Emphasis on the former came from both sides of the continuing struggle in the pre-revolutionary period, while populist historians of the nineteenth century anticipated their Soviet counterparts by stressing the latter. For Robert O. Crummey, Old Belief after 1667 was 'an indistinguishable blend of opposition to the liturgical reforms, foreign cultural influence, bureaucratic centralism, and social injustice. Antichrist was the symbol of all that was new and oppressive in Muscovite society. His power had to be resisted'.[16] Soviet historians showed most interest in the movement's social variation (the aristocrat Prince Khovanskii being one of its first leaders and the *streltsy* providing many of its most stubborn adherents) and in the contradictoriness of its aims and methods (the lack of agreement about whether to commit suicide or to rise up in protest).

Avvakum himself was burnt at the stake in 1681, and between 1675 and 1695, up to 20,000 Old Believers threw themselves into the flames in expectation of the imminent end of the world. At the same time there were old Believer revolts against the reform, those of the *streltsy* being at least partly definable thus, and the monks at the Solovetskii Monastery on the White Sea waged a long battle against the government from 1667 to 1676. At the beginning of the revolt, when the news of the Nikonian reform first reached the Solovetskii Monastery, the monks are reported to have said 'Brothers! Brothers! Alas, alas! Woe, woe! The faith of Christ has fallen in Russia, just as in other lands. ...' The monks were referring to the decline of Orthodoxy elsewhere, but one may be at least permitted to speculate if they did not also have in mind the great religious upheavals of non-Orthodox Europe. Certainly, later historians have put forward the hypothesis that the Old Believer movement could well have been part of a Pan-European phenomenon, France and to a lesser extent Scotland both being cited as states in which parallel developments took place.[17] Throughout the continent, the established Church made a compromise with the state, while sectarian groups sacrificed themselves in the vain attempt to adhere to what they believed to be former standards of pure devotion.

If religious currents were able to cross the frontiers of localism and prejudices as the old culture started to disintegrate, the more liberated spirit of the new culture could well be expected to cross them too. And so it proved, although the numbers directly affected by it in each state were small, and although even they had not yet made the clear distinction between the world of God and of man. In Russia, for example, contemporary petitions and other documents show that many members of the upper classes and even some ordinary townspeople and peasants had at least crossed that first important threshold and mastered the art of making their own signature. However, the first printed grammar of 1634 left no doubt that the main aim of primary education was to enable people to understand Holy Writ.

At a somewhat higher level, an education was being acquired from private tutors and, before the end of the century, in a small number of institutions. Simeon Polotskii from the Kiev Academy, an important percolator of advanced ideas, was engaged by Alexis to teach his children, and boyars and other prominent members of society soon followed the tsar's example. Polotskii was put in charge of a theological school in Moscow in 1666, and, although its activities were soon curtailed, another school fashioned after the Kiev Academy was opened under one of Polotskii's pupils in 1682. This school, in which the basic emphasis was on Latinism, was soon merged with another founded at about the same time as the Moscow printing press, where Hellenism was the predominant influence, to form the Slavono-Graeco-Latin Academy. From the mid-1680s onwards, the Academy was not only an institution of higher learning but also the guardian of educational respectability. New subjects such as foreign languages or philosophy and physics were undertaken in conditions of strict security and only with sworn professions of Orthodoxy by both teachers and students. Emerging from these oppressive conditions before the end of the century were men such as A. L. Ordin-Nashchokin, A. S. Matveev and V. V. Golitsyn, whose libraries reveal them to have been men of considerable breadth, conversant with works not only in Russian, Greek and Latin but also in Polish, German and other foreign languages. Poland was the most important conveyor of the new culture.[18]

And so a new humanity was apparent, even in icon-painting, while church song moved away from unison towards polyphony. Some specialists in architecture talk of a Russian baroque. Parallel developments have been noted in verse and prose.[19] At a lower social level, too, popular tales began to concern themselves with such mundane subjects as the corruption of judges and other day-to-day vicissitudes of ordinary life.

Perhaps the arrival of the new as well as the persistence of the old are best represented in the example of a single person. Kliuchevskii said that many of the ideas of Peter the Great were anticipated by Ordin-Nashchokin. Much the same may be said about V. V. Golitsyn, of whom a French visitor of the late seventeenth century, Foy de la Neuville, wrote, albeit not completely accurately:

> He had built a very magnificent stone College, invited a score of doctors in from Greece, as well as a quantity of good books, exhorting the great men to educate their children, and permitting them to send their children to Latin Colleges in Poland while advising that Polish tutors should be brought in for the others. He accorded to foreigners the entry to and exit from the realm, which had never been practised before him. He also wanted the nobility to travel and learn how to make war in foreign countries, since his design was to change into good soldiers those legions of peasants whose land remained uncultivated when they were led to war. And instead of such service which was useless for the state, he wanted to impose on each head a reasonable sum, to maintain Ministers in the principal courts of Europe, and to allow liberty of conscience in the country.[20]

This same Golitsyn usually slept in an old wooden bed and ate from wooden plates, even though he had a magnificent bedroom and silverware to show off to his guests. In this and many of the other features of his outlook as reported by the French visitor, he resembled Peter the Great. Peter was distinguished by his wholehearted submission to a wider range of foreign influences, first in Moscow's German Settlement and then in Western Europe, and above all by the tireless authority which he commanded for over a quarter of a century, and used in the attempt to shake all his fellow-countrymen out of that Muscovite exclusiveness and suspicion from which only a few Russians had fully emerged before the consolidation of his power in 1698.

However, as always, we must be careful not to overpersonalise. And so let us conclude this chapter by noting that Russia could not have entered Europe entirely before the reign of Peter the Great because the continent as a modern secular entity did not fully exist before about the end of the seventeenth century. Until then, the emphasis had been on Europe as Christendom, Russia's Orthodoxy underlining its apartness.[21]

5   The Completion of the Structure, 1698–1761

In 1698, Peter I hastily returned from his first visit to Western Europe determined to crush the *streltsy* along with their adherence to the old ways and to put into practice his new ideas for the transformation of Russia. As well as cutting off the heads of the *streltsy*, he cut off the beards of his courtiers, the outward symbols of their adherence to Muscovite tradition. From 1 January 1700, Russia moved closer to the West by adopting the Julian calendar and starting to record time from the birth of Christ rather than from the dawn of creation. Later on in that year, Russia suffered a great defeat in the battle of Narva at the beginning of the Great Northern War against Sweden, and the long journey which then began back to reconstruction of the armed forces, complete victory and a secure foothold on the Baltic has often been seen as the major theme of Peter the Great's reign. As Pushkin put it, Russia entered the ranks of the great powers like a launched ship with the knock of axes and the roar of cannon.

In adulthood, Peter was nasty, brutish and extremely tall. He liked sick jokes, and since he was an Emperor, could make them come to life. The well-organised centre of his merry pranks was 'The Most Drunken Council of Fools and Jesters', dedicated to the worship of Venus and Bacchus, and specialising in the elaborate ridicule of Church and court ceremony.[1] Possibly, such antics developed a 'rational political purpose' – the debasement of the Patriarch's dignity and the thawing of Byzantine tsarist ritual, but they may also be seen as the reflection of a 'possibly tragic flaw', of a persistent and insensitive tendency 'to regard those who were thereby offended as obstinate children who would not see that most things western or new were better than most things Russian or old, that in Russia radical reform had become urgently necessary'.[2]

Peter's own childhood had been very disturbed, and this circumstance probably explains much of his bizarre temperament. For example, at the age of ten, in 1682 he was obliged to witness the execution of two uncles and several other kinsmen. For reasons such as this, his childhood games of soldiers were attended by a precocious element of seriousness, and his irregular education at the hands of Scots, Dutch and other foreigners in the German Settlement possessed from the first an unusually practical element. His upset youth also made him into something of a nervous wreck, with frequent convulsions of the head and acute insomnia. Before his final collapse, however, constantly on the move, shaking people at all levels of society into action with his oak club, Peter stormed throughout Russia and Europe as like a colossus as anybody else in history.

It is little wonder, therefore, that such a man has been a subject of great fascination for historians for more than two hundred years. Kliuchevskii detected many contradictions making it 'difficult to paint one painting … even his good actions were accompanied by disgusting methods.' Perhaps Peter was best likened to 'the impetuous showers of spring, which strip branches from the trees, but none the less refresh the air, and by their downpour bring on the growth of the new seed.' For their part, Soviet historians praised Peter for the progressive character of his reforms, but censured him for the exploitation of the popular masses. They admired him for his tremendous will-power, but condemned his neglect of the individual and his cruelty. The torture and execution of his own son, the Tsarevich Alexis, in the summer of 1718, is an outstanding example, even if accompanied by charges of complicity with internal reactionaries and foreign enemies.

L. G. Beskrovnyi and B. B. Kafengauz saw Peter as:

… one of the greatest ideologues of absolutism. Together with his assistants he gave it a theoretical basis … Peter I considered autocracy to be 'the bastion of justice'. The state was seen by him as a most powerful force, capable of transforming society on the basis of reason.[3]

Taking a different tack, the post-Soviet historian E. V. Anisimov writes:

It was in the varied forms of coercion, which became the regulator of the system Peter created, that its totalitarianism was exhibited. Of course, it would be wrong to simplify everything. The Petrine reform had roots in the past. … Peter sharply intensified the processes under way in the country; he forced it to make a gigantic leap. … At the same time, all of Peter's revolution possessed, however paradoxical it may sound, a distinctly conservative character.[4]

Voltaire, in the history of her father first commissioned by the Empress Elizabeth, was one of the first analysts to see Peter as an early version of the enlightened absolutist. He then somewhat flatteringly asserted that the reformer's work was carried on after his death by four women, 'who have maintained, in full vigour, all the great designs he accomplished, and completed those which he had begun'.[5] The fourth of these women, Catherine II or Great, was remarkable enough for her reign to be considered separately in the next chapter. Here, we will attempt to sketch the other three, less remarkable women, Catherine I, Anna and Elizabeth, as well as the men whom Voltaire neglected to mention.

At Peter's death in 1725, the succession was unsettled. In 1722, he had issued a decree giving the tsar the right to appoint his successor. But he himself did not act upon the decree, and so his widow was declared Empress by a group of officials supported by the Guards. Ekaterina or Catherine I (1725–7) had been a good companion and second wife for her husband, but by herself was capable of nothing more than the continuation and extension of their drunken debaucheries. The real ruler quickly became Peter's close associate A. D. Menshikov. To encourage the support of other men in high places, Menshikov was forced to accept the establishment of a new organ of central government, the Supreme Privy Council. At Catherine's death in 1727, Menshikov and the others declared that the throne would go to Peter, the son of the son of Peter the Great, the Tsarevich Alexis. The eleven-year-old Peter II was affianced to Maria Menshikov and her father appeared to be within reach of new heights of power. But then the fall of Menshikov was engineered by the Dolgorukii family, who supplanted him as the protectors and prospective in-laws of the young Emperor.[6] On the day appointed for his wedding, however, Peter II died of smallpox, and the male line of the Romanovs died with him.

In the confusion which followed his death in 1730, the Supreme Privy Council haggled among themselves, finally deciding to offer the crown to Anna Duchess of Courland, a daughter of Peter the Great's sometime co-ruler, Ivan V. Their offer was attended by certain 'Conditions', but Anna succeeded in tearing them up, overwhelming the Supreme Privy Council and introducing a new establishment, largely but not wholly of German origin, which formed her Cabinet.[7] The most outstanding favourite was named Biron, and so her reign (1730–40) has often been called the *Bironovshchina*, although such a title neglects the importance of other individuals in Anna's establishment, including some Russians. The Empress was a passionate huntswoman, and was at least as fond of weird entertainments as Peter the Great. She had a particular taste for freaks and dwarfs; one of her greatest entertainments was the marriage of one of her jesters in a palace made of ice on the frozen river Neva. An interesting case study in the psychopathology of Russian monarchs, she did not herself make much impact on the government's policies, and need not therefore detain us any longer.

On her deathbed in 1740, Anna declared that Biron should be regent during the minority of her niece's son, who was to become Ivan VI. After her death, Biron was ousted and the niece herself, Anna Leopoldovna, assumed the regency. The Germans along with some Russians continued to squabble among themselves, with some encouragement from France and Sweden, until a coup was staged by the Guards on behalf of the daughter of Peter the Great, Elizaveta or Elizabeth. She herself preferred guardsmen to power, but would probably have lost the first if she did not gain the second, and then have been confined in a nunnery. For her this would have been a fate worse than death, and so she allowed herself to be made Empress. As Empress, Elizabeth (1741–61) was able to indulge her insatiable liking for clothes, both men's and women's, hardly ever wearing the same outfit twice and leaving about fifteen thousand dresses at her death. Like her father, she was always worried about her security, and for this reason was often afraid to sleep, allegedly ordering her ladies to talk to her while tickling the soles of her feet to keep her awake. She paid more attention to the business of government than had Anna before her, but still left most of it to her favourites. Towards the end of her reign, a Conference was formed to replace the defunct Cabinet, and formed a convenient focus for the confluence and clash of the interests of the favourites.

While none of the monarchs between 1725 and 1761 had anything like Peter the Great's drive and acumen, some of their ministers were capable enough to continue his work, which itself was a culmination of a process inaugurated before his effective reign. Absolutism remained progressive during its ascendant phase, which lasted in Russia approximately down to the end of the eighteenth century. Granted that Peter's contribution to the completion of the structure of the Empire was far greater than that of most of his predecessors and successors, it is nevertheless surely misleading to persist with any variation of the idea summarised in a Russian pastiche of Alexander Pope's epitaph on Sir Isaac Newton:

> Russia for many years lay hid in night,
> God said, Let Peter be! and all was light.[8]

Political

The neat row of colleges, first constructed for Peter's bureaucrats in the new capital city of St Petersburg and now part of the University, give the impression of an order and probity which in fact were at least as lacking in the Russian administration as in any other in Europe during the eighteenth century. People were not intrinsically more inefficient or corrupt at this time than in later periods of history, but were influenced by the social circumstances in which they found themselves. In the Russian case, the salient features of the situation were a largely enserfed peasantry, a small and weak bourgeoisie, and a small but strong nobility. Hence, as the state became more unified, its government took the form of a bureaucracy responsive to the wishes of the nobility and prone to be a clumsy tool of class oppression as well as a focus for the interplay of personal rivalries and individual ambitions. On such a foundation, Peter superimposed an edifice constructed according to contemporary theoretical principles. Although in many respects, the edifice was to survive until the Revolution of 1917, the tension between it and its unstable underpinning resulted in cracks soon appearing both literally in the marshes of St Petersburg and metaphorically in the great swamp of the Russian Empire.

Peter's reforms in government as elsewhere were improvised rather than carefully planned, particularly in the beginning. The first of them were tinkerings with the *prikaz* and *voevoda* system bequeathed to him by his Romanov forebears, and need not be detailed here. The first of the comprehensive reforms, which was introduced in the years 1708–10, aimed at the improvement of social good order and financial efficiency. The whole country was divided into eight large provinces: Moscow, Ingermanland (later St Petersburg), Kiev, Smolensk, Kazan, Archangel, Azov and Siberia. All of these, except Moscow, contained part of the Empire's troublesome frontiers, and they were all entrusted to governors from among Peter's close associates. In the governor's hands was committed the judicial, administrative, police and financial power of the huge area under his jurisdiction. The *prikazy* were struck a mortal blow, but the *voevoda* gained new strength at the expense of the municipalities and other provincial officials below the level of governor.

Meanwhile, at the centre, the Boyar Duma was virtually dead on its feet, and the Privy Council, manned by eight of Peter's trusted underlings, was handling the most important business of state although legally subordinated to the Duma. And then in 1711, while the tsar was away on the campaign of the Prut, the Senate was set up to take care of business. At first envisaged as a temporary replacement for the sovereign, the Senate was entrusted with those tasks currently occupying Peter's attention. Thus it was instructed to consider some leases for the sale of salt, trade with China, the attraction of young nobles into service, and so on. Gradually, however, deliberations about the service of young nobles led to a general supervision of the army and navy, concern for the Chinese trade grew into management of trade in general, and activity connected with one aspect of the tsar's income soon became the control of all the state's finances. In such a manner, the Senate became a permanent body and its nine members came officially to be the most important government functionaries. However, none of the members was a close henchman of Peter, and all of them, like everybody else in the land, were kept under close scrutiny by a network of supervisory officials known as fiscals.

With the introduction of the Senate and the fiscals, the first period of Peter's political reforms came to an end; the second consisted of the creation of the colleges and some new officials, and a further reform of local administration. The idea of the institution of colleges had been with Peter for some years before its final implementation; they were widely accepted in Europe as the best available bureaucratic system. Foreign experts were consulted, and many recruited to come to St Petersburg either to help with the planning of the colleges or to man them. They came into existence on paper in 1717, but by 1718 only the top three, War, Admiralty and Foreign Affairs, were in actual operation. By 1720, the six others had been created, three dealing with finance, and three dealing with industry and trade. None of them functioned for long on the co-operative collegial principle, however, even though their functions were spelled out comprehensively in a General Instruction of 1720. The most important of the new officials was the procurator-general, at first Pavel Iaguzhinskii, whom Peter considered to be his own private eye and Russians at large believed to be the second most important man in the Empire. The procurator-general was to be in charge of the secret police and to supervise the government, including the Senate, to which in Peter's later years were added a number of offices, notably the herald-master's. The reform of the local administration from 1718 onwards, like the new arrangement of town government in 1721, was too elaborate to be transplanted from Swedish, Prussian and other European soil to the vast spaces of the Russian Empire. The personnel were just not available to fulfil the aims projected.

Soon after Peter's death, decrees of 1727 and 1728 restored a simplified control of fifty provinces by governor and *voevoda*. Together with local army units, and a growing number of nobles living locally, this system worked reasonably well, if harshly, for the time being. Central government, as already noted, experienced a number of sudden changes after 1725, with fluctuations in the fortunes of the Senate and other parts of the machinery, and the creation of a succession of advisory bodies to the sovereign. A point of greater importance, according to some contemporary observers and later analysts alike, was the nature of the personnel in the entourages of the various sovereigns. For this reason, the palace revolutions of the period take on no small significance.

The most interesting of them was that which brought Anna to the throne in 1730. The traditional interpretation of the succession crisis following the death of Peter II is that the members of the Supreme Privy Council, particularly D. M. Golitsyn, presented Anna with restrictive conditions, because they sought to introduce an oligarchic form of government into Russia. But the mass of the nobility, preferring the rule of one to many, persuaded Anna to tear up the 'Conditions' and were at least in the short run content to see the restoration of autocracy. Several reservations must be made to this traditional interpretation. Firstly, it is doubtful that Golitsyn ever had the constitutional dreams that have been attributed to him; at least none of them is known to be in existence on paper.[9] Secondly, the opponents of the councillors included some nobles of very high rank who had previously been in office, and so the clash should be seen less as an ideological clash than as a simple struggle between 'ins' and 'outs' who agreed on the basic forms that the government should take. As Lenin said of 1730 and the other coups of the eighteenth century, they 'were ludicrously easy, when it was a question of taking power from one clique of nobles or feudal lords and handling it over to another'.[10] The whole process was assisted by the greater cohesion achieved by the nobility in the eighteenth century, a circumstance that stands out in stark relief when we contrast its coups with the bloody struggles of the seventeenth century. This is not to say that the structure of the *dvorianstvo* did not contain strains and weaknesses, but they were obviously of a less profound nature than the tensions between the upper and lower classes.

These revealed themselves in a numbers of revolts, the greatest of which was the third 'peasant war' under the leadership of Kondratii Bulavin. This broke out soon after the first large-scale incident of civil disturbance in the eighteenth century, the revolt of 1705 centred on the town of Astrakhan at the mouth of the Volga and involving *streltsy* and soldiers many of whom were Old Believers. In 1707, the major conflict erupted on the Don, where the Cossacks were aggrieved at encroachments on their freedom by the centralising government. Under the leadership of Bulavin, a local hetman, or commander, Cossacks from the Don and the Dnepr joined with peasants from a large number of places, and prepared to go 'to Rus to kill the boyars'. Negotiations were carried on with various tribesmen and with Turkey, and some vain attempt was made to reach accommodation with the tsar. Bulavin was assassinated in the summer of 1708 by some dissident Cossacks, but it was early 1709 before the revolt was brought to an end. Cruel reprisals followed, and the people were cowed into passivity. Bulavin's revolt, according to the Soviet historian V. V. Mavrodin, resembled the other three peasant wars 'in such traits as the leading forces ... (above all the peasantry, the Cossack rank and file, the poor townspeople), its anti-serf ideology, its aspiration to a struggle for power, the wide territory seized by the incursions of the insurgents, the existence of a general centre for the movement'.[11] Until the fourth peasant war under the leadership of E. I. Pugachev in the 1770s, there was no revolt of comparable size, although the serfs of the field and the factory and the tribesmen were by no means completely quiescent. For example, at the end of the 1750s and the beginning of the 1760s, there were more than sixty violent outbreaks on noble and monastic estates. In 1755 there was a culmination of much unrest in a large-scale rising of the Bashkirs and other tribesmen along the Volga. Small-scale brigandage and flight were problems of great concern to the authorities and their supporters at all times.

The reasons for such troubles are not hard to find; social and racial inequalities were perpetuated and even aggravated by a government primarily responsive to the property-owning classes. Peter's policy, which was continued under his successors, strengthened the bonds of serfdom and intensified the process of the incorporation and russification of the nationalities, while contributing to the cohesion and strength of the bour-geoisie and particularly of the nobility. Not only did Peter recruit a vast number of peasants for his army and navy: the construction of St Petersburg and the improvement of canals also made great demands on the Empire's manpower, 120,000 workers being requisitioned for the new capital during each of several years following 1704. A further consider-able quantity of peasants were given away to the tsar's favourites. The introduction of the poll tax in 1718 and of compulsory internal passports in 1724 were only two of a whole series of decrees burdening and restrict-ing the peasantry at large. A sample decree from the post-Petrine era was that of 1760 permitting landlords to send their serfs into Siberian exile. Such laws were more likely to be implemented than that of 1721 con-demning the break-up of families and the piecemeal sale of peasants 'like cattle'.

Meanwhile, the embryonic bourgeoisie was nurtured by the govern-ment, although not to the extent recommended by such spokesmen as Ivan Pososhkov, a passionate mercantilist who wanted his country to be self-sufficient and his class to receive, among other concessions, exclusive rights to commerce.[12] Legislation encouraging guilds and municipal gov-ernment constituted a graft which could not find suitable Russian roots, but merchants and manufacturers certainly received material subsidies from the government, enough to achieve a level of prosperity at which many of them could aspire to membership of the nobility.

Undoubtedly, the nobility received the greatest wedge of the national cake, although the slices were by no means equitably distributed among the individual members of the class, the poorest of which were miserable clients aspiring to nothing more than a few crumbs given to them by their richer brethren. The cohesion of the *dvorianstvo*, already encouraged by such networks of patronage in the armed forces and the civil service, was increased in a statutory manner, notably by the introduction of the Table Ranks in 1722. Deriving partly from earlier Muscovite evolution and prepared also by a thorough study of the arrangement of other nobilities, particularly the German and Scandinavian, the Table guaranteed ennoblement, hereditary or personal, to those reaching certain levels in the hierarchy. The principle of rank as a reward for service was to remain a basic element of the Russian imperial state until its overthrow. However, an attempt made in 1714 to introduce from abroad the concept of single succession in estate ownership was never really accepted and had fallen into disuse long before its repeal in 1736.

Entry to the nobility could also still be achieved by the personal grant of the monarch or through the translation of non-Russian ranks. One of the first to go through the former procedure was the industrialist N. I. Demidov; several of those to take the latter route came from the upper class of the peripheral nationalities. During the first half of the eighteenth century, not only Ukrainians and Balts but also representatives of the Bashkir and other peoples along the Volga and beyond were adopted in such a manner, thus assisting the russifying drive of the central government. Future candidates for such assimilation would come from the Caspian littoral, Transcaucasia and Central Asia, into all of which areas the Russian influence was penetrating during the period, as indeed it was into Siberia too.[13]

The demands made on the armed forces for the support of such expansion, the maintenance of domestic security and the prosecution of foreign wars were even greater than before and demanded a higher degree of modernisation than that achieved by the first Romanovs. Peter discovered in his Azov campaigns and even more at the disaster of Narva that the forces at his disposal were insufficient for the tasks that he wished to pursue, and he therefore introduced a more developed recruitment system as well as widening the regimental structure and publishing new regulations. The regular army reached a size of 130,000, with between 200,000 and 300,000 men being called to take their turn with the colours during the first ten years of the war against Sweden. Meanwhile, the navy was created out of virtually nothing, some 800 ships being manned by nigh on 30,000 sailors by the end of Peter's reign. After the death of Peter, the navy declined somewhat in importance, but the army was larger during the Seven Years War than during the Great Northern War, and probably by then the largest in Europe.

Such changes were partly the consequence of changes in the priorities of foreign policy, a shift of emphasis to the sea and then back again to land. At the beginning of his reign, Peter concentrated his energies against the Turks, attempting vainly to revive a Christian coalition during his first trip abroad. However, he did succeed in reaching agreement with the Poles for a joint attack on Sweden, and from 1700 until 1721, the struggle for a firm foothold on the Baltic became his major preoccupation. The Great Northern War developed ramifications throughout Europe. Polish and other support was fitful; Britain, alarmed at the self-assertion of what she previously considered to be something of a client state, generally supported Sweden against Russia. For his part, Peter often became embroiled in the petty dynastic affairs of German princes, as well as having to fight the Turks at the same time as the Swedes. Having recouped much of the morale lost at Narva in 1700 with the victory of Poltava in 1709, Peter believed it necessary to pursue Charles XII of Sweden and his Ukrainian henchman, the hetman Mazepa, down into the Turkish domains, where he found himself surrounded on the river Prut by the Turks. He was forced to return Azov and make other concessions to the Turks in the treaty of 1711. In the end, after further victories on land and sea, Russia acquired a large part of the Baltic littoral and the grudging recognition of Europe through the Treaty of Nystadt of 1721. By the end of Peter's reign, then, the window on the West was firmly established, with extremely important consequences for Russia and for the whole continent. For the most part, Russian historians, both Soviet and non-Soviet, view the reformer's foreign policy as consistent with Russian national needs, even when he led an expedition from 1722 to 1724 to take some of the littoral of the Caspian Sea, possibly with a view to an expedition to India.

In the 1730s wars against Persia and Turkey deprived Russia of the shore of the Caspian, but regained for her the possession of Azov, albeit with the fortress destroyed, and a large amount of southern Russia. Throughout the period after 1725, relations with the rest of Europe were usually uneasy, as the power balance was upset not only by the more positive assertion of Russian interests but also by the rise of Prussia. Already revealing itself in wars concerning the Polish and Austrian succession and against Sweden, this latter development was the central circumstance leading to the outbreak in 1756 of the Seven Years War. The struggle between Great Britain and France for overseas dominance was another major theme of the war, the British for the most part supporting Frederick II and the Prussians against the French and their Austrian and Russian allies. Possibly, the continental initiative for the war came from Russia, with the Empress Elizabeth herself showing an unusual amount of bellicosity. If so, it was all the more surprising when, after a series of victories over the Prussian army leading to a brief occupation of Berlin itself, the Russian troops found themselves at the death of Elizabeth in late 1761 not only withdrawn from the war against Frederick but put back into it on Frederick's side. This *volte-face* has normally been seen as a clear example of the new ruler Peter III's insane Prussophilia. However, there is at least the common-sense argument in favour of it that a completely dismembered Prussia would have been almost as dangerous for Russia as a Prussia all-powerful. This historic struggle between Germany and Russia for a balance of interests in central and eastern Europe undoubtedly reached a new intensity as a consequence of the Seven Years War, with serious implications for the states separating them, particularly Poland.[14]

Economic

Before the reign of Peter the Great, there was no adequate estimate of the Russian population, and even the eighteenth-century censuses were probably unreliable. From the first census begun in 1719, a total may be inferred of just over $15^1/_2$ millions, with the most thickly peopled regions being the centre around Moscow, and then, a long way behind, the Left-Bank Ukraine, the Middle Volga and the north-west focused on St Petersburg. By the second census, begun in 1744, the total had risen to nearly $18^1/_4$ millions, the steepest rise having occurred in peripheral areas such as the Lower Volga, the Northern Urals and Left-Bank Ukraine.

Some of this rise would betoken an extension of the basic economic pursuit, agriculture, although as before this was not accompanied by much intensification. The three-field strip system still predominated, particularly in the centre, and a simple plough with only the share made of iron continued to make shallow furrows, while harrows usually consisting of a wooden frame with pegs or even a bunch of branches lashed together barely scratched the surface. Under Peter and to a lesser extent his successors, attempts were made to increase fertilisation, to introduce better ploughs and harrows and to discourage sickles in favour of scythes, and to encourage the cultivation of crops that could boost exports or reduce imports such as flax, hemp and tobacco. The silk industry was fostered by the government, with experts being persuaded to come for this purpose from Italy. Silesian and Spanish strains of sheep were imported to improve the domestic flocks, which were to be found mostly in the south and the Ukraine, and special military stud-farms were developed at Kazan, Kiev and Azov. The government also made attempts to protect Russia's timber resources and to promote bee-keeping.

For all such attempts at change and progress, rye remained the predominant crop and traditional farming methods persisted. The flavour of rural life is caught by the instruction for the estate of the Dutch family Vinius near Moscow. In February the steward was to see to it that brushwood was put down on the arable land, so that it would be dry and be ready for burning by spring. In March manuring should be carried out as well, and by May ploughing and sowing were to be in progress. The steward was to make sure that the peasants did not steal seed, to check that stones were placed on the harrows so that they would bite deeper, and to stop time being wasted, since late sowings in previous years had meant harvests spoiled by frost. Work for the landlord was naturally made a priority, the peasants being allowed two days for themselves. Disobedient peasants were to be beaten with rods or receive other corporal punishment. In August, after the harvest, seed had to be collected from the peasantry in return for what had been lent them in the spring. Vegetables and berries were to be collected too. In the autumn and winter months buildings were to be repaired, flax processed, and the peasants given yarn so that they could produce cloth.

The Vinius peasants worked on the *barshchina* corvée labour basis rather than making *obrok* quitrent payments to their landlords. Roughly speaking, *barshchina* was to be found in the black-earth region and *obrok* in the centre and the north where the land was less fertile. While about half the peasants belonged to the nobility, about a quarter were the property of the Church and most of the remainder in the charge of the state. In each category of peasant, there were those who managed to achieve a comparatively high level of prosperity, at least in good times, as well as some in the depths of poverty, particularly in bad.

With the extension of agriculture in the first half of the eighteenth century went a growth of petty manufacturing. This could include iron-working, as well as the smithery of silver and gold, but textiles of various kinds would be more typical products. Furriers, shoemakers, soap manufacturers, tailors and carpenters were in business in most towns of any size, while luxury specialists producing such goods as wigs, chairs, carriages and gowns were to be found primarily in the capitals. In Moscow there were about 2500 such petty manufacturers and in St Petersburg around 7000 of them, about half of whom in both cases were of peasant origin, a not insignificant number of foreign extraction, and the majority self-employed. In other towns there would be fewer foreigners and more peasants. Government policy towards this sector of the economy wavered, on the whole aiming at the encouragement of guilds and higher standards. For example, the width of certain kinds of cloth was regulated, and the use of tar in shoemaking forbidden. But it was very difficult to enforce such policy.

Large-scale industry, as is well known, flourished with official support during the reign of Peter the Great. It is rather less well known that it continued to flourish after his death. Now, however, there was less active state participation, fewer public works programmes, and not so many imaginative gestures such as Peter's invitation to the Chinese government to send over some experts in bridge building. The grand total of large-scale enterprises from the death of Peter the Great to the accession of Catherine the Great, which has been variously estimated according to definitions used, probably rose from something approaching 200 to nearly 700.[15] Families such as the Stroganovs and Demidovs were making vast industrial fortunes during the period.

While the extent of Russia's industrialisation during the early eighteenth century must not be exaggerated, it was already sufficient to make an international impact, a British writer of the period fearing that: '... the sound of the Forge in the next Generation will not be heard or known among us. We need not call in the *Americans* to their Assistance: the *Swedes* and *Russians* alone are sufficiently able to subdue the British Woods and Iron-works.'[16] In other words, Russia was by about 1752 already exporting a not insignificant amount of iron, as well as a considerable amount of linen, along with hemp and flax, leather and naval stores. Her major imports at this time were woollen goods, dyestuffs and wines. The balance of trade was in her favour, and the government's trading policy protectionist. The major trading partner in the West was Britain, followed by Holland; the Eastern trade was with a number of places from Persia to China, silk being the most important single item. In commerce as well as industry, there was both growth and an essential continuity after Peter's death, although Soviet historians condemn Anna's government for its treaty of 1734 which gave Britain most favoured nation privileges with regard to the Persian silk trade and made other concessions.[17] Throughout the period, the government attempted to adhere to its own version of mercantilist principles, although even Peter's energy was not enough to create a Russian mercantile marine. In 1757 protectionist tariffs were raised on many items to a higher level than in Peter's list of 1724.

The growth of domestic trade was most clearly reflected in the abolition of internal customs in 1753 for all regions except Siberia. The all-Russian market was now taking on a firmer shape around such centres as St Petersburg, Moscow, Novgorod and the fair of St Macarius near Nizhnii Novgorod. Links with the Ukraine and other peripheral regions were strengthened.

Quite naturally, the government was interested not only in promoting the expansion of the economy, but also in extracting from whatever prosperity there was as large a share as possible. 'Money is the artery of war', wrote Peter the Great to his Senate, and even after the end of the Great Northern War nearly 75 per cent of state expenditure went on the army and navy. By this time, over half the state's income came from the poll tax which was levied on all males in the common populace and replaced the household tax, and was fully introduced by 1723. A further third came from the indirect sources of the state trade in vodka and salt and the levies on trade in general. Debasements of the coinage were a much-used traditional method of increasing revenues, and resulted in a loss of half the purchasing power of the rouble during Peter's reign. But even this was not enough to keep the artery pumping properly, and further stimulants had to be applied, including all sorts of ingenious taxes thought up by a group of 'profit-makers', such as those on boots, watermelons and blue eyes. Of course, in Peter's reign and after it, a vast amount of state money went into the pockets of corrupt officials. In the later period there were some half-hearted attempts to reduce government expenditure, but also some great rises in it, during the Seven Years War, for example. The distinct social bias in the financial system became if anything more apparent with the institution in 1754 of a State Bank which lent money primarily to members of the nobility.[18]

Cultural

The reign of Peter the Great marked a significant step forward of a Russian secular culture, marked by the move from Moscow to St Petersburg. The first lay education institutions were set up, the Church was brought firmly under state control, and the language, literature and the arts and sciences began to focus their attention more on earth and less on heaven.

By a decree of early 1701, a School of Mathematics and Navigation was set up, staffed by Henry Farquharson of Marischal College, Aberdeen, and two youthful graduates of the Royal Mathematical School at Christ's Hospital, London, on which the Moscow School was largely modelled.

The curriculum was to include arithmetic, geometry, trigonometry, navigation, astronomy, fencing, reading and writing. The inaugural years were very difficult, because teachers and pupils could not understand each other, there were no Russian textbooks, and the preparatory education of the students had often been inadequate. The situation improved after a Russian mathematician, L. F. Magnitskii, joined the organisation, and soon the School was producing not only navigators but also civil servants and teachers, artillerymen and engineers, topographers, hydrographers and architects. In 1715 the Moscow School closed to be re-opened as the Naval Academy in St Petersburg, and other navigation schools were set up in several towns. Specialist schools were also set up for Artillery (1701), Engineering (1712) and Medicine (1707). A different kind of school was the Glück Gymnasium opened in Moscow in 1705, and specialising in such subjects as languages, philosophy and politics, and 'compliments in the French and German manner'. Before its closure ten years later, the Gymnasium had succeeded in sending out into the world some 250 graduates, including bureaucrats and diplomats as well as soldiers and sailors.

An attempt at the introduction of a general network of primary schools was made with the creation in 1714 of the cipher or mathematical schools. The decree projected two such schools for each province, with a simple curriculum of reading, writing, arithmetic, geometry and trigonometry. In fact, by 1716 only 12 such schools had been opened, and by 1722 only 30 more. By 1744, a mere eight were still in existence, and only the three largest of them were retained, merged with garrison schools. These, a second type of general school, were just starting in Peter's reign and were expanded in the 1730s. A third category, the most successful, were the diocesan schools. There were nearly 50 of them with about 3000 students by 1727, at Novgorod, in the Ukraine, and elsewhere. These and other Church schools were often plundered for their students by ailing secular educational institutions.

This was so with the Academy of Sciences, founded in 1724 as a repository and propagator of higher learning and opened in 1725 by Peter the Great's widow, the illiterate Catherine I. European savants such as Leibniz and Wolff made a considerable contribution to the St Petersburg Academy, as did several of their lesser-known colleagues in the university and gymnasium attached to it. The great ideas of Newton and others were received, while the work of the Academicians became known abroad.[19] But the teaching side of the Academy's activities did not prosper and had virtually ceased before the opening of Moscow University in 1755. Soviet historians stressed the participation in this project of Mikhail Lomonosov, while the initial impetus appears to have come from one of Elizabeth's favourites, Ivan Shuvalov. Another institution of some importance was the Noble Military Academy, founded in St Petersburg in 1731. Here, most obviously, the ever-present element of class discrimination in education was apparent, although it could be argued that young nobles were given the best facilities because of the key role that they were expected to play in the armed forces and in the bureaucracy.

Nobles and commoners alike often received some kind of education at the hands of private tutors, and many young Russians were sent abroad for training of various kinds, the emphasis being practical under Peter the Great, less so under his predecessors. Many of the tutors were themselves barely educated, and were often appointed solely on the basis that they were German or French and could therefore teach their own language. At least one of the Russian tutors was a widow who could not read, but recited passages that she had learned by heart from Church books for her pupils to make of what they could. As for the journey to Western Europe, the young Russians were at first terrified at the prospect, and then naïvely impressionable when they actually arrived at their destination. Gradually, the visitors from Eastern Europe came to take a deeper interest in aspects of Western European life, although not many Frenchmen would have agreed with the appraisal made of Louis XIV's France by one of the visitors, who could see only order and the absence of arbitrary government.[20] Ignorance and misunderstanding were mutual, of course, and many foreigners were hopelessly inaccurate in their observation of eighteenth-century Russia.

The gap between the two extremities of the continent must not be exaggerated, for a broad conformity to a general pattern of cultural development may be discerned in Russia. This is so with regard to education and to the Church, about which Miliukov wrote: 'The entire ecclesiastical policy of Peter can be summarized as a consistent development of two ideas: the elimination of the Patriarch, who could become a Russian Pope … and the subordination of the Church to the reigning monarch.[21] In 1700, the Patriarch Adrian died, and Peter did not hurry to appoint a successor. The *locum tenens* Stepan Iavorskii soon embroiled himself in controversy with the tsar, and thus contributed to the abolition of the Patriarchate. And then, in 1721, the Ecclesiastical Regulation was introduced, setting up the Holy Synod as the basic governor of the Russian Church, with a layman as its chief procurator keeping it in order. Peter himself had a soldier's bluff faith, which encouraged him to concentrate on the morality and loyalty of his subjects rather than on niceties of doctrine. For this reason, he considered it necessary to subject the Church itself to the discipline of his all-pervasive bureaucratic state. For example, a decree on a seminary's daily routine stated that: 'like soldiers at the beat of a drum, the seminarists will, at the sound of a bell, proceed to the performance of whatever is appointed for that hour.' Historians of the Russian Church are divided in their interpretation of the effect of Peter's reform, some seeing it as a liberation for clerics who could now concentrate exclusively on spiritual matters, while others look upon it as a victory for encroaching secularism. Either way, ecclesiastical matters will henceforth be of smaller concern up to 1917.[22]

The second of these two directions is certainly more apparent in the linguistic and literary developments of the period. During the reign of Peter the Great, when a large amount of translation was carried out, particularly of technical books, the written language based on Church Slavonic had to be adapted to the needs of the new age. This task, which was reputed to have driven at least one translator to attempt suicide on several occasions, prepared the way for the poets and prose writers of the period after his death. While popular tales and ballads similar to those of the seventeenth century continued to be composed in the eighteenth, the more ordered world of the ode and the drama was establishing itself. This involved the transplantation to Russian soil of Western verse forms and classical models. The work was carried out by such men as A. D. Kantemir, V. K. Trediakovskii, A. P. Sumarokov and M. V. Lomonosov.

Lomonosov was a man of many parts, producing scientific and historical treatises as well as poetry. Another historian of note was V. N. Tatishchev, who also produced a mature piece of political thought at the time of the constitutional crisis of 1730, a rational defence of autocracy as the most suitable form of government for the Russian Empire. Scientific voyages of discovery through Siberia and over to North America were made by such individuals as Vitus Bering and Aleksei Chirikov.

Before the accession of Catherine the Great, then, the way had been prepared for the cultural flowering usually associated with her name, not only in literature and the sciences but also in the arts. The reign of Elizabeth was a clear precursor as the dominant foreign influence turned from German to French. Painters such as I. I. Vishniakov and A. P. Andropov, and architects such as I. F. Michurin and D. V. Ukhtomskii, received Elizabeth's patronage, which was also given to the portraitist François Tocqué and the Paris-born creator of the Hermitage Palace, Bartolomeo Francesco Rastrelli. In such a manner, the regularisation of Russian art and architecture embodied in the creation of the new capital was subjected to modification.[23]

Russia by 1761 had in all three principal areas under our consideration – political, economic, cultural – made the effort to adapt to herself the most advanced ideas of Europe, and had thus effected the completion of much of the structure of the Russian Empire on the foundation laid during the second half of the seventeenth century. This process, it must be remembered, was made possible by imperial expansion. Without the assimilation of first the Ukraine and then the Baltic provinces, the edifice would have been rickety indeed.[24]

On 22 October 1721, to celebrate the end of the Great Northern War, the victorious tsar was awarded the title of 'Peter the Great, Emperor of All the Russias and Father of his Country.' A rationale for the new stage in Russia's emergence combining the injunctions of Holy Writ with such concepts as the 'general good' was devised by Feofan Prokopovich and adapted later by Vasily Tatishchev and others as the young Empire made its presence known more widely throughout Europe and beyond.[25]

6 Enlightened Absolutism, 1761–1801

'Peter gave Russians bodies, and Catherine – souls', declared a contemporary poet, thereby expressing in a personalised manner some of the differences between the two phases of absolutism. Peter's emphasis was indeed on the practical and Catherine's on the intellectual. The two phases may also be separated according to the major Western influences on them: Peter was struck mainly by the scientific movement and the rationalism of the late seventeenth century, while Catherine was more receptive to the somewhat more rarefied arguments of the eighteenth-century *philosophes*. At the same time, there was at least a little continuity between the two phases, as there was between the sources of their inspiration and between the problems that they aimed at overcoming.[1]

Along with Ekaterina, Catherine II – or Catherine the Great (1762–96) as she is more normally known – we must consider her husband Petr or Peter III and her son Pavel or Paul I. Peter III reigned for little more than six months, yet this period saw quite an amount of legislative action which has been the subject of considerable discussion among historians. A not insignificant feature of the discussion is the personality of Peter himself. Born in Kiel in 1728, Peter had arrived in Russia from Germany soon after the accession of his aunt Elizabeth. He was declared the heir of Elizabeth after being received into the Orthodox Church. Catherine came from Germany in 1745 to be married to him, and, although the young couple soon decided that they did not care much for each other, they both agreed to find consolation elsewhere and were able to enter into something like a stable state of peaceful co-existence. Unfortunately for Peter, however, one of the major sources of information concerning him is the *Memoirs* of Catherine, in which she showed much more devotion to self-justification than to objective truth. Other sources suggest that Peter was not the childish imbecile, not the 'permanent patch upon a very beautiful face' that Catherine made him out to be. He spoke three languages – in ascending order of fluency, Russian, French and German – although he wrote them all rather incorrectly. He liked his large library, and was probably no less an intellectual than many of his predecessors, if not the equal of his wife. His passion for playing the violin, which he did badly, and for coarse merry-making, at which he was an accomplished master, again hardly set him far apart from most of his forebears. While some analysts have found the key to an understanding of his policy in his psychological make-up, others have discovered it in his great admiration for Frederick the Great of Prussia. Certainly he had a taste for drill which might be called Prussophile, as he forced even high-ranking officers to turn out on the parade ground, and changed army regulations and uniforms according to Prussian models. Undoubtedly too, he did have great personal respect for Frederick the Great. But as we shall see below, to explain his short reign exclusively by the quirks of his personality would be to exaggerate his importance and to under-estimate the part played by other individuals.[2]

Sophia Augusta Frederika, an obscure German princess born in 1729, was about sixteen years old when she came to Russia to marry Peter, and became Ekaterina Alekseevna with her conversion to Orthodoxy.[3] The major influences on her early life are considered to have been her father and her governess: from the former she acquired a serious interest in politics as well as a certain tomboyish masculinity; from the latter she gained a great curiosity if not so much the means of satisfying it. These traits were to stand her in good stead during the frustrating years from 1745 to 1762, as she read widely and imbibed a considerable amount of ancient and modern wisdom. Her correspondence with Voltaire and most of the other great men of the age shows her to be well-informed and lively if not profound or original. Allowing her to lead her notorious private life in her off-duty hours, we shall give our primary attention here to her public policies.

Catherine has not received from posterity anything like the adulation that she received from flatterers while she was alive. Pushkin called her a Tartuffe in skirts, and her vainglorious hypocrisy has come under attack from many other quarters. A more balanced appraisal came from Kliuchevskii, who wrote that, after the failure of an early liberal idealism, she consoled herself with the thought that 'after me they will follow my principles', and concentrated on educational and propagandist activity. Making herself a famous personage of Europe, she also assisted some members of society to feel a new self-confidence: 'From Peter, hardly daring to consider themselves people and still not considering themselves proper Europeans, Russians under Catherine felt themselves to be not only people, but almost the first people of Europe.' For this reason, they forgave her for the mistakes of her foreign policy and for her persecution of various internal foes, for her profligacy and perpetuation of social injustice. In a

similar manner, Isabel de Madariaga has observed that Catherine's great-
ness is to be found 'not much in her territorial acquisitions but in the new
relationship between rulers and ruled which she fostered.'[4]

However, many of her contemporaries, especially from the lower
orders, showed what they thought of Catherine by joining in the Pugachev
Revolt. In such a tradition was the dismissal of her worth by Marx and
Engels. Moreover, neither the fact that she was born a foreigner nor that
revolutionary thought first arose towards the end of her reign helped to
acquire for her anything more than the coolest of receptions from Soviet
historians. However, her particular brand of enlightened despotism was
seen by at least some of them as a move towards the formation of a bourgeois ideology, and her personal qualities have also been given some
recognition. I. A. Fedosov wrote, 'Without doubt Catherine was one of
the outstanding figures on the Russian throne – clever, and educated, and
capable, and successful.' In post-Soviet Russia, she has received a greater
measure of rehabilitation, A. B. Kamenskii looking upon her as 'bright
and extraordinary' and her reign as stable and consolidative.[5]

Her son has received a greater measure of rehabilitation. It is true that
Fedosov considered Paul I to have been a crazy despot who 'threatened
to discredit the very idea of absolutism'. On the other hand, a few pre-
revolutionary historians argued that he could be called some kind of
enlightened absolutist; and some Soviet historians believed that he was
at least in some respects progressive. For his Western biographer R. E.
McGrew, Paul was 'the first of a series of Russian rulers to attempt to
cope with a radically modernising world through an essentially conservative ideology.'[6]

Paul was born in 1754. Some doubt that his father was Peter III, but
certain physical and psychological resemblances give support to the evidence that he was born in grand-ducal wedlock. He spoke the same
languages as his father and spelled them as badly, and like Peter was fond
of his large library. Like Peter too, he admired Prussia and disliked
Catherine. His education under the supervision of Nikita Panin, one of
Catherine's chief advisers, appears to have been sound, but he was kept
well away from actual business of government. He paid two visits to
Western Europe, one of them after the death of his first wife, a German
princess; during this second visit, he found another to be his second wife.
He then settled down on the Gatchina estate near St Petersburg. He was a
solicitous landlord and a good if disciplinarian garrison commander. His
relations with his second wife were clouded, however, by one of her
ladies-in-waiting, who developed a close if chaste connection with the
future Emperor and encouraged the mysticism which had already been

kindled by an earlier acquaintance with Freemasonry. Around Paul gathered an entourage which was to take full advantage of the opportunity offered to it in 1796 at the death of Catherine.

During the last decades of the eighteenth century, 'the Russia of Catherine II, by virtue of the number of its factories and work-shops, the volume of its production and the part it played in European trade, took its place among the great economic powers.'[7] The Empire consolidated itself on the Black Sea and swallowed a large slice of Poland. Its army won great victories in Eastern and Western Europe, its navy triumphantly asserted a presence in the Mediterranean. Europe gained the impression that Russia had become one of the great laboratories of the Enlightenment. All this was achieved at enormous social cost, and led to the outbreak of the Pugachev Revolt, the fourth, last and largest of the 'peasant wars'. And then, with the impact of that even greater civil disturbance, the French Revolution, absolutism became unenlightened and reactionary. Having at least to some degree assisted the development of the Russian Empire in the first century or so of its existence, tsarism now became, to be sure not without some echoes of liberalism, a dead weight on progress in all the major sectors of the national life.

Political

Although the reign of Peter III has often been looked upon as a crazy six months unconnected with very much that went before or came after, it may in fact be considered as a busy transitional period. To take its most celebrated decree, the so-called Emancipation of the Nobility of 18 February 1762, research has revealed a close connection with the ideas put forward in the later years of Elizabeth's reign. And of course the implementation and significance of the decree depended on Catherine. In such a light, the Emancipation does not stand out as a radical alteration in the service prescriptions of Peter the Great, but rather appears as a modification of their rigours. Kliuchevskii rightly observed: 'The law said: be so good, serve and teach your children, and nevertheless, he who does neither the one nor the other will be driven from society.' More generally in the informed words of Marc Raeff: 'In no sense was the legislation radical, nor did it introduce any notions and practices that were alien to the Russian polity of the eighteenth century.'[8] The question therefore naturally arises, why was the reign of Peter III so brief? Again to follow the interpretation of Raeff, an important reason was that Peter chose a new entourage which threatened to form an exclusive government, demeaning the Senate and other parts of the administration as it did so. In this respect as well as in others, the reign of Peter was in the tradition of Anna and Elizabeth, and so some weight must be given to the traditional verdict that one of Peter's greatest mistakes was the alienation of the Guards, whom Anna and Elizabeth had been careful to patronise.

Catherine II seized the supreme power in the summer of 1762. Her current lover, Grigorii Orlov, and his brothers were sufficiently popular among the Guards to gain sufficient support for the removal of Peter III and the installation of his wife, soon, if none too soon for her, to be his widow. While Peter and other threats to Catherine's position were eliminated, the Orlovs and their associates received considerable rewards for their endeavours. In the 1770s, another Grigorii, Potemkin, became Catherine's first favourite and, like his predecessors and successors, made large material if not moral gains. Potemkin continued to influence the policies of the Empress even when he became a less frequent visitor to her bed. Of her later lovers, only Platon Zubov, the last of the long line, enjoyed any political significance; no other affair of the heart can really be called an affair of state. In an informal manner, both her favourites and her advisers in general were broadly responsive to the class from which most of them sprang, the nobility. This tacit alliance between the autocrat and the ruling class became more marked as the reign wore on, particularly after such disturbing events as the Pugachev Revolt and the French Revolution. Catherine's policies concerning both local and central government clearly reflected such a social background.

From soon after her accession onwards, Catherine was presented with a series of memoranda on the subject of local government. A suggestion contained in many of them, for the introduction of an elective noble element, was repeated many times by assemblies of nobles in their instructions to deputies at the Legislative Commission of 1767. Although Catherine did not read all the instructions, the message got through to her. And then she was impressed by her reading in French translation of Sir William Blackstone and her consequent understanding of the English system of local government, especially the part played in it by the J. P.'s. Further reports of the methods of administration employed in the Baltic provinces, where officials elected by the nobility were dominant, also struck forcibly. The Pugachev Revolt of 1773–5 probably clinched the reform and accelerated its completion.

The decree of 1775 implementing the reform lamented the disorder of Russian local government and hoped to replace it with efficiency through the following four changes: the increase in the number of provinces, making them less unwieldy; decentralisation of several important powers concerning police, justice and finance; division of these powers among separate agencies; and introduction of officials elected by various classes, with the nobility predominant. Although the reform was imperfectly carried out, it put the seal on the control of the provinces by the nobility that had been developing since the death of Peter the Great; at the top there were such governors as Potemkin, near the bottom many less notable but still important district captains of police supervising the affairs of commoners. The fifty or so provinces in existence at the end of the eighteenth century were thus considerably prepared for the important reform of local government which was to take place in the 1860s.

Meanwhile, during the reign of Catherine, the government's bureaucracy grew larger and partly changed its nature. In 1763 there were about 16,500 officials on the establishment, all given a salary increase to encourage efficiency and reduce corruption. With the reform of 1775, up to 18,000 men now staffed the civil service and nearly a tenth of the total expenditure of the state went on its upkeep. At first encouraging a limited democratisation of the bureaucracy by facilitating the rise from the lower to the higher ranks in the table, Catherine reverted in her later reactionary mood to the aristocratic exclusiveness of earlier times, now reinforced by the introduction of the elective element. This restriction eliminated even some of the lesser members of the *dvorianstvo* from the civil service, particularly after the Charter of the Nobility of 1785, which allowed only landed proprietors to vote, and only those of them with the rank of commissioned officer and an income of not less than 100 roubles to be elected to office. Thus, at the end of Catherine's reign, the civil service was dominated by the upper and middle nobility, which looked upon the income derived from its state service as a supplement to that from its estates – a governor-general could earn as much as 600 roubles per annum in this manner, a middle-ranking councillor from 200 to 600 roubles. The lower echelons of the provincial bureaucracy were staffed by nobles who also depended on their salaries to make up the deficiencies of their income as landlords, and there was of course a whole ever-growing stratum of professional bureaucrats helping to swell the volume of paper in the governmental archives.

Apart from the reform of 1775, there were some other significant changes made by Catherine in the formal structure of government. First, a State Council was inaugurated in 1769, manned by an inner circle of officials who had worked as a less formal advisory group since the beginning of her reign. Although the Council was given a more defined constitutional position in the reign of Alexander I, the earlier version appears to have functioned well enough as an intermediary power between the Empress and the Senate. At the same time, it would certainly be wrong to see either in the formation of the State Council or in the preliminaries to it an aristocratic threat to the formal status of the autocrat. Second, the Senate itself was reorganised in 1763, neither for much better nor much worse as far as can be judged. With the reform of 1775, the Senate retained its administrative and judicial control of the provinces, but its ancillary Colleges were largely atrophied with the decentralisation of functions that the reform had entailed. They were soon abolished, except for the Colleges of Foreign Affairs, the Army and Navy which were directly responsible to the autocrat. Third, the office of procurator-general, which had lost much of its importance during the years before 1764, regained all that had been lost in the person of Prince Alexander Viazemskii, who was an important assistant to Catherine from 1764 to 1792. His hands were on the purse strings, his thumb was firmly on the network of secret police, and he had a finger in everything of importance. Fourth, along with the Charter of the Nobility of 1785, there was a Charter of the Towns and an unpublished charter for the state peasants. Neither of these schemes got far off the ground, especially the second of them. Catherine's dreams of a self-reliant peasantry and a flourishing middle class never approached realisation.

A few words must be said about Catherine's other shattered dreams. At first a pupil of Montesquieu, Beccaria and the *philosophes*, later of Blackstone, the Empress did not succeed in adapting the ideas of Western Europe into any coherent rationale of absolutism. In the first few years of her reign, however, she made a considerable effort, with her Legislative Commission of 1767 and her *Instruction* for it, to give her adopted country a new enlightened code of laws. Although the Commission failed to provide a code, it did give the Empress a clearer picture of what needed to be done to reform the Empire. The *Instruction*, which was banned in France and severely restricted in circulation in Russia, gives us an impression of the theoretical framework in which such a process would be carried out. The political philosophy that emerges from it is a modification of the balance-of-power concept of Montesquieu coupled with the German cameralist idea of social welfare achieved within the framework of the bureaucratic state. Catherine rejected Montesquieu's libertarian views and could not even accept the independent role that he suggests for the nobility, but she did agree with him that the separation of the legislative, executive and judicial powers subordinate to the monarch would prevent her absolutism from becoming despotism. Restrained from excesses by this and other measures adapted from Montesquieu, her government would address itself to the protection and prosperity of her people in the Christian cameralist manner suggested by such writers as Baron de Bielefeld. Those who still broke the law would be punished in the humane manner recommended by Beccaria. Such an exercise in self-justification was not without ingenuity, but Catherine's essential philosophy of government was expressed in a more succinct and accurate manner at the time of the Pugachev Revolt. Writing to the Kazan nobility, she declared herself to be a 'proprietress of Kazan' and emphasised that the security and well-being of the nobility were indivisible from her own and her Empire's.[9] Such a belief became more fervent with the onset of the French Revolution.

Paul's political vision, characterised by Florinsky as 'a thoroughly disciplined policy over which a wise absolute monarch exercised a quasi-paternalistic rule within the framework of the law', did not differ substantially from Catherine's.[10] At the same time, he gave more emphasis to service than to privilege, to coercion than to example, threatening dissident nobles with corporal punishment. The local elective governmental functions of the nobility were suppressed, and centralist control was asserted in a simplified provincial administration. The central government itself was largely unaltered, although a beginning was made towards the replacement of the Colleges by ministries. In 1797, he issued a 'Statute on the Imperial Family and succession to the Throne', regularising the order made imprecise by Peter the Great in 1722.

While the general tendency of Paul's governmental policy was to reverse the centrifugal trend of his mother's, his policy towards the nationalities inclined towards a reversal of her centripetal russification. For example, he restored the local rights and privileges of the Ukraine, Poland and the Baltic provinces that she had taken away. Near the beginning of her reign, Catherine wrote to her newly appointed procurator-general that the Ukraine and the Baltic provinces 'should be gently reduced to a condition where they can be russified and no longer, like wolves, look to the woods'.[11] Some twenty years later, with the application of the 1775 local government reform to these areas, this gentle reduction was brought to its culmination, the Ukrainian and Baltic nobilities being reconciled by their adoption into the *dvorianstvo* – with all the attendant opportunities for advancement in the service – and by the reinforcement in their regions of the institution of serfdom. The Poles, brought into the Empire by a series of partitions from 1772 onwards, were russified less but protested more, notably in the early nineties. The extension of Russian influence in other directions brought even greater problems. The occupation of the Crimea and establishment of a protectorate over Georgia in 1783 contributed to further wars against Turkey, and infiltration into Central Asia stimulated rebellions in Kazakhstan in 1783 and 1797. The consolidation of Russian interests in Siberia was attended with less violence, and the Empire's involvement in Alaska was marked by the formation in 1799 of the Russian–American Company.[12]

Catherine's policy of the firm incorporation of the outlying provinces and of their russification was one of the major reasons for the greatest outbreak of civil disturbance of the eighteenth century, the Pugachev Revolt, or fourth and last peasant war, of 1773–5. Dissident Cossacks rising on the Iaik River were joined by tribesmen and factory-workers as the movement spread to the Urals. While the main band was led by Emelian Pugachev, a Don Cossack claiming to be Peter III, other detachments and groups wrought havoc throughout a wide area. Having suffered several reverses, Pugachev was able to recover sufficiently to take Kazan except for its Kremlin. Defeated again, Pugachev swept down into the Volga region, where more than sixty peasant armed companies were formed. The threat to Moscow and St Petersburg seemed real enough to Catherine for a month or so, but then, overcome yet again by government forces, Pugachev took flight, only to be betrayed by some of his erstwhile supporters and handed over to the authorities. Taken to Moscow, Pugachev was executed there in January 1775. Stern reprisals were taken against all participants in his movement, and the government attempted literally to erase its memory by changing the name of its place of origin from the Iaik to the Ural river. While Soviet historians conceded the weaknesses of the ideology and organisation of the insurgents, they also adduced an impressive amount of evidence to show that these weaknesses can be exaggerated and to indicate that the fourth peasant war was the most worthy of the name. At least one of the Western historians who have lately turned their attention to the event is reluctant to typify it as much more than a 'frontier jacquerie'.[13]

Certainly, the Pugachev Revolt and some of the other civil disturbances of the period, such as the widespread peasant movement of 1796–8 which flared up in more than thirty provinces, would not have posed such a serious threat if the government had not been engaged in a busy period of international relations. At the beginning of her reign Catherine had to arrange Russia's final withdrawal from the Seven Years War after Peter III had taken his troops from the anti-Prussian side to the pro-Russian. The argument that there was some *raison d'état* in this *volte-face* draws support from Catherine's continuance of friendly relations with Frederick the Great, encouraged by her chief adviser Nikita Panin. The royal pair set about carving up Poland between them after some initial self-restraint, but the suspicion of Austria and France was aroused and the enmity of Turkey provoked.

Strongly aroused in addition by Russian probes towards the Black Sea and the Balkans, Turkey opened hostilities in 1768. The resulting war brought mixed results on land, and some famous victories on sea, where Russia asserted a firm presence in the Mediterranean, notably at the battle of Chesme off the Anatolian coast in 1770. The Pugachev Revolt brought the war to a somewhat hurried conclusion, the Treaty of Kuchuk–Kainardzhi of 1774 giving Russia parts of the Crimea and of the Black Sea littoral, the right of free passage through the Straits for her merchantmen, and an ill-defined protection over Turkey's Christian subjects.

Meanwhile, the first partition of Poland along with Russia and Austria in 1772 guaranteed the continued suspicion of Turkey and her European supporters. After a Russian Declaration of Armed Neutrality in 1780 had made no small impact on the American War of Independence,[14] Catherine was encouraged to think again of expansion, Potemkin's 'Greek Project' involving nothing less than the revival of the Byzantine Empire. Her occupation of the Crimea and infiltration into Transcaucasia goaded Turkey into action, and a second Russo–Turkish war broke out in 1787. This war brought about the triumphant assertion of the power and skill of the Russian forces, particularly the army under Suvorov[15] and the navy under Greig and Ushakov. It was also very complicated in its international ramifications. At first an ally of Russia's, Austria was persuaded in 1790 to leave the war by Prussia and Britain, who had also instigated a Swedish attack on Russia in 1788, brought to an end in 1790 with a recognition of the *status quo ante bellum*. For its part, the Russo–Turkish War was concluded by the Treaty of Jassy at the end of 1791; the terms of Kuchuk–Kainardzhi were confirmed, and more Black Sea littoral, notably between the rivers Bug and Dnestr, ceded to Russia. Later plans for revival and extension of the 'Greek Project' under Catherine's last lover, Platon Zubov, who wanted to move towards India as well as Constantinople, were abandoned at Catherine's death in 1796.

Before then, the outbreak and intensification of the French Revolution had brought about *rapprochement* with Austria, Prussia and Sweden, as well as good cover for the further dismemberment of Poland. The Poles took advantage of Russia's Turkish preoccupations and Prussian encouragement to adopt a new constitution in the spring of 1791, only to bring upon themselves the second partition of 1793, in which Russia and Prussia joined together, using as an excuse their fear that the spirit of the French Revolution was threatening Poland. Proof that such a fear was justified came in 1794 with the outbreak of a radical insurrection led by Tadeusz Kosciuszko, who had participated in the American Revolution and was imbued with many of the ideas of the French. The revolt was crushed, and was followed by the third partition, finally agreed between Russia, Prussia and Austria in early 1795. The Russian share consisted largely of White

Russia, Lithuania and other provinces, enabling Soviet historians to call it a reunion rather than a robbery, while condemning Catherine for her acceptance of the division of Poland proper between Prussia and Austria. However they are appraised, the Partitions of Poland certainly introduced into Russia the Jewish 'Pale of Settlement'.[16]

Paul's foreign policy included such eccentric moments as the Emperor's adoption of the knights of Malta and some brilliant campaigns by Suvorov, including a rapid crossing of the Alps. These and other moves were in the shadow of the rise of Napoleon, who was to constitute Russia's primary problem of international relations during the first decade and a half of the nineteenth century. Paul also formally annexed Georgia in 1801, and was preparing a grandiose campaign for the conquest of India at the time of his assassination in the same year.[17]

The second half of the eighteenth century produced a foreign policy at least as glorious and successful for tsarism as that of the first. Although the cost was crippling, such a policy could hardly have been undertaken at all if the Russian Empire had not been able to command an impressive amount of men and materials by the standards of the century. As Russia fell behind the rate of development of other nations in the nineteenth century, so her foreign policy became less successful, declining from the tremendous triumph over Napoleon to the humiliating disaster of the Crimean War.

Economic

At the beginning of her reign, Catherine was a keen proponent of economic progress. For example, she encouraged in 1765 the institution of the Free Economic Society for the Encouragement of Agriculture and Good Husbandry. In the first number of the Society's *Works*, the editor announced that everything possible would be done to improve Russian farming, which he looked upon as the basis of the Empire's prosperity. In the same year, the Society announced a Prize Essay Competition on the advisability of allowing the peasants to own property. The attitude of the bulk of the landlords to the question was possibly expressed by an ironic entry which declared that the abolition of serfdom would be possible when:

> Russia becomes as populous as the kingdom of Holland, when our priests are as literate as foreign priests, the nobles such sharp-witted fellows as the English and the French, the peasants know their ABC and are consequently honest and obey more the wrath of God and go to church more often than to the drinking houses, do not stave in the

barges on the Volga, and our rabble has a better understanding of foreign crafts, and becomes more intelligent.

The message of the winning entry, which proposed the grant to the peasants of a token amount of property, was summarised in its observation that 'It is a pleasure to see your dog following you everywhere ... can it be compared with the burdensome labour of leading a bear?' Even such unexceptionable remarks as these were published only after the intercession of the Empress, who also made some remarks which were very guarded – even more so after her advisers had expressed their shock – about the limitation of serfdom in her *Instruction* to the Legislative Commission of 1767. At the same time she spoke out more openly for the improvement of agriculture as well as of industry and trade. Enacting what she preached, she issued decrees in the first five years of her reign promoting the immigration of foreign colonists, the cultivation of potatoes and the execution of a general survey; weakening guild control and allowing people of every rank to engage in various kinds of manufacturing enterprise; and fostering trade with Great Britain and other foreign customers. While such policies as these certainly advanced the interests of the bourgeoisie, they were not necessarily to the detriment of the nobility, whose support Catherine always recognised as fundamental to the maintenance of her own power. Such a priority may be even more clearly observed through the rest of her reign.[18]

Although her personal and legislative contribution was small, Catherine was pleased to see the rise in the population from about $23^1/_4$ millions in 1762 to nearly $37^1/_2$ millions in 1795. This steep climb was partly natural and partly the consequence of imperial expansion. The incorporation of Lithuania and White Russia brought in more than 5 million people and that of the Right-Bank Ukraine nearly $3^1/_2$ millions. Peripheral areas became much more populous as the Empire became consolidated, New Russia tripling its numbers to well over a million and the Lower Volga nearly doubling them to just under a million. The more settled central provinces also grew demographically, and altogether by the end of her reign, Catherine might have been wondering if what had appeared to be a dearth at the beginning of it had now become an excess, at least in the heart of the Empire.

The social division of the Russian people remained roughly the same at the end of the eighteenth century as it had been at the middle, although perhaps with more local variations. That is, more than 90 per cent of them were peasants, and more than 50 per cent of the peasants were the serfs of the nobility rather than attached to the state. The percentage of town dwellers has been placed variously from 3.6 per cent to 8.3 per cent, depending on the definitions and figures used. The clergy, armed forces and nobility accounted for most of the rest of the population. Quite obviously, a Siberian tribesman, a New Russian peasant and a Baltic factory-worker would have much to differentiate them as well as the designation of peasant and a fundamental class interest to keep them together. Another link would be agriculture for, as in most of the world at that time, even those not engaged in farming would never be far from it. This sector of the economy was slow to change as well as all-pervasive. In spite of all the efforts of the Free Economic Society and government decree, for example, 'earth apples' or potatoes were still rarely grown. Another comparatively new crop, wheat, spread more rapidly, with Ukrainian and other southern farmers beginning to realise its market possibilities as their colleagues in the Baltic provinces and the north-west increased their profits from the more traditional cultivation of flax and hemp. Technical improvements such as improved ploughs or harrows were mostly to be found on the estates of the noble landlords, to whom also went the lion's share of the new lands and redistributed peasants. But merchants and peasants were also taking some of the fresh fields; for example, officially, peasant homesteaders were each allowed sizeable plots in some of the southern regions, unofficially, they were often procuring more and even securing the services of some of their poorer fellows. Such incidents encouraged some Soviet historians to discuss the stratification of the peasantry and the emergence from among them of a rural bourgeoisie and proletariat, but others have issued words of warning about the antedating of capitalism and pointed out the persistence of the basic, feudal three-field strip system in many provinces.[19]

Such words of warning must be borne in mind as we turn to consider the contemporary situation in industry and trade. Between the middle and the end of the eighteenth century, the number of factories and plants doubled from over 600 according to some accounts, tripled from a higher figure according to others. Iron production rose from something over 30,000 metric tons in 1750 to more than 160,000 in 1800, so one estimate suggests. The Urals had undoubtedly become the most important metallurgical centre, with local tribesmen used as labour along with Russian peasants. Textile production also appears to have climbed steeply, with other areas removing some of Moscow's earlier predominance and hired workers forming an embryonic industrial proletariat.

The importance of Russian metals, textiles and other goods to Britain, still the major trading partner remained significant after the renewal of the 1734 treaty in 1766. It was described by Mr Foster, the agent of the Russia Company, in the following manner at the House of Commons in 1774:

The articles we bring from Russia, our hemp, our iron, our flax, are so indispensably necessary to us for every purpose of agriculture and of commerce, that, had we no export trade, it would be very expedient we should attentively cultivate the friendship of Russia on account of our import trade only ... without them our navy, our commerce, our agriculture, are at end; without them, where would be our wealth, where our naval honours? ... You will never, Sir, think that trade a prejudicial one, which brings home the materials, without which commerce could neither be undertaken nor protected.

Mr Foster also said that Russia's linen exports to Britain, although not of good quality, were much used by the poor, and 'the want of them could not be supplied by our home manufacturers'. As far away as the United States, Russian exports, particularly hemp, were in considerable demand before the end of the eighteenth century. Imports continued to consist largely of sugar, cloth of various kinds, dyestuffs and luxury items such as coffee, wines and fruits. St Petersburg was by far the most important port, but the foundation of Odessa in 1794 helped the Black Sea trade well on its way, while Astrakhan retained its importance in the trade with the Orient. The tariff of 1766 was moderate, in line with the liberal trend of Catherine's early economic policies; an increase came in 1782, and then the rates were raised to a formidably high level in the mid-1790s. Although the general direction was towards protectionism, foreign trade almost quadrupled in total value between 1759 and 1798. To some extent, such growth was a reflection of the expansion and consolidation of the internal market.[20]

Economic advance gave the state the opportunity to extract more money from its subjects, and the state income rose from just over 24 million roubles in 1769 to 56 millions in 1795, a formidable increase even when allowance has been made for the inflation that set in towards the end of the century. As before and after, the bulk of the burden fell upon the peasantry, who paid most of the direct poll tax and the indirect taxes on salt and vodka. Expenditure began to exceed income, and the paper assignats issued to cover the deficit accounted for much of the inflation. Between a third and a half of the expenditure went on the armed forces, and from a quarter to a third of it on administration. The court consumed 10 per cent or more of the total, while less than 1.5 per cent was invested in education and welfare. Banking policy continued to favour the nobility, branches of the State Bank being set up in the provinces most severely struck by the Pugachev Revolt in 1775, for example.[21]

Although the Emperor Paul attempted to tax the landed estates of the nobility and to suggest a three-day limit on the *barshchina* services, the people were no more happy with his economic policies than with his mother's. And after a wave of revolts second only in seriousness to the Pugachev Revolt had broken out in the first year or so of his short reign, Paul ordered ruthless suppression. In such conditions, the rank-and-file peasants could hardly be under the impression that enlightened absolutism had percolated down to their level.

Cultural

During the reign of Catherine, there comes to an end that period which Miliukov calls 'the official triumph of critical elements'.[22] In other words, absolutism ceases to be enlightened, and the torch of progressive thought is handed to members of the nascent intelligentsia. For most Soviet historians, absolutism had never really held the torch at any time.

At the beginning of her reign, Catherine was very keen to see the spread of education, proclaiming in her *Instruction*: 'order it so, that the *Light of Knowledge* may be *diffused* among the People'. But reports from all provinces, with the partial exception of the Ukraine and the Baltic area, revealed a very gloomy school situation at the time of the Legislative Commission of 1767. And Catherine's educational reforms in her first few years had been mostly piecemeal rather than wholesale, along lines partly suggested by Peter III's legislation in the field and partly elaborated by I. I. Betskoi, a collaborator with a broad cosmopolitan outlook. Catherine and Betskoi projected development in two directions in their decree of 12 March 1764: towards the rearrangement and enlargement of special schools in St Petersburg and Moscow; and towards the introduction into the Empire as a whole of a modern system of general schools. Understandably enough, more progress was made with the first and easier aim. The cadet and other military schools in the capitals were reorganised, with their curricula made less specialised; schools for girls and for orphans were created. As far as the second aim was concerned, several skeletal projects such as that drawn up on the basis of the British educational system were formulated, several good principles such as reduction of corporal punishment were enunciated, and even some dreams such as the creation of a 'new human being' were indulged. But not one positive practical step was taken.[23]

Miliukov wrote: 'Influenced by the theories of enlightenment, full of enthusiasm, the Catherine of the sixties could dream of the creation of this new race. Cooled down by experience of life and disappointed, the Catherine of the eighties could see how insufficient for the execution of this grand scheme were the means within her hands'.[24] For her second bout of education 'legimania', then, Catherine concentrated not so much on the universal diffusion of light as on the narrower inculcation of some sound ethical concepts and a basic primary and secondary education. For several years a new collaborator, F. I. Jankovich de Mirievo, a Serbian graduate of the University of Vienna who had assisted in the establishment of schools of a Prussian type in Hungary, worked on the project with several associates. And then, on 5 August 1786, a Statute of Popular Schools was promulgated. Drawing on foreign models and adapting several special texts, the Statute proposed the institution of two main kinds of school: major or secondary, and minor or primary. The models included Prussia and Austria, while the texts included such unexceptionable statements as 'In each rank it is possible to be happy. People often think that tsars, princes, nobles and aristocratic individuals alone have a happy life; but this, however, is incorrect.' Just after Catherine's death, there were approximately 7000 students with 270 teachers in 50 major schools and 15,200 students with 490 teachers in 240 minor schools. Although these figures are minute, they compare favourably with the 2000 figure for attendance at the cipher schools just after the death of Peter the Great. Schools run by the Church and the army had a student population of over 20,000 and 12,000 respectively towards the end of the eighteenth century, and the special schools of the capitals and private schools mainly for the nobility accounted for several thousand more. The grand total was nearly 62,000 students in 550 institutions. To that must be added the large numbers of nobles and other ranks who received some kind of education from private tutors or even from waiting at their masters' tables.[25]

While Russian figures pale before others such as the 8000 elementary schools in contemporary France or the 250,000 students in attendance at the English Sunday schools of the period, there were enough culturally aware Russians for it to be possible to talk of an intelligentsia drawn from the nobility, from the middle class and even from the peasantry. The third of these was probably the smallest, and certainly least is known about it. Most of the peasants would gain their world view from songs, proverbs and legends, all strongly intermixed with Orthodox teaching and Slavonic superstition. A clear political attitude is discernible in the Razin and Pugachev legends and in the following piece of popular verse:

The ox did not want to be an ox
And so he became a butcher.
When the butcher went to hit him on the head,
He knocked the blow aside with his horns,
And butted the butcher in the side.

Then the ox managed to snatch the axe from him,
Cut off his arms and hung him up by his legs,
And started to pull out the guts and lights.[26]

Common sense rather than concrete evidence tells us that there were at least a handful of peasants with some awareness of more advanced thought in politics and other fields. As far as the middle-class or democratic (as Soviet historians – notably M. M. Shtrange[27] – called it) intelligentsia is concerned, such men as M. V. Lomonosov and S. E. Desnitskii were highly educated and in some senses critical of the tsarist establishment, although it is too early to talk of groups of them.

Even the noble intelligentsia was composed less of organised cells than of bold individuals. Outstanding among them was A. N. Radishchev, who in his *A Journey from St. Petersburg to Moscow* laid bare the wretchedness of the peasantry. Through what Allen McConnell has called his 'sensitive moral vision', Radishchev saw clearly the inequity of an Empire based upon such an institution as serfdom. Radishchev incurred Catherine's deep displeasure, as did N. I. Novikov, satirist and publicist. The first Russian journals had been published during the earlier phase of absolutism, especially in the 1750s, but the early 1770s saw the first real wave of them. Catherine and Novikov both had their own vehicles of satirical comment, but while the Empress concentrated on evil in the abstract, Novikov's barbs were more pointed. A Freemason, like many other members of the intelligentsia, Novikov later devoted himself to good works and general publishing activities.[28] A critic of the Empress from the right was Prince M. M. Shcherbatov, who in his best-known but then unpublished work, *On the Corruption of Morals in Russia*, accused Catherine of undermining the rigorous governmental system set up by Peter the Great and in particular of bringing to ruin the backbone of society, the nobility.[29]

The ideas of the Enlightenment were disseminated by such men and by such translations as that of some five hundred articles from Diderot's *Encyclopedia*. Even the provincial nobles gained a veneer of Voltairism, and would bear comparison with their foreign peers. At the same time at the highest level, without being as critical as Radishchev, Novikov and Shcherbatov, a few Russians were making considerable contributions to literature and learning. G. R. Derzhavin was the finest lyric poet, and D. I. Fonvizin wrote two good lightly satirical comedies, *The Brigadier* and *The Minor*. A. P. Sumarokov created some less memorable pseudo-classical tragedies, while N. M. Karamzin was active as publicist, historian and prose writer. Most of these, particularly Karamzin, made contributions to the formation of the Russian literary language, and to international movements such as neo-classicism and sentimentalism. Karamzin was also among those writers affected by the widespread vogue for the Ossianic revival promoted by the Aberdeen student James Macpherson.[30] Meanwhile, students from Russia continued to go abroad for the completion of their education and Russian scientists and savants were in increasing touch with their counterparts throughout the Western world. If the foreign names Leonhard Euler and Peter Pallas are the most celebrated, their indigenous colleagues included such worthy men as Lomonosov, whose experiments in atmospheric electricity parallelled those of Franklin,[31] the naturalists I. Lepekhin and N. Ozeretskovskii, the astronomer S. Rumovskii, the mineralogist V. Severgin and the mathematician S. Kotelnikov. A contemporary Scot wrote: 'The Russians, hitherto, have made but an inconsiderable appearance in the republic of letters; but the great encouragement given by their sovereigns of late, in the institution of academies, and other literary boards, has produced sufficient proofs, that they are in no way deficient as to intellectual abilities. The papers exhibited by them, at their academic meetings, have been favourably received all over Europe.'[32] Several academic expeditions were sent to Siberia and the Pacific during the period. Historiography was advanced by I. Boltin as well as by Shcherbatov and Karamzin. Russian artists such as F. Rokotov, D. Levitskii and V. Borikovskii produced fine portraits, while architects such as V. Bazhenov and M. Kazakov extended the Kremlin and constructed new buildings in Moscow, doing for the old capital what the Italian G. Quarenghi, the Scot C. Cameron and the Russian I. Starov did for the palaces of St Petersburg.

In literature, science and art, Catherine was patron and often participant. But most of the cosmopolitan enlightenment had gone from Russian absolutism by the time of her death. Although at the beginning of her reign she had carried through the secularisation of the monastic estates, she increasingly leant on the Church as a preacher of imperial peace and cohesion. Even the toleration that she extended to Old Believers and Muslims could be the cover for their assimilation.[33] And then, under the impact of the French Revolution, both Catherine and Paul after her turned towards the conservative ideology of the nineteenth century – Orthodoxy, autocracy and nationality (i.e. Great Russian patriotism.).[34]

7   Russian Nationalism 1801–1855

For Kliuchevskii, during the period from the end of the eighteenth century to 1855, there was no basic change in Russia, but there were some new ideas and aspirations. Internally, there were hopes for a movement towards collaboration, towards general rights and obligations. But while the nobility lost some of its power, the gainer was not the peasantry, but the bureaucracy. Meanwhile, oposition to the established order grew. The frontiers expanded as the old business of the unification of the Russian lands and people neared completion, while fellow Slavs and others in the Balkans were summoned to existence.[1]

In the 'classic' Soviet view, the first half of the nineteenth century marked the ripening of the crisis of the serf order. A weakening feudalism and strengthening capitalism faced each other; measures were taken to maintain the old order, but the industrial revolution was nevertheless in full spring flow. Contradictions abounded. Imperial expansion was continued to shore up the weakening power of the nobility, but also served to accentuate internal social divisions through such results as the free peasant colonisation of the new regions. Moreover, the nationalities in the Empire began to get together as they carried on their mutual anti-tsarist struggle, assisted by the closer links which were now established with the people of Great Russia. Similarly, while the great victory over Napoleon in 1812 gave a great boost to nationalism and fostered the belief that the army was invincible, it also intensified the motivation of the members of the intelligentsia, particularly the Decembrists, or first revolutionaries. Increasing its influence throughout Europe and Asia, tsarism found itself helping the national-liberation movement in Germany, the Balkans and the Caucasus, and accelerating the disintegration of the outdated Turkish Empire, but also promoting reaction in the Holy Alliance. Not only the tsars found friends abroad, so did the radicals of the post-Decembrist phase such as A. I. Gertsen or Herzen and V. G. Belinskii. As a Soviet view had it: 'The role of Russia in world history grew as the elements of the revolutionary situation in it ripened. The more actively tsarism showed itself as the gendarme of Europe and its own country, the greater the international significance obtained by the liberation struggle of the Russian people and the other peoples of Russia.'[2] Even before the shocks of the 1848 revolutions and the Crimean War, the gendarme strove rigorously to censor and control the creativity of its writers and artists. Such obstacles notwithstanding, Russia made its first outstanding contributions to modern world literature through such persons as Pushkin, Lermontov and Gogol.

To many Western historians, the principal emphasis should be given not to the revolutionary movement which was still small, but to the mainstream of tsarist activities which may be subsumed under the general heading of the growth of the Russian species of that general nineteenth-century European genus, nationalism. The distinguishing characteristics of the species are formed during the reigns of Aleksandr or Alexander I (1801–25) and Nikolai or Nicholas I (1825–55), both tsars making a significant personal contribution. Catherine the Great wanted her eldest grandson Alexander, who was born in 1777, to be educated according to Rousseau's principles of reason and nature, and took him away from his father Paul for the purpose, entrusting him to a very talkative Swiss liberal named La Harpe. Combined with the influence of this tutor and some other (Russian) tutors was the impact of weekly visits to his father at Gatchina, where the atmosphere was that of the barrack room rather than that of the classroom. Further confusion was brought upon Alexander by his marriage at the age of fifteen to a German princess, Louise of Baden (Elizaveta or Elizabeth as she became called in Orthodox Russia). Since the marriage occurred at a time when the principles inculcated into him in childhood were producing the French Revolution, it did not make his development any easier. And if all this was not enough to create a personality of some complexity, the manner of his elevation to the throne, through the assassination of his father, added yet another dimension to the enigma. For Allen McConnell, a searching Western analyst, Alexander did not want Paul killed and felt himself betrayed by his trusted associates who carried out the deed. And so it was partly because those who had murdered his father favoured a constitution that Alexander at first rejected it. He became a strict paternalist because he could trust neither the Russians at the top of society nor those at the bottom of it.[3]

While Alexander had a tendency towards daydreaming, mysticism and infatuation, Nicholas was more down to earth and practical. This was partly because he was not at first expected to become tsar, since another brother Konstantin or Constantine was his senior. The manner of his accession is intimately connected with the Decembrist movement, and will therefore be considered below. Nicholas had been born in 1796 and married to a German princess, Charlotte of Prussia, later Aleksandra or Alexandra after her removal to Russia. Kliuchevskii believed that his cast of mind and the sum total of his early impressions led Nicholas to the conviction that it was not enough to have a plan, the plan had to be fulfilled in detail. Whereas Alexander had looked at the state from above, Nicholas viewed it from below. He was therefore interested in improvement rather than innovation, revision rather than reform, systematisation of laws rather than legislation. In the year of his death, 1911, Kliuchevskii was more dismissive: 'Alexander I related to Russia like an alien diplomat, cowardly and cunning. Nicholas I was both alien and frightened, but because of his fear a more resolute police spy.'

Engels said that Nicholas had the outlook of a company commander, and, enlarging upon such an observation, The Soviet historian N. M. Druzhinin wrote that:

> The political wisdom of Nicholas I amounted to the ideal of an autocratic monarch, who was guided by 'the descendants of the ancient nobility' and paternally concerned himself with the welfare of his humble subjects; the army, schooled by the disciplinary cane, and the bureaucracy, fettered by the feeling of service duty, had to serve as the weapons of a powerful authority watching over the people.

Such a philosophy, pointed out Druzhinin, was a variation of the 'patriarchal-feudal absolutism' which Marx and Engels saw dominating Eastern Europe until the middle of the nineteenth century. To Druzhinin and his colleagues, it was more profitable to consider Alexander in such a light rather than as the crowned Hamlet of some of the more romantic Western biographies. Like his younger brother, if not perhaps quite to the same extent Alexander was a thoroughgoing autocrat and a lover of military order, a 'paradomaniac'. Both of them could therefore readily assist in the formation of that feudal-military nationalism which was to provide a rationale for tsarism down to the end of its existence.[4]

Political

At his accession, the twenty-three-year-old Alexander proclaimed that he would rule 'according to the heart and the laws' of Catherine II.[5] Since such a sentiment was vague and Alexander had no great liking for his grandmother, his policy was not immediately clear, but the frenzied activity of the first few months of his reign soon revealed its main drift. As well as liberal measures releasing from exile or jail thousands of citizens who had been arrested without trial under Paul, abolishing the Secret Chancellery and restoring the right to publish freely, Alexander's early actions also included the reaffirmation of the 1785 Charter of the Nobility. Such support for the *dvorianstvo* was to be a much more lasting theme than respect for the rights of the individual, and long before Alexander's death in 1825, arbitrary police activity and the censorship were back in full swing. In fact, the Emperor was as much an absolutist as his successor, and equally interested in the maintenance of noble support for his throne.

And so, although a Permanent Council was set up in 1801 to replace the State Council instituted by Catherine in 1769 and to discuss and confirm with the sovereign decisions regarding state affairs, it in fact enjoyed little freedom of deliberation. An attempt to restore the Senate to its previous high position ended in failure. Similarly, although the tsar's 'unofficial committee' enabled him to use much of the language he had learned from La Harpe about the rights of man, he agreed with his eloquent friends that such a step as the emancipation of the serfs must be considered only as a remote possibility. The committee dissolved in a flood of meaningless chat, and even such a measure as the 1803 law on free farmers (of which more below) arose from a private project via the Permanent Council.[6] The reactionary Arakcheev, who had begun his career under Paul, returned to a position of prominent power in the important War Ministry, and the comparatively liberal Speransky, who devised an ingenious constitution and promoted other progressive measures, incurred the enmity of the nobility and the displeasure of the tsar, and was sent into exile in 1812.

Mikhail Speranskii, or Michael Speransky, was the son of an ordinary village priest. His outstanding abilities secured him an early transfer from an ecclesiastical to a bureaucratic career. He then demonstrated considerable administrative talent and capacity for hard work, and by 1809 rose to become the tsar's right-hand man. He had already in 1803 produced a draft of constitutional reform during a period when the great task of law codification, which had been unsuccessfully attempted several times during the eighteenth century, was under consideration. And then in 1809, after a request from Alexander himself, he presented a general plan for constitutional reform, including the separation of powers – legislative, executive and judicial – under the Supreme Power, and the election of a State Duma. Franchise was to be restricted by a property qualification, and no provision was made for the eventual enfranchisement of the working people. In the context of its time and place, however, Speransky's plan was forward-looking, and not surprisingly it got nowhere. In the rearrangement of the central government carried out in 1810–11, there were no more than distant and distorted echoes of Speransky's proposals: a State Council, appointed by the tsar to help him with legislation and substituting for the Permanent Council of 1801; and a group of ministries, their number increased and their functions rationalised in comparison with their first arrangement in 1802, when they were first introduced to replace Catherine's colleges.

Little can confidently be said about the improvement of standards of administration resulting from the reforms of 1810–11. In conjunction with another of Speransky's brain-children – a decree of 1809 which laid down that civil service promotions above a certain rank should be by examination or through the possession of a university degree – they perhaps made for the procedural improvements noted by some pre-revolutionary constitutional historians. Certainly, they did not present such a threat to the privileges of the nobility and the prerogative of the tsar as some contemporaries believed, clamouring in their dismay for Speransky's removal. Alexander's own suspicion of Speransky grew, and he was more than ready to drop his pilot by 1812.[7]

Meanwhile, Arakcheev was in the ascendancy. Powerful enough during the preceding years, he was in virtual control of the government from 1815 to 1825. As he himself put it, 'I am the friend of the tsar and complaints about me can be made only to God.'[8] The situation of the people was unhappier than usual after the departure from Russia of Napoleon. A. A. Bestuzhev, later active in the Decembrist Revolt, wrote at this time that: 'Negroes on the plantations are happier than many of the landlords' peasants.'[9] Disturbances were frequent if mostly local, and discontent was also to be found in the army, even in the Guards. In 1820 the soldiers of Semenovskii Regiment mutinied against a cruel commander, and in the Preobrazhenskii Regiment a leaflet was circulated expressing sentiments against both the tsar and the nobility. Arakcheev's formula for the maintenance of the peace was rigid control. In 1815 a decree was issued which forbade peasants to seek their freedom, and another of 1822 assured to the landlords the right to send serfs to Siberia without trial. In 1823 the monopolistic right of the nobles to serf ownership was confirmed, and the government continued to reinforce it by the distribution of land and serfs. On the other hand, peasants in the Baltic provinces were emancipated from 1816 onwards, albeit without land.

In more than any other measure, the general tenor of Arakcheev's policy was expressed by the extension from 1816 onwards of the institution of military colonies, even though the project appears to have been first conceived by Alexander rather than by his minister, who was originally opposed to it. The basic idea was to combine farming with soldiering in a manner that would improve the lot of the rank and file; in fact, the close supervision considered necessary made things far worse for them. To carry on agriculture by numbers and with spit and polish – as one commentator put it 'for both soldier and cow, one and the same exact schedule for their daily routine' – rendered the life of the colonists an over-regimented hell on earth.[10] By the end of Alexander's reign, there were about 375,000 unfortunates, roughly one-third of the peace-time army, in such settlements, mostly in the provinces of St Petersburg, Novgorod, Kherson and Kharkov. Worst off of all were the peasants on Arakacheev's own estate Gruzino near Novgorod, where the master required the women to produce at least one child a year each and ordered all cats to be hanged because he liked nightingales. Assessing the significance of such a system, A. P. Bazhova and A. V. Fadeev commented:

It would be incorrect to think that the drill and the canes were the consequence of some kind of pathological cruelty of Arakcheev or some other individual military commander. No, the Arakcheev regime in the army was the expression of a definite political line, consciously created by the tsarist government with the support of the higher aristocracy and the military bureaucracy.[11]

To be sure, many members of the nobility objected to the military colonies on the ground that, if successful, they would produce 'free' peasant proprietors. Meanwhile, the smaller number of members of the nobility who had hoped that Alexander would bring reform to Russia could only become alienated from the system as a whole when they realised that his early promise was not to be fulfilled. The roots of the Decembrist movement may be traced back to the late eighteenth century, when the first noble members of the intelligentsia aspired to apply the ideas of the Enlightenment and the French Revolution (and to a lesser extent the American Revolution) to their own fatherland. Strong elements are also to be found in it of Freemasonry and mysticism, and of early nineteenth-century German idealistic philosophy and French utopian socialism. The Decembrist movement was not then apart from the mainstream of European development but very much in it; parallels are to be found in the German *Tugenbund*, the Italian *Carbonari*, and the Spanish liberal organisations.[12] These opposition groups (as well as those supporting the government) may be best seen as reflections of the age of nationalism which followed the end of the Napoleonic era in 1815. Looking back, one may see the Decembrists as the last purely noble movement and the distant heirs to D. M. Golitsyn and other projectors of the eighteenth century.

In 1816 in St Petersburg the Society of True and Faithful Sons of the Fatherland, or the Union of Salvation, was founded. Formed by Guards officers returning from abroad and other members of the nobility, the Union aimed at the emancipation of the peasants and the introduction of a constitutional monarchy. Already divisions were apparent between those who wanted a wide or narrow membership, and between those who were for moral propaganda or political, even revolutionary action.

By and large, these divisions were reflected in the two principal groups to emerge out of the ashes of the Union of Welfare, which had replaced the Union for Salvation in 1818, only to destroy itself by 1821. The Southern Society was led by Colonel Pavel (or Paul) Pestel, whose ideas were expressed in his *Russian Justice*, written between the years 1821 and 1825 as 'the obligations to be imposed upon the Provisional Government'. Pestel wanted Russia to be a unified, one-class republican state. Everybody would own a plot of land, although some land would also be retained by the state for its own support and profit. A Provisional Supreme Administration would gradually introduce a system of representative government, Pestel declaring that 'The fear that the so-called populace will shake the state if it participates in the elections is completely unnecessary and groundless.' To win over the people to their cause, an associate of Pestel's in the Southern Society produced an 'Orthodox Catechism' which included the following question and answer: 'Why are the Russian people and army unhappy? Because the Tsars robbed them of their freedom.'[13] Meanwhile, the Northern Society developed a more moderate programme, Nikita Muravev drawing up a plan for constitutional monarchy, not republicanism, for the abolition of serfdom, but no mass hand-over of land, for civil liberties and voting rights, but limited by property qualifications.

The two societies and their allies attempted to use the occasion of the sudden death of Alexander I in December 1825 to carry out their revolt. Tsarism itself experienced a moment's hesitation as it was not clear who would succeed to the throne; Constantine had secretly given up his right to the succession, but had not yet publicly declared that the imperial inheritance belonged to Nicholas. For their part, the Decembrists themselves were hesitant and disorganised, and their movement soon collapsed. Five leaders were executed, and became martyrs to the revolutionary cause. The Soviet atittude was certainly that the Revolt was progressive, but that its leaders were a long way from the people. The link between the revolutionary intelligentsia and the proletariat would not be formed before 1890.[14]

With the accession of Nicholas, little change could have been expected in tsarist policy. Indeed, during the aftermath of the Decembrist Revolt, if there was any change, it was for the worse. A considerable number of peasant disturbances ensued, particularly in the Right-Bank Ukraine and central industrial provinces, and in 1826, out of 178 such incidents, 104 involved considerable numbers and 54 were put down by military force.[15] Some of the insurgents appear to have misunderstood the Decembrist Revolt, believing that it stemmed from the nobility's outrage at Constantine's wish to give the serfs freedom, and several impostors purported to be Constantine or his emissary. (There were further calls for Constantine at Nicholas I's death in 1855.) Being under no illusion about the implication of such developments, Nicholas moved energetically to quell them.

Trusting nobody, he tried to do everything of importance himself. He personally supervised the investigation of the Decembrists. Learning from that experience, if he was not already sufficiently aware of the fact, that some rearrangement of the Empire's affairs was long overdue, he instigated a series of political discussions among a circle of close advisers. Among the contributors was Speransky, who had returned from exile towards the end of Alexander's reign and played a leading part in the prosecution of the Decembrists. His modest ideas of representative government abandoned, Speransky now suggested that the best means of maintaining law and order was through a reinforcement of the existing class hierarchy, as well as through continued technical readjustments of the administration.

The suggestions of Speransky and his colleagues on class hierarchy were to some extent followed up. The *dvorianstvo*, which Nicholas called the first support of the throne, was shored up by making it more exclusive. A decree of 1831 disqualified those with less than five serfs or 400 acres of land from voting in the provincial assemblies, and restricted the rights of all but the top members of the class. From 1845 onwards, hereditary nobility was to be reserved for army staff officers and civil officials in the highest five ranks, and prominent noble families were again encouraged to entail their estates. In 1832 a rank of 'honorary citizen' was introduced to help keep the *dvorianstvo* free from bourgeois infiltration and to boost the official middle class. A further move in this direction was the decree of 1846 on the government of St Petersburg, with the top stratum of town society being reserved for hereditary nobles, and the second being composed of personal nobles (or life peers) and 'honorary citizens'. In such a manner, there was some hope that social involvement in the government of the capital would be broadened.

As far as technical readjustments of the administration were concerned, Speransky was still keen on the division, if not of powers, then at least of functions. He wanted the State Council to concentrate on legislation and the Senate on executive and judicial business, while a comparable arrangement was to be worked out for the lower echelons of government, where there were also to be a certain number of elective officials. Almost nothing came of these proposals, but Speransky was able to find an outlet for his talents and energy in an enterprise that amounted to something more than technical readjustment, the collection and codification of the laws. It will be remembered that such a task had defeated several commissions and committees in the eighteenth and early nineteenth centuries, and that the Code of 1649 was still in whatever operation a law code could be in such a lawless society. In 1830 and 1833 Speransky and his aides produced fifty-one volumes of the *Complete Collection of Laws of the Russian Empire* – in fact not quite complete, then fifteen volumes of a systematic *Code of Laws of the Russian Empire* – supposedly of those still in operation. This work was followed by the promulgation of a new Criminal Code in 1845, and the extension through the early 1840s of the Russian Code to the Polish, White Russian and Ukrainian provinces of the west and south-west.

Changes in the official governmental structure and judicial framework meant less than usual during the reign of Nicholas since his rule was so personal. This did not mean that he could dispense with the traditional bureaucracy which was becoming more of a self-perpetuating professional caste during the first half of the nineteenth century, with its upper echelons firmly ensconced in the nobility. But the regular processes of the bureaucracy were for the most part cumbersome and corrupt.[16] And so the most important day-to-day work of administering the Empire was done not by the State Council or Senate but by His Majesty's Own Chancery, an all-pervasive web, stretching out to envelop all His Majesty's subjects. Chief spider was at first General Benckendorff, in charge of the Chancery's notorious Third Section. Supposedly dealing with important police matters, the Third Section under Benckendorff interpreted its brief broadly to include everything under the sun and moon, and the general himself was more than a prime minister, although keeping himself in the background. With Nicholas taking a close personal interest in the Section's activities, it sweated to amass a vast heap of paper for his scrutiny. More sinisterly, it also produced for him a considerable amount of his often innocent subjects' tears and blood.[17]

Although Benckendorff's gendarmes looked for trouble where there was none and often found it, they also had plenty of real trouble to busy themselves with. At least 400 disturbances occurred among the peasants during each five-year period following 1826, and from 1844 to 1849 the number rose to 605. None of these was on a large scale, but accompanied by mass flight to the frontier and other forms of passive resistance, they were enough to alarm the tsar and his associates. Nor was Russia's growing industry without its problems. Recognising these, the government issued in 1835 a decree to regulate relations between workers and their employers, and another in 1845 sought to restrict the night work of minors. Such paternalistic gestures did little to improve the conditions of the factory labourers, who sought to redress their grievances by collective complaint, mass refusal to work, insubordination and violence. During and after an incident at a metalworks in the Urals in 1841, 33 people were killed, 50 heavily wounded and 300 corporally punished. Such an event was rare, so many Western historians would be suspicious of N. M. Druzhinin's declaration that 'the disturbances of the workers of Russia achieved the significance of a serious social factor, undermining the bases of feudal-serf relations and simultaneously creating conditions for the class struggle of the industrial proletariat against the capitalists which developed after the abolition of serfdom.'[18]

Of further concern to Russia's gendarmerie was the circumstance that its most busy periods of activity tended to coincide with those of its brother organisations abroad, in 1830–31 and 1848–9. True, domestic circumstances such as harvest failure and cholera were of importance at these critical times, and so was the nature of serfdom, but the international revolutionary movement was a cause of at least as much concern, and possibly more. The tsar himself wrote the famous manifesto of 14–26 March 1848, in which he lamented that rebellion and lawlessness were rampant in Prussia and Austria and menacing 'our holy Russia'. He summoned the people to arouse themselves for 'faith, tsar and country', assuring them that God was with them. An army of 400,000 was drawn up at the borders, and, according to some accounts, Nicholas intended to march it to the Rhine, a move which would no doubt have alarmed the monarchs of Europe more than the words and actions of their domestic revolutionaries. Nicholas contented himself with acceptance of an Austrian invitation to help suppress the nationalist Kossuth and his followers in Hungary.[19] The success of this measure in 1849 no doubt enabled Nicholas to breathe more easily, at least for a short time. No doubt too, some of the forces that had been unleashed in 1848 and described by Marx and Engels in their *Communist Manifesto* were beyond his comprehension. To the last, nevertheless, he worked at his command, hoping to make his garrison state impregnable against threats both domestic and foreign.

For such a purpose he needed an efficient army, and personally spent much time and effort trying to drill his forces into the proper shape. Unfortunately for him, the commanders he chose to help him in his task were nonentities. More fundamentally, Russia's social system was inadequate for the provision of an army fit to fight the battles of the nineteenth century. Among the insoluble problems was that of providing an adequate reserve in conditions of serfdom. Although the military colonies lingered on until 1857, Nicholas himself admitted right at the beginning of his reign after a tour of them that they presented 'a most distressing picture', and that they could not fulfil the purpose for which they had been set up. On the other hand, a serf who entered the army became a free man, and so universal service would have completely upset the social system. Even the reduction of the length of service from twenty-five to fifteen years was anathema to many landowners and officers from the nobility. A general feared that the result would be that the Russian villages would be 'filled with people without work and without means for livelihood, from which we may expect great disorders'.[20]

All such problems notwithstanding, a large army was kept up throughout the first half of the nineteenth century not only to counter subversive influences at home and abroad, but also to extend the peripheral regions of the Empire and to keep them quiet, as well as playing its more normal part in international war. The majority of Finland was taken to add to a previously acquired slice in 1809 after war with Sweden, and the whole was then given some autonomy as a grand duchy. Georgia was finally incorporated into the Empire in the first decade of the century, much to the annoyance of the Persians and the Turks, with both of whom war broke out. As a consequence, Russia made further gains in the Transcaucasian regions of Azerbaidzhan and Armenia, and at the west end of the Black Sea – first Bessarabia and later considerable if temporary rights in Moldavia and Wallachia. In the twenties, thirties and forties, the tsarist forces moved into Central Asia, beginning to encounter the British thrust up from India. For Soviet historians, the Russian assimilation of the Middle East and Central Asia saved the local peoples from feudal disunity and dismemberment at the predatory hands of Turkey and Persia. Economic and cultural benefits accrued, too, although these were restricted by the nature of the tsarist establishment.[21] At the same time, Siberia was infiltrated further and the island of Sakhalin off its Pacific coast was gradually acquired. Reforms of the Siberian government in 1822 and 1827 improved its administration and the arrangement for collecting taxes there. Russian settlers increased in number, but were still very few for such a huge area.[22]

While Siberia posed few problems to the maintenance of good order, other peripheral regions were seldom trouble-free, by no means all of their inhabitants believing in the benefits of imperial incorporation. The tribesmen of Central Asia were seldom completely at peace, and Muslim resistance in the Caucasus led by the legendary Imam Shamil did not die out until the early 1860s, although Shamil himself was captured in 1859. In Belarus and the Ukraine there were peasant disturbances in the twenties and thirties, and similar outbreaks occurred in the Baltic provinces in the early forties. An intellectual nationalist movement in the Ukraine, centred round the Kiev Brotherhood of Cyril and Methodius, caused alarm in the later forties and several of its more radical leaders, including the artist and poet Shevchenko, were arrested and punished. The biggest single source of trouble, however, was Poland, which rose against Russian domination in 1830 only to find itself made 'an indivisible part' of the Empire in 1832 after the uprising had been crushed.[23] Russification was applied here as elsewhere through such agencies as the Russian language and the Orthodox Church.

Poland was of capital importance to tsarism as a barrier against the potentially hostile powers of Central and Western Europe. The retention of its loyalty was therefore a necessary aim in the conduct of foreign policy, as was the satisfactory settlement of what came to be known as the Eastern Question. During the reigns of Alexander I and Nicholas I, the central events were the great triumph of the defeat of Napoleon and the great disaster of the failure to win the Crimean War.

War with France appeared remote when Alexander and Napoleon made their unexpected accommodation at Tilsit in 1807, but the agreement was not popular with the Russian nobility, who saw in Napoleon the child of the French Revolution and a threat to the existence of serfdom. Merchants and nobles were worried by the adherence of Russia to the French Continental System, which crippled international trade and thus curtailed their grain exports. Influential members of society wanted to retain Poland and acquire the Dardanelles. Napoleon, for his part recognised the vital importance of both Poland and the Dardanelles as well as understanding that the Continental System had to be enforced if his plans for the domination of Europe were to succeed.[24] He believed that he would achieve mastery of the universe if he could defeat Russia in one good battle. His chance came at Borodino, after the Russians had avoided head-on collision following earlier disasters.

Just as it would be wrong to ascribe the beginning of the War of 1812 to the personal rivalry of the French and Russian Emperors, so it would be over-simplifying the battle of Borodino to see it as a showdown between Napoleon and Kutuzov. Even the cool strategical account of Clausewitz declares that: 'Kutuzov, it is certain, would not have fought at Borodino where he obviously did not expect to win. But the voice of the Court, of the Army, of all Russia, forced his hand.'[25] The truth of this statement may be seen reflected in the size of the casualties at Borodino, both the French and their allies on the one hand and the Russians on the other losing more than 50,000 killed and wounded. The same kind of spirit of national resistance saw Russia through the evacuation of Moscow and the burning of the capital, which were carried out with the connivance, even the encouragement of the governor, Count Rostopchin. And when Napoleon and his forces set out on the long retreat they were harried not only by the weather but by the Russian regular forces and by partisans. The fears of the nobility that the serfs would be enticed by French offers of emancipation turned out to be false. Undoubtedly, the War of 1812 was a great patriotic war, even though it has sometimes been celebrated in too intoxicated a fashion by Soviet historians.[26]

The defeat of Napoleon and the arrival of Russian troops in Paris made Alexander one of the principal arbiters of Europe at the Congress of Vienna. Under the mystical banner of his Holy Alliance, his chief minister Count Nesselrode strove to protect the interests of Russia in particular and of absolutism in general.[27] On the whole this was not a great problem, although there were points of tension between the Russians and their fellow-absolutists, the Austrians, guided by Metternich. The most tricky question arose when the Greek War of Independence broke out in the early 1820s. If Alexander followed his religious affiliation, he would support the Greeks, but this would weaken the Turks and upset the Balkan equilibrium, at the same time alarming the Austrians and others with the threat of the expansion of Russian infiltration into the area.

Alexander's death in 1825 occurred at a time when the Eastern Question was no more than posed for Russia and the other powers. Nicholas had to attempt to solve it in the least painful manner possible, with the continued dutiful assistance of Nesselrode. He took a more positive interest in Greece than had his brother, partly through fear that the British would become the major influence in the region if the Russians did not. In 1827, a combined Anglo-Franco-Russian naval force destroyed a Turkish fleet at Navarino off the Greek coast. This led Russia into a war with Turkey, which lasted from 1828 to 1829 and enabled Nicholas by the Treaty of Adrianople to acquire the mouth of the Danube and further influence in its hinterland, as well as passage for Russian merchant ships through the Dardanelles. But Turkey's loss was not completely to Russia's advantage, for Egypt now followed Greece in seeking its independence, and the problem of the 'sick bear' of Europe as Nicholas called it arose in threatening clarity. The Treaty of Unkiar–Skelessi of 1833 sealed the friendship of Turkey and Russia, but the other great powers were suspicious, and the Treaty of London of 1840 and the Straits Convention of 1841 brought Britain, France, Prussia and Austria together with Russia to protect the Dardanelles. It was from this situation that the Crimean War arose in 1854.

To describe in all their complexity the negotiations and the misunderstandings leading up to that fateful war would be an impossible task here, although it would be wrong to accept without strong qualification the assertion of a Soviet textbook that: 'The Crimean War was brought about by the aggravation of class conflicts inside European states and the intensification of the struggle for external markets, linked with the development of capitalism.'[28] All we can say here is that the personality weaknesses of such people as Napoleon III, Nicholas I and Palmerston certainly played their part as immediate reasons for the outbreak of hostilities, and that such underlying circumstances as the British desire for a protected route to India and the Russian wish for an outlet for her grain were important too.

The war itself was as full of error as the period leading up to it. 'Folly and blunder' were by no means the monopoly of the British Light Brigade. Although the Russian defence of Sevastopol moved an artillery officer there named Leo Tolstoy to write about 'The Sevastopol epic, the hero of which was the Russian people',[29] the Russian troops found themselves armed with smooth-bore muskets while their enemies had rifles, and the Russian sailing ships confronted hostile steamers. Railway and other communications were so poor that the home forces were at least as badly supplied as the foreign invaders. And so the Crimean War revealed to an ailing Nicholas I that his reign was ending in failure and probably accelerated his death. Alexander II came to the throne determined to fight on but soon faced the necessity of accepting the humiliating Treaty of Paris (1856) by which Russia was forced to withdraw from the mouth of the Danube, to cease to protect the Orthodox under Turkish rule, and even to give up its fleet and fortresses on the Black Sea. For the next fifteen years or so, Russia aimed at the revision of the Treaty of Paris.[30] The failures of the war also impressed upon Alexander II the necessity of introducing long-overdue reforms into the Russian Empire itself.

Economic

From the economic point of view, the first half of the nineteenth century may be looked upon in two principal ways. On the one hand, this is the period when, slowed down by such institutional features as serfdom and such environmental features as the maldistribution of natural resources, one of the leading powers of the late eighteenth century fell behind the growth rate of most of its European neighbours. On the other hand, 'Many

economists have noted that periods of quick and massive industrial development are usually preceded by longer periods of preparation, of slower,
less dynamic, less comprehensive change.' Certainly, some adaptation was
necessary before the great spurt ahead could take place towards the end of
the nineteenth century. In the all-important iron industry, for example, the
Russia which had led the world when smelting was performed with the aid
of charcoal had to lose its primacy before it could start to catch up again
making use of coking coal.

Most Western and Soviet analysts also agreed that it was necessary for
serfdom to be undermined before a properly modernised economy could
start to grow. However, a minority group of Western historians imply that
servile labour was not necessarily a serious deterrent to industrialisation,
and that the institutional reason for the slow progress of the reigns of
Alexander I and Nicholas I is therefore principally to be found in government policy, which tended to be formed around the idea of Russia's
national apartness based on peasant agriculture.[31]

Certainly, there was no shortage of peasants, as the population continued to rise with the proportions remaining much as before. From a total of
37.5 millions in 1795, the population climbed to 61.5 millions in 1838 and
69 millions in 1851. The greatest areas of growth were the central agricultural regions, New Russia and the Lower Volga to the south and the
Northern and Southern Urals to the east, but nowhere was there not an
increase of some kind. The peasants in private hands, although declining
in numbers, totalled more than 22 millions by the middle of the century
and those under state control, rising in numbers, more than 20 millions.
Crown peasants accounted for 1.5 millions and free peasants less than 0.5
million. The urban population was well above 5 millions and approached
10 per cent of the total. St Petersburg topped the half million mark and
Moscow approached it, with Warsaw, Odessa, Kishinev, Saratov and Riga
a long way behind in that order. Registered urban categories amounted to
something over 3.5 millions, and the balance of the urban population
would be made up of itinerant peasants and the nobles, clergymen and
other non-taxable citizens who also went to make up the balance of the
population as a whole. Broadly speaking, Russians were almost twice as
numerous as Frenchmen and thrice as numerous as the British and
Americans. At the same time, while about 55 per cent of Frenchmen,
22 per cent of the British and 65 per cent of Americans were engaged in
agriculture, the equivalent Russian figure approached 90 per cent.

Russian labour was generally more extensive than that of other nations,
and the pressures for its more intensive exploitation would not be felt nearly
as strongly as in, say, Britain. Nevertheless, the arrival of the new order

was signalled by an increasing realisation of the market possibilities of agriculture and by the expansion of industry to near the point of industrial revolution. Landlords, to take them first, were attracted by the trade in grain for internal and external consumption. There were many more mouths to feed in the Empire, particularly in the towns. The demand from abroad increased in size, especially from Britain after the repeal of the Corn Laws in 1846. The average annual export of grain rose, not without considerable fluctuations, from about 325,000 metric tons at the beginning of the 1830s to nearly 1,140,000 metric tons by the end of the 1850s, when it amounted to almost a tenth of total production and a third of all exports. Ports such as St Petersburg, Riga and Odessa flourished, agricultural societies expanded and exhibitions were held. New implements were put to use, if not enough, and the cultivation spread of non-traditional crops such as sugar beet, tobacco and potatoes, if slowly. An important social reflection of these changes was that in the mid-fifties in 33 provinces there were 270,000 households among the state peasants farming a total of a million or so hectares (about 3 million acres), and in the same decade there were 300,000 peasants for hire in the South Ukraine, 150,000 in the Volga region, 120,000 in the Baltic provinces and up to 150,000 elsewhere. Most peasants would still be in the middle category, tending towards neither bourgeoisie nor proletariat, but this majority would not be completely untouched by the sturdy growth of the money economy, even when they were still enserfed, mostly farming by traditional methods or increasingly subject to *barshchina* services. The resultant contradictions led to a real crisis of the old order, even if it did not yet approach revolutionary intensity.

Agricultural progress would probably have been most noticeable near the Baltic and in the Ukraine, around Moscow and St Petersburg. These also were the centres of embryonic industrial revolution, indicated by a three-fold increase in the number of both enterprises and workers between the mid-twenties and late fifties. In 1825, according to one scale of measurement, there were some 5000 units of production with a total work force of about 200,000; by 1860, these figures had risen to about 15,000 and more than 550,000 respectively. During the same period, the production of cast-iron nearly doubled to reach a total of over a quarter of a million tons. The relative backwardness of Russia's iron industry by this time, however, is reflected in the calculation that while Britain produced nearly 140 kilograms of iron per head and Belgium something over 70 kilograms, the Empire managed a *per capita* rate of hardly more than 4 kilograms. The iron industry was still largely based on the Urals and serf labour, although by 1860 about a fifth of the workers were hired. Four-fifths was the equivalent proportion in light manufacturing, which was situated in the regions listed above and consisted primarily of textiles, although sugar and vodka were also important items of production. The captains of Russia's growing industry were mainly from the middle class, but included many nobles and some rich peasants. The most forward-looking among them were becoming aware of the advantages of mechanisation.

Mechanisation was creeping into transport and communications too; with some reluctant help being given by the government, there were in existence by the end of the reign of Nicholas more than 5000 kilometres of highway and 1500 kilometres of railroad, not much of a beginning but a beginning nevertheless. The tsar himself was something of a supporter of the iron horse, deciding that the prosperity of his subjects would gain most from it if the first line were constructed from St Petersburg to his palace at Tsarskoe Selo! This was finished by 1837, and the next line, from St Petersburg to Moscow, was completed in 1851. According to unsubstantiated anecdote, Nicholas took a hand in this line as well, fixing its route with a bold stroke on the map. Some of his advisers were less enthusiastic railwaymen, one of them, Kankrin arguing that trains endangered 'public morals' through their encouragement of 'the restless spirit of our age'. Later lines from Warsaw to Vienna and Warsaw to St Petersburg were begun largely for reasons of security and strategy. State support was useful in the necessary collection of large amounts of capital, while foreigners contributed not only some of the money but not a little of the engineering skill. River transport was improved during the period; by 1860 there were about 400 steamboats in the Empire mostly on the Volga. Toll, another adviser, asserted that waterways would pose less of a threat to social stability than railways.[32]

The growing land and water network assisted the expansion of domestic trade, which rose to a value of about 900 million roubles by the end of the period. Only 10 per cent was in manufactured goods, the main items being grain, foodstuffs, lumber and cattle. In the mid-forties, Russia's external trade was about one quarter the size of the domestic, the Empire occupying sixth place among the trading nations of the world. Grain was still the most important export, followed by hemp and animal fats; cotton thread and dyes were the most important imports, followed by luxury goods and foodstuffs. While tariffs were high, prohibitions and restrictions were gradually lifted, and Russia became more involved in the commerce of the world, principally with Britain and the continent of Europe, but also with Asia and the U.S.A.

Generally speaking, the attitude of the government to the changes that were going on was one of reluctant adaptation rather than of enthusiastic promotion. Such an attitude was personified by Count Kankrin, who believed above all in a stable fiscal situation.[33] Hence, little money was spent on the advancement of agriculture or industry, while very much, as always, was spent on the army and navy, the bureaucracy and the court. The financial reform of 1839–43, which reduced the influence of paper money and phased out the assignats which had been introduced by Catherine II, helped to achieve the desired balance. Financial policy as a whole, however, was strained by the necessity of aiding the nobility, which had mortgaged two-thirds of its serfs for 425 million silver roubles by 1859.

This central problem of serfdom was only partly tackled by a series of measures ranging from the free farmer law of 1803 to the measures associated with the name of Kiselev. The law of 1803 allowed landlords to make arrangements for the liberation of individual serfs, but very little use was made of it. Between 1816 and 1819, peasants in the Baltic provinces were emancipated, but without land. General P. D. Kiselev, in charge of a new Ministry of State Lands from 1837 onwards, attempted to give the state peasants a reasonable amount of land and to protect them with a far-reaching welfare scheme, but he allowed them very little initiative or freedom of movement. Much of the scheme remained on paper, as did the decree of 1842 on 'obligated' peasants, which bore some resemblance to the decree of 1803. For all their ineffectiveness, or restricted application, such pieces of legislation were looked upon by many landlords as writing on the wall of great danger to their continued possession of the serfs.[34]

Cultural

The first half of the nineteenth century is a period of considerable progress in the development of Russian culture, but also of deep contradictions. Thus, there was a numerical expansion in education and great achievement at the higher academic level, but attended by too little financial support and too much bureaucratic control. Russian literature experienced its golden age and Russian music first began to make an international impact, but in conditions of harsh censorship and restriction. Revolutionary ideology came near to formation with the emergence of socialism, but tsarism also developed the political philosophy that was to see it through to the end of its existence, continuing to make great use of Orthodoxy.

To consider each of these cultural spheres in turn, we begin with the question of the schools. At the end of the eighteenth century, it will be recalled, there were about 60,000 students; by 1856 the total had grown to nearly 400,000. Just after the beginning of the reign of Alexander I, a Ministry of Education was set up in 1802, and soon announced plans in

1803 for a network of universities, and schools at the provincial, county and parish level throughout a Russia divided into six regions. Three new universities were necessary to supplement those developing on old foundations, a Russian in Moscow, a Polish in Vilno and a German in Dorpat. Universities were duly founded in Kazan, Kharkov and St Petersburg, the last named starting its new life as a teachers' training college. The universities were theoretically autonomous, but in fact increasingly brought under governmental control to make sure that bad ideas, particularly political, were not fostered and that good ideas, particularly religious, were. Many of the professors were foreign and lectured in Latin, which many of their students could not properly understand. By the end of the reign there were 1700 university students in the Empire proper (that is, excluding Poland and Finland), nearly half of them at Moscow. A large proportion of the graduates probably went into the civil service, encouraged by the decree of 1809 which offered regular promotion prospects to entrants with a university degree. The grand total for state education by the end of the reign was 2118 institutions with 263,223 students, the military schools accounting for over 100,000 of them and the rest shared by schools under the Ministry of Education (or Public Instruction as it was officially called) and special and technical schools. As before, many of the nobles would go to private schools or be educated by tutors, and various commoners would learn in an informal manner at least to read and write.

The restrictions on education introduced towards the end of the reign of Alexander I were extended during that of Nicholas I, both in theory and in practice. Whereas the reform of 1803 aimed at the progress of the individual student throughout the hierarchy from parish school to university, at least in theory, each type of school was now specifically aimed at the satisfaction of the needs of that social group from which it expected to attract most of its students. Decrees of 1828 and 1835 spelled out the new theoretical approach in some detail. Among other reforms, streaming was introduced into the provincial schools or gymnasia, with those intending to go on to university being given a strong dose of classical languages. The administration of the schools was adapted to their new separation. Numerically, there was growth in the second quarter of the nineteenth century as there had been in the first quarter. The university population increased to 3659 by 1855, that of state schools in general to about 400,000. Moreover, in Riasanovsky's considered view, 'the government of Nicholas I made some significant contributions to the development of education in Russia'. Count S. S. Uvarov, Minister of Education from 1833 to 1849 and coiner of Russian nationalism's slogan 'Orthodoxy, autocracy and nationality', applied himself energetically to this task.[35]

Not only this, at the highest level Russian academic life was producing scholars of world stature. Outstanding among these was the mathematician N. I. Lobachevskii, who taught mathematics at the University of Kazan and who devised a non-Euclidean geometry. Moreover, some significant discoveries were made in physics, especially electricity, chemistry and biology, while one fortunate result of great cholera outbreaks was an advance in medical training.[36] Voyages of discovery and exploration continued into Siberia and beyond. In 1821, Antarctica was discovered by an expedition under the leadership of Thaddeus Bellingshausen, for example. And N. M. Karamzin's multi-volumed *History of the Russian State* enjoyed a wide popularity among a growing reading public.[37]

However, in case this is presenting too bright a picture of Russian education and its achievements, we should remember that the schools cultivated monarchist and religious ideas. 'The schools are crushed by supervisors and priests', Herzen complained. The University Charter of 1835 was an attempt to institute military discipline into the universities; a similar system was introduced into the newly founded railway and forestry institutes. Half-educated generals were often appointed as supervisors of schools districts. 'I do not need educated people, I need loyal subjects', Nicholas I is reputed to have said. Benckendorff, the head of the Third Section, wrote that 'there must not be too much of a hurry with enlightenment, lest the people come to the level of understanding of monarchs and thus encroach upon their power'. Because of the dangers inherent in the subjects, the teaching of philosophy, natural law and political economy in the universities was brought to a halt.[38]

So it was also in literature, which experienced a golden age in spite of the clumsy censorship and foolish restrictions. (One censor said that, according to the law of 1826, the Lord's prayer would be under suspicion as a revolutionary document.) While the most familiar names internationally speaking are Pushkin, Lermontov and Gogol, others such as Griboedov and Krylov are among the great figures of literature to Russians and quotations from them are household sayings throughout Russia. And then there is a whole host of writers at least known to most Russians who have never even been heard of by Western students of literature. This would be even more the case with the national bards and story-tellers of the non-Russian-speaking regions, who will be completely unsung and unrelated here.

Even the great giant of the first half of the nineteenth century, Alexander Pushkin, has diminished in stature somewhat when exported. This is partly because of the cultural egocentricity of other nations, and partly because the poetry which forms such a significant amount of his work does not translate at all easily. Marshak has done something creative with Burns, and Pasternak with Shakespeare, but no Western poet has really got to grips with Pushkin. Vladimir Nabokov has made one of the bravest of attempts with his rendering of *Evgenii Onegin*. Through the international language of music, foreigners have been able to achieve some sort of an appreciation not only of the narrative verse of *Evgenii Onegin* and the evocative prose of the short story of *Queen of Spades* in the operas of Tchaikovsky, but also of the poetic drama *Boris Godunov* in the opera of Mussorgsky. Whether applying himself to great historical and philosophical themes as in the long poems *Poltava* and *The Bronze Horseman*, or revealing a more private world in his love lyrics, Pushkin exerts great power through his complete use of the inflections and nuances of the language which he brought to a new peak of expression.

Like Pushkin, Mikhail Lermontov excelled in prose and poetry as well as, like him, being killed in a duel. His most accessible work is probably the short novel *A Hero of Our Time*, which some critics consider to be a better social and individual analysis than Pushkin's *The Captain's Daughter*. To call Lermontov as many have done 'the Russian Byron' may not be fully appropriate, but there is no doubt a lowering spirit of romantic doom in his tales as well as his poems. He was also capable of a penetrating directness and simplicity; since he was only twenty-six at the time of his death, however, his development was cut short before it could take him towards a more mature realism.

Nikolai Gogol breaks through the language barrier best, even though his Russian is more difficult to read than that of Pushkin or Lermontov. His satirical play, *The Inspector General*, has often been successfully done on the Western stage and even been made into an entertaining Hollywood film with Danny Kaye, himself of Russian descent, as the hero, a simpleton mistaken for a government inspector in a remote provincial town. And the novel *Dead Souls*, which tells of the purchase of the records of dead serfs to be used as surety for a mortgage, has caught the attention of many foreign readers who do not begin to understand the legal complexities of the story, but who immediately appreciate the grotesque denizens of remoter parts of European Russia so well etched by Gogol. To communicate his living power to Soviet citizens not so long ago, one need only refer to items in the Soviet press referring to latter-day recreations of Gogol's classic situations in a railway buffet, where a bewildered traveller was given the red-carpet, several-course treatment laid on for a visiting inspector, and on a Moscow construction project where an enterprising 'foreman' managed to draw the wages for a non-existent shift: Other works of great interest by Gogol include *Taras Bulba*, about the Ukrainian

Cossacks, and a number of short stories, of which the most important is *The Overcoat*, which tells of an obscure government clerk's shattered dreams and which was considered by Dostoevsky to be the source of all later Russian fiction.

Griboedov's play *Woe from Wit*, a social satire, became a standard part of the Russian classical repertory, Krylov wrote colourful fables full of homely wisdom, and writers such as Zhukovskii, the romantic poet, are among many of whom much could be said. There is no such problem with contemporary exponents of the pictorial and plastic arts, who do not appear to merit much discussion, for most of the exhortations and attempts to found a national style produced either a stilted mock-heroism or a cumbersome monumentality. But there were individual fine buildings such as the Admiralty in St Petersburg by A. Zakharov and a few excellent paintings such as *The Last Days of Pompeii* by K. P. Brüllow. In music, however, the distinctive voice of Russia was widely heard in a formal structure for the first time. The great name is Mikhail or Michael Glinka, whose *Ivan Susanin* (renamed *A Life for the Tsar* at the censor's request) founded the national school of Russian opera and whose musical adaptation of Pushkin's *Ruslan and Liudmila* inaugurated a long line of operas on rustic magical tales. His arrangement of folk tunes is best typified by his symphonic piece *Kamarinskaia*, which might be said to do for Russian music what Gogol's *The Overcoat* did for Russian literature; indeed, Tchaikovsky called it the acorn from which the oak of Russian music grew. Aleksandr Dargomyzhskii (Dargomyzhsky) also made use of popular themes in his operas, and attempted to put stress on words as well as music. Mussorgsky called him 'a great teacher of musical truth'.

By the end of the reign of Nicholas I, without much positive contribution by him or his elder brother, a Russian national style had asserted itself in literature and the arts. All kinds of cultural cross-currents moved across Europe and Asia in a complex manner which it would take a multilingual critic of uncanny perception to describe properly. All that can be said here with confidence is that at the beginning of its golden age, Russian culture was giving as good as it got, so to speak, and had arrived at a new level of maturity.

A problem of comparable complexity faces us as we move on to consider the third theme of this section, the ideological developments of the first half of the nineteenth century. Again we are confronted with elusive questions of originality and borrowing of ideas, of the main flow of concepts across continents finding their concrete expression within the national context. Broadly speaking, it may be said that the period before the death of Alexander I in 1825 was the seedtime, and the period after it contained the flowering. This change of season was undoubtedly affected by domestic developments, but was also intimately connected with events abroad such as the revolutionary outbreaks of 1830–1 and 1848–9.

Much of the thought of the preparatory period is connected with the Decembrists, and the gap between them and Radishchev was bridged in an undistinguished manner which was at least partly the result of the preoccupation of many thinking people with the impact of Napoleon. After the Decembrists, whom we have discussed above, radical thought was kept alive by various circles formed mainly at the universities of Moscow and St Petersburg. The students attempted little action, but talked at great length under the influence of German idealistic philosophers from Schelling to Hegel and French utopian socialists from Saint-Simon to Louis Blanc. It was from these circles that the principal radical figures of the thirties and forties sprang, notably Alexander Herzen (Aleksandr Gertsen) and Vissarion Belinskii. Herzen was sent into exile after graduation, Belinskii sent down before graduation. Herzen left Russia, while Belinskii stayed at home. Herzen is best remembered for his autobiography *My Past and Thoughts* and for his editorship of the *émigré* journal *The Bell*, while the best-known example of Belinskii's wide-ranging critical journalism is his denunciatory letter to Gogol, lamenting the conversion of a realistic writer to religious conformity. Herzen, like his associate N. P. Ogarev, came from the nobility; Belinskii is one of the first radicals to spring from the *raznochintsy* or commoners of the intelligentsia.[39] While their origins and careers are somewhat different, Soviet observers put them together as socialists who were non-scientific, although they were familiar with Marx's earlier writings. They did not appreciate the part that would have to be played by the urban proletariat, and increasingly believed that the main force for change in Russia would be the peasant commune. Nevertheless, they realised the importance of the class struggle and saw the necessity of revolution. Such extremism separated them from the liberal group broadly known as the Westerners, who placed their emphasis on constitutional government and peaceful development towards capitalism. An eccentric version of the negative part of their argument was put by Petr Chaadaev, who saw the root of Russia's predicament in its reception of the cultural influence of 'decadent Byzantium'. Further to the right were the Slavophiles, whose doctrine was a strange mixture of progressive and reactionary ideas. In favour of the gradual emancipation of the serfs, they also extolled the virtues of the village commune. In favour of free speech and the re-assembly of the *Zemskii Sobor*, they also gloried in the apartness of Russian history, in Orthodoxy, autocracy and nationality, if by no means in the same way as Uvarov and the 'official nationalist' apologists for Nicholas I. They often incurred the displeasure of the censor and the police, and have been praised by Soviet historians for their 'great and fruitful work' on 'the Russian national culture, way of life and creativity of the people' which 'objectively encouraged the growth of the democratic tendency in the development of cultural life'.[40]

The 1848 revolution brought a new intensification of the development of the revolutionary movement. Fifteen members of a discussion circle, the Petrashevtsy group (which included Dostoevsky) were condemned to death for nothing more than 'a conspiracy of ideas'. Although these sentences were commuted at the last moment, the gendarmes were obviously becoming more alarmed. Even Uvarov, who had contributed so much to the formation of the ideology of Russian nationalism, found it necessary to resign in protest at their excesses.[41]

8 The Emancipation, and After, 1855–1894

On 19 February 1861 the emancipation of the serfs was decreed, although, owing to a last minute pause at the brink by the government, it was not announced until 5 March. In common with their fellows throughout Russia, the peasants of the Spassk region not far from Kazan looked for somebody to interpret the manifesto for them. In the nearby village of Bezdna, they found Anton Petrov, a barely literate Old Believer. According to his own account, Petrov mysteriously misinterpreted the figure '0.0.' to mean that freedom had been given to everybody, and then fabricated further details in order 'to attract the peasants to my side, reasoning that the more peasants there were, the sooner I should gain freedom'. He told them that the landlords would retain only one-third of the land, that they themselves would no longer have to give labour services nor money payments. Petrov's imagination fired his oratory, as may be seen in the following report of one of his speeches:

> You will have true liberty only if you defend the man who finds it for you. … Young men and old will come to you; do not let them reach me; do not hand me over to them. They will cheat you by saying that they have come from the Tsar; do not believe them. The old men will come with smiles; middle-aged men will come; both bald and hairy men will come; and every kind of official; but you must not hand me over. And in due time, a young man will come here sent by the Tsar. He will be seventeen years old, and on his right shoulder he will have a gold medal and on his left shoulder a silver one. Believe him, and hand me over to him. They will threaten you with soldiers, but do not be afraid; no one will dare to beat the Russian, Christian people without orders from the Tsar. And if the nobles buy them, and they fire at you, then destroy with your axes these rebels against the will of the Tsar.[1]

Such eloquence did much to build up a movement around him, but could do little to protect him when the troops did come. After the revolt at Bezdna was put down, Petrov was tried by a military tribunal and then shot. But his name lived on, and legends grew up about him among the peasants to such an extent that the nobles of Kazan feared a new Pugachev. Herzen described the revolt fully in *The Bell*, and A. P. Shchapov, Professor of Russian History at Kazan University made a speech about it at the requiem mass organised by the students of the University and the Theological Academy on Palm Sunday. Addressing those who had fallen, Shchapov declared:

> Friends killed for the people ... In Russia for about a hundred and fifty years there have begun to appear among the bitterly suffering dark masses of the people, among you, peasants, your own Christs – the democratic conspirators. From the middle of the last century they have been considered prophets, and the people has believed in them as atoners, emancipators. Here again has been such an atonement, and you friends are the first to fall at its summons as sacrifices to despotism expiating the freedom long expected by the whole people. You are the first to destroy our sleep, you have destroyed by your initiative our unjust doubt about our people not being capable of initiative in political movements ... The land, which you worked, with the fruits of which you have fed us, which now you wanted to obtain as your property and which has accepted you as its martyrs into its bowels – this land summons the People to revolt and freedom ... Peace to your dust and eternal historical remembrance to your self-sacrificing deed. Long live the democratic constitution.[2]

Shchapov's speech may be looked upon as one of the first steps towards the foundation of the populist movement which was to develop for most of the rest of the reign of Alexander II, and then to split up just before his assassination in 1881 in two principal directions, towards liberalism on the one hand and Marxism on the other. About the time of the death of Alexander III in 1894, the emergence of the proletarian phase in the revolutionary movement may be discerned. The stages in the growth of the opposition to tsarism thus neatly coincide with the reigns of Alexander II (1855–81) and Alexander III (1881–94), a coincidence to some extent reflected in the personalities and outlooks of the respective monarchs.

    Alexander II was born in 1818, the eldest son of the future Nicholas I and his Prussian wife. Not surprisingly, Alexander grew up with that love for most things military shared by the majority of his predecessors, although like them he found the spit and polish of the parade more to his taste than the blood and filth of actual war. The tsarevich was not much of a student, and his tutors complained of his lack of attention. Alexander preferred the open air to stuffy classrooms, and soon developed a lasting passion for hunting. He nevertheless managed to pick up several languages, and was able to put them into practice on a grand tour of Europe which followed a progress around the Russian Empire in the late 1830s. His German helped him in Darmstadt to fall in love with the Princess Mary, the fifteen-year-old daughter of the local duke. 'She is the woman of my dreams,' he told his companions, 'I will never marry anyone but her.' Although one of the objects of Alexander's grand tour had been to find a wife, Princess Mary was far from the ideal choice since, while recognised by the duke as his lawful daughter, she had in fact been sired by another man, even by a commoner. But Alexander insisted that he would rather give up the throne than Mary, and Nicholas finally acquiesced. In 1841 Alexander Nicholaevich married his Maria Alexandrovna, as she had now become according to Orthodox custom, and they were happy, if not for ever after, for at least a dozen years or so. Then, in the inevitable welter of court intrigue, Alexander took a mistress. On the whole, however, he would rather chase bears than princesses, and was a good father if not an exemplary husband.[3]

As tsar, Alexander II was idle rather than tolerant, weak-willed more than liberal. He admired his father's system of government, but lacked the energy and persistence to maintain it. Undoubtedly, the situation bequeathed to Alexander was already deteriorating, and the difficulty of the choice between resistance and accommodation explains much of the waywardness of his character. The fact that he did show exceptional determination in the great debate on emancipation could indicate not only a flash of the same personality trait that had gained him his wife but also the narrowness of his choice on this occasion. The general indecision of the Emperor was to some extent the reflection of the contradictory advice that he received from conservatives like D. A. Tolstoi and K. I. Palen on the one hand and comparative liberals like D. A. Miliutin and P. A. Valuev on the other.

If the crisis after the Crimean War called for concessions to the demands of the people, that after the assassination of Alexander II invited reaction. Alexander III responded to this challenge with enthusiasm, making no secret of his belief in autocracy and of his distrust of foreign forms of government. To him, that of France was 'vile', that of the United Kingdom was 'hardly a monarchy'[4] – Queen Victoria would not have been amused. Such crude ideas as these received intellectual support from the tsar's advisers, notably K. P. Pobedonostsev, officially Procurator of the Holy Synod, unofficially 'vice-emperor'; Count Dimitry A. Tolstoi (Tolstoy), Minister of Internal Affairs from 1882 until his death in 1889; and M. N. Katkov, editor of the establishment newspaper *Moscow News*, whose foremost reader was the Tsar himself. Although such a trio should have been united, it was in fact rent by differences of opinion and mutual suspicion, recalling to at least one contemporary's mind the fable of the swan, the pike and the crab, who could never agree on how to get the cart that they were supposed to be pulling in motion. Where he could not find solid support from his three closest adherents, however, the Emperor found it in the three main principles of his grandfather – Orthodoxy, autocracy and nationality.

Stern, even cruel with his people at large, the 'little father' was at home a corpulent, jovial family man, with none of his father's irregularities in his private life. He had married a Danish Princess called Maria Fedorovna in Russia, and their five children included the future Nicholas II. Alexander was born in 1845, the second son of Alexander II, and was not therefore thought of as tsarevich until the death of his older brother Nicholas twenty years later. As a result, his education had been somewhat neglected, and he himself had certainly not pursued it with any enthusiasm. His spelling was deficient, and so was his grammar. Such faults did not deter him from doing his job conscientiously, and he wrote dutiful annotations on reams of state papers, but he did increasingly prefer to spend his time away from the capital in rural retreat at his estate, Gatchina. There perhaps was the safest place to make a stand against the changes symbolised by the emancipation, changes which sufficiently impressed Engels for him to write in 1883: 'Russia, this is the France of our century. To her rightly and properly belongs the initiative of the new socialist reconstruction.'[5]

Political

The reign of Alexander II, like that of his father, Nicholas I, began and ended in crisis; nor was it exactly plain sailing in the middle. For too long, Nicholas had kept to his policy of 'holding on to everything', and now, to use the oldest of historical clichés, it was perhaps too late to right the ship of state. Not all Western historians have been so pessimistic, some of them considering that the Great Reform could have been the beginning of a relatively painless process of modernisation. Among the more cautious of them, W. E. Mosse has written that a wiser, more liberal course of action in the latter part of Alexander II's reign '*might*, if adopted, have led Russia along the road of peaceful constitutional development'.[6] Other such 'optimists' have put forward an argument like this for a period as late as that following 1905. For their part, looking at society from the lower levels upwards, many Soviet historians wondered why the situations at the beginning and end of the reign were not ripe enough for completely successful revolutions to take place. They, like Western historians, argued among themselves about the emphasis to be placed on their fundamental assertion.

As far as the years following the end of the Crimean War are concerned, M. V. Nechkina declared that 'What happened in Russia at the end of the fifties and the beginning of the sixties was only a part of the great world-historical movement of democratic character.' Unrest in Poland, an upsurge throughout the whole continent of Europe, the Taiping Rebellion in China and the end of Negro slavery in the United States were the other principal parts of this movement. Far from being a reform from above, then, the emancipation of the serfs was forced on a reluctant government by an irresistible progressive wave of global proportions, taking the form in Russia of widespread peasant unrest. To this extent, it was a revolution from without.[7]

In 1858, a year in which considerable progress was made towards reform, 378 peasant disturbances took place according to Soviet calculation, and in the first four months of 1861, before and after the emancipation decree of 19 February, there were 1340 disturbances. Such figures are impressive, yet even some Soviet scholars criticised the exaggeratedly statistical approach of their colleagues. Only forty-six of the total for 1858 are sufficiently documented for the numbers of their participants to be known. Sometimes, a very small incident such as illegal tree-felling is included along with more serious occurrences such as the murder of landlords. And the disturbances of 1861 came too late to influence the nature of the emancipation itself. P. A. Zaionchkovskii pointed out that the military needed to be used to suppress the peasants in no more than 4 per cent of the villages of Russia during the critical years, and that the Bezdna uprising led by Anton Petrov was most exceptional. Hence, taking a different line of approach from Nechkina, he suggested that the government was moved more by the fear of what might happen than by the threat of what actually did happen. Moreover, the fear of what the peasants might do had to be weighed against the necessity of maintaining the support of sufficient numbers of the landlords. Thus, there was neither a strong enough will on the part of the oppressed nor a weak enough will on the part of their oppressors for the situation to be truly revolutionary.[8]

The contradictory nature of Alexander II's policy, which his Minister of the Interior, P. A. Valuev, characterised as 'a system of impossible diagonals',[9] revealed itself not only in the emancipation but also in the reforms which formed its sequel. Leaving the emancipation for later discussion, we turn now to look at the measures which followed it. Although the conservative 'planters' were in the ascendant after 1861, a momentum built up since the 1850s maintained the swing of the pendulum in the 'liberal' direction. At the very beginning of 1864 a local government reform was introduced, the first such reform to be comprehensive since that of Catherine II in 1775. Now assemblies and boards were to be elected at various levels of local administration by three major categories of voters: landowners; town property-owners; and peasants in communes. These new *zemstvo* organisations were to deal with a wide range of local problems including health and education, roads and famine relief. But police and administrative control were to remain with the central government, and the *zemstvo* was given only extremely limited rights to tax. While some Western commentators have argued that the experience of the *zemstvo* helped to create politicians ready for action in later years, Lenin took a dimmer view, declaring that 'the *zemstvo* was doomed from the first to be the fifth wheel on the cart of the Russian state administration, a wheel *allowed* by the bureaucracy only as long as its exclusive power was not destroyed, and the role of the deputies from the people was limited in actual practice to the simple technical execution of a sphere of tasks drawn up by the bureaucracy itself.'[10] Certainly, the nobility dominated the *zemstvo* from the first: in 1866, out of 1180 officials in thirty-three provinces, 854 were *dvoriane*. Moreover, for good or ill, the reform was applied first to the provinces of Russia proper, leaving out the borderlands.

A new system of local government had been made necessary by the emancipation. Some assemblies of the nobility believed that the time had come for the reform of the central government, too, the Tver group asking for the convocation of a constituent assembly in 1862, and the Moscow *dvorianstvo* voting by 270 votes to 36 for the summons of a general duma in 1863. Such appeals met with little response from Alexander II and his advisers. They did, however, take another important step beyond the introduction of the *zemstvo*, with the reform of the judicial system, which had also been made necessary by the emancipation. Many nobles felt that if labour were now to be free, legality would have to be ensured, and Valuev echoed such sentiments in a memorandum to the tsar at the end of 1861, declaring that it was necessary 'to intensify activity and to encourage enterprise in all branches of industry. The essential obstacle to this has long been recognised in the short-comings of our court system and judicial process'.[11] Drawn up by a group of learned enthusiasts, the reform borrowed heavily on Western theory and practice. Such principles as the independence of the judiciary, equality of all before the law and the right to trial by jury for criminal offences were proclaimed in the statute of 20 November 1864. A reorganised Senate was to be at the apex of a unified system of courts, and lawyers, previously little employed in Russia, were to play a much bigger part in court proceedings. While the new arrangements were undoubtedly superior to the old, and the expressed wishes of Valuev and the nobility largely fulfilled, Riasanovsky's verdict on the reform, that 'almost overnight it transformed the Russian judiciary from one of the worst to one of the best in the civilized world', is perhaps too enthusiastic.[12] Some peasant courts, church courts and military courts were still to maintain their competence. The reform was introduced into peripheral regions of the Empire in an incomplete and slow manner, not being implemented in the Caucasus before 1871, for example, and then only partially. The social situation being what it was, in a system of classless courts some classes would be effaced less than others.

For the greatest possible success of the administrative changes of the early 1860s, there were at least two prerequisites: a sufficient number of trained personnel; and the continued enthusiasm of tsarist ministers. The first desideratum was to a considerable extent fulfilled. While in 1840 as few as six of the hundred or so of the top secretarial staff of the St Petersburg branch of the Senate had enjoyed higher education, by 1850 50 out of the 80 of these in the judicial sections had studied at such institutions as the universities, the School of Jurisprudence (founded in 1835), and the Lycée first at Tsarskoe Selo, later in St Petersburg. In 1856 more than 200 of the 300 chancellery officials in the judicial sections of the St Petersburg and Moscow branches of the Senate had been educated in such a manner. There was, then, no shortage of competent civil servants in at least some parts of the central bureaucracy. But there was a lack of leadership. By the middle 1860s the failures of the Crimean War and the threats of the ensuing years seemed remote. The Polish Insurrection of 1863 had been quelled. And so, when the ex-student Dmitrii Karakozov made an unsuccessful attempt on Alexander II's life on 4 April 1866, the advisers in favour of reaction and the dismissal of liberal ministers did not find it difficult to catch the tsar's ear. A contemporary anecdote had it that if Karakozov's bullet missed the the tsar, it hit several of those around him, for ministers did indeed now find themselves dismissed. A new head of the Third Section, P. A. Shuvalov, moved to take control of the situation. Provincial governors were empowered to close private societies or clubs if they appeared to constitute any danger to the state. In 1867 the *zemstva* were forbidden inter-provincial organisation, and prohibited from publishing their decisions or accounts without the permission of the governor.

The judicial arrangements of 1864 were changed, too, judges being subordinated to the governors in 1866. Count K. I. Palen, who became Minister of Justice in 1867, made no secret of his support for such measures, going so far in 1871 as to suggest to the tsar the radical alteration of the 1864 reform. Alexander is reported to have replied: 'You have not understood me, I instructed you only to discuss changes for the conduct of political cases.' As before, then, some of his advisers were prepared to go further than the tsar himself wanted to.[13]

This is not to imply that Alexander was a frustrated liberal, but there were comparatively progressive pressures on him as well as reactionary even after the 'massacre' of 1866, and some further reforms were introduced in the 1870s. A new form of city government was announced in 1870, for example, doing for the town roughly what the *zemstvo* had done for the country. Municipal councils were to be elected, although voters were to be divided into three groups according to the amount of taxes that they paid. As it was applied in Moscow, this system meant that two-thirds of the council were elected by 13 per cent of the taxpayers. An advance on the previous arrangement nevertheless, the reform was gradually brought into the whole of the Empire by the end of the 1870s, with the exception of Poland and Finland, which retained their own form of municipal government.

The most important reform of the 1870s, and arguably second only to the emancipation for the whole reign, was the universal military service law of 1874. All Russians were now bound to serve from six to seven years, although reductions and exemptions could be obtained through educational qualifications or family commitment. In theory at least, the so-called emancipation of the nobility of 1762 was now rescinded, and the conditions were created for a professional rather than a class-ridden army. The architect of the law of 1874, Dmitrii Miliutin, was Minister of War from 1861 to 1881 and was responsible during that period for a whole series of measures, including the abolition for soldiers of corporal punishment, the readjustment of the local and central military administration, the improvement of education, training and conditions of life off duty, the modernisation of armaments and regulations, and the realignment of military justice with the civil changes of 1864.[14]

Miliutin skilfully adapted Prussian innovations to Russian soil. He was also a diplomatic and strategic thinker of some distinction, and his memoir of 1878–9, which forcefully argued the case for defence rather than attack should war break out in the West, remained the basis of Russian thought on the subject down to the First World War. More than any other individual, Miliutin helped the Russian army to recover its confidence and efficiency after the fiasco of the Crimean War. Its performance in the

Russo-Turkish War of 1877–8 was by no means great but already an improvement. Ironically, it is arguable that Miliutin did his job too well, since Russian generals obviously had too much confidence in their army in the years leading up to 1914, or at least up to the disastrous encounter with Japan in 1904. Praising the Miliutin reforms as a whole, Florinsky writes that 'it was in the army, that stronghold of tradition and conservatism, that Russian democracy scored one of its first modest, yet real, successes'. Forrestt Miller writes enthusiastically of Miliutin as 'among the greatest statesmen of the Russian Empire'.[15] On the other hand, Lenin had no more time for these reforms than for the *zemstvo*, calling even the reformed army 'a school of wilfulness and violence'.[16]

The ebb and flow of reform and reaction were still very much in evidence at the end of Alexander's reign, the years of the second 'revolutionary situation' of 1878 to 1882. Zaionchkovskii, who devoted a major work to this crisis, again saw it as a crisis of leadership rather than as an all-Russian confrontation embracing every class. In so far as it went beyond a loss of confidence on the part of the government, the threat could certainly be discerned in popular disturbances in town and country, but was centered mainly on the revolutionary Land and Freedom Movement and Party of the People's Will. Inaugurated by the shooting of the military governor of St Petersburg, General Trepov, by Vera Zasulich in 1878, a wave of terrorism brought a vigorous reaction from the government but also some serious soul-searching, particularly when large sections of the public made no secret of their pleasure at the acquittal of Zasulich and, albeit to a lesser extent, of their sympathy for the actions which followed hers. A liberal, Count M. T. Loris-Melikov, who had been governor-general of Kharkov province, was in February 1880 placed at the head of a Supreme Executive Commission, which was entrusted with the task of putting an end to the civil upsets. An optimist, Loris-Melikov took his appointment as an excuse to further his previously expressed preference for 'measures, which would facilitate the soothing of the trustworthy elements of society, and, defending their lawful interests, revive their weakened trust in authority'.[17] Little came from the Commission, although some unpopular ministers were dismissed and the notorious Third Section was dissolved. So was the Commission itself soon after, and Loris-Melikov now took control of an enlarged Ministry of Internal Affairs, to which was subordinated a new police department. As well as making a few further concessions, Loris-Melikov also devised a project for reform which rejected both Western and old Russian models of government as too dangerous. Rather he proposed a convocation of representatives from the *zemstva* and larger municipalities to give advice on legislative measures before they were passed on to the State Council. Such a 'constitution' found some favour with Alexander II, who asked for it to be discussed by his ministers just a few hours before the People's Will succeeded (after at least seven failures) in assassinating him on 13 March 1881.

Although Alexander III and his advisers were manifestly shaken, it was rather the revolutionaries who wilted, having exhausted themselves with the assassination. And so the Loris-Melikov project was abandoned by the Council of Ministers, one of whom, Count S. G. Stroganov, declared that it would have transferred power 'from the hands of the autocratic monarch, who is now absolutely necessary for Russia, into the hands of various good-for nothings'.[18] The new tsar himself agreed with Stroganov that the acceptance of the project would be the first step towards a constitution. While some later analysts have tended to dismiss the project as not likely to have made a significant impact even if accepted, we have the authoritative opinion of Zaionchkovskii that while it 'did not violate the principle of autocratic power, ... in the conditions of an increasingly complex situation it might, given the specific inter-relation of forces, have been the beginning of the establishment of a parliamentary system in Russia'.[19] Here Zaionchkovskii came near to the evaluation of Mosse and other Western scholars.[20] If a constitution was what the government most feared, it was probably well-advised to reject the proposals of Loris-Melikov and to proclaim the confirmation of autocracy in the manifesto of 29 April 1881, which was written by Pobedonostsev and M. N. Katkov. Loris-Melikov and Miliutin went into retirement, and the new administration set about restoring order according to its own recipe.

The new Minister of Internal Affairs was N. P. Ignatev, dubbed by Lenin 'a diplomat with the assignment of covering the retreat of the government to complete reaction'.[21] A 'Statute on reinforced and extraordinary security' of 14 August 1881 gave the government powers which according to the French observer A. Leroy-Beaulieu were appropriate for the commander-in-chief in an enemy country, and which according to Lenin formed 'the Russian constitution in fact'.[22] Brought in originally for three years, the Statute was still in effect at the time of the fall of the monarchy. It allowed, for example, the arrest of suspects and the sequestration of their property in an extra-judicial manner, and the sentence of five years' exile without trial.

Against such a background, there were not likely to be many reforms, before or after the crisis had passed. The most immediate legislation, however, did attempt to do something to relieve the plight of the peasants. In 1881 arrangements were made for many peasants to be included in the redemption payment network with the rates scaled down. In 1882 a

Peasant Land Bank was set up, although its charges were higher than those of the open market and the Bank was therefore of little use. In the same year a beginning was made to the final abolition of the poll tax, the process being completed by 1 January 1887. To crown such work, Ignatev, who was closely connected with the Moscow Slavophiles, pressed for the summons of the *Zemskii Sobor* to mark the coronation of Alexander III set for 1883. Pobedonostsev said that this would lead to 'revolution, the ruin of government and the ruin of Russia', and his fellow-reactionary M. N. Katkov said it would mean 'the triumph of sedition'.[23] The suggestion was unanimously rejected at a meeting of the tsar's advisers, and Ignatev was sent into retirement.

His successor as Minister of the Interior, Count D. A. Tolstoy, became known as the 'Minister of Conflict', a nickname earned by dint of opposition to progress and energetic prosecution of the interests of the landlords, who included himself. 'Your ancestors created Russia', he said to the tsar, 'but they created it with our hands.'[24] To strengthen these hands, a Land Bank was set up for the nobility in 1885, with a lower rate of interest and therefore about six times more business than the Peasant Land Bank. In 1886 the dissolution of peasant households was made more difficult, and in 1893, restrictions were placed on the re-partition of peasant lands. In 1889 a new noble official, the *zemskii nachalnik* or land captain, was introduced to consolidate the provincial grasp of the *dvorianstvo*. He was to appoint local judges, and the decisions of the peasant assemblies were to be submitted to him for approval. He was empowered to levy fines or imprison suspects without trial. In brief, as Florinsky puts it, 'nothing pertaining to the financial, economic, social, and cultural welfare of the rural community escaped the jurisdiction of the land captains'. Although Tolstoy died in 1889, his spirit lived after him as the property qualifications for voting in *zemstvo* and municipality elections were raised in decrees of 1890 and 1892.[25]

A note or two of paternalist concern can be detected in some of the legislation of Alexander III's reign as the labour question posed itself more clearly. For example, a law of 1882 forbade the industrial labour of most minors under the age of twelve and another of 1885 prohibited female nightwork. But more in the mainstream of the tsar's policy was the decree of 1886 which set punishments for refusal to work and disallowed complaints. Moreover, in 1890, deterioration in the industrial sector was recognised, and some exceptions which had been made to the earlier protective decrees on a temporary basis were now declared permanent. Generally speaking, the difference between the domestic policies of Alexander II and III is that, while the father had some notions which were at least partly liberal, the son had none.

Such a difference may be considerably explained by personal character-istics, as we have seen, and by the changing nature of the economic and political situation. It must also be taken into account that the world was shrinking and becoming more interdependent throughout the nineteenth century, and that Russia's attempts at imperial expansion and self-assertion were bound to bring repercussions at home and abroad. Fears for domestic stability could thus dissuade the government from too heavy an involve-ment in foreign problems which did not directly affect tsarist interests.

In any case, Russian patriots did not for the most part envisage their flag being carried overseas. Since the huge mass of the Empire stretched half-way round the world and the sun already hardly ever set on it, there seemed to be no need for seaborne extensions. Indeed, there was a certain amount of seaborne contraction. In 1867 the government folded up its American colony with the sale of Alaska to the United States for $7,200,000. And then, in 1875, Russia exchanged its Kurile Islands with Japan for the southern part of the island of Sakhalin. On mainland Asia, however, far from weakening, the drive for more territory and consolidation became more intense. In the Far East Count Nikolai Muravev, the governor-general there from 1847 to 1861, brought the two-headed eagle into the valleys of the Amur and Ussuri rivers. China, weakened by foreign incur-sions and the Taiping Rebellion, was forced to accept these losses in the Treaty of Aigun of 1858 and the Treaty of Peking of 1860.[26] Russian expansion in the Far East was far from controlled and some of Muravev's lieutenants exceeded their orders to near the point of court-martial. But the government needed consolidation for the failures of the Crimean War, the losses to China of the Treaty of Nerchinsk in 1689 had been more than recovered, and so, instead of being chastised for the over-enthusiasm of his men, the governor-general was awarded the title of Muravev–Amurskii in 1858. A new city founded by the Russians in 1861 near the southern extremity of their new possessions left little doubt about their intentions in the area. Its name was Vladivostok, which means 'Rule over the East'.

Further slices of land were later taken from China in Central Asia, where Russian generals such as Cherniaev, Kaufmann and Skobelev found plenty of room for the realisation of their ambitions. Before the end of the reign of Alexander II, the khanates of Kokand, Bukhara and Khiva had been taken and the eastern shore of the Caspian annexed. As in the Far East, the men on the spot by no means listened carefully to every word of command from St Petersburg. As David Mackenzie puts it,

The saga of Russian expansion in Central Asia during the mid-1860s reveals that the advances, initiated by government decisions, greatly exceeded its plans or intentions. The Foreign and Finance ministries envisioned cautious, limited expansion largely to promote commerce with the Orient and promote Russia's security. Their public opposition to unchecked imperialism was sincere, but they proved impotent against the generals and their supporters.

In Mackenzie's evaluation, 'What eventually set limits to Russian expansion in Central Asia were not ministerial resolutions but mountain barriers and British power.'[27]

Consolidating Caucasian areas previously annexed, Prince Aleksandr Bariatinskii finally succeeded in 1859 in capturing the legendary Shamil, who had been leading Muslim resistance to the infidel invader for twenty-five years. It was nearly all over now, even if the Caucasus never became completely tame. Conversion in the Caucasus was not as forced as in other colonial cases, in which some tribesmen found the Orthodox Church extremely enthusiastic about the salvation of their souls, particularly during the reign of Alexander III. In the so-called Multanskoe case, which ran from 1892 to 1896, a group of Udmurty were accused of sacrificing human victims to heathen gods. While not condoning such behaviour, some observers saw the trial as part of a ruthless attempt to introduce rigid standardisation. Soviet historians, examining this and other elements of Russian imperial policy, made a distinction between the actions of tsarist administration at the top and the sympathetic development lower down of the 'friendship of peoples'. However, such groups as the Jews could well be forgiven for denying that the hand of friendship was extended towards them at any level, especially at such times as the first pogroms from 1881 onwards.[28]

At the time, the general line of his government's policy was vigorously defended by Chancellor Gorchakov, who compared it in 1864 to that of other expanding powers. He declared: 'The United States in America, France in Africa, Holland in her colonies, England in India, were all forced to take the road of expansion dictated by necessity rather than ambition, a road on which the chief difficulty is to know where to stop.' Russification, then, was considered no worse than Americanisation or Anglicisation. Indeed, in the nineteenth century, Russians thought it was far better, many of them clothing their beliefs in the ideas of Panslavism, which had its heyday during the period under discussion. It could be used to excuse the suppression of other Slavonic cultures such as the Ukrainian and the Polish, most notably after the failure of the Polish insurrection of 1863.[29] Panslavism also gave impetus to Russian efforts to expand in the

Balkans, where the humiliation of the Crimean War had to be found compensation. Neither their fellow Slavs in Bulgaria and elsewhere nor their uneasy allies, the Habsburgs, were completely happy with Russian attempts to solve the Eastern Question, and, of course, the Turks were very much alarmed. War could not be far away.

The Panslavists' chance came when revolts against Turkish rule broke out in the Balkans in 1875 and 1876. International attempts were made to avert hostilities between the major powers, but finally met with failure as Turkey rejected a Russian ultimatum. In the war of 1877–8 the forces of the tsar were in the end successful, but not before several reverses had been inflicted upon them by the troops of the Porte, notably at the important fortress of Plevna. The Treaty of San Stefano in the spring of 1878 made Bulgaria virtually independent and extended freedom widely throughout the Balkans. But fears for the balance of power were raised throughout Europe, and the Congress of Berlin in the summer of 1878 produced a revised Treaty which reduced the independence of Bulgaria and the gains of the Slavs in general. Russian nationalist crusaders were disappointed that Constantinople had not been taken and that the Empire was obliged to be content with Bessarabia and more minor acquisitions. Bulgarians and others wondered if their qualified release from the thrall of the Turk was going to be limited further by increased control exerted by their big brother. Smirnov commented: 'Although the tsarist government pursued expansionist aims in the fight against Turkey and the burden of the war was borne entirely by the people of Russia, the war nevertheless played an important part in liberating the Balkan peoples from the Turkish yoke.'[30]

The war of 1877–8 also brought tension with the Habsburgs. Rivalry with Austria combined with anxiety at the rise of Germany to make the Three Emperors' League a fragile and mostly ineffective alliance of the reactionary crowned heads of Europe against change and progress. In the pursuit of security, Russia found it necessary to seek a new ally in France. Her fresh course was marked by a diplomatic agreement of 1894, when a military convention of 1892 was also ratified. Expressly though secretly directed against the Triple Alliance of Germany, Austria and Italy, which had first been set up in 1882, the Franco-Russian accord marked a further step towards the diplomatic alignment of the period leading up to the First World War.

Economic

In the stages of the development of capitalism, Russia might be said to have reached the mercantile by the middle of the seventeenth century, the manufacturing by soon after the middle of the eighteenth century, and the industrial in the years following the emancipation of 1861. By no means all economic historians would accept such a scheme, and even those who would accept it might well disagree among themselves about its exact chronological application. 1830 was preferred to 1861 as the third transitional date by some Soviet historians, while Western experts have tended to favour the 1880s or even later. In the broad sweep of the centuries, perhaps, fifty years is not such a long time, particularly when the subject under discussion cannot be exactly defined. In such a perspective, Russia's notorious backwardness does not appear so great. But, in the short run, the timing of Russian change was all-important in comparison with, say, German or American. Russia's apartness may be clearly seen not only in the slow pace of her capitalist development but also in the persistence of socio-economic features antipathetic to it. In other words, the Russian Prometheus was less unbound than his counter-parts in the other modernising nations.

This circumstance is plainly on view in the event which is often said to launch imperial Russia on the path of industrialisation, the emancipation of 1861. Alexander II showed his awareness of the situation in his famous speech in 1856 to a section of the nobility, 'the mainstay of the throne'. The tsar declared: 'It is better to abolish serfdom from above than to wait for the time when it will begin to abolish itself spontaneously from below.'[31] Throughout the long discussions preparatory to the decrees of 1861, the ministers were conscious of the twin calls of progress and reaction. And when the announcement finally came, the illiterate peasants at Bezdna and elsewhere were able to read enough between the lines to understand that they had been cheated, while the conservative 'planters' believed that the floodgates of anarchy had been opened and that the downfall of the throne and its mainstay was now inevitable. The contradiction continues clearly visible through the wording of the 'Great Reform' and the sequel to it.

The aspiration of the emancipation edict of 1861 was that the peasants 'should understand that by acquiring property and greater freedom to dispose of their possessions, they have an obligation to society and to themselves to live up to the letter of the new law by a loyal and judicious use of the rights which are now granted to them'.[32] The serfs were to be personally free, that is not only to acquire property rights, but also to marry without the lord's permission, to engage in trade or litigation. While newly created agencies relieved the lords of most of their supervisory functions, they were nevertheless charged with the duty of preparing during the course of the following year inventories of the lands, services and payments of their former charges. After a further year, the peasants were to be 'temporarily obligated' according to these inventories until redemption payments were agreed with the lords. After agreement had been reached, the landlords were to receive from the state interest-bearing securities amountmg to between 75 per cent and 80 per cent of the total cost of the redemption debt, which was calculated on the basis of the serfs' previous dues. The peasants were to have paid back the redemption debt with interest over forty-nine years. Redemption agreements, the option for which was to be more with the former masters, did not become compulsory throughout the Empire until 1881 (1886 for state peasants), and would still not have been completely paid off by 1950 if the whole system had not been recognised as entirely broken down by 1905. To facilitate developments, as we have seen above, a Peasant Bank was set up in 1882 and a Nobles' Land Bank in 1885.

For such a system to have worked, however, the peasants would have needed a sufficient amount of land or unrestricted opportunities to make money in non-agricultural employment. Neither desideratum was attained. While maximum and minimum norms were established for different zones, they were not always realised or adequate in all cases even when they were realised. The peasants often lost land, particularly in the black-earth region – in Saratov and Samara more than 40 per cent of what they had previously worked. In such provinces, they were often forced by economic circumstances if not by law to continue working for their masters (*otrabotka* replacing *barshchina* in technical terms). In less fertile regions near the centre and in the north, it is true, they often gained land, but here the *obrok* form of payment had long been more profitable for the landlords than labour services, and therefore land was not as important to the erstwhile masters as cash. In 36 provinces of European Russia as a whole, more than 5.7 million hectares were cut off from the lands previously used by the peasants – 31.8 million hectares. Moreover, the retention of the commune, its incorporation into a new unit of local administration, the township or *volost*, and the continued exercise of a large amount of their power by the landlords, made it very difficult for the enterprising peasants to make their way in the world at large.

Arrangements were somewhat different for other categories of peasant such as those previously attached to the state and for other areas such as the Transcaucasian and Western Provinces. Such complications make it very difficult to give with any accuracy a brief description of the emancipation, or to evaluate its impact on society. But its significance is not to be found only in the small print of the twenty or so decrees which put it in the statute book, since emancipation was very much a worldwide phenomenon in the middle of the nineteenth century. In theory, the ideas of Adam Smith and others had been widely discussed for fifty years or more, and now the intellectual movement within Russia which had started with the Prize Essay Competition of Catherine II almost a century before could be said to have borne its fruit. In practice, the awareness that serfdom was incompatible with an industrialising economy was gradually forced upon a reluctant government. Just possibly, this was a false awareness. Closer examination of the profitability of the peculiar institution might show what some experts have claimed it demonstrates for the American South: that slavery is not necessarily unprofitable in an expanding capitalist economy. Such an exercise would put in bolder relief the environmental features of Russia's comparative backwardness. The climate and quality of the soil, the vast distances and remoteness from the major commercial centres kept the Russian economy in their thrall almost as much after the emancipation as before it. The further exercise of comparing the Russian emancipation to the American 'day of Jubilo' would no doubt clearly show that both 'black' peoples were robbed of what they believed to be their due, but that capitalism in both economies received something of a boost. The peculiarities of the Russian case, where unrestrained industrialisation was anathema to tsarism, were described by N. M. Druzhinin in the following manner: 'the task of the government and the class of landlords standing behind its back was ... by means of the reform to direct the economic life of the country along the peaceful path of gradual agro-capitalist development, favourable for the nobility, but tormenting for the working mass of the peasantry'.[33]

Even if the government and its supporters had wanted to force the pace, their power to goad the mass of the peasantry into action would have been too limited. Harry Willetts points out that the latter

... had a static and archaic view of their calling. Where land was plentiful they tilled part of it to near exhaustion, then moved on to long-fallow soil. Elsewhere, they observed a three-field rotation, leaving one field fallow, scratching the others with their wooden ploughs, and planting them, for the most part, with 'grey' cereals – rye and oats. Between the short, back-breaking periods of ploughing, sowing and reaping, their preference was to wait God's will in patient lethargy. These primitive procedures, wasteful enough at any time, were suicidal in the decades of rapid population increase and growing land-hunger. Peasants from the more advanced Western provinces might comment caustically on the 'lordly' mentality of their Russian brothers, those 'gentlemen at the plough' who, short as they were of land, kept a third of it permanently 'on holiday'.

As Willetts goes on to say, only 'generous help and patient indoctrination', which would have included a greater share of the land and advice on how to use it, could have brought a real change to the time-honoured practices of the *muzhiks*.[34]

Not that all agriculture was stagnant when a large amount of grain was sold abroad. Between the 1850s and the end of the century the average annual amount of exports of wheat and other grain rose from over a million to over seven million metric tons. The greatest increase occurred in the 1880s, even though this decade was in the middle of a period of depression in the world grain market, with prices at the time being nearly halved. The government laid great stress on grain exports to help Russia's international trade and credit balance, and such a policy certainly made a contribution to the Empire's growing reputation as Europe's granary. Most of the outward flow went westwards from the Ukraine through the Black Sea, although nine-tenths of the cultivation in European Russia as a whole was of grain. But no more than a fifth of the total grain production went abroad; most of it was produced either for the home market, national and local, or for subsistence purposes.

On the whole, the larger landlords, including many from the nobility, had their eyes on the export market, while the focus of the smaller farmer tended to be nearer home where, with industry growing, demand was often high. The stratification of the peasantry was intensified by this expanding commerce. While the majority of them were as unenterprising as in Willetts' description, a small but growing number were taking advantage of the changing situation. Opportunities for them were greater in the periphery, where Russia was taking the American or freer road to capitalism in agriculture, than in the centre, where the Prussian or *Junker*-dominated mode was more in evidence. In the outer regions, too, some cultivators were being caught up in the new developments, wines and fruits going to the urban markets from Transcaucasia, and beet grown in the Ukraine helping to make the manufacture of sugar second in importance only to that of textiles, whose cotton spindles were increasingly fed by Turkestan.

By the end of the century there were more cotton spindles active in Russia than in France and not many fewer than in Germany. In the thirty years following the emancipation, cotton-goods production centred mainly around Moscow increased fourfold. Heavy industry, as might be said to befit it, moved forward at a more deliberate pace. Having fallen steeply from the supremacy that they had enjoyed in the late eighteenth century, Russian metalworks produced only 4 per cent of the world's cast iron in 1860 and an even smaller 2.5 per cent in 1880. In the late 1870s, however, a British immigrant named Hughes opened up the Donbass, where a town – Iuzovka – was named in his honour, and most of Russia's coal was soon produced there in a region not far from Krivoi Rog, where iron deposits were at last beginning to be properly exploited. Ukrainian smelting was now twice as important as that in the older Urals metalworks, and by the end of the nineteenth century, Russian iron production had risen to 7 per cent of the world's total. By this time, not only Mr Hughes but many other foreigners had invested in Russia's growing industry. Among other contributions, they helped with the much-needed mechanisation, which resulted in a threefold growth of machines in use in the 1890s, a half of them admittedly in trains and ships, and a 25 per cent increase in industrial productivity during the same decade. To conclude a paragraph full of statistics, which were much beloved by the Soviet historians who supplied most of them, a further indication of the increasing mechanisation of industry is that, whereas in the 1880s there was in Russia little more than 0.09 horsepower of steam for each industrial worker, by the end of the 1890s the figure had risen to 0.65.

The establishment of industrial capitalism goes hand in hand with an improvement in communications. Metal makes the iron road and its rolling stock, the trains burning coal transport minerals and other goods more quickly and efficiently than has been previously possible. By 1871 railway lines had been completed from Moscow to Nizhnii Novgorod, to Voronezh, to Kharkov and to Brest via Smolensk and Minsk. The last of these joined Russia by rail to Europe, even though the change of gauge that was (and still is) necessary en route detracted somewhat from the journey's smoothness. By 1871, too, there were rail connections from the centre to both Black and Baltic Seas. At the end of the decade, however, the war with Turkey gave the Russian railway system an examination which it failed. Partly for this reason, partly because the government-assisted state companies were profligate and corrupt, the state decided to take over. In 1880, only 4 per cent of the railroad belonged to the state, by 1900, more than 60 per cent. Meanwhile, in the 1890s, nearly 30,000 kilometres (20,000 miles) of track were added to the approximately 30,000 kilometres (20,000 miles) already in existence. Transcaucasia, the Donets Basin, the Urals and Siberia were now penetrated. During the later years of the nineteenth century, water traffic also remained important, particularly along the Volga. The number of steamboats on that and other rivers and canals grew two and a half times in the 1860s and 1870s, and by the same amount again in the 1880s and 1890s. By the end of the century, about 70 per cent of the Empire's internal transport was handled by trains, 30 per cent by boat. Roads remained primitive, carriages and carts finding them impassable except in summer. During the same period, the government-controlled postal and telegraph services were expanding. Stamps were introduced for internal deliveries in 1857 and for foreign in 1864. Nearly two million letters were handled by the end of the 1870s. Between the years 1855 and 1880, the telegraph network's size grew from over 2000 kilometres (1300 miles) to nearly 80,000 kilometres (50,000 miles). Four years before the Atlantic cable was laid in 1869, an American group sought to join North American and Russia with a cable across the Bering Strait. One of the proponents of the project declared: 'Thus the commerce of the world will find its path across this continent, awakened into life by a new power; for the telegraph is to precede all, rapidly and cheaply we press it forward as the swift-running courier. First the adventurous merchant seeks the channel opened by this messenger; then the stately ship, soon to make way for the more rapid steamer; finally the iron way joins the circle, and girds the world with steam and electricity.'[35] Neither the narrower hopes for the Bering Strait nor the wider ones for the world in general were to be realised as quickly as the group believed possible, particularly when faced by the intractability of the climate, size and government of the Russian Empire.

And as always, Russian merchantmen fared abroad but little; less than a fifth of the ships in Russian ports were of indigenous origin during the second half of the nineteenth century, by 1900 little more than a tenth of them. Nevertheless, Russia was able to acquire a share of the rapidly expanding international trade of the period. In millions of gold roubles, the value of her exports rose from something over 225 in 1861 to more than 620 in 1895, while that of her imports climbed from about 205 to around 460. As before, the major exports were grains and raw materials, while machines constituted an important part of the imports. A significant change in the foreign trading pattern was the replacement of Britain as the major partner by Germany. It is also noteworthy that after a liberal tariff policy in the 1850s and 1860s, there was a return to stringent protectionism in the late 1870s and 1880s. In this manner, the government would maintain the rouble exchange rate, and maintain its budget control.

This reversion was encouraged by the war with Turkey, which also made difficult the attempts being made by the government to stabilise the currency and to balance the budget. Most of the state's income continued to come from indirect taxation, particularly the excise on spirits which replaced the previous farming-out system in 1863, while the most important direct tax was the poll tax until its abolition in the mid-1880s. But there was not enough money to pay for the heavy expenditure on the army and navy, and the national debt rose from 2180 million gold roubles in the late 1850s to 6 billion in 1881 and 7 billion in 1892. Successive ministers made strenuous efforts to clean up the financial mess, and to adjust the economic administration of the Empire as a whole to the arrival of industrial capitalism, which followed in the wake of the emancipation of the serfs. The most comprehensive of these efforts was made by Sergei Witte after the accession of Nicholas II in 1894. By this time, factories and mines were well on their way to superimposing themselves on the vast Russian landscape, even though its spaces were so vast that they almost swallowed up the appurtenances of modern civilisation. But the social consequences of the change – a larger urban population, a more stratified arrangement of the classes – were clearly revealed in the census of 1897, which will be subjected to analysis in the next chapter, when we shall consider Russian industrial capitalism at its highest stage, that of imperialism.[36]

Cultural

The emancipation of the serfs and the development of industrial capitalism exerted considerable influence on the various spheres of Russian cultural life during the reigns of Alexander II and Alexander III. Neither tsar made any significant impact himself, although Alexander III had something of a taste for the theatre and music, and sometimes played the trombone. It was rather such trends as the growth of the city that affected education, literary and other forms of creation, and the revolutionary movement. A widespread phenomenon throughout the industrialising world, urbanisation in Russia was marked by the decline of the nobility-dominated culture and the rise of the part played by the *raznochintsy*, people of various ranks who formed an intelligentsia of middle-class origin. Held back by upperclass prejudice, the censor and an obscurantist Church led by such reactionaries as Pobedonostsev, progressive creativity could not be stifled, whether in the shape of a peasant teaching himself to read or a universitytrained intellectual forming an idea of his revolutionary duty. At the end of the period under discussion, the all-important proletarian consciousness began to show clear signs of formation.

To begin with the most simple indicator of modern cultural advance, the growth of literacy. While in the 1860s, the ratio of literates to illiterates was about 1:15, by 1897 it had risen to near 1:5, for the age groups ten to thirty-nine to 1:4 or even 1:3. The urban population was about two and a half times more literate than the rural, and men more literate than women by nearly the same amount. There was regional variation as well, with no more than 12 per cent of the people being able to read and write in the Caucasus and Siberia, and 5 per cent in Central Asia.

Some, but not all, of the growth of literacy was attributable to the advance in elementary education, in Sunday schools and other establishments run by the Church, and in state institutions in which the Church also had considerable influence. Proponents of secular enlightenment were in constant conflict with the ecclesiastical authorities, the clerics being in the ascendancy, particularly during the reign of Alexander III, and progressive pedagogic thinkers such as K. D. Ushinskii achieving little immediate impact. Class prejudice was running at a high level then, too, as was graphically indicated in the notorious circular sent out in 1887 by the Minister of Education, Count Delianov, who ordered candidates for admission to gymnasia to be carefully examined for social and financial adequacy. The effect of gymnasium education on 'the children of coachmen, footmen, cooks, laundresses, small shopkeepers and other similar people' was 'contempt for parents, dissatisfaction with their own station, and bitterness towards the existing order and, in the nature of things, inevitable inequality in the financial position of various social groups'.[37] Such prejudice combined with financial pressure to restrict somewhat severely the movement from elementary to secondary education. At the upper level, too, the dead hand of obscurantism applied its baleful pressure, as in the so-called 'Greco-Roman bondage' to which Count D. A. Tolstoy, Minister of Education from 1866 to 1880, subjected the gymnasia. Through Tolstoy's influence, study of the classics was intensified at the expense of such subjects as history and geography, literature and even Russian. Emphasis on the classics was, of course, a phenomenon common to all Europe at this time, rather than Tolstoy's eccentricity. Moreover, a spirited defence has been made of Tolstoy's record in such fields as peasant education and teacher training, asserting his contribution to the advance taking place through the reigns in question.[38] The number of boys in gymnasia and progymnasia rose by nearly three times up to 70,000, and by the 1890s, their number in secondary education as a whole, that is including those at technical, commercial, military and church schools at this level, exceeded 150,000. By the same decade, about half that number of girls were in their gymnasia and other middle-level schools. These figures derive from a base in 1896 of about 3,500,000, the number of boys and girls in 65,000 primary schools, of which more than half were church schools.

Meanwhile, the number of students at universities and other institutions of higher learning slowly increased, while the conditions in which they did so fluctuated according to the political situation. At the beginning of Alexander II's reign, for example, they were treated rather liberally: the uniforms enforced by Nicholas I were no longer obligatory; freedom to travel was restored; and certain prohibited courses such as philosophy and European constitutional law were allowed back into the curriculum. But then, just after the emancipation, there were disturbances which led to the temporary closure of St Petersburg University and to trouble at the universities of Moscow, Kiev, Kharkov and particularly Kazan. A new university charter of 1863 was comparatively enlightened, but the attempt on the life of Alexander II by the ex-student Karakozov in 1866 led to a further reaction. And so on, with reaction more in evidence than progress, the number of students rising to approximately 14,000 in ten universities by the mid-1890s, and to 29,000 in the sixty or so institutions of higher learning in general. Four per cent of the 29,000 were women, whose acceptance by the universities in particular was slow and impeded by arguments such as that their presence would have 'a pernicious effect upon the studies of young men'. Commoners tended to be excluded as well as females, Katkov arguing that higher education should be reserved for 'the upper class which decides the fate of the nation and charts its future'.[39] Nevertheless, there was some democratisation in the social as well as the sexual, if not the racial, directions. While special arrangements were made for women to complete their education at St Petersburg, Moscow, Kazan and Kiev before the end of the nineteenth century, in the late 1890s a third of the students at St Petersburg University and three-fifths of them at Kharkov came from outside the upper class. At the same time, however, quota restrictions were imposed at the higher and secondary levels on Jews.

In spite of the difficulties with which it confronted them, Russia was producing scholars and scientists of the first world rank during the second half of the nineteenth century, such as the historians S. M. Solovev and V. O. Kliuchevskii, the chemists A. M. Butlerov and D. I. Mendeleev, the botanist K. A. Timiriazev, the biologist I. I. Mechnikov and the physiologist I. P. Pavlov. Such savants joined young people escaping from their Greco-Roman bondage, self-taught workers and peasants, to help form a quickly growing reading public. Although the censorship and other forms of restrictions were more rigorous in Russia than in most modernising countries, there were still some 350 periodicals in existence by the 1870s and more than 1000 of them by the end of the century. Bookshops multiplied sixfold from the 1860s to the 1890s, and many libraries were opened during these decades.

At its most enduring level, Russian literature of the period was the equal, and arguably the superior, of any other. In Turgenev, Tolstoi

(Tolstoy) and Dostoevskii (Dostoevsky), it produced three masterly writers of prose fiction. For some Dostoevsky is the greatest, with his profound psychological insight and heights of emotional frenzy. For others, the breadth of Tolstoy's world, particularly in *War and Peace* and *Anna Karenina*, has greater attraction. Yet others would argue that Turgenev is at least as remarkable as his two contemporaries for his closely analytical descriptions of a society rent by the generation gap and social divisions. Certainly, what Lenin said to Tolstoy, that he was the 'mirror of the Russian revolution', has been a label equally not only for Turgenev and Dostoevsky, but also for Goncharov, whose *Oblomov* became a synonym for 'feudal parasitism, passivity and stagnation', and to Saltykov-Shchedrin, who in *The Golovlev Family* and other works 'exposed the autocracy, the serf-owners, the predatory capitalist profit hunters and the thick-skulled and wilful civil servants'.[40]

In an age of realism, poetry could not flourish as prose did: N. A. Nekrasov came nearest to capturing the predominant spirit of the times in verse, while Fedor Tiutchev and particularly Afanasii Fet pointed the way forward towards the flourishing of the 'art for art's sake' movement at the turn of the century. Meanwhile, the drama prospered, although the works of the greatest playwright of the period, Aleksandr Ostrovskii, have not translated well. The more direct and international language of music, on the other hand, has permitted due recognition to the remarkable composers produced by Russia in the second half of the nineteenth century. In the sixties and seventies, the Moguchaia Kuchka or 'Mighty Handful' – consisting of Balakirev, Borodin, Kiul, Musorgskii or Mussorgsky and Rimskii or Rimsky-Korsakov – was more active in its attempts to follow in the footsteps of Glinka and Dargomyzhsky and bridge the gap between folk legends and songs and the more ordered world of the opera and the symphony. The most powerful result was Mussorgsky's *Boris Godunov*, the most colourful either Borodin's *Prince Igor* or one of Rimsky-Korsakov's *opéras fantastiques*. Mussorgsky's use of the *leitmotiv* and of folksong was to influence Stravinsky and many other composers. Not so successful in the symphonic sphere, although such works as Borodin's Second Symphony have undoubted impact, the Group was clearly surpassed here by P. I. Chaikovskii or Tchaikovsky, whose genius survives without difficulty the charges of self-indulgent sentimentalism levelled at it by his detractors. Tchaikovsky's music for ballet and his operas have also deserved their lasting, world-wide popularity.

With another means of international communication, that of the graphic and plastic arts, Imperial Russia under Alexander II and III made a far less effective impression. Although several of them broke away from the pseudo-classicism of the Academy in 1863 to pursue nationally and socially conscious aims, artists did not for the most part achieve a high level of expression. The best known of them, I. E. Repin, perhaps makes his greatest impact in such historical portraits as *Ivan the Terrible*. The epic canvasses of V. I. Surikov and V. V. Vereshchagin can also hardly fail to catch the eye in the Tretiakov Gallery in Moscow and elsewhere. The sculpture of the period is less memorable than the graphic art, and the prevalent Imperial style of architecture more monumentally tedious than its counterparts elsewhere. This is not to say that the sculptors and architects fully deserve the lack of mention that they receive here. This would also be the case with the writers and artists of the national regions, whom linguistic and cultural barriers have consigned to local fame.

Similarly, as we turn to consider the history of revolutionary and other forms of political ideology, we shall be able to consider only the most outstanding figures and the most salient of their ideas. Without too much distortion, the development of the revolutionary movement after the emancipation until the consolidation of industrial capitalism may be equated with the rise and fall of populism. From the late 1850s until the middle 1860s, the chief vehicle of progressive ideas was *The Bell*, published in London by Alexander Herzen with the collaboration of N. P. Ogarev. At first hailing the emancipation as a great step forward and Alexander II as the tsar-liberator, *The Bell* soon became disillusioned with both, and declared that the people had yet to be granted their greatest needs, 'land and freedom'. With the curtailment of universities' activities towards the end of 1861, students were urged to take themselves 'to the people'.

But *The Bell* was by no means the only voice to call to anti-tsarist dissidents. During the 1860s and early 1870s, ideas for action were put forward by several outstanding individuals, most notably perhaps by Mikhail Bakunin, Petr Lavrov, Sergei Nechaev, Petr Tkachev and Nikolai Chernyshevskii. Like Herzen and Ogarev, these were all moving, albeit in widely different ways, from the influence of German idealistic philosophy to something more materialistic, thus to some degree acting out the roles of the young generation in Turgenev's *Fathers and Sons*. Bakunin, more than anybody else the creator of revolutionary anarchism, forcefully argued his case against the more disciplined views of Marx in the First International. Expelled from it in 1872 during the great debate which followed the fall of the Paris Commune, he nevertheless exerted a large influence on later revolutionaries, continually proclaiming his belief in the readiness of the masses to rise and of the peasants in particular to play an important part in any upheaval. Lavrov put forward his mature views in the *Historical Letters*, published first in 1868–9. These talked of the obligations to society as a whole of that small group of people who are capable of critical analysis of their environment. If properly aware, they can be the principal engine of historical progress, influencing the rest of society through their propaganda. Nechaev was a fanatical preacher of strict organisation and political terror, prepared to go to the length of murder to preserve party discipline. His ruthlessness alienated Marx and Bakunin, but attracted others. Those who plotted the assassination of Alexander II were spurred on by Nechaev, who rejected their alternative plan of assisting his own break from jail. Tkachev followed Blanqui, the nineteenth-century French revolutionary, in his belief that the government could be overthrown by the determined conspiracy of a small group; for which reason Tkachev has been called a Jacobin and even a Bolshevik. Chernyshevskii was most influential through his journal *The Contemporary* and political novel, *What Is To Be Done?*, written in the Peter and Paul Fortress during the years 1862–4. Believing that tsarism should be overthrown, and that the peasants could make an important contribution to this overthrow, he argued that conditions in Russia would lead to the immediate establishment there of socialism based on the commune without the intervening stage of capitalism.[41]

Such beliefs were shared by most members of the amorphous populist movement which gathered momentum in the late sixties and early seventies. But there were many debates among them about the best means of achieving their ends. How long would the revolution process take to mature, and how if at all could it best be accelerated? These important questions were hotly discussed, with the works of Chernyshevskii and the others frequently cited in support of the views put forward. Actions varied as well as words. While Karakozov made his celebrated attempt on the tsar's life in 1866, unsung idealists were attempting to put their ideas across on the grass-roots. Soon, according to R. E. Zelnik, they were operating at the factory-floor level too, making contact with factory-workers by 1870.[42] Proselytism reached a climax in the 'crazy' summer of 1874, when thousands of crusaders attempted to take the message to the people, often dressing as peasants and attempting to clothe their arguments in similarly homespun garb. But the people were not receptive, and the authorities moved in to suppress the agitation before it could become dangerous. All but the most dedicated populists lost their enthusiasm.[43]

From the hard core sprang a new group, organising itself in 1876 and reviving the name Land and Freedom. The members could not agree on the methods to be adopted to reach their eponymous objectives, and the group split in 1879 into two, the People's Will and Black Partition.

Terrorism preoccupied those who sought to express what they believed to be the tacit desire of their fellow countrymen, and they met with their greatest but final success by the assassination of Alexander II. Pressure for distribution of all the land to the peasants, or 'black' people, was the major concern of the other splinter group, one of whose leaders was Georgii Plekhanov. This group too was soon dissolved, and Plekhanov took a new path along with other former members of Black Partition, such as Paul Akselrod and Vera Zasulich. In 1883 they brought about the formation in Geneva of the Marxist Liberation of Labour organisation. Meanwhile, the workers were beginning to form their own unions, and the strike at the Morozov Cotton Mills near Moscow in 1885 compelled even reactionary newspapers to admit that the 'labour question' had arrived in Russia. The connection between Marxist intellectuals and progressive workers, however, was not made until the mid-1890s.[44]

By no means all disillusioned populists followed such an extreme course as Plekhanov. Rather more of them probably preferred to cultivate liberal ideals, pressing at the time of the crisis at the end of the seventies as they had during that of the early sixties for freedom of the press and other forms of expression of a public opinion. Such views were politely put forward by a few *zemstva*, and in 1879 a secret congress of liberals made an abortive attempt to form a united movement.[45] The dominant voice in the *zemstva*, however, was the same as that in respectable society at large, conservative, even reactionary. Pobedonostsev, with his rejection of the 'parliamentary sham', defence of autocracy and assertion of Orthodoxy, articulated the unspoken assumptions of all those who saw in the government of Alexander III not the worst in Europe but the best.[46]

While its opponents cried out in desperation from jail or exile, the supporters of tsarism declaimed their triumph over the populists and early Marxists. But appearances were deceptive. Zaionchkovskii summed up the period thus:

The political reaction of the eighties and the beginning of the nineties, directed at the conservation and strengthening of the remains of serf feudalism, held back to a considerable degree the development of social life in the country as it brought about a series of reactionary laws and the massive arbitrariness of the administration and police. But it could not change the general process of socio-economic development, could not hold back the development of Russian progressive social thought, in spite of the repressions of the censor and other reactionary measures.

However, the long period of reaction, characterised by the persecution of everything progressive, and also by massive political arbitrariness, aroused in the social organism such reserves of hatred for autocracy that could only spill out in a revolutionary outburst.

The period of reaction also clearly brought about a crisis in the system of the autocratic order, the decomposition of its upper stratum, from the imperial family right down to some representatives of local authority.

Thus, the political reaction of the eighties and beginning of the nineties was one of the reasons for the revolutionary events of 1905 to 1907.[47]

For Kliuchevskii, who came to maturity during this period, Alexander II could be compared with Alexander I, granting reforms with one hand while appointing ministers who ruined those reforms with the other. As for Alexander III, he was easily persuaded by the smart-witted lackeys of his court that a premature liberalism was a great danger for Russia. But the balance between progress and reaction was delicate since, more generally, Kliuchevskii lamented that 'The law of the life of backward states or peoples among those which have outstripped it is that the need for reform arises earlier than the people is ready for reform. The necessity for accelerated movement in pursuit leads to the over-hasty adoption of the ways of others.' Moreover:

The nearer we have approached Western Europe, the more difficult has become the appearance among us of popular freedom, because the means of Western European culture, falling into the hands of some narrow strata of society, have been turned to their defence rather than the advantage of the country, strengthening social inequality, have been changed into a weapon for the many-sided exploitation of the culturally defenceless masses, lowering the level of their social consciousness and strengthening their class animosity, by which they are prepared for revolt rather than freedom.

Meanwhile, the tragedy of the opposition was that 'the patriot enlightened at government expense was struggling against his own country, while not believing in the power of enlightenment or in the future of the motherland.'[48]

Applicable enough to the reigns of Alexander II and Alexander III, these remarks would have even greater significance for the reign that followed.

9 Russian Imperialism, 1894–1917

At the end of the nineteenth century, wars throughout the world clearly showed the desire of the advanced industrial nations to extend or consolidate their overseas empires. In 1898 the United States fought Spain to protect its predominance in the Caribbean and to establish more firmly its influence in the Pacific. A year later in South Africa, Britain commenced a bitter struggle with the Boers for the retention of some of the finest jewels, both literal and metaphorical, of its great Empire. Then, in 1900, the U.S.A, Britain, Germany, France, Austria–Hungary, Italy, Japan and Russia sent their troops into China to crush the Boxer Rebellion, thus guaranteeing their continued influence there.

While the struggle for colonial and other forms of control throughout the world is usually known as imperialism, Lenin and others also applied the term to the underlying reasons for this rivalry among the industrialising powers. To him, 'Imperialism is capitalism at that level of development, when the dominance of monopolies and finance capital is established, in which the export of capital has acquired pronounced importance, in which the division of the world by the international trusts has begun, in which the division of all the territories of the globe by the biggest capitalist powers has been completed.' The understanding of the final period of tsarist history in Soviet works is normally based upon such an understanding, while many non-Soviet analysts tend to ignore it.[1]

In the 'traditional' Soviet view, Russia possessed some of the general characteristics of imperialism, but was also weighed down by less advanced economic features often characterised as oriental. Like other advanced countries, Russia moved into the monopoly-capitalist phase of development at the beginning of the twentieth century, and then, after 1914 until 1917, into military state monopoly-capitalism. The next stage of development was to be socialist. In the Russian case, however, the great banks and industrial monopolies coexisted with a backward agriculture and near serfdom. Russian imperialism was distinguished from most other varieties of the genus by its military-feudal nature and its application in areas contiguous to the metropolis rather than overseas. The bourgeoisie was still held back by a government more responsive to the interests of the powerful landed nobility, and thus was still carrying on the struggle for complete emancipation long after this had been achieved elsewhere. Its first task was therefore the overthrow of autocracy and the semi-feudal system of land possession which supported it.

The Revolution of 1905 did something towards the achievement of this priority. With land reforms, Russia took more positively the Prussian road to capitalism in agriculture. With the establishment of the Duma, tsarism took a further step towards transformation into a bourgeois monarchy. But such progress intensified rather than diminished the contradictions inherent in the peculiarities of Russian imperialism. The bourgeoisie found itself forced into an alliance with the landed aristocracy, and thus contributed to the maintenance of the system that it was attempting to overthrow. The alliance, in any case uneasy, was the sole focus of the rising revolutionary attack which had brought it about. Granted some respite at the beginning of the dénouement of world imperialism, the First World War, the ruling classes were then subject to a new and more vigorous onslaught from those whom they exploited. With the downfall of tsarism in February/March 1917, the weak bourgeoisie was soon virtually deserted by its expiring partner, the *dvorianstvo*, and was now at the mercy of the other class produced by industrialisation, the proletariat. The threat posed by the proletariat was all the greater because of Russia's geographical situation and late development, which presented the industrial working class with two firm allies in the shape of the oppressed nationalities and the downtrodden peasantry. Nevertheless, this new progressive combination against the bourgeoisie would not have been successful in the October Revolution and might not even have been formed in a few months of the year 1917 had it not been for the galvanising effect of the Bolsheviks, themselves dependent on the theoretical insights and strategic skill of Lenin. Such, briefly, is the 'traditional' Soviet historians' view.[2]

To a large group of non-Soviet historians, on the other hand, the reign of the last tsar has been of greatest interest not as the final stage in the relentless march towards revolution but as a period during which there were many opportunities for the old régime to reform itself by peaceful means and thus to avert destruction at the hand of fanatical opponents. The downfall of Nicholas II is seen as a tragedy, and the overthrow of President Kerensky in October as a disaster. As already mentioned, those who think that there were chances for non-violent transformation have been called the 'optimists', those who take the opposite side in the debate without agreeing with the Soviet interpretation – the 'pessimists'.[3] From the 'optimist' point of view, there were several routes to salvation open to tsarism in its last years: reforms introduced by Witte and Stolypin might have succeeded; a Duma ministry might have been formed in 1906 or 1915; entry into the First World War might have been avoided; the conquest of illiteracy might have produced a more responsible people. These and other crucial question will be examined below.

Central to most of them stands the tsar, Nicholas II. Some of the 'optimists' think that if he had been cast in a sterner mould, one of the safety routes would have been taken. To them, he was a good family man, but not the stuff that tsars should have been made of.[4] At the other end of the spectrum of interpretation, Trotsky argues that Nicholas II possessed the same fundamental characteristics as Charles I of England and Louis XVI of France, and with a wife as unsuitable for the situation as Henrietta-Maria and Marie-Antoinette. More than coincidence, these similarities revealed, not that a stronger man than Nicholas was necessary to suppress the Revolution, but rather that the Revolution was so relentless that the man attempting to stem it was bound to appear weak.[5]

Nicholas was born the eldest son of Alexander III in 1868. Tutors educated him, and he learned several languages. Before his accession in 1894, he travelled widely within Russia and around the world, but was given little practical training for the position he came to occupy at the age of twenty-six. Here we will not indulge in any attempt at character analysis, mostly because the exercise has become one of the most familiar themes of Russian history through book and film. Everybody knows about the closeness of the royal couple, Nicholas and Alexandra; about the evil influence of Rasputin brought about by the haemophilia of the tsarevich; and about the final execution of the whole family, and the disputes surrounding it. Suffice it here to note that sentimentality and romantic nostalgia have often been taken too far, and that to many contemporaries, the last of the Romanovs were by no means completely lovable. To quote one of the most distinguished members of the opposition, Leo Tolstoy, Nicholas II was to him as Nicholas I had been to Herzen, 'Chingis Khan with the telegraph'.[6] More succinctly, from the Revolution of 1905 onwards, people at large thought of their tsar less as the 'little father' and more as 'Bloody Nicholas'.

About a year after the outbreak of the war, 'Nikky' left his 'Sunny' to go to the front to take up the duty of leading the armies in the field. 'Sunny' or 'Alix' now began to assert her views about the government even more confidently than before, listening even more closely to the 'mad monk' (in fact, Rasputin was neither mad nor a monk).[7] On her role at this time, the Empress made the revealing remark, 'I am wearing invisible trousers'.[8] It would not be long before the workers and their comrades would see that the Empress and her husband, like the emperor in the fairy tale, wore no clothes at all.

Political

The reign of Nicholas II began quietly enough; right from the start, however, he made clear what his attitude would be to any question of reform. In a famous address to a meeting of deputies from the *zemstva* and municipalities at the beginning of 1895, he declared that all hopes for their participation in central government were 'senseless dreams', and that he would protect 'the principles of autocracy' as firmly and consistently as had his father.[9] He soon showed clearly what this policy would involve by expressing openly his support for those who had shot some troublesome workers in Iaroslavl, and by attending a ball after his coronation in 1896 even though over a thousand people had just died in a panic which followed the collapse of a viewing stand. The influence on Nicholas of his father and also of his tutor, Pobedonostsev, revealed itself in the further limitations which were placed on the *zemstva* and municipalities; the continued russification of the nationalities, including bloody suppression of such disturbances as the Central Asia Andijan Rising of 1898; the vigorous retention of the 'temporary regulations' of 1881; and the persecution of religious minorities, particularly the Jews, and of dangerous individuals, such as revolutionary radicals and other outsiders, notably Leo Tolstoy, who was excommunicated in 1901.

During this first half of the reign of Nicholas II, the *dvorianstvo* remained the most powerful political class, for all the efforts of Count Witte, Minister of Finance from 1892 to 1903, to develop the industrial economy and thus the bourgeoisie. Foreign policy, like domestic policy, was therefore most responsive to the needs of the landlords and the generals. While maintaining the alliance with France and aiming for peace, or at least rules of war, at the First Hague Conference which he instigated in 1899, Nicholas was also striving for the protection and extension of tsarist interests in the Balkans, the Middle East and Far East. Fearful after the Boxer Rebellion that Japan was gaining too much in the scramble for China with its seizure of Korea and infiltration of Manchuria, Nicholas moved his troops along the nearly completed Trans-Siberian Railway. They arrived just in time to be involved in the war which followed a sneak attack by the 'yellow monkeys' on Port Arthur in February 1904. While the bitter battle of Mukden in February 1905, which involved more than half a million men, ended in defeat for Russia, there was no rout on the land and the real humiliation came on the sea. The Pacific fleet, weakened by the unexpected Japanese descent on Port Arthur, was virtually annihilated while trying to break through to Vladivostok in late July 1904. Worse was to come when the powerful Baltic fleet set out to circumnavigate the world in a quest for vengeance. Nearly provoking war with Britain after mistaking fishing vessels in the North Sea for its Japanese enemies, it met the real thing at the Straits of Tsushima in May 1905 and was totally crushed.[10]

By this time, the débâcle of the war had combined with the unrest of the workers, peasants and nationalities to produce the first Russian Revolution. Ironically, Pleve, the Minister of the Interior, had at first welcomed the conflict with Japan, saying. 'To hold back the revolution, we need a small victorious war.'[11] Ironically too, the middle class, whose spokesmen had been pressing for representative government throughout 1904, soon discovered that the revolution that they had done more than a little to foment, went much further than they would have wished. Before the situation returned to something like normal in early 1906, the Revolution had spread wide enough and deep enough to fully justify Lenin's appraisal of it as a 'dress rehearsal' for the second and third Revolutions of February and October 1917.[12]

The first Revolution of 1905 broke out on 9 January with the notorious incident remembered as 'Bloody Sunday'. A peaceful procession of strikers from the Putilov Works and sympathisers was marching to the Winter Palace under the leadership of a priest, Father Gapon, in order to petition the tsar for 'justice and protection'.[13] The crowd, which numbered about 150,000 and included women and children, carried icons and portraits of the tsar. Suddenly, tsarist troops opened fire, killing more than a hundred and wounding more than a thousand. The impact of the mass murder was great and immediate. By evening barricades were up in many parts of St Petersburg. Strikes of sympathy were soon organised in Moscow and other towns. The peasants, their traditional faith in the 'little father' strongly shaken, increased the scale of revolt already in progress, the unrest reaching as far as the border provinces. A climax was reached in the summer with the celebrated insurrection on the battleship *Potemkin* in the Black Sea. The government, which had made a number of concessions and announcements, issued a manifesto on 6 August outlining the arrangements for elections to the State Duma which had first been promised in February. The public was far from ecstatic in the reception that it gave to the manifesto, nor was it happy with the terms of the Treaty of Portsmouth ending the war with Japan published in the same month. Witte's able diplomacy and Theodore Roosevelt's moderation had overcome the Japanese demands for indemnity, but Russia was forced nevertheless to acknowledge the supremacy of Japanese interests in Korea and to hand over to the 'yellow monkeys' Port Arthur and the peninsula on which it stood as well as the southern half of the island of Sakhalin.

More labour troubles led to a nationwide general strike from 7 to 12 October. Smirnov commented that it was 'on a truly gigantic scale with about two million people participating; it was the greatest mass strike that had ever taken place in Russia, or, for that matter, anywhere in the world. The military and police forces of the tsarist government were, to a certain extent, paralysed'.[14] Soviets, or Councils, of workers were organised in St Petersburg and elsewhere, and started to publish their own journal, *Izvestiia* or *News*. In the face of such opposition, persuaded by Witte that the alternatives were a constitution or a military dictatorship, Nicholas issued a manifesto which set Russia on the former course.[15]

The October Manifesto met with a mixed reception. The extreme right was appalled and became even more determined to smash all Jews and other such 'traitors' with its terroristic 'Black Hundred' gangs. The extreme left was completely unimpressed, Trotsky declaring that it was a 'scrap of paper' which could be torn up by the government as easily as by him.[16] The attitude of those in between varied from guarded suspicion to wild enthusiasm. Most certainly, the Revolution was not yet over. There were more strikes in the towns, culminating in an armed uprising in Moscow in December, which lasted for about ten days and resulted in nearly a thousand fatalities. Renewed outbreaks of violence broke out among the peasants in European Russia and the Baltic Provinces. The Finns and the Poles pushed their grievances, the Finns receiving considerable redress, the Poles none. There was more trouble in the armed forces, with a navy lieutenant named Schmidt leading the largest revolt at Sevastopol and soldiers from the defeated army of the Far East taking over a large section of the Trans-Siberian Railway for almost three months.

By the beginning of 1906, the tsarist government had restored order, Trotsky commenting 'la révolution est morte, vive la révolution'. Trotsky's wish was to be granted. As John Keep says, 'It is difficult to appreciate the extent of the psychological shock administered by the events of 1905 to men brought up on a diet of pious maxims and ancient superstitions'. He describes a political meeting which took place at Kazan University, where the speech of a Bolshevik propagandist was interrupted by an old worker shouting, 'How simple all this is! Why, brethren, did we not work this out for ourselves?' The others shouted in reply that it was because they were always drunk, but the point had got home, and at the end of the meeting, a cab-driver who belonged to the Old Believer sect called for a holy war against capital. According to Keep, the impact of the

Revolution was similar in other towns, as well as among the peasants and national minorities. Its influence spread beyond the boundaries of the Empire, too.[17]

The Revolution of 1905 gave much encouragement to political parties on the left and at the centre. Of those on the left, the Bolsheviks have since become the most celebrated, but at the time they were one faction among many. The Russian Social Democratic Labour Party was formed in 1898 out of a number of groups started up in previous years in the capitals and other towns. But government interference sent some of its members to prison and some into exile, and the Party did not take on much shape before the celebrated split at the London Congress of 1903. Disagreements over the extent to which revolution should be immediately pursued and membership narrowly restricted led to the rift between the 'extremist' majority Bolsheviks and the 'moderate' minority Mensheviks. Legends have developed about these early historic moments and were encouraged in Soviet popular history. But the documentary record appears to show that at the beginning of the twentieth century affiliation to either wing of the R.S.D.L.P. did not necessarily mean complete adherence to its principles. Organisation and doctrine were both often weak and confused. Similarly, the Socialist Revolutionary Party, founded in 1901, with Viktor Chernov as its best-remembered leader, was neither neatly constituted in membership nor programme. Broadly speaking, we may say that the S.R.s were the heirs of the populists, but they differed among themselves about the emphasis to be placed on terrorism and the degree to which they should concentrate on the peasant problems. Undoubtedly, S.D.s and S.R.s alike gained considerably from their first experience under fire in 1905.

The left-wing radicals were not the only busy politicians in the aftermath of revolution. Before the end of 1905, the two principal middle-class parties had been founded, and had prepared themselves for their self-appointed task of leading Russia along a peaceful road to constitutional monarchy. The Constitutional Democratic, or Cadet (after the initials Ka and De, not to be confused with army cadets) Party, was led by the historian Pavel Miliukov and became the main hope of Russian liberals. The Union of 17 October, or Octobrist Party, proclaimed its belief in the principles of the October Manifesto and was led by the businessman A. I. Guchkov. It was to the right of the Cadet Party, whose avowed beliefs in land expropriation were too much for landlords such as M. V. Rodzianko. Cadets and Octobrists came together with other deputies, such as those from the Trudovik or Labour Group (mainly peasants, left-wing but anti-revolutionary), the nationalities representatives and a few left-wing and right-wing radicals. With such party alignments, and a tsarist establishment opposed to constitutional progress, the chances for success were slim indeed.[18]

The First Duma was convened in St Petersburg in April 1906. Elected on a suffrage which divided a restricted number of electors into four groups – landowners, townspeople, peasants and workers – and was then weighted in favour of the nobility and bourgeoisie, boycotted by the Bolsheviks and others on the left, the Duma was made even less dangerous by the Fundamental State Laws announced just before its first session. These retained for Nicholas the title of autocrat and complete control over the armed forces and foreign policy, which between them accounted for 40 per cent of the state budget. The State Council, which now became the upper legislative chamber, was to be half chosen by the tsar and half by various groups selected mainly from the nobility and bourgeoisie. If these limitations were not enough to render the Duma innocuous, Nicholas retained the power of veto over legislation and the right to issue emergency decrees when the Duma was not in session, although such decrees supposedly had to be confirmed during the first two months of the next session of the Duma, which was to meet every year.

The First Duma lasted just over seventy days. Its main party, the Cadets, attacked the Fundamental Laws and insisted on the implementation of its land policy, which included compensated expropriation of the landlords. While asking for an amnesty to be extended to political prisoners, the Cadets refused to condemn terrorism. In such circumstances, the failure to form a party-based ministry and the dissolution of the Duma came as a surprise to nobody.[19] Soon afterwards, about two hundred of its deputies, mostly Cadets, met at Vyborg in Finland to attack the government and call on the people to resist its requests for army recruits and taxes until the Duma was reconvened. The signatories of the Vyborg Manifesto were given three-month jail sentences and excluded from participation in the new elections.

The composition of the Second Duma, which convened in March 1907, was to the left of the First. The S.D.s and S.R.s did not boycott the elections and gained some representation, along with a reduced number of Cadets, more Trudoviks and more right-wingers. With Stolypin firmly in the saddle, and his controversial land bill introduced under the emergency Article 87 of the Fundamental Laws and now before the Duma for confirmation, there was much less chance of success for the Second Duma than the First. Again there was some talk of a party-based ministry, but it had come to nothing by the time that Stolypin used the refusal of the Duma to surrender the immunity of its S.D. members to dissolve it on

3 June. On the same day new electoral arrangements were announced which restricted the popular vote and led to the election of the much more compliant Third and Fourth Dumas.

From 3 June 1907 to the outbreak of war, Russian political life experienced what Soviet historians called a Bonapartist phase, the Bonaparte in this case being P. A. Stolypin. Perhaps the most interesting discussion of the phase was by A. Ia Avrekh, who began one of his books on the subject with a discussion of what he called the Stolypin Terror.[20] In 1908, he claimed, there were in tsarist jails more than 200,000 inmates, twice the number of places available. Many were tortured, and more than 5000 death sentences were passed for political offences between 1907 and 1909. No fewer than one and a half million people were affected by oppressions ranging from investigation to execution during the years 1904–9. In a somewhat different period, 1906–12, more than 600 unions were forced to disband and as many were refused registration: 978 newspapers and periodicals were put out of action, with 174 of them being fined a total of 112,000 roubles. Meanwhile, the government connived at the activities of the anti-Semitic Black Hundreds and corrupt elections. The tsar himself sent congratulations to the leader of the *Union of the Russian People* and both he and his son wore the badges of this organisation of the radical right, to which Church leaders also lent their support.[21] Meanwhile, in 1909, some liberals showed their hand with their collective publication of *Vekhi*, or *Landmarks*, expressing their clear opposition to socialism. Lenin denounced *Vekhi* as the encyclopedia of liberal renegades. From the other side, *Vekhi* has been defended, even praised, as a thoughtful and perspicacious series of essays.[22] Western appraisals of Stolypin have been mixed, although even those antipathetic to him have not usually been as denunciatory as those of Avrekh and his colleagues.[23] The essence of the defence of Stolypin has been that extraordinary times demand extraordinary measures. If he meted out terror, it was in response to the terror directed at him and other tsarist officials. According to government statistics, more than 1500 of them were killed by terrorists in 1906 and more than 2500 in 1907. Against a background of disturbances among the workers and peasants, a group of terrorists bombed Stolypin's summer home in the summer of 1906, killing more than thirty people and wounding more than twenty, including his son and daughter. Stolypin himself escaped unhurt, but his reprieve was temporary; he was assassinated in September 1911, probably not at the orders of the tsar, as was rumoured, but by a double agent acting on his own initiative.[24]

In the Third Duma, elected in 1907 by about 15 per cent of the population, the Octobrists replaced the Cadets as the centre party. They enjoyed

no absolute majority, but could be the dominant members of two majorities, to the left with the Cadets for reform, or to the right with the conservative deputies for stabilisation. According to Avrekh, such a situation
was no accident, but rather the manipulation of tsarism and its chief minister to retain power in conditions of Bonapartism. Stolypin nevertheless
needed a considerable amount of skill, since he and his associates were
themselves often manipulated by the real government, the court camarilla.
Using the formula pacification, then reform, and making patriotic appeals
such as 'no second Tsushima', Stolypin persuaded the Duma moderates to
give out tens and hundreds of millions of roubles to the army and navy,
the police and other organs of the state apparatus while conceding 'legislative cud' to their appetite for liberal measures. An example of such
'reforms' scornfully dismissed by Avrekh was a bill 'On the institution at
the Erevan Teachers Seminary of 20 stipends for Tatar students, with the
issue from the treasury of 2600 roubles a year, on the supplementary consignment of 140 roubles a year as payment for a teacher at the said seminary and on the transformation of the one-class elementary school at this
seminary into a two-class structure with a supplementary consignment for
his upkeep of 970 roubles a year'.[25] More meaningful measures which
passed the Duma, such as some projects on religious toleration, were
turned down either by the State Council or the tsar. When attempts to
restrict the power of the second chamber or to assert its own power
appeared to be making even the conservative Third Duma something of a
real threat, Stolypin crushed such impudence with the full support of the
court camarilla. In such a context, Avrekh argued, Miliukov's ideas of
'parallel activity', the struggle for democratic constitutionalism in the
Duma at the same time as popular pressure outside it, acquire their real
empty meaning. For Geoffrey Hosking, Stolypin's programme is best
called a kind of 'constitutional nationalism', a mixture 'similar to that
which Joseph Chamberlain had been preaching in Britain a few years
earlier: an Empire for the common man'. Meanwhile, 'Germany was the
model to which the centre and right in Russian politics tended to look as
an example of the successful integration of an authoritarian monarchy, an
imperial patriotism and parliamentary institutions'. In Hosking's evaluation, it was the latter right-wing Octobrist model which stood the better
chance of adoption in the Third Duma, Avrekh exaggerating the importance of Miliukov and the Cadets.[26]

    At the cost of his position and perhaps his life, Stolypin was able to put
through the Duma much of his legislation concerning the difficult problems of the peasants, the workers and the nationalities. On the agrarian
question, his formula was first the citizen, then citizenship. He secretly

said to a meeting of the Council of Ministers in July 1907, 'a strong rich peasantry permeated with the idea of property serves everywhere as the best stronghold of order and quiet, and if the government manages to achieve this aim through the implementation of its land measures, there will be an end once and for all to dreams of a state and socialist revolution in Russia'.[27] After much debate and some anxiety, Stolypin received the support of the Duma for his land programme. As far as the workers were concerned, there was a considerable amount of talk and some action, on insurance projects for example, but only enough to persuade liberal members of the Duma that they were taking some steps at least to solve the growing proletarian predicament. On the nationalities question, Stolypin undoubtedly took the Great Russian point of view, but his western *zemstvo* project did not go far enough for some patriots and he was running into trouble with it from several sides at the time of his assassination.

The Fourth Duma, which first met at the end of 1912, was weaker and more to the right than its predecessor and controlled by a similarly endowed minister, V. N. Kokovtsov. As he came to power, he received advice from the royal couple. Nicholas said, 'Don't follow the example of Petr Arkadevich, who tried to overthrow me', and Alexandra said, 'You must not try to continue blindly what your predecessor had done ... Do not seek support in political parties; they are so insignificant with us. Depend on the trust of the sovereign.'[28] On the whole, Kokovtsov took the advice, but was removed at the beginning of 1914 for taking a stand against corruption and Rasputin. He was replaced by the ineffectual reactionary I.L. Goremykin, a seventy-five-year-old sycophant.

Bonapartism was more than a governmental system, as far as the historian Avrekh and his Soviet colleagues were concerned. To them, it also reflected the social system, the unsteady alliance between the landed aristocracy and the industrial bourgeoisie. Stolypin was able to control the Duma, to put it in an oversimplified manner, because he was able to exploit the tensions between the two classes which were demonstrated in the two majorities capable of being formed by the Octobrists. With the outbreak of the First World War, and the shift from monopoly capitalism to military state monopoly capitalism, the alliance between the aristocracy and the bourgeoisie moved into a new phase. Against such a background, the last political manoeuvres of the tsarist period were played out. Thus, the attempt of Miliukov and the Progressive Bloc to achieve 'a ministry enjoying the confidence of the public' in 1915[29] and 'the ministerial leapfrog' of 1916 (as Commander-in-Chief Nicholas at the front and the Empress Alexandra behind his back tried to find a man enjoying the confidence of their 'Friend', Rasputin), reveal tsarist society at successive stages of its dissolution.

Some Western historians would agree to some extent with the Soviet interpretation of the government and its social setting between 1905 and 1917. For example, Leopold Haimson comes close to an acceptance of the Soviet view of social stability in urban Russia from 1905 to 1917, except concerning the part played by the peasants coming into the towns and the extent to which the Bolsheviks were losing touch with the worker movement on the eve of the outbreak of war.[30] On the other hand, Miliukov's biographer, Thomas Riha, argued that Russian constitutionalism had several solid achievements to its credit and weathered the storm well until 1914.[31]

While the Duma debated, the revolutionary movement was quiet from 1907 until 1910. Resistance to tsarism was passive on the whole, one of the most evident forms that it took being emigration. Between the beginning of the century and 1910, roughly a million and a half people went from the towns and villages of European Russia, the Ukraine, Belarus, Poland, Lithuania, Latvia and the Jewish Pale to the New World. Between 1896 and 1914, about three and a half million colonists moved from these older areas of settlement to Siberia. But the 'safety-valve' of the domestic and transoceanic frontier was not enough to relieve the Empire's social tensions. A new strike movement gathered momentum in 1911 and moved on to a new level after the massacre in April 1912 of more than 250 strikers at the Lena Goldfields in Siberia. There were sympathy strikes in Moscow and St Petersburg, the Ukraine and the Baltic provinces, and in towns along the Volga. And then in 1913, 250,000 workers came out to press for the reprieve of some revolutionary sailors who had been condemned to death for plotting an abortive uprising in the fleet. 40,000 people demonstrated over the Beilis Affair, the rigged trial of a Jew for the supposed ritual murder of a young Russian. Altogether, there were nearly 1,000,000 strikers in 1912, 1,270,000 in 1913 and 1,300,000 in the first six months of 1914.[32] A new revolution was in the air, in the towns if not in the countryside. The outbreak of war brought tsarism some respite, with only a handful of demonstrators incurring the wrath of Russian patriots, but a new upsurge set in early in 1915 and continued, albeit with some fluctuation, right up to the February Revolution. The biggest outbreak of violence was in central Asia, where a revolt by the inhabitants against their mobilisation in 1916 cost the tsarist army more casualties than the entire conquest of Turkestan.[33]

The internal collapse of the Empire was inextricably connected with the failure of its foreign policy to avoid war. Stolypin had realised clearly enough that Russia could deteriorate in such a manner. 'Our internal situation does not permit us to pursue an aggressive foreign policy', he once declared. 'Peace at any price' was his motto. A reactionary adviser of the tsar, P. N. Durnovo, argued in a memorandum of early 1914 that Russia's probable defeat in a European war would fling the Empire into 'hopeless anarchy, the issue of which cannot be foreseen'. A voice even closer to the tsar's ear, that of Rasputin, proclaimed that 'with the war will come the end of Russia'.[34] Why was it then that Russia became involved in the first World War?

The answer to this vexed question does not lie in the Far East, except in the negative sense that *rapprochement* with Japan after 1905 allowed tsarist ministers to concentrate their attentions elsewhere. In the Middle East and Central Asia, there was further tension with Britain before, and, to a lesser extent, after the Anglo-Russian Agreement of 1907, which divided Persia into spheres of influence. But tension did not lead to crisis and Russia, already tied to France, joined the Entente Cordiale between France and Britain as the European situation deteriorated.[35] As the weakest of the imperialist powers, Russia was obliged to follow the lead of its stronger partners; in the last resort, the decision for war would be taken in London, Paris or Berlin. But we cannot evade the question of Russia's involvement. Why was it that Russia was sucked into the vortex by way of the Balkans? Was her rivalry with Austria–Hungary and Germany so great that skilled diplomats such as Izvolskii and Sazonov could not avoid the ultimate confrontation?

At times, it appeared that the Three Emperors' League would be revived to supplant the Triple Entente. Germanophilia possessed an influential group of reactionary landowners and some members of the court camarilla. The tsar himself was very fond of the kaiser, and embarrassed his ministers by signing a bilateral treaty with Wilhelm at Björkö in the summer of 1905 while the two Emperors were cruising together on the Baltic in their yachts. And then, at the very brink, the 'dear cousins' exchanged an unsuccessful series of telegrams. However, the circumstances making for war were bigger than both of them.

If A. J. P. Taylor is justified in calling the dénouement of 1914 'war by timetable', there were still necessary great powers keen to abide by the schedule. As far as Germany is concerned, Fritz Fischer has most thoroughly documented its grasp at world power. In his view, the generals and their allies in business and government were aiming at a huge empire stretching from Hamburg to Constantinople. At the very least, as even Fischer's critics would concede, a line of defence would be drawn to the east of Germany's frontiers and large parts of Eastern Europe looked upon as a sphere of German commercial and diplomatic influence.[36] As for the

Russians, far from wanting to accede to the reduction of their Empire and interest without a fight, many of them harboured dreams of expansionism hardly less ambitious than those of their German counterparts.[37] According to such Soviet analysts as I. V. Bestuzhev, a powerful segment of bourgeois-landlord opinion was in favour of the firm protection of Russia's power and of its extension too. They increased their demands through the series of Balkan crises until they were making loud cries for a showdown in the summer of 1914. In the West, Dominic Lieven has caught the ambitions and aims of the Russian elite, while Dietrich Geyer has given most emphasis to their apprehensions and anxieties. L. C. F. Turner sees the Russian mobilisation of July 1914 as the decisive moment.[38] More generally, with his emphasis on socio-economic factors, Bestuzhev claimed that the July crisis was 'not an accidental catastrophe, but the consequence that was bound to follow from the objective conditions reflected in the policies of the imperialist powers'.[39]

In the early days of the war, German pressure on Paris was very great indeed, and the Russians were asked to afford relief by attacking from the east. The Russians took the French chestnuts out of the fire, but at the cost of putting their own in it. As Smirnov put it, 'The famous Battle of the Marne, that saved Paris, was won at the cost of the blood of Russian soldiers in East Prussia'.[40] Those not killed, wounded or captured were exhausted and wretchedly supplied. Little resistance was offered to a determined attack by the Central Powers in 1915 as the original plan of campaign, named after Schlieffen and concentrating on the Western front, was reversed. By the end of that year, all of Poland and Lithuania had been lost, as well as part of Latvia and Belorussia. Many important economic resources were no longer available to the Russians. Moreover, their total losses in manpower, including prisoners, were nearly three and a half millions. In March 1916 the Russians again attacked to relieve pressure on the Western front, this time on Verdun. Losses were as high as before. Then in May an army under General Brusilov attacked the Austro-Hungarians on the south-western front and advanced all summer, thus keeping beleaguered Italy in the war and virtually knocking the Habsburg Empire out of it. But the success was not followed up on other fronts, nor was Nicholas II encouraged by Rasputin and the Empress to pursue it. In any case, the Russian forces were by now thoroughly weak. By the end of 1916 the Russian Empire's western flank was almost as fragile as its insides.

In return for its efforts in the war, which included some successful operations and some failures in minor theatres such as Transcaucasia, Russia received large amounts of aid from the Allies and the U.S.A. Because of inadequate transport facilities and sometimes because of the reluctance of businessmen to support a bad risk, by no means all the aid promised to Russia reached it or was even sent. Moreover, the tsarist régime found itself increasingly treated as a junior partner of the Entente, with its place at the conference tables by no means secure. In such a manner, a military and diplomatic legacy was built up too heavy for its successor to bear. The war broke President Kerensky as surely as it had broken Tsar Nicholas.

Economic

At the turn of the century, Russia was an inseparable part of the world capitalist economy. She shared in the prosperity of the later 1890s, in the crisis which struck about 1900, and to a lesser extent in recovery from 1904 to 1907. Set back by another depression in 1907, she moved on from 1909 to 1913 to a new and greater recovery. The dislocation brought about by the First World War was greater for the Russian imperial economy than others, and it succumbed in 1917.

Before we take a closer look at this process, we must briefly consider the demographic trends of the period, as previously promised. This may conveniently be done by looking at the following analysis of the class composition of the population in 1913 compared with that in 1897 and set out in tabular form, putting urban and rural dwellers together:

	Whole population: Both sexes in millions		Proportion in percentages	
	1897	1913	1897	1913
Large-scale bourgeoisie, landlords, higher officials	3.0	4.1	2.4	2.5
Wealthy small proprietors	23.1	31.5	18.4	19.0
Poor small proprietors	35.8	42.0	28.5	25.3
Semi-proletariat	41.7	55.6	33.2	33.6
Proletariat	22.0	32.5	17.5	19.6
Total	125.6	165.7	100.0	100.0

As far as native language indicated, in 1897, nearly 45 per cent were Great Russians, 18 per cent Ukrainians and 11 per cent Turkic peoples. Of the hundreds of other peoples who went to make up the polyglot Empire, the largest groups were the Poles, more than 6 per cent, the Belarusians, nearly 5 per cent, and the Jews, just over 4 per cent of the total. Thirdly, the urban population was about 17 millions in 1897 and grew by 1914 to about 22 millions, by 1916 to about 28 millions. Both St Petersburg and Moscow had over 2 million inhabitants by 1917. The urban proletariat, which was to have a significance far beyond its numbers, increased from $1^1/_2$ millions in 1897 to nearly $4^1/_4$ millions in 1913, over half of the workers being employed in large-scale enterprises. But Teodor Shanin, who considers that the 1897 census possessed 'the virtues of a well-executed snapshot of Russian society', points out that the editors of the census themselves stressed that peasants and their like constituted 'nearly 90 per cent of all mass of the population'.[41]

Although the most significant features of the Russian economy from the imperialistic point of view may be found in the industrial sector, we can readily see that most of the people were still involved in agriculture, and that the most influential class in late tsarist society was the landed nobility, even if it was in steep decline. Grain was by far the most important export at the beginning of the twentieth century, and the Stolypin land reforms are often considered by 'optimists' and even by 'pessimists' to have been the basis for Russia's best chance of achieving a peaceful path to modernisation.

While the landlords sold nearly 27 million acres of land through the Peasant Bank in the years 1906–16, and nearly as much more was mortgaged through the Noble Bank in the same period, there were still in existence on the eve of the February Revolution more than 75, 000 estates of the nobility covering more than 7 million hectares (about 19 million acres), with less than 10,000 of the estates accounting for more than half the area. Just before the First World War broke out, from a total grain production of more than 80 million metric tons, about 12 per cent of the total still came from the estates of the landlords. Nearly 50 per cent of the landlords' wholesale grain production was sold in the market, and landlords were also very busy with the manufacture on their estates of sugar, vodka and flour. On the whole, the profitability of their agriculture was higher than that of the peasants.

This comparative prosperity was achieved through the maintenance of the backward semi-serf labour system of agriculture known as *otrabotka*. Even when not subjected to a landlord, peasant farming was often held back by the stranglehold of the commune and the persistence of strip farming. Discussions of reform made some if limited progress before the Revolution of 1905, but, with provisions made in November of that year for the cancellation of the redemption payments, the way was now open for comprehensive reforms such as those envisaged by Stolypin. Legislation of 1906 permitted each householder to demand a private plot from his village in exchange for scattered strips, while from 1910 all communal land not redistributed since the 1880s was to become hereditary property. More than two million individual applications for consolidation of holdings had been approved by 1915. Whereas to Mosse, the success of the Stolypin reform was greatest where it was least needed, and the programme of the Socialist Revolutionary Party posed a far greater threat to Lenin's chances of success, Tokmakoff quotes with approval a Soviet verdict that, with the reform, 'the Russian pre-revolutionary village considerably moved forward on the road of a rapidly developing capitalism'.[42]

Soviet historians generally noted the boost that the reforms of 1906 and 1910 gave to capitalist farming, but also stressed that the rural proletariat rose in numbers to reach four and a half millions by 1913. They also pointed out that, while co-operative farms increased eighteen times from 1900 to a figure of 23,841 in 1915 and the gross annual harvest rose by about two-fifths in roughly the same period, more than half the peasant farms still used primitive ploughs at the time of the February Revolution. To show the relative backwardness of Russian agriculture as a whole, they presented such statistics as, for example, the ratio in 1914 between population and head of cattle – 1000:293 in Russia, 1000:622 in the U.S.A. and 1000:888 in Denmark.

For an industrial revolution to succeed without foreign assistance, indigenous capital must come ultimately from the rural sector of the economy. This was the necessity which drove the Soviet government towards collectivisation. In the pre-1917 case, the foreign capital was forthcoming, and so the need was not so great. Of importance here was the work of Sergei Witte, Minister of Finance from 1892 to 1903. To T. H. Von Laue, Witte was a far-sighted, energetic statesman trying 'to rally both government and people to one common, almost superhuman effort'. For Smirnov, he was 'a militant monarchist'.[43] Certainly, by the time that the Stolypin reform was under way, a considerable capital base had already been formed in the Empire, and so the pressure was not on it for immediate success. At the commencement of the advance of 1909–13, there was twice as much railroad as in 1893, when the previous leap forward had occurred. The railroads were still insufficient for Russia's industrialising needs, as we shall see below, but, coupled with such increases as a doubling of heavy industrial production and a 50 per cent rise in the number of workers during the same period, they provided a more substantial foundation for growth than there had been at the beginning of Nicholas II's reign. A further advance could now take place towards monopoly capitalism.

During the years 1909–13, the annual growth rate of Russian industry was about 8.8 per cent per annum as opposed to 9 per cent per annum in the years 1893–1900. This rate was broadly similar to that of other industrialising countries during the same years. Although the Russian tempi were sometimes higher than the Western (for example, world production of cast-iron, 1909–13, up by 32 per cent: U.S.A. up by 20 per cent; Germany up by 50 per cent: Russia up by 64 per cent), Russia produced fewer machines than the U.S.A., Germany or Japan, if more than France. As a consequence of this, in 1912 the import of industrial machinery equalled domestic production, while that of agricultural machinery exceeded it. While capital also came from abroad (about 126 million roubles per annum on average from 1908 to 1913), domestic investment now rose above foreign (225 million roubles per annum on average in the same period).[44]

The industrial advance in the years leading up to the First World War took place for the most part in six regions: the central in and around Moscow; the north-west in and around St Petersburg; the Baltic in Riga, Tallin and other towns; the southern in the Donbas and Krivoi Rog; the Polish at Dombrova and elsewhere; and the Urals. In 1911 more than 75 per cent of all large-scale production took place in these regions, and nearly 80 per cent of all large-scale enterprise workers were employed in them. In the comparatively new southern region alone, more than 80 per cent of Russia's coal and more than 70 per cent of her cast-iron were produced. Baku on the Caspian, the most important centre for oil, was the only town not in the six regions that could properly be called industrial. The advance was strictly regional, then, and so it was possible to visit parts of the Empire in 1913, as it still was possible to visit parts of the Soviet Union many years later, without noticing the level to which industrialisation had climbed. But in 1912 there were more than 250 metallurgical works and in 1911 more than 550 coal mines. In 1913 there were nearly 850 cotton factories, with 9 million spindles and more than 200,000 looms. By 1914 $4^1/_2$ million horse-power was being applied in industry by machines, a rise from something over 2 million horse-power in 1908. For each worker, there was now $1^1/_2$ horse-power, as opposed to less than 1 horse-power per worker earlier.

For all this advance, the structure of Russian industry in the period of imperialism was very different from that of other advancing countries. In 1913 more than 40 per cent of Russian workers were in textiles and food processing, while about 35 per cent of them were in the mines, metal extraction and smelting or machine-making. In Germany the comparable figures were something less than 25 per cent and something more than 40 per cent respectively. True, in concentration of industry, Russia outstripped Germany and the other developed countries, but this was a reflection of the insufficiently intensive industrial development of the Empire as a whole, and was for the most part accompanied by a lower level of specialisation and less technical equipment.

Growth in large-scale industry was accompanied by growth in the small-scale and peasant sectors. On the eve of the war, out of a grand total of about 800,000 such enterprises, there were about 150,000 of them with 2–15 workers in each. There were also about 600,000 small tradesmen working by themselves or with one worker. Meanwhile, peasant crafts supplemented the income of up to 4 million semi-proletarianised tradesmen during the winter months. In under-developed regions workers employed in small-scale industry outnumbered those in large-scale concerns. On the whole, however, Soviet historians said that after 1900 the part played by large-scale industry became marked. It 'determined the level of industrialisation of the country at large and could serve as the material-productive basis for the transition to socialism'.[45]

Such a basis could have been more substantial if there had been a commensurate expansion of communications and transport. But between 1908 and 1913, railroad construction reached its lowest level since the 1880s: about 4500 kilometres of track being added to those already in existence to produce a grand total of about 65,000 kilometres. Even in European Russia, the railways were considerably less widespread than in Western Europe or the U.S.A. The state continued to dominate this principal artery of communications and transport, along with six large private companies in the 1890s. It was government policy, then, for railroad construction to be curtailed, for reasons that will be considered below. Even those lines already in existence were not adequately kept up, and about 40 per cent of the Empire's locomotives were out of date in 1913. The average freight carried by a Russian wagon was about 15 metric tons while a German wagon could carry up to 50 metric tons. Moreover, the government's priorities, partly at the bidding of its foreign creditors, were military and strategic rather than commercial. Perhaps the most noteworthy of those enlargements of the system that did manage to be achieved during the last years of tsarism resulted in the extension of the Trans-Siberian Railway to Vladivostok in 1916.

A sizeable amount of inland freight was carried by waterways, particularly the Volga network, which accounted for about 60 per cent of all waterborne traffic. There were more than 30,000 river-boats in operation in 1912, including more than 5500 steamboats. Telegraph and telephones were other forms of communication to show some advance from 1900 onwards. However, there were very few properly metalled roads, and the cart was the standard means of transport along most of them. Baedeker's *Handbook for Travellers* in Russia for 1914 advises motorists: 'The great national highroads connecting St Petersburg, Moscow, Warsaw, and Kiev are admirably adapted for motoring and are kept in good condition … The roads maintained by the provincial authorities are of a very different character, and the traveller is advised not to try any of them until he has made enquiries at a local motor club'.[46] Except for oil freighters on the landlocked Caspian Sea, Russia's mercantile marine was negligible in size. Foreign ships, then, carried most of her growing external commerce. By 1913 this had doubled from the 1890s, and was now worth more than 2.5 billion roubles. But her share of the world's trade had not grown nearly as much, from about 4 per cent at the end of the nineteenth century to 4.25 per cent in 1913. This was about half France's share, twice that of Japan at the time. Unlike the more developed countries, Russia continued to export grain and other agricultural produce, and to import mainly industrial goods. By 1913 grain exports had risen one and a half times in quantity and twice in value from the 1890s, and most of the other exports by at least as much, butter, eggs and timber by three or even four times. During the years leading up to the war, Russia's annual exports were valued at 1.5 billion roubles per annum, of which grain comprised 44 per cent, and cattle and forest products 22 per cent. Industrial exports did not reach 10 per cent, and nearly all of them went east to Asia. Imports also doubled during the same period, reaching an average annual value of 1.2 billion roubles from 1909 to 1913. The principal items of import were textile raw materials – cotton, wool and silk, coal for the north-west and Baltic industrial regions, chemicals and non-ferrous metals, machines and technical equipment, tea and luxuries for the consumption of the ruling classes. While the balance of trade was favourable to Russia, her balance of payments was under strain from the burden of the payment of percentages and dividends on foreign debts and investments, and from the considerable expenditures of prosperous Russians travelling abroad. Germany continued to take first place in Russia's foreign trade – 30 per cent of exports and 50 per cent of imports in 1913, Great Britain was second and France a long way behind in third place.

The internal trade was much more valuable than the foreign, reaching a total of 18 billion roubles in 1913, which was one and a half times the 1900 level. According to Soviet calculations, her internal trade network consisted of 1,118,000 units in 1913 compared with 854,000 in 1900. Among them were 183,000 wholesale and large retail firms, and more than 1.2 million shopkeepers, stallholders, traders and distributors. With hired workers added, the total number of people involved in domestic commerce approached 2 millions. Their activities were partly capitalist, partly pre-capitalist. They were distinguished by a strong seasonal and fluctuating character because of their agricultural emphasis. Although in decline, fairs were still important. The standards of internal trade were low. Payments were often late, contracts poorly observed and specialisation lacking. Russian backwardness was clearly demonstrated in her grain trade. There were not many elevators or proper collection points. Conditions at the ports were bad, and much grain was spoiled. Large-scale operations were few, and credit facilities undeveloped, constant peasant indebtedness causing perpetual troubles.

Nevertheless, trade as a whole was more profitable than industry, accruing 788 million roubles in 1913 as opposed to 510 millions from large-scale industry and 142 millions from small-scale industry. And so commercial-mercantile capital, based mostly on Moscow, was very important during the imperialist period. The growth of capitalist enterprise in general was reflected in the expansion of the banking system. Not only did the State Bank and the joint-stock commercial banks mainly centred on St Petersburg increase their operations during the period under discussion, local banks also were either founded, or expanded their already existing business. From 1908 to 1913 the resources of all commercial banks grew two and a half times to 7 billion roubles, and their active operations expanded in approximately the same degree. The State Bank was the central issue bank, looking after the gold reserves, regulating the circulation of money and putting out gold-backed notes ever since 1897 when Witte put Russia on the Gold Standard. It also kept the state income, which was the basis of its loan operations. The State Bank of Russia was distinguished from that of most other countries through its close connection with the state budget and the Ministry of Finance. It was thus able to keep a close watch on the financial operations of the Empire as a whole. Mutual credit and co-operative banks expanded in number and activity in the pre-war years, and the Land Bank system was still in active use. In 1914 the Land Banks had a total capital of 5.3 billion roubles, of which just under a third belonged to the bourgeoisie. Even in Junker-bourgeois Germany, the urban share in such mortgage operations was considerably more than twice that of rural proprietors. Here, as elsewhere, comparative Russian backwardness was clearly revealed.

Such backwardness was to an appreciable extent the result of the government's priority of financial stability. It saw railroad construction as the basic lever of economic growth, but restricted it to keep the budget steady. It favoured the protection and expansion of industry, but the latter only at a moderate pace. Thus, having approached the economic level of other countries in the 1890s, Russia fell behind in the early twentieth century. The budget was balanced, but at great cost, particularly since it included a state debt increasing from 7.9 billion roubles in 1900 to 12.7 billion roubles in 1913. 5.4 billion of the latter figure were of foreign origin, and

400 million roubles had to be sent to France and elsewhere every year to repay the debts of the state and of private commerce. Tsarist Russia was the greatest international debtor in the world. For this reason, taxes had to be squeezed as much as possible out of a recalcitrant public, more than a quarter of the state's income actually coming from the state's monopoly on spirits.

Backward though it was in some aspects of its financial arrangements, Russia was very advanced in others. By the outbreak of the war, its industry had entered the stage of monopoly capitalism. The stock exchange, which had previously been used mostly for the floating of state and land loans, was now very much interested in industrial stock, particularly in St Petersburg, where it was dominated by the large banks. The joint-stock capital of all companies, including non-industrial enterprises and banks, had grown to 2.1 billion roubles, of which 64 per cent was floated in Russia itself, and most invested in heavy industry. While the first monopolistic amalgamations had been brought about in the late nineteenth century, and a second group of them achieved during the crisis at the beginning of the twentieth century, the third and most decisive stage took place in the immediate pre-war years, when a wide range of trusts, cartels and syndicates was set up. Glass, cable and agricultural machinery were just three of the items covered by the new organisations, which spread throughout the provinces as well as expanding their activities in the capitals. For example, *Prodamet*, which had been originally set up in 1902 to manage the all-Russian sale of ferrous metals, came by 1912 to control 76 per cent of the Empire's rails and 95 per cent of her girders. In 1910 *Prodamet* consisted of about 30 enterprises, including 16 to the south, 8 in Poland, 3 by the Baltic, and 1 each in the centre, the Urals and along the Volga. The syndicate had a complex accounting and distributive network, with central and provincial branches. It would undercut competitors and compensate by high prices where no competition existed.

The banks played an important part in *Prodamet* and other syndicates, and were extending their operations to the peripheral regions of the Empire. The railway was reaching into Central Asia and Siberia, too, and Russians were going to live there in increasing numbers. Colonies of the settlement type, similar to Canada and Australia, were being formed in Siberia and Kazakhstan, while subject colonies, similar to India and Algeria, were being developed in Uzbekistan and Transcaucasia. About four million Russians moved into the new lands between 1896 and 1916, and many raw materials were produced by them. For example, cotton production rose from about a quarter of a million metric tons in 1907 to a figure approaching half a million metric tons in 1914. About a third of the total requirements of Russian industry were supplied from such a source in 1900, more than a half by 1913.

On the eve of the war, then, the Russian Empire possessed the most advanced form of financial–industrial management on the one hand and primitive nomadic forms of economic organisation on the other. As a whole, it was a country of middle-level economic development, its means of production having risen sevenfold from 1890 to 1913. In the latter year, Russia was fifth overall in world industrial production, in some branches fourth. However, as far as her share was concerned, it amounted to only 4.2 per cent of the world's total. Russia was in an advancing but precarious international position, then, when the war broke out.[47]

The immediate impact on Russia of the war was tremendous. The cornerstone of her financial policy, the Gold Standard, was abandoned almost immediately. Without gold backing for its notes, the currency was undermined by rampant paper inflation. Foreign loans increased to a level which meant more than 6 billion roubles going on repayment and relevant orders just before the February Revolution. Even more than before, Russia had become the client of foreign powers, Britain, France, the United States, Japan and Italy in descending order of importance. An additional burden was placed on the Empire's strained financial resources by the introduction of prohibition. Moreover, the break with Germany meant the loss of Russia's major trading partner. While the decline was not always immediate or continuous, crises had set in by 1916 in transport, metallurgy, fuel, and other branches of industry as well as in agriculture.[48] Social dislocation had been brought into the city and the village.

On the other hand, the concentration of the economy brought about by the war had moved it into a new and higher stage, that of military-state monopoly capitalism. War Industrial Committees and Special Consultative Councils for defence, fuel, supply and transport, brought government and business closer together. There are two ways of looking at this development, as there are of considering Russian economic progress during the age of imperialism as a whole. Von Laue, Carr and other 'pessimists' in the West join Soviet historians to assert that it was making revolution more unavoidable. Gerschenkron is perhaps the most ingenious exponent of the 'optimist' point of view, which argues that Russia was moving towards the patterns of the Western industrialising powers, and nearing the point when revolution would have been superfluous. Even most 'optimists', however, find it difficult to persist in their argument when considering the years after 1914. And that war cannot be dismissed as a blow from outside, since the Russian Empire was as heavily involved in the crisis leading up to the First World War as its allies and enemies. If the

Russian economy had grown in the last half century or so of tsarism, it was largely because the government had been able for the most part to maintain peace.[49]

Cultural

'Not only the body but the soul of Russia as well was growing stronger and healthier during the decade which preceded the World War', argued the émigré Michael Karpovich, finding striking progress in cultural activity as well as in the economy.[50] In his view, education took important strides forward. With a relaxation of censorship, the daily press, including opposition newspapers, came to occupy a significant position in Russian life, and religious toleration grew, even though the Orthodox Church remained a central part of the tsarist establishment. Now that the Duma was an outlet for political expression, many intellectuals were able to turn more exclusively to the sciences or the arts, to both of which Russians made exciting new contributions. In the 'traditional' Soviet view, on the other hand, while many of the artistic and scientific achievements are to be celebrated, other developments reveal the sickness of a society on the point of collapse. Above all, this was the period which saw the formation of the revolutionary and post-revolutionary outlook. As S. S. Dmitriev put it:

> Russian culture of the epoch of imperialism is not only our yesterday, but also something of today. The ideas of Lenin illumine the world. They are the zenith of Russian culture at the beginning of our century. The literature and art of socialist realism were born in our country in the years of the first Russian revolution, and developed in the difficult time between the two revolutions. Many achievements of contemporary science are rooted at the beginning of our century. The war of ideas by Marxists for progress in science, against decadence in literature and art, for the correct understanding of national pride and respect for the revolutionary and democratic traditions, campaigns against apostasy, for socialist optimism, for a scientifically based belief in a bright future are still timely and instructive.[51]

While recognising the cultural progress of the other nationalities soon to be members of the Soviet Union as well as the Russian move forward, Dmitriev noted the opposition of Lenin to the bourgeois, often Black Hundred clerical slogan of 'national culture' and his substitution for it of the international culture of the democratic movement of the workers of the world.

In our discussion of these 'optimistic' and 'pessimistic' appraisals of the last stage of tsarist culture, we may make a division, as in our political discussion, between a pre-1905 and a post-1905 period. We may also notice that during this period Russia was not unaffected by new phenomena which were beginning to fill the earth and sky – the train, the automobile and the aeroplane. On 27 August 1913 N. N. Nesterov revealed a previously unrealised aspect of the potential of the aeroplane by performing the first loop-the-loop in the history of mankind, Dmitriev proudly told us. Before the outbreak of the war, both the army and the navy were using radio. By that time, too, there were nearly 1500 cinemas in Russian towns, of which both St Petersburg and Moscow as well as others such as Kiev, Odessa, Riga and Tiflis, were taking on all aspects of a modern shape. Baedeker's *Handbook for Travellers* in Russia for 1914, for example, gives information on the electric tramways as well as on the horsedrawn vehicles in all these cities, among others.[52] Even the appearance of many villages was changing, with the replacement of at least some wooden buildings by stone.

According to some 'optimists', Imperial Russia was at last in sight of a solution to the age-old problem of illiteracy by the time of its collapse. A growing debate in the 1890s, intensified by the revelation of the 1897 census that barely a fifth of those for whom information had bee gathered could read and write, and given new emphasis by the Revolution of 1905, led to the law of 3 May 1908. While more progressive legislation was turned down by the State Council, the Duma believed that through this law it was still making provision for the complete application by 1922 of compulsory education to all children between the ages of eight and eleven. The problem was barely half solved for such children by 1914, and is made to appear much more formidable if a wider age bracket is considered or a more regional emphasis is given. In such a case, the problem would be more like a bare quarter on the way to solution. Nevertheless, progress was marked from 65,000 primary schools (including church schools) with about $3^1/_2$ million pupils in 1896 to 122,000 schools with more than 8 million pupils in 1915. State appropriations for these schools increased from just over 3 million roubles in 1900 to more than ten times that amount by 1914, while *zemstvo* expenditure on education rose about eight times by 1914, from an 1891 figure of rather more than 5 million roubles. Even though they concede that the target for 1922 was unlikely to be reached even if the war and the revolutions had not intervened, the 'optimists' consider that the delay would not have been great. On the other hand, Lenin declaimed in the pre-war period that 'Such a savage country, in which the mass of the people are so robbed in the sense of education, enlightenment and knowledge, – there is no such country in Europe as Russia'.[53]

Such an assertion could be supported to some extent at the secondary school level by the comparative ratio of students to population for a number of modernising countries halfway through the 1890s: U.S.A. 1:83; Prussia 1:122; England 1:202; France 1:300; and Russia 1:564. To this, an 'optimist' would point out that by 1914 figures for secondary schools of all types and students of both sexes had approximately doubled from the beginning of the reign of Nicholas II, when they had been about 900 and 225,000 respectively. The number of university students also at least doubled between 1900 and 1913, reaching approximately 36,000 in the latter year, even though only one new university – at Saratov in 1909 – was founded during the period. If higher institutions of education as a whole are taken, that is, if engineering and technical colleges and the like are included, the total enrolment increases from just under 30,000 in the mid-1890s to a figure variously estimated from 90,000 to 150,000.[54]

If the educational advance, according to some figures at least, appears greatest at the highest level, it was also here that the tensions between the government and those involved in the educational process showed themselves to be most strained. After the series of troubles at the turn of the century, including the first all-Russian University strike in 1899, more than 340 academics in a *Memorandum on the Needs of Education* produced for the one hundred and fiftieth anniversary jubilee of Moscow University on 12 January 1905 declared: 'The threatening condition of enlightenment in the fatherland does not allow us to remain inactive and forces us to express our deep conviction that the contemporary state order of Russia is not compatible with academic freedom. For its achievement partial corrections of the existing order are insufficient, and its complete and thorough reformation is necessary'.[55] During the ensuing Revolution of 1905, the tsarist régime relaxed somewhat its regulations of 1884–5 and restored a certain amount of self-government to the universities. But more disturbances in 1910–11 led to several 'undesirable' staff members of Moscow University being driven from their posts; more of their colleagues resigned in protest, and relations between the universities and the government remained strained up to the outbreak of war, to some extent up to 1917.

Somehow, through all these tribulations, not only the academics just mentioned but also their colleagues in their own and other fields managed to produce work of the highest quality, both in institutions of higher learning and outside them. A just roll of honour would be long and contain many names that should be known in the West. But since they would mean little without a full explanation of their contributions, just a few representatives must be chosen here: Petr Lebedev, a great physicist; Nicolai Zhukovskii, the mechanical mathematician, whom Lenin called 'the father of Russian aviation'; Konstantin Tsiolkovskii, expert on rocketry, who predicted space travel; and Ivan Pavlov, continuing his outstanding work in physiology, not to mention Kliuchevskii and others in the humanities.

Open lectures managed to communicate some of the achievements of Russian savants to the public, who were also able to read about them and everything else in a growing number of books, journals and newspapers. In 1913 in the Russian language alone, more than 100 million copies of books to a value of more than 40 million roubles were sold. Two-thirds of them were produced in Moscow and St Petersburg, where the first millionaire publishers based their activities, but the provinces were also becoming more active, both in Russian and regional languages. In 1912 of the more than 2000 registered periodicals well over half were in Russian, but the rest were divided among thirty-two different languages. Among all these publications, many were political, even revolutionary in tone. Lenin wrote that after the Revolution of 1905, 'Millions of cheap editions on political themes were read by people, by the masses, by the crowd, by the "lower orders" more greedily than ever before in Russia … Merchants stopped dealing in oats and began a more profitable trade – the popular cheap pamphlet. Popular books became a *market* product.' Among the newspapers were those of the Mensheviks and Bolsheviks, about which a member of the Cadet Party commented respectively: '*Luch* (The Ray of Light) and *Pravda* (the Truth) are powerful not because they write about workers and for workers, but because in them workers write about themselves. No other party could achieve this, not from the right, or the left.' It was also during the reign of the last tsar that Lenin, in exile and out of it, wrote some of his most solid works, notably, *What Is To Be Done?*, *The Development of Capitalism in Russia, and Imperialism, the Highest Stage of Capitalism*. Lunacharsky and Plekhanov were others among a growing number of socialist critics and analysts.[56] Needless to say, Lenin was just one among many of varied Marxist persuasions, while liberalism and other movements were also in fairly full flow in the early twentieth century.[57]

Even those writers with more purely literary intentions, if such existed, found it difficult to avoid politics completely in this turbulent period. The patriarchal Tolstoy increasingly turned from realism to didactic preaching, determined to drive as many people as possible from the evils of tobacco, alcohol and sex back to the simplicities of the life of the commune, where, as Tolstoy must have known, there was in fact as much smoking, drinking and fornicating as in other sections of society. Of his later large-scale works, perhaps the novel *Resurrection* most completely exercises his genius. Although no supporter of the new parties, the excommunicated Tolstoy was a sympathetic figure to young radicals, and the neglectful reception of his death by officialdom did much to promote the university disturbances of 1910–11.

Anton Chekhov, critical of Tolstoy's lack of understanding of scientific and other forms of progress, was broadly liberal rather than specifically committed to any political programme. Although he broke with a patron over the Dreyfus affair, Chekhov even denied that he was a liberal. Such commitment he rejected as likely to damage the artistic creativity which he prized above everything else and which he believed could be kept apart, or perhaps rather above. Western critics would therefore argue that Soviet commentators have exaggerated Chekhov's progressive beliefs, and that the alienation and melancholy of his short stories and plays are a reflection on the human condition in general rather than a condemnation of tsarist society in particular.

About Aleksei Peshkov, that is Maxim Gorky, there can be less dispute. A man of the people, Gorky writes about the men and women from *The Lower Depths* in a manner which starkly lays bare the life of the poor along the Volga and in St Petersburg. Among other prose writers, V. G. Korolenko, A. I. Kuprin, Leonid Andreev and Ivan Bunin have met with lasting critical approval from Western and Marxist critics alike, albeit with different emphasis from each side. What can be seen as a new approach from one point of view might be looked upon as a blind alley from the other. On the whole, the Western estimate of this period sees it as one of interesting experiment, of renaissance, a Silver Age or even a Second Golden Age.[58] From the Soviet side, A. Ia. Avrekh talked of a decadent literature being produced around 1910 and after, its main themes being death, disintegration, eroticism and individualism.[59] Similarly, the two attitudes differ to the principal poetic movements of the period, symbolism and futurism. Soviet critics were less happy about the stamp of 'symbolist mysticism' on Aleksandr Blok, Andrei Belii, Valeri Briusov and others, regret that Vladimir Maiakovskii (Mayakovsky) started his career in the escapist world of futurism, and are much happier when 'motifs of social and civic significance' appear in their work in a reasonably straightforward manner.[60]

Both the symbolist and futurist movements were influenced by developments in France, Italy and elsewhere. They also partly stemmed from the group centered around the review *Mir iskusstva*, or *World of Art*, which was published between the years 1898 and 1904 and edited by A. N. Benua (Alexander Benois) and Sergei Diagilev. The group was agreed on total commitment to creation, but realised their commitment in ways which differed considerably. Isaak Levitan, an impressionist, has been called 'the poet of the Russian landscape'. Valentin Serov was perhaps the best portraitist of the modern school. M. Larionov and N. Goncharova became well known abroad as cubists and then as futurists. More radical movements developed in the second decade of the twentieth century, taking such names as *Knave of Diamonds* and *Ass's Tail* and including such abstract painters as V. Kandinskii (Kandinsky) and K. Malevich. A combination of styles received distinctive treatment at the hands of Marc Chagall. The sculptors and architects of the period made far less of an impact.[61]

The last years of tsarism were great years for Russian performing artists. The plays of Chekhov, Gorky and others received the best possible production at the Moscow Arts Theatre from the method of Konstantin Stanislavskii (Stanislavsky). But these names are only the best known of a large number of talented people working in the drama, as Pavlova, Nidzhinskii (or Nijinsky) and Diagilev are the most famous of those who made Russian ballet known throughout the world. Shaliapin and others did almost the same for Russian opera. Obviously in such a period, there were many opportunities for musical composers to apply their talents, although the work of Rimsky-Korsakov, Glazunov, Rakhmaninov, Skriabin, Stravinskii (Stravinsky) and Prokofev (Prokofiev) often goes far beyond the simple needs of orchestral accompaniment.

All the new developments in the arts passed by the majority of the people, whose tastes were more traditional. Folk motifs from all parts of the Empire were used by the artists, but the exchange was hardly mutual. In the pre-revolutionary period, the gap did not worry those who were interested in art for art's sake. After the Revolutions of 1917, it would become a problem of considerable dimensions.

Back in 1891 for Kliuchevskii, Russia was a medieval knight in armour, appearing powerful but in fact easy to knock over; by 1898, it was staggering on the edge of a precipice. As early as 1895, the great historian observed, 'Nicholas II will end the Romanov dynasty; if he has a son, he will never rule', and then in 1905, a few days after Bloody Sunday, he declared: 'Nicholas II is the last tsar; Aleksei will not reign'. Still in January 1905, he wrote in his diary: 'The Russian intelligentsia beats against its own ideas like a fish floundering on ice after coming up for air.' Nevertheless, he participated in a meeting chaired by Pobedonostsev to discuss the August Manifesto before losing his confidence about the future more completely by 1906 when for him 'There is no Russia now, only Russians' and the only recourse was 'practical patriotism'. Kliuchevskii had also lost confidence in the past. It was not only illness leading to his death in 1911 that stopped him from completing the fifth volume of his *Course of Russian History* which was due to take the national story from the accession of Catherine the Great to the reforms of Alexander II.[62]

Part Three

Contemporary Russia: The U.S.S.R. and After

Introduction

The First World War acted as a mighty accelerator of many historical processes: in general, it contributed to the decline or collapse of European empires while giving a tremendous boost to the influence of the United States of America; in particular, it was a major factor in the overthrow of tsarism and the institution of the Soviet Union. The latter event, which was the result of the Russian Revolution of 1917, made a profound impact around the whole of the earth. Few Western historians would deny this, although not many of them chose to agree with their Soviet colleagues that 'The Great October Socialist Revolution inaugurated a new era in the history of the Soviet peoples and of all mankind, and marked the beginning of the transition from the old, exploiter society, to the new, socialist system.[1]

The Union of Soviet Socialist Republics was the first major society to announce its creation according to a coherent ideology. From about 1924 to 1991, the claims of this ideology, Marxism–Leninism, to be not only a scientific, global and progressive explanation of history but also a guide to its transformation were widely accepted in the U.S.S.R. and beyond. The events of 1917 and subsequent years have therefore been a subject of great controversy among both supporters and opponents of Marxism–Leninism.[2] The account of those momentous events that follows here will probably

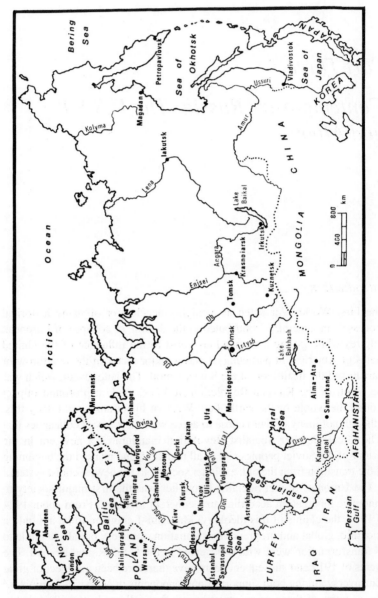

3 The U.S.S.R., 1917–1991

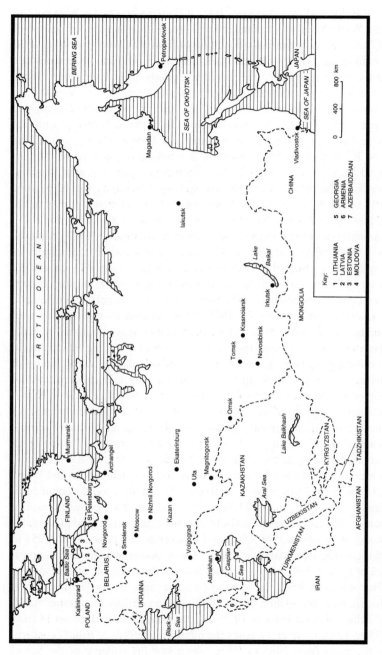

4 Post-Soviet Russia

not be welcomed by either side, since it borrows arguments from both of them. While based on the fundamental proposition that the Revolution of 1917 was part of the organic evolution of Russian history and in no sense an unfortunate accident or avoidable tragedy, it will seek to demonstrate that the modern and even the medieval periods of development weighed very heavily upon the new society and, in conditions of a continued European 'civil war', and a by no means peaceful wider world, prevented it from fully realising the great hopes laid upon it. Steering a middle course between savage condemnation and lyrical glorification of the U.S.S.R., this explanation is aimed at a balanced appraisal of the part played by the Soviet Union in the contemporary phase of world history. Here, as in the medieval and modern sections, objectivity will be pursued partly by taking a comparative approach, before attention is turned to the collapse of the U.S.S.R. and the post-Soviet phase of Russian history.

An analysis of the February and October Revolutions of 1917 and of the Civil War and Intervention that formed their sequel is the subject of Chapter 10, opening this contemporary section. Chapter 11 covers the period 1917–29, during which the energy of the government was concentrated on the consolidation of the Soviet Union in a largely unsympathetic international atmosphere. By 1929, after tremendous effort along with some bracing experimentation, little more had been accomplished than the approximate restoration of the economic level of 1914, the establishment of political unity at home and credibility abroad, and the near conquest of illiteracy. Between 1929 and 1941 (the opening and closing dates of Chapter 12), the construction was achieved at enormous cost to Soviet socialism, a variant of the species so mutated that some commentators believe that it is better called state capitalism. Although many terrible events occurred during the 1930s, the advances that were made in an international atmosphere even more hostile than that of the preceding decade were solid enough for the U.S.S.R. to triumph in the Second World War. The Great Patriotic War (to give the Soviet title) and the commencement of its sequel, the Cold War, 1941–53, are the central themes of Chapter 13, which also discusses their devastating impact and the arduous process of reconstruction. Chapter 14, covering the period from 1953 to 1964, considers the assertion of Soviet superpower, which made the presence of the U.S.S.R. felt not only throughout the world but also in space.

But widening horizons made the maintenance of Soviet superpower difficult, then impossible: Chapters 15 and 16 consider in turn the 'stability' achieved from 1964 to 1975, and the 'stagnation' which set in from 1975 to 1985. Chapter 17 poses the question 'Reform or Ruin?' concerning the years from 1985 to 1996, which saw the collapse of the Soviet

Union and the creation of a new Russia. Finally, in Chapter 18, a brief summary is presented of the course of Russian history through its major phases, and some attention is given to the direction that post-Soviet civilisation could take in the future. Throughout Part Three, some evaluation is made of the parts played by Lenin, Stalin, Khrushchev, Brezhnev, Gorbachev and Yeltsin and other outstanding figures. Nevertheless, although the terminal dates of the chapters often coincide with periods of their power, history will not be personalised and simplified to the extent that Soviet and post-Soviet successes and failures will be attributed to them alone. As far as possible, the deeds and thoughts of the Russian and other peoples will be noted, as will their context both socialist and otherwise, both before and after 1991.

10 The Russian Revolution, 1917–1921

I The February Revolution

For Soviet critics, Western historians gave too much emphasis to the fall of tsarism rather than to the necessity for its overthrow in the February Revolution, and exaggerated the degree of social harmony in general while underestimating the role of the proletariat led by the Bolsheviks at the beginning of 1917. Moreover, the charge continued, there has been too much talk of the democratic gains of a spontaneous February being liquidated by the totalitarian reaction of an engineered October, when in fact the two Revolutions are complementary rather than antagonistic.[1] In fact, however, West and East have been moving closer together in their interpretation, to such an extent that the two basic views overlap.[2]

In a real sense, the events of 1917 had been prepared by the whole previous course of Russian history, and to emphasise out of proportion 'turning points' at which tsarism could have righted itself is to distort that course. The accidents of history, such as the haemophilia of the tsarevich, may delay or advance the arrival of a crisis, but they cannot completely avert it. If this were not the case, then the study of history could not be attempted in any rational manner, since random events would assume such importance that explanation would be rendered impossible. On this premise, which will by no means satisfy everybody, we shall now proceed to an examination of the February Revolution.[3]

After an intensification of the burdens of the war had led to a wave of strikes in October 1916 and January 1917, the government made a number of arrests and separated the Petrograd military region from the Northern front as a whole, hoping to isolate any threat posed in the capital by the internal enemies of the state. The Petrograd garrison commander, S. Khabalov, prepared his plans, placing his trust for the suppression of any serious disturbances in the police and the Cossacks. While Miliukov and most of the future members of the Provisional Government attempted to retain the Duma as the chief vehicle of opposition and protest, left-wing politicians and the workers were thinking more in terms of demonstrations in the factories and on the streets.

Such demonstrations led to the outbreak of the Revolution on Thursday 23 February (8 March New Style). The initiators of the movement in many cases were the women who had particularly suffered from the hardships imposed on their families by the bread shortage – appropriately enough, 23 February was International Women's Day. The movement quickly spread to the Vyborg working-class district in the north-east of the city and to the Putilov metal-works in the south-west, where a lockout had already brought about a critical situation. While the radical leadership gave no clear directive, rank-and-file Bolsheviks, Mensheviks and S. R.s undoubtedly played an energetic part in organising bands of demonstrators in the various localities. Moreover, the boiling over of dissatisfaction into revolution must at least to some extent be seen as the result of years of propaganda and political education. The radical workers, many of them already on strike, were the heart of the movement.

Crowds poured on to the Nevsky Prospect, the traditional assembly place for demonstrations. When the police closed the main bridge from the Vyborg side, the insurgents came over the ice. Well over 100,000 people appear to have joined in. There were many meetings throughout the capital. Many of the slogans were still moderate; there were clashes with the police, but only a score or so of arrests and few causalities. The government was surprised by the demonstration and by its size, but was not unduly downhearted on the evening of 23 February. For their part, many members of the Duma believed that it would still be possible to make some accommodation that would avert revolution. Meanwhile, educated by their experiences and discussions since 1905, the workers and the radical politicians were beginning to realise that they were on the brink of the final showdown with tsarism.

On Friday 24 February the number of striking demonstrators grew to about 200,000 and the clashes with the authorities became more intense. Crowds sang the *Marseillaise* and cries of 'Give us bread!' were mixed with 'Down with the tsar!' and 'Down with the government!' By Saturday 25 February, another 100,000 had joined the movement, and the police, Cossacks and dragoons became more irritable. The number of casualties and arrests mounted. But the demonstrators grew bolder and freed some of those arrested. While the Duma leaders still talked of action within the law, and the government was still not unduly alarmed with Nicholas at Army Headquarters believing that the worst was over, revolutionary leaflets circulated around the capital and revolutionary politicians discussed how best to achieve the disaffection from tsarism of the troops.

This central question was largely decided on 26 February, one of history's many Bloody Sundays. During the night more than a hundred members of radical parties were arrested. All was relatively quiet in Petrograd during the morning, but this was the proverbial lull before the storm, for the crowds were gathering in the working-class districts, and poured into the Nevsky Prospect in the early afternoon. The clashes with the troops were even sharper, and scores of demonstrators were shot, machine guns being used as well as rifles. At the same time, the Duma president M. V. Rodzianko still believed that, if only the tsar would create a 'ministry of confidence', all could be well. As for the workers and the students and their other supporters, their resolution was increased by the bloodshed. The revolutionary parties intensified their activity. And most significant of all, soldiers from the reserve battalion of the Pavlovsky Guards Regiment started to defect.

On Monday 27 February this trickle became a flood, particularly after the shooting of an unpopular officer, and many soldiers of the capital's garrison deserted the cause of tsarism. Among the exceptions was a battalion of bicyclists, who after all had more to lose than their chains; but even those who did not defect no longer actively supported the government. Encouraged by their successes and by more revolutionary leaflets, the crowd stormed the Bastilles of Petrograd, and freed thousands of prisoners. Khabalov was becoming powerless, and his urgent telegrams to tsarist headquarters met with no response. Considerably to their surprise, the Duma leaders at the Taurida Palace found themselves being hailed as the prospective revolutionary government. The reasons for this are difficult to isolate, but have been said to include the following circumstances. Firstly, the Duma had just been prorogued by the tsarist Council of Ministers, and by deciding in some confusion to stay in session informally, had moved however gently to the side of illegality. Secondly, the soldiers who had broken their oath of loyalty were looking for a new source of authority. Thirdly, while the Bolshevik and other revolutionary leaders hesitated, orators such as Kerensky of the Socialist Revolutionary Party and Chkheidze, the Menshevik, were doing all they could to get mass support for the Duma. Fourthly, the Revolution, like most of its predecessors, had to pass through a moderate phase before it became radical, in this case through a bourgeois phase before it could become proletarian. And so, the provisional committee of the conservative Fourth Duma was inching its way towards becoming the Provisional Government of the Russian Revolution.

But already Miliukov noted that the Duma members felt that they were not alone in the Taurida Palace, that they were already not complete masters of it. There were in fact squatters in the Palace, the members of a Soviet or Council similar to that created in 1905. Labour leaders and revolutionary intellectuals and politicians, some of them just freed from jail, gathered together from 24 February and on the afternoon of 27 February elected a Provisional Executive Committee of the Soviet at the Taurida Palace. N. Chkheidze was elected chairman and A. Kerensky (strictly Kerenskii) one of the vice-chairmen. Two Bolsheviks were in the Committee – A. Shliapnikov and P. Zalutskii – but the membership consisted predominantly of their Menshevik opponents. Immediately, the Committee began to consider the important questions of the war and supply, of Soviet and militia organisation. The decision was taken to publish the newspaper *Izvestiia* daily. At the same time, the moderate leadership of the Committee, supported by some elements in the rank and file, was deferentially seeking a compromise with the Provisional Committee of the Duma, of which Chkheidze and Kerensky were also members. When a plenary session of the Soviet obliged the Executive Committee to pass on 2 March a resolution forbidding socialists to be members of a future bourgeois cabinet, Ckheidze obeyed. But Kerensky became Minister of Justice and the only link between the Soviet and the provisional Government.

On the same day the citizens of Petrograd were informed that 'the Provisional Executive Committee of the members of the Duma, with the aid and support of the garrison of the capital and its inhabitants, has triumphed over the dark forces of the Old Régime to such an extent as to enable it to organise a more stable executive power'.[4] Some of the limitations on the accuracy of this declaration we have already seen. It is also true that, before triumphing over the dark forces of the Old Régime, the Duma leaders made some last-ditch attempts to come to terms with them.

Tsarism was still not completely lost by 28 February. As his ministers were being arrested in Petrograd, the tsar finally decided to yield to the entreaties of Rodzianko and others and to return to the capital. But he found his way blocked and his train diverted to Pskov. There he spent a couple of days giving impotent orders for the suppression of the Revolution and discussing the question of his abdication with his generals. At least some of these were among members of an elite 'ready to dump Nicholas in order, so it was hoped, to stem the tide of revolution'.[5] The Soviet, for its part, stopped Rodzianko from going to Pskov, but two other emissaries did manage to get through to the tsar. Nicholas was finally persuaded that his departure from the throne might save it for his son or his brother, and he abdicated on 2 March, first to Alexis and then to the Grand Duke Michael. After talking the matter over with the Duma leaders, Michael said that he would accept the crown only if it were offered to him by a Constituent Assembly and if his personal safety could be guaranteed. And so, like a good old soldier, the monarchy did not die but rather faded away. The constitutional framework of Russia, if that were of any importance in a time of complete upheaval, passed into an uncertain limbo until Kerensky belatedly declared it to be a republic on 1 September. Even then, the objection was put forward that Kerensky was arrogating to himself the powers of the Constituent Assembly, the convocation of which was widely looked upon in 1917, as it had been in 1905, as a matter of central importance.

The form of political organisation that in fact emerged from the February Revolution is best described as the 'dual power' of the Provisional Government and the Soviet. On the one hand, the leading members of the Duma and a few outsiders such as Kerensky strove for the 'legitimate' succession. The first president of the Provisional Government, Prince G. E. Lvov, was a rich but liberal landowner, who expressed his estimate of the extent of his administration's control over events towards the end of April in the statement: 'We are tossed about like flotsam on a stormy sea.' He resigned in July. Made of sterner stuff, but for that reason remaining in office for an even shorter period, were P. N. Miliukov, leader of the Cadets, and A. I. Guchkov, leader of the Octobrists. Having been alone in urging Michael to take the crown, they were now the most uncompromising ministers in their dealings with the Soviet and in their conduct of the policies put to their charge, foreign affairs and the army and navy respectively. A much more adaptable minister, an eloquent and impassioned piece of flotsam, was A. F. Kerensky, who declared himself 'sent by the revolution'.[6]

By the middle of March, the other component of the 'dual power', the Petrograd Soviet of Workers' and Soldiers' Deputies, as it had come to be called, numbered about 3000, the soldiers outnumbering the workers by more than two to one. Since the soldiers tended to be less extreme in their political outlook than the workers, the Soviet was weighted against revolutionary policies, a trend reinforced by the lack of radical resolution on the part of its leaders. Moreover, the Soviet was a somewhat undisciplined and vacillating body, and would have made it difficult for the Executive Committee to carry out consistent policies even if the leaders had attempted to do so. Nevertheless, the cry 'All power to the Soviets!' was already heard in early March, albeit soon to die down for several months. The number of such bodies grew by the end of March to nearly a hundred and by the end of the summer to about six hundred in many parts of the former Empire, and so there was an enormous amount of potential waiting to be tapped when the cry rose up again.

During the first two months of its existence, the 'dual power' already showed signs of breakdown. While the Provisional Government put through such liberal measures as civil rights and set up committees to consider such important problems as land reform, the Soviet at times moved in a more radical direction. This was particularly so with Order No. 1, which Trotsky called 'the single worthy document of the February revolution'.[7] Published on 2 March in *Izvestiia*, the order declared that committees should be elected in every army unit and that deputies to the Soviet should be elected by all regiments. These and other concessions to the new democratic spirit began to undermine the army discipline that was already shaky enough. Guchkov and the Provisional Government attempted to take further limitations on the order which the Executive Committee of the Soviet itself imposed, but the damage was done.

Even more serious disruption of the 'dual power' was caused by disagreements about the conduct of foreign policy. For the most part Miliukov and the Provisional Government attempted at the outset to continue the foreign policy of tsarism, the prosecution of the war to a 'victorious conclusion'. Miliukov argued that the February Revolution had excited Russia's fighting spirit rather than revealing its complete exhaustion, and that the army could now press on to the realisation of historic objectives such as the annexation of Constantinople. Meanwhile, the Soviet called for war 'without annexations or indemnities', for a defensive war which would result in a democratic peace and the establishment of international unity. The Provisional Government declared its acceptance of such a policy, but Miliukov still talked of the necessity of the pursuit of decisive victory and of adherence to wartime agreements with the Allies. Demonstrations against Miliukov led to his resignation and that of Guchkov around the end of April.[8] At the same time, the Executive Committee of the Soviet agreed to let its members join the Provisional Government, and a coalition set up on 5 May deceptively appeared to make for a new stability. In fact, nothing had been gained except a short breathing space.

For the coalition to succeed, it would need either to solve or appear to be solving the severe problems which faced Russia in the spring and summer of 1917. The greatest of these, which permeated all the others, was the war. The depth of feeling on this subject has just been hinted at; if peace were not established, then fresh purpose would have to be injected into the prosecution of hostilities. Hardly less vital to the continuance of the coalition than the support or at least acquiescence of the army was that of the peasants and the workers. Something had to be done about the hunger for land of the rural inhabitants and the hunger for bread of those who lived in the towns. A further difficulty for the government was the control of the centrifugal forces which were threatening to get out of hand in many of the peripheral regions of the former Empire. A solution real or apparent to these problems would call for a correct analysis of them and for the highest political skill and willpower. In the end, such desiderata could be supplied from one source only.

II   The October Revolution

On 3 April 1917 Lenin arrived at the Finland Station in the Vyborg working-class district of Petrograd. A large crowd greeted him, and Chkheidze, the chairman of the Executive Committee of the Soviet, delivered an address of welcome. Then Lenin spoke. A sympathetic eye-witness later recollected that Lenin declared that:

> the workers and soldiers had heroically overthrown the autocracy and had, within a few days, turned Russia from a politically backward country into one of the freest democratic states. 'And now they want to palm off on us another tsar – capital', he continued. 'But the factories and mills must belong not to the capitalists but to you, and the land must not belong to the landowners but to the peasants.' Lenin finished his short speech with the words: 'long live the socialist revolution!' It seemed as though the workers and soldiers were spellbound. They were not used to hearing such words. Then they broke their silence and applauded and cheered.[9]

On 7 April the Bolshevik newspaper *Pravda* published the essence of Lenin's more theoretical elaboration of the message contained in his speech at the Finland Station, the *April Theses*. They began with the argument that fraternisation with the soldiers of the Central Powers should be encouraged and that the war could be carried on only if it became a war against imperialism as the revolution was carried a stage further. The *Theses* then put forward the contention that such a development was possible, since the situation existing in Russia at that time could be characterised as 'the transition from the first stage of the Revolution, which gave power to the bourgeoisie as a result of the insufficient class consciousness and organisation of the proletariat, to its second stage, which must give power into the hands of the proletariat and the poorest classes of the peasantry'. The transition involved the 'maximum of legal toleration' and the 'absence of violence against the masses' on the part of the government and the 'ignorantly trustful attitude of the masses toward the Government of the capitalists, the worst enemies of peace and socialism' on the part of the governed. In such special conditions, the Bolsheviks must not support the Provisional Government in any way, but rather patiently work for the establishment of a revolutionary government by the Soviets. This would not be a parliamentary republic but a truly democratic polity in which the police, army and bureaucracy would be eliminated and their functions taken over by elected and removable officials from the people, none of whom would be paid more than a good worker. At the same time, the land and banks would be nationalised, while the party would change its name to become the Communist Party in order to escape the opprobrium deserved by the compromising European Social Democrats, and its programme would be changed to fit in with the new circumstances. Finally, a new revolutionary International would be created.

Lenin spelled out his views further in his most substantial work of 1917, written in hiding during the lull before October, *The State and Revolution*. Here, following Marx and Engels, he described at some length the necessity for the complete dismemberment of the old bourgeois state before the construction of the new proletarian state would be possible. While many Western analysts have seen this work as essentially visionary, Marc Ferro has suggested that the process described by Lenin was actually occurring in 1917. The peasants and workers were already governing themselves as the government lost its grip on them, and the process of disintegration had already reached an advanced stage. Thus, *The State and Revolution* was 'as much the pertinent diagnosis of the situation as the utopian exposition of a theoretician'.[10] In a more literary manner, a similar analysis is to be found in Konstantin Paustovsky's description of a young writer's account of a tour round Russia at about this time:

> He discovered the strangest, ancient, moth-eaten little towns – Khvalynsk, Sarapul, Serdobsk – so remote and so cut off from Moscow that it was hard to believe in their existence except as a myth.
>
> Russia seemed once more to be split up into small fiefs, separated by the lack of roads, the breakdown of the post and telegraph, by forests, swamps and demolished bridges, by distance grown immeasurably longer.
>
> In these God-forsaken corners of the country, autonomous republics were proclaimed and banknotes printed by the local printers (though more often postage stamps were used for money).
>
> It was all mixed up with remnants of the past – balsam in the window-boxes, bell-chimes, wedding feasts with drunken salvoes from sawn-off shotguns, and weed-choked fields of straggly corn, and talk about the end of the world when nothing would be left of Russia but 'black night and three pillars of smoke'.[11]

In such dislocated conditions, the coalition government attempted to impose some kind of order and sense of direction while the Bolsheviks and other disaffected elements sought to increase the disruption and to take advantage of it. Until the left-wing demonstrations of the July Days, which brought the first coalition to an end, and even to some extent up to the Kornilov Revolt at the end of August, many people on the right also believed 'the worse, the better', since the government would be given the excuse for crushing the revolutionary groups and parties. After the utter failure of Kornilov's attempt to institute a military dictatorship, the remnants of the right still vainly hoped that the centre could somehow hold. Thus, a renewed threat from the left, more powerful since more organised than in July, could be resisted. These phases of development were intimately linked with the rise and fall of Kerensky, and mostly centred around events taking place in Petrograd. But they will also have to be considered against the background of the problems posed more widely to the workers, peasants, nationalities and soldiers. And the general context will have to be established of Russia's continued involvement in the war and the attitudes to it of the other belligerents.

In the first coalition formed at the beginning of May Kerensky was Minister of War and Navy. The new Foreign Minister was M. I. Tereshchenko, a rich industrialist who had previously been Minister of Finance. Although Lvov remained President, the cabinet in general may be said to have taken a move to the left, with such appointments as the S. R. leader V. M. Chernov as Minister of Agriculture. Apparently at an end, the 'dual power' was soon shown to be still in existence as members of the new government and of the Soviet expressed their disagreement on a number of important issues, both foreign and domestic. At the same time, support grew for the Bolsheviks and other extremists outside the Soviet, making it possible to talk of the 'triple power'. The split between the Soviet and some of its erstwhile supporters became apparent in mid-June when the Executive Committee decided to hold a demonstration in support of the coalition as a response to an earlier march, planned but never in fact taking place, on behalf of the Bolsheviks. Participating in full force in the Soviet demonstration of 18 June, the Bolsheviks and their supporters were able to give the impression of more opposition to the policies of the coalition than support for them. But this and some other minor incidents involving anarchists were small in their significance compared with the crisis that broke out at the beginning of July.

Soldier and worker discontent which had been building up for some time came to a head on 3 July when the First Machine-Gun Regiment led an untidy march on the Taurida Palace to demand that the Executive

Committee of the Soviet replace the Provisional Government. At the peak of the demonstration on 4 July, according to Miliukov, a worker shook his fist in the face of the S.R. Minister of Agriculture Chernov while screaming 'Take power, you son of a bitch, when it's given to you'. The Bolshevik leadership was divided on the response that it should make to such encouragement, Lenin believing that the time for the armed struggle for power was not yet ripe and categorising the event as 'more than a demonstration and less than a revolution'.[12] In the aftermath of the 'July Days' Lenin was forced into hiding in Finland and others such as Trotsky were temporarily arrested. The Bolsheviks in general were branded as traitors in the pay of the Germans, a charge previously levelled at the court camarilla. With the Executive Committee again expressing its confidence in the government, a new coalition was formed with Lvov resigning and Kerensky becoming Prime Minister while remaining Minister of War and Navy. Confident and rhetorical, Kerensky moved into the Winter Palace and appealed to the Russian people to achieve 'a new, free and great Russia' through submitting themselves to an 'iron rule'.[13]

While Kerensky toyed with the idea of 'iron rule', discussing what needed to be done in small groups and large conferences, there were those who believed that it should be made an immediate reality. Among them was the commander-in-chief, General L. G. Kornilov, a man of plain speech and strong character, to his supporters, while to Trotsky a man with the heart of a lion and the brain of a sheep. Proclaiming that he wanted nothing more than the salvation of the motherland and the preservation of Great Russia, Kornilov was quite possibly using the encouragement of right-wing business and patriotic organisations to aim at the assumption of power for himself. The debate still rages about the Cossack general and his contorted relations with the Prime Minister. Two points can be made with some certainty. Firstly, when Kornilov attempted to move to Petrograd to crush Bolshevism, his troops were reluctant to follow him and in any case had their way blocked by resolute railway workers. The 'Kornilov Revolt' quickly fizzled out. Secondly, in order to avert the threat to his power that Kerensky himself had rightly or wrongly discerned, he appealed on 27 August for the support of the Bolsheviks and the workers' militia or Red Guard. Soon Trotsky and other imprisoned leaders were freed, and the right having been revealed as powerless, the left was in the ascendancy. Even Miliukov argued that the choice was between Kornilov and Lenin, and the choice had now been made.[14] Assuming yet another office, that of commander-in-chief, Kerensky appeared to be reaching a new pinnacle of power. In fact, on the crest of a wave, the biggest piece of flotsam thrown up by the February Revolution was about to be hurled to the depths.

The Provisional Government was on the point of collapse because it had been unable to solve the problems bequeathed to it by its tsarist predecessor. The attempts at solution, however unsuccessful, must briefly be considered along with the exacerbation of the problems before our consideration of the actual events of the October Revolution. To start with the centre of the revolutionary movement, the proletariat, the organisation of the workers, the extent of their demands and the seriousness of their plight all grew in the months following the February Revolution, particularly from May onwards.[15] Trade Unions and the more militant factory committees staged important strikes in the textile, leather printing and metal industries, and in the Donets mines. While the strikes amply demonstrated that the workers would have liked more to eat, as well as higher wages and shorter working hours, the political content of their demands grew, and proposals for the introduction of labour control, limitation of profits and nationalisation of industry were now common. The government attempted to arbitrate and conciliate, and gave some support to such concessions as the widely demanded eight-hour day. But with inflation rampant and food in fluctuating supply, the workers could not be satisfied by such palliatives and turned increasingly to the parties with more radical policies while applying pressure to the Soviet for more vigorous action. Although the proletariat was small in numbers, it provided the vanguard of the Bolshevik revolutionary movement.

At the same time, the vast masses of the peasantry were to help create conditions in the provinces which would make more likely further action at the centre. Fluctuating in their intensity after February, rural disturbances reached a new climax towards October, especially in the fertile Black Earth region. The peasants wanted the land which they had believed to be theirs from time immemorial and which they now had the real chance of acquiring. But they were impatient with the land committees of the Provisional Government, even when Chernov tried to speed up their work and to make it more effective. Stories about the ignorance of the peasants were frequently told by the officials sent out into the countryside. A peasant was said to have cried out at an agitator: 'Hey, you! You've got such long nails, aren't you the Antichrist?' And he and his friends assaulted the man from the city to find out if he was covered in hair and had a tail. Another anecdote was that when asked to vote, the peasants whispered in hushed tones about whether to cast in favour of the tsar or the undergraduates. But the 'dark people' were making their intentions clear enough with their axes and sickles. Although some observers were too condescending or too aloof to see the point, Trotsky forcefully argued that if the peasants had not read Lenin, Lenin had clearly read the thoughts of the peasants.[16]

In the peripheral regions the problems of the peasantry were often compounded with those of centrifugal nationalism, which also exercised the
local bourgeoisies and sometimes peoples at the feudal or even pre-feudal
stage of development. The answer of the Provisional Government to the
nationalities was roughly the same as to the workers and peasants –
pending the decisions of the Constituent Assembly or the government
chosen by that Assembly, nothing much could be done except to collect
preliminary information. But often they were not prepared to wait. The
Finns argued that their ties had been with the tsar, the Grand Duke of
Finland, and that if he had gone, so could they. Sometimes they were not
allowed to wait. Particularly was this the case with the Ukraine, where the
Central Council or Rada was forced into a separatist position. In some
instances the question was at least temporarily solved in fact by the invasion of the armies of the Central Powers, for example into Poland and the
Baltic provinces. In a few of the outlying areas, it is true, 1917 was a comparatively quiet year. The Armenians in Transcaucasia, their brethren
across the border massacred by the Turks, were not keen to break away
from Russia at that time. In other Asian areas, however, there was considerable violence. As Richard Pipes puts it: 'In the second half of the year,
while a class struggle was taking place in Russia proper, an equally savage
national conflict developed in the vast eastern borderlands of the Empire:
Chechen and Ingush against Russian and Cossack: Kazakh–Kirghiz
against the Russian and Ukrainian colonist; Bashkir against the Russian
and Tatar.' Sometimes, strong Muslim feeling revealed itself in the borderlands, a leader in the eastern Caucasus declaring: 'I am spinning a rope
with which to hang all engineers, students and in general all those who
write from left to right.' Many years would pass before such turbulent
areas would be brought back to a condition of quietude.[17]

A further problem that could not be left unsolved for so long was that of
the soldiers, two million of whom deserted in 1917, voting for peace, as
Lenin put it, with their feet. However, the picture presented by the army
during the inter-revolutionary months was not one of complete disintegration. On the whole in the region near the theatre of war, the further west
and south a unit was from turbulent Petrograd, the greater was its stability,
and the further north and east from the front, the more complete was its
demoralisation. But such a picture has to be built up from reports given by
various observers ranging from members of the government and the generals to members of the rank and file and political agitators, and not all of
these described exactly what they saw. For example, while an ex-general,
Golovin, talks of official optimism as a result of a fear of pessimism being
looked upon as defeatism, Trotsky argues that the highest officers some-

times exaggerated the signs of demoralisation among the troops in order to provoke some decisive action from the government against agitators.[18] Certainly, although there were many incidents of fraternisation, some of the generals were still confident that the morale of the troops, at least at the front, was sufficiently high for a new offensive, which would not only drive the Germans and the Austrians back, but also raise the spirits of the army, possibly those of the navy also, and of the people as a whole.[19]

A new offensive might be additionally welcomed by the Provisional Government as a means of keeping faith with the Allies and retaining their support. By no means a client of the Allies, often indeed demonstrating irritation at the neglect of Russian interests in strategic decisions and at the reluctance to discuss with the Russians the aims for which the war was being fought, the Provisional Government nevertheless was as fundamentally loyal to the cause of the Allies under Tereshchenko as it had been under Miliukov. The difference was that the cause was for a just peace rather than for imperial expansion. In such a spirit a new offensive was launched in mid-June, Kerensky having talked himself to new heights of patriotism and having even aroused some of the soldiers. But the offensive soon collapsed, and the disillusionment of the army in its aftermath had some influence on the nature of the July days. The restoration of the death penalty and of military tribunals, far from restoring anything like good order or military discipline, accelerated new collapse and the army fought no more. Although the Americans made some efforts to restore morale, the Allies in general were soon virtually writing the Russians off.

American dollars came too late to save the Provisional Government, German marks (if they ever came, and it has not been conclusively proven that they did come) were unnecessary to ensure the success of the Bolsheviks.[20] The day after the Kornilov Revolt was crushed, the Petrograd Soviet passed its first Bolshevik resolution. On 5 September the Moscow Soviet followed suit, and during the course of that month, Bolshevik majorities were achieved in a considerable number of Soviets, mainly in towns and industrial areas. The cry 'All Power to the Soviets!' was raised with new fervour and with unprecedented coherence. In desperation, Kerensky rushed forward the elections to the Constituent Assembly which he had previously been delaying.[21] He called together a 'Democratic Conference' which in turn produced a 'Council of the Republic'. But all to no purpose. Lenin decided that the moment had come for the Red Guards, who had been building up their strength since the Kornilov Revolt, and other Bolshevik supporters to be led into armed insurrection. With some reluctance, the Party's central committee came round to agree with him.

The immediate victory of the October Revolution was achieved with surprising ease. It was at first led largely by Trotsky, who was chairman of both the Petrograd Soviet and the Military Revolution Committee, which had been set up in early October for the revolutionary defence of Petrograd against any surviving Kornilovists and the advancing Germans. Lenin returned from hiding on the evening of 24 October, and assumed command for the overthrow of the Provisional Government. During the night of 24–5 October, insurgents took such important points as bridges, railways and the telephone exchange. The Winter Palace had not fallen, but Kerensky could see that his hour had come, and made a getaway escorted by an American Embassy car. Ostensibly he was looking for support, but in fact making his final exit. After a blank shell had been fired at it by the cruiser *Aurora* and some real shells fired at it from the fortress of Peter and Paul, the Winter Palace was deserted by the Cossacks and army cadets who had been acting in its defence and a stubborn women's battalion then decided to surrender. The remaining members of the Provisional Government were arrested. With far less bloodshed than the February Revolution, the October Revolution had triumphed.

But bloodshed is not the only indicator of the significance of a revolution. The influence of October was to be felt on a very wide scale indeed, and John Reed was quite correct to celebrate it as *Ten Days that Shook the World*. Of course, as with all revolutions, October soon acquired its own mythology and distortions. A decade later, Lenin had already been made a revolutionary saint, and Eisenstein's cinematic celebration of October 1917 was in some ways more epic than the event itself. More seriously, the factional disputes of the Communist Party in the twenties and thirties resulted in the exaggeration of the part played by Stalin and the virtual suppression of the part played by Trotsky and some of the other leading Bolsheviks. On the other hand, Trotsky overcompensated for this suppression in his own writings on the Revolution and its sequel.

Nevertheless, those who argue that the October Revolution was no more than a coup or that it can in no proper sense be said to have followed the Marxist pattern are demonstrably incorrect. If the February Revolution was in any sense bourgeois, there was nothing unorthodox about a proletarian sequel following hard on its heels. In *The Manifesto of the Communist Party*, Marx and Engels had written:

The Communists turn their attention chiefly to Germany, because that country is on the eve of a bourgeois revolution that is bound to be carried out under more advanced conditions of European civilisation and with a much more developed proletariat than that of England was in the seventeenth, and of France in the eighteenth century, and because the bourgeois revolution in Germany will be but the prelude to an immediately following proletarian revolution.

While the eyes of Communists were still very much on Germany in 1917 and the years immediately following, there was an argument in this passage about the accelerated process of revolution that could be applied to Russia as well. Such an application was indeed made by Marx and Engles themselves to the Russian edition of *The Manifesto of the Communist Party* in 1882, in the preface to which they said that a Russian revolution could become 'the signal for a proletarian revolution in the West'.[22] This is what Lenin and his supporters fervently believed in the aftermath of October, and many people afterwards came to see October as a signal for both West and East. In the short run, such an attitude was to have an influence of no small significance on both the Civil War and the Allied Intervention.

III   The Civil War and Intervention

October was not the end to the Russian Revolution; in some ways it was more of a beginning. True, there was immediate celebration, tumultuous applause for Lenin when he made his first public appearance since July at the All-Russian Congress of the Soviets which had just convened. However, when Lenin declared: 'We shall now proceed to construct the socialist order!',[23] few of his supporters could have realised, as they renewed their roars of approval, how painful a process that construction was going to be. The ease with which the takeover of power had been accomplished in Petrograd was deceptive. Almost immediately, the Bolsheviks were under attack from domestic opponents – the Whites and dissident S.R.s – aided by foreign interventionists. Several years were to elapse before the attack was fully overcome, and the Soviet Union could be constituted.

The White forces took on embryonic shape after the collapse of the Kornilov Revolt, imprisoned officers and others looking for an opportunity to crush the radical left as soon as possible. Kerensky aroused no enthusiasm among them, it is true, and an attempt at a Cossack counter-attack against the Bolsheviks under General Krasnov got nowhere. But a group including Kornilov (who was soon to be killed by a shell while sitting in his headquarters) were released from prison by General Dukhonin who assumed the position of commander-in-chief after Kerensky's departure. Dukhonin was killed by infuriated soldiers; the others escaped to the Don where they were joined by Krasnov and began to organise from various disaffected elements a counter-revolutionary Volunteer Army. In loose alliance with this first nucleus of the White opposition were the Cossacks – for the most part unattracted to the new régime. Springing up in European Russia and Siberia were various large and small groups of brigands and partisans who sometimes supported the Whites and sometimes opposed them.

At the beginning of 1918, Red forces established themselves in the Ukraine and drove the Whites from the Don. But their victory was short-lived since the Treaty of Brest-Litovsk transformed the Baltic provinces and Ukraine into German satellites in March. By May the Finns had achieved their independence, with German assistance, and German troops had reached the Don, protecting the Whites as they prepared themselves for further action. At the same time, with support from the British, French and particularly the Japanese, General Semenov was initiating anti-Communist action in the Far East. About 40,000 Czech prisoners being shuttled along the Trans-Siberian Railway revolted. Their action encouraged the S. R.s to form two régimes in June, one at Samara and the other at Omsk. In June, too, Allied forces were established at Murmansk to the north and a revolt against the Tashkent Soviet broke out in Central Asia. Throughout the summer of 1918, the Reds found it difficult to contain such opposition, which showed itself in the capitals as well as the periphery. The Czechs and S.R.s advanced into the Urals and along the Volga, capturing Kazan. The Communists were driven from Archangel, and Allied forces occupied it. Japanese troops in Vladivostok were joined by Americans after Woodrow Wilson overcame some initial hesitancy, and along with the Czechs and Semenov's followers they together drove the Reds from the Far East and Siberia. British assistance came to the aid of the Central Asian insurgents, F. D. Volkov asserting that General Malleson was aiming there at the establishment of a Turkestan Republic which would be a British colony.[24] The British presence was so well imposed upon Transcaucasia that several street signs in Baku were in English. A short-lived commune in that city was liquidated in September.[25] The Volunteer Army began to move forward from the Don. The outlook for the Communists was gloomy.

But then from the autumn of 1918 to the spring of 1919 the Red fortunes revived. At the end of the First World War the Germans left the Ukraine and the Communist forces moved in, although Odessa was taken over by an Allied detachment under French control. Kazan was recaptured and the Communists advanced on Siberia. True, a new leader arose in Siberia, Admiral Kolchak, who made himself Supreme Ruler of the region and inflicted reverses on the Reds. Moreover, the Volunteer Army in the Caucasus recouped some of its losses. But the secret decision taken by the Allies in March 1919 to withdraw their troops meant that the complete defeat of the Whites could only be a matter of time.

To take the various sectors in turn, the British left Murmansk and Archangel by September 1919 after a limited offensive to cover their evacuation in the late summer. The situation was more serious in the Baltic region, where troops of various nationalities took Riga in May. They neared Petrograd by October with the assistance of British naval detachments, although they were soon repelled. In the south Red hopes were high in the spring after the French had left Odessa and Bela Kun had carried out a Communist coup in Hungary. They even began to contemplate a revolutionary drive into south-east Europe, but defections and squabbles with a local peasant guerrilla army under the anarchist Nestor Makhno caused them to change their minds. Moreover, White forces under Denikin launched a major offensive from the south which approached Moscow in the late summer. But the Whites had over-extended themselves and were in confused retreat by November. On the lesser Transcaspian and Transcaucasian fronts, the Reds encountered no great difficulty, while in the east Kolchak fell back after some initial successes and was executed by the Bolsheviks in Irkutsk.

At the beginning of 1920, after months of anxiety and near-crisis, all seemed to be over, but then at the end of April without much warning the Poles launched an invasion reaching Kiev by early May, and the Volunteer Army now under Baron Wrangel broke out from the Crimea in June. After fluctuating fortunes, and more thoughts about extending the revolutions particularly into Germany, the Reds agreed with the Poles on an armistice in the Treaty of Riga of October and the Whites evacuated the Crimea in November. The Far East remained a problem until 1922, when the Japanese finally left Vladivostok, the Americans having done so in 1920. To most intents and purposes, however, the Civil War and Intervention were over by the winter of 1920–21, even though they left wounds which would take many years to heal and whose scars still show.

Our brief survey of the campaigns of 1918–21 completed, we may now turn to some analysis of them in order to discover the reasons for the Red victory and the nature of their legacy. The first question is the less difficult to answer. The Reds possessed certain strategic and ideological advantages. They had the active sympathy of many towns and at least the indifference of the peasantry, possibly the balance of their support. They were able to exploit the inner lines of the battle fronts, and gained much material and moral benefit from their possession of Petrograd and Moscow.

Moreover, although there was undoubtedly dissension among the Red leaders about plans for defence and attack, the direction of their war effort was both more co-ordinated and more efficient than that of the Whites. Lenin, in this sphere as in every other, was at the centre – 'a one-man political-military staff'.[26] A keen student of Clausewitz, Lenin discarded much but always retained the view that 'war is politics continued by other means'. His first object was therefore to preserve and extend the revolution, by any means that came to be necessary. Such a policy involved departures from traditional means of making war on the one hand and theoretical orthodoxy on the other. A good example is the organisation of the Red Army. In the beginning, Lenin believed that a militia of workers and peasants would be the best force for fighting the Civil War, but he soon came round to the recognition that a regular conscript army had to be created. 'Bourgeois specialists', particularly former tsarist officers, would have to be used, and at critical moments, more general use was made of members of the middle class as cannon fodder for the workers and peasants. At the same time, more than customary attention was paid to the upkeep of revolutionary morale and political orthodoxy. An indispensable figure here was Trotsky, dashing everywhere in his armoured train to encourage and instruct Red Army units. At a lower level, there were many dedicated commissars and ordinary soldiers. More than for any other reason, the Reds won the Civil War because they believed in their cause.[27]

For their part, the Whites had no concerted drive or clear positive purpose. True, they mostly aspired to the overthrow of the Communist régime and the institutions of a military dictatorship, but they could not agree about who should be dictator and what policies he should pursue. Even towards the conclusion of hostilities, Wrangel had arrived at no clearer ideology than that contained in the following declaration of June 1920:

Hear me, Russian People! For What Are We Fighting?
For violated faith and desecrated shrines.
For the liberation of the Russian people from the yoke of the
Communists, tramps and criminals, who have completely ruined
Holy Russia.
For the cessation of civil war.
So that the peasant, who has acquired the land which he farms as
his own property, may engage in peaceful labour.
So that the honest worker may be assured bread in his old age.
So that the real freedom and justice may rule in Russia.
So that the Russian people may choose for itself a *master*.
Help me, Russian people, to save the Motherland.[28]

Bravely and well though White units often fought, they rarely persisted sufficiently to drive home the initiative. And they were at least as much harmed as helped by the fitful nature of the Allied intervention.

Lloyd George, as ignorant as most Western politicians about the realities of the Russian situation (for example, referring at one point to the town of Kharkov as one of the revolutionary leaders) was at least shrewd enough to observe that to make war on Lenin was to play into his hands. The error of intervention was compounded by the half-hearted nature of its commission. At least as confused as the Whites about their motives for sending men and materials to aid the anti-Communist cause, the Allies agreed that Communism was an evil influence. But they had no idea what they would do if the White cause should turn out to be victorious, and did far too little anyway to ensure such an eventuality.

The principle legacy of the years of Civil War and Intervention was harmful to the cause of national and international harmony. The Russian traditions of xenophobia and security mania became intensified, while the Russophobia of foreigners took on a more virulent and widespread form as fear and hatred of Communism. Arguments with individuals, and even with whole classes, notably the peasants, became old scores to be settled a decade or so later. Separatist nationalism in such areas as the Ukraine and Transcaucasia was as exploited by the enemies of the Soviet Union as it was feared by the Communists.[29] Moreover, the declared aims of world revolution on the one hand and of the suppression of that revolution on the other could hardly lead to immediate amity between the Bolsheviks and capitalist governments. True, by 1921 these aims were recognised as incapable of immediate realisation. But the experiences of the years 1917–21 were to give the antagonism between the Soviet Union and the ex-interventionist powers an intensity that was to blind both sides to some of the realities of the situation that developed in the ensuing decades.

11 The Consolidation of the Soviet Union, 1917–1929

After the October Revolution, Lenin pointed out that the new order would have to be constructed from the bricks of the old. If the tsarist government had condoned primitive savagery, the Communist successor which he now headed could not immediately enjoy completely civilised brotherhood. Many concessions would have to be made to the inertia of the past. The transformation was made even more difficult through the circumstance that the embryonic Soviet Union found itself continually surrounded by hostile powers which wished its great experiment no success at all. And so, while it never forgot the major cause of the international revolution, Lenin's government was mortally afraid for its own survival and brought the historic Russian fear of invasion to a high pitch of intensity. Moreover, since the Civil War and Intervention weakened the proletariat before it was able to fully establish its dictatorship, the Communist Party found itself increasingly bound to act as a substitute for it. In this substitution, as well as in the later neglect of the international revolution, many critics find the beginning of the bureaucratisation which was in their view completely to negate the dictatorship of the proletariat in favour of the Party and then of a single individual, Stalin.

In this chapter, we shall consider the first two phases of Soviet history which brought about the consolidation of the U.S.S.R.: War Communism and the New Economic Policy, or N.E.P. We shall see how, with a mixture of experiment and improvisation, the economic, political and cultural policies of the Communist government took shape. For the first half of the period, Lenin was in control. Before his death at the beginning of 1924, he undoubtedly discovered that to lead a revolution, difficult enough though that was, could hardly be considered more of an exertion than to administer the state that emerged from it.

The central figure is still the subject of heated controversy. Anathema to those who dislike him, Lenin for others came as near to deity as it was possible for adherents of dialectical materialism to allow. Before any attempt at assessment here, an outline of his earlier career needs to be given. Vladimir Ilich Ulianov was born on 22 April 1870 in the small, provincial town of Simbirsk on the Volga. He was the second son in a family of six children, his mother being a doctor's daughter and his father the local school inspector. Lenin's childhood and early adolescence were free from any obvious trouble and the Ulianov family life was boisterous but on the whole harmonious. But then, in 1886, the father died and in 1887 the eldest son Alexander was executed after an attempt on the life of Tsar Alexander III. Far from deterring Lenin from a revolutionary course, his brother's execution appears to have placed him more firmly on it. Graduating top of his class from Simbirsk gymnasium a month after that shocking event, Lenin was able to use a favourable reference from the gymnasium's director whom his father had designated as the family guardian (by a coincidence stranger than fiction, the father of Kerensky) to gain entrance to the nearby University of Kazan. Almost at once, however, he was drawn into political activity and expelled. At his mother's intercession, Lenin was allowed to take an external law degree from St Petersburg University, but while reading for the bar he was also reading Marx and organising clandestine political discussions. Passing his examinations with honours in 1891, he devoted more and more time to political activity in the provinces, being particularly enraged by a famine which swept along the Volga in 1892. He then moved to the capital in 1893. In St Petersburg Lenin quickly became a member and then the leader of a secret Social Democratic circle known later as the Elders. Deeply involved in revolutionary agitation and writing, Lenin was arrested at the end of 1895 after his return from a visit to Western Europe where he had met and talked with Plekhanov. From prison he went to exile in Siberia, where he vigorously continued his publicist work and took his revolutionary pseudonym from the river Lena. There too he married Nadezhda Krupskaia, who was to be his closest collaborator until his death. The principal events in his life from the end of the Siberian exile in 1900 sufficiently belong to history for them to have been recorded in earlier chapters.

One of the best portraits of Lenin after October 1917 was drawn by Arthur Ransome, most remembered for the stories he wrote for children after his return from Soviet Russia where he was correspondent for the *Manchester Guardian* in 1919. Ransome later remembered a meeting with Lenin in the following manner:

> More than ever, Lenin struck me as a happy man. Walking home from the Kremlin, I tried to think of any other man of his calibre who had a

similar joyous temperament. I could think of none. This little, bald-headed, wrinkled man, who tilts his chair this way and that, laughing over one thing or another, ready any minute to give serious advice to any who interrupt him to ask for it, advice so well reasoned that it is to his followers far more compelling than any command, every one of his wrinkles is a wrinkle of laughter, not of worry. I think the reason must be that he is the first great leader who utterly discounts the value of his own personality. He is quite without personal ambition. More than that, he believes, as a Marxist, in the movement of the masses which, with or without him, would still move. His whole faith is in the elemental forces that move people, his faith in himself is merely his belief that he justly estimates the direction of those forces. He does not believe that any man could make or stop the revolution which he thinks inevitable. If the Russian revolution fails, according to him, it fails only temporarily, and because of forces beyond any man's control. He is consequently free with a freedom no other great man has ever had. It is not so much what he says that inspires confidence in him. It is this sensible freedom, this obvious detachment. With his philosophy he cannot for a moment believe that one man's mistake might ruin all. He is, for himself at any rate, the exponent, not the cause, of the events that will be for ever linked with his name.[1]

A full and balanced Western judgement comes from Robert Service, writing: '… the intellectual range of Lenin's interests deserves respect … . But the final result was analytically uneven and, when assessed as a pro-grammatic whole, unsuccessful'. Moreover, 'Lenin was a political giant; he was never an ordinary figure in the array on the Bolshevik tapestry … . And yet the latitude for political action to occur was not boundless. Most general books on Lenin overrate his practical authority.'[2]

From the other side, Academician I. I. Mints asserted that in the years of the Civil War and Intervention, 'Lenin showed himself to be not only a wise political leader and statesman but also a strategist of genius … Under the control of V.I. Lenin the Party demonstrated the flexibility, patience and skill to wait and prepare for a change in the attitude of the broad masses.' But a decline and collapse of Lenin's reputation has set in since 1991.[3]

During much of the rest of this chapter, we shall be noting the policies which Lenin advocated and the recommendations which he left at his death. Towards the end of the 1920s, another leader arose in the shape of Joseph Stalin. We shall leave to Chapter 12 a description and appraisal of this even more controversial figure.

Political

Lenin and the Bolsheviks came to power without any experience of government. Just a few months before October, Lenin had been an obscure refugee in Zurich, Trotsky another in New York. Because of their lack of practice, they necessarily turned where their inclination would have taken them anyway, to theory.

While Lenin's major work of the pre-October months, *The State and Revolution*, contains a view of Russia in 1917 that is in many ways realistic, its vision of the future undoubtedly possesses elements of wishful thinking. Lenin does not foresee the replacement of the government by another similar to it in any basic way: while the withering away of the state is not to be immediate, it will be progressive and continuous, and while it will have to be strong enough to repress the old order, no special machinery will be necessary, rather just the simple organisation of the masses. No bureaucracy or army in the traditional sense will be needed, and the Soviets will provide whatever new apparatus is called for. In production and distribution too, the people will take over. Lenin declares:

> Thus, when *all* learn to administer and in fact independently administer socialised production, and independently carry out the checking and control of the boneheads, lordlings, sharpers and such like 'defenders of the capitalist tradition', then evasion of this checking and control by the whole people will inevitably become so immeasurably difficult, so rare an exception, and will in all probability be visited by such swift and condign punishment (since the armed workers are practical people and not sentimental intellectuals, and will not allow themselves to be trifled with), that the *necessity* of observing the uncomplicated fundamental rules of very human society will soon become a *habit*.

Torn between such ultimate aims and the demands of practical politics, Lenin was able for the most part to bridge the gap, although subject to some doubts and fears about the future towards the end of his life. He argued that the state could hardly be expected to wither away while the Soviet Union was under attack from hostile internal and foreign forces. Moreover, although the dictatorship of the proletariat had been established, the working class was weakened by the extraordinary efforts that it had been called upon to make during the troubled times from 1917 to 1921, and the Communist Party would therefore have to substitute for it. At the same time, bourgeois engineers, bureaucrats, army officers and other experts would have to be used in the struggle to build up the economy, the administration and the armed forces. Far from being persuaded that such developments necessitated a considerable change in his aims, Lenin considered that they made it all the more urgent to train all citizens, so that the 'government of men' could be transformed into an 'administration of things'. In Lenin's tradition, most Soviet ideologists asserted that there was no compromise with the fundamental aims of the Communist Party and that the nature of Communist society itself has none of the utopian elements ascribed to it by some Western analysts. But they, Lenin and Lenin's self-appointed heirs at least shared the view that revolutionary theory was much more than a superficial frivolity during the 1920s: that the debates that took place then involved far more than a naked struggle for power. Equally, there would be widespread agreement that actual experience also governed the manner in which the Council of People's Commissars, or *Sovnarkom*, installed by the Second Congress of Soviets after the October Revolution, on the one hand, and the Central Committee of the Bolshevik Party, on the other, jockeyed for power along with other groups and bodies.[4]

Lenin's active life in government falls into two main periods, from October to the adoption of N.E.P. in the spring of 1921, and from then up to his final incapacitation two years later. In the succession crises that followed, policy and personality were both involved. By 1926 fundamental decisions had been taken about the planned economy and the government that was to carry it through, and these were elaborated and confirmed up to 1929 when a shattering dénouement took place. Let us consider each of these phases in turn.

The Decree on Peace of 26 October 1917 abolished secret diplomacy, annulled annexations, declared an armistice and called on the workers of Great Britain, France and Germany to support the movement for peace. Its influence spread across the Atlantic to the United States, where Woodrow Wilson had it in mind when composing his Fourteen Points. However, if the Decree on Peace had certain bourgeois-democratic overtones, the first People's Commissar for Foreign Affairs had none. Describing his policy as 'active internationalism', Leon Trotsky announced: 'I will issue a few revolutionary proclamations to the people of the world and then shut up shop.'[5] And Trotsky was not alone in his uncompromising attitude towards the continuance of the war in conjunction with the Allies, while they in their turn would have little to do with the peace feelers put out by the Soviet government at the end of 1917 and the beginning of 1918.

With one nation, however, business had to be done. This was with Germany, which was bearing down upon the new and fragile state arising from the wreck of its erstwhile tsarist enemy. Protracted negotiations between the imperialists and the Communists took place at Brest-Litovsk. The Russian delegation argued among itself about what to wear, how to deal with its token peasant representative who spent more of the time under the table than round it, and, much more seriously, whether or not to accept the extremely harsh terms demanded by Germany. Some delegates agreed with Bukharin's demand for a 'revolutionary war'; others supported Trotsky's formula of 'neither war nor peace'; Lenin argued for acceptance of the terms as an appalling necessity. After much inter-party and intra-party dispute and threats of resignation from Lenin as well as further loss of land, the Treaty of Brest-Litovsk was finally signed on 3 March 1918 and then ratified at an emergency Party Congress.[6] Poland and the Ukraine had been lost as well as the Baltic provinces, Finland and Bessarabia. The isolation and weakness of the Red position was felt all the more keenly as appeals for support from the workers of other lands were not answered nearly as much as hoped for, although the response was by no means negligible.

Meanwhile, the government moved to Moscow in mid-March 1918, its dynamic force acquiring a new name – the Communist Party – to dissociate it from the renegade social democrats of Western Europe, and its timescale being adjusted – to gain thirteen days – in order to catch up with the modern calendar. While the Red Army was being organised to fight the military opposition, the All-Russian Extraordinary Commission for the Suppression of Counter-Revolution, Sabotage and Profiteering (*Cheka*) had been set up in December 1917 under Feliks Dzerzhinskii to deal with civil enemies. These probably became more numerous after the government dissolved the Constituent Assembly with its Socialist-Revolutionary majority after a single session on 5 January 1918, Lenin putting forward the argument that 'a republic of Soviets is a higher form of the democratic principle than the customary bourgeois republic with its constituent assembly'.[7] On 10 July the creation of the R.S.F.S.R. (Russian Soviet Federated Socialist Republic) was the first step in the new direction. Meanwhile, dissident S.R.s and their allies attempted through political murder and insurrection to oust the Communists, and the summer of 1918 was tense. The assassination of the German ambassador, Mirbach, brought about a diplomatic crisis, and Lenin himself was seriously wounded. However, by the autumn of 1918, the immediate danger was past and the Red Terror was in full swing. Many of the S.R.s and Mensheviks who had first been adherents of Lenin's government were now removed from power; some went into exile, others went over to the Bolsheviks.

As the Civil War was being won, and peripheral regions were being occupied, decisions about self-determination had to be taken. Many Ukrainians were hoping that they would be able to govern themselves, but the option was not given to them. Transcaucasians had a brief experience of separate government, but they were harshly disciplined by Stalin. Among the Muslim and other peoples of Central Asia and Siberia, there was some desire for independence, although often of a pre-nationalistic variety. To encompass such a wide variety of race, creed and level of civilisation within his ideas on the dictatorship of the proletariat was a difficult task for Lenin, but he just about succeeded. Broadly speaking, his pre-October argument was that bourgeois nationalism or even more rudimentary centrifugal force was progressive because it weakened the rule of the tsar or of Kerensky. But after October all such threats to social cohesion became reactionary, as educated workers would realise. Since educated workers in the peripheral regions were few and usually Russian, there were dangers in Lenin's argument – of Great Russian chauvinism and 'substitutional' bureaucratisation – that he himself was worried about before his death.[8]

Nearer the centre, a clear focus for many of the government's problems towards the end of the Civil War was the Kronstadt Revolt of March 1921. Peasants were already in revolt in the provinces and workers already on strike in Petrograd factories when the Kronstadt sailors petitioned for re-elections to the Soviets and relaxation of many of the controls that had been introduced during the years of fighting. Their revolt was ruthlessly suppressed, the workers' opposition and peasant insurgency overcome. And so, as the compromise policies of N.E.P. were being introduced at the Tenth Party Congress, Party controls were being tightened; with a ban on 'factions' or 'groupings'.[9]

Lenin argued that the true meaning of the Kronstadt Revolt was to be seen in the nature of its support from abroad. If enemies of the October Revolution were in favour of the sailors, the sailors were wrong. If their 'petty-bourgeois anarchist' ideology triumphed, the Russian Revolution would go the way of the French Revolution, and Russia would be given over to capitalism like France before it.[10] While clearly still determined to work for the world socialist revolution and to judge everything in that perspective, Lenin was nevertheless coming to realise by 1921 that some form of compromise was necessary in the international as well as in the internal sphere. From the other side, there was the beginning of the realisation that some form of *rapprochement* was possible now that the German revolts of 1918–20 had come to nothing and the *cordon sanitaire* against the spread of Bolshevism created at Versailles appeared to be holding fast. And so, while the flag of international revolution was kept flying by the Third International set up in 1919, the Soviet Union and other powers were developing something like normal relations. A trade agreement with Great Britain in March 1921 was followed by similar deals with other bourgeois nations, and the opportunity was taken during the Genoa Conference on European problems in April 1922 to arrange a *rapprochement* with Germany at nearby Rapallo. And so the powers excluded from

Versailles came together.[11] Treaties with Turkey, Iran, Afghanistan and Mongolia in 1921 showed that the Soviet government was taking a considerable interest in the affairs of the Near and Far East.

Before the onset of his final illness, Lenin was able, on 30 December 1922, to supervise the official creation of the Union of Soviet Socialist Republics, which replaced the Russian Soviet Federated Socialist Republic. The original federation of Russia, the Ukraine, Belorussia and Transcaucasia was later joined in 1925 by the Turkmen and Uzbek republics and in 1929 by the Tadzhik republic of Central Asia. Among his last instructions, Lenin stressed the necessity of the equitable treatment of all nationalities within the Soviet Union.

Another prime concern for Lenin was the cohesion of the Communist Party which was to continue to be the motor of government in the U.S.S.R. as it had been in the R.S.F.S.R. Before his death, Lenin suggested enlarging the size of the Central Committee to include a hundred members. Such a measure would serve 'to raise the prestige of the Central Committee, to do a thorough job of improving our administrative machinery and to prevent conflicts between small sections of the Central Committee from acquiring excessive importance for the future of the Party'. Among those chosen to enlarge the Central Committee should be rank-and-file workers who by attending all its meetings and reading all its documents, as well as going to sessions of the supreme Party body (the Politbureau), could constitute 'a cadre that would be loyal to the Soviet system and able, firstly, to impart stability to the Central Committee itself and, secondly, really work on renewing and improving the apparatus'.[12] In fact, the early Party leadership was predominantly middle class and highly educated, with proportionately many members of non-Russian origin. But if those born between 1868 and 1874 are compared to those born between 1883 and 1891, a process of democratisation can be detected, the younger men tending to be provincial Russians from the lower classes.[13] And so there was some reason for thinking that the new blood coming into the Party leadership would provide the anti-bureaucratic transfusion that Lenin believed to be necessary. Ironically, the leadership of the younger men was to go to a non-Russian born in 1879, Iosif Vissarionovich Dzhugashvili, alias Stalin.

Recognising the rising power of Stalin, the dying Lenin was not happy about it, declaring:

> Comrade Stalin, having become General Secretary, has concentrated boundless authority in his hands, and I am not sure whether he will always be capable of using that authority with sufficient caution ... Stalin is too rude and this defect, although quite tolerable in our midst

and in dealings among us Communists, becomes intolerable in a General Secretary. That is why I suggested that the comrades think about a way of removing Stalin from that post and appointing somebody else differing from Comrade Stalin solely to the extent of being more tolerant, more loyal, more polite and more considerate to the comrades, less capricious etc.[14]

Lenin's warning was read out at meetings of separate delegations arriving for the Thirteenth Congress of May 1924; Stalin confessed his faults and promised to correct them. The delegates gave him a vote of confidence, looking upon Trotsky and 'petty-bourgeois deviation' as the greatest threats to Party unity. A believer in 'the natural selection of accidents' in the great process of historical evolution, Trotsky had already lost ground to his opponents after catching a fever at an important moment in the autumn of 1923. As he put it in his autobiography, 'one can foresee a revolution or a war, but it is impossible to foresee the consequences of an autumn shooting-trip for wild ducks'. Accident though this may have been, its importance became magnified as Trotsky employed faulty tactics in the period following Lenin's death. Meanwhile, with quiet cunning, Stalin was making his bid for the succession. The flavour of his approach was revealed in an oration on the death of Lenin in January 1924. While others talked in the usual Bolshevik manner, Stalin introduced a quasi-religious tone, putting his remarks in the form of Leninist precepts and liturgical responses, the first of which was 'leaving us, comrade Lenin enjoined on us to hold high and keep pure the great calling of member of the party. We vow to thee, comrade Lenin, that we will fulfil this thy commandment.' As the mummified body of Lenin was moved to its mausoleum under the Kremlin wall, those observers who detected neo-Slavophile elements in the Soviet outlook must have received encouragement for their views. Undoubtedly, Stalin was attuned to the cultural wavelength of many of the Party members.[15]

Moreover, Stalin was able to make use of his position as General Secretary to gauge the mood of the Party and to manipulate it through appeals to its loyalty as his opponents were outmanoeuvred in the great debate whose main contours we have already sketched. Trotsky and the pro-permanent revolution Left Opposition were thrown out of the Party in 1927 after some street demonstrations in their favour, and Trotsky was banished to Alma Ata, and as far as Soviet chronicles were concerned, until after 1985 to the 'dustbin of history'. Trotsky's recent allies Zinovev and Kamenev recanted and lived to be purged another day, while

Bukharin, who had been the most radical of the Bolsheviks after October, now led the right-wing opposition in its campaign for the continuance of N.E.P., increasingly expounding his concept of 'socialism in one country'. Stalin finally overcame Bukharin and his associates through an adoption of similar policies by the spring of 1929. Although the debate naturally centred around personalities, its theme transcended them, as we shall see in the next sections.

In the international sphere, the early years of 'socialism in one country' meant the comparative neglect of the world revolution, arguably its betrayal. G. Chicherin, who was chief Foreign Commissar from Trotsky's resignation after Brest-Litovsk in 1918 to his own virtual replacement by M. Litvinov in 1928, brought about to a considerable degree the normalisation of relations with foreign powers. Great Britain's recognition of the Soviet Union in 1924 was followed by that of most other Western states, the most important exception being the U.S.A. Closest relations, in the short run at least, were established with Germany. At the same time, the Third International or Comintern was pursuing a 'united front' policy of infiltration rather than confrontation. This policy led to some curious episodes. In 1924, for example, the first Labour administration was brought down soon after its recognition of the U.S.S.R. at least partly by the Zinovev letter, a forgery urging British Communists to work for the forcible overthrow of the government and thus helping to achieve the objective of whoever wrote it in a peaceful manner. The Comintern's attitude to the British General Strike in 1926 amply demonstrated that its bark was far worse than its bite. Nevertheless, mutual suspicions were still great enough in 1927 for Anglo-Soviet diplomatic relations to be broken off and the threat of war to arise. At the same time, the Soviet Union was subscribing to the principles of the Kellog–Briand Pact renouncing war as a means of settling international differences.[16]

Soviet policy towards what was to become known as the 'Third World' continued throughout the 1920s to involve compromise with bourgeois nationalism, much to Trotsky's disgust. To take China as an example, the Soviet government co-operated from 1923 onwards with Chiang Kai Shek, a course of action which led in 1927 to the slaughter of the Chinese Communists. Relations with Japan were stabilised in 1925, and further treaties established with states in the Middle East.

Support for bourgeois nationalism abroad was combined with ruthless suppression of the same phenomenon at home. As Commissar for Nationalities, Stalin demonstrated unwonted severity towards his native Georgia in 1921, and his dislike of counter-currents to the consolidation of the Soviet Union was hardly milder towards the end of the decade.

Economic

From the economic point of view, the argument has been put forward that 'the October Revolution marked a complete break with the past'. Although the fact that many of the basic conditions had not changed suggests 'a natural continuity between the Russia of 1914 and the Russia of the First Five-Year Plan', appearances are deceptive since 'this continuity did not extend to forms of organisation, or to the structure of industrial life, or to the working of the system'. It is true that Sergei Witte had written in his secret memorandum of 1899 that 'Every measure of the government in regard to trade and industry now affects almost the entire economic organism and influences the course of its further development', and that he had argued from such premises that governmental policy for trade and industry be carried out 'according to a definite plan, with strict system and continuity'. It is also true that measures taken under the pressure of war by the tsarist government, and then under the pressure of war and revolution by the Provisional Government, appeared to be along the road mapped out, if not for the most part actually constructed, by Witte. Moreover, even before Witte, the tradition was well established in Imperial Russia of the state playing an important part in economic life. But the virtual disappearance from the scene of large-scale private capital, of huge foreign loans and of the landlord and bourgeois classes combined with the arrival of a much stronger belief in planning, aimed this time at the creation of socialism, to produce a clear break in continuity.[17]

And so after December 1917 the Provisional Government's Economic Council, which had never been very active and was now moribund, was finally killed off. In its place, the Supreme Council of the National Economy (*Vesenkha*) was set up to supervise and to give special attention to industrial development. *Vesenkha* became the keystone of War Communism, the title which somewhat flattered the hand-to-mouth policy of the government during the critical days of the Civil War and Intervention. By the summer of 1918, most branches of industry and the banks had been nationalised, compulsory labour introduced, and private trade largely replaced by government-supervised rationing. The land, which had been socialised in February, was expected to be used by the peasants for the general benefit. Compulsion was soon brought into agriculture as well as into industry, and a food levy attempted to oblige farmers to hand over most of their produce to the hungry workers and soldiers. What had been intended to be fraternal co-operation and mutual sustenance soon degenerated under the pressure of events into severe control. This is not to say that there were fewer examples of selfless heroism than of vicious egocentricity during these dark days. And the government survived.

Scientific organisation of the country's economy continued to be the aspiration, and the Ninth Party Congress in the spring of 1920 supported the principle of a single unified plan. Provisions were to be made in it for the restoration of the transport system and the collection of reserves of grain, fuel and raw materials. Heavy industry was to be developed first, then light industry, with comprehensive electrification as the fundamental guarantor of success. It was towards the end of 1920 that Lenin made his famous pronouncement that 'Communism is Soviet power plus electrification of the whole country'.[18]

After a considerable amount of debate about the optimum extent of planning, the General Commission on State Planning (*Gosplan*) was set up by a decree of 22 February 1921. For the first few years *Gosplan* was 'little more than a consultative organisation on the economic problems of the moment'. It did, however, collect studies and statistics, in 1925 began to publish its 'control figures', and in 1926 was instructed to work out a 'long-term' plan for five years.'[19] But before the Herculean efforts of the Five-Year Plans, a breathing space was necessary.

Just after the creation of *Gosplan*, in the spring of 1921, the Tenth Party Congress accepted the decision to adopt N.E.P. in place of War Communism. Lenin and his colleagues had little choice, in face of the desperate situation which confronted them as the Civil War and Intervention drew to a close, but to push through the N.E.P. Industrial output had fallen to less than 20 per cent, possibly less than 15 per cent of its pre-First-World-War level, with the metal, fuel and textiles sectors all nearly destroyed. The number of workers in large-scale industry had declined steeply. In agriculture, cultivated land had shrunk to less than two-thirds of the pre-First-World-War acreage, and the harvest yield to little above a third of the contemporaneous total. Two roubles could be exchanged for an American dollar in 1914; now 1200 roubles were necessary. Territorial and demographic losses in general had been great. Finland, the Baltic Provinces, Bessarabia and Poland had gone. About ten million people had died through starvation, epidemic, war and Terror, Red and White, before the end of 1921. Small wonder that from September 1920 onwards peasant and worker unrest grew as the army began to demobilise, and tens, even hundreds, of thousands of ex-soldiers were turning to banditry. And then, to confirm to the Tenth Party Congress the need for N.E.P., the Kronstadt Revolt broke out soon after its assembly.

In his speech to Tenth Congress recommending the adoption of N.E.P., Lenin reiterated an argument that he had advanced as long before as 1905. In a country like Russia, where well over 80 per cent of the population were peasants, socialist revolution would be successful only on two conditions: support from further socialist revolution in other countries; and a compromise between the proletariat and the peasant majority. Although Lenin did not specifically say so, the emphasis in the world situation of 1921 would obviously have to be on the second condition, or thus it was soon claimed by the advocates of 'socialism in one country'. At the time, the essence of N.E.P. was put succinctly by the Communist theoretician Riazanov who called it 'a peasant Brest': a forced withdrawal in face of economic problems reminiscent of the military pressure of 1918.[20] The main feature of N.E.P. was the reduction of the compulsory deliveries of grain by the peasants from the whole of their surplus to a fixed quantity paid as a tax. The balance could be sold on the open market, and even the compulsory deliveries were later commuted to a tax in money rather than in kind. Small-scale industry as well as small-scale trade was less tightly controlled, although the government was to retain the 'commanding heights' of the economy, that is large-scale industry and trade, including foreign trade, modern transportation and finance. The currency, which some Communist economists thought had gone for good with War Communism, was stabilised by 1924 as the lubricator of the partly capitalist, partly socialist 'transitional mixed system' as Lenin called it – for a brief period, as a symbol of new directions, there was an attempt to introduce a new monetary unit – the *chervonets*.

At first, N.E.P. made little impact. The year 1921 brought harvest failure and terrible starvation, which would have been far worse if it had not been for the work of the American Relief Administration; then the situation took a turn for the better in 1922. However, Lenin declared in 1922 that:

> Russia cannot be saved only by a good harvest in a peasant economy – that is not enough – or only by the good condition of light industry which supplies articles of consumption to the peasantry – that also is not enough; *heavy* industry is also indispensable. Heavy industry needs state subsidies. Unless we find them we are lost as a civilised state – let alone, as a socialist state.[21]

While economic recovery continued apace throughout the mid-1920s, the problem of heavy industry was not completely solved. Moreover, in 1923 the 'scissors' revealed themselves in high manufacturing and low agricultural prices, and the blades were largely closed by state order in 1924, continuing that way until the end of N.E.P. Here obviously were trends that some members of a government committed to socialist industrialisation could not accept.

A great debate took place among the Party leadership about what needed to be done. On the right, there was Bukharin, who argued that the Soviet Union should ride to socialism on the back of the peasant donkey or proceed in the same direction with the steps of the tortoise, i.e. continue

N.E.P., albeit with more state intervention. Another spokesman of a similar point of view was the neo-populist A. V. Chayanov, whose works on peasant farm organisation published in the 1920s put forward the thesis that the individual family should remain the basic unit in the countryside, although simple forms of co-operation attractive to the peasants should also be encouraged.[22] On the left there was Trotsky, giving strong emphasis to the need to continue the international revolution and to press forward more quickly towards industrialisation. On this side of the debate, although not entirely in agreement with Trotsky, was E. A. Preobrazhenskii, whose book *The New Economics* came out in 1926 to stress that 'primitive socialist accumulation' could only be carried out through peasant investment in the socialised sector of the economy.[23] In the middle of the argument, as we shall see below, was Stalin.

In 1927 an American delegation which included such future New Dealers as R. G. Tugwell visited the Soviet Union and found a peaceful but poor community that was beginning to conquer its difficulties and establish a new civilisation. Industry was back to the pre-First-World-War level and agriculture had surpassed it. Little sense of urgency or impending crisis was detected. But the government was not happy that the 'Nepmen' had taken three-quarters of retail trade into their private hands and that the 'capitalist kulaks' should be enriching themselves from the proceeds of agriculture while the co-operative, socialist sectors of the economy were enjoying less prosperity. Exports of grain, oil, timber and other resources were not earning enough capital for full industrialisation, and dependence on foreign assistance was too great.[24] For a complex mixture of motives, which we shall be examining in Chapter 12, the First Five-Year Plan and the attack on the kulaks were launched in 1928 and then intensified in 1929. Thus came the end of the New Economic Policy and the beginning of a period of Soviet history that nobody in the government or outside it appears to have foreseen.[25]

Cultural

Cultural revolution was a constituent part of Communist ideology, entailing the creation of a new co-operative outlook generally. In Lenin's view, the cultural revolution was to be closely linked with that in political and economic life. To maintain the connection between factory, farm and school, for example, education would be polytechnical. But 'to pay the cultural debt of many centuries', as he put it, would perhaps take longer than was first thought by those celebrating the October Revolution or by those who later believed that they had found much progress where there was little. With Stalin in mind, Lenin said in late 1922: 'People dilate at great length and very flippantly on the notion of "proletarian culture". We would be satisfied with real bourgeois culture for a start, and would be glad if we could dispense with the cruder types of bourgeois culture, such as bureaucratic or serf culture.'[26]

Among the obstacles to be overcome was religion. Before the people could properly imbibe the new culture, they would have to stop taking the old opium. If further excuse for its persecution were needed, the Orthodox Church gave the new régime plenty. Already upset by such moves from the Kerensky government as the secularisation of the parish schools, the Church leaders were incensed by the Soviet confirmation of this move, as well as by the nationalisation of church lands, removal of financial support and introduction of civil registration of births and marriages. Separated from the state that had for so long been its chief bastion, the newly reformed Patriarchate moved into the counter-attack under Tikhon. Tikhon condemned the Bolsheviks and called on the faithful to resist them. Encouraging those who appeared in mass demonstrations in Petrograd and Moscow towards the end of January 1918, the Church in Council declared: 'It is better to shed one's blood and win a martyr's crown, than to abandon the Orthodox faith to be abused by the enemy. Take heart, Holy Russia. Go to thy Calvary!'[27]

The Communist Party was not slow to respond to the challenge, its atheism made all the more energetic by the Patriarch's dismissal of Brest-Litovsk as a 'shameful peace' and the open support of many church leaders for the White cause in the Civil War. While some party members remained clandestine believers and the Central Committee adopted a policy of at least limited toleration, others wanted to take the fight for scientific materialism against superstitious idolatry in a more positive direction. Although Tikhon and some of his followers made an accommodation with the government, others sought and suffered martyrdom, thus further encouraging persecution. A vehicle for such activity was the League of The Godless formed in 1925, becoming the League of the Militant Godless in 1929. Propaganda from this and other organisations through their journals and campaigns made some headway, but surveys towards the end of the 1920s amply demonstrated that religion was still deeply entrenched. For example, graduates of atheist schools were said to be in attendance at church services, and it was alleged that monasteries were continuing their existence under the guise of 'collective farms'.

The principal positive means of spreading secular enlightenment during the first years of Soviet power was through educational advance. Nothing seems to have struck foreign visitors so forcibly in these early days as the struggle to teach everybody to at least read and write. Two by no means completely sympathetic Canadians wrote:

Nobody could be ten days in Russia, if he were really listening, and not sense how keen the people are for education. They are just like a people who have long had an intense craving, and suddenly have found the means of slaking their thirst. It comes out at every turn ... . They have a phrase constantly on their lips – 'the liquidation of illiteracy'. At first it seemed to be humorous, but soon it took on another colour as one sensed the eager effort behind it.[28]

Progress was difficult at first; in the schools, the factories and the huts, teachers and teaching materials were hard to find. A decree of 26 December 1919 declared that all citizens between eight and fifty years of age should be obliged to learn to read and write either in Russian or their native language, but the difficulty of implementing the decree was clearly shown in a manual published in the same year containing a section 'how to make do without paper, pen, ink and pencils' – pieces of wood, glass and coal were among the substitutes recommended. A further contemporary illustration may be taken from the memoirs of a young woman teaching soldiers on the southern front how to read. On hearing the first phrase from an old primer, 'Masha ate her kasha', a loud mocking voice shouted out, 'We had kasha, and we had Masha, but now we don't have kasha and we don't have Masha.' But the young woman did not lose her grip: her training as a political agitator did not let her down. Before the laughter died away, she sternly said: 'Please answer for me the questions, why in our country, which occupies one-sixth of the world's land surface, is there no kasha? Why do your mothers, wives, sweethearts, sisters lead such a miserable life alone? Why aren't you doing peacetime work? What are you fighting for now in the front lines of the Civil War?' Silent seriousness returned to the soldiers as one of them answered that if they did not carry on the fight, the landlords and the capitalists would come back and make the peasants slaves again, but they were not slaves. And so the young woman started to compose a new primer beginning with the words 'We are not slaves, we shall overcome'. Filled with such ideas, the primer was printed on wrapping paper by the press of the political department of the southern front.[29]

Towards the end of 1919, there were nearly 4000 schools for Red Army soldiers. With these and other special institutions for workers and peasants, some 8 million adults were taught to read and write in the first ten years of Soviet power. But the U.S.S.R. was still in nineteenth place for literacy among the nations of Europe. Moreover, although just over half the people as a whole were literate, the figure for the peasantry was less than 50 per cent and for the outlying region of Tadzhikistan less than 4 per cent.

In the basic schools there were more than 10 million children at primary and secondary level in the academic year 1925–6 as opposed to less than 8 million just before the outbreak of the First World War. In the cities there was a considerable amount of exciting experiment with new curricula, student participation in the administration of the schools and co-education. But complaints developed about the anarchism growing up in the reformed schools, and the Young Communist organisation, the *Komsomol*, was increasingly taken over by the Party to maintain political conformity. In the villages teaching and learning were often carried out in the most primitive of conditions where there could be little thought of progressive experimentation. At the higher level of education, there were in 1925 145 universities and institutes with 167,000 students, compared to less than 100 and 120,000 respectively in 1914. In 1923 nearly half of the intake into higher education was of peasant or worker origin. Some of these students became distinguished scholars, and they largely compensated for the losses brought about by emigration.[30]

During these early years, the writing of history became dominated by M. N. Pokrovskii (Pokrovsky), who defined his craft as 'politics projected into the past', and who reduced Russia before the Revolution to a somewhat schematic arena for the class struggle.[31] The break with tradition was not so noticeable in the field of the natural sciences, where outstanding work was done by such men as the biologist Ivan Michurin, the metallographer Dmitrii Chernov and the still-active physiologist Ivan Pavlov. In the world of learning, as elsewhere, Lenin was anxious to see the Soviet Union taking the proper path: one of his early directives was for the nationalisation of the works of Kliuchevskii, while one of his last polemics was against a deviating intellectual; as early as April 1918 he had prepared a scientific and technical plan linking research closely to production needs so that natural resources could be properly exploited.

A large part of the cultural revolution was the discovery of literary and art forms which would properly represent Soviet man and his aspirations at the same time as being comprehensible to him. Lenin made clear his views on the subject in an interview with Klara Zetkin, stressing that a proletarian culture would take a long time to develop. Although he pointed out that efforts were being made to take enlightenment to the provinces, he also made the observation that 'at the very time when here in Moscow a few tens of thousands of people are enjoying a brilliant theatrical performance, throughout the country millions are still striving to spell their names, and have to be told that the earth is not flat but round and that the world is governed by the laws of nature instead of by witches and sorcerers jointly with the Heavenly Father'. At the same time Lenin confessed that he himself had little appreciation for some of the newer forms of expression and declared himself a barbarian. Nevertheless, Lenin did not interfere very much with artistic freedom, as Stalin was to do. As for Trotsky, he went

244 CONTEMPORARY RUSSIA: THE U.S.S.R. AND AFTER

even further than Lenin, pointing out that since bourgeois culture required no less than five centuries for its creation, the proletariat would have to follow the one possible path of apprenticeship for many years to come, concentrating the bulk of its immediate energy on the proletarian world revolution. Meanwhile the leading members of the class could not through 'laboratory methods' build the proletarian culture by themselves.[32]

Such good sense as this was too sober for writers and artists wishing to celebrate the arrival of the Revolution. The poet Vladimir Mayakovsky proclaimed: 'Only the proletariat will create new things, and we, the Futurists, are the only ones to follow in the footsteps of the proletariat.' Fellow futurists declared that bourgeois artists had concentrated their attention on subjects such as landscapes of which the reality far surpassed the imitation. With the Revolution, 'Factories, mills, and workshops are waiting for artists to appear and supply them with new models of objects never seen before'. His eye roving wider, Mayakovsky cried 'Streets are our brushes, squares our palettes', and some of his colleagues forcefully expressed their agreement with him. For one celebration, all the grass, trees and flowers in front of the Bolshoi Theatre in Moscow were painted red and purple. Streets, trams and buildings were also covered in dazzling geometrical patterns of paint. In something like the same spirit, the architect Tatlin proposed the following plan for the 'dynamomonumental' building of the Third International in Petrograd. As Miliukov describes this huge edifice, it was to consist of:

...three stories built in the shape of a cube, a pyramid, and a cylinder, each in turn to revolve perpetually, yearly, monthly, and daily. The ground floor was intended for meetings of legislative institutions and congresses of the Comintern, the second for executive agencies, and the third for press and propaganda. Double walls were to provide even temperature. A gigantic spiral, which coiled round the entire building, was the symbol of the new spirit of Communist dynamics in contrast to the bourgeois horizontal, which was the symbol of the spirit of greed. Steel and glass, materials created by fire, symbolised the power of a sea of flame.

With similar exuberance, musical works such as *Engine c 15* and *Komsomol Leap Frog* attempted to catch the new spirit. So did a symphony orchestra, formed in 1922 without a conductor, who they believed would restrict their freedom of expression.[33]

During the first years of Soviet power, a thousand flowers bloomed, including some that were not revolutionary but produced through the spirit of 'art for art's sake'. Among the more perennial of the flowers of the Revolution have been the poems of Blok, Esenin and Mayakovsky, the prose writings of Maxim Gorky, Nikolai Ostrovskii, Isaak Babel, Mikhail Bulgakov and Evgenii Zamiatin. The satirists Mikhail Zoshchenko and Ilf and Petrov persuaded people to laugh at the mistakes and shortages of the N.E.P. period. Miaskovskii was the most successful musical composer of the time. The cinema, called 'the most important of all the arts' by Lenin, made a wider impact than the theatre, with directors such as Pudovkin, Dovzhenko and above all Eisenstein making films of high excellence. Special trains and boats became mobile cinemas for the provinces, while widespread use was made of the political poster. Experimental movements involving the drama and all the arts, such as Constructivism (of which it was said that 'it must not reflect, imagine or interpret, but really build') flourished for some years. But at the same time a beginning was made to the creation of the heroic-revolutionary style of Stalinist times, and of its more sinister rigid controls.[34]

And so in the U.S.S.R. during the 1920s there was on the one hand an attempt to create a new culture worthy of the proletariat revolution, on the other a realisation that even the basis for such a culture – consisting of literacy and the eradication of superstition – had still to be constructed. In its social aspect, Alexandra Kollontai was calling for the abolition of the family and the emancipation of women at a time when the reality throughout most of the Soviet Union was a household ruled by a stern and even cruel husband and father.[35] Some people would take a step in the fresh direction by choosing a revolutionary name – Vladlen, Diamat, Oktiabrina or Elektrifikatsiia – for their children, but even this move would make them worry about incurring the wrath of the Church at a time when a large number of Soviet citizens would agree with the peasant who said that 'Religion is your only comfort: you tell yourself that only God knows what is good and bad, and that is some consolation'.[36] Much of the peasant belief would still be pre-Christian, the world full of evil spirits and demons. The predicament was neatly set out by the ex-shepherd Esenin who not long before committing suicide confessed 'I am not a New Man. With one foot in the past, I try to catch up with the army of steel but I stumble and fall.' Something similar to what happened to Esenin in particular in 1925 was to occur in rural Russia as a whole in 1929.

Could the great change have been avoided? Was it possible to continue N.E.P. along lines variously recommended by Bukharin and Chayanov, Trotsky and Preobrazhenskii, and others? Or are historians, considering the alternatives, reluctantly obliged in the end to agree with Igor Klyamkin: 'Sober Reason is implacable: no, it could not have been. But how I wish that Reason was in error!'?[37] Certainly, there was 'Reason', or at least pressure, both national and international, for the change of course in 1929, which we must now investigate.

12 The Construction of Soviet Socialism, 1929–1941

The period 1929–41 makes great demands on E. H. Carr's assertion that the historian should not make moral judgements.[1] Most Western analysts of the period have been far away from such a standard of objectivity, many of them over-simplifying it with explanations centring around the characterisation of Stalin as an omnipotent dictator, enslaving millions of people to satisfy his own persecution mania and sadistic perversity. However, as the period has receded in time, some of them have managed to play the part of the historian as described by Carr, and look for explanations of its principal developments beyond the 'cult of personality', as well as giving proper weight to its more constructive aspects. Nevertheless, hardly anybody would yet choose to make an assessment more neutral than Carr's own, that 'seldom perhaps in history has so monstrous a price been paid for so monumental an achievement'.[2]

For their part, the Soviet commentators who first used the term 'cult of personality' did not succeed in giving a fully Marxist interpretation of the significant events of the 1930s. To attribute all the errors to Stalin alone was unsatisfactory; to go further than that involved some fundamental criticism of the whole Soviet system. One worthy attempt at a balanced objectivity was made by the 'unofficial' Soviet historian Roy Medvedev in his *Let History Judge*, as well as later writings, while since 1985, even more since 1991, floodgates have opened on a wide variety of denunciations of Stalin, several of them including rehabilitation for previous 'enemies of the people' such as Bukharin and even Trotsky.[3] Trotsky's own conclusion was that 'the crushing of Soviet democracy by an all-powerful bureaucracy and the extermination of bourgeois democracy by fascism were produced by one and the same cause: the dilatoriness of the world proletariat in solving the problems set for it by history. Stalinism and fascism, in spite of a deep difference in social foundations, are symmetrical phenomena. In many of their features they show a deadly similarity.'

Nevertheless, Trotsky emphasised that Soviet Russia even under Stalin was separated from Hitler's Germany and Mussolini's Italy by 'the difference between a workers' state and a capitalist state'.[4]

Before describing the period during which Stalinism arose, we must pay some lip-service to the 'cult of personality' by saying something about the early career of the man who came to embody it. Iosif Vissarionovich Dzhugashvili was born in 1879, the son of a Georgian shoemaker and his young wife Ekaterina. Both parents were of serf origin, and living in poor circumstances in the town of Gori, about a hundred kilometres from Tbilisi (Tiflis). Iosif or Joseph was their fourth child, but the first to survive infancy. Even he had smallpox at the age of six or seven, which made him pock-marked for life, and he later suffered a serious blood infection of the left arm, which he could thereafter never properly bend. The father had to go off to work in Tiflis and died there when his son was eleven, leaving the mother to care for him while working as a washer-woman. Hard-working and deeply religious, Ekaterina struggled to keep her son at the ecclesiastical academy at Gori, to which she had first sent him at the age of nine. A precocious pupil, Joseph was able to move on in 1894 to the Theological Seminary in Tiflis, and he remained a student there until the spring of 1899. Even in the barrack-like atmosphere of the Seminary, Joseph picked up extra-curricular reading such as Darwin and Hugo and developed a social conscience as well as Georgian patriotism. A combination of these influences took him into an underground local political party in 1898, and out of the Seminary in disgrace a few months later. Soon a full-time political agitator, he took the pseudonym Koba, the name of a legendary outlaw. A few months' work in the oil town of Batumi gained for Koba his first jail sentence.

In the 'university' of prison and Siberian exile, Koba developed his political consciousness, becoming a Bolshevik in a predominantly Menshevik area soon after his return to Tiflis in 1904. During the Revolution of 1905, he was an energetic and loyal advocate of Lenin's standpoint and thus first came to the Bolshevik leader's attention. Congresses in Finland, Stockholm and London put Koba more in the wider limelight, although most of his attention was given to activities in Georgia, including liaison work with local 'fighting squads' who raised funds for the party by robbing banks. Leadership of strikes in the oil-fields around Baku took Koba back to jail in 1907 and then to exile in European Russia. He escaped for a time, but was then recaptured and sent back to complete his sentence. On his release in 1911 he did not go back to the Caucasus, but still directed his energies towards the revolutionary end nearer the centre of the movement. There has been some allegation that at about this time he was working as a double agent, undermining the socialist cause as he worked for it. But the evidence here is inconclusive. By the beginning of 1913, he had acquired a new revolutionary pseudonym – Stalin, taken further 'business trips' abroad to Krakow and Vienna, written an article on the nationalities and helped to edit *Pravda*. For such activities, he gained another sentence to Siberian exile, in which he appears to have spent some comparatively idle years until the February Revolution of 1917 brought him back to Petrograd. Compared to Lenin and Trotsky, Stalin played a minor part in the events of 1917, devoting himself mostly to further editorial and propagandistic activity. During the Civil War, he ruthlessly held Tsaritsyn, the important town on the Volga which was later named after him and then after the river on which it stood. (Tsaritsyn – Stalingrad – Volgograd: an interesting discussion of Soviet history could be based on these changes alone.) Stalin's official posts in these early years included Commissar for Nationalities after October, Commissar of the Workers' and Peasants' Inspectorate in 1919, and General Secretary of the Party in 1922. For all its modest title, this last position more than any other was to carry him to power.

Before 1929 Stalin had already shown the psychological traits that were to be more fully exhibited during the next quarter-century. As well as demonstrating considerable capacity for leadership and administration, he had also revealed those negative characteristics that Lenin complained of in his 'last testament'. But from his fiftieth birthday in December 1929 onwards, both sides of Stalin were to be forgotten in the Soviet Union as he became elevated into the super-human titan of the 'cult of personality', referred to as Lenin's 'most outstanding disciple and comrade-in-arms' who as far back as the pre-October period had 'stressed and defended the Leninist principles of the possibility of building socialism in one single, backward country'. Stalin was the 'only theoretician' apart from Lenin and 'the great strategist of the Leninist school', 'the perfect prototype' of the leader who 'combines Russian revolutionary fervour with American efficiency'.[5]

We shall return to the problem of the explanation of the 'cult of personality' after an examination of the period in which it became firmly established. For the moment, the final emphasis in these introductory remarks must be given to the major achievement of the 1930s which the 'cult' must not be allowed to overshadow, the construction of Soviet socialism. Such a concept would itself appear a reckless distortion to those who prefer to describe the Soviet system as state capitalism. Undoubtedly, the crude compromises that were made between aspiration and reality produced a society that few of those who died in the struggles of the post-revolutionary years would recognise as that for which they had made their final sacrifice. Moreover, there is no doubt that the Soviet Union borrowed heavily from the experiences of those capitalist societies which had undergone the process of industrialisation before it. Nevertheless, experimentation was to more than a sufficiently high degree and on more than an adequate scale for it to deserve a title which differentiates it from anything that had gone before.

Political

The years of the first Five-Year Plan are most commemorated in the West for the not unrelated developments of the final imposition of Stalin's dictatorship and the elimination of the opposition to it, both real and imagined. Let us begin then with the familiar, and the alternative explanations of it that have been put forward in Soviet, post-Soviet and foreign analysis.

In the first place, there was the official pronouncement given at the time, that various opponents of Leninism – Trotskyists, Zinovievites, Bukharinists and others – were agents of the international bourgeoisie and had to be destroyed if the world's first socialist state was to survive. Hardly anybody would now accept such an assertion, although to many it was acceptable enough at that time. Rather more plausible is the account given by Khrushchev at the Twentieth Party Congress in 1956. Allowing some part of the earlier persecution to be right and necessary, Khrushchev condemned Stalin for excesses committed in the cause of guaranteeing and boosting his own security and power. A Soviet general history argued that 'the fact that people had faith in Stalin made it difficult to struggle against illegality and arbitrary rule. Any acts against him were not supported by the people and were regarded as acts against socialist construction'.[6] While there is obviously something in both Khrushchev's and the text-book's account, neither of them comes near to a full explanation from a Marxist or any other point of view.

More satisfying is the analysis made by Isaac Deutscher, which merits considerable attention. Beginning with one of his illuminating comparisons between the courses of the French and Russian Revolutions, Deutscher observes that Robespierre's 'reign of terror' was much closer to the commencement of the Revolution than Stalin's, that it lasted for a much shorter time, and ended with the execution of its leading instigator, while Stalin survived. The Russian revolutionaries constantly had in mind French precedents, and were anxious to avoid those that appeared less agreeable, particularly Thermidorean reaction and Bonapartism.[7] And so at first many oppositionists, including Trotsky, were allowed to emigrate, although the 1920s were not completely bloodless.

In exile Trotsky published tracts which contained much inside information about developments in Soviet Russia and exerted some influence there, his avid readers probably including Stalin himself. Suspected of adhering to the Trotskyist or lesser branches of opposition, hundreds of thousands of members were thrown out of the Party during the early 1930s. According to Deutscher, the opposition now disagreed among itself about the response to be made to this early purge, one of the clearest cleavages of opinion reflecting the generation gap. While the old men grumbled, sometimes arguing that a change in the system was more important than the persecution of individuals and that such a change could perhaps be achieved in co-operation with Stalin, the young thought of the terrorist heroes of the nineteenth century and how to act in such a tradition. One of them, named Nikolaev, assassinated Sergei Kirov in Leningrad on 1 December 1934.

Kirov was immensely popular in the Party, and some observers have believed that his assassination was instigated by Stalin, as anxious as ever to remove a potential rival.[8] The ruthless Andrei Zhdanov was appointed in Kirov's place as Party head in Leningrad, and tens of thousands of 'enemies of the people' including criminals and Party members, old and young, were deported to Siberia from Leningrad and other cities. There they were joined in the spring of 1935 by about forty members of the Leader's own bodyguard, two of whom were executed. In Siberia 'Kirov's assassins', as the Leningrad contingent was called, and the other political prisoners found themselves subjected to a harsh régime aimed at rendering impossible the revival of the practice of tsarist times for prisons and places of exile to be used as 'universities' of the opposition.

Further explanation of this excessive retaliation, and of the even greater political purges which followed it, is to be found in Russia's previous history. As Deutscher puts it, 'the cruelty with which the past oppressed the present was proportionate to the determination with which the revolution had set out to repudiate the past'. In the construction of socialism, a new aim, the Soviet government was obliged to resort to an old method, coercion from above. And so Deutscher sees Stalin as part Nicholas I, part Alexander I, part Peter the Great and part Ivan the Terrible, and the Leader himself appears to have concurred with the second pair of comparisons, if not the first pair. Stalin put the predicament of the U.S.S.R. in historical perspective in a famous speech made on 5 February 1931:

To slacken the tempo would mean falling behind. And those who fall behind get beaten. But we do not want to get beaten. No, we refuse to be beaten! One feature of the history of the old Russia was the continual beatings she suffered because of her backwardness. She was beaten by the Mongol khans. She was beaten by the Turkish beys. She was beaten by the Swedish feudal lords. She was beaten by the Polish and Lithuanian gentry. She was beaten by the British and French capitalists. She was beaten by the Japanese barons. All beat her – because of her backwardness, because of her military backwardness, cultural backwardness, industrial backwardness, agricultural backwardness. They beat her because to do so was profitable and could be done with impunity. You remember the words of the pre-revolutionary poet: 'You are poor and abundant, mighty and impotent, Mother Russia.' These gentlemen were quite familiar with the verses of the old poet. They beat her, saying: 'You are abundant', so one can enrich oneself at your expense. They beat her, saying: 'You are poor and impotent', so you can be beaten and plundered with impunity. Such is the law of exploiters – to beat the backward, and the weak. It's the jungle law of capitalism. You are backward, you are weak – and therefore you are wrong; hence you can be beaten and enslaved. You are mighty – therefore you are right; hence we must be wary of you ... We are fifty or a hundred years behind the advanced countries. We must make good this distance in ten years. Either we do it, or we shall go under.[9]

The style of the speech itself, as well as the content, is a mixture of nationalist and socialist rhetoric. Containing a digest of Russian history which is in some ways inaccurate – more battles were won than lost between Poltava in 1709 and the Crimean War of 1854 – the speech is still a powerful argument for the patriotic and ideological necessity of forcing the pace.

From coercion to persecution had always been and was still now a small step, and there were several additional reasons for taking it in the 1930s. Scapegoats could be found for errors and excesses in the implementation of the Five-Year Plans. In the increasingly unstable international atmosphere of the period, enemy agents were feared to have permeated even the innermost ranks of the Party. There were old scores to settle from the infighting of the 1920s. Such thoughts did not occur to Stalin alone. Indeed, a 'lynch law' psychosis pervaded Soviet Society as a whole.

In the second half of 1935 and the first half of 1936, the situation was fairly peaceful. However, under the surface, all was far from well. It was at about this time that Trotsky claimed that his Fourth International – founded in 1933 – already possessed 'its strongest, most numerous and most hardened branch in the U.S.S.R.'. *Pravda* and *Izvestiia* were publishing stories about clandestine opposition groups and about 'sabotage' and wilful resistance to the introduction of new production methods. The outbreak of the Spanish Civil War, Hitler's move into the Rhineland, and the conclusion of the Nazi-Japanese Anti-Comintern Pact were giving rise to concern. In such an atmosphere, the great purges began.[10]

There were four major trials: of the 'sixteen', Zinovev, Kamenev and others, in August 1936; of the 'seventeen', including Piatakov and Radek, in January 1937; of the 'twenty-one', among whom were Rykov, Bukharin and Yagoda, in March 1938; and (in secret and very summary fashion, if at all a 'trial') of Marshal Tukhachevskii and a group of the highest generals in the Red Army in June 1937. Among those arraigned were every surviving member of Lenin's original Politbureau except Stalin and Trotsky, two heads of the political police department, ambassadors, generals and other high functionaries. All were accused of attempting to assassinate Stalin and wreck the Soviet Union in collusion with various foreign powers. While few if any of the charges were substantiated, the defendants without exception pleaded guilty. Some appear to have seen their false confession as a last service to the Party for which they had worked for much of their lives, others might have been more concerned to save their wives and families. Certainly, the recantations became as much a part of the ritual of the trials as the denunciation made by the chief prosecutor Andrei Vyshinskii, 'Shoot the mad dogs!'. At the lower Party levels, and outside the Party, millions of others were purged, often without ceremony. J. Berger, E. S. Ginzburg, A. V. Gorbatov and N. Ia. Mandelshtam were among those who lived through the harrowing experiences of the period to tell the sorry tale of its less famous victims. No level of society or area of the Soviet Union was left untouched: millions died, and millions more were kept in the GULAG concentration camps.

Stalin and many of his entourage were themselves able to escape the firing squad or the concentration camp largely because they themselves believed and were able to persuade others to believe that their course of action was one of the harsh necessities on the road to the establishment of 'socialism in one country'. Savage means were justified by the glorious end, in the way of which neither internal nor external opposition must be allowed to stand. The unity of the Party and of its allies abroad thus gained its rationale, and would be the basis for all branches of domestic and foreign policy. Moreover, the new élite, which included the secret police, often had a vested interest of a more personal kind in the maintenance of the régime. Not that individuals were safe even there, as the personal histories of two heads of the secret police, Yagoda and Ezhev, show.

As a centre piece or symbol of the order that was being created, a formal framework for it was set up in the mid-1930s. A Soviet history described the process in the following manner:

The time had now come when it became possible to lift all limitations to Soviet, socialist democracy.

A decision to draft a new Constitution was passed at the Seventh All-Union Congress of Soviets in 1935. In 1936, it was published in the press for nation-wide discussion. Nearly half of the adult population took part in the discussion. The new Constitution was adopted in November 1936 by the Eighth Extraordinary Congress of Soviets of the U.S.S.R. in Moscow.

It recorded the triumph of socialism and provided the foundation for broad socialist democracy, stating that a socialist economic system and ownership of the means of production were the economic basis of the Soviet Union, while the Soviets of Working People's Deputies were its political foundation. It removed the remaining restrictions in elections to the Soviets, replaced multi-stage elections by direct elections and established the election of all Soviets on the basis of universal, equal and direct suffrage by secret ballot. Citizens of the U.S.S.R. received equal rights to elect and be elected to the Soviets.[11]

While many analysts have seen the Constitution of 1936 as little more than an empty propaganda gesture, pointing out that in fact it received very little mention of either a direct or an indirect kind in later legislation, some of them also put the argument that it performed the vital function of giving the Soviet Union a considerable amount of social cohesion. In such a case, there was at least a grain of truth in Stalin's claim that it was a legislative embodiment of what had already been achieved. Furthermore, what was established for the Soviet peoples in general was particularly granted to those of Kazakhstan and Kirgizia, which became Union republics, and for the members of the Transcaucasian Federation, which was now split into three such republics – Armenia, Georgia and Azerbaidzhan. The constituent parts of the Soviet Union were thereby increased from seven to eleven. The addition of Moldavia and the Baltic States in 1940 brought the number of republics up to sixteen (including the Karelo-Finnish, which existed from 1940 to 1956). Undoubtedly this process was attended, for the individuals and groups involved, by extreme discomfiture, the nature and intensity of which possessed features peculiar to the larger process of the construction of Soviet socialism. At the same time, it is worth recording that industrialising societies everywhere show little mercy to those who stand in their path. Thus, some of the tribesmen of Central Asia and the Caucasus who were overcome at this time might be compared to the native 'Indians' of North and South America. There was indeed a 'frontier' element in the great Soviet changes of the 1930s. Returning to the

Constitution but retaining the same area for analogy, we could point out that the Federal Constitution of the United States is broadly comparable with that of the Soviet Union in this one respect, that its cohesive influence has often been greater than its literal interpretation.

This is not to suggest that constitutional comparisons can be taken anywhere near the point of identity or to deny that the specific historical conditions obtaining in the Soviet Union were a major influence on the development of the C.P.S.U. during the 1930s. Throughout the course of that momentous decade, there were significant changes in the Communist Party, both quantitative and qualitative. As far as the numbers were concerned, the total rose from just over 1 million to nearly $2^1/_4$ millions in the first hectic years of the Stalinist forced pace from 1929 to 1933. From 1933, there was an annual decline down to about $1^1/_2$ millions in the later years of the decade, the total climbing again to almost $2^1/_2$ millions by 1941. Such fluctuations in the figures were attended by variations in age and occupation. The official intention was that workers should provide the bulk of the party membership, and indeed they did so, although from the ranks of those who were classified as workers there were many who were employed in the office rather than on the factory floor. The new intelligentsia was a vital constituent of the Party. Other distinguishing characteristics of the Communists of the 1930s were their comparatively youthful age and their male sex. Here, then, was the new élite, with many 'little Stalins' and their own minor 'cult of personality' in central and provincial government, all joined together in a gigantic network with the Leader.[12]

Apart from the Party, another major constituent part of the Soviet polity was the army, something over half of whose officers in the 1930s were members of the C.P.S.U. The general tendency of the decade was towards the professionalisation of the army, while keeping it under strict political control. This involved the restoration of ranks and of privileges which had at first been abolished after the October Revolution. In such a manner, military developments paralleled those in many other spheres of the national life. At the same time, the armed forces were being mechanised. The outstanding figure of the period was Marshal Tukhachevskii, whose purge along with many other senior and junior officers was largely responsible for the initial poor performance of the Red Army after the outbreak of war in 1941.[13]

Before 1939, the Red Army had been involved in little action since the end of the Civil War. Although the threat of international conflict had been constant, the only actual fighting of any consequence was in the Far East, where in 1938–9 the Japanese were engaged on a fairly large scale near the Soviet borders. This area had been causing concern ever since the

Japanese moved into Manchuria in 1931, and the U.S.S.R. attempted to guarantee its security there through treaties with both Mongolia and China. The second of these two treaties implied the continued neglect of the Chinese Communists led by Mao Tse-tung. The signing of the Anti-Comintern Pact by Japan and Nazi Germany in 1936 amply demonstrated that there could be no clear distinction between East and West, and revived old fears of trouble on two fronts or even something approaching virtual encirclement. Such fears were intensified as the Anti-Comintern Pact was joined by Italy in 1937 and by Spain in 1939. They constitute much of the explanation of the Soviet foreign policy in the 1930s.

For these and other reasons, the Soviet Union's Foreign Commissar, Maxim Litvinov, played a vigorous part in international attempts to secure disarmament and collective security. But the efforts of Litvinov and his associates met with little success. For example, at the World Conference on the Reduction and Restriction of Armaments at Geneva in 1932, the Soviet proposals for the partial and then complete destruction of the weapons of war were welcomed by the major Western powers no more than the Soviet delegates looked with approval upon the Western suggestions. However, the U.S.S.R. had now shown itself to be an important enough force for the U.S.A. to recognise it in 1933 and for the League of Nations to invite it to become a member in 1934.

The principal Soviet aim in the mid-1930s was the transformation of this recognition into an alliance against Fascism, to the rising threat of which the U.S.S.R. itself had mistakenly made a contribution by discouraging early opposition to Hitler. Non-aggression treaties with most of the states of Eastern Europe were consolidated by 1934, and mutual defence treaties, albeit of a limited nature, were arranged with Czechoslovakia and France in 1935. Italy's aggression against Ethiopia in 1935–6 was condemned by the Soviet government, which also gave republican Spain some if by no means enough moral and material support after it had been attacked in 1936 by Franco with the encouragement and *de facto* intervention of both Italy and Germany. The Western Allies could not agree to any firm stand against Fascism, and then appeared to be making every attempt to conciliate it in the Munich agreement of 1938. The traditional Soviet interpretation of this appeasement is based on the by no means unsupportable hypothesis that the French and British governments were assuming that the major Fascist strike would be to the east against Communism and for *Lebensraum*.

In the aftermath of Munich, the U.S.S.R. made its last desperate attempts at securing collective security. Firstly, it did everything possible to arouse public opinion abroad through its policy of reducing the emphasis on the

Comintern and increasing its encouragement for the 'popular front', without any great degree of success. Secondly, after the Nazi takeover of the whole of Czechoslovakia in March 1939, it initiated talks with the French and British governments on the question of concerted action against any further Nazi moves. But the Western Allies treated the question with little urgency, sending low-ranking missions in a tardy manner, and in desperation the Soviet government, in the person of a new Foreign Commissar, Viacheslav Molotov, turned to Germany (with whom discussions had been in progress for some time, albeit in secret), and signed a non-aggression pact with its chief potential adversary in August 1939. Like the Tilsit Peace with Napoleon more than one hundred years previously, the pact was recognised by both sides as nothing more than a breathing space. Like Tilsit, too, the Nazi-Soviet agreement contained secret protocols creating spheres of influence. Taking as full advantage as possible, the Red Army moved into areas contiguous to the Soviet Union, incorporating much of the Baltic States, Moldova (Bessarabia) and parts of Poland as the Nazi Army invaded Poland on 1 September to start the Second World War. But Finland was not prepared to make concessions to her powerful neighbour and the Winter War of 1939–40 which brought about these concessions by force inflicted both military and diplomatic reverses on the Soviet Union. The Western Allies were completely alienated by the Soviet non-aggression pact with Hitler and the attack on Finland, and for more than a year there seemed even less prospect of an anti-Fascist coalition than in 1938–9. However, the speedy successes of the German armed forces in western and central Europe throughout the year 1940 encouraged Hitler to turn to his major purpose of the defeat of the Soviet Union and persuaded the remnants of the Western Allies to be less fastidious about the political philosophy of potential anti-German friends. Meanwhile the Soviet government made sure that its eastern flank was reasonably secure by concluding a neutrality pact with Japan in April 1941.

The debate still continues about the errors and miscalculations of international diplomacy in the years leading up to 1941 and the entry of the Soviet Union into the Second World War. Munich of course has become a notorious example of appeasement, although Soviet apologists could be forgiven for complaining that the later reputation of Chamberlain's fateful step has been used against the Soviet Union almost as much as the step itself. On the other hand, so some arguments run, Stalin and his advisers should have been able to see that their best interests lay in declaring at an earlier stage that they wholeheartedly wished to work for an anti-Fascist alliance and even as late as 1939 in engaging the German forces on the eastern European front at the same time as France and Great Britain moved in from the west. Either of these commitments would have necessitated a degree of trust considerably higher than the Soviet experience since 1917 was capable of achieving.[14]

Economic

The economic construction of Soviet socialism consisted basically of two interconnected processes: the development of heavy industry and the collectivisation of agriculture. The first of these measures was carefully prepared, the second hastily improvised; both of them produced severe dislocation, but there was at least some success by the time of the Soviet entry into the Second World War in 1941.

The First Five-Year Plan was launched in the spring of 1929, 'backdated' to the autumn of 1928 after some years of debate and preliminary calculation. Samsonov's Soviet textbook described its aims in the following manner:

> The overall target of the First Five-Year Plan was to modernise industry, turn the Soviet Union from an agrarian into a powerful industrial country that would be economically independent of the capitalist states, and strengthen its defence potential.
>
> The socio-economic relations in the country had to be changed, industry and agriculture had to be developed on a single socialist foundation, and a considerable proportion of small peasant farms had to be merged into socialist, collective farms. It was planned to draw some 4–5 million peasants into collective farms and enlarge their crop area in the country. It was planned to improve the standard of living, introduce universal elementary education, and so forth.[15]

Immediately after the commencement of the implementation of the plan, trouble arose in the agricultural sector. Already in the winter of 1927–8 there had been a grain crisis, with deliveries by the peasants to the towns falling short of expectation if not of absolute need. The refusal of some farmers – the well-to-do kulaks were blamed in particular – to sell their surpluses at fixed prices below the market level stung the government into precipitate action, and what started off as an attempt at the forced collection of grain became an all-out war on the kulak and a drive to solve Russia's age-old farming problems once and for all.

The reasons for this change of tact are still hotly debated. Certainly, it was annoying for a government embarking on the construction of a modern planned economy in strained international circumstances to have to worry about inadequate or even critically short food supplies, for the new socialist administration to be hampered by the kind of difficulty which most capitalist societies had apparently long overcome. Moreover, as revolutionaries steeled in the harrowing experiences of the years following October, who had not hesitated to introduce the rigorous controls of War Communism, Stalin and his associates would not stop short of further compulsory measures where necessary. Since the link between the proletariat and the peasantry seemed to be breaking down in the relaxed conditions of N.E.P., the only course now open was the forcible re-establishment of the link. Socialist industry and capitalist agriculture could no longer co-exist. Proper socialist planning required scientific arrangement of all branches of economy. Such was the argument for the great change. A further and later pressure was exerted from outside the Soviet Union: with the onset of the Depression in the capitalist world, prices for grain, the Soviet major export, declined more steeply than those for machines and other imports.[16]

Encouraged by early successes, the government had swung into a programme of full collectivisation by late 1929. The scale of the process is indicated by the fact that the number of households in collective farms rose from 1 million at the beginning of July to nearly 5 millions at the end of December 1929 and to almost 15 millions by the beginning of March 1930. In some areas, almost all the households were collectivised. Stalin attempted to exculpate himself in a speech of 2 March 1930 entitled 'Dizzy with success'. He complained about 'excesses', and suggested that further introduction of the new system be carried out in a more moderate manner, with the peasants being allowed to choose for themselves. Within a few weeks, the level of collectivisation fell from nearly 60 per cent to less than 25 per cent; more than 10 million households had left the collectives by the autumn of 1930. With pressure being re-applied to the peasants in 1931, about 14 million households (that is, approximately 75 per cent of the total), were in the system by the end of the First Five-Year Plan. At the end of this process, an eye-witness in the North Caucasus in 1933 found 'something like a wilderness – fields choked with weeds, cattle dead, people starving and dispirited, no horses for ploughing, not even adequate seeds for the spring sowing.'[17]

Most survivors were put in the type of organisation known as a *kolkhoz*; that is, a collective farm normally controlled by its members, who were jointly responsible for the delivery of certain quotas but who were allowed to spend the rest of their time on their own small private plots. Some worked for wages in the other basic form of arrangement called a *sovkhoz*, or state farm. During the 1930s, a number of attempts were made to raise incentives in agriculture. Another important ingredient in farming progress was its modernisation. To transform rural Russia into a part of the economy worthy of inclusion in the Five-Year Plans, it would have to be mechanised. The focus of the effort in this direction was the M.T.S. or Machine-Tractor Station, which was looked upon not only as an accelerator of such processes as ploughing and harvesting but also a means of maintaining party discipline and promoting cultural enlightenment. But since there were only a few thousand M.T.S.s and about a quarter of a million collectives, the hopes held out for them could not be realised, and the problem of bringing rural Russia up to date was to remain with the Soviet government long after the initial difficulties of setting up heavy industry had been overcome.[18]

By the end of 1932, with considerable exaggeration, the First Five-Year Plan was proclaimed as complete in four years and three months. The major emphasis had been on heavy industry, about 85 per cent of all industrial investment going in that direction, and a large number of new large-scale enterprises had been completed. New branches of industry – machine, chemical, electrical – were now set up, and new towns built as centres of industrial activity. Describing the construction of a metalworks at Kuznetsk in Siberia, an eyewitness wrote:

People streamed to us from all parts of the country. In addition to Russians and Ukrainians there were Kazakhs and Kirghizes. These formerly illiterate people who had never seen a real factory in their lives performed incredible exploits. Instead of their quota of 150 mixes, the concrete-mixers produced 408 ... . The rivetters drove 266 rivets home during a shift instead of their quota of 105. The navvies sometimes fulfilled ten quotas during a single shift. YCL members braved temperatures of –50°C to continue rivetting at a great height. Bricklayers each laid up to 15 tons of refractory brick during a shift. Nothing, neither snowstorm nor rain, could dampen the labour enthusiasm of the builders.[19]

An American at Magnitogorsk in the Urals compared his experiences there to a battle involving more casualties than some of the engagements of the First World War. Undoubtedly, the great progress was achieved at enormous sacrifice, some of which was voluntary, much of which was enforced. A great amount of assistance, voluntary and purchased, came from abroad: bourgeois specialists of various kinds were employed; capital and other goods were imported.[20]

Dependence on such outside sources declined during the Second Five-Year Plan from 1933 to 1937 and the initial stages of the Third Five-Year Plan from 1938 onwards. Progress during the 1930s set the seal on the construction of a largely self-reliant modernised economy. In comparison with the level reached in 1913, production in heavy industry, in machines and metal and in electricity grew many times over. Claims were made that 9000 new enterprises were in operation and that the Soviet Union was the first industrial power in Europe and second only to the United States in the world. Not all targets were reached but even agriculture, which remained a problem, was making some progress.

Overall, in the authoritative estimation of Alec Nove:

> Despite all errors and waste, the U.S.S.R. did succeed, in the ten years beginning in 1928, in creating the industrial base for a powerful arms industry. But this base was still too weak to enable the civilian investment and consumers' programmes to survive the effects of a redoubling of arms spending.

A necessary component of the great transformation was a steep rise in the mileage of communications, particularly railroads. The most solid achievement of the First Five-Year Plan was the completion of the Turksib Railway, nearly 1500 kilometres of track bringing Central Asia firmly into the Union network. Altogether about 5500 kilometres of track were laid during the period, and transport by rail nearly doubled. Advances of a smaller kind occurred in the minor Soviet sectors of road and water transport. Such growth continued if more slowly during the Second Five-Year Plan, with the emphasis still being given to the eastern regions. A consequence of such concentration was the creation of a unified Soviet economy which at last began to make real use of vast natural and human resources.

The staggering costs of all the agricultural and industrial enterprises were met internally, by socialist accumulation which by 1941 had ceased to be primitive even if it was by no means refined. From 1930 onwards the turnover tax – a mixture of excise, purchase and processing tax – was the major source of state income. In theory equitable, the burden of the turnover tax fell mainly on the peasants. The state budget ran into increasing difficulty as expenditure on rearmaments necessarily but unexpectedly increased in the years immediately preceding the Second World War.

The social dislocation involved in the fulfilment of the First and Second Five-Year Plans was tremendous. From 1926 to 1939 the urban population increased in size from something over 26 millions to more than 56 millions, that is roughly from less than 18 per cent to 33 per cent of a total climbing from just under 150 to about 170 millions. The number of towns grew from just over 700 in 1926 to more than 1200 in 1940. During the same period, the rural population – about 114 millions in 1939 – fell from more than 80 per cent to less than 70 per cent of the total. The blood, sweat, toil and tears involved in these statistics would be hard to convey. A widely celebrated 'peak of labour heroism' was said to have been reached on 31 August 1935 when a miner named Aleksei Stakhanov allegedly cut more than 100 metric tons of coal in one shift, thus overfulfilling his quota by 1300 per cent. Stakhanovites, 'shock' workers and forced labour using machines and bare hands maintained productive and statistical output in sufficient flow for the Soviet Union to withstand many if not all the blows of the Nazi invasion of 1941 on its own resources. But before 1941 Soviet citizens had not experienced much of the fruits of the modernised economy in the shape of good housing and ample consumer goods. Queues and the black market were much in evidence in peacetime and were to become even more so after the outbreak of war.[21]

Cultural

An integral part of Stalinism, although one of its often neglected aspects, is the cultural revolution which took place during the 1930s. Accompanying the forced pace of the industrialisation and collectivisation programme and the imposition of strict political controls, this cultural revolution most clearly marked the painful reconciliation between socialism and Russian tradition which is the most characteristic feature of the period as a whole. So great was the incubus of the past that progress in several directions was restricted enough for cultural counter-revolution rather than revolution to suggest itself. Nowhere was this more the case than in the field of religion, although appearances were at first deceptive.

As Fainsod described the initial process:

> The abandonment of the N.E.P. marked a new turn in Soviet policy towards religious organisations. In the eyes of the regime the church interposed an obstacle to the successful fulfilment of the new pro-gramme of collectivisation and rapid industrialisation, and a frontal assault was launched to diminish the power and influence of all forms of religious organisation. The campaign took the form of discriminatory penalties against the clergy, of tightening restrictions on religious activ-ity, and, most important, of the closing of churches on a mass scale.

Jews, Muslims and Buddhists fared no better than Christians, in fact prob-ably worse, as the campaign mounted.

The Second Universal Congress of Atheists, which met in June 1929, heard from one of its speakers that no more than 250 out of 600,000 members of the Union of Atheists came from rural areas, and that therefore a long and bitter struggle would be necessary before the Union's aims were achieved. Even in the towns, religion was in no more than a slow decline, apparently. In 1930 the members of a Party cell in a Smolensk factory shop were revealed by an investigation to be far from atheistic in their outlook: 70 per cent still hung icons in their homes, and more than 10 per cent had children who were baptised after their fathers had joined the Party, one of the baptisms taking place in celebration of the father's survival of a purge. In 1937 a census taken of the people as a whole was widely believed to reveal that 40 per cent of them were still religious in their outlook, even after years of much propaganda, some persecution and not a little announcement of positive progress towards atheism. For example, the local Soviet of Iaroslavl claimed in 1930 that it had abolished the ringing of church bells at the request of 80,000 people[22].

These and other impressive statistics could not disguise the persistence of religion, in recognition of which the government moved, not without some backtracking, towards partial accommodation. Demonstrations against the celebration of Christmas and Easter were curtailed in the mid-1930s, although clergymen and some of their charges fell in the purges of 1937–8. The additional circumstances of a deteriorating international situation appear to have contributed to the introduction at the beginning of 1939 of a new general religious policy. Not only did the government now admit that its attempts at the liquidation of religion had been over-zealous, it also argued that it was wrong to condemn religion as being solely an instrument of class oppression. Christianity, for example, helped to preserve the family and boost morality. Its historic significance had at times been progressive, too. Commenting on the absence of the Orthodox Church from the film *Alexander Nevsky*, the League of Militant Atheists declared that there was 'no reason to be afraid of objectively showing the role of the Church in Russian history. Anti-religious propaganda is permissible in films of this kind; however, it must be directed not against the Orthodox clergy but against Catholic monks and the Roman Pope.' Such evidence of accommodation with Orthodoxy was to become much more marked after the Nazi attack on the Soviet Union in 1941[23].

Compromise between aspiration and reality was noticeable at an earlier stage in education. While the persistence of prayer did not necessarily interfere with the realisation of the Five-Year Plans, lack of skill and knowledge often did present obstacles, as other industrialising societies had discovered previously. And so the tendency away from experimentation and improvisation towards regularised inculcation of basic skills, already noticeable in the mid-1920s, now became much more pronounced. A decree of 5 September 1931 pointed out, as a basic defect of the current system, 'the fact that school instruction fails to give a sufficient body of general knowledge'. Thus, there was a dearth at the higher educational level of 'fully literate people with a good command of the basic sciences'. Although the decree did not cease to emphasise the importance of the polytechnical approach, at the same time it stressed the fact that 'Every attempt to separate the polytechnisation of the school from a systematic and firm mastery of the sciences and of physics, chemistry, and mathematics in particular ... constitutes the most flagrant perversion of the ideas of the polytechnical school.' To ensure that future progress would be along the correct lines, such lines were to be clearly drawn. By 1 January 1932 the educational authorities in the constituent republics of the Soviet Union were to work out and implement revised programmes which would ensure the inculcation of 'a strictly defined body of systematic knowledge (native language, mathematics, physics, chemistry, geography, history)'. Such a curriculum was to be uniform for virtually all children undergoing the first ten years of education. Moreover, teaching methods were to be characterised by 'decisive warfare against irresponsible projectorising and the introduction on a mass scale of methods untested in practice', although 'attempts to go back to the bourgeois school' were to be resisted at the same time as 'extreme left tendencies'. A further series of decrees restored traditional methods of discipline and assessment, while textbooks were reintroduced in contradiction to the assertion of Krupskaia and other early Soviet educators that 'life must be the textbook'[24].

Against such a background, numerical advances were clearly made. While the final conquest over illiteracy was brought several stages nearer, from the beginning of the 1930s, four-year primary education was made compulsory for all young Soviet citizens, seven-year for those living in towns, these figures being increased to seven and ten respectively by 1941. At the outbreak of war, there were more than 35 million pupils being taught in Soviet schools by nearly 1,250,000 teachers. At university level, there were more than 800,000 students, at least half of whom were women.

The rise in the general educational level was reflected in the fact that there were more than 70,000 public libraries in existence by the late 1930s. In 1937 the total of books published in the Soviet Union approached 700 millions in at least a hundred different languages. Of course, it goes almost without saying that most if not all of this reading matter was subject to a severe censorship before publication and that the breadth of choice open to library users was strictly limited. Somehow, in spite of similar difficulties and under the almost constant threat of the purges, Soviet scholars managed to continue to produce work of real worth. For example, among outstanding scientists, the mathematician I. M. Vinogradov developed a new analytical method for the theory of numbers; the physicist P. A. Cherenkov discovered an aspect of the luminosity of liquids under the action of gamma-rays; and the chemist N. N. Semenov devised a theory of chemical chain reactions. In biology progress was retarded by the official support given to the genetic views of T. D. Lysenko.[25] Arctic and other scientific expeditions continued to provide useful information for many branches of natural science.

Historians such as B. D. Grekov and M. N. Tikhomirov made research advances and fresh syntheses in Russian medieval history, while E. A. Kosminskii did the same for the medieval history of England. While both history and other social sciences were held back by the dead hand of institutionalised error, Pokrovsky's views of the past were renounced, and a Soviet patriotic interpretation, reviving some of the pre-revolutionary glories, was put in their place. A new edition of Kliuchevskii's *Course of Russian History* was published in 1937. In no field perhaps was rigidity so great as in linguistic theory, where the crude assertions of N. Ia. Marr were enthroned with the approval of Stalin.

A similar bureaucratic degeneration occurred in literature and the arts. During the 1930s the unions for writers, musicians and other artists increasingly imposed their control over the creative output of their members, many of whom disappeared temporarily or for ever during the purges. Somehow or other, even in such straitened circumstances as these, work of real merit was produced. Leaving aside for other fuller discussions the question of what exactly constitutes real merit in a culture dedicated to the basic principle of socialist realism, even readers untutored in theory as most of us are have been impressed by such works as Mikhail Sholokhov's *And Quiet Flows the Don* and *Virgin Soil Upturned*; Nikolai Ostrovskii's *How the Steel Was Tempered*; Valentin Kataev's *Time Advance!* and *Lone White Sail*; Konstantin Fedin's *Cities and Years* and *The Brothers*; and Leonid Leonov's *Soviet River* and *Russian Forest*. While these novels dealt with twentieth-century subjects, others which went much further back in history also achieved considerable popularity. Among these were Viacheslav Shishkov's *Emelian Pugachev* and Aleksei Tolstoy's *Peter I*. This list could be extended without much difficulty.[26] At the same time, although nothing of commensurate length could be written about contemporary painters, sculptors and architects, a full appreciation of Stalinist art is still inhibited by awareness of the circumstances in which it was produced.[27] In cinema, such directors as Eisenstein, Dovzhenko and

Kosintsev were continuing to produce remarkable films, if by no means so many as in the 1920s. Composers such as Prokofiev, Shostakovich, Miaskovskii, Kabalevskii and Khachaturian were composing some memorable music as well as some that might be best forgotten. In music, as well as in the other arts, it might be said that creativity flourished best when untrammelled by pressure or directives from the union's bureaucrats. For example, we do not hear so much today of pieces written specifically to commemorate various aspects of the Five-Year Plans as of those written to a less specific order, although some of them, such as Mossolov's *Symphony of Machines*, make an undoubted impact.

But such an argument would take us back to the consciously abandoned 'art for art's sake' position, which no Soviet worker in any creative field was allowed to adopt in the 1930s. Granted that the emergence of a proletarian culture could not be much more apparent than in the previous decade, most of the novelists, film directors and musical composers who have been mentioned here as representative distinguished figures would inevitably be responding in part to the growth of a larger audience brought up to at least some appreciation of that culture's distinguishing features. It could be argued that such interaction impeded these artists from moving down some of the blinder alleys of arid experimentation. True, this possibly beneficial effect would be counter-weighed by the oppressions of untalented bureaucrats and by the imposition of the 'cult of personality'.

The Soviet Union had set out to construct socialism with hope and vision. The spirit of the times was caught in a primer written near the beginning of the Five-Year Plans for the illiterate of all ages: 'We must root out uncouthness and ignorance, we must change ourselves, we must become worthy of a better life. And this better life will not come as a miracle: we ourselves must create it. But to create it we need knowledge: we need strong hands, yes, but we also need strong minds.'[28]

A decade later, the material task was nearly completed, but much of the spirit had been dashed: much if by no means all, for the 'Stalin Revolution', political and economic as well as cultural, was far from the work of one man. As Nadezhda Mandelshtam pointed out, '"Unanimity" did not fall from the skies ... It was eagerly created by crowds of active, energetic supporters of the new order.' Moreover, there was a real sense of urgency brought about by worsening international circumstances. To some extent, Stalinism was the consequence of Fascism.[29]

13 War and Reconstruction, 1941–1953

The dominant theme of Soviet history from 1941 to 1953 is war. By far the most bloody battles of the Great Patriotic War, as the Second World War is still known in Russia, were fought on Russian soil and up to forty million soldiers and civilians lost their lives. And then, soon after the return of peace, the Cold War arose to make the task of reconstruction an even more painful task than it already would have been. At the death of Stalin in 1953, the Soviet Union was struggling to fulfil the difficult roles of the world's second superpower and the titular leader of international socialism.

During this period, Stalin took on the guise of a firm if unemotional leader of the Soviet peoples in the fight against Fascism. In 1943 he became Marshal Stalin, and the uniform that became his most remembered attire recalled in its dress form the splendour of pre-revolutionary days. Such a reversion was soon apparent in his speech, too. On 6 November 1941 at the meeting to commemorate the Revolution held in the Mayakovsky metro station, Stalin appealed to the soldiers not only to recapture the spirit of the dark times of the Civil War when 'three quarters of our country was in the hands of foreign interventionists' but also to fight with the spirit of the heroes of modern and medieval Russia. He declared: 'Let the manly images of our great ancestors – Alexander Nevsky, Dimitry Donskoy, Kuzma Minin, Dimitry Pozharsky, Alexander Suvorov and Mikhail Kutuzov – inspire you in this war!'[1] And so the collision of tradition and socialism that had brought much of the suffering of the 1930s as well as their triumph now emerged at a time of greater crisis in a clearer form.

Stalin was both a figurehead and much more. Although he never personally visited the front line, the image of the leader watching over the people from the Kremlin helped to boost an often flagging morale and was still strong enough at the beginning of the seventies to draw spontaneous applause from cinema audiences of the war epic 'Liberation'. Even by the nineties, his popularity had not waned completely. Moreover, although caught napping at the beginning of the war, Stalin became something of a strategist as well as a manager while the fighting progressed. At the same time, his energies were mostly directed towards logistical problems. Born in 1879, the Leader had led a hard life and was getting old by the end of the Second World War. Although he could be considered to be one of the instigators of the ensuing Cold War, he appears to have had little understanding of the wider implications of the new conflict, but rather to have degenerated into a tired tyrant driven mostly by a powerful persecution mania. Purges, if not so great, and other forms of oppression, if anything more suffocating, again became a common feature of Soviet daily life. However, even in his final phase, the Leader reflected something of a wider mood as well as his own psychopathology. Now as before, the 'cult of personality' possessed sociological as well as personal characteristics, and therefore needs to be seen against the background of contemporaneous political, economic and cultural developments. While Stalin remained aloof from the Soviet peoples, he and they were largely isolated from the outside world.

Political

At the beginning of the period, Nazi Germany launched its attack on the U.S.S.R. Stalin was taken by surprise and the Soviet peoples as a whole were woefully unprepared. Some analysts believe that Stalin trusted Hitler too much and the Western Allies not enough. In a post-Soviet evaluation:

> Having occupied the position of earthly God, his perception of the sur- rounding events became so distorted that Stalin did not want to believe anything could happen that would contradict his forecast and his wishes.[2]

Premature from the Soviet point of view, the German attack may well have been too late from that of the Nazis. If Stalin has been blamed for thinking that the invasion came too soon, Hitler has been blamed for not launching it soon enough. But the extent of the delay caused by action in the Balkans has been exaggerated as well as that resulting from the eccentricity of the Führer; it was physically impossible for the German war machine to mobilise the necessary huge army of more than 150 divisions much before the fatal day of 22 June 1941, whatever the other circumstances. Even so, the German generals were gambling on a quick end to hostilities.[3]

Plan Barbarossa entailed a three-pronged offensive against Leningrad, Moscow and Kiev. The Nazi forces were most successful in the south: Kiev managed to hold out for nearly three months, but the Soviet army then fell back towards the Don. Neither Moscow nor Leningrad fell in 1941, or indeed at any time. Perhaps the war was already lost as the policy of *Blitzkrieg* failed for the first time, but a great amount of effort would be expended before that possibility was made certain. As morale sagged in Germany itself, the campaign was stepped up against Jew and Slav as preparations were made for the Holocaust with the extermination of millions of Soviet prisoners of war and the ruthless pursuit on Soviet soil of a 'war of Race Annihilation'.[4]

In 1942 the Nazis increased their strength on the Russian front to 266 divisions of which 193 were German. (The relative importance of this theatre of war at the time was reflected in the fact that there were no more than 4 German and 11 Italian divisions in North Africa.) Stalin believed that the main drive would be made for Moscow and made provision accordingly, but Hitler decided rather to strike for the Volga and the Caucasus, where he would be able to acquire much-needed oil supplies. By the end of July Rostov-on-Don had fallen and the approaches to Stalingrad on the Volga were under attack; by mid-September the outskirts of Stalingrad were occupied and the Caucasus threatened. But neither the river nor the mountains were taken in the end. The holding of the Volga line through the heroic defence of Stalingrad was one of the great epics of the war, with such individuals as Sergeant Pavlov and the small detachment who held out in a single building becoming justly famous. However, at least some of the heroism may have been imposed by Stalin's uncompromising Order No. 227 of 28 July 1942, which demanded: 'not a step backwards without an order, from the superior command.' Officers who fell short of these requirements were to join penal battalions at the front, where they would be able to 'atone for the crimes against the Motherland'. While, as is normal in war, there was chaos and short shrift, Academician Samsonov, a war veteran as well as leading historian, observed: 'The Order was extreme, but it was necessary in those terrible times. It was necessity, and not ruthlessness that people saw in it. For the first time in many years people heard the truth.' On the other side, sticking to their task at the insistence of their High Command, Field-Marshal Paulus and nearly 100,000 men were forced to surrender in February 1943. In January of that year the appalling blockade of Leningrad, during which as many as a million people died of starvation, was finally broken, and the spring saw the Soviet troops pushing back the Germans on all fronts while partisans harried the enemy rear. In July a large-scale counter-offensive was mounted by the Germans with tanks and self-propelled guns in the Kursk region; once this was broken, the enemy moved back towards the Dnepr, harried by partisans.[5]

All was not yet over, for 70 per cent of the German forces were still on the eastern front, while the Western Allies pushing up through Italy rejected as impracticable the Soviet pressure for the opening of a second front through the invasion of France. Soviet historians argued that the D-Day operation was finally undertaken on 6 June 1944 mainly because the Allies were becoming alarmed at the speed of the Red Army's success in eastern Europe at the beginning of that year, a spring offensive clearing the Crimea and the Western Ukraine and considerable advances taking place in most sectors.

With further successes achieved in the summer and autumn of 1944, everything was ready for the European war's final phase. In January 1945 a large-scale winter offensive was undertaken at the request of the Western Allies, hard pressed in the Ardennes by German forces, whose government was hoping to secure a negotiated peace before being driven to the point of unconditional surrender. The Red Army moved forward on a wide front extending from East Prussia to the Carpathians to liberate the whole of eastern Europe. Many commentators would, of course, argue that this last advance was actually to subject a large part of the continent to a new and more terrible occupation. To take the Polish case as an example, the Red Army had massacred the Polish officer corps at Katyn in 1941, and now allegedly delayed the recapture of Warsaw in 1945 until the partisans involved in the uprising had been wiped out by the Germans.

Charges have flown in the other direction, since Soviet historians argued that the Allies were acting in an unfriendly manner before the end of hostilities and that the part played by the Soviet forces in the final phase of the war both in Europe and Asia was misunderstood. One of the allegations was that the Western Allies made a point of destroying cities previously assigned to the Red Army – among them Dresden. Another was that the entry of the U.S.S.R. into the fight against Japan was misrepresented; it was claimed that the promise was made to effect this entry three months after Victory-in-Europe Day, and then scrupulously carried out. V.E. Day was 9 May 1945, and the declaration of war against Japan was made on 8 August. Red forces attacked the Japanese in the Transbaikal, Amur and Maritime regions, adding to the predicament that was already critical enough with the dropping of atom-bombs on Hiroshima and Nagasaki on 6 and 9 August respectively.

These terrible events have been looked upon as not so much the final blows against Imperial Japan as the first blows against the Soviet Union in what has become known as the Cold War. Further early evidence is sought in the exclusion of the U.S.S.R. from the peace negotiations with Japan, even though Japan's long-held aggressive intentions towards the Soviet Union, the Red Army's involvement in the Asiatic war and Allied agreements concerning its outcome all pointed to the U.S.S.R.'s inclusion. While the Red Army remained in Sakhalin and the Kurile islands, great pressure was exerted to push it back from Manchuria.

To understand fully the Cold War, some observers have argued that it is necessary to commence discussion not with the varied interpretations of the events of 1945, but with an analysis of the Russian Revolution and the Allied Intervention. In a sense, the whole of Russian and American history needs to be studied as a prerequisite for a proper appreciation of the Cold War. Here, while there is no need to retrace ground already covered, it is indeed necessary to glance back at the conferences held during the war, which developed the policy of unconditional surrender and unwittingly, or at most semi-consciously, prepared the ground for later disagreement and severe tension.

The most celebrated or most notorious of these conferences was that held at Yalta in the Crimea in February 1945. An essential insight was revealed about the agreement reached there by Roosevelt's chief of staff, Admiral Leahy, when he observed that it was 'so elastic that the Russians can stretch it all the way from Yalta to Washington without ever technically breaking it'. Moreover, the sad fact needs to be recalled that in the international sphere of law, as in most others, possession comprises nine-tenths of the whole. Furthermore, having experienced two German invasions in less than half a century, the Soviet government could hardly be blamed for wanting to ensure security in eastern Europe. Its response to the situation at the end of the Second World War would have been one of criminal folly if it had not largely consisted of the attempt to erect as strong a barrier as possible against any future invasion from Europe or Asia. Any analysis which takes no account of factors such as these may be dismissed as worthless.

This is not to accept the more extreme version of the revisionist thesis which attaches all the responsibility for the Cold War to the United States and its European allies. Few conflicts where the participants are of roughly comparable strength can be attributed solely or even predominantly to one of them, although as the stronger power, in this case the United States had at its disposal more of the initiative.[6] Moreover, it should not be forgotten that the creation of the United Nations Organisation in 1945 held out at least a glimmer of hope for lasting world peace.

A year of great significance was 1947, which saw the launching of the Truman Doctrine and of the Marshall Plan. Both these measures are usually interpreted in the West as counters to the ringing down of the 'Iron Curtain', first named during the period of the Civil War and Intervention after 1917 and then again by Churchill in his Fulton speech of 5 March 1946. The Truman Doctrine aimed at the protection from subversion by Communism of any government accessible to American aid, the first two recipients being Turkey and Greece. As Walter Lippmann and other distinguished commentators pointed out at the time, such a choice was not made because Turkey and Greece were shining examples of democracy but rather because of their strategic position by the Black Sea and in the Balkans.[7] The Marshall Plan, for its part, was advertised as a selfless gesture of assistance to war-torn Europe in its enormous task of reconstruction. While an element of idealism was almost certainly present in the minds of those who conceived it, the Plan could hardly avoid increasing the strength of the donor power, which already controlled something like two-thirds of the world's industrial capacity. Although they took a close look at the offer, Stalin and his entourage came to believe that acceptance of the Plan would place the Soviet Union and the rest of Eastern Europe in a client relationship to the United States and that the only alternative open to them was a return to 'socialism in one country' which could now at least be extended to several countries. Left to themselves, the other governments of Eastern Europe might well have decided to accept the American offer, but in the atmosphere that the Truman Doctrine reflected and intensified, their choice became increasingly restricted to the extremity of non-existence. In September 1947 the Cominform was created to replace the Comintern, and the satellites were all brought into closer orbit to the Red Star. In 1949 the Council for Mutual Economic Aid, or Comecon, was set up as an alternative to the American-dominated Western European arrangement.

In 1948, the split between East and West widened, the Communist coup in Czechoslovakia reflecting and intensifying the division of Europe. The conflict between the Soviet Union and Yugoslavia increased the suspicion of both sides. A more serious conflict arose over Berlin. The agreements made about Germany at the Yalta conference and at the Potsdam conference which followed it never worked smoothly, and discussions about a more permanent settlement ended in deadlock, each side blaming the other. Against a similar background of mutual recrimination, the Soviet government impeded access to Berlin, arguing that a unilateral devaluation of the mark by the Western powers was undermining the East German economy. As a response, the Western powers organised the 'air lift'. In May 1949 freer access to Berlin was restored, but the division of Germany had by this time become solidified, both Republics – the Federal (Western) and Democratic (Eastern) – being created in that year. In 1949, too,

NATO was founded just in time to counter the ending of the Western monopoly of atomic weapons.

1949 also brought a victorious end to Mao's long struggle for power with the proclamation on 1 October of the People's Republic of China. Although the fact that Soviet assistance to the Chinese Communists was never anything like wholehearted had already sowed some of the seeds of later dissension, at the time it appeared that a vast Red monolith of 800 million people had been created. Concern about this new combined threat led to the American-sponsored UNO intervention in Korea in June 1950. The war widened with the injection into it at the end of 1950 of Chinese troops. World conflict again appeared possible, and the Korean War was not brought to its untidy halt until some months after Stalin's death in 1953. Elsewhere in Asia the Vietnam War was a minor but persistent cause of international tension, the French forces becoming more and more bogged down in their attempt to retain a hold on this outpost of empire.

By 1953 not only Europe and Asia were caught up in the global rivalry of Soviet socialism and American capitalism; all parts of every continent were affected. The influence of the Cold War became inextricably involved with the process of Decolonisation that was dismantling the old empires of Europe and encouraging the growth of the spheres of influence of the new superpowers peripheral to it. Many of the new leaders of the Third World proclaimed themselves socialist, although their views and policies would often be more accurately characterised as 'bourgeois nationalist'; ironically, even Ho Chi Minh in Vietnam at first modelled his ideology on the American and French Revolutions rather than on Marxism–Leninism. While concentrating its major energies on domestic reconstruction and European security, the Soviet government found itself increasingly concerned with developments from Indonesia to Iceland.[8]

The 'cult of personality' in the war and post-war years was in some ways a more, in others a less, baneful influence on Soviet political life than in the pre-war period. The greatest improvement in the situation was the cessation of mass purges, even though the brink of such a horror seemed to be near in 1949 and 1953. During the Second World War, while Beria and the N.K.V.D. were far from unemployed, their major attentions appear to have been directed less towards dissident Party members and Great Russians than to centrifugal nationalities. The Crimean Tatars, the Kalmyks, Karachai–Balkars and Chechen–Ingush from the Caucasus region, and the Germans from the Volga were all deported to Central Asia, the Far North or Siberia, and many of them were executed. A similar fate might have been meted out to the Ukrainians if there had not been so many of them.[9] At the end of the war in 1945, more than 4 million Soviet citizens returned to the fatherland, many of them unwillingly. While over half of them were allowed to return to their homes, albeit under suspicion, many of the others found themselves assigned to forced labour battalions, or sent to the GULAG.

As far as all Soviet citizens were concerned, there was a reaction almost immediately after the war under the slogan 'back to class vigilance'. Rigid adherence to Party orthodoxy was restored under A. A. Zhdanov, who had been governor of Leningrad during the siege and was now to give his name to the repressions of the years 1946–8. After his death, many of his associates fell from power; the so-called 'Leningrad case', indicating new apprehension about the U.S.S.R.'s second city and, involving allegations of intrigue with Yugoslavia and other crimes, accounted for most of them. At about the same time, an anti-Semitic tinge became apparent in Soviet political persecution, charges of Zionism being widely flung after the creation of Israel in 1948, for which the U.S.S.R. had nevertheless been a sponsor. Many of those arrested in the 'doctors' plot' which was 'discovered' by Stalin as an attempt to murder him in 1953 were Jewish. Not only Jewish doctors but also several Gentile members of the Politburo were more than apprehensive about their future at the time of Stalin's death. But in fact only one of them, N. A. Voznesensky, head of *Gosplan*, was executed in the years 1945–53.

A convenient focus for a discussion of developments in party and government in the last years of Stalin is the Nineteenth Party Congress which met in 1952, nearly fourteen years after the previous congress, a delay infringing party rules. Between 1939 and 1952 the membership had nearly trebled from less than $2^{1}/_{2}$ millions to more than $6^{3}/_{4}$ millions. But greater size did not necessarily mean more mobility; particularly at the higher levels, there does not appear to have been much change in personnel in the years leading up to 1952. At the same time party and government were coming even closer together than before, with the dominance of the former being clearly marked. In other words, the terror of continuous purges was already ceasing to be the main motor of political progress before the death of Stalin. A somewhat more stable life for top Soviet politicians was taking shape, even though not yet discernible either to the individuals concerned or to foreign observers. The arrival of the new phase was to some extent symbolised by the change in title from the All-Union Communist Party (Bolsheviks) to the Communist Party of the Soviet Union, and the replacement of the Politburo by the Presidium.[10]

Economic

Although the launching of the Nazi plan Barbarossa came as a surprise, the U.S.S.R. was able to adapt itself with considerable speed. A Soviet account declared that 'The conversion of the Soviet Union into a close-knit military camp and the phenomenal rate at which the economy was reshaped along wartime lines laid the foundation for ultimate victory'. During the first three months of hostilities, more than 1500 enterprises were moved to safe regions behind the lines. On the other hand, many important natural resources and some of the industrial plant that could not be moved were soon lost to the invading forces.

To supervise the migration of industry and to solve all the problems posed by the war, a State Committee of Defence was set up. By the spring of 1942 the monthly production of artillery weapons had risen to 6000, of tanks to 1690, and of aeroplanes to 1650. Most of these figures were achieved in the Urals and Western Siberia, some of them in Central Asia. New sources of raw materials were exploited in these regions, and better assembly procedures and techniques were used. By a decree of 26 December 1941, labour was mobilised to an unprecedented degree, with forced overtime and directed employment; productivity rose by 19 per cent in 1942 and 7 per cent in 1943. And so the workers made an enormous contribution to the war effort. With recaptured areas being brought quickly back into action, annual production rose to 120,000 artillery weapons, 30,000 tanks and armoured cars, and 40,000 aeroplanes. Such totals were supplemented by Allied Lend-Lease. (On 11 June 1994 *Pravda* acknowledged the receipt of nearly 9000 aircraft, more than 3000 tanks and over 3700 anti-aircraft guns.) In addition, large supplies of food and clothing were delivered by the Allies, whose part in the Soviet economic offensive was certainly important if not decisive.

Transport was severely hit by the Nazi attack, 15,000 locomotives and 400,000 wagons being destroyed during the war and railroad use in general falling by 40 per cent before the beginning of 1943. Yet 10,000 kilometres of track were constructed on average during each wartime year, mostly in the east, and many important lines were kept open through the great heroism of the railroadmen, for example at Stalingrad. Sea and river traffic was also as active as possible, and the 'road of life' brought about 350,000 tons of truck-borne cargo to Leningrad during the winter of 1941–2. On the other hand, chaos was endemic in all forms of transport, and supplies were by no means distributed in the most rational manner.

Such dislocation was intensified through the loss in the first year or so of the war of 40 per cent of the pre-war sown area. More than a hundred thousand tractors were put out of action and millions of cattle and pigs were killed. But decline in production was halted to some extent in various ways: collective farm-workers reported for duty on about 350 days in 1942 as opposed to 250 days in 1940; new regions were opened up behind the lines, in Siberia, Central Asia and the Far East; and women and young people were mobilised as labourers and mechanics. Such measures, combined with strict rationing and price control, and wide use of kitchen gardens and small plots, ensured something like a reasonable supply for most of the people most of the time. And as occupied regions were retaken, they were quickly brought back into production, thus alleviating the problem still further.

Like any other wartime economy, that of the Soviet Union could not dispense with a budget. Soviet historians argued that, whereas the tsarist government needed to resort to large foreign loans and rapid paper inflation to acquire the money to fight the First World War, the Communist government was much more self-reliant and self-controlled during the Second. Roughly a half of the necessary income came from the turnover tax and socialist profits; new taxes were levied and much money contributed in loans and collections by the people. In the years 1941–5, expenditure amounted to 1146 billion roubles, of which 582 billion were devoted to military expenditure, but an increasing percentage was devoted to social and economic purposes. At the same time, the value of money fell, although Soviet historians claimed that the inflationary rate was still lower than in the First World War, even after it had been accelerated by the Fascist injection of forgeries. Western historians tend to take less sanguine a view, but few war histories of any origin manage to escape entirely a patriotic bias.

Nobody could deny that Soviet losses during the war were enormous; the most tragic of them was in population – as many as forty millions were lost. Such mortality defies the imagination. Material losses were correspondingly enormous, including thousands of large and small settlements and millions of buildings. Soviet calculations claimed that one-half of the destruction in Europe during the war years was suffered by the U.S.S.R.[11]

The daunting task of reconstruction was tackled by the Fourth and Fifth Five-Year Plans. The aim of the Fourth Plan was to restore and surpass pre-war levels of production during the years 1946–50. The emphasis was to be on heavy industry, but it was not intended to neglect either light industry or agriculture. Soviet appraisal of the degree of success was mixed. Undoubtedly, big steps forward were taken in heavy industry. For example, by 1950 iron smelting was up to 19.2 million tons and steel smelting up to 27.3 million tons, 29 per cent and 49 per cent more respectively than the totals for 1940. Coal and oil were also being produced in larger quantities than ever before, and electric power nearly doubled the rate for 1940. New regions had been opened up and new methods brought into use. However, the timber and construction industries lagged behind, the latter reaching little more than half of its target increase. Labour productivity in general barely reached its expected level.

Light and food industries grew comparatively slowly. Clothing and footwear were in desperately short supply. The food problem was exacerbated by the fact that the plan for agriculture was fulfilled in non-comestible production only. While rationing was abolished after a bad harvest in 1946 had caused some delay, a decree of that year made no secret of the failures of collective farming: improper adherence to working hours; neglect of collective fields in favour of private plots; abuse of collective property; and 'destruction of the democratic bases of collective government' or maladministration. Additional problems recognised during the course of the Fourth Five-Year Plan were: the inadequate fixing of prices; the improper arrangement of incentives; and insufficient application of mineral fertilisers. To combat these huge difficulties, the average size of collective farms was increased and the system of collective farming was introduced into new areas; some special attention was paid to each of the specific problems. A rise in tractor and other machine production was of some benefit to the farmers. But neither the Fourth Plan nor the first years of the Fifth came near to achieving for agriculture the degree of success attained by heavy industry. Indeed, the lot of the farm worker differed little from that of the forced labourer, and these was widespread famine to the south from Moldova to the Volga in 1946–7 at a time when city-dwellers were able to acquire at least the basic necessities. Such a disparity was to contribute to the rise of Nikita Khrushchev. Before the death of Stalin, trade was mainly restricted to the Eastern bloc.

Transport in the post-war period faced a problem the size of which is reflected in such data as the destruction of some 13,000 bridges and the disablement of 26 railway lines. As early as 1944, however, 60 per cent of the disabled lines were restored, and the task of the reconstruction of the railroads was wholly completed in the three years after 1945. By 1950 railroad capacity was 44 per cent up over 1940, with several new lines being built in Siberia and Soviet Asia. Twelve times the number of pre-war diesel trains were brought into use, but both diesel and electric trains were still much less in operation than steam trains. Other forms of locomotion were of little significance; although both water and road transport increased in size, the latter accounted in 1950 for no more than 2.8 per cent of the total.

A final economic aspect of consideration for the period of Stalin's last years is the financial. Of central importance here was the monetary reform of December 1947, by which ten old roubles were to be exchanged for one new rouble. The measure was aimed at the inflation of the war and post-war years and at the black-market and other speculators who had been exploiting it. Savings of up to 3000 roubles were exchanged one for one, with a declining rate for larger sums. The government's aims were by no means completely realised since, even with the new rate, retail prices of 1950 were 86 per cent above those of 1940. In the same ten-year period, the national income went up by 64 per cent, more than half the total coming from the turnover tax, while the national expenditure included 38 per cent spent on the economy and 24 per cent on defence. These figures would be disputed by many Western economists, who would also dispute the general Soviet assertion that international socialism prospered as international capitalism weakened. The revaluation of the rouble against the dollar is seen by them as a meaningless gesture.[12]

Cultural

Under the pressure of the Second World War, several traits of Soviet cultural development now became more marked. Such a tendency is discernible in all three of the major areas of our consideration, religion, education, and literature and the arts. Broadly speaking, the tendency may be characterised as the further reconciliation of the weight of Russian tradition to the new impetus of Soviet socialism.

In the previous chapter it was noted that the 'new religious policy' launched in 1939 had very much reduced the militancy of the drive towards atheism. This relaxation paid dividends during the war, since the Church was able to play something like its pre-revolutionary part in assisting social cohesion. On the very first day, 22 June 1941, the Acting Patriarch condemned the 'Fascist bandits' and blessed the people 'with heavenly grace for their heroic battle'. On 26 June a 'Te Deum' was sung for the victory of the Soviet Union at the Cathedral of the Epiphany in Moscow with an estimated congregation of 12,000 in attendance. On 8 August the Metropolitan Nikolai spoke about 'the well-known fact that Hitler brings with him his atheist world view and his cult of the pagan god Wotan', and on 14 October the Acting Patriarch complained that some Orthodox clergy were enrolling 'under the shadow of the pagan swastika instead of the holy cross'.[13]

These last remarks were a prelude to one of the most important activities of the Orthodox Church during the war years. Its officials continued to condemn those who had gone over to the other side and to make appeals to the faithful not only within the borders of the Soviet Union but as far away as Greece and Yugoslavia. As the occupied lands were retaken, the

Church hierarchy assisted the task of sorting out the faithful from the treacherous.

Meanwhile, the Church was carrying further its reconciliation with the Soviet state. On 5 January 1943 Stalin thanked it for arranging among its congregations the collection of money to pay for a column of tanks to be named after the medieval hero-saint, Dmitri Donskoi. This, Fireside says, was the first official communication to the Church since the Revolution of 1917. In August 1943 the Church leaders met Stalin and were allowed to elect a new Patriarch. And then, on 14 September an official Council for the Affairs of the Russian Orthodox Church was set up under an atheist chairman who was soon dubbed 'Narkombog' and 'Narkomopium' (People's Commissar for God or Opium). During the war as a whole, according to an eye-witness, Alexander Werth, a considerable religious revival occurred in the Soviet Union, and for some people the Church became the centre of the Russian national consciousness.[14]

At the end of the war, the Church called Stalin a 'God-given leader' and proceeded to help him consolidate the control over Eastern Europe while participating energetically in the various congresses and appeals for peace. At his death, the Church lamented his passing and talked of his 'eternal memory'.[15] Quite clearly, in carrying out such policies, the Church hierarchy was torn between spiritual duty and political pragmatism, as it had been for centuries. Some believers considered that the compromise had gone too far and sought outlets for their belief in sectarianism. Age-old and new elements were inextricably linked in certain policies: for example, the continuance of the attack on Roman Catholicism and on the Vatican in particular for their toleration and even alleged support of Fascism; and the proposition of the argument that bourgeois religion in general was to be condemned, while a newer, more enlightened religion could take an undisturbed place in a Communist society. Even Party members, including possibly Stalin himself, still retained something of a religious belief, and the less elevated of them could exercise it fairly freely until the revival of positive if not quite militant atheism in 1954.

A similar mixture of the traditional and innovatory can be detected in the educational history of the years 1941–5. Already before the outbreak of the Second World War, one of the chief tasks of the schools had become the inculcation of Soviet patriotism. While this was not supposed to involve nationalism in the usual sense but rather more the brotherhood of peoples with a common Communist aim, a Great Russian element certainly crept in. With medieval as well as modern history summoned to help in the process, the emphasis was placed on the central development from Kiev through Muscovy to the Empire.

After the beginning of the war, new ingredients more directly connected with the fighting were brought into the curriculum. The youngest children were evacuated whenever possible, and taught the dangers of the times through rhymes and riddles. A special effort had to be made to stop their older brothers and sisters from losing all interest in school subjects in the midst of so much turmoil. This problem often ceased at the age of fourteen, for then many adolescents, particularly boys, were drafted into industrial or agricultural work. Polytechnical ideas were therefore brought into practice in a very real way indeed, even if much of the earlier experimental theory was by this time left far behind.

During the war, the move towards traditional methods and organisation begun in the 1930s now became more pronounced. From 1943 onwards, boys and girls were increasingly catered for in separate classes, and earlier methods of examination including the five-point scale were adopted still more widely.[16]

A great problem of educational rebuilding confronted the Soviet government at the end of the Second World War. The official estimate was that 84,000 schools and colleges had been destroyed as well as 43,000 public libraries with 110 million volumes. Thousands of teachers had been killed, and all kinds of disruption created problems. Nevertheless, the Fourth Five-Year Plan aimed at consolidating the primary base and extending secondary education by 1950. Samsonov recorded that:

Between 1946 and 1950, inclusive, the nation built 18,500 schools seating 2,500,000 pupils, including premises for 1,300,000 pupils partially or wholly built on money contributed by the collective farms. In the first ten years after the war the country built or restored more than 30,000 educational establishments, with accommodation for 5,000,000. Obligatory seven-year schooling was enforced throughout the country in 1949 and the stage was set for universal ten-year education in the capitals of Union republics and the big cities. In the early 1950s all children of school age regained the opportunity to go to school. By 1952 the Soviet Union had, in the main, enforced universal, free seven-year schooling.[17]

The polytechnical approach was encouraged, if by no means as much as it would be during the Khrushchev years; there were still complaints about the divorce between practical life and communicated knowledge. Additional criticisms included the weak training of teachers; the deficient nature of curricula and textbooks; and the pursuit of formal achievement at the expense of general education.

At the highest level, too, all was not well with the programme, even though more than half a million students were being catered for by 1950. Great difficulties lay in the way both of inculcating and, even more, of advancing learning during the last years of Stalin. After the Second World War, Party control became more rigid rather than less, and the whole range of academic disciplines was at least partially crippled by directives which were often impossible to fulfil. Most notorious were the fields of biology and philology, where the dominant figures were Lysenko and Marr. Lysenko argued that acquired characteristics could be passed on genetically, a suggestion useful for the development of Communist society but of great harm to scientific research. Stalin personally sided with Lysenko when argument broke out in 1948. Marr had died in 1934, but his views about the origin of languages and their future direction lingered on long after him. Stalin intervened in 1950 to denounce Marr's interpretation but to substitute his own. As Deutscher put it: 'Stalin, uninhibited by the scantiness of his own knowledge – he had only the rudiments of one foreign language – expatiated on the philosophy of linguistics, the relationship between language, slang, and dialect, the thought processes of the deaf and dumb, and the single world language that would come into being in a remote future, when mankind would be united in communism.'[18]

In a less optimistic manner, Stalin gave warning in his *Economic Problems of Socialism in the U.S.S.R.*, published in 1952, that there were limits to the transformation that could be carried out from above, that in particular the slow development of Soviet agriculture was acting as a brake on the progress of the economy, and that problems would take a long time to solve. But time was not on the U.S.S.R.'s side, since international capitalism was in deep crisis which would lead to further war. While there were some pieces of common sense in these and other propositions, Stalinism in its last phase continued on the whole to act as a cruel and clumsy clamp on creative work in the natural and social sciences, and in party ideology. With Einstein still denounced as 'petty bourgeois', with no official admittance of cybernetics and other new concepts, fertilising ideas from home or abroad were severely curtailed.

A similar kind of straitjacket was imposed upon artistic creativity during the *Zhdanovshchina*[19] and afterwards, although controls had been to some extent relaxed during the Second World War. Then it was possible to forget for a while the strict tenets of socialist realism in favour of passionate declamations of love of country and family, of hatred for the Nazi enemy, even of hatred for the German race as a whole. Literature produced in such a framework certainly fulfilled its temporary purpose, but little of it would receive a very high critical evaluation today. Many of the writers of the period became simply war correspondents, putting the bravest face possible on the retreats and celebrating in triumphant tones the advances. Ilya Erenburg was a popular practitioner of the genre, particularly adept at denouncing the invaders. Konstantin Simonov made an impact in a number of different literary fields: his sentimental poem 'Wait for Me' was very widely known; his plays on war themes caught the attention at the time; and his novel *The Living and the Dead*, published in the early 1960s, was welcomed for saying something about the darker 'cult of personality' side of the fight against the Nazis as well as about its heroism. The enthusiasm of the 'common man' was perhaps most aroused by Aleksandr Tvardovskii's creation Vasilii Terkin. Other noteworthy prose writers of the time include Vasilii Grossman and Leonid Leonov. Much emphasis was placed on the great writers of the past, Pushkin, Tolstoy, Chekhov and Gorky, names to inspire the soldier at the front and the civilian behind the lines.

But after the war was over reaction set in. Writers came in again for Party criticism; some of them were expelled from the Union of Soviet Writers in 1946. Among them were Anna Akhmatova, denounced by Zhdanov as half whore half nun, dividing her interests between 'bedroom and chapel', and Mikhail Zoshchenko, held guilty of abandoned satire and pathological introversion. Formalism, aestheticism and cosmopolitanism all came under attack during the following years, and few writers could successfully avoid these pitfalls at the same time as reconciling the demands for socialist realism with the necessities of the 'cult of personality'. Much of the worthwhile literature of the period came from the pens of Konstantin Paustovskii, Petr Pavlenko and Konstantin Fedin. A sure note to success for lesser men was the vilification of debased foreign bourgeois cultures and the proclamation of the superiority of the exalted Soviet socialist culture. The United States and its unreformed citizens were favourite targets of attack, much praised works including a play about the evils of Harry S. Truman, entitled *The Ill-Fated Haberdasher*.

Other creative artists had even less to show for the period 1941–53 than the writers. Shostakovich's poignant Seventh Symphony written during the Leningrad siege was among the musical exceptions, but they were drowned in a brash and vacuous march towards victory and the reconstruction of socialism. Even more tedious to foreign eyes are most of the stilted Stalinist paintings, sculptures and buildings of the period.

To sum up, the 'cult of personality' probably exerted an even more harmful influence on scientific and artistic creativity after 1945 than it had before 1941. To some observers, the cumulative damage inflicted by the years of Stalinism was revealed as irreparable in the years following his death. To others, the rising educational level contributed to the development of both the imagination and the power to appreciate what the imagination produced.

In general, the harm done by the 'cult of personality' was dwarfed by the destruction wrought by the Second World War, the consequences of which remained with the Soviet Union for the rest of its existence.

14 The Assertion of Soviet Superpower, 1953–1964

In the years following the death of Stalin, the Soviet Union reached a new peak of confidence as the world was astonished by the launching of the the first earth satellite in October 1957 and a further row of space successes culminating in the first manned orbital flight by Iurii or Yuri Gagarin in April 1961. Years of anti-Soviet propaganda about technological backwardness and inefficiency now met with a triumphant response. Less spectacular successes in the economy encouraged the government to talk of the completion of the construction of socialism and a move forward towards the full-scale building of Communism. In such an atmosphere, the severe cultural controls of the previous period were to some extent relaxed, although it was not at all difficult for individual artists to find themselves in disgrace for taking the process of thaw too far. In the governmental organisation, there was an immediate return from the 'cult of personality' to collective leadership, although a new less powerful cult arose from it in turn. In the international sphere, the Soviet Union showed its self-possession by talking less of a final showdown between socialism and capitalism and more of the peaceful coexistence between the two systems. But this did not mean that the world rivalry would be discontinued, only that it would not have to be solved by military means; this was a point made completely clear in one of the best-remembered Soviet utterances of the time, 'We shall bury you'.

This phrase, as well as many other colourful statements of the time, came from the mouth of Nikita Sergeevich Khrushchev, whose rise and fall are demarcated by the dates 1953–64. Some would say that Khrushchev's own peculiar version of the 'cult of personality' was one of the many justifications for the observation of Karl Marx that history does repeat itself, first as tragedy, then as farce. But such an assertion would be to mistake appearance for reality; Khrushchev's period in power possessed its own deep significance, and the man himself was much more than a clodhopping clown. A brief survey of his career will readily show that he had necessarily developed political skills of a very high order indeed.

Khrushchev was born in 1894 in a small village in Kursk province near the Ukraine. His father was a poor peasant making seasonal journeys to earn money in the coalfields of the Donets Basin, some three hundred miles to the south. Khrushchev himself followed this pattern in adolescence, having picked up a rudimentary education at a local school. Quite soon, although in a minor capacity, Khrushchev was involved in the working-class movement. Avoiding war service in 1914 as a skilled worker, he joined the local Soviet and Military-Revolutionary Committee at the time of the Revolution of 1917, although he did not become a Bolshevik until the Civil War was well under way in 1918. This decision, like many others later, appears to have been taken for practical rather than theoretical reasons – Lenin's party stood out to him as the most likely victor over the Whites and Interventionists.

During the Civil War, Khrushchev was a junior commissar, working at the maintenance of the cohesion of various Red Army units. He returned to the mines during the terrible famine of 1921, which took from him his first wife and left him with a young son and daughter. In 1922 he was sent to the local technical college, where he became party secretary and listened to lessons that, according to his own later account, made him think that Karl Marx had been at the mine where his father and he had worked. In 1924, just before leaving the college, he married his second wife Nina, who was to play an important part in his life beyond presenting him with two more daughters and one more son.

Khrushchev rose with Stalin through a connection with Lazar Kaganovich, who was made Ukrainian Party Leader in 1925. With Kaganovich, Khrushchev went to Moscow in 1929 and by 1934 became the Moscow Party leader. He spent a large amount of time and energy on the detailed and resourceful modernisation of the capital city, particularly on the Metro underground railway, which was seen as a showpiece of the potential of socialism. He survived the purges in the same way as most other survivors, by praising Stalin, abusing Stalin's enemies and hoping for the best. In 1938 he was sent to the Ukraine with the dual mission of purging the Party of nationalism and other deviations and getting the economy moving more rapidly. He quickly succeeded in earning one of his nicknames – 'butcher of the Ukraine' – and was well on the way to deserving another of them – 'Nikita Kukuruznik' (Man of Corn or Maize) – when the crisis leading up to the Second World War captured his major attentions.

During the war, Khrushchev retreated from Kiev to Stalingrad and then advanced back again to Kiev via Kursk. As always, he played his part with great vigour, although some of his exploits as political adviser to the army were somewhat romanticised during his period of power. Returned to the Ukraine, he started where he had left off, keeping the Party 'clean' and cajoling workers and particularly peasants into higher production. His situation was very precarious during the disastrous harvest failure of 1946, but he negotiated this and more than one later hazard to be back in Moscow from 1949 well placed for the succession after the death of Stalin.

The differences between Khrushchev's style and Stalin's were well caught by Milovan Djilas: 'Unlike Stalin's humour, which was predominantly intellectual and, as such, cynical, Khrushchev's humour was typically folksy and thus often almost crude, but it was lively and inexhaustible'. Djilas considered that the clichés of Khrushchev's conversation were 'the expression of both real ignorance and Marxist maxims learned by rote'. Nevertheless, Djilas believed, 'He was the only one of the Soviet leaders who delved into details, into the daily life of the Communist rank and file and the ordinary people.' Moreover, 'he did not do this with the aim of changing the system, but of strengthening and improving things under the existing system. He did look into matters and remedy them, while others issued orders from offices and received reports.'[1]

A more succinct characterisation of Khrushchev would be that of a vigorous N.C.O. who increasingly while in power devised policies as well as trying to make sure that they were carried out. In such a manner, although he was clearly a man of strong personality and individual character, he was also very much the representative of a generation or even of a wider group of Soviet citizens. His career reflected the common experience of many who had moved from peasant agriculture to proletarian industry, through wars and purges to responsible Party positions. Thus he was well fitted to play the part called for when the death of Stalin left such a void in the political consciousness of the people at large. As J. P. Nettl aptly put it:

Khrushchev represented the often inchoate wishes and sentiments of the Soviet population and particularly of the Party. The new contact with the outside world, even with the arch-imperialist United States, was genuinely welcomed everywhere. The doctrine of peaceful co-existence, according to which communism would succeed by demonstration of superiority instead of the revolutionary or military destruction of its opponents, was only a theoretical justification for the determination of the newly educated and professional groups in positions of power not to live any longer in an inbred, isolated world of their own. The incessant call for reform and modernisation, for the exploitation of the enormous industrial potential of the Soviet Union, struck a deep chord among all these groups. Above all, the self-confident articulation of Soviet power challenging American technological and political domination contrasted favourably with the fearful and defensive isolationism of Stalin. In all these directions Khrushchev represented the future, and had the support of the most progressive groups in Soviet society.[2]

However, in the Soviet Union as in other societies, political survival depended on the maintenance of the support of the centre, and Khrushchev therefore found it necessary to change his tack more than once while in power. What finally brought him down appears to have been the loss of support on all sides through the over-hurried pursuit of easy palliatives and solutions for ills and problems which were in fact of some seriousness and complexity.

Political

Peaceful coexistence in the foreign sphere directly depended on domestic stability and development. In a rapidly changing and shrinking world, such interconnection was more clearly pronounced than in any previous period of history. Successes in both major sectors brought him to power, and failures in both of them removed him from it. However, for the sake of convenience and clarity, we shall consider his rise and fall firstly from the internal, and secondly from the international, point of view.

At the death of Stalin, according to several accounts, Khrushchev wept. As Averell Harriman reported his words, Khrushchev explained his tears in the following manner: 'After all, we were his pupils and owed him everything. Like Peter the Great, Stalin fought barbarism with barbarism but he was a great man.'[3] Undoubtedly, a huge gap had been left, and now the pupils had to decide among themselves who was going to fill it. The heir apparent was Georgii Malenkov, who at first assumed the leading role in a restored collective leadership without very much obvious difficulty.

The only immediate obstacle to temporary fraternal harmony was Lavrentii Beria, Stalin's last secret police chief and, according to his daughter Svetlana, the source of many of the Soviet leader's woes. Beria was now continuing to make full use of the apparatus at his disposal, and was conceivably making a bid for the supreme power. But in June 1953 he was arrested and, after an interrogation, was shot, as were six of his henchmen[4].

The removal from power of Malenkov took place rather more gradually, and appears to have occurred for three main reasons. Firstly, the very fact that he had been assigned the succession by Stalin told against him. Secondly, he concentrated on the governmental side of the Soviet power base to the increasing neglect of the more important Party side. Thirdly, his over-optimistic assessment of the agricultural situation and his emphasis on consumer goods production aroused the opposition of many of his colleagues in the Presidium, the renamed Politburo. At the beginning of 1955, Malenkov resigned from his post of Chairman of the Council of Ministers, which was now filled for a short period by Nikolai Bulganin.

Meanwhile, Khrushchev had become Party Secretary in 1953, and, like Stalin before him, had built up a considerable network of patronage. He was now poised for the final assumption of power, and fully seized the opportunity presented to him by the Twentieth Party Congress at the beginning of 1956. This Congress is best remembered, of course, for the attack launched at it by Khrushchev and others on the Stalin cult. Samsonov put it this way:

The Central Committee exposed the gross violations of socialist legality and abuses of power that occurred in Stalin's time, and decided to tell the Party and the people about them from the rostrum of the Twentieth Congress. It knew that this might create bitterness, even some discontent, among a certain section of people. It knew too that its candid criticism of errors may be used by enemies for anti-Soviet ends. But it had no choice, because it had to eliminate the conditions in which violations of democracy and of the principles of collective leadership, the abuses of power and other acts alien to Soviet society had been possible. Valid guarantees had to be created that such things would never recur within the Party and the country.

While criticising the errors and distortions made by Stalin, the Party gave him due credit for his previous services to the country and the international working-class movement. The Twentieth Congress produced a model of Party criticism, whose ultimate goal was to strengthen socialism and encourage the creative initiative of the masses in communist construction.[5]

Foreign observers to both left and right of the political spectrum agreed to reject such an explanation as a weak excuse; Soviet apologists argued that those who were actually faced with the task of running the government had to live with their own past and could not therefore reject it as being completely worthless. While some foreign socialists remained fervid supporters of Stalin, many others believed that the attack on him had not gone far enough and that it was a monstrous distortion to talk of the architect of socialism in one country as a performer of creditable services to the international working-class movement. Stronger talk than this would be necessary to return the Soviet Union to the true Leninist path. For their part Kremlinologists argued that Khrushchev was primarily anxious to save his own face at the same time as isolating his opponents in the Presidium who were about to be unmasked as an anti-Party group. As a further explanation which leads on to a more complete exculpation, adherents to the Party's general line would claim not only that to condemn Stalin unreservedly would be to deny the achievements of the years during which he was in power, but also that those who saw the Twentieth Party Congress solely in terms of Stalin were helping to perpetuate the cult rather than dismantle it. They are anxious to point out that great efforts were made at it to consolidate the restoration of Party democracy at all levels.

Some support for the latter argument could be gained from the manner of the overthrow of the anti-Party group in 1957. Defeated in the Presidium by the votes of Malenkov, Molotov, Bulganin, Kaganovich and others, Khrushchev appealed to the Party Central Committee of some three hundred members for support. With the assistance of Marshal Zhukov, who brought members to Moscow from all parts of the Soviet Union in military aircraft, Khrushchev won a vote of confidence. He then proceeded to remove his opponents from power and without violence, completing the process by his own replacement of Bulganin as Chairman of the Council of Ministers in March 1958. By this time, Zhukov had also been demoted. However, the point must be emphasised that it would be wrong to see the political events of 1956–8 solely as a struggle between the individuals just mentioned. They also marked an increased trend towards the professionalisation of the Party at the top and its democratisation at lower levels. About two-thirds of the members of the new Presidium were full-time Party secretaries, while worker and peasant recruitment rose to over half as the Party doubled in size from 6.8 million members in 1952 to 11.8 million in 1965.[6]

After the extraordinary Twenty-First Party Congress which met in early 1959 to endorse the Seven-Year Plan, the Twenty-Second Party Congress was convened towards the end of 1961. Given the unofficial title of the 'Congress of the Builders of Communism', the meeting addressed itself to the consideration of a New Party Programme, to replace the second Programme, the prime aim of which, of the construction of socialist society, was now considered to have been completed. The new Programme therefore mapped out the course that was to take the Soviet people to Communism within a generation. Khrushchev concluded the Congress by declaring:

> Comrades, never before have our forces, the forces of world socialism, been as great as they are today. The new Programme opens before the

Party and the people the most radiant, breathtaking vistas. The sun of communism is rising over our country. Let us do everything to hasten, by our tireless labour, the day when this sun will flood with its light the boundless spaces of our wonderful country! Let us devote all our forces, all our Bolshevik energy, to the triumph of communism! Under the leadership of the glorious Leninist Party – forward to the victory of communism![7]

For some sceptics, the sun would rise over an horizon defined as a vague and indistinct line which retreated as it was approached. These would include dissidents from the outlying Union republics, where there was increasing resentment at Russification, both real and imagined. In Russia itself, there were protests against what was seen as favourable treatment of the other republics, as well as against many aspects of the Soviet system as a whole.[8] Others were fired with enthusiasm, fortified by much agitation and propaganda (*Agitprop*).

For Khrushchev in particular the Congress should have meant the seal on his triumph. De-Stalinisation was taken further with the removal of the Leader's body from the Lenin Mausoleum in Red Square, while the words of the First Secretary and Chairman were frequently and widely quoted. In fact, however, Khrushchev's power was already on the wane. His introduction in 1961 of an obligatory rotation of from a half to a third of all offices at each Party election and division of the Party according to the 'production principle' in 1962 increased the awareness of his waywardness, lack of ideological sophistication and, worst of all perhaps, his insensitivity concerning the need for Party cohesion. His promises were becoming bigger and his delivery of the goods smaller. Both the Presidium and the Central Committee were alienated, and Khruschev was unable to out-manoeuvre the opposition when it moved against him in October 1964. In a sense, as Mark Frankland says, Khrushchev's dismissal 'was his finest hour: ten years earlier no one would ever have imagined that Stalin's successor would be removed by so simple and gentle a process as a vote'.[9] And generally speaking, his years in office were marked by distinct if limited progress towards legality, including the release of millions of prisoners from the GULAG.

Khrushchev's rise and fall may be traced through international as well as internal developments. In these as well as in the others, however, the ebullience of the dynamic protagonist must not blind us to the significance of the general shifts in the position of the Soviet Union which occurred during the years 1953–64: not just the split with China or the crisis over Cuba which made the greatest impact at the time, but also its contribution to the formation of what has become known as the 'Third World'. At the same time, we must recognise that, if peaceful coexistence had not been firmly established as a policy, there would never be a perspective in which such an observation could be made. We must also recognise that, without armed forces equipped for the deadly game of nuclear rocket strategy, the Soviet Union could not establish itself as a superpower.[10]

Soon after the death of Stalin, the first steps were taken in such a direction in the shape of *rapprochement* with Turkey, Iran, Afghanistan and India. An armistice was finally reached in Korea during the summer of 1953, with the Soviet Union giving its support to North Korea and China. Nearer home, there was trouble in the shape of riots in Czechoslovakia and East Berlin, all of which were nipped in the bud through the uncompromising intervention of the Red Army. Such irksome embarrassments were forgotten as Soviet diplomacy moved back to the wider stage in an attempt to solve general European and Asiatic problems.

The foreign ministers of the U.S.S.R., U.S.A., Great Britain and France met in Berlin at the beginning of 1954 and vainly tried to come to some agreement about the Vietnamese and European security problems. Transferring to Geneva and joined by China in the spring, the foreign ministers appeared to get some way nearer agreement on Vietnam, but unwittingly prepared the way for later troubles in South-East Asia. As far as Europe was concerned, late 1954 and early 1955 was a period of retrogression rather than progress. From the Soviet point of view, the most unwelcome developments were the Paris agreements of October 1954 on a Western Alliance including the Federal Republic of Germany and the commencement in 1955 of the build-up of the armed forces in the Federal Republic, which joined NATO in May. A counter-move in the same month was the Warsaw Pact, which committed the states of Eastern Europe to a twenty-year term of 'Friendship, Co-operation and Mutual Assistance'. In the same month the situation took a turn for the better with the agreement on the evacuation and neutralisation of Austria. In July 1955 the 'Big Four' met in Geneva at a summit conference, which was conducted in a friendly atmosphere and did much to indicate the real possibilities of peaceful coexistence even though nothing like a concrete agreement was reached. In August the Soviet government stated that it was reducing its armed forces by more than half a million men, and in September a friendship treaty with Finland was signed. At about the same time, however, a further meeting of foreign ministers confirmed the impossibility of the major powers coming to any firm arrangement about the vexed questions which divided them.

During the winter of 1955 the first of the 'B. and K.' visits beyond Eastern Europe took place, on this occasion to India. Apart from the rich pabulum that Bulganin and especially Khrushchev supplied for the news media, the visit clearly indicated the new attitudes that had developed in the Soviet Union towards the Third World. Stalin travelled little abroad and was suspicious of 'bourgeois nationalists' everywhere. Khrushchev and his advisers clearly believed that the experience of the world's first socialist state could be fruitfully passed on to emerging 'bourgeois nationalist' states along with certain amounts of material aid. Later trips by Soviet emissaries took in several other Asian, African and Latin American states, and were reciprocated by the journeys of a considerable number of Third World visitors to Moscow. (It was partly in response to such a widening of Soviet vistas that the South-East Asia Treaty Organisation (SEATO) was created by the Manila Pact of September 1954 and the Central Treaty Organisation (CENTO) was set up soon afterwards to guarantee the collective security of a large part of the Middle East.) China was a special case. While the Soviet Union supported Mao's government over the issue of the off-shore islands of Quemoy and Matsu, which flared up in the winter of 1954–5, and provided aid in technical expertise and material goods, the fraternal relations between the two greatest socialist powers were already by no means completely harmonious. Among the reasons for this was Chou En-lai's bid for Chinese leadership of the Third World at the Bandung Conference in April 1955.

Troubles back in the 'Second World' pre-empted much of the Soviet Government's attentions during the year 1956. A limited *rapprochement* which was gradually being arranged with Yugoslavia and the dissolution of the Cominform in April seemed to be the prologue to some relaxation of Soviet control over Eastern Europe. While such was certainly the long-term trend, the immediate direction was in reverse owing to outbreaks of violence in Poland and Hungary. Scores of Poles were killed in the riots which broke out in Poznan in June, and thousands of Hungarians fell in the uprising which commenced in Budapest in October. Severe repression was the order of the day in both cases, although in the aftermath the Gomulka régime in Poland and the Kadar régime in Hungary necessarily resorted to some concessions in order to restore the greatest possible approach to harmony. Luckily for Khrushchev, the West was busy with the Suez Crisis at the time.

There were echoes of the disturbing events of 1956 after the celebration of the fortieth anniversary of the October Revolution in 1957. Communist leaders from more than sixty countries came to a conference in Moscow, which appeared to confirm the U.S.S.R.'s leadership of the worldwide movement and to condemn 'polycentrism'. But cracks in the monolith soon began to show themselves again, particularly in Chinese policy.

Differences of attitude to Middle Eastern and Far Eastern crises could be discerned in 1958, with China taking a less compromising, harder line than the Soviet Union. A meeting between Khrushchev and Mao in the summer of that year did little if anything to iron out these differences. In 1959 they became wider as Khrushchev's famous visit to the U.S.A. increased Chinese suspicion that the U.S.S.R. was going soft on capitalism, particularly after the friendly exchanges between Khrushchev and Eisenhower at Camp David.

Détente with America and alienation from China looked even more likely as another summit meeting was arranged for the summer of 1960 in Paris. Although the shooting down of the U-2 reconnaissance plane and the capture of the pilot Gary Powers gave Khrushchev little alternative but to break off the meeting before it had really begun, the immediate aftermath to the disruption, as well as the meeting with Kennedy and the proclamations of the Twenty-Second Party Congress in 1961, demonstrated that the Soviet government was still firmly committed to the policy of peaceful coexistence with the capitalist states of the West. Meanwhile the withdrawal of Soviet experts from China and the increasingly sharp words exchanged between the Soviet and Chinese leaders revealed that the split of the two great Communist states was near completion.

Such a trend continued throughout the last few years of Khrushchev's power, for all the many appearances to the contrary. The two most important events were the crises over Berlin and Cuba of 1961 and 1962 respectively. The Soviet version of the first crisis was that the Western powers had rejected all attempts to settle the question of Germany in general and of Berlin in particular, while transforming the former capital into 'a nest of spies and the seat of subversive activities'. And so, on 13 August 1961, the wall was hastily constructed to impede such contamination. The Western response of 'war hysteria' was countered with firm resolution.[11] It goes almost without saying that such an account would have appeared ridiculous to most Western observers, who believed rather that the Communist governments simply could no longer bear the embarrassment of the juxtaposition of an outpost of freedom and prosperity on the one hand and a citadel of captivity and exploitation on the other. What could be noted with certainty is that this storm was weathered somewhat more easily than its predecessors. By any standards, the Cuba incident of October 1962 was more serious. Again, the Soviet interpretation was in almost diametrical contradiction to the Western: rockets were sent to the Caribbean not for offensive purposes, but to defend Cuba against the repetition of any invasion such as that in the Bay of Pigs. And then, although the rockets were withdrawn to avert the threat of war, the Soviet action had secured from the American government a guarantee that it would cease its 'export of counter-revolution' and therefore abandon the 'gunboat diplomacy' traditional to imperialist powers for more than a century. For their part, Western analysts talked of Khrushchev's reckless adventurism and saw the removal of the rockets as a setback for him.[12]

In international relations as in domestic politics, a year can be a long time, and August 1963 saw the representatives of the Soviet Union, United States and Great Britain signing the nuclear test ban treaty in Moscow; but further discussions on disarmament were getting nowhere because of disagreement about what constituted adequate safeguards. China (like France) would not sign the treaty, and there were those in the Soviet government who believed that Khrushchev was taking peaceful coexistence with the Western capitalist bloc too far. On the whole, however, as far as their international aspects were concerned, probably the increasingly individualist manner of Khrushchev's policies rather than their essential content led to his downfall. Changes of emphasis rather than direction were most noticeable after 1964.

Economic

At the death of Stalin, according to the Soviet view, a high-enough level of economic development had been reached for new methods to be tried by a restored collective leadership. Since socialism was now moving beyond one country towards a world scale, this new phase was to assume a very wide significance indeed. The opportunities presented by it were considerably restricted, however, by the harmful effects of the 'cult of personality' on the economy, particularly on agriculture. The standard Western view would be far less sanguine, arguing that all branches of the economy showed signs of maladjustment to the stage of full industrialisation, that assertion of superpower with vast military expenditure caused great distortion, that failure rather than success necessitated reform, and in its extreme version that Soviet socialism had shown itself to be fundamentally unworkable.

At least, there were more people now to experience both the failures and successes of the Soviet economy. In 1956 the total population was 220,200,000, and life expectancy was approaching seventy. Between 1950 and 1954 the town population rose by 17 million, something less than a half of which was brought about by influx from rural areas. The urban population as a whole was 43.4 per cent of the total by 1956, 53.3 per cent by 1965.

Undoubtedly, the problem singled out for special attention by the new administration was agriculture. Decrees of 1953 and 1954 attempted to isolate the problem and to suggest a cure for it. In 1953 a Party directive talked of the over-concentration on heavy industry as opposed to agriculture, the inadequate incentives given to farm-workers and the inferior personnel and equipment of the Machine Tractor Stations. Electrification of rural areas was proceeding too slowly. In 1954, in order to solve the central problem of grain production, the Party announced its decision to increase the area under the plough by up to 30 million hectares during the following two years, the figure being later raised to more than 35 million hectares. Most of this new area was to be in previously uncultivated regions in Kazakhstan, Siberia, the Northern Caucasus and the Urals. The 'virgin lands' scheme was supported by a large amount of propaganda. Young Communists and others were exhorted to lend a hand to the land, and more than 350,000 of them were already on the job by the summer of 1954. More than 200,000 tractors were injected into the new scheme, too. Agriculture as a whole was given a boost through the improvement of technical standards; the Machine Tractor Stations were dismantled and replaced temporarily by Repair Technical Stations, with individual collective farms soon assuming primary mechanical responsibility. Material incentives were raised, food prices becoming higher to cover the necessary costs. Undoubtedly, there were considerable successes resulting from the new arrangements. Between 1953 and 1958, grain production went up by more than 70 per cent. Dairy produce did not achieve the same spectacular results, but Khrushchev was sufficiently encouraged to talk of catching up and overtaking American agriculture.

During the last years of the Fifth Five-Year Plan and the first years of the Sixth Five-Year Plan (which was later withdrawn to accommodate newly discovered mineral resources and to scale down some over-optimistic targets), industry also moved forward, albeit in a somewhat more moderate manner. The emphasis here was still on the side of heavy industry, of course, and many of its sectors steadily continued their advance. However, the Twentieth Party Congress of 1956 noted that some items such as cast-iron, certain non-ferrous metals and gas had not reached their expected levels, and that productivity had climbed by 44 per cent rather than by the envisaged 50 per cent. Consumer goods output was even more disappointing. While 3000 kilometres of railroad were constructed between 1953 and 1958, and there was a large growth in rail transport, conversion to electric and diesel power was slow. Transport by sea still accounted for only 6.6 per cent of the total and by river for about 5.3 per cent, that by road being little more than negligible. Here, Khrushchev attempted to make a virtue out of necessity by arguing that Soviet citizens had no need for private cars and would prefer to use taxis.

In response to economic disappointments, the Twentieth Party Congress decided on a decentralisation of the administration. A law passed in 1957 largely replaced the central ministry organisation by regional councils. Individual republics played a large part in the reorganisation, and an Economic Commission was formed in which they would all coordinate their activities.

The Twenty-First Party Congress of 1959 confirmed the tasks of the next period which were to be carried out in a Seven-Year Plan running from 1959 to 1965. These were: to create the material-technical basis of Communism; to develop and complete socialist productive relations; and to educate Soviet citizens in the spirit of Communism. In practice, the emphases were much as before. With priority being given to heavy industry, industrial output by 1965 was to be 80 per cent greater than in 1958. Some stress was to be put on the growth of the chemical industry, particularly on polymer-plastic materials. Electrification of the economy was to near completion, and the transport network was to be consolidated. Agricultural and consumer goods production were to rise by up to 70 per cent.[13]

The Twenty-Second Party Congress of 1961 was informed in the Report of the Central Committee that all was going well. Khrushchev triumphantly declared: 'Let those who prophesied the failure of our plans think of a way out of the bog into which they have floundered, that is not our headache.' Claiming that production in the U.S.S.R. now amounted to more than 60 per cent of that in the U.S.A., he went on to say:

I would remind you that a mere ten or eleven years ago Soviet industrial output was less than 30 per cent that of the U.S.A. At the present time the U.S.S.R. has already outstripped the United States in the extraction of iron ore and coal, the production of coke, prefabricated concrete elements, heavy diesel and electric locomotives, sawn timber, woollen textiles, sugar, butter, fish, and a number of other items.

Our country now accounts for almost a fifth of the world's industrial output, or more than Britain, France, Italy, Canada, Japan, Belgium and the Netherlands combined. Yet these are all highly-developed countries with a total population of 280,000,000. The fact that our country with a population of 220,000,000 has surpassed them in total volume of industrial production shows how swiftly and surely socialist economy is progressing.

The implementation of the Seven-Year Plan will bring our country up to such a level that little more time will be required to outstrip the United States economically. By fulfilling this basic economic task the

Soviet Union will achieve an historic victory in the peaceful competition with the United States of America.[14]

This was Khrushchev at his most confident, but in fact the situation was not nearly as happy as he claimed. Those foreign analysts who accepted his quantitative claims could point out that many of the items which the Soviet Union was now producing at a greater rate than the United States were no longer priorities in the American economy. After the fall of Khrushchev, the following inadequacies in industrial production were noticed by Soviet critics: plan targets were not being reached in electricity and gas, plastics, turbines, diesel engines and some consumer goods; light industry in general was progressing more slowly than heavy; and productivity, planning and technical progress were insufficient in both sectors. The major extractive industries, coal and oil, were managed in an inefficient, wasteful and even dangerous manner. And the old problem of incentives, with or without profits, remained. For such reasons, even before 1964, the decentralisation policy inaugurated in 1957 was severely modified.[15]

Life for the average Soviet citizen undoubtedly improved during the years 1953–64. From 1959 to 1962 alone, wage rates rose by 18 per cent, and income tax (never an important feature of the Soviet system admittedly) fell. A six- or seven-hour day became standard, and housing and consumer conditions were to some extent eased. In a sense, it was possible to interpret complaints about houses and consumer goods as a reflection of the rising expectations that the improvement was bringing about. On the other hand, prices were rising as well as expectations, although a new monetary reform of 1961 exchanged ten old roubles for one new rouble (without any real devaluation, or so it was officially claimed). High prices and shortages were noticed particularly in agricultural produce.[16]

Khrushchev's agricultural policy had undoubtedly brought about a rise in production, but 80 per cent of this had come from the extension of the area under cultivation rather than intensification. The Soviet Union produced only one-third as much wheat per hectare as Western Germany, for example. While the mechanisation of Soviet agriculture was reasonably well advanced, the plan of replacing the M.T.S. by the R.T.S. had proved a failure. Fertilisation, particularly by chemicals, was still at an abysmally low level. The incentives to collective farm-workers and the administration of collective farms continued to be inadequate.

Khrushchev's response to such problems was as varied and pragmatic as ever. His agro-town project which was to give farm-workers a proper social centre was not forgotten. A campaign was launched against private plots which still produced more efficiently than the collective fields. Meat and milk prices were raised; fertilisers were produced and stronger efforts made to get them used. And Nikita Kukuruznik persisted in his belief that the answer to many of the Soviet Union's problems was a development of corn (maize) growing. So important was the agricultural sector to Khrushchev that he attempted to divide the Party into two halves, one to deal with industry and one with farming. And so, as we have seen, his economic policies were inextricably connected with his political programme, and with his downfall.

Cultural

The word most used to describe cultural developments between 1953 and 1964 is 'thaw'. While certainly not inapplicable, the word needs to be used with care; indeed, at some times and from some points of view, the temperature went down rather than up. Moreover, as always, there is no point in applying somewhat idealised Western standards to the concrete Soviet situation.

Governmental policy towards religion is an apt example here. In the summer of 1954, after a brief lull, the campaign against the Church was stepped up. Then, militancy was reduced, some observers believing that this was because of Khrushchev's intervention, others claiming that it was the result of the fact that Khrushchev was not yet completely his own master and could not therefore continue the campaign as he would have liked. Certainly, towards the end of the 1950s atheistic propaganda resumed an intense form. To quote an American authority on the subject, 'by 1960 this modest beginning had spread over into the anti-religious campaign which was to become the dominant feature in the lives of all denominations, legal and illegal, throughout the succeeding decade'.[17]

In 1960 the Party Central Committee declared that anti-religious propaganda should be intensified. Both G. G. Karpov, who had been chairman of the Council for the Affairs of the Russian Orthodox Church since its creation and the Metropolitan Nikolai, his contemporary, were removed from their posts. And then at the Twenty-Second Congress in 1961 Khrushchev observed that the battle with survivals of capitalism in the consciousness of the people, the changing by the cultural revolution of the habits and customs of millions of people built up over the centuries, would be a prolonged and not a simple matter. 'Survivals of the past are a terrible power that weigh on the minds of people', he declared. 'Communist education implies the emancipation of the mind from religious prejudices and superstitions, which still prevent some Soviet people from displaying their creative ability to the full.'[18] In other words, with the return to the Leninist path, the transition from socialism towards Communism and the creation of the 'new Soviet man' required the more energetic extirpation of the old morality and more positive inculcation of the new.

Under various kinds of direct and indirect pressure, the number of active monasteries appears to have declined from about seventy to just over thirty, and the number of churches certainly dropped steeply, although estimates of the exact figure vary widely. Known believers were harried and sometimes found it difficult to find employment or entrance to educational institutions. While baptism by immersion was discouraged through a decree making it illegal to jeopardise health in the name of religion, a Communist 'baptism' ceremony was encouraged which gave the child a 'commemorative certificate' to read and follow on growing up. Among the injunctions was 'Walk firmly on the path of life indicated by the great Lenin. Be honourable, diligent, and orderly in great and small matters. Respect parents and elders.' Also during the early 1960s, the first 'palaces of marriage' were set up to compete with the impressive church ceremonies. Films, radio and television contributed to the campaign. At work and at school, Soviet citizens found themselves confronted with various programmes of 'scientific atheism'. Many special texts were prepared, including some providing expressly atheistic methods of teaching such subjects as agriculture and algebra.[19]

But the creation of the 'new Soviet man' involved more than the injection of atheism. Khrushchev himself placed heavy emphasis on the polytechnical aspects of education, his own experience obviously influencing his attitude to a considerable extent. Reflecting such an attitude, which was at the same time very much in the Soviet socialist tradition, the new Party programme of 1961 asserted that:

> The system of public education is so organised as to ensure that the instruction and education of the rising generation are closely bound up with life and productive labour, and that the adult population can combine work in the sphere of production with further training and education in keeping with their vocations and the requirements of society. Public education along these lines will make for the moulding of harmoniously developed members of communist society and for the solution of a cardinal social problem, namely, the elimination of substantial distinctions between mental and physical labour.[20]

Some analysts believed that the vocational training given to students who were attempting to concentrate on more theoretical or academic subjects impaired their scholastic progress at the same time as doing little to create unity between hand and brain. Partly for this reason, the polytechnical element in education was somewhat reduced after the fall of Khrushchev, although by no means abolished.

While the qualitative nature of some aspects of Soviet education is debatable, there can be no argument about its quantitative advance. By the mid-1960s there were more than 20 million students at each of the first two levels, primary and junior high. High school attendance was approaching the 10 million mark, and about 6.5 million students were undergoing higher education, nearly half of them at university or advanced institutes. Such figures put the Soviet Union near the top of the international comparative education table. Moreover, as always, the Soviet Union had at least its fair share of outstanding scientists. Such engineers as Sergei Lebedev, such physicists as Igor Kurchatov and such mathematicians as Ivan Vinogradov, to name just a few, achieved a wide international reputation. Historians such as P. A. Zaionchkovskii and B. F. Porshnev impressed their foreign colleagues, while Pokrovsky was to some extent rehabilitated. An eight-volume edition of the works of Kliuchevskii including his *Course of Russian History* was published between 1956 and 1959. But the difficulties experienced by the editorial board of the periodical *Problems of History* during the mid-1950s were just one example of the limited nature of the 'thaw' in the intellectual world.

The Thaw was the title of a novel by Ilya Erenburg, the first part of which was published in 1954, and gained for its author a reprimand from the Writers' Union. The Twentieth Party Congress rehabilitated some writers and subjected others to attack, Mikhail Sholokhov declaring that 'the last twenty years had produced no more than a handful of good books'. In the eight years after the Congress, that handful hardly increased to a huge pile, partly because the 'thaw' was so limited and partly because there was not a large number of talented writers around. From the point of view of the Western reader, appreciation of Soviet literature was restricted by the circumstances that both prose and poetry were examined more for their political message than for their artistic value. Thus it was that good poets such as Evgenii Evtushenko and Andrei Voznesensky were appreciated outside the U.S.S.R. more for their daring them their muse, and prose writers such as Konstantin Paustovskii and Vladimir Soloukhin were little known abroad while the most internationally famous works of the period included Vladimir Dudintsev's *Not By Bread Alone* (1956), Boris Pasternak's *Doctor Zhivago* (1957) and Alexander Solzhenitsyn's *One Day in the Life of Ivan Denisovich* (1962). The first of these was noted for its attacks on the bureaucracy and the somewhat woolly-minded idealism of its hero, the inventor Lopatkin. *Doctor Zhivago*, which needs no introduction, was published in the West, not the Soviet Union, and helped to gain for its author the Nobel Prize, a distinction which not every Western critic believes to have been deserved by literary merit alone.[21] An interesting point about *One Day*, which also needs no introduction, is that Khrushchev himself gave its publication his support. Soon afterwards, the Chairman appears to have realised that he had gone too far in relaxing controls and made his celebrated remark at a Moscow Art Exhibition about certain modernistic paintings that a donkey could do better with its tail.

Even this would have been a welcome change to most of the 'official' art and architecture produced at the time. Radio and television, the cinema, theatre and ballet all achieved at least some worthwhile productions, however, and Soviet performers impressed foreign audiences throughout the world. In this respect as in others, the Soviet Union was moving out from the Eurasian heartland into all quarters of the globe.

Tremendous progress had been made by 1964. The Soviet Union was now the only state which could claim along with the United States to be a superpower. Soviet rockets could not only move out into space but also deliver nuclear bombs throughout the earth in sufficient numbers to destroy mankind. However, in other respects, economic as well as cultural, Soviet qualifications for superpower were more than a little suspect. As the process of globalisation intensified, shortcomings would be more clearly revealed.

15 Stability and Relaxation, 1964–1975

After the removal from power of Khrushchev in October 1964, two new leaders emerged in the ample shape of L. I. Brezhnev and the more slender figure of A. N. Kosygin. Their order of precedence turned out to be more than alphabetical (unlike the earlier B. and K.), and a new if at first minor 'cult of personality' was erected around the substantial figure of Mr Brezhnev. Having occurred once as tragedy with Stalin and once as farce with Khrushchev, the 'cult of personality' now appeared to be making a bid to become a long-running serial. Was the need for an outstanding individual so deeply embedded in the political culture of the Russian and other Soviet peoples that such a role was now thrust upon Mr Brezhnev whether he liked it or not?

As he became accustomed to the part, there were many indications that he did indeed like it. At the beginning, however, he could be placed in the category of skilful but not very colourful bureaucrats, a man with a 'grey flannel face', to use a label applied at the time to such a person in the Western world. Possibly there was a wider trend towards 'managerial' government enveloping the Soviet Union too. But there were also internal reasons for such an appearance. In the first place, Brezhnev and Co. no doubt wanted to exhibit behaviour in contrast to the unpredictable antics of Khrushchev. Secondly, and more profoundly, they were playing the parts for which much of their careers had prepared many party activists of their generation.

Khrushchev had been born in 1894, the year in which Nicholas II ascended the throne. Leonid Ilich Brezhnev followed him into the tsarist world just after the throne had been threatened by revolution, in 1906. The village of Kamenskoe in the province of Ekaterinoslav, Little Russia, where he first saw the light of day, was to become the town of Dneprodzerzhinsk in the Dnepropetrovsk *oblast* of the Ukrainian Soviet Socialist Republic. The young Brezhnev could not have been actively involved in the initial stage of that transformation, the Russian Revolution of 1917 and Civil War, even though he must have been exposed to the attendant dislocation and discomfort during adolescence. His advanced education in Kursk was technical, with emphasis on the surveying and reclamation of land, and he found appropriate, varied employment after graduation in 1927. But an alternative career had already been indicated by his entry into the Young Communist League, or Komsomol, in 1923, and he held several party posts before returning to his birthplace as chairman of a trade union committee involved in the completion of the Dneprostroi hydroelectric scheme.

The transformation of the First-Year Plan was well under way, and although many succumbed, others prospered, including the energetic activist Brezhnev, who became a full member of the C.P.S.U. in 1931, a year after his return to Dneprodzerzhinsk. Throughout the 1930s, he studied engineering and did military service at the same time as continuing political work which culminated in his appointment as First Secretary of the Dnepropetrovsk *oblast* Party Committee in 1939. He now became a client of the Ukrainian First Secretary, N. S. Khrushchev, co-operating with him in the local purges.

During the war, Brezhnev performed meritorious party services, and he contributed to the 'cleaning-up' and reconstruction which took place after 1945. Further advancement led by 1950 to his appointment as First Secretary of the C.P. in Moldavia, a republic recently retaken from Romania. Here too, building was accompanied by purges. Still under the patronage of Khrushchev, Brezhnev became a candidate member of the Presidium of the Central Committee of the C.P.S.U. in 1952 at the Nineteenth Congress. Then, with the rise of Khrushchev after the death of Stalin, Brezhnev was given a series of important military and civilian appointments such as head of the political department of the Soviet armed forces and director of the 'virgin lands' scheme in Kazakhstan. In 1957, he became full member of the Party Presidium, in 1960 its chairman. From 1962, he was also chairman of a committee drafting a new constitution, and was also by now senior manager of Soviet heavy industry, with responsibilities for the equipment of the armed forces and of the space programme. Widely tipped as the heir apparent to Khrushchev, he was called upon, in October 1964, to bite the hand that had fed him. Married with a daughter, Brezhnev was also in a position to extend the influence of his political 'family' from Dnepropetrovsk and at large. The former client had now became the leading patron.[1]

Political

Brezhnev worked hard to maintain his reputation as a guardian of the interests of its members. On the very day of Khrushchev's removal, the

Central Committee decided to separate its first secretaryship from the chairmanship of the Council of Ministers so that one person could not gather 'excessive power'. In 1965, the Committee of Party-State Control set up by Khrushchev was replaced by a Committee of People's Control, which omitted the Party from its scrutiny. Although, like its predecessor, it was to be set up at all administrative levels, it did not achieve as widespread an influence as its structure might suggest. And, at the Twenty-Third Party Congress in 1966, another Khrushchevian innovation, a compulsory percentage turnover in C.P.S.U. committee membership varying from a quarter to as much as a half, was dropped.[2] Moreover, Brezhnev re-assumed the title of general rather than first secretary, and the Party Presidium became again the Politburo.

By this time he himself was sixty years old, but more than half the total membership of the C.P.S.U. was under forty. In 1973, out of a total membership of nearly 15 millions (14,821,031), almost three quarters (10,853,904) were under fifty.[3] The generation strain between those who had come to political consciousness during World War Two and after on the one hand and those who remembered the first Five-Year Plans on the other must have been considerable, but Leonid Ilich managed to keep the extended 'family' together in his increasingly avuncular manner. As with the C.P.S.U., so with the Soviets and the Ministries, the aim appears to have been stability. By the early 1970s, the 'family' numbered about 750,000 persons, nearly 3 million if their wives and actual families are included. These were the people on the *nomenklatura*, or list of top jobs from the general secretary himself down to secretary of local party organisation or village Soviet.[4] Most of them appear to have believed that the best way to keep the boat on an even keel was to avoid rocking it. In other words, while paying lip service to slogans involving greater effort and self-sacrifice, they worked mostly to preserve their positions of privilege. These, then, were the members of the 'new class' or bureaucratic stratum identified by Milovan Djilas and well described by Alec Nove.[5]

The *nomenklatura* stretched out into all fifteen Soviet republics, thus making a major contribution to the Union's cohesion. Nevertheless, stability in these republics was far from complete. For example, in the mid-1960s, there was a campaign against nationalism in the Ukraine. Fears of its resurgence led to the decision to invade Czechoslovakia in 1968. Lithuania, especially its Roman Catholicism, was another source of local protest and central concern. There were signs of nationalism in Transcaucasia and resentment against Russian dominance in Central Asia. While a government decision of 1967 to rehabilitate peoples deported during the Second World War brought relief to most of those concerned, partial exceptions were made for Georgian Muslims, Crimean Tatars and Volga Germans.[6]

Stability appears to have been one of the main aims in foreign policy, too. With the fall of Khrushchev, the new collective leadership denounced 'hare-brained schemes' and adopted the steadier approach of the tortoise. At first, a lower priority was placed on 'peaceful coexistence', at least partly to demonstrate that the government was not going soft on capitalism. There was an attempt to decrease the speed of *rapprochement* with the Federal Republic of Germany and of the rupture with the People's Republic of China. For this reason among others, emphasis was placed on closing the missile gap through increased production of I.C.B.M.s (intercontinental ballistic missiles). This aim was achieved by 1969, according to many Western analysts, although some were sceptical about quality equalling quantity. While the Soviet preponderance of conventional forces in Europe was increased, and their strong presence in the Far East was maintained, the Red Navy established constant patrols in the Indian Ocean by the late 1960s. In the early 1970s, the first Soviet aircraft carrier was commissioned, while the airforce in general was not neglected. The superpower asserted by Khrushchev was becoming more of a reality under Brezhnev.[7]

Like its counterpart in the West, however, Soviet strategic wisdom was to maintain a high level of armament while being prepared to talk of arms control. The new leadership did not seek intensification of the Cold War. Indeed, after a suitable pause, it took up again the path of negotiation with the rival superpower, the U.S.A. At the same time, of course, it strove for order and progress in the socialist camp, including some accommodation of China, and hoped that its influence would spread into the developing countries. For this reason, national liberation movements would be supported outside the camp (while any similar tendencies within it would be summarily squashed). The ultimate aim of world Communism was still firmly held, but probably more as a basis for ideological cohesion within the camp than as an item on the immediate agenda for policy beyond it. For the Soviet government, then, 'détente' meant a relaxation of tension while adhering to its basic set of values and purposes. In this respect again, it was not so very different from its Western rival, which sometimes went so far as to assert that 'détente' would only become meaningful when the Soviet government gave up its own ideology and adopted the West's.[8]

The most significant relationship was probably with the rival superpower, the U.S.A. In spite of many differences over events in Europe,

Asia and elsewhere, there was some progress made throughout the 1960s towards a better understanding. By the end of the decade, there was some movement forward from the 'Hot Line' Agreement and Partial Test Ban Treaty achieved in 1963 after the Cuban missile crisis. Economic collaboration was added to the items in the relationship, and was given considerable emphasis at the Twenty-Fourth Party Congress in 1971. And a high point was reached with the visit to Moscow in May 1972 of President Nixon. The American and Soviet leaders signed some Basic Principles of Mutual Relations concerning prevention of war, limitation of arms – notably S.A.L.T. I (Strategic Arms Limitation Agreement I) and extension of economic and cultural contacts. They also signed an A.B.M. (antiballistic missile) Treaty, an Interim Agreement on Offensive Missiles and a number of other encouraging documents. Further summits followed with President Nixon and then with President Ford, but, unfortunately, they promised more than they delivered. Stumbling blocks included the vexed question of the emigration of Soviet Jews and the extension of human rights to all the citizens of the U.S.S.R. As we shall see, Soviet–U.S. relations took a turn for the worse from 1975.[9]

The bipolar U.S.S.R.–U.S.A. confrontation was affected deeply by developments in the triangular relationship between the U.S.S.R., the U.S.A. and the People's Republic of China. The split between the two leading Communist powers was intensified by disagreements over the attitude and action to be taken on the escalating war in Vietnam and the Indo-Pakistan War of 1965, while the Chinese Cultural Revolution that began in 1965 led to denunciation of the U.S.S.R.'s conduct as 'social imperialism'. Heated words almost led to open conflict in March 1969, when about thirty Soviet border guards and an unknown number of their Chinese adversaries were killed along the disputed frontier of the Ussuri River. A visit from Kosygin to Beijing (Peking) in September helped to smooth the troubled waters, but suspicions remained. Two superpowers had been something like company: three would be a crowd.

In June 1969, the Soviet government made an effort to re-establish its global influence in the Conference of Communist and Workers' Parties meeting in Moscow. But Soviet proposals for peace and collective security were hampered by the absence of delegates not only from China, but also from North Korea, North Vietnam, Yugoslavia and Albania. An observer only came from Cuba, which continued to be a drain on Soviet diplomatic patience as well as economic resources. Elsewhere in the Third World, the U.S.S.R. had given a large amount of support to Egypt up to the Six-Day War with Israel of June 1967 and beyond. But the Egyptian expulsion of Soviet military advisers in 1972 was a considerable reversal for Soviet policies in the Middle East. In the same year in the Far East, the U.S. President Nixon's visit to Beijing was watched with alarm by the Soviet ambassador, who had arrived there in 1970 as a consequence of Kosygin's mollifying visit in 1969.

While the Middle and Far East were areas of great concern to the Soviet Union, it still gave top priority to Eastern Europe, where, as in other parts of the world, by no means all was going the Soviet way. From 1965, Romania under Ceausescu developed an independent line in foreign policy. Much more threatening to the Soviet Politburo was the Prague Spring of 1968, when a new Czechoslovak government led by the Slovak Anton Dubček appeared to be undermining the control of the Communist Party by lifting the censorship and paying too much attention to the rights of national minorities. Fearing a 'domino' effect throughout Eastern Europe, the Soviet government made several attempts to dissuade Dubček and his associates from their bold new initiatives, and then sent in Warsaw Pact forces in August 1968. There were few casualties (and probably more among the invaders than the invaded) but much outrage throughout Europe and beyond. There was more trouble in Poland in 1970, where the direction of subsequent reform was closely monitored. In *Pravda* on 25 September 1968 was published the announcement of what came to be known as the 'Brezhnev Doctrine', the assertion that the socialist states would intervene in the internal affairs of any of their number which exposed the rest of the collective to the danger of anti-socialist activity.

The assertion of the 'Brezhnev Doctrine' did little to reduce Western European fears of further Soviet encroachment. Soviet attempts to allay such fears and to promote a European conference on security broke down amid the events of 1968 not only in Czechoslovakia but also in the states of Western Europe, which nearly all experienced student demonstrations and industrial unrest. Nevertheless, the arrival of the S.P.D. (Social Democrats) as the government of the Federal Republic of Germany with a fresh policy of *Ostpolitik* towards the German Democratic Republic led to some relaxation of the tension in 1969. The emergence in Western Europe of a more flexible 'Eurocommunism', after 1968, also gave some hope to Brezhnev and his associates that relations between the two halves of the continent might be improved. Ensuing treaties in 1970 recognised formally the existence of the two German states, and various agreements on trade and technology paved the way for the opening in 1973 of the Conference on Security and Co-operation in Europe (C.S.C.E.) and the commencement of negotiations on mutual balanced force reductions (M.B.F.R.) in Europe. And so, by the mid-1970s, the prospect of war had receded from Europe, even if it was to be found too frequent and wide-spread in other continents.[10]

Economic

Under its new management, U.S.S.R. Incorporated's slogan could be interpreted as 'business as was usual'. However, it is always difficult to turn the historical clock back, especially in a rapidly changing world, and Brezhnev and Kosygin soon found it necessary to attempt change and adjustment, if at nothing like the hectic pace introduced by Khrushchev.

For agriculture, Brezhnev announced guidelines in March 1965: no more reorganisation, except the restoration of the previous state and party apparatus; no more grandiose 'campaigns' in the 'virgin lands' or anywhere else; no more pressure on private livestock; and more money through higher subsidies, incomes and investments. By 1975, agriculture was receiving more than a quarter of total Soviet investments, a staggering amount when higher prices and costs are taken into consideration. Large sums were spent on the production of chemical fertiliser in particular. Production certainly rose to a considerable extent, but problems of organisation and distribution, machinery and personnel, fodder and even fertiliser, all persisted, and considerable amounts of the basic commodity, grain, continued to be imported. The blame for shortcomings was placed on the collective farm (*kolkhoz*) in particular; there had been in any case a tendency to replace it by the state farm (*sovkhoz*), so that by the mid-1970s, the *kolkhoz* accounted for less than a quarter of all cultivated land. A number of experimental mini-projects were launched. But critics continued to argue that there could not be substantial progress until there was a more thorough overhaul of the whole system, with more incentives for the individual worker or team of workers, and more toleration, even encouragement, for the private plot.[11]

Many would say the same about the organisation of industry, where there was a similar attempt to achieve fresh aims with unchanged methods. There was – especially from Kosygin late in 1965 – much talk of incentives, profits and other 'economic levers', but there was later a reversion to the previous arrangements, from ministry via specialised administration to individual enterprise. The middle tier was officially abolished in 1973, but retained an existence in actuality.

As in other countries, there was a call for industry to adapt itself to what the British Prime Minister Harold Wilson called the 'white heat of technology'. There was a tacit abandonment of Khruschev's call for Communism within a generation, and some further attempts to adapt

Marxist theory (e.g. the labour theory of value) to the demands of the new age. Therefore, the amount of machinery imported from the West, helped by a rise in the price of gold and oil which were the major exports, rose considerably in the early 1970s. But closer contact between East and West beyond long-term credits would be necessary for technology transfer to be a complete success. Such contact could also lead to lower expenditure on the armed forces.

The Eighth Five-Year Plan (1965–70) called for ambitious, but not extravagant, targets to be met, with a higher relative emphasis on consumer goods. As always, official results probably contained elements of optimism and even exaggeration. Oil output rose above expectation, much of it flowing from new wells in remote parts of Siberia, but electricity, gas and coal fell short of projected figures. So did fertilizer, cement, motor vehicle and tractor production, as well as steel and, indeed, most items apart from footwear. 620 million pairs were called for and 676 million were deemed to have been made. Since it was easier to fulfill the plan with lower amounts of leather if smaller sizes were manufactured, it is possible that the needs of Soviet citizens with larger feet were relatively more difficult to meet!

The Ninth Five-Year Plan (1971–5) maintained approximately the same overall target as its predecessor – just a few points below 50 per cent, with consumer goods now overtaking producer goods. Oil now joined gas and electricity in shortfall, although coal overfulfilled the set figures. Every other major item, including footwear, fell short of plan, except for fertiliser, the recipient of a disproportionate amount of investment. In general, the sums poured into agriculture and the armed forces made it difficult for other totals to be met. This is not to say that a peasant serviceman would feel himself especially privileged.

The degree of overall economic prosperity has been difficult to measure, especially in any comparative manner, owing to the non-convertibility of the rouble and fundamental differences between the Soviet socialist and Western capitalist systems. If an average Soviet salary in 1973 was less than half its French counterpart and little more than a quarter of the American, this disparity would have to be balanced against the respective expectations. The queues for consumer goods and even for basic foodstuffs found widely throughout the Soviet Union would have been intolerable in France and the U.S.A. Equally, Soviet citizens would have not easily accepted European and transatlantic concepts of self-reliance including the threat of unemployment. The Soviet tempo of labour was slower than in the West, in spite of all the government's encouragement to increase it (partly as a consequence, industrial productivity was about a half, agricultural about a quarter, of their American equivalents). But the most idle American worker, even the most desperate American searcher after work, would have found it difficult to accept the conditions in Soviet factory and farm.[12]

Many of these differences would have to be explained, like nearly everything else, in a long historical perspective stretching back way beyond 1917. So would the persistence of a second, unofficial economy accompanying the official first, a phenomenon already existing in the early nineteenth century (see p. 141 above). *Blat*, an impossible word to translate – roughly speaking, it means 'undercover influence', was so much ingrained into Soviet culture that it was continually satirised in the public media. A good example was provided by the comedian Arkadii Raikin in a sketch about a citizen whose simple desire for a theatre ticket leads to the construction of a long chain of obligations and favours involving goods, services and jobs. In a more similar manner, networks of patronage involving the misappropriation of vast amounts of money coexisted with the apparatus of government and even threatened to replace it. Altogether, bribery and corruption were probably the greatest growth industries.

As far as population growth was concerned, there were three significant trends: the rate of growth was in decline; the move to the city on the rise; and the proportion in the Slavic core to the peripheral nationalities changing in favour of the latter. From 1964 to 1974, the total population rose from 226.7 to 250.9 millions. The steepest rises were in Central Asia and Transcaucasia. In the Volga–Viatka and Central Black-Earth regions, on the other hand, the population actually fell. Similarly, in the same period, the rural population fell from 109.0 to 101.3 millions. The move to the city with an attendant housing shortage was one of the reasons for the fall in the birth rate. Another was more female employment. A third was the attainment of higher educational levels. In other words, the movements in population statistics were brought about by cultural as well as economic considerations.[13]

Cultural

Picking its way between traditional impulses and official directions, the Soviet government worked towards flexibility in the cultural sphere. This meant, to take religion first, applying the brake to militant atheism. In 1965, indeed, there was a fairly open debate on the most appropriate policy to be adopted, one atheistic lecturer going so far as to assert:

Insults, violence and the forcible closing down of churches not only fail to reduce the number of believers, but they actually tend to increase their number, to make clandestine religious groups more widespread, and to antagonise believers against the state.[14]

While church closure and wholesale imprisonment now ceased, laws passed in 1966 indicated that the way forward for believers would not be easy. Generally speaking, congregations could meet if they were registered with the state, but they could not proselytise or publish, and these kinds of activity were given a broad interpretation. A subsequent law on marriage and the family introduced in 1968 obliged parents to bring their children up 'in the spirit of the moral code of the builder of communism'.[15] Along with such restrictions on the flocks, the government also attempted to find compliant shepherds, to give the leaders of the various churches at least a little room for manoeuvre in return for strict political loyalty.

Such prescriptions were most easily followed by the Orthodox Church, which had a long history of close association with the state. They were most difficult for the Roman Catholics in Lithuania, impossible for the Uniates of the Ukraine who were not legally recognised. Baptists, Evangelicals and Pentecostals sometimes found it difficult to achieve registration, and often encountered harassment. More than thirty million Muslims were now to be found in the Soviet Union, and their adherence to patriarchal society and other traditional practices made it difficult to make of them Soviet men, let alone Soviet women. Buddhists, among the Buriats and other Far Eastern peoples, were subject to a greater measure of persecution, partly because of their small number, partly because of their proximity to China. Jews attracted less attention for their desire to practise their religion within the Soviet Union than for their desire to leave it. The number of synagogues was probably about sixty, but their rabbis were for the most part not taken seriously as spiritual leaders among the international Jewish community.[16]

If stability in religious policy required a relaxation of the screw, in literary policy it seemed to the government to require tightening. Limits were set by the trial of two writers, Andrei Sinyavsky and Yulii Daniel, early in 1966. The charge against them, the dissemination of anti-Soviet propaganda and slander, was based on their publication in the West of satirical short stories. The inevitable verdict of guilty led to sentences of seven and five years respectively in labour camps, but also to some official protest from their fellow writers and unofficial comment in an expanding *samizdat* (literally self-publication; that is, carbon-copied typescripts). From 1968 onwards, a 'Chronicle of Current Events' attempted to record infringements of human rights, and there was also an insistence on the implementation of the less illiberal aspects of 'Soviet socialist legality'. For its part, along with continued repression, the government adopted a new stratagem – enforced emigration – applied most notably to the poet Iosif Brodsky in 1972, and the novelist Alexander Solzhenistyn in 1974.[17] The latter in particular was greeted in the West as a great prophet, at least until he began to predict the downfall of the West and the supremacy of the Russian national spirit.

In spite of restrictions and difficulties, worthwhile literature was still produced in the U.S.S.R., notably among the *derevenshchiki* (villagers), writing about traditional life and its passing in the provinces – Rasputin, Shukshin, Soloukhin and others.[18] The most popular writers of the period in polls conducted by Soviet periodicals included Paustovsky, Solzhenitsyn, Simonov, Aksenov and Sholokhov. The publication of the works of Kliuchevskii continued throughout the Brezhnev period, although living historians were still subject to ideological restraint.[19] Meanwhile, the best known poets such as Evtushenko, Rozhdestvenskii and Voznesenskii continued to excite adulation and execration, with crowds at their public performances sometimes reaching the emotional levels of those at football matches. On the whole, those writers were most successful who could give the most imaginative treatment to the officially encouraged themes of Soviet patriotism, socialist realism and internationalism, or who even managed to evade them. The 'guitar poets', Okudzhava, Vysotsky and Galich, were wildly popular in public performances, which amateur recordings preserved in *magnitizdat* (tape-recorded copies) when, as was usual, state recordings were not made.[20] Sport and the cinema remained among the most important leisure activities (if drinking and sinking into lethargy are to be excluded). The cinema was a place to keep warm and to meet friends in the winter, and remained popular as somewhere to go in the summer. However, most films were not very remarkable, light romances, heavy epics and so on, while the film-makers' film-maker Andrei Tarkovsky was probably a minority taste. By 1973, television was well on the rise towards saturation level, 70 per cent of the population regularly watching an average hour and a half a day, with rural figures far exceeding those for the city.[21]

The reading public grew along with the numbers of those undergoing a higher level of education. Khruschev's emphasis on the polytechnical was reduced by the new government. In 1965, there was a return to the competitive selection system, with a quota for each category. The percentage of *proizvodstvenniki* (students with productive experience) declined steeply, and access to higher education became that much easier for the children of the intelligentsia. Indicative figures in thousands were as follows:

	secondary 7–8 years	10–11 years	tertiary full-time	part-time
1960	2383	1055	257.9	333.4
1970	4661	2591	500	411.0

For some observers, it was these higher numbers of those undergoing secondary and tertiary education that were to bear the most significant implications for the nature of future Soviet society.[22]

Primary school dropout or university graduate, the Soviet citizen did not find it easy to survive. Figures for infant mortality were higher, for life expectancy lower, than in most parts of the Western world. Spiritual uplift was more often gained from religion or vodka than from the exhortations of the Party. How many listeners were fully convinced by Brezhnev's assertion at the Twenty-Fourth Party Congress in 1971 that 'total victory for the socialist cause in the entire world is inevitable. And we will not spare efforts to achieve that triumph'?[23] For every explicit dissident, there were probably dozens of implicit opponents of the government, perhaps even a silent majority. The stability which had been welcome in 1964 was turning to stagnation by 1975, and the overthrow of the 'cult of personality' of Nikita Sergeevich Khruschev was now being followed by the full erection of another around Leonid Ilich Brezhnev.

16 Stagnation and Tension, 1975–1985

In January 1975, the U.S. Senate made specific Soviet concessions on emigration a condition of acceptance for the U.S. – Soviet Trade Bill. As a consequence, the Soviet government abandoned the Trade Agreement of 1972, and détente started to slip away. There was no clean break, however, or immediate dramatic shift in policy.

The Soviet leadership continued for the next decade to present as resolute a stance as possible in difficult, somewhat extraordinary circumstances. Brezhnev himself appeared to be going from strength to strength. In 1976, his position was consolidated at the Twenty-Fifth Party Congress in February, and he became a Marshal of the Soviet Union in May. In December, his seventieth birthday was the occasion of widespread and fulsome panegyrics. Yet in that very year, according to some observers, he suffered a stroke which actually 'killed' him for several minutes, and he had to be restored to life. Now, the cult of personality threatened to be replaced by the cult of the living dead, and the cosmetic resources of the Soviet government almost needed to be replaced by the taxidermic. The government in fact was carried on behind the scenes by members of the Politburo, while Brezhnev made occasional public appearances as a figurehead, and continued to accumulate powerful positions. For example, in 1977, he became Commander-in-Chief of the armed forces and Chairman of a new Committee on State Defence, as well as of the Presidium of the Supreme Soviet of the U.S.S.R. As Marshal of the Soviet Union, he wore sixty decorations on his dress uniform. He produced books and records of his speeches in large editions, although sales were in fact less than brisk.[1]

The early 1980s presented an odd spectacle of an ageing Soviet leadership coming to the end of its tenure of office only with the loss of its tenure on life itself. In 1980, Kosygin died less than two months after taking retirement for ill-health. At the beginning of 1982, M. A. Suslov, the party ideologue, also died. Brezhnev himself had another stroke just before making a formal T.V. appearance, and, when sufficiently revived to make another, read several minutes from the wrong speech. In November 1982, he departed definitively, and made a last, posthumous appearance on T.V. in a bizarre funeral given wide international coverage. His successor, Iurii Vladimirovich Andropov, was already a sick man, but made a powerful enough impression while supported by renal dialysis throughout 1983. He died in February 1984, to be followed by yet another invalid, Konstantin Ustinovich Chernenko, who also succumbed in little more than a year. In March 1985, a younger, fitter General Secretary was at last elected in the energetic shape of Mikhail Sergeevich Gorbachev, while the last surviving leading member of the gerontocracy, A. A. Gromyko, became President.

More of Gorbachev later. As for Andropov and Chernenko, although there was much discussion of them at the time, especially of Andropov, there seems to be less of a case now for discussing them and their policies in detail. Andropov's career had been spent largely in the K.G.B., but he was also ambassador to Hungary during the time of the uprising of 1956. Nevertheless, he was able to establish something of a reputation as a liberal, although puritan, intellectual. Chernenko, a party man from start to finish above all, had been Brezhnev's right-hand man from 1950, and came over as little more than a colourless functionary.[2] In general, the years 1975–85 appeared to show that the Soviet régime could survive without strong leadership. Yet all kinds of difficulties and weaknesses were revealed, and at least some of the ways of improving the situation were already apparent, before the arrival of Mr Gorbachev.

Political

The C.P.S.U. continued to form the principal link between leadership and people, but what had on earlier occasions been an accelerator of progress now acted more like a brake. Stability was becoming stagnation.

The number of party members rose from 14.4 millions in 1971 to 15.6 in 1976 and 17.4 in 1981. This meant the maintenance of approximately a 9.5 per cent representation of all adults in a growing population. The percentage of members and candidates under fifty years of age fell somewhat from nearly three-quarters (73.3 per cent) in 1973 to just over two-thirds (66.9 per cent) in 1981, while during the same period the percentage which had completed higher education rose from 21.7 to 28.0. The proportion of women in these figures rose slightly, of representatives from the non-Russian nationalities rather more.[3]

The aged top leadership showed a palpable tendency towards collectivity through fairly frequent meetings of the Politburo and Secretariat of the

Central Committee. Frequency in this case did not necessarily mean vitality, however, and the output of significant decisions was not impressive. The Twenty-Fifth Party Congress in 1976 and the Twenty-Sixth in 1981 heard bold claims regarding the nature of 'developed or mature socialism', with continuing emphasis on the leading role of the C.P.S.U. Brezhnev declared in 1976: 'Only the party, armed with Marxist–Leninist doctrine and the experience of political organisation of the masses, is capable of determining the main lines of social development.' For some outsiders, these main lines would include a one-track concentration on the privileges as well as the power of those included in the *nomenklatura* lists of the most-favoured positions in Soviet society.[4]

The adoption of a new Constitution in 1977 after fifteen years of preparation did not bring much political or social progress, but it merits at least a summary description. The preamble declared that the Revolution of 1917 had created a new kind of state, and that humanity had therefore begun 'the epoch-making turn from capitalism to socialism'. By 1977, there was in existence:

> a society of mature socialist social relations, in which, on the basis of the drawing together of all classes and social strata and of the juridical and factual equality of all its nations and nationalities and their fraternal co-operation, a new historical community of people has been formed – the Soviet people.

A number of rights – for example, to health protection, old age maintenance, housing, cultural benefits – were guaranteed, but Article 39 pointed out that: 'Enjoyment by citizens of their rights and freedoms must not be to the detriment of the interests of society or the state, or infringe the rights of other citizens.' Similarly, Article 60 indicated that:

> It is the duty of, and a matter of honour for, every able-bodied citizen of the USSR to work conscientiously in his chosen, socially useful occupation, and strictly to observe labour discipline. Evasion of socially useful work is incompatible with the principles of socialist society.

And while education was universal, Article 25 made clear that: 'In the Soviet Union, there is a single educational system, which serves Communist education.'

The U.S.S.R. was defined as 'an integral, federal, multinational state' composed of fifteen Republics, each of which 'shall retain the right freely to secede from the USSR'. All power belonged to the people, and Article

6 pointed out that, 'the leading and guiding force of Soviet society and the nucleus of its political system' remained the Communist Party of the Soviet Union, which 'exists for the people and serves the people'.[5] For some analysts, the people in the C.P.S.U. itself were served better than others. Scepticism about the Constitution was probably widespread, not only in the Russian Republic but also in its fourteen partners, where there were many citizens who would have liked to assert freely their right to secede from the U.S.S.R. Of growing concern to the Party leadership was the possibility of a rise of Muslim fundamentalism in the Central Asian republics, reinforced by a population growth throughout the 1970s of between a quarter and a third.[6]

Beyond the Soviet frontiers, the important superpower relationship, already in decline from about 1975 onwards, deteriorated further two years later when President Carter committed the U.S.A. to a harder line on foreign policy, with more emphasis on human rights. An American proposal in 1977 for strategic arms reduction was rejected as disadvantageous to the U.S.S.R. and departing from previous agreements. The road to S.A.L.T. II was long and arduous, and when the Treaty was signed in the summer of 1979 at a Carter–Brezhnev summit in Vienna, the U.S. Senate would not ratify it. The invasion of Afghanistan in December 1979 and the threat of invasion of Poland, in December 1980 and March 1981 respectively, set the scene for an even harder line from President Reagan in 1981 and after. Relaxation had given way to tension.

The superpower relationship was affected by developments in all corners of the world. Europe, still the most important region for the inhabitants of that continent, was no longer quite as crucial, and to some extent, benefitted from its comparative demotion. The Helsinki Final Act of 1975 set the seal on existing frontiers, and thus removed a principal source of previous tension. However, two later meetings in Belgrade (1977–8) and Madrid (1980–1) did little to advance European harmony as arguments broke out concerning inadequacies in cultural contacts and observation of human rights.[7] As the 1980s unfolded, tension was revealed not only between the Soviet Union and its East European clients, but also between the U.S.A. and its junior partners in Western Europe. Later, the Reagan administration attempted to limit co-operation on the construction of a natural gas pipeline from the U.S.S.R. to West Germany. There was some apprehension that a wedge would be driven between Western Europe and the U.S.A., and that the influence of the U.S.S.R. would spread in an extension of 'Finlandisation' reducing the sovereignty of European states. But continued tensions in Poland and elsewhere reduced such a possibility to a minimum.[8]

As far as Asia was concerned, the U.S. *rapprochement* with China continued to disconcert the Soviet Union, which made some effort to restore harmony in the Communist camp. But the People's Republic of China was set on modernisation, for which purpose relations with the leading capitalist powers were more important than ideological purity. And so in 1978, it finalised a Treaty of Peace and Friendship with the other Far Eastern great power – Japan. Soviet attempts to obstruct this move through a treaty on 'Good Neighbourly Relations and Co-operation with Japan' failed because the Japanese continued to believe that Soviet armed forces should leave the four Kurile Islands that they had occupied in 1945 while they were not yet convinced that adequate returns would accrue from any participation in the development of Siberia.[9]

The Soviet difficulty was not eased by problems in South-East Asia, where in 1978, Vietnam which was aligned with the U.S.S.R. invaded Kampuchea (Cambodia) which was a client of China. Early in 1979, China launched a brief punitive invasion of Vietnam, but nevertheless, under Vietnamese occupation, Kampuchea came over for the time being to the Soviet side. In the southern subcontinent. India was associated with the Soviet Union while Pakistan was close to the U.S.A. and China. This alignment, along with repercussions from other parts of Asia, no doubt contributed to the decision of Brezhnev and his associates to launch an invasion of Afghanistan in December 1979. Anxiety about Muslim fundamentalist or other infiltration across frontiers combined with concern about the régime in Afghanistan itself to bring about the fateful step.[10] In retrospect, a Soviet ambition to use Afghanistan as a stepping stone towards the Persian Gulf appears unlikely, although the U.S.S.R. certainly continued its traditional interests in the Middle East region.

Africa was of more recent importance, both as a continent of interest to the Soviet Union and as a source of tension between the U.S.S.R. and the U.S.A. In 1975, Soviet material and Cuban military assistance was vital for the victory in Angola of the M.P.L.A. over rivals supported by the U.S.A., China and South Africa. In 1977, the same Soviet–Cuban combination helped the Ethiopian government to defeat Somalia (which had moved away from earlier Soviet patronage) and to suppress revolt in Eritrea. Here too, there were suspicions of Soviet expansionist aims, as there were indeed also in Latin America, through the exploitation of insurgent forces in El Salvador and elsewhere, and of the Sandanista government in Nicaragua. Even the Arctic and Antarctic regions were not free from superpower rivalry.[11]

In October 1979, a Soviet spokesman divided the world into four zones consisting of: 'developed socialism' – the U.S.S.R. itself; 'fraternal countries' – in Eastern Europe and beyond; 'progressive regimes' such as

Nicaragua; and the capitalist camp. In 1978, Afghanistan was deemed to have entered the third zone with the coming to power of the local Communist Party. The Soviet invasion in December 1979 was aimed at maintaining Afghanistan as a 'progressive regime', and helping it to enter the second zone as a 'fraternal country'.[12] Fear of Chinese or other infiltration contributed to the fateful decision, which also had echoes of the 'great game' of empire of the nineteenth century. Certainly, like the U.S.A. in Vietnam, the U.S.S.R. was to discover that it was easier to begin an intervention than to bring it to a successful conclusion.

Economic

Agriculture continued to be a hardy annual problem. It remained difficult to find a sufficient amount of skilled labour and to provide appropriate incentives, to avoid bureaucratic interference and to provide appropriate fertilisers and machinery, communications and transport, to care for harvested crops, especially fodder grains. As always, the question was posed, what to do with the private plots? A worker could not take great pride or interest in the daily round of activity on a large collective or state farm, especially when rewards were poor, instructions from high had little to do with circumstances in the fields, when tractors lacked spare parts, roads were almost impassable and trucks scarce, when phosphates or fodder were ruined by improper storage or exposure to the elements.

The government allowed a few more decisions to be taken locally, and gave a little more encouragement to the private plot. In 1977, an academic analyst pointed out that 28 per cent of the U.S.S.R.'s gross agricultural output came from *sovkhoz, kolkhoz* and urban private plots, although the plots accounted for about 1 per cent only of the cultivated land total. As a consequence of this and other evidence, a decree was issued in 1978 allowing private plots in rural and urban regions, and encouraging both civilian enterprises and army units to develop auxiliary farming for their own purposes. The government continued to invest an enormous amount of money in agricultural production and food subsidies. But short of a miraculous improvement in the climate, or an almost as unlikely overhaul of the collective and state system, sympathetic critics feared that a marked degree of progress would be elusive. In November 1981, Brezhnev asserted: 'The food problem is on the political as well as the economic plane, the crucial question of the Five-Year Plan'. But could the Eleventh such plan succeed where its ten predecessors had failed? Generally speaking, the Tenth Five-Year Plan (1976–80) had failed to meet targets. In the short run, grain and other foodstuffs were imported, mostly from the

U.S.A., in even greater bulk than before – no less than 25 million metric tons in 1979.[13]

In the industrial sector, too, the Soviet Union relied heavily on foreign collaboration, and there were fears, especially in the U.S.A., that in such a manner capitalist powers were assisting the expansion of the Communist armed forces. Western credits reached large proportions, too, 50 billion dollars by 1978 and rising, with British banks lending the most, followed by their French and German, and then by their U.S. counterparts.

By the end of the 1970s, of course, most of the world's nations, with the prominent exception of Germany and Japan, were debtors, including to an ever more alarming extent, the senior superpower, the U.S.A. Other Soviet indices, including a drop in the annual growth rate of industry during the eighteen years of Brezhnev from more than seven (7.3) to less than 3 (2.8) per cent, would find parallels elsewhere, if not often such steep ones. The most glaring difference between the Soviet economy and those of its fellow superpower and other industrialised powers was its persistent relative backwardness. Even after eleven five-year plans, nearly 40 per cent of all fixed capital and labour resources were devoted to extracting and processing raw materials and fuel, while a similar proportion of Soviet labour remained manual and unmechanised. In 1983, the chairman of the State Committee on Science and Technology confessed that 'quite a few of today's enterprises are in need of radical reconstruction. Transport and communications are lagging behind the growing demands of the economy. Capital construction is also in need of better organization'. In 1982, an article in *Pravda* heavily criticised the rigidity of central planning, and the lack of managerial incentive, initiative and responsibility.

Failing wholesale reform, which would have tampered with the *nomenklatura* and other established arrangements, the Soviet economy could continue its space activities and strengthen its armed forces only by giving them preferential priorities which detracted from other spheres of activity. And joint activities with foreign enterprises remained vital. For example, in the early 1980s, contracts to the value of 16.5 billion dollars were drawn up for a Soviet–West German commission to develop energy resources, while most notably perhaps, an agreement was made with companies of several foreign nationalities for the construction of a gas pipeline from the U.S.S.R. to Western Europe, with an estimated annual profit for the U.S.S.R. of 5–8 billion dollars. Across the Atlantic, the Reagan administration was not best pleased. Was the pipeline driving a wedge between NATO partners?[14]

While it was increasingly apparent that isolation from the world economy would bring further ruin to the Soviet Union, such disaster would not be the exclusive responsibility of the central government and its planning failures. The climate could not be controlled, for example, and the poor harvests of 1972, 1975 and 1979, to take just one decade, were largely the result of plain bad weather. Secondly, both the human and natural resources of the Soviet Union were far from ideally distributed. The highest birth rates were to be found in Central Asia, where a work force was in low demand. Meanwhile, the proletariat of the industrial areas had almost ceased to increase, with a consequent labour shortage, especially of skilled workers, even if there was some overmanning, especially of the unskilled variety. As for natural resources, many of them were to be found in naturally inhospitable areas far to the north of the Trans-Siberian Railway. Even though the vital line of communication and transport was vastly improved by the construction of BAM (the Baikal–Amur *Magistral* or main line), long distances had to be covered by many commodities in order to reach it. Natural gas, ever more important as a source of energy, was on the whole less accessible than oil. Furthermore, although this point is elusive, the whole traditional culture of the Soviet Union, stretching far back into tsarist times, was not easily compatible with the 'mature or developed socialism' that was deemed to have arrived by Brezhnev and his associates. Such a declaration was in fact almost as utopian as the predictions of the imminence of Communism by Khrushchev. Attitudes to work, and the place that it occupied in life in general, were not conducive to the adaptation of the command economy to the demands of the last decades of the twentieth century. Nor were bribery and corruption.

Old attitudes were one thing, new incentives could be another, and it might have been possible to make upwardly mobile consumers of the Soviet peoples if the appropriate rewards could accrue to individual enterprise. But as the whip became less appropriate, it was difficult to supply the carrot. In most lists of priorities, top place was taken by separate accommodation with creature comforts, that is a flat or apartment with bathroom and heating. The official target in the late Brezhnev years was 15–20 square metres of living space per person by the year 2000. This would fall somewhat short of the amounts already available to citizens in some Comecon countries twenty years before (for example, 24 metres in the G.D.R.), and there could be no guarantee that the target would be reached. Already there were widespread complaints about the jerry-built nature of many of the square metres that had been completed.

A second aspiration of Soviet citizens was for a private car, with Khrushchev's claim that a proper supply of trains, buses and taxis would make such an aim redundant long forgotten (not that this proper supply had been forthcoming). 1.5 million private cars per annum were to be built by 1985, but such a quantity would hardly begin to satisfy the long waiting lists, even when the official prices were extremely high, amounting to several years wages for the average worker. Around the year 1980, only 6 per cent or so of Soviet households owned a car (as opposed to about 40 per cent in the G.D.R.). Consumer durables of the household variety, radio and television sets, refrigerators and washing machines, were in much better supply, although quantity as well as quality again lagged behind most Comecon countries, not to mention the El Dorado of the capitalist West. The problems encountered in that far-off part of the world would hardly have been easily understood in the Soviet Union – the envies and anxieties, and so on, of the advanced consumer society being alien from both traditional and more recent points of view. However, already questions were being asked by academic investigators about how demands might be more appropriately channelled. Expenditure tended to be too high on food and drink, particularly alcohol, and too low on services. To redirect the behaviour of the more prosperous members of society was considered to be the most advantageous first step, since they could lead the way for the others. To raise living standards under socialism involved 'educating people to a reasonable demand structure and a meaningful way of using their leisure.' But could they begin to think green before they had become fully red?[15]

Cultural

Perhaps the most remarkable feature of Soviet culture during the later Brezhnev years was the more explicit revival of old traditions and attitudes. This is not to say that attempts at creating the 'New Man' had completely ceased. In 1979, for example, an all-union seminar conference on socialist ceremonies (the second, following the first in 1964) considered ways of eclipsing 'the illusory sun in the minds of believers' with the more truly enlightening 'Soviet sun'. Appropriate rites and ceremonies were considered, and could be viewed by the foreign visitor around the Kremlin walls in Moscow. Not far from the never-ending line to pay respects to the embalmed Lenin in his mausoleum, brides and bridegrooms would arrive from local wedding palaces to pay their respects at the eternal flame commemorating the glorious war dead, for example. A secular faith was asserted from space by a succession of cosmonauts with variations on the theme that ours is a wonderful but small earth in a vast, still to be fathomed universe.

At the Twenty-Fifth Party Congress in 1976, Brezhnev declared that Soviet society was dominated by concepts of science and materialism, but nevertheless he and his colleagues recognised that there was a survival of religious beliefs which, according to some rumours, were still to be found in the highest echelons of the C.P.S.U. It is difficult, even impossible to calculate the numbers of those adhering to ancient faiths throughout the population as a whole: Soviet calculations of something over one in ten were not likely to be over-estimates, while the claims sometimes made in the West that nearly all Soviet citizens were hungering for religion probably exaggerated both their appetites, and the famine.[16]

In 1975, there were just over 7000 Orthodox 'working' churches and nearly 6000 clergymen, according to government statistics. If several of the bishops and priests collaborated with the secular authorities, this would reflect a relationship firmly established before the Revolution and to some extent resumed after it. The situation continued to be less comfortable for some Roman Catholics in Lithuania and some evangelical Protestants in Estonia, Latvia and the Russian Republic itself, while the very existence of the Ukrainian Uniates was still not recognised.

The 50 million or so Muslims in Central Asia and Transcaucasia were tolerated although viewed with some apprehension. Fundamentalist movements could be welcomed when they were part of foreign national liberation struggles, but the possibility of their emergence within the Soviet frontiers conjured up potential nightmares. In spite of the prognostications of some Western analysts, however, the years of Brezhnev, Andropov and Chernenko passed without holy war, even without any major disturbance. Conceivably, Soviet Muslims looked at developments in Iran and elsewhere, and came to the conclusion that any attempt at repetition was best avoided. Similarly, Buddhists in the Near and Far East appear to have come to the conclusion that they stood the best chance of free exercise of their faith by keeping a low profile. Jews, especially those wanting to emigrate to Israel or the U.S.A., took a much more self-assertive position.[17]

Meanwhile, the secular Soviet soul remained in the charge of the varied range of writers and artists, who were still expected to make use of their technical expertise to provide ideological guidance within the broad framework of 'socialist realism'. The way forward in this direction, as in others, was indicated by Leonid Ilich Brezhnev, of whose works there were up to 20 million copies in print by his death. These included not only his speeches and political thoughts, but also his autobiography. At the alleged request of the proletariat, this exercise in self-glorification received the Lenin Prize for Literature in 1979, while the Chairman of the Union of Soviet Writers characterised it as an embodiment of 'the science of victory'. In more fulsome fashion, the well-established writer Valentin Kataev had declared in 1977:

We have all been accorded the greatest honour and confidence, and I would like to thank with all my heart the Soviet people, the Communist Party, its Central Committee, and the chairman of the Constitution Commission, our dear comrade and friend, Leonid Ilich Brezhnev. He has accomplished a truly titanic job in the creation of the new Soviet constitution. History will never forget his feat.[18]

However, unsold heaps of books by Brezhnev and his most enthusiastic supporters gave ample testimony to the fact that an insufficient number of the Soviet reading public shared the extravagant views of Valentin Kataev. At his death, they were barely removed from the shops before they were followed by others from the pen of Andropov, then from that of Chernenko. On the other hand, those new books which gained any measure of genuine praise, as likely to be unofficial as official, even reprints of Russian and foreign classics, could sell like hot cakes. The 'village writers' in particular retained their popularity, as did other celebrants of the old ways. And art reflected literature in the work of Ilya Glazunov, whose studio was full of icons gathered from derelict churches throughout rural Russia, and whose portraits and landscapes often reflected themes from the national past. While the voice of Old Russia was still sometimes muffled within the Soviet Union, it was proclaimed loud and clear in exile by Alexander Solzhenitsyn and others.[19]

Popular entertainment grew in importance through traditional Soviet media such as the radio and cinema, newer such as television, which was also official, and the tape-recorder, which often was not. The gospel of rock and roll was now established far and wide among Soviet youth, and domestic imitators could be found in out of the way places. The also adulated voices of the guitar poets were dimmed by the enforced emigration of Galich in 1974 – he died in 1977 – and the death in his homeland of Vysotsky in 1980. Only Okudzhava of the great ones was left to sing on.[20]

Many Soviet citizens continued their diversion and education by way of *samizdat* and *magnitizdat*. Meanwhile, formal education continued to expand in the following manner (in thousands):

	completion of secondary		entry into higher	
	7–8 years	10–11 years	full-time	part-time
1970	4661	2591	500	411
1980	4270	3996	640	412

The numbers for more lengthy secondary, and full-time higher, education showed a considerable increase, which was to help produce a positive reception for the great changes occurring in the Soviet government's policies after 1985.[21]

Before then, the problems of the growing Soviet intelligentsia were clearly set out in 'official', not to mention dissident literature. For example, in the story 'The Boarded-Up Dachas' by Galina Shergova, published by the journal *Novyi Mir* in 1978, a successful painter and regular broadcaster is asked by an influential party official to criticise on his programme the work of a fellow-artist and friend that has fallen into disfavour. Although the story is set in the year 1964, the dilemma would have been recognised as applicable in later years, too, and in many areas of creative and academic endeavour. From the early to mid-1970s, for example, historians with suspect outlooks were often ostracised by many colleagues, and several lost their positions. There was something of a mild thaw in the later 1970s, but it did not last, a resolution of the party Central Committee on 23 July 1982 declaring that 'it is impossible to tolerate the publication in certain journals of works in which events of the history of the fatherland, the socialist revolution and collectivisation are presented with serious departures from the living truth.' However, as R. W. Davies points out, 'While the press maintained a grey silence about all the sensitive historical issues, away from the official world the Soviet past continued to be hotly debated in private. Neo-Stalinists and Russian nationalists contended with democrats, liberals and dissident Communists.'[22]

The problems of the Soviet intelligentsia were by no means entirely internal to the whole social stratum or visited upon it by the party. Further, age-old difficulties were the gap that separated the intelligentsia from the broad masses of the people, and the other gap that divided generations, fathers and mothers from sons and daughters. These lent the long discussions an almost nineteenth-century atmosphere as a whole range of 'vexed questions' were tackled far into the night. Certainly the necessity for 'living truth' was never forgotten, even if there was little agreement about what it comprised. These and other considerations serve to remind us that, throughout the years of 'stagnation', still pools were running deep. In other words, 'new thinking' was in active if not always obvious preparation.

17 Reform or Ruin? 1985–1996

From the vantage point of the middle 1990s, Russian history seemed to be uncomfortably placed at one of its many critical points. Parallels suggested themselves with the Time of Troubles at the beginning of the seventeenth century, or the collapse following the Russian Revolution of 1917. To optimists, this was the birth trauma of a new age, to pessimists the death-throes of the old. Fortune-tellers and mystics abounded, offering a wide variety of future and other worlds. In a more down to earth manner focused mainly on the present, this chapter will attempt to put the simple question (although without a simple answer): Reform or ruin?

In the later 1980s, appearances (which might have been deceptive) were more of reform, as new thinking received official approval in the Soviet Union, and many aspects of the present and past were opened up to fresh scrutiny with a new slogan – *glasnost* and *perestroika*. What did it mean? *Glasnost*, like so many Russian words, is difficult to translate. To look at it in its adjectival form, a *glasnyi sud* is a public trial, while a *glasnyi* used to be a member of the town Duma. In the form of a noun, then, there are implications not only of openness but also of activity, which are taken further in the other term. But again, *perestroika* conveys meanings other than the literal 'reconstruction'. It can mean not only rebuilding but also ideological reorientation, thus becoming more closely associated with *glasnost* and helping to form an almost inseparable pair.

New thinking was much more to the fore than fresh action in the years immediately following 1985, and the question arose: Would the new leader most closely associated with *glasnost* and *perestroika* manage to remain in power if he could not more effectively use it? Moreover, his health might be undermined, or some unforeseen accident bring his life to an end. On the other hand, the contrast between him and his immediate predecessors, Andropov and Chernenko, was so striking that such eventualities seemed remote. According to some observers, his significance was more than personal, since he represented the arrival to a position of influence in Soviet society of a whole generation. As one of them has argued:

> Since the 1950s the country has continued to become increasingly urbanized, educated, professionally differentiated, and politically, ideologically and culturally diversified ... . A huge class of educated specialists has emerged, and different elites, previously so heavily brutalised, have had time to recreate themselves or to recover. Or, at least, an educated pool of talent from which elites can be quickly composed and recomposed, is now at hand.[1]

Even up to the end of the Stalin period, the majority of the Soviet peoples were rural dwellers: until then, Soviet culture was still up to a point a peasant culture. But could a new outlook be created in little more than thirty years?

The confident focus of many hopes, together with not a few fears, was Mikhail Sergeevich Gorbachev, whose rise to power had been unusually rapid. This was partly because the old guard had to give way at some point, however delayed, and partly because he was linked with it through his own parents, who were both peasants. In this sense, Gorbachev was near the end of a line running back through Brezhnev and Khrushchev: but of course, he was also to reveal some formidable talents of his own. He was born on 2 March 1931 in a village not far from Stavropol, in the Northern Caucasus, between the lower reaches of the Rivers Don and Volga. Old Cossack country, the region still had much virgin soil to upturn in the forced collectivisation of agriculture, in which Gorbachev's parents and grandparents were arduously involved. At first, while completing his schooling at the end of the appalling experience of the Second World War, Mikhail followed his father Sergei's calling as a tractor driver, but then was nominated by the local party to enter the Law Faculty at Moscow State University in 1950. There he was a Komsomol activist, joining the C.P.S.U. in 1952 and broadening his outlook, not least by meeting students from Eastern Europe as well as from other parts of the Soviet Union. He married one of the latter, Raisa Titorenko, in 1953, returning to Stavropol on graduation in 1955, and gaining promotion through the ranks of the Komsomol. With fortunate affiliations and hard work, he rose to become first secretary of the regional party committee by 1970. His contacts with Moscow now grew closer through even better patronage as well as continued application after he became a full member of the Central Committee in 1971, and he moved to the Soviet capital at the end of 1978 as a member of the Central Committee Secretariat. Although showing more energy than success as managing director of the most difficult sector of the economy – agriculture, – he soon became a candidate of the Politburo in 1979 and a full member in 1980. He was now well placed to pick his way through the political complications of the early 1980s to emerge as the new General Secretary in March 1985, just after his fifty-fourth birthday.[2]

There followed a dazzling series of events on the domestic and international stages. Talking, even listening to a wide range of people throughout the Soviet Union, Gorbachev appeared on TV as the first Soviet leader to have mastered that deceptively simple medium. Viewers at home and abroad could see him encouraging in the workplace more competition and efficiency, promising in the market place better supplies and services while asking for yet more patience. Proposals were soon made for changes in the C.P.S.U. and the Soviets, while Gorbachev himself received a number of promotions before becoming President of the U.S.S.R. in 1990. Foreign travel also showed Gorbachev to favourable effect, most notably in a series of summits with President Reagan in Geneva and Reykjavik, with President Bush in Malta and Helsinki, and with both in Washington, D.C. and Moscow. As the Soviet peoples hoped for improvements in their standard of living accompanied by further changes in their way of life, the peoples of the world began to wonder if they were perhaps after all to be granted peace in their time. But then, surprisingly, *perestroika* and *glasnost* turned sour, and Gorbachev himself was quickly transformed from tomorrow's man to yesterday's.

We will introduce this process after a summary description of the career of the man who supplanted him. At first ridiculed as an ignorant and clumsy buffoon by many of his opponents, Boris Nikolaevich Eltsin or Yeltsin was to rise above them all for the last laugh (at least in the short run, since there is no absolutely last laugh in politics.) Like Gorbachev, Yeltsin was born in humble circumstances in a village, in his case in the province of Sverdlovsk (later to revert to the pre-revolutionary Ekaterinburg) on 1 February 1931. According to his own account, he was nearly drowned in the baptismal font by a drunken priest, who observed 'if he can survive such an ordeal it means he's a tough lad'. This, and a succeeding period of immersion in atheism, did not deter him from conceiving it his later duty 'to restore the church's rights'. For the first ten years of his life, young Boris lived with his grandfather, parents and two other children in a single room in a draughty wooden barracks along with twenty other families but no creature comforts. The Yeltsins moved then to the nearby Perm province, where his father became a factory worker until arrested at the peak of Stalin's purges in 1937. At school, Boris was awarded top marks for scholarship but lowest marks for conduct. He enjoyed sports, especially volleyball, but had to spend much of his time working from quite an early age. He began his career as a bricklayer, before becoming site foreman and then chief engineer. By the early 1960s, he was manager of a large construction enterprise in Sverdlovsk, joining the Party in 1961.

In the belief that he was helping to build communism both literally and figuratively, he laboured hard and long, rising in the party ranks as more and more houses were erected. In 1976, he was asked by Brezhnev to become First Secretary in Sverdlovsk, and carried out his duties in an apparently exemplary manner for nine years. Then, in 1985, he was asked to move to Moscow to work for the Central Committee, and, before the year was out, requested to become head of the party organisation of the Soviet capital by the new General Secretary himself. Mikhail Gorbachev soon came to rue that decision as Boris Yeltsin became a dissident, then an opponent, and finally a replacement, albeit as President of Russia rather than of the Soviet Union. This process is part of the political history of the years following 1985, to which we will soon turn.[3]

From August 1991 onwards, Boris Yeltsin quickly discovered that power could be more onerous than opposition. Far from enjoying tastes of his own medicine, the Russian President found criticism so hard to take that he proclaimed it treason, and attacked the seat of the Russian Congress, the White House, in October 1993 after dissolving it in September with as much determination as he had defended it two years before. To be sure, the Constitution of December 1993 gave him an almost dictatorial role which he used to the full. But opposition parties did well in elections at the end of 1993 and 1995, while his personal popularity sank lower and lower, and his prospects for re-election in the summer of 1996 looked bleak indeed. But against all the odds, with all kinds of promises, even bribes and not a few warnings, he triumphed over his Communist opponent Gennadii Zyuganov, only to reveal that the state of his health was even more parlous than the health of his state. Question marks were coming into greater prominence. In the international arena, Yeltsin was far less an accomplished player than Gorbachev. He was either too little at ease, or, under the influence of alcohol, too much. Moreover, the hope and excitement that had seized the world in the first years of *glasnost* and *perestroika* had been replaced by disillusion and apathy.

Political

Essentially, Gorbachev's aim was to reform the old system, not to create a new one. As his aim began to fail, he was pushed towards more complete change, but, by then, he had lost the power to control it.

At the Twenty-Seventh Party Congress early in 1986, about a year after his appointment, the General Secretary declared that 'democracy is the wholesome and pure air without which a socialist public organism cannot live a full-blooded life'.[4] As he brought in *glasnost* and *perestroika*, he talked in the summer of 1987 about 'socialist pluralism'. Then, in a speech to the Central Committee of the Communist Party he proposed the removal from the Soviet Constitution of that section of Article 6 which declared that the Party, 'armed with Marxism–Leninism', was the 'leading and guiding force of Soviet society and the nucleus of its political system'. While stopping a long way short of dissolution of the C.P.S.U., General Secretary Gorbachev was undoubtedly moving towards a broader pluralism attended by 'democratisation'. Quite rightly, his defenders have pointed out that such democracy as the West possesses has evolved over the course of more than a century, and that, while there may be some democratic elements in the Russian tradition, they were not sufficiently strong at the end of the 1980s and beginning of the 1990s for Gorbachev to be able to propose a comprehensive changeover. On the other hand, his critics charge that this was a time for boldness, and that he should have taken a leap from the still familiar into the unknown.[5] Might he have survived the ups-and-downs of 1991 if he had put himself up for election as President just a year earlier?

To a considerable extent the challenge was to Soviet, and indeed to Russian, ideology. Arguably, Marxism-Leninism satisfied an old craving for an all-enveloping completeness which could also be found in Christian Orthodoxy.[6] Most of the dissidents of earlier years favoured either a purer form of the Soviet ideology, or an updated version of the pre-revolutionary. Much of the instability of the years after the reduction of the 'leading and guiding force' of the C.P.S.U. resulted from the failure to find any adequate replacement for its basic idea. Early in 1988, Gorbachev himself reiterated that Marxism–Leninism was 'the scientific basis of the party's approach to an understanding of social development and the practice of Communist construction'. But he also went on to say that 'there cannot and must not be any limitation of scientific inquiry. Questions of theory cannot and must not be decided by any kind of decrees. The free competition of intellects is essential'.[7]

The Nineteenth Party Conference in the summer of 1988 turned out to be an indicator of how much progress had been made, but also of how much more was necessary. By this time, there had been a considerable reshuffle from top to bottom: about half the Politburo, Secretariat and membership of the Central Committee were new; more than half of the powerful provincial Party Secretaries had been replaced. (Meanwhile, about two-thirds of government ministers had also lost their jobs, and the number of bureaucrats in the ministries reduced.) Moreover, by this time, the Communist Party was not the only vehicle of political expression: tens of thousands of civic groups had been set up for a whole range of purposes, including the extension of democracy. And cracks had begun to appear at the top of the edifice of the Communist Party itself. Most notably, Boris Yeltsin had been ejected from control of Moscow in November 1987 and his place on the Politburo in February 1988 as his increasing criticism of the shortcomings of *perestroika* and of its major architect Mikhail Gorbachev was denounced as 'political adventurism'.[8] From the right, an attack on the excesses of *perestroika* in the guise of a letter to the press in March 1988 condemning attacks on Stalin and the spread of Western popular culture had become prescribed reading at Party meetings.

At the first Party Conference to meet since 1941, talk flowed freely and with passion, and from all quarters. The most important proposal for more democracy (and yet more speeches) was a new two-level legislature: a Congress of People's Deputies, a third of whose members would be chosen by 'social organisations' including the Communist Party and the trade unions; and a Supreme Soviet elected by the Congress, but with a Chairman who would 'normally' be the General Secretary of the Communist Party. For better or worse, however, any semblance of 'normality' was about to depart from the Soviet scene.

In spite of a variety of attempts to control the outcome of the elections to the Congress in March 1989, they produced at least some outspoken People's Deputies including Boris Yeltsin. When the Congress met from May to June, there was a series of radical suggestions such as the removal of Lenin's body from its Mausoleum, and of refusals to accept proposals from Chairman Gorbachev, for example for a ban on strikes. But there was too much procedural wrangle and apparently aimless chat for the proceedings to maintain their hold on the attention of the general public: the actors remained on the stage, so to speak, after most of the audience had left the theatre.

Too late already by March 1990, the producer attempted to recast and rewrite. General Secretary and Chairman Gorbachev persuaded the Congress to elect him as President as it ratified his suggestion that Article 6 of the Constitution concerning the ' leading and guiding' role of the party be reformulated. Throughout the rest of that year, there were other developments beyond his control: the Communist Party was to find that it was far from alone as a political organisation; and there was a great stir around the U.S.S.R., with the Soviet and Socialist ingredients in the Republics weakening in the face of a mounting nationalism. Was the Union itself in danger?

At first, problems appeared in the periphery. The Baltics – Estonia, Latvia and Lithuania – spoke up for themselves first, from soon after 1985, and demonstrations and declarations led to all three Communist Parties breaking away from the C.P.S.U. by 1990. On 11 March 1990, just days before Gorbachev took the oath as President of the U.S.S.R., it began to break up with a Lithuanian declaration of independence; a year later, Latvia and Estonia also confirmed their breakaway. On the whole, the wayward sisters were allowed to depart in peace by September 1991, although twenty or so lives were lost in confrontations with Soviet tanks and troops. Relatively speaking, the Slavic siblings were less disturbed, although there were some rumblings in Belarus and even more in the Ukraine, especially to the west, where the Uniate church and other traditions produced a considerable degree of Russophobia. Beyond the River Dnestr, Russians physically clashed with Moldovans from the end of 1989 onwards, and there were some signs of disintegration. Meanwhile, in Transcaucasia, there were more serious internal tensions as well as centrifugal forces contributing to a considerably higher level of mortality. For example, hundreds of Armenians died along with not a few Azeris, while there were thousands of refugees, after trouble flared up in the autonomous region of Nagornyi Karabakh in Azerbaidzhan at the beginning of 1988. This problem contributed to the upsurge of nationalism – linked in part to religious fanaticism – in both Christian Armenia and Muslim Azerbaidzhan. In nearby Georgia, a distinctive difficulty arose in the autonomous republic of Abkhazia, which resisted more complete incorporation into the Georgian republic even though less than a fifth of its population were Abkhazian. After about a year of violence, beginning in April 1989 with the shooting, beating and gassing of a peaceful demonstration in Tbilisi and continuing in that capital city, Abkhazia and elsewhere, a 'national forum' came together in May 1990 to decide on a concerted move towards independence which was to be formally declared on 9 April 1991. In August 1990, another nationality to be found on both sides of the frontier, the Ossetians, asserted their own independence from Tbilisi. Further fighting erupted there, as well as between government troops and dissidents nearer the capital. The total mortality in the Caucasus is difficult, even impossible, to calculate, but amounted to at least hundreds and was possibly thousands. Viewed from the centre, the impending secession of the Caucasus and its manifold problems seemed to some welcome. So would be that of the Central Asian Republics, but it seemed slower in coming. Before the end of 1991, only a minority were in favour of the dissolution of the Soviet Union, many more seeking self-assertion, with local leaders. There was some internal friction with local minorities, notably in Uzbekistan and Kyrgyzstan, and some emphasis on cultural autonomy, with Islam most to the fore in Tadzhikistan. There was little or no violence in favour of the complete cutting of ties to Moscow. Nevertheless, by about the end of 1990, Kazakhstan, Turkmenistan and the three other Central Asian republics had all declared their sovereignty, if not yet their independence.[9]

In the Soviet capital, President Gorbachev claimed that he did not authorise a crackdown in the Baltic, Georgia or anywhere else. Arguably, he should have made it his business to know what was going on. Certainly, he appears to have underrated the importance of the problem of nationalism, retaining to the end too much confidence in a cohesive Soviet patriotism, and neglecting the new upsurge not only in the outer parts of the structure but also and particularly at its very centre. Here, an indication of the relative size of the populations of the Republics in an all-Union total for 1989 of 285,743,000 could be helpful (in descending order in thousands as in 1989, with their post-Soviet names and percentages of major nationalities):

Russia	147,022	Russians 81.5, Tatars 3.8, Ukrainians 3.0
Ukraina	51,452	Ukrainians 72.7, Russians 22.1, Jews 1.0
Uzbekistan	19,810	Uzbeks 71.4, Russians 8.4, Tadzhiks 4.7
Kazakhstan	16,535	Kazakhs 39.7, Russians 37.8, Germans 5.8
Belarus	10,152	Belarussians 77.9, Russians 13.2, Poles 4.1
Azerbaidzhan	7,021	Azeris 82.7, Russians 5.6, Armenians 5.6
Georgia	5,400	Georgians 70.1, Armenians 8.1, Russians 6.3
Tadzhikistan	5,093	Tadzhiks 62.3, Uzbeks 23.5, Russians 7.6
Moldova	4,335	Moldovans 64.5, Ukrainians 13.9, Russians 13.0
Kyrgyzstan	4,258	Kyrgyz 52.4, Russians 21.5, Uzbeks 12.9
Lithuania	3,675	Lithuanians 79.6, Russians 9.4, Poles 7.0
Turkmenistan	3,523	Turkmenians 72.0, Russians 9.5, Uzbeks 9.0
Armenia	3,305	Armenians 93.3, Azeris 2.6, Kurds 1.7
Latvia	2,667	Latvians 52.0, Russians 34.0, Belarussians 4.5
Estonia	1,566	Estonians 61.5, Russians 30.3, Ukrainians 3.1

Numbers alone do not tell the whole story, of course. We have just seen that the smallest of them, in Latvia and Estonia, played a disproportionate part in the events leading up to the end of 1991. Moreover, as shown above, the figures give no indication of small national minorities. Soon, especially after the break-up of the U.S.S.R. in December 1991, from Sakhalin and Kamchatka to the Kola peninsula and the Crimea, all kinds of peoples would be clamouring for more recognition for themselves, sometimes with less recognition of their neighbours. Feelings ran especially high near the Caucasus, among the Chechens, for example. There were clamorous Russian inhabitants in some of the republics, from Estonia to Kazakhstan, among a total Russian expatriate population of about 25 millions.[10]

In Russia itself, the majority natives were restless. Extremists among them were against all foreigners, especially Asiatics. At least some were in favour of a Russian (as opposed to the Soviet) Communist Party. Most seemed to be seeking new democratic directions. But which? From the late 1980s onwards, a bewildering number of parties, fractions and blocs arose and fell. Attempting to remain aloof from such confusion, but increasingly sucked into it, was the Union President Mikhail Sergeevich Gorbachev, uncertain how to deal with Russia in particular. Meeting from May to June 1990, the Congress of People's Deputies of the Russian Soviet Federative Socialist Republic elected in March voted in favour of national sovereignty, and chose as the chairman of its Supreme Soviet Boris Yeltsin, who increasingly realised the possiblities of his new power base. In July, at the Twenty-Eighth and last Congress, he resigned from the C.P.S.U., and argued that the U.S.S.R. should become a looser union. But if the Russian Federation might leave the U.S.S.R., might not Chechens, Tatars and others want to secede from the Russian Federation?

Towards the end of 1990, his mind made up partly perhaps by an attempt on his life at the anniversary parade of the Russian Revolution on 7 November, Gorbachev appears to have decided that the threat of dissolution had gone far enough. He appointed conservatives to the Ministry of the Interior and other key posts. On the other hand, there were street demonstrations and new organisations in favour of further reform in several towns including Moscow and Leningrad (which was to revert to its former name St Petersburg on 1 October 1991). For his part, Gorbachev hoped that a new sense of united purpose would be achieved by a referendum on 17 March 1991, asking the question: 'Do you consider necessary the preservation of the U.S.S.R. as a renewed federation of equal sovereign republics, in which the rights and freedom of the individual of any nationality will be fully guaranteed?' To say no to a question like this would be almost to favour sin; to say yes could be considered a vote for cloud-cuckoo land. Moreover, while more than 75 per cent of the 80 per cent of the electorate who responded did say yes, the significance of their response for Gorbachev was lessened by an additional question tacked on by his rival: should Russia have its own President? Again, there was a yes, if not quite so resounding.[11]

The rivalry between Gorbachev and Yeltsin now became almost a duel. Conservatives arranged for an extraordinary session of the Russian Congress towards the end of March 1991, and attempted to pass a resolution of no confidence in Boris Yeltsin, the chairman. But not only did a sufficient number of Communists and others reject this resolution, they also gave the chairman special powers to be retained until the election of a

Russian President in June, from which he emerged triumphant. While President Yeltsin moved to restrict the activities of the Communist Party in Russia, President Gorbachev made his last attempt to adapt it to the rapidly changing situation throughout the U.S.S.R. But the conservatives could not accept a Soviet Union of ten rather than fifteen republics, nor more departure from state control of the economy. While their leader was on holiday in the Crimea, on 19 August a Committee of State Emergency announced that he was ill and that they were taking over from him. Tanks rumbled into Moscow, and the cause of reform appeared lost. But if the wider world moved towards recognition of the new situation, Boris Yeltsin showed that he was made of sterner stuff, mounting a tank and donning a flak jacket to address the defenders of the Russian White House in the full glare of the world's TV cameras. In fact, barely a shot was fired, and there were just three fatalities. But the Russian President was now in the ascendancy, while the Soviet President survived rumours of illness and even death only to return from the Crimea virtually finished as a politician. The duel was virtually over, and, fortified with the grant by the Russian Congress of emergency powers, the victor evidently enjoyed the final thrusts as the loser was obliged to witness the prohibition of the C.P.S.U. and the collapse of the U.S.S.R. before the end of 1991.

These events shook the world, but the world in its turn was at least partly responsible for the shake-up. Arguably, the Soviet Union and the ruling Communist Party were brought down by their insistence on their superpower: for too long, in the international arena, they had bitten off more than they could chew. Certainly, as Archie Brown has pointed out, Gorbachev 'saw more clearly than any of his predecessors the links between domestic and foreign policy'.[12] Thus, to cease the persecution of Andrei Sakharov and other dissidents and to introduce a measure of democracy would improve relations with the West. Equally, to reduce the heavy emphasis on defence would help to remove imbalance in the economy and reduce the influence for the military–industrial complex.

In a sense, then, the nine summit meetings with U.S. Presidents (five with Ronald Reagan and four with George Bush) in the less than seven years of his own leadership were a cover-up for a failing superpower. But they also promoted world peace, and Gorbachev's personal contribution here was considerable. For example, Ronald Reagan, who had not so long before been denouncing the Soviet Union as an 'evil empire' and support-ing an escalation of the arms race in 'Star Wars' (the Strategic Defense Initiative, or S.D.I.), was partly persuaded by the 'man-to-man chemistry' between himself and Mikhail Gorbachev to go further than his predeces-sors down the long road of strategic arms reduction. Thus, in 1987, an

Intermediate-Range Nuclear Forces (I.N.F.) Treaty (to be formalised in June 1988) was signed in Washington DC at 1.45 pm on 8 December. This time was set by Nancy Reagan's astrologer, and therefore made the agreement a 'Star Peace' in one sense at least: in fact, however, it was more down to earth, achieving the elimination from Europe of a whole class of nuclear weapons, the Soviet SS–20s and the Western Cruise and Pershing missiles.[13]

There were even more dramatic developments in 1989, the collapse of the erstwhile 'evil empire' in Eastern Europe and the Soviet withdrawal from Afghanistan. In 1989, too, Gorbachev visited China, suggesting that Sino-Soviet relations were entering a 'qualitatively new stage'. Demonstrations in support of his *glasnost* and *perestroika* contributed to the later wave of unrest culminating in the bloody crushing of Chinese dissidents in Tiananmen Square. But the leaders managed to establish the normalisation of relations between themselves, their parties and their countries, and a reciprocal visit by President Jiang Zemin to Moscow in the spring of 1991 sealed the reconciliation. Also in 1991, Gorbachev did what he could to improve relations with Japan, but the vexed question of the Kurile Islands impeded closer agreement. The Soviet President appeared ready for compromise, but only succeeded in arousing suspicion back home, where his position was already weakening, without being able to conclude a deal. Nearby on the Pacific Rim, Gorbachev was able to strengthen relations, both diplomatic and economic, with South Korea, and to assist the withdrawal of the Soviet Union from its over-extended presence in the Third World. But his critics charged that he had gone too far and too quickly here, too, adhering too closely to the United Nations resolutions leading to the Gulf War early in 1991. In the last of his summits, in July 1991 in Moscow, Gorbachev agreed with President Bush a Strategic Arms Reduction Treaty (S.T.A.R.T.) to the order of 30 per cent on both sides. Again, the suspicion arose of too much deference to the other side.[14]

New directions in international relations needed ideological justification. And so, Gorbachev abandoned Marxist–Leninist insistence on a class war between proletarians and capitalists for a newly conceived 'Humanistic universalism'. More than once, he argued, Lenin himself had spoken about 'the priority of interests common to all humanity over class interests'.[15] Here, not for the first time nor the last, Gorbachev alarmed diehards, and there was a more widespread apprehension that he was making too many concessions to the West in his pursuit of world peace, and of personal popularity. His foreign policy, therefore, probably made its contribution to the decision of the State Emergency Committee to make its fateful bid for power in August 1991.

Exit Gorbachev and enter Yeltsin. But this was much more than a simple change of leadership; not for the first time in Russian history, the personalities of the rulers were to blend with the phases of their rule. Thus, if Gorbachev had no more than belatedly dallied with the democratic system, Yeltsin embraced it from the first with a bear hug, squeezing much of the life from it almost as soon as it was born. In other words, while Gorbachev used as many of the rules of the old game for as long as possible in order to preserve his own position via the rule of one party, Yeltsin bent the rules of the new game amid a plethora of parties to preserve *his* power. And if Gorbachev sought ideological consistency, within the Soviet framework, Yeltsin was among the first to realise simply that:

> Russia never had its own voice and it did not argue or disagree with the center … . It was clear to me that the vertical bureaucratic pivot on which the country rests had to be destroyed, and we had to begin a transition to horizontal ties with greater independence of the republic states. The mood of the people, the democratization of society, and the growth of people's national self-awareness led directly to this.[16]

Thus, on 25 December 1991, President Yeltsin officially changed the name of the Russian Soviet Federal Socialist Republic to the Russian Federation (adopted officially along with just Russia by the Congress of People's Deputies in April 1992). In January 1992, both the U.S.A. and the European Community recognised the R.F., which also occupied the Soviet seat in the United Nations Organisation. In March, a new Federal Treaty was signed between the Moscow government and the autonomous republics, with the exception of Tatarstan and Chechnia, which both insisted on their independence (Tatarstan making a later accommodation, while Chechnia was to break away more completely).

Throughout 1992, there was much talk of a new constitution amid energetic jockeying for position by the President, the government and the legislature. By December, Yeltsin was obliged to jettison the reformer Egor Gaidar as Prime Minister in favour of the more conservative Viktor Chernomyrdin.

Then, after agreement had been reached to hold a referendum on the basic principles of a new constitution in April but other attempts at compromise had failed, the Congress met in special session in March 1993 to rescind the emergency powers granted to the President in late 1991 and to declare itself 'the supreme body of state power'. In response, the President proposed a 'special form of administration' in a TV address of 20 March 1993, and confirmed a referendum for April. Although the Constitutional

Court declared this 'special rule' illegal and the Congress came very near to impeaching him on 26 March, the President received majority support for the continuance of his own term of office and of socio-economic reform if not for new elections in the referendum of 25 April. Immediately, he submitted the draft of a new constitution to the deliberations of a Constituent Assembly and other bodies. Meanwhile, the Congress continued to impede economic and other reforms until the President dissolved the legislature in September and announced new elections. In response, dissident members of the Congress formed their own government and occupied the White House. In October little over two years after he had defended this building, he ordered the army to attack it, also forestalling an attempted coup, most notably at Moscow's (and Russia's) television centre.

Once his hold on power was assured, Yeltsin placed restrictions on those sections of the television, radio and press media which had been implicated in the coup, and suspended the Constitutional Court. A referendum on a new constitution was held on the same day as elections to a new Federal Assembly in December 1993. The voters elected to the lower house or State Duma 450 deputies including 70 candidates of the pro-government Russia's Choice, 64 of the ultra-nationalist Vladimir Zhirinovskii's Liberal Democratic Party, 48 of the Communist Party and 33 of the C.P.'s ally, the Agrarian Party.[17]

This was far from the result that the President would have liked, but his concern was tempered by the fact that the new Constitution gave him sweeping powers: he could declare martial law, war or a state of emergency (although the upper house or Federation Council would have to confirm the declaration); control foreign and defence policy; veto parliamentary legislation and even dismiss the parliament, among other powers. He could be impeached on the grounds of treason or other serious crime, but only after rulings by the highest judicial bodies – the Constitutional and Supreme Court and a two-thirds majority in both houses of the parliamentary legislature – the State Duma directly elected by popular vote, and the Federation Council with two members chosen by each of the 89 members of the Federation.

Throughout the ensuing years, 1994 and 1995, there was no shortage of disagreements between the executive head and the legislative bodies but no return of crisis, largely because the President was too powerful to worry about it. However, as 1995 came to an end, Yeltsin must have been concerned about his own very low popularity ratings in the increasingly significant public opinion polls, and by the comparative failure of the party that supported him in the elections to the State Duma compared to the success of those which opposed him: 55 seats for Our Home is Russia as opposed to 157 seats for the Communist Party, 51 for the Liberal Democratic Party, out of a total of 450.[18]

We must be careful here not to equate the Russian parliamentary process with that to be found in a 'normal' Western democracy. In the elections of 1993 and 1995, there were a bewildering number of parties and combinations presenting candidates for election. For example, in 1995, the voters were asked to express a preference for one out of no less than 43 electoral units or blocs, of various hues and sizes, including The Party of Beerlovers, or to register a negative reaction to all of them. Moreover, behaviour in the legislature could be far from parliamentary and the rulings of the judiciary could appear less than impartial, while the executive subjected the other two branches of the constitutional order to severe manipulation.

While the debate continued at the centre, there was ongoing war at the periphery, against not a foreign enemy, but the breakaway Chechen republic. Having refused to sign the Russian Federal Treaty in March 1992 after an earlier declaration of independence in November 1991, Chechnia resisted all attempts to bring it back into the fold throughout 1993. Then, as violence escalated, the President launched a military operation in December 1994, and 40,000 deaths ensued by the summer of 1996.

This was the major theatre of action for the Russian armed forces in the years following the collapse of the Soviet Union, but the potential for larger-scale activity was far from lost, the total personnel amounting to more than 1,700,000, more than 900,000 of whom were conscripts. Tens of thousands of Russian servicemen were to be found in several of the former Soviet republics as 'peacekeepers', while just under 170,000 members of the Strategic Nuclear Forces still had at their disposal about 700 nuclear missiles. But chains of command and lines of communication were often substandard, while equipment was by no means always ready for use. Hair-raising stories abounded of all kinds of neglect and abuse, ranging from nuclear submarines dangerously rusting away to tanks being used on mushrooming forays, with anything and everything up for illegal sale.[19]

Against such a background, was it possible to pursue a credible foreign policy? And what indeed constituted a foreign policy, now that the Soviet Union had collapsed? To take an important example, all the former fraternal republics of the former Soviet Union, with the exception of the three Baltics, were associated with Russia through the Commonwealth of Independent States first set up in late 1991 before the formal dissolution of the U.S.S.R. in December. But relations with all the countries of the 'near abroad' had their difficulties as far as economic and other questions were concerned. None of these constituted such a headache as Chechnia, however, which would enter the realms of foreign policy if it achieved its independence.

Fraternal ties stretched beyond the C.I.S., and while there remained different levels of regret concerning the collapse of the Warsaw Pact and other connections with fellow Slavs, the strongest waves of sympathy were for the Serbs cast in the West as the villains of the chaotic dismemberment of Yugoslavia, where a token Russian force was part of the U.N. peacekeeping operation. Apart from that ongoing problem, all was fairly harmonious in Europe, although there were apprehensions about the possible inclusion of Central and Eastern European countries in N.A.T.O. The summits continued with the U.S.A. For example, in January 1993, Presidents Yeltsin and Bush signed another Strategic Arms Reduction Treaty (S.T.A.R.T. 2). There was no significant condemnation of Yeltsin's assault on the White House from West, or East, President Jiang Zemin of China signing treaties with his Russian counterpart in September 1994 for the demarcation of their mutual frontiers and the retargeting away from each other's territory of their nuclear weapons. So great was their preoccupation with problems at home that the Russian peoples as a whole appeared less concerned with problems in the wider world. On the other hand, a reflection of the apprehension that Russia was playing second fiddle among the great powers was the President's expression of dissatisfaction with foreign minister Andrei Kozyrev, leading to the latter's resignation early in 1996.[20]

Economic

In 1985, the Soviet government published a draft of *Guidelines for the Economic and Social Development of the USSR for 1986–1990 and for the Period ending in 2000*. It asserted that: 'The next fifteen years will be a historic period for our country on the road towards perfecting socialism and building communism'. The central objective of the Twelfth Five-Year Plan was:

> ... to increase the growth rates and efficiency of the economy on the basis of accelerating scientific and technological progress, the technical modernisation and re-equipment of production, intensive utilisation of the created production potential, perfecting the system of management and the economic mechanism and achieving on this basis a further rise in the Soviet people's well-being.

Unfortunately, however much they promoted the lumber and paper-making industries, the publication of such words led to less general prosperity. Indeed, the gap between hope and reality turned out to be much greater than in the past: Five-Year Plans had always gone awry, but none as much as the Twelfth, which duly turned out to be the last. And the *Guidelines* appeared more and more like fantasy.[21]

The radical divergence from them may be followed through four stages, as follows.

(1) From 1985 to 1989, there was an attempt at adjustment of the Soviet system; that is, to improve its efficiency without the wholesale introduction of the market or the lowering of living standards. At the same time, Gorbachev called for further sacrifices, notably of the time-honoured thirst for strong drink, as part of an attempt to continue management of the economy through political means. Prohibition had been introduced once, disastrously, by the tsarist government at the outbeak of the First World War. After the Revolution, while there had been a puritan streak in the Soviet government from the beginning, Stalin had argued in 1925 that it could not build socialism in white gloves, and that the alternative to slavery to Western capitalists was the revenue accruing from the vodka monopoly. By the late Brezhnev era, during the years of the Eleventh Five-Year Plan from 1981 to 1985, the turnover tax on alcoholic beverages brought in nearly 170 billion roubles, and Gorbachev conceded early in 1988 that if the income from sales at home of strong drink and sales abroad of another liquid, oil, were deducted from the Soviet budget, there had been no significant economic growth for about twenty years, and even, from 1981 to 1985, some decline. But now, through example and precept, abstinence and restriction, he hoped to improve the health and prosperity of the people and the economy.[22]

(2) From 1989 to 1991, there ensued an increasing number of reforms pointing towards the end of the Soviet system: for example, the legalisation of small private businesses in August 1990; the reduction of state control in October 1990; and further denationalisation and privatisation in July 1991. Widespread dissatisfaction was reflected in strikes, for which not the least cause was the anti-alcohol campaign which one opponent declared to amount to 'the castration of the working class'. Gradually, the campaign was relaxed, and by the early 1990s the Russians were catching up and even overtaking the world's other leading drinkers.[23] Meanwhile, all kinds of advisers flocked in from the Harvard Business School and other repositories of the accumulated wisdom of the capitalist West, offering all kinds of cures, partial and more complete, for the Soviet Union's economic problems: generally speaking, the lower the level of understanding of those problems, the higher the level of optimism concerning the cure.

(3) From 1992 to 1994, with the departure from the scene of Mr Gorbachev and the Soviet Union, there was radical reform, but with alter-

nate leaps forward and back. In May 1992, most state subsidies and price controls were abolished. Later in the same year, more complete privatisation was announced in August, while in October, all Russian citizens were given vouchers to enable them to buy shares in denationalised industry. This was the heyday of Egor Gaidar, bold advocate of the short, sharp shock: apparently, the Russian people were to be thrown in at the deep end of the free market pool so that they would all the more quickly learn to swim in it. But unfortunately, too many sank, before he himself sank in December 1992. Nevertheless, halfway through 1993, more than two thousand large firms with about 3 million employees had been privatised, and more than 30 thousand smaller enterprises had been set up. Nearly 200 thousand agricultural holdings had been privatised during the same period. However, land could not yet be bought and sold without restriction. This was hardly surprising: just a decade earlier, hardly anybody dared suggest the need for any reform of ownership relations.[24]

Just days after the abolition of the central distribution system scheduled for 1 January 1993, Prime Minister Chernomyrdin reintroduced several price controls. In July 1993, after the Central Bank had agreed in May to restrict the money supply and credits in order to restrain inflation, a further move for the same purpose through restriction of credit by other banks failed because of popular opposition.

(4) From 1994 to 1996, the intended emphasis was on stabilisation. A considerable degree of control was achieved over inflation, particularly after the government gained control of the Central Bank and the money supply in October 1994, while reducing subsidies to both industry and agriculture. On the other hand, the Chechen war threatened economic as well as social stability.

Generally speaking, from 1985 to 1996, the rich got richer and the poor got poorer, while a new middle class based on private rather than state activity did not emerge as clearly as advocates of the free market would have hoped. The exact extent of these three tendencies, however, is difficult to measure, not because of a shortage of statistics, but rather because of their conflicting nature. And it was not just statistics which had gone awry – a report of the Academy of Sciences early in 1994 stated that 'the concept of the state's abandonment of the regulation of economic and social processes has resulted in a general loss of governability'.[25] Accustomed to being taken care of from the cradle, however uncomfortably, to the grave, however prematurely, Russian citizens found it difficult to fend for themselves, especially those of working age who were unemployed, or unpaid even if employed, and more especially those who had entered the ranks of senior citizens.

Having often been stop-gap disguised as planned, government policies now seemed hand-to-mouth rather than providing the promised prosperity, which replaced communism on the horizon defined as a vague and indistinct line which retreated as it was approached. But old Russian virtues of resilience had not disappeared. At least some citizens were almost proud of their minimalist existence, and, while they could be envious of the new rich, they could also despise them, reminding themselves as they looked at the luxurious houses being built around most cities of the old Russian proverb – From honest toil you do not build stone palaces.

On the other hand, the soup, cucumbers and kasha of the simple life could well be poisoned. For the all-important basic human rights of clean air, earth and water were under threat throughout Russia and beyond, threatening agriculture and life itself. Pollution knows no frontiers: the Chernobyl nuclear catastrophe of 26 April 1986 might have happened in the Ukrainian republic, but its effects were felt throughout large parts of the Soviet Union and Europe. And, tragically, this was just the most notorious of many incidents accompanying continuous seepage. Industrial areas were normally submerged in a dirty haze while water was often undrinkable: in the countryside, the soil was often polluted.

Alerted to the encroaching danger of natural disaster, like human beings elsewhere, Russians took action in various ways ranging from local protests to governmental adherence to the Action Plan for Central and Eastern Europe approved by the European Conference of Ministers on the Environment meeting in Lucerne in 1993. The Federal Ecological Foundation set up in 1992 supported various programmes such as the sound management of the natural resources of the world's largest repository of fresh water, Lake Baikal; the revival of the Volga river; the conservation and restoration of the species diversity of wildlife and vegetation; and the preservation of the biota gene pool.[26]

While Russians themselves struggled to survive and even prosper, large amounts of advice as well as money were injected from outside. Free the market, following Western example, said many. Do not worry about other freedoms, said some, recommending the example of China, with its severe social control. However, if Red Square had followed the bloody lead of Tiananmen Square after 1989, there might well have been less enthusiasm for this Asiatic model. In prevailing conditions of such uncertainty, financial support came mainly from the International Monetary Fund (I.M.F.), with private capital showing a certain amount of reluctance: full exploitation of the country's greatest natural assets, especially its oil and gas, was limited by the reluctance of the multinational companies to have their fingers burned.[27]

Emerging from the many promises of the Presidential election of 1996, citizens of Russia resumed enormous economic and social tasks. If they were among the prosperous few, they nevertheless had problems: for example, they could hardly avoid coming into contact with networks of bribery and corruption, and would therefore need a *krysha* (literally a roof); that is, to be connected with an unofficial, often illegal protection organisation. With enough money, however, they had no need to worry about the absence from Russia of civil liberty traditions going back as far as the Magna Carta of 1215: as the writer Saltykov-Shchedrin had pointed out in the nineteenth century, the law too had its price. As for the less prosperous majority, they too would find it difficult to survive alone. But their hopes for a better life were reinforced by their knowledge that they, and/or their parents, grandparents and friends, had known worse.

Cultural

In apparent harmony with such contemporary theory as Postmodernism and Chaos, Russian culture turned topsy-turvy during the years following 1985. As we have already seen, previously daring ideas such as democracy in the political and the market in the economic sphere came out from the underground towards a new orthodoxy while the monopoly of one party and central planning fell apart. Dissidence gained acceptance, and prohibited literature, for which the reading public had been hungry for many years and could only consume through *samizdat* or foreign editions, was now openly published at home. Sakharov and Solzhenitsyn could now be read freely, along with a number of less worthy authors. But soon indigestion ensued, and a withering away of the appetite. Similarly, television could now operate in a more truthful manner, but the purity was soon under threat from two main sources: the soap opera and 'pop'; and the influence of the new régime. Now that entry was unrestricted, attendance at church increased, but then fell away again: moreover, hot gospel and cultism joined the more traditional rivals of Orthodoxy. The new dissidents were communists or extreme nationalists. And all this occurred in the context of globalisation.

To adjust to these cultural developments, as has already been observed about the years following 1985, 'at least, an educated pool of talent from which elites can be quickly composed and recomposed, is now at hand'. While the size of that pool did not necessarily diminish, the waters were muddied, or at least stirred up by new thinking about education in particular. Criticisms of the old uniform system led to a more informal arrangement put forward in a Russian Federation Law on Education of 1992 devoted to the following principles: decentralisation and regionalisation; democratisation; humanisation; diversification; 'humanitirisation' – that is, giving emphasis to what the Minister for Education Evgenii Tkachenko called 'the enrichment of the spiritual world of each individual', noting that up to 70 per cent of the Japanese curriculum in senior grades was devoted to the study of cultural subjects. The 'right impression' would have to be conveyed about the past, for example.

However, as in earlier periods of radical reform such as the 1920s, there soon arose questions about the nature and pace of change. Tkachenko himself, more cautious than his predecessor, wondered if the region was becoming too strong for cohesion and control, expressing the fear that 'the destruction of education will lead to the destruction of the notion of the state'. Democracy in school life had led to some student councils voting for the abolition of difficult subjects such as mathematics, and further worries about too much emphasis on individuals and their spiritual needs. So by 1995, there was a considerable amount of pressure for a return to the comprehensive arrangement and a core curriculum.

And, as always, there was the all-important question: Who is going to pay? In President Yeltsin's first decree of June 1994, he proclaimed that the salaries of workers in education should be maintained at a level above those in industry, but in fact teachers have turned out to be among the low paid if paid at all. Early in 1995, no more than 13 per cent of expenditure on education came from the federal government, unlucky for the regions that had to provide the remaining 87 per cent. There were estimates of a six-figure shortfall in required teacher numbers in the mid-1990s in the state system, while many turned to the more remunerative private sector. By the end of 1994, there had been set up 447 private schools and 1160 state *litsei* and *gimnazii*; that is, alternative schools, often on pre-revolutionary or foreign models, usually in Moscow or St Petersburg. But these could cater for a mostly fee-paying minority, and many of the students in the remainder of Russia's 67,000 or so secondary schools would feel decidedly under-privileged, especially when the Constitution of 1993 confirmed a decree of 1992 that free education would be provided up to the age of 15 only. After much agitation by those concerned with such matters, although without widespread public debate, the age of 17 for free education was restored. But this did not mean the absence from Russian streets of unemployed, undereducated and non-motivated teenagers such as could be found throughout Europe and some parts of the wider world.[28]

Primary education struggled on, probably with fewer problems than at the higher level. In connection with what was deemed to be the 'catastrophic condition' of science and culture, a group of academics issued a manifesto in October 1995 complaining that 'egoistical aims have led to the eradication of the higher directions of the evolution of society'. But Russia could not be a 'Great country' without a 'Great culture'. And it was not only a question of learned people, writers, poets, musicians, architects and artists both creative and performing: 'If we do not want to fall in the twenty-first century to the level of medieval armed forces facing an up-to-date fighting machine, we do not have the right to allow the destruction of our scientific potential.'[29]

Some complaints would be more strident. As for the most famous dissidents from the late Soviet period, Andrei Sakharov had died in 1989, while Solzhenitsyn had returned to his homeland only to fade into the background after a brief hold on the educated public's attention. In any case, both their outlooks were now dated, although taking an honoured place in the distinctive Russian traditions. Sakharov was the Westerner, post-Petrine, the advocate of a 'Union of Soviet Republics of Europe and Asia' and of a political convergence leading towards world government. Solzhenitsyn was the Slavophile, pre-Petrine, calling for a spiritual renewal of the Orthodox universal outlook. Neither view retained many adherents by the mid-1990s, although in such a fragmented condition as it was, the basic outlook or outlooks of the Russian intelligentsia could not be determined. The basic task, charting Russia's path into globalism, remained unfulfilled.[30]

Meanwhile, what of the imagination and creativity? In 1991, a critic complained that the only themes to be found in Russian literature were 'the camps, the Jews, the KGB and sex'. Just one of these, the last, could be considered a perennial source of inspiration, but now, as in the West, it made a more explicit appearance on the printed page and in other media. Failing state patronage, and there were at least a few signs of its revival, the artist had to become a *biznesmen* or a *biznesmenka*, and sex sells. However, as Rosalind Marsh observed in 1993:

What of Russian literature as a whole? It is worth recalling that Russians have an apocalyptic propensity for announcing that Russian literature is dead: in 1834, for example, the critic Belinsky said 'We have no literature' shortly after the publication of Pushkin's *Evgenii Onegin* and *The Queen of Spades*. It could also be argued that ever since Stalin's death, long before the Communist Party had been officially disbanded, much literature produced in the U.S.S.R. had already been transformed from 'Soviet' to 'Russian' literature, since it had ceased to be the handmaid of the party. Nevertheless, it is certainly true that Russian literature will never be the same as it was before Gorbachev's accession. The map of twentieth century Russian literature has completely changed; new literary values and new literary authorities have replaced the old false ones. Rumours of the death of Russian literature would seem to be greatly exaggerated ... .'[31]

Can Russian education fulfil even its most basic functions in conditions of financial deprivation? Will the reputation of Sakharov and Solzhenitsyn decline further, or revive? What of other writers and artists, conformist and dissident, from the Soviet as well as the post-Soviet period? Will it come to pass that even Stalinist architecture will come to be celebrated for its intrinsic worth?

Looking to the guardians of the past, we find historians in as much disarray as colleagues in other academic disciplines. As surprised as anybody by the collapse of the Soviet Union, they found it almost impossible immediately to suggest lines of continuity running through the twentieth century. Some of them, avoiding the problem altogether, went back for such lines before 1917 and ignored the Soviet period completely. Others attacked the problem centrally; for example, the journal *Istoriia S.S.S.R. [History of the U.S.S.R.]* changed its name early in 1992 to *Otechestvennaia Istoriia [History of the Fatherland]* with a minimum adaptation of its programme set out in 1990, and publication of interesting discussions of future tasks for Russian historiography. Senior historians put forward broad interpretations, for example discussing the advantages and disadvantages of Russian spaces, and the context of the aspirations of nationalities for statehood. And the continued relevance of V. O. Kliuchevskii was not forgotten in 1991, the 150th centenary of the great man's birth.[32]

18 The Limits of Russian History, 1996–

Following the presidential election of 1996, there were many echoes of the past, both recent and more remote. The loudest and most persistent of them is that the course of Russian history never has run smooth, for major upsets in the shape of internal disturbances and/or invasions from outside have occurred in every one of its centuries. On many previous occasions, the question of reform or ruin has hung over the whole land, and the bells have rung out in alarm rather than celebration. Indeed, the tocsin sounds back through to the dawn of Kievan Rus, and we could find analogies with the present predicament even there.[1]

A second major reverberation is that Kliuchevskii's choice of the continuous process of colonisation as the major theme of Russian history retains a kind of validity 85 years after his death. Let us remind ourselves of the great man's words:

> The history of Russia is the history of a country in process of colonisation. The area of colonisation has broadened together with the territory of the state. Sometimes falling, sometimes rising, this movement continues to our own day.

Since the collapse of the Soviet Union, millions have moved on or back, and millions more would choose to do so if they could. But an attribute of colonisation even more in evidence is the moving frontier: one calculation has been that the boundaries of Russia have never remained fixed for more than fifty years.[2] In the twentieth century alone, Finland, the Baltics and a large part of Poland left what had been the tsarist empire after the Russian Revolution, before they were brought back into the Soviet Union as a whole or in part (in the case of Finland a very small part) with the onset of the Second World War. Most, if not quite all of this territory, was lost again by the end of 1991. There have been other significant differences between the shape of the tsarist empire and the Soviet Union, and within the Soviet Union, too. There have also been important lines of continuity. Most notably, the Chechen revolt or war for independence of 1994–6, however it is described, could be clearly seen as the latest in a long series of centrifugal movements in or near the Caucasus. Without a doubt, although they cannot be predicted specifically, changes are in store for Siberia and Central Asia.

More particularly, to personalise the point, both Gorbachev and Yeltsin have claimed historical continuity for themselves through comparisons of their own policies with those of outstanding predecessors, notably Peter the Great.[3] It is interesting to note in addition that neither Gorbachev nor Yeltsin looked with such favour on the contribution of Ivan the Terrible as had Stalin. Unlike Yeltsin, however, Gorbachev also sought consistency with the principles of Lenin.

To return to the presidential election of 1996, while possessing post-Soviet characteristics, it also recalled deeper-seated attitudes towards the question of popular choice. This curious amalgam was reflected in the campaigns of both Boris Yeltsin and his principal opponent, the Communist Gennadii Zyuganov. Like other politicians determined to hold on to power, President Yeltsin littered his campaign trail with promises that he knew he could not keep, in such profusion indeed that he gave some posthumous vindication to the criticisms of parliamentary democracy made by the adviser to the last tsar a century ago, in 1896. Considering 'The Great Falsehood of Our Time' to be 'the principle of the sovereignty of the people, the principle that all power issues from the people', Konstantin Pobedonostsev wrote:

The people loses all importance for its representative, until the time arrives when it is to be played upon again; the false and flattering and lying phrases are lavished as before; some are suborned by bribery, others terrified by threats – the long chain of manoeuvres spun which forms an invariable factor of Parliamentarism. Yet this electoral farce continues to deceive humanity, and to be regarded as an institution which crowns the edifice of State. Poor humanity![4]

Poor humanity indeed, and a great strain on our basic belief that democracy is the worst system of government apart from every other.

But up to a point, the President's progress through the provinces also recalled times back beyond the American and French Revolutions when the principles of popular sovereignty were first clearly enunciated, not so much of a candidate putting himself up for election as of a ruler distributing gifts among his faithful subjects. As for Gennadii Zyuganov, the post-

Soviet message which he purveyed was partly Eurocommunist, but at least as much patriotic–populist (indeed, after the election, the Communist Party joined with nationalists in an alliance of parties and groups). He touched on a nostalgia less for the Soviet concrete apartment than for the Russian wooden house in which he also grew up and featured in as much of the media coverage as he was able to snatch from the President, whose hold on TV in particular would have made a Western media baron envious in the extreme. Not surprisingly, Zyuganov found his major support away from Moscow and St Petersburg, where Old Russia was more in evidence and city-slicker spin doctors were less effective.

Events immediately after the election continued to resonate with echoes from the past, the most powerful of which came from little more than a decade ago. As soon as his victory appeared assured, Boris Yeltsin virtually collapsed, and his health gave as much cause for concern as that of Andropov and Chernenko in the years immediately preceding the attainment of power by Mikhail Gorbachev. But the scene was not only a reminder of the persistence of the latter-day 'cult of personality': it also recalled the terminal illness of a tsar with would-be successors jockeying for position, as, for example, in Pushkin's *Boris Godunov*.

As we move towards the year 2000, then, we must not forget the previous millennium. In other words, in order to understand the varied interpretations of the Russian situation towards the end of the twentieth century, we need to think again of ten and more previous centuries. Such a controversial history of so vast a country is not easy to summarise. Nevertheless, the attempt must be made, and at least a few suggestions for overall comprehension may then be put forward. The first of them is that the division of the subject, as throughout this book, into three main phases and three principal themes provides a basic framework. But we must recognise that even before the medieval period begins, many of the influences on it and its modern and contemporary successors were already formed – the geographical circumstances and distinctive types of human organisation, for example. These comprise much of the material for the debate which still rages about the nature of the Kievan state and its legacy to the Muscovite sequel. The temperature of that debate is probably raised by the lack of appropriate evidence. The 'Dark Ages' preceding the medieval period are obscure indeed at the Eastern extremity of Europe. And then, as we have seen, even with the chronicles and other documents to guide us, we still find it difficult to find answers to certain basic questions: what was the composition of the Kievan ruling class and how do we typify the society which it dominated; what were the predominant elements in its economy; and which of its major cultural constituents, the traditional Slavic or the imported Byzantine, was in the ascendancy? The points at issue are equally controversial when we move on from Kiev to Moscow. On the one hand, we may quarrel about the manner in which the movement from the south-west to the north-east took place. On the other hand, we must consider the breadth and depth of the Mongol impact. Even when we come to the fifteenth century and the establishment of the supremacy of Moscow over rival principalities, can we be certain even yet about the main thrust of political, economic and cultural developments?

For although appearances are now clearer, they might be deceptive. Ivan III, the Great, and later Ivan IV, the Terrible, are establishing the rule of one, the autocrat or tsar, making use of a centralising tradition and an ideology adapted from Byzantium and the Holy Roman Empire. But do they actually rule in isolated splendour, or are they dependent upon the boyars and other members of the nobility? Old problems, such as the balance of agriculture and commerce, are intensified by the arrival of the European world economy. Was Russia on the semi-periphery or periphery to the Western European core? And now, it was not just the Old Slavic versus the Byzantine-Christian aspects of Russian culture. Even if the answer is to be mostly in the negative, there has to be some investigation of the extent of the impact on the Eastern extremity of Europe of such movements as the Renaissance, Reformation and Counter-Reformation.

For all the reservations and controversies, however, certain assertions can be made with some confidence about the Russia that was emerging from the medieval world and becoming modern from about the middle of the seventeenth century onwards. It was European, or at least frontier European, rather than Asian, or Eurasian, and therefore bears comparison more with developments to the West than to the East. In other words, while from the inside of Europe, especially from the Western centre, which enjoyed this status in a political and cultural as well as economic manner, Russia might look exceptional, the view from Asia makes it adhere firmly to the rule. For example, Muscovite socio-political arrangements may be characterised as feudal, even though they do not conform to the norms set in France. From the entourage of the prince to that of the tsar, there may have been a lack of formality in the reciprocal relationship of the individual members of the ruling class, but the mutual aspects of an at least tacit contract were undoubtedly there. Indeed, for some analysts, from about the late fifteenth century onwards, there was more give and take in Moscow than in Paris or London (each of themselves to a considerable degree an exception measured by the rule of the other, although from Rheims to Paris or from Winchester to London was neither such a long distance nor such a cultural adjustment as from Kiev to Moscow).

Russia becomes even more feudal when emphasis is given (as it was by Soviet historians following Marx) to the socio-economic rather than the socio-political aspects of the situation. The ties developing among the forests and steppes of the expanding Muscovite principality between landlords and peasants were not fundamentally dissimilar from those to be found in the more compact fields of Western Europe. The most striking divergence, the emergence of Russian serfdom at a time when serfdom had disappeared from the European core, becomes less significant when we consider it as a reflection of the aforementioned European world economy. That is, the core had no need of serfdom as it consolidated modes of acquiring wealth in a manner that was less labour intensive through closer relationship with the continents beyond Europe, while finding alternative labour supplies in considerable numbers of slaves and dependents in Asia, the Americas and Africa. Without such wider opportunities Russia (along with Prussia, Austria, and other states in Central Europe) necessarily turned inwards for the early modernisation of its economy. Similarly, early modernisation of Russian culture at the time of the Renaissance, Reformation and Counter-Reformation appears less exotic if we recall the divergent nature of its experience within the more general sphere of the classical inheritance and the Christian tradition of the continent as a whole. Emphasis on Eastern Orthodoxy and Greco-Byzantine learning, although grafted, possibly no more than superficially, on to pre-literate native Slavic folkways, constituted the particular application of more general principles, embodied in the concept of the 'Third Rome'.

In summary, then, while recognising that the ultimate measure of historical objectivity must be global, but also that the present state of such awareness is not well advanced, we must locate medieval Russia at the edge of feudal Europe. Does this placement remain the same throughout the modern period of history, that is, from about the middle of the seventeenth century to 1917? Or is it rather the case that the shrinkage of the world towards the end of that period makes the position less clear-cut? Certainly, as far as Russia is concerned, the period may be described most succinctly as that of the rise and fall of absolutism within a framework still containing many of the features of feudalism. With Ivan the Great and Ivan the Terrible, arguably, there was the rise and fall of what we may call proto-absolutism, with the aspiration being greater than the reality. That is, the two tsars completed the process of the in-gathering of the Russian principalities while beating back external threats, but could never really exert full control over their thus expanded dominions. The impossibility of the completion of the task that they had set themselves was revealed quite starkly in the bizarre stratagems adopted by Ivan the Terrible, and even more, soon after his death, in the Time of Troubles breaking out at the end of the sixteenth century. Then, from 1613 onwards, the administration of the first Romanov could aim at little more than the recapture of what had been lost. The socio-political foundations for a more complete absolutism, we have argued, were laid during the second half of the seventeenth century, after Russia, like many other parts of Europe, was struck by a severe political crisis at the end of the Thirty Years War. Ensuing legal, administrative, military and ecclesiastical reforms prepared the way fairly fully for the much more celebrated policies of Peter the Great, whose degree of success may be measured by the relative degree of their continuance and amplification during the reigns of some far less remarkable successors. Meanwhile, from the Great Northern War to the Seven Years War, Russia was asserting a more positive presence in Europe.

A third and final ascendant phase for Russian absolutism is associated with the reign of Catherine the Great, who energetically promoted an overhaul of the governmental machine while pursuing ambitious cultural objectives with equal zest. We must not exaggerate the degree of Catherine's success or that of Russian absolutism's in general. Nevertheless, by the standards of the time as well as in its own estimate, the Russian Empire cut an impressive figure, reinforced by further military victories. Why, then, was Russian absolutism now to move into decline? The shortest answer is in a word – modernisation. That is, the process marked by the French and Industrial Revolutions – the 'dual revolution' as it has been called – left Russia behind. Alarmed by the implications of the first, the tsarist administration drew back from the second. And then, the victory over Napoleon in 1812 persuaded Alexander I that his own system needed no reform, while his successor Nicholas I, shocked by the abortive Decembrist Revolt led by dissident nobles at the beginning of his reign, did all he could to resist fundamental change at home and abroad, in, for example, the year of revolutions, 1848. Soon after that, however, defeat in the Crimean War hastened the death of Nicholas I and persuaded Alexander II that reform could no longer be avoided. Hence, the emancipation of the serfs and other considerable new departures.

After some progress, the assassination of Alexander II in 1881 brought reform to an end, and the last two tsars, Alexander III and Nicholas II pursued policies that were as reactionary as possible. To be sure, at the very end of the nineteenth century and the beginning of the twentieth, an impressive amount of economic growth was achieved, in a highly competitive imperialist world. Then, the shame of further defeat in the Russo–Japanese War of 1904–5 led to the Revolution of 1905 and a limited amount of political reform: at last, Russia had a parliament – the

Duma. Although this Duma, like the German Reichstag, has been considered by some no more than the fig-leaf covering the nakedness of absolutism, it has been looked upon by others as evidence for an optimistic appraisal of tsarism in its last years. Had the outbreak of the First World War not ensued, the argument runs, Russia could have continued along the path of peaceful modernisation. The contrary, pessimistic analysis would include the observation that, as the dénouement of decades of imperialistic rivalry in which Russia was a full, enthusiastic participant, the First World War can hardly be looked upon as an unfortunate, extraneous accident.

It would be an over-simplification to ascribe tsarist backwardness in the process of modernisation to absolutism alone. After all, another absolutist power, Imperial Germany, was a world leader in the later stages of that process, and was therefore held up by some reformers as the model to follow. Others, looking further afield to find a basis for comparison and emulation, lighted upon the U.S.A. Lenin himself talked about the Prussian and American paths to modernisation as the choices that could be made. But the October Revolution led by Lenin in 1917 helped to usher in a new historical phase, the contemporary, and by the end of the First World War in 1918, absolutism had fallen in Austria and Germany, too. However, just as Hitler's Third Reich was to some extent the heir to Bismarck's Second, so the Soviet Union of Lenin and Stalin did not mark a completely clean break with the tsarist past. As Lenin himself observed, the new order would have to be constructed with the bricks of the old.

But before we look more closely at the new order, we must examine more closely these old bricks. What was the nature of absolutism? In summary form, its characteristics may be presented as follows: an all-powerful figurehead, usually a monarch; and ideology, basically 'divine right' with a growing secular component, for example 'the general good'; an accommodation with the Church, or assumption of superiority over it; a tendency towards a unified system of law and permanent bureaucracy; the coalescence of the empire from older provinces and newer acquisitions; a standing army, and often a fleet in being; the nobility as a ruling class, counterbalanced by a bourgeoisie or even by a huge peasantry and/or an embryonic proletariat; a national market and taxation network, with a basically agrarian economy necessarily making some adjustments to the necessity for industrialisation; and some awareness of the necessity for education, at least a basic literacy, and for the encouragement of a broader cultural development. Altogether, these characteristics appeared in a positive fashion during the ascendancy of absolutism, in a negative fashion during absolutism's decline.

If the Revolution of 1917 constituted a break with tsarist absolutism, some observers would argue that Soviet power was equally absolutist. Indeed, the argument has been put forward many times in various ways that continuity was almost complete. Bearing this argument in mind, let us look more closely at the features of absolutism as listed above and as emulated after 1917. Certainly, there remained an all-powerful figurehead, in fact if not in theory, with a 'cult of personality' as great in its own way as that assumed by the tsars, evolving from Lenin to Gorbachev. The ideology, becoming more pervasive than Orthodoxy or its secular accompaniments, emerged as Marxism–Leninism, with the Church itself in fuller subservience: Soviet law, at least in theory, encompassed the Soviet Union more fully than tsarist law the empire (while there were major actual infringements of the law in both cases). Similarly, Soviet bureaucracy became even more permanent and pervasive than its tsarist predecessor. For its part, imperial coalescence was forced into reverse in the short run, as Finland, Poland and the Baltic states all achieved their independence; to a considerable extent, 'Socialism in One Country' and other inter-war policies were brought about by the exclusion of the Soviet Union from a large slice of Europe. To be sure, much of the territorial loss was made up with the arrival of World War Two, as a consequence of which Stalin and his adherents were able to exercise an influence over Eastern and Central Europe scarcely dreamed of by the Romanovs, while maintaining a firm grip on the U.S.S.R. in Asia, too.

Meanwhile, the Red armed forces were as obtrusive as their imperial counterparts, if remaining, like them, obedient to the civil government. After some early discussion of a new 'people's militia', many of the old distinctions returned, including an officer caste. Moreover, if the nobility disappeared, many Red officers joined with most leading Soviet civil officials to form a new ruling class in the Communist Party with some others included in the *nomenklatura*, a new Table of Ranks. But the landed basis for eminence, enjoyed by the majority of the *dvorianstvo* in earlier years, had gone, and in most respects, the new class was aggressively urban. And since there was no middle class in the traditional sense, the new Soviet ruling class was deemed by many analysts to exceed in power and influence the *dvorianstvo* – even if Stalin, like Ivan the Terrible before him, eliminated many individuals, he did not change the system, indeed even strengthened it. As for the most numerous class before the Russian Revolution, and for many years after it, the peasantry declined in numbers and significance during the years of Stalin – to a considerable extent being reduced by force, and some would say to a new serfdom. As for the proletariat, much smaller in 1917 and for some years afterwards than the theoretical influence assigned to it might suggest, it certainly rose steeply in numbers from the 1930s onwards, if never actually achieving the preponderance suggested in Marxism–Leninism. By the arrival of 'mature socialism' in more recent years, the social basis of the Soviet Union, including also a larger share of the total population from the non-Slavic republics, came to differ markedly from that of tsarism a hundred or even fifty years before.

Most certainly, the transformation brought about by the Five-Year Plans involved the concepts of a national market and taxation network, although forcing the pace and controlling the nature of industrialisation to an extent never attempted before 1917, even if some tsarist policies during and before World War One could be deemed precursors. The drive to eliminate illiteracy was also more concerted and accelerated than before, while cultural revolution was aimed at reinforcing throughout society the change of outlook already completed in the world views of the leading Bolsheviks.

With this update of the leading features of absolutism, we have indicated that there are limits to the argument of continuity from the imperial period into the Soviet. Generally speaking, we might summarise the differences by observing that the task of modernisation that had defeated the tsarist régime in its decline was taken up by the Communist régime in its ascendancy. Moreover, the wider circumstances of the contemporary period, from World War One to World War Two to the Cold War, were of increasing influence as governors of internal developments. In particular, the central process of industrialisation was under way with still a considerable distance to travel before it reached the point at which its major rivals had arrived before the end of the nineteenth century. But the world did not stand still, for while old empires collapsed or began to fade away in Europe, the U.S.A. in particular had taken giant strides forward during the First World War, and was now the leading financial and industrial power. After Lenin's death, Stalin described Leninism as Soviet power plus American efficiency. To catch up with and overtake the U.S.A. became the top priority as the Five-Year Plans were launched at the end of the 1920s with widespread discomfort, dislocation and death. But the forced pace was not brought about solely, or even principally, by the Soviet government's desire to achieve world power. There was a much more pressing need: in the unstable conditions even preceding the Great Depression, Stalin and his adherents believed that the very existence of the Soviet Union was under threat from outside, and from inside. Intervention was feared on a much greater scale than that which had occurred during the Civil War years following the Russian Revolution. Traitors to the Soviet cause were detected at all levels of society, especially in the Party. In the most fraught conditions, the fundamental process of the creation of heavy industry was completed during the 1930s.

Modernisation was not just a matter of industrialisation. Beyond the liquidation of illiteracy, a whole new cultural outlook had to be created and while some of his followers talked about the possibility of a proletarian culture, Lenin himself said that he would be satisfied at first with the achievement of a bourgeois culture. Even to reach this second goal was difficult in a society still mostly composed of peasants. Therefore, after a brief period of exciting experimentation, artists and writers were called upon to help create a 'New Soviet Man' through implementation of the principles of 'Socialist realism'. Within their new constraints, creative people managed a few masterpieces and a considerable number of works that were impressive enough, but as often as not through employing old rather than new methods. Even Eisenstein's films, especially *Alexander Nevsky* and *Ivan the Terrible*, were a celebration of the traditional in an upstart medium. By the end of the 1930s, the compromise between pre- and post-1917 culture was near completion, and in the ensuing Second World War, it was taken even nearer, especially as far as the Orthodox Church was concerned.

The Second World War was a watershed as great at 1917 and 1929, and, as with them, the impact was both internal and international. As the epic victory over Nazism was won, and the Red Army liberated and then occupied Eastern Europe, the U.S.S.R. gained recognition as a world great power; indeed it was soon placed along with the U.S.A. in the unprecedented category of superpower. However, the domestic economy was in ruins, and more rigorous controls were superimposed on society in order that this weakness should not be exposed at the same time as stability was maintained. Enormous tensions were created as the leading characteristics of the mature contemporary world took shape. Along with the culmination of the emergence of the superpowers, these were: the creation of atomic weapons; a new industrial revolution – the scientific–technological – with a steep rise in world production; a demographic explosion; decolonisation; transfer from the Atlantic to the Pacific rim of the economic core; culmination of the full arrival of a post-printing culture based on television and radio, recordings and computers; and a neo-totalitarianism making use of electronic surveillance and databases. Of course, these characteristics were not all formed simultaneously, but over a period of several decades, with the Soviet Union lagging behind at a time when, with the shrinkage of the world and the pace of change, it was ever more difficult to catch up.

Although the U.S.S.R. was deemed to be a superpower after 1945 and possessed the atomic bomb from 1949 onwards, the last years of Stalin were devoted to reconstruction after the devastation of war, and the U.S.A., which had gone from strength to strength during the war years, was in almost every respect far ahead. From 1953 onwards, under Khrushchev, and then from 1964, under Brezhnev, the gap between the two superpowers scarcely narrowed, in spite of some appearances to the contrary. For example, the launching of the first Sputnik and then Gagarin's first manned space flight gave the Soviet Union a brief, illusory lead in the space race. In nearly all other respects, the U.S.A. led the way in the new industrial revolution even if Japan and West Germany emerged as rivals in this field. Neither superpower was severely affected by the demographic explosion and the decolonisation movement, but the repercussions from Asia, Africa and Latin America could not go unobserved or unfelt. At times, it seemed that the Third World had become a surrogate battlefield for Soviet and U.S. arms and ideologies. The transfer of the core from the Atlantic to the Pacific was a comparatively late development of the post-war years. However, there was little evident prospect of Vladivostok and its hinterland emulating California, even if the Soviet government gave considerable priority to building up its Far Eastern defences against threats from China overland and from the U.S.A. across the sea. The post-printing culture, arriving in the West from the 1960s, reached the U.S.S.R. more than a decade later; even then, it was apparent that some time would elapse before the Soviet Union would be swamped with computers, video recorders and the other indices of the new culture, even if virtually the whole of its population could now catch sight of television. Finally, and perhaps most surprisingly, it could at least be argued that the Soviet Union was finding it very difficult to catch up with and overtake the West in new techniques of surveillance and what were still called 'cloak and dagger' operations, even if now carried out by electronic means. All in all, then, the problem of comparative backwardness remained at least as great during the process of 'contemporisation' as it had been throughout that of modernisation.

In this latest period, comparison was made most appropriately with the Soviet Union's fellow superpower, the U.S.A. By the late 1980s, the competition between them had exhausted so much of their treasure (if not of their blood) that a comparison was now being made not of their rise, but of their decline. A Soviet spokesman observed in May 1988, by no means facetiously, that the U.S.S.R. was in danger of becoming a developing country, the U.S.A. – a 'semi-colony' of Germany, Japan and possibly South Korea. Earth's proud empires had passed away in earlier years, and while few analysts would adhere rigidly to a cyclical view of history, there did appear to be the distinct possibility that neither superpower could make adequately a readjustment to the global demands of the end of the twentieth century. And then, indeed, the Soviet Union collapsed in 1991.[5]

Both the U.S.A. and the U.S.S.R.'s predecessor, the tsarist empire, were among the great powers involved in the imperial rivalry of the years before 1914. Both therefore form part of the comparative basis for a balanced appraisal of the process of modernisation, in so far as it was completed before the outbreak of the First World War. The powers that failed that supreme test did so either because they lagged behind in that process or because they had overstretched themselves in the rush to complete it. Tsarist Russia was in the first category, the kaiser's Germany was an example of the second. The U.S.A. was the principal beneficiary of the great imperial struggle. If we go back to the medieval period, we can observe the process of the development of the centralised state, the emergence of Muscovy lending itself to comparison with the like process in France or England. We should also bear in mind that, although the U.S.A. was not formed before 1776, its medieval and early modern roots in England, Scotland and elsewhere must not be neglected in any attempt at a full appraisal of the weight of history that lay upon the two superpowers, and helped to bring about the downfall of the U.S.S.R.

To appraise that weight on Russia today, two inseparable questions must be asked: What is the legacy of the past, and how is it perceived? The two answers merge into each other, for the problems of human societies, like those of the individuals within them, can be psychosomatic. To put it another way, today's realities include a large measure of our perception of yesterday. To take the second question first, although there are an infinite number of answers, they can perhaps be reduced to two groups, those from inside, and those from outside. Generally speaking, national histories can be over-celebratory, and a foreign appraisal can therefore add a corrective. In the eighteenth century, Adam Smith suggested that:

> This self-deceit, this fatal weakness of mankind, is the source of half the disorders of human life. If we saw ourselves in the light in which others see us, or in which they would see us, if they knew all, a reformation would generally be unavoidable.[6]

Let it be said immediately that no foreign investigator of Russian history has ever known all, since the barrier of language is just one of many that has to be crossed in order to make any meaningful contribution to the subject. Perhaps the most difficult preliminary is the achievement of a degree of sympathy for a subject with more than its fair share of violence and injustice. Sympathy, we must emphasise, however, does not mean in this case encouragement, support or even acceptance of infringements of accepted norms of human behaviour, but rather the imaginative comprehension of the circumstances in which the infringements took place. To repeat the point with an adaptation of an old French saying – to understand is not necessarily to forgive. A further obstacle in this difficult exercise is the application of idealised foreign national or international standards to the actual Russian situation. Has any society ever observed completely the aforementioned 'accepted norms of human behaviour'? In other words, the outside observer as well as the peoples perceived should be influenced by Adam Smith's dictum. Moreover, while many Russian citizens echo a point made to foreigners by many of their pre-revolutionary predecessors that the experiences since 1917 or before are so unique that they can be understood only by those who have undergone them, it needs to be said that a completely unique experience would be understood by nobody, since all human comprehension proceeds by comparison.

The inside view of Russian history may be approached most conveniently by a summary of its evolution. The medieval chroniclers were the factual counterparts of the monk Pimen from Pushkin's *Boris Godunov*, writing not only to supplicate God but also to justify the actions of a dynasty:

> so that the future generations of the Orthodox may know the bygone fortunes of their native land, remember their great tsars for their labours, their glory, their good actions, and humbly implore the Saviour for their sins, their dark deeds.[7]

After their own fashion, similarly, their modern successors concentrated on the story of the Great Russian state and its rulers. However, towards the end of the imperial period, as that state was clearly in danger of dissolution, the problem arose of continuing the story in a progressive and forward-looking manner. This process has been illustrated above in the interpretation of the pre-revolutionary historian V. O. Kliuchevskii.

With the arrival of the contemporary period following the Revolution of 1917, some of the first Soviet historians rejected an analysis of the past based on the tsars and their state, concentrating instead on the development of the class struggle and the rise and fall of capital. With Stalin, there was a partial return to patriotic history in which Lenin was deified and at least some of his predecessors were partly rehabilitated. Ivan the Terrible and Peter the Great, for example, were both seen by the Leader as working with ruthless determination in the same direction as Lenin and himself. A sign of these times was the republication of some of the works of a historian who had never been completely ignored, V. O. Kliuchevskii, a process continued and expanded without lengthy interruption ever since. After the death of Stalin in 1953, there were movements towards wholesale revision within a more flexible Marxist–Leninist framework, although before 1985 some of the more adventurous spirits found themselves in trouble. With the arrival of the new Russia, the opportunity may have arisen for a completely open reconsideration of Russian and Soviet history, in which foreign colleagues may have their part to play.[8]

How far revision might go it is difficult to say. Unless a dissolution of the Russian Federation is seriously contemplated, however, it will not be easy to reject all previous accounts describing the manner in which its principal antecedents, the imperial tsarist empire and the Soviet Union, were built up from the foundation of the centralised Muscovite state. In other words, it will be difficult to view the policies of Ivan the Terrible and Peter the Great, or even of Stalin, in a completely negative manner. One can hardly expect Russian historians to abandon their contribution to socio-political cohesion when most of their counterparts abroad are doing no such thing.

However, in a world radically different from that which existed, say, a quarter of a century ago and is changing fast, perhaps all historians everywhere need to apply themselves more energetically to the task of approaching objectivity, resisting as much as possible all interpretations of the past that are romanticised, partial or distorted. In this way, we will move together towards a more accurate picture of the medieval, modern and contemporary history not only of Kievan Rus, Muscovy, the tsarist empire, the Soviet Union, post-Soviet Russia and the other successor states but also of the whole world.

This does not mean the abandonment of patriotism, especially as defined (and contrasted with nationalism) by Academician Dmitrii Likhachev:

> True patriotism means enriching others while enriching oneself spiritually. But nationalism, while fencing itself off from other cultures, spoils and dries up one's own culture …. Patriotism is the most noble of feelings … [while] nationalism is the meanest misfortune of the human race.[9]

On the other hand, some might argue that the higher stage of patriotism cannot be reached without a preliminary stage of nationalism, or more specifically in the post-Soviet case, that it is easier for Russians to be patriotic than others, while at least a few would want to insist that Russians have never been able to achieve true self-fulfilment. Patriots and nationalists alike, especially the historians among them, would have no difficulty in agreeing with another of Likhachev's observations, that our past and our present will remain in our distant future.

Looking to the future, social scientists have been encouraged to investigate the manner in which the creation of industrial society forces states with differing backgrounds into similar moulds: capitalist democratic; socialist democratic; communist; bureaucratic; fascist; 'environmentalist'. Such constructs, which may conveniently be identified by colour – blue, pink, red, grey, black and green – obviously vary in their appeal. Social scientists can be as guilty of wishful thinking and of unwarranted gloom as their fellow human beings, and none of them can yet forecast what will happen with any certainty. Writing as optimistic a scenario as possible for post-industrial society, one might hope for a global convergence with the creation of a world government with an appropriate multicoloured ideology. In any such development, positive and negative aspects of the Soviet experience might not be irrelevant; moreover, an important part might be played both by the U.S.A and what is left of its former fellow superpower, especially if the observation made by Alexander Herzen about their large slice of the Northern hemisphere a century and a half ago be held still to retain its relevance:

> The North-American States and Russia represent two solutions which are opposite but incomplete, and which therefore complement rather than exclude each other. A contradiction which is full of life and development, which is open-ended, without finality, without physiological discord – that is not a challenge to enmity and combat, not a basis for an attitude of unsympathetic indifference, but a basis for efforts to remove this formal contradiction with the help of something broader – if only through mutual understanding and recognition.[10]

Who knows what new frontiers could be opened together?

Historians, like social scientists, analyse the development of Russia and other states according to their own world outlook. Worthwhile work can be produced by the devoutly religious and militantly atheistic, the most stubborn conservative and the most dedicated progressive. But this does not mean that academic analysis is a completely random activity. Apart from accepted conventions of scholarship, which enforce their own demanding restrictions, and the guiding principles of whatever philosophy possesses the researcher, there is the relentless governor of time itself. As far as has been possible, this book has attempted to be consistent with the canons of historical research and writing, and with the definition offered by E. H. Carr: 'History is the long struggle of man, by the exercise of his reason, to understand his environment and to act upon it'.[11] As to the value of this definition for man and woman alike, as to the thoroughness of its implementation here, time alone will tell.

Notes

Full publication details, where not supplied here, will be found in the relevant sections of the Select Bibliography.

General Introduction

1. Kliuchevskii, *Sochineniia*, I, p. 47.
2. R. J. Kerner, *The Urge to the Sea: The Course of Russian History – The Role of Rivers, Portages, Ostrogs, Monasteries and Furs* (New York, 1971).
3. See G. V. Vernadsky, *Ancient Russia* (New Haven, Conn., 1943); P. P. Tolochko *et al* (eds), *Drevnie slaviane i Kievskaia Rus* (Kiev, 1989).
4. See K. Hannestad and others., 'Varangian Problems', *Scando-Slavica*, Supplement 1 (Copenhagen, 1970). See also the controversial study by O. Pritsak, *The Origin of Rus* (Cambridge, Mass., 1981). 'Normans' are usually said to be settlers of later generations, but all four terms – Normans, Norsemen, Varangians and Vikings – have been used here interchangeably.

Part One   Medieval Russia: Kiev to Moscow

Introduction

1. Kliuchevskii, *Sochineniia*, I, pp. 360–1, finds feudal obligations less binding in Russia than in the West. Martin, *Medieval Russia*, pp. 372–99, has a chapter on 'Conclusions and Controversies'. See also T. Kuryuzawa, 'The debate on the genesis of Russian feudalism in recent Soviet historiography' in T. Ito (ed.), *Facing Up to the Past: Historiography under Perestroika* (Sapporo, 1989).

Ch. 1   The Construction and Collapse of Kiev, 882–1240

1. Cross, *The Russian Primary Chronicle*, p. 59. See T. S. Noonan, 'Why the Vikings first came to Russia', *Jahrbücher für Geschichte Osteuropas*, vol. 34 (1986).
2. Kliuchevskii, *Sochineniia*, I, p. 204. P. P. Tolochko, *Drevniaia Rus: ocherki sotsialno–politicheskoi istorii* (Kiev, 1987) gives a judicious summary view of early Kievan developments. On the 'aristocratic diaspora', see Robert

Bartlett, *The Making of Europe: Conquest, Colonization and Cultural Change, 950–1350* (London, 1994), pp. 24–59.
3. Tolochko, *Drevniaia Rus*, pp. 26–7. On Riurik and Oleg, see Franklin and Shepard, *The Emergence*, pp. 57–8.
4. Rybakov, *Early Centuries*, p. 4.
5. Ibid., p. 42.
6. See A. N. Sakharov, *Diplomatiia Sviatoslava* (Moscow, 1991).
7. Vernadsky, *Kievan Russia*, pp. 73–4.
8. See, for example, Poppe, *The Rise of Christian Russia*. See also *Kak byla kreshchena Rus* (Moscow, 1988).
9. Martin, *Medieval Russia*, pp. 373–80. Franklin and Shepard, *The Emergence*, pp. 265, 275, 369–71, are unhappy about the application of the words 'state' and 'federation' to Rus, tentatively preferring 'collegiate cousinhood' and suggesting that 'The idea of an emerging political culture is more appropriate to the times than that of a fixed political system'; 'there was no "state", but perhaps there were the beginnings of a nation'.
10. Tolochko, *Drevniaia Rus*, pp. 80–3; Franklin and Shepard, *The Emergence*, pp. 257–8.
11. Cross, *The Russian Primary Chronicle*, p. 142.
12. Tolochko, *Drevniaia Rus*, pp. 89–90.
13. Cross, *The Russian Primary Chronicle*, p. 187.
14. Franklin and Shepard, *The Emergence*, pp. 275–7; 369–71. Tolochko, *Drevniaia Rus*, p. 223, argues that the disintegration of the eleventh and twelfth centuries has been exaggerated.
15. Kliuchevskii, *Sochineniia*, I, pp. .239, 247–9; V. O. Kliuchevskii, *Boiarskaia duma drevnei Rusi* (Moscow, 1909), p. 12.
16. Ibid., p. 13.
17. Grekov, *Kiev Rus*, p. 70. See also, for example, P. P. Tolochko, *Drevnerusskii feodalnyi gorod* (Kiev, 1989), pp. 79–99.
18. Vernadsky, *Kievan Russia*, pp. 103–5.
19. Blum, *Lord and* Peasant, p. 25; Vernadsky, *Kievan Russia*, p. 133.
20. Grekov, *Kiev Rus*, p. 347.
21. Cross, *The Russian Primary Chronicle*, pp. 308–9.
22. Tikhomirov, *The Towns*, p. 149; B. A. Rybakov, *Remeslo drevnei Rusi* (Moscow, 1948).
23. Vernadsky, *Kievan Russia*, pp. 121–30.
24. In his *Kievskaia Rus* (Leningrad, 1980) I. Ia. Froianov rejects the predominance of elite landholding, and thus plays down the feudal nature of Kievan society. The Grekov view is updated by M. V. Sverdlov, *Genezis i struktura feodalnogo obshchestva v drevnei Rusi* (Leningrad, 1983).
25. Grekov, *Kiev Rus*, p. 497.
26. Rybakov, *Early Centuries*, pp. 66–77.
27. Fedotov, *The Russian Religious Mind*, I, p. 412.
28. Franklin and Shepard, *The Emergence*, pp. 238–43.
29. Fedotov, *The Russian Religious Mind*, I, pp. 84, 94, 244, 380–1. On Vladimir Monomakh, see the study by D. Obolensky in *Six Byzantine Portraits* (Oxford, 1988). The name 'Monomakh' came from his Byzantine mother.
30. See, for example, J. L. I. Fennell, 'The Recent Controversy in the Soviet Union over the Authenticity of the *Slovo*', in L. H. Legters (ed.), *Russia:*

Essays in History and Literature (Leyden, 1972); D. S. Likhachev, '*Slovo o polku Igoreve'*: *istoriko–literaturnyi ocherk* (Moscow, 1982). Scc also D. S. Likhachev, *The Great Heritage: the Classical Literature of Old Rus* (Moscow, 1981).

31. See, for example, M. W. Thompson (comp.), *Novgorod the Great: Excavations at the Medieval City* (London, 1967). See also Simon Franklin, 'Literacy and Documentation in Early Medieval Russia', *Speculum*, 60 (1985).
32. Fedotov, *The Russian*, I, p. 380.
33. Seaman, *History*, p. 1.
34. Franklin and Shepard, *The Emergence*, p. 355. V. N. Lazarev is sceptical in *L'Art de la Russie medievale et l'occident: XI–XV siècles*, XIIIe Congrès International des Sciences Historiques (Moscow, 1970) pp. 21–2. See also Hamilton, *The Art*, pp. 35, 49.
35. Obolensky, *Byzantium*, p. 35. See also A. N. Konrad, *Old Russia and Byzantium: The Byzantine and Oriental Origins of Russian Culture* (Vienna, 1972); J. Meyendorff, *Byzantium and the Rise of Russia* (Cambridge, 1981).
36. Rybakov, in Pletneeva *et al.* (eds), *Istoriia SSSR*, I, p. 682; Grekov as in note 25 above.
37. Franklin and Shepard, *The Emergence*, p. xvii.

Ch. 2   Invasion and Disunity, 1240–1462

1. Grekov, *Kiev Rus*, p. 642.
2. R. V. Viatkin and S. L. Tikhvinskii, 'Some Problems of Scholarship in the CPR', *Soviet Studies in History*, vol. 2, no. 4 (1963–4) p. 53.
3. Vernadsky, *The Mongols*, p. 1.
4. Fennell, *The Emergence*, pp. 9–10.
5. Zenkovsky, *Medieval Russia's Epics*, p. 18.
6. J. J. Saunders, 'Matthew Paris and the Mongols', in *Essays in Medieval History Presented to Bertie Wilkinson*, T. A. Sandquist and M. R. Powicke (eds) (Toronto, 1969).
7. Smirnov, *Short History*, p. 59; Fennell, *The Crisis*, pp. 120–1.
8. Vernadsky, *The Mongols*, p. 338.
9. Ibid., p. 90. Charles Halperin, *Russia and the Golden Horde*, pp. 60, 102–3, 119, 125. See also V. V. Trepavlov, 'Eastern Influences: The Turkic Nobility in Medieval Russia', *Coexistence*, vol. 32, no. 1 (1995) pp. 9–16. Kliuchevskii, *Sochineniia*, II, p. 43, suggests that 'the power of the khan gave an illusion of unity to the fragmented and mutually alienated Russian principalities'.
10. Crummey, *The Formation*, p. 40.
11. Kliuchevskii, *Sochineniia*, II, pp. 5–27.
12. Presniakov, *The Formation*.
13. Fennell, *The Emergence*, p. 110.
14. L. V. Cherepnin, *Obrazovanie russkogo tsentralizovannogo gosudarstva v XIV–XV vekakh: ocherki sotsialno–ekonomicheskoi i politicheskoi istorii Rusi* (Moscow, 1960). For a different interpretation, see V. A. Kuchkin, *Formirovanie gosudarstvennoi territorii severo-vostochnoi Rusi v X–XIVvv* (Moscow, 1984).

15. M. K. Liubavskii, *Obrazovanie osnovnoi gosudarstvennoi territorii veliko-russkoi narodnosti: zaselenie i obedinenie tsentra* (Leningrad, 1929). See also O. P. Backus, 'The Problem of Feudalism in Lithuania, 1506–1548', *Slavic Review*, vol. 21 (1962); 'The Problem of Unity in the Polish–Lithuanian State', *Slavic Review*, vol. 22 (1962); and *Motives of West Russian Nobles in Deserting Lithuania for Moscow, 1377–1514* (Lawrence, Kansas, 1957). See also Martin, *Medieval Russia*, pp. 389–93.

16. Smirnov, *Short History*, p. 56. See also, for example, Gavin Hambly (ed.), *Central Asia* (London, 1969) pp. 151, 162, 172.

17. Vernadsky, *The Mongols*, pp. 216–19.

18. R. A. French, 'The introduction of the three-field agricultural system', in Bater and French, *Studies*, vol. 1, pp. 65–81, points out the difficulty of trying to be precise.

19. G. F. Kochin, *Selskoe khoziaistvo na Rusi v period obrazovaniia russkogo tsentralizovannogo gosudarstva: konets XIII–nachala XVIv* (Moscow–Leningrad, 1965) p. 434. See also A. M. Sakharov, 'Rus and its Culture in the Thirteenth to Fifteenth Centuries', *Soviet Studies in History*, vol. 18, no. 3 (1979–80) pp. 28–34. Smith, *Peasant Farming*, p. 1, believes that 'lack of earlier data compels us to concentrate on the period from the fifteenth century.'

20. Cherepnin, *Obrazovanie*, chs 2 and 3. See also A. M. Sakharov, 'The Town-Center of Feudal Dominance', and 'The Urban Population', *Soviet Studies in History*, vol. 18, no. 3 (1979–80). Some Soviet historians considered it inappropriate to apply the term 'feudal' to Russia before the fourteenth or even the fifteenth century. See also E. Levin (ed.), 'Studies of Medieval Novgorod', *Studies in Soviet History*, vol. 23 (1985), and Martin, *Medieval Russia*, pp. 393–7.

21. M. N. Tikhomirov *et al.* (eds), *Istoriia SSSR*, II, pp. 81–2; Janet Martin, *Treasure of the Land of Darkness: The Fur Trade and Its Significance for Medieval Russia* (Cambridge, 1986).

22. Florinsky, *Russia*, p. 129.

23. Miliukov, *Outlines*, I, p. 10.

24. A. M. Sakharov, in N. A. Smirnov (ed.), *Tserkov v istorii Rossii IXv–1917g; kriticheskie ocherki* (Moscow, 1967) pp. 74–8.

25. Vernadsky, *The Mongols*, p. 380.

26. V. N. Lazarev, *Andrei Rublev* (Moscow, 1960) p. 23. D. Likhachev, *Reflections on Russia* (Oxford, 1991) p. 125, deems the *Trinity* 'our greatest treatise of the beginning of the fifteenth century.'

27. A. A. Zimin *et al.*, in Tikhomirov *et al.*, *Istoriia*, II, pp. 357–8.

28. See generally, Sakharov as in number 19 above and R. R. Milner-Gulland, 'Russia's Lost Renaissance', D. Daiches and A. Thorlby (eds), *Literature and Western Civilization*, vol. 3 (London, 1974).

29. The Eurasian school after the Revolution of 1917 and, more recently, individuals such as Lev Gumilev would put their emphasis firmly to the East. See, for example, L. V. Ponomareva *et al.*, *Evraziia: istoricheskie vzgliady russkikh emigrantov* (Moscow, 1992); N. V. Riasanovsky, 'The Emergence of Eurasianism', *California Slavic Studies*, 4 (1967); B. Naarden, '"I am a Genius, but no more than that": Lev Gumilev (1912–1992): Ethnogenesis, the Russian Past and World History', *Jahrbücher für Geschichte Osteuropas*, vol. 44 (1996). See also *Rodina*, no. 9 (1996).

Ch. 3   Consolidation under Moscow, 1462–1645

1. See Parker, *An Historical Geography*, p. 17.
2. See Berry and Crummey (eds), *Rude and Barbarous Kingdom*, for this and similar descriptions.
3. H. Morley (ed.), *The Discovery of Muscovy: From the Collections of Richard Hakluyt* (London, 1889), p. 109.
4. See, for example, Mazour, *The Writing of History*, pp. 35–45.
5. Von Herberstein, *Notes*, X, pp. 24–5.
6. M. Cherniavsky, 'Ivan the Terrible as Renaissance Prince', *Slavic Review*, vol. 27 (1968) p. 208.
7. Kliuchevskii, *Sochineniia*, II, pp. 198–9.
8. Ibid., III, p. 23; Florinsky, *Russia*, p. 250.
9. Smirnov, *Short History*, p. 84; Kliuchevskii, *Sochineniia*, II, p. 116.
10. G. Alef, 'Reflections on the Boyar Duma in the Reign of Ivan III', *Slavonic Review*, vol. 45 (1967) p. 108.
11. Ibid., p. 107. See also S. O. Shmidt, 'Mestnichestvo i absoliutizm: postanovka voprosa' in his *Stanovlenie rossiiskogo samoderzhavstva* (Moscow, 1973). See also H. W. Dewey, 'The 1497 Sudebnik', *Slavic Review*, vol. 15 (1956). Nancy Shields Kollmann, *Kinship and Politics: The Making of the Muscovite Political System*, pp. 186–7, concludes that 'Muscovy was a minimally governed society in most ways, far more similar to [earlier] medieval European states than its European contemporaries', less bureaucratic than patrimonial.
12. G. Alef, 'The Adoption of the Muscovite Two-Headed Eagle: A Discordant View', *Speculum*, vol. 41 (1966) argues that the Habsburg example was a more immediate influence than the Byzantine. For a more general and conventional view, see M. Szeftel, 'The Title of the Muscovite Monarch up to the end of the Seventeenth Century', *Canadian–American Slavic Studies*, vol. 13 (1979).
13. T. Esper, 'Military Self-Sufficiency and Weapons Technology in Muscovite Russia', *Slavic Review* vol. 28 (1969) pp. 188–91. See also John Keep, *Soldiers of the Tsar*, pp. 13–79.
14. A. N. Grobovsky, *The 'Chosen Council' of Ivan IV: A Reinterpretation* (Brooklyn, N.Y., 1969), believes the council should be seen rather as an undefined moral influence.
15. Esper, 'Military Self-Sufficiency', pp. 193–4.
16. R. G. Skrynnikov, *Tragediia Novgoroda* (Moscow, 1994) p. 105; and his *Tsarstvo terrora* (St Petersburg, 1992) p. 527. For a more positive view, see D. N. Alshits, *Nachalo samoderzhaviia v Rossii* (Leningrad, 1988); and see more generally Richard Hellie (ed.), 'Ivan the Terrible: A Quarcentenary Celebration of his Death', *Russian History*, vol. 14 (1987). See also M. Perrie, *The Image of Ivan the Terrible in Russian Folklore* (Cambridge, 1987); A. Yanov, *The Origins of Autocracy: Ivan the Terrible in Russian History* (Berkeley, Calif., 1981).
17. Smirnov, *Short History*, p. 104
18. Quoted in Mazour, *The Writing*, pp. 68–9.
19. See, for example, S. O. Shmidt, *Stanovlenie*, pp. 129, 260–1.
20. Berry and Crummey, *Rude and Barbarous*, pp. 140, 152–3. For another early account, see G. E. Orchard (trans., ed. and intro.) I. Massa, *A Short History of*

the Beginnings and Origins of These Present Wars in Moscow ... (Toronto, 1982).

21. Platonov, *The Time of Troubles*, pp. 43–4.
22. Ibid., p. 159. See also the works of R. G. Skrynnikov, and Perrie, *Pretenders*.
23. J. L. H. Keep, 'The Regime of Filaret, 1619–1633', *Slavonic Review*, vol. 38 (1959–60).
24. B. F. Porshnev, *Muscovy and Sweden in the Thirty Years' War, 1630–1635* (Cambridge, 1995).
25. Vernadsky, *The Tsardom*, pp. 745–6.
26. See, for example, A. G. Mankov, *Tseny i ikh dvizhenie v russkom gosudarstve XVI veka* (Moscow–Leningrad, 1951), p. 99. See also Crummey, *The Formation*, pp. 15–26.
27. Zernov, *Eastern Christendom: A Study of the Origin and Development of the Eastern Orthodox Church* (London, 1961), p. 140.
28. Ibid., p. 141.
29. Platonov, *Moscow and the West*, p. 23.
30. See, for example, A. I. Klibanov, *Reformatsionnoe dvizhenie v Rossii v XIV–pervoi polovine XVI v* (Moscow, 1960). See generally, Crummey, *The Formation*, pp. 116–42.
31. D. S. Likhachev, *Chelovek v literature drevnei Rusi* (Moscow–Leningrad, 1958), p. 5.
32. Zernov, *Eastern Christendom*, p. 143.
33. See A. M. Sakharov, 'Historical Knowledge in the Sixteenth Century', *Soviet Studies in History*, vol. 18, no. 3 (1979–80); and see more generally D. C. Waugh (ed. and intro.), *Essays in Honor of A. A. Zimin* (Columbus, Ohio, 1983). See also C. J. Pouncy (ed. and intro.) *The Domostroi* (Ithaca, N.Y., 1995).

Part Two   Modern Russia: The Tsarist Empire

Introduction

1. Kliuchevskii, *Sochineniia*, III, pp. 6–7.
2. Richard Hellie, 'The Structure of Modern Russian History: Toward a Dynamic Model', and comments, *Russian History*, vol. 4 (1977); Edward L. Keenan, 'Muscovite Political Folkways', *Russian Review*, vol. 45 (1986) and comments, vol. 46 (1987). See also R. Pipes, *Russia under the Old Regime* (London, 1977); M. Raeff, *Understanding Imperial Russia: State and Society in the Old Regime* (New York, 1984); G. Yaney, *The Systematization of Russian Government: Social Evolution in the Domestic Administration of Imperial Russia 1711–1905* (Chicago, 1973); *The Urge to Mobilise: Agrarian Reform in Russia, 1861–1890* (Chicago, 1982).

Ch. 4   The Foundation of the Russian Empire, 1645–1698

1. See E. N. Williams, *The Ancien Regime in Europe: Government and Society in the Major States, 1648–1789* (London, 1970), p. 17, and G. Parker, *The General Crisis of the Seventeenth Century* (London, 1978). For an interesting

interpretation of the Muscovite variation of this process. see J. L. H. Keep, 'The Muscovite Elite and the Approach to Pluralism', *Slavonic Review*, vol. 48 (1970). See also P. Dukes, *October*, Chapter 1.

2. Kliuchevskii, *Sochineniia*, III, pp. 327–9; P. Longworth, *Alexis: Tsar of All the Russias*, p. 244; L. Hughes, *Sophia: Regent of Russia*, pp. 268, 275–6.

3. R. Hellie (trans. and ed.), *The Muscovite Law Code (Ulozhenie) of 1649* (Irvine, Calif., 1988).

4. Klyuchevsky, *The Rise of the Romanovs*, p. 258.

5. Collins, *The Present State of Russia*, p. 258; G. Miege, *A Relation of Three Embassies to the Great Duke of Muscovie* (London, 1669) pp. 290–5. See J. Keep, 'The Decline of the Zemsky Sobor' and 'Afterword', *Power and the People*, pp. 51–85, and Crummey, *Aristocrats and Servitors*. See also N. F. Demidova, *Sluzhilaia biurokratiia v Rossii XVIIv i ee rol v formirovanii absoliutizma* (Moscow, 1987).

6. L. G. Beskrovnyi *et al.*, *Istoriia SSSR*, III, p. 98: and see P. H. Avrich, *Russian Rebels* (New York, 1972), pp. 118–19.

7. See A. P. Bogdanov, 'Fedor Alekseevich', *Voprosy istorii*, no. 7 (1994). These measures were consolidated during the regency of Sophia.

8. Keep, *Soldiers of the Tsar*, pp. 88–9; Hellie, *Enserfment and Military Change*, pp. 21–5, 181–5.

9. See B. F. Porshnev, *Frantsiia, Angliiskaia Revoliutsiia i Evropeiskaia politika v seredine XVII v* (Moscow, 1970). In the wider context see also M. Mancall, *Russia and China: Their Diplomatic Relations to 1728* (Cambridge, Mass., 1971); G. V. Lantzeff, *Siberia in the Seventeenth Century* (Berkeley Los Angeles, 1943); and Stephan M. Horak, 'Russian Expansion and Policy in the Ukraine', in M. Rywkin, *Russian Colonial Expansion*.

10. See, for example, R. H. Fisher, *The Russian Fur Trade, 1550–1700*, University of California Publications in History, vol. 31 (1943).

11. Beskrovnyi *et al.*, *Istoriia*, III, pp. 28–30.

12. Collins, *The Present State*, p. 60.

13. See, for example, S. H. Baron, 'The Weber Thesis and the failure of Capitalist Development in "Early Modern" Russia', *Jahrbücher für Geschichte Osteuropas*, vol. 18 (1970); R. O. Crummey, *The Old Believers and the World of Antichrist: The Vyg Community and the Russian State, 1694–1855* (Madison, Wisc., and London, 1971) pp. 135–7; Gerschenkron, *Europe in the Russian Mirror*, pp. 11–47. And see P. Kolchin, *Unfree Labor: American Slavery and Russian Serfdom* (Cambridge, Mass., 1987); R. E. F. Smith, *The Enserfment of the Russian Peasantry* (Cambridge, 1968).

14. Olearius, *The Travels*, pp. 139, 159, 160.

15. Lenin, *Collected Works*, I, pp. 154–5. Richard Hellie has about 100,000 pieces of evidence broadly in support of the Lenin thesis. From his paper 'Price Trends in the Seventeenth Century' and subsequent discussion at V World Congress of Central and East European Studies, Warsaw, 6–11 August 1995.

16. Crummey, *The Old Believers*, p. 16. See also M. Cherniavsky, 'The Old Believers and the New Religion', *Slavic Review*, vol. 25 (1966).

17. Crummey, *The Old Believers*, p. 10; P. Pascal, *Avvakum et les débuts du raskol* (Paris, 1938) pp. xx–xxv; C. B. H. Cant, 'The Archpriest Avvakum and his Scottish Contemporaries', *Slavonic Review*, vol. 44 (1965–6);

W. Palmer, *The Patriarch and the Tsar*, 6 vols (London, 1871–6); Paul Bushkovich, *Religion and Society in Russia: The Sixteenth and Seventeenth Centuries* (Oxford, 1992).

18. See, for example, L. W. Lewitter, 'Poland, the Ukraine and Russia in the 17th Century', *Slavonic Review*, vol. 27 (1948–9).

19. See L. A. J. Hughes, 'The West comes to Russian Architecture', *History Today*, September (1986); A. M. Panchenko, *Russkaia stikhotvornaia kultura XVII veka* (Leningrad, 1973); A. N. Robinson (ed.), *Russkaia literatura na rubezhe dvukh epokh XVII–nachala XVIIIv* (Moscow, 1971).

20. Foy de la Neuville, *Relation curieuse et nouvelle de Moscovie* (The Hague, 1699) pp. 175–7. See the translation by J. A. Cutshall (London, 1994). See, in general, L. A. J. Hughes, *Russia and the West: The Life of a Seventeenth-Century Westernizer, Prince Vasily Vasilevich Golitsyn, 1643–1714* (Newtonville, Mass., 1984).

21. Peter Burke, 'Did Europe exist before 1700?', *History of European Ideas*, vol. 1 (1980).

Ch. 5   The Completion of the Structure, 1698–1761

1. See R. Zguta, 'Peter I's "Most Drunken Synod of Fools and Jesters"', *Jahrbücher für Geschichte Osteuropas*, Band 21(1973); Zguta believes that Peter's merry pranks should not be taken too seriously.

2. Cracraft, *The Church Reform*, pp. 14, 21. Cracraft cites Reinhard Wittram on the 'rational political purpose'.

3. Klyuchevsky, *Peter the Great*, pp. 270–2.

4. Quoted in Beskrovnyi, *Istoriia SSSR*, III, pp. 249–50; E. V. Anisimov, *The Reforms*, pp. 297–8. See, generally, Riasanovsky, *The Image of Peter the Great*.

5. F. M. A. de Voltaire, *The History of the Russian Empire under Peter the Great*, English trans. (London, 1837), p. 324.

6. On Menshikov's subsequent trial, see R. V. Ovchinnikov (ed.), 'Krushenie poluderzhavnogo vlastelina' (dokumenty sledstvennogo dela kniazia A. D. Menshikova), *Voprosy istorii*, no. 9 (1970). See, more generally, J. P. LeDonne, 'Ruling Families in the Russian Political Order, 1689–1825', *Cahiers du monde russe et soviétique*, vol. 28 (1987).

7. For documents concerning the accession of Anna, see Raeff, *Plans*, pp. 41–52.

8. V. Ulanov, 'XVII vek i reforma Petra Velikogo', *Tri veka*, 111, 14. For a late Soviet view of the post-Petrine period, see E. V. Anisimov, *Russia v seredine XVIII veka: borba za nasledie Petra* (Moscow, 1986).

9. See Raeff, *Origins*, p. 42.

10. Quoted in Beskroynyi, *Istoriia*, Ill, p. 253. See also S. M. Troitskii, 'Istoriografiia "dvortsovykh perevorotov" v Rossii XVIIIv', *Voprosy istorii*, no. 2 (1966); Meehan-Waters, *Autocracy and Aristocracy*; LeDonne, 'Ruling Families'.

11. Beskrovnyi, *Istoriia*, III, p. 294. For Avrich's verdict, see *Russian Rebels*, pp. 174–7.

12. See A. P. Vlasto and L. R. Lewitter (trans. and ed.), Ivan Pososhkov, *The Book of Poverty and Wealth* (London, 1987).

13. For the long process of incorporation which contributed to the rising, see A. S. Donnelly, *The Russian Conquest of Bashkiria, 1522–1740: A Case Study in Imperialism* (New Haven, Conn., 1968). See, more generally, Rywkin, *Russian Colonial Expansion*.

14. For a different perspective on the Great Northern War, see A. Rothstein, *Peter the Great and Marlborough: Politics and Diplomacy in Converging Wars* (London, 1986). For the later conflict, see H. H. Kaplan, *Russia and the Outbreak of the Seven Years War* (Cambridge and Berkeley, Calif., 1968); for a patriotic Soviet view, see N. Korobkov, *Semiletniaia voina, I 756–I 762gg* (Moscow, 1940).

15. R. Portal, *L'Ourale au XVIIIe siècle* (Paris, 1950); Blum, *Lord and Peasant*, p. 294; Kahan, *The Plow*, p. 4 and throughout.

16. Anon., 'The Interest of Great Britain in Supplying Herself with Iron', *Journal of the Iron and Steel Institute*, vol. 2 (1985).

17. See D. K. Reading, *The Anglo-Russian Commercial Treaty of 1734* (London and New Haven, Conn., 1938).

18. B. B. Kafengauz, *Ocherki vnutrennego rynka Rossii pervoi poloviny XVIII veka* (Moscow, 1958); E. V. Anisimov, *Podatnaia reforma Petra I* (Leningrad, 1982); Kahan, *The Plow*.

19. See V. Boss, *Newton and Russia: The Early Influence, 1698–1796* (Cambridge, Mass., 1972); and, for example, Dukes, *October*, pp. 29–30.

20. See A. D. Liublinskaia (ed.), *Russkii diplomat vo Frantsii: Zapiski Andreia Matveeva* (Leningrad, 1972) pp. 199–200; and Max Okenfuss (trans. and ed.), *The Travel Diary of Peter Tolstoi: A Muscovite in early modern Europe* (DeKalb, Ill, 1988). See also A. G. Cross, *By the Banks of the Thames: Russians in Eighteenth-Century Britain* (Newtonville, Mass., 1980) and *By the Banks of the Neva: Britons in Eighteenth-Century Russia* (Cambridge, 1997).

21. Miliukov, *Outlines*, I, p. 130.

22. Cracraft, *The Church Reform*, p. 267. See also A. V. Muller (trans. and ed.), *The Spiritual Regulation of Peter the Great* (Seattle, Wash., 1972).

23. J. Cracraft, *The Petrine Revolution in Architecture* (London, 1989).

24. Thaden, *Russia's Western Borderlands*, Chapter 1. A major contribution came from the people as a whole, on aspects of whose lives, see L. N. Semenova, *Ocherki istorii byta i kulturnoi zhizni Rossii: pervaia polovina XVIII veka* (Leningrad, 1982).

25. See A. V. Lentin (trans. and ed.), *Peter the Great: His Law on the Imperial Succession in Russia, 1722* (Oxford, 1996).

Ch. 6   Enlightened Absolutism, 1761–1801

1. Kheraskov, quoted in Kliuchevskii, *Sochineniia*, IV, p. 202. O. A. Omelchenko, *Zakonnaia monarkhiia Ekateriny II: Prosveshchennyi absoliutizm v Rossii* (Moscow, 1993) separates the Petrine and Catherinian phases of absolutism more completely.

2. Catherine II, *Memoirs*, trans. K. Anthony (New York, 1935), p. 264. See generally R. N. Bain, *Peter III: Emperor of Russia* (London, 1902); Leonard, *Peter III*; and M. Raeff, 'The Domestic Policies of Peter III and His Overthrow', *American Historical Review*, vol. 75 (1970).

3. P. Petschauer, 'Catherine the Great's Conversion of 1744', *Jahrbücher für Geschichte Osteuropas*, vol. 20 (1972).

4. Kliuchevskii, *Sochineniia*, V, pp. 309–71; Madariaga, *Russia*, p. 587.

5. I. A. Fedosov, 'Prosveshchennyi absoliutizm v Rossii', *Voprosy istorii*, no. 9 (1970) p. 38; A. B. Kamenskii, *Pod seniiu Ekateriny: vtoraia polovina XVIII veka* (St Petersburg, 1992) pp. 428–34.

6. Fedosov, 'Prosveshchennyi absoliutizm', p. 52; McGrew, *Paul I*, p. 356. See also H. Ragsdale (ed.), *Paul I: A Reassessment of his Life and Reign* (Pittsburgh, 1979); N. Ia. Eidelman, *Gran vekov: politicheskaia borba v Rossii konets XVIII – nachalo XIX stoletiia* (Moscow, 1981).

7. R. Portal, 'The Industrialisation of Russia', in H. J. Habbakuk and M. Postan (eds), *The Cambridge Economic History of Europe*, vol. 6 (Cambridge, 1966) p. 802.

8. Kliuchevskii, *Sochineniia*, VIII, p. 277; M. Raeff, 'The Domestic Policies', p. 1302.

9. Quoted in Alexander, *Autocratic Politics*, p. 89. For a full description of Catherine's reforms, see LeDonne, *Ruling Russia* and *Absolutism*; and for an important example of her collaboration, see R. E. Jones, *Provincial Development in Russia: Catherine II and Jakob Sievers* (New Brunswick, N.J., 1984).

10. Florinsky, *Russia*, pp. 612–13. See also Ransel, *The Politics*, pp. 282–9; Ragsdale, *Paul I*, generally. Eidelman, *Gran vekov*, pp. 73, 139, 160, writes of 'a definite programme, idea, logic' based on a 'conservative utopia' embodying the courtly codes of the medieval past.

11. Dukes, *Catherine the Great*, p. 55.

12. A. W. Fisher, *The Russian Annexation of the Crimea 1772–1783* (Cambridge, 1970); Rywkin, *Russian Colonial Expansion*; Thaden, *Russia's Western Borderlands*.

13. J. T. Alexander, 'Recent Soviet Historiography on the Pugachev Revolt: A Review Article', *Canadian–American Slavic Studies*, vol. 4 (1970) p. 617. See also J. T. Alexander, *Autocratic Politics in a National Crisis:The Imperial Russian Government and Pugachev's Revolt, 1773–1775* (Bloomington, Ind., and London, 1969); Avrich, *Russian Rebels*, pp. 246–54; P. Longworth, 'The Last Great Cossack Rising', *J. of European Studies*, vol. 3 (1970); M. Raeff, 'Pugachev's Rebellion', in R. Forster and J. Greene (eds.), *Preconditions of Revolution in Early Modern Europe* (Baltimore, Maryland, 1970). For some Soviet views, see contributions by A. L. Shapiro and A. P. Pronshtein to *Soviet Studies in History*, vols 5 and 6 (1966–8).

14. I. de Madariaga, *Britain, Russia and the Armed Neutrality of 1780: Sir James Harris's Mission to St Petersburg during the American Revolution* (New Haven, Conn., and London, 1962); N. N. Bolkhovitinov, 'Russian Diplomacy and the American War of Independence of 1775–83', *Soviet Studies in History*, vol. 3 (1964–5); D. M. Griffiths, 'Nikita Panin, Russian Diplomacy, and the American Revolution', *Slavic Review*, vol. 28 (1969).

15. See P. Longworth, *The Art of Victory: The Life and Achievements of Generalissimo Suvorov, 1729–1800* (London, 1965). V. A. Zolotarev *et al.*, *Vo slavu otechestva rossiiskogo* (Moscow, 1984) p. 46, tell us that the Russian army, including regulars and irregulars, grew in size from 331,000 in the early 1750s to 502,000 in 1795.

16. See H. H. Kaplan, *The First Partition of Poland* (New York, 1962); L. R. Lewitter, 'The Partitions of Poland', *New Cambridge Modern History*, vol. 8 (1965); R. H. Lord, *The Second Partition of Poland: A Study in Diplomatic History* (Cambridge, Mass., 1915); R. H. Lord, 'The Third Partition of Poland', *Slavonic Review*, vol. 3 (1924–5); Smirnov, *Short History*, p. 184; Thaden, *Russia's Western Borderlands*. And see J. D. Klier, *Russia gathers her Jews: The origins of the 'Jewish Question' in Russia, 1772–1825* (DeKalb, Ill., 1986).

17. N. E. Saul, *Russia and the Mediterranean, 1797–1807* (Chicago, 1970) pp. 32–9; H. Ragsdale, *Detente in the Napoleonic Era: Bonaparte and the Russians* (Lawrence, Kansas, 1980).

18. Dukes, *Catherine the Great*, pp. 93–9.

19. See M. Confino, *Domaines et seigneurs en Russie vers la fin du XVIIIe siècle: Etude de structures agraires et de mentalités économiques* (Paris, 1963); A. Kahan, 'The Costs of Westernisation in Russia: The Gentry and the Economy in the Eighteenth Century', *Slavic Review*, vol. 25 (1966); N. L. Rubinstein, *Selskoe khoziaistvo Rossii vo vtoroi polovine XVIIIv* (Moscow, 1957). See also R. P. Bartlett, *Human Capital:The Settlement of Foreigners in Russia, 1762–1804* (Cambridge, 1979).

20. *Hansard's Parliamentary History of England* (London, 1913) XVII, 1142, 1137. See more generally Blum, *Lord and Peasant*, pp. 293–5; Beskrovnyi, *Istoriia*, III, pp. 407–10. On trade with the U.S.A., see A. W. Crosby, Jr, *America, Russia, Hemp and Napoleon: American Trade with Russia and the Baltic, 1783–1812* (Columbus, Ohio, 1965).

21. For full details, see S. M. Troitskii, *Finansovaia politika russkogo absoliutizma v XVIII veke* (Moscow, 1966); Kahan, *The Plow and the Hammer*. See also I. Blanshard, *Russia's 'Age of Silver': Precious Metal Production and Economic Growth in the Eighteenth Century* (London, 1989). B. N. Mironov, 'Vliianie revoliutsii tsen v Rossii XVIII veka na ee ekonomicheskoe i sotsialnoe–politicheskoe razvitie', *Istoriia SSSR*, 1 (1991) argues that Russia experienced a price revolution a century and a half after the West, strengthening serfdom and the position of the nobility while weakening the bourgeoisie and not helping the government.

22. P. N. Miliukov, *Ocherki po istorii russkoi kultury*, III (Paris, 1937) p. 369ff.

23. See J. L. Black, *Citizens for the Fatherland: Education, Educators and Pedagogical Ideals in Eighteenth-Century Russia* (Boulder, Col., 1979).

24. Miliukov, *Ocherki*, II, pp. 75–8.

25. Dukes, *Catherine*, pp. 241–5.

26. A. V. Kokorev, *Khrestomatiia po russkoi literature XVIII veka* (Moscow, 1961). And see M. D. Kurmacheva, *Krepostnaia intelligentsiia Rossii (vtoraia polovina XVIII-nachalo XIX veka)* (Moscow, 1983). Many historians, Soviet as well as Western, have been sceptical about Kurmacheva's assertion of a 'serf intelligensia'.

27. M. M. Shtrange, *Demokraticheskaia intelligentsiia Rossii v XVIII veke* (Moscow, 1965).

28. A. McConnell, *A Russian Philosophe: Alexander Radishchev, 1749–1802* (The Hague, 1964) p. 208. See W. G. Jones, *Nikolay Novikov* (Cambridge, 1984).

29. See A. Lentin (ed. and trans.), M. M. Shcherbatov, *On the Corruption of Morals in Russia* (Cambridge, 1969).

374   NOTES TO CHAPTER 6-7, PAGES 120-126

30. See A. G. Cross, *N. M. Karamzin: A Study of his Literary Career, 1783–1803* (Carbondale, Ill., 1971); H. M. Nebel, *N. M. Karamzin: A Russian Sentimentalist* (The Hague, 1967); J. L. Black (ed.), *Essays on Karamzin* (The Hague, 1975). See more generally G. Marker, *Publishing, Printing, and the Origins of Intellectual Life in Russia, 1700–1800* (Princeton, N.J., 1985) and Jones, *Nikolay Novikov*.

31. N. N. Bolkhovitinov, 'Beginnings of the Establishment of Scientific and Cultural Relations between America and Russia', *Soviet Studies in History*, vol. 5 (1966–7); and generally, see N. N. Bolkhovitinov, *The Beginnings of Russian–American Relations, 1775–1815* (Cambridge, Mass., 1975); N. N. Bashkina *et al* (eds), *The United States and Russia: The Beginnings of Relations, 1765–1815* (Washington, D.C., 1980).

32. W. Guthrie, *A New System of Modern Geography* .. (London, 1782), p. 118.

33. A. W. Fisher, 'Enlightened Despotism and Islam under Catherine II' *Slavic Review*, vol. 27 (1968); Iu. Ia. Kogan *et al.* in N. A. Smirnov, *Tserkov v istorii Rossii* (Moscow, 1967) pp. 203–5. See also Madariaga, *Russia*, pp. 503–18; G. L. Freeze, *The Russian Levites: Parish Clergy in the Eighteenth Century* (Cambridge, Mass., 1977).

34. See Dukes, *October*, Chapter 2. K. A. Papmehl, *Freedom of Expression in Eighteenth-Century Russia* (The Hague, 1971); A. Narotchnitski *et al* (eds), *La révolution française et la Russie* (Moscow, 1989).

Ch. 7   Russian Nationalism, 1801–1855

1. Kliuchevskii, *Sochineniia*, V, pp. 186–8.

2. A. P. Bazhova *et al.*, *Istoriia SSSR*, IV, p. 11.

3. A. McConnell, 'Alexander I's Hundred Days: The Politics of a Paternalist Reformer', *Slavic Review*, vol. 28 (1969) pp. 375–6. See also McConnell, *Tsar Alexander*; Palmer, *Alexander I;* and Hartley, *Alexander I*.

4. Kliuchevskii, *Sochineniia*, V, pp. 263–4; and his *Pisma, dnevniki, aforizmy i mysli ob istorii* (Moscow, 1968) p. 317; Bazhova, *Istoriia*, IV, pp. 259–60. See also Lincoln, *Nicholas I*.

5. McConnell, *Tsar Alexander*, p. 21.

6. Bazhova, *Istoriia*, IV, p. 69.

7. M. Raeff, *Michael Speransky: Statesman of Imperial Russia, 1772–1839* (The Hague, 1957); J. Gooding 'The Liberalism of Michael Speransky', *Slavonic Review*, vol. 64 (1986) argues that Speransky was a liberal forerunner of the Decembrists. See also D. Christian, 'The Political Ideals of Michael Speransky', *Slavonic Review*, vol. 54 (1976). Speransky's verdict on Alexander I was that he was 'too feeble to reign and too strong to be governed'. Quoted by Hartley, *Alexander I*, p. 91.

8. Bazhova, *Istoriia*, IV, p. 168.

9. Ibid., p. 161.

10. McConnell, *Tsar Alexander I*, p. 143.

11. Bazhova, *Istoriia*, IV, p. 172. For a less critical view, see R. E. Pipes, 'The Russian Military Colonies, 1810–1831'; *J. of Modern History*, vol. 22 (1950). See also M. Jenkins, *Arakcheev: Grand Vizier of the Russian Empire* (London, 1969). Arakcheev's personal influence was in decline before the accession of Nicholas I.

12. I. de Madariaga, 'Spain and the Decembrists', *European Studies Review*, vol. 3 (1973).
13. Raeff, *The Decembrist Movement*, pp. 155, 121. On Pestel, see also A. E. Adams, 'The Character of Pestel's Thought', *Slavic Review*, vol. 12 (1953); contrast catechism with page 118 above: educational text. See also P. O'Meara, *K. F. Ryleev: A Political Biography of the Decembrist Poet* (Princeton, N.J., 1984); N. Eidelman, *Conspiracy against the Tsar: A Portrait of the Decembrists* (Moscow, 1985).
14. Bazhova, *Istoriia* IV, pp. 216–17.
15. Ibid., p. 258.
16. H. J. Törke, 'Continuity and Change in the Relations between Bureaucracy and Society in Russia, 1613–1861', *Canadian–American Slavic Studies*, vol. 5 (1971), and in colloquium with J. Keep, vol. 6 (1972). See also W. B. Lincoln, *In the Vanguard of Reform*; J. T. Flynn, 'The Universities of the Gentry, and the Russian Imperial Services, 1815–1825', *Canadian–American Slavic Studies*, vol. 2 (1968); W. McK. Pintner, 'The Social Characteristics of the Early Nineteenth-Century Russian Bureaucracy', *Slavic Review*, vol. 29 (1970). See also Orlovsky, *The Limits of Reform*; Pintner, *Russian Officialdom*.
17. See S. Monas, *The Third Section: Police and Society in Russia under Nicholas I* (Cambridge, Mass., 1961); P. S. Squire, *The Third Department: The Establishment and Practices of the Political Police in the Russia of Nicholas I* (Cambridge, 1968).
18. Bazhova, *Istoriia*, IV, pp. 300–6. For a balanced view of peasant unrest in its context, see D. Moon, *Russian Peasants and Tsarist Legislation on the Eve of Reform: Interaction between Peasants and Officialdom, 1825–1855* (London, 1992).
19. Florinsky, *Russia*, pp. 851–4.
20. J. S. Curtiss, *The Russian Army under Nicholas I, 1822–1855* (Durham, N.C., 1965), p. 112. See, more generally, L. G. Beskrovnyi, *Russkaia armiia i flot v XIX veke: voenno–ekonomicheskoi potentsial Rossii* (Moscow, 1973); Keep, *Soldiers of the Tsar*, pp. 323–50.
21. Smirnov, *Short History*, pp. 191–2.
22. See M. Raeff, *Siberia and the Reforms of 1822* (Seattle, Wash., 1956).
23. See R. F. Leslie, *Polish Politics and the Revolution of November1830* (London, 1956; Westport, Conn., 1973); See also Rywkin, *Russian Colonial Expansion*; Thaden, *Russia's Western Borderlands*; and J. D. Klier, *Russia gathers her Jews: The Origins of the 'Jewish Question' in Russia, 1772–1825* (De Kalb, Ill., 1986).
24. See V. J. Puryear, *Napoleon and the Dardanelles* (Berkeley, Calif., 1951).
25. C. von Clausewitz, *The Campaign of 1812 in Russia* (London, 1843) p. 142. See also M. and D. Josselson, *The Commander: A Life of Barclay de Tolly* (Oxford, 1980).
26. B. Hollingsworth, 'The Napoleonic Invasion of Russia and Recent Soviet Historical Writing', *J. of Modern History*, vol. 38 (1966); M. Raeff, 'The 150th Anniversary of the Campaign of 1812 in Soviet Historical Writing', *Jahrbücher für Geschichte Osteuropas*, vol. 16 (1964). On the burning of Moscow in particular, see V. M. Kholodovskii, 'Napoleon li podzheg Moskvu?', *Voprosy istorii*, no. 4 (1966).

27. P. K. Grimsted, *The Foreign Ministers of Alexander I: Political Attitudes and the Conduct of Russian Diplomacy, 1801–1825* (Berkeley, Calif., 1971).

28. N. S. Kiniapina, *Vneshniaia politika Rossii pervoi poloviny XIX veka* (Moscow, 1963) p. 244; qualified agreement with Kiniapina would be found in V.P. Puryear, *International Economics and Diplomacy in the Near East, 1834–53* (Stanford, Calif., 1935). For other views, see J. H. Gleason, *The Genesis of Russophobia in Great Britain: A Study of the Interaction of Policy and Opinion* (Cambridge, Mass., 1950); G. B. Henderson, *Crimean War Diplomacy and Other Historical Essays* (Glasgow, 1947; New York, 1973); N. Rich, *Why the Crimean War? A Cautionary Tale* (London, 1985).

29. Quoted in Smirnov, *Short History*. See also J. S. Curtiss, *Russia's Crimean War* (Durham, N.C., 1979).

30. See W. E. Mosse, *The Rise and Fall of the Crimean System, 1855–1871* (London, 1963).

31. Blackwell, *The Beginnings*, pp. 3, 138–48, 205–11. S. L. Hoch, *Serfdom and Social Control in Russia* (Chicago, 1986), p. 187, finds serfdom 'far more socially oppressive than economically onerous'.

32. R. Haywood, *The Beginnings of Railway Development in Russia in the Reign of Nicholas I* (Durham, N.C., 1969) p. 180.

33. See W. McK. Pintner, *Russian Economic Policy under Nicholas I* (New York, 1967), pp. 184ff.

34. See N. M. Druzhinin, *Gosudarstvennye krestiane i reforma P. D. Kiseleva*, 2 vols (Moscow–Leningrad, 1946, 1958). Most of the figures and much of the information in this section are taken from the contributions by Druzhinin and P. G. Ryndziunskii to Bazhova, *Istoriia*, IV.

35. Riasanovsky, *A History*, p. 351. See, generally, C. H. Whittaker, *The Origins of Modern Russian Education: An Intellectual Biography of Count Sergei Uvarov, 1786–1855* (DeKalb, Ill., 1985). J. T. Flynn, *The University Reform of Alexander I, 1802–1835* (Washington, D.C., 1988) takes a more optimistic view. Universities were founded or reformed as follows: Dorpat, 1802; Vilna, 1803; Kazan and Kharkov, 1804; Warsaw, 1816; St Petersburg, 1819.

36. Smirnov, *Short History*, p. 207. R. E. McGrew, *Russia and Cholera, 1823–32* (Madison, Wise, 1965).

37. J. L. Black, *Nicholas Karamzin and Russian Society in the Nineteenth Century: A Study in Russian Political and Historical Thought* (Toronto, 1975) p. 155.

38. Smirnov, *Short History*, p. 207.

39. See H. E. Bowman, *Vissarion Belinsky, 1811–1848: A Study in the Origins of Social Criticism in Russia* (Cambridge, Mass., 1954); M. Malia, *Alexander Herzen and the Birth of Russian Socialism, 1812–1855* (Cambridge, Mass., 1961); E. Acton, *Alexander Herzen and the Role of the Intellectual Revolutionary* (Cambridge, 1979).

40. Bazhova, *Istoriia*, IV, pp. 333–8. For Western views, see Riasanovsky, *Russia and the West*; and his *Nicholas I and Official Nationality* and *A Parting of the Ways*; P. K. Christoff, *An Introduction to Nineteenth-Century Slavophilism: A Study of Ideas* (The Hague, 1961); A. Walicki, *The Slavophile Controversy: History of a Conservative Utopia in Nineteenth-Century Russian Thought* (Oxford, 1975). Monas, *The Third Section*, p. 192, argues that Nicholas I 'felt it as part of the mission of enlightened absolutism

... to encourage the flowering of letters'. See also M. T. Choldin, *Fence around the Empire: Russian Censorship of Western Ideas under the Tsars* (Durham, N.C., 1985); C. A. Ruud, *Fighting Words: Imperial Censorship and the Russian Press, 1804–1906* (Toronto, 1982). See also D. Saunders, *The Ukrainian Impact on Russian Culture, 1750–1850* (Edmonton, Alberta, 1985).

41. J. H. Seddon, *The Petrashevtsy: A Study of the Russian Revolutionaries of 1848* (Manchester, 1985). For a late Soviet view, see B. G. Egorov, *Petrashevtsy* (Leningrad, 1988).

Ch. 8   The Emancipation, and After, 1855–1894

1. F. Venturi, *Roots of Revolution*, p. 5. See more fully D. Field, *Rebels in the Name of the Tsar* (Boston, Mass., 1976).

2. S. B. Okun and K. V. Sivkov (eds), *Krestianskoe dvizhenie v Rossii v 1857–mae 1861gg: sbornik dokumentov* (Moscow, 1963) pp. 364–5. In his inaugural lecture in November 1860, Shchapov had spoken of a concern 'not with the thought of statehood, not with the idea of centralisation, but with the idea of nationality and of regionality'. In prison after his speech on Bezdna, he wrote 'The history of the Russian people fills our heart with the belief and hope that sooner or later a time must come for the Russian people when it acquires politcal self-consciousness and, as a result, political self-government.' Saunders, *Russia*, p. 240.

3. Mosse, *Alexander II*, p. 34.

4. S. S. Volk *et al.*, *Istoriia SSSR*, V, p. 355.

5. Ibid., p. 11. H. W. Whelan, *Alexander III and the State Council: Bureaucracy and Counter-Reform in Late Imperial Russia* (New Brunswick, N.J., 1982)

6. Mosse, *Alexander II*, pp. 178–9. See also A. J. Rieber. 'Alexander II: A Revisionist View', *J. of Modern History*, vol. 43 (1971).

7. Cited by C. C. Adler Jr, 'The "Revolutionary Situation": The Uses of an Historical Conception', *Canadian–American Slavic Studies*, vol. 3 (1969) p. 386.

8. Ibid., pp. 392–6. See also Field, *Rebels*.

9. Volk, *Istonia*, V, p. 95.

10. Quoted in ibid., p. 100. See Starr, *Decentralization*, pp. 352–4. See, generally, T. Emmons and W. S. Vucinich (eds), *The Zemstvo in Russia: An Experiment in Local Self-Government* (Cambridge, 1982); T. Pearson, *Russian Officialdom in Crisis: Autocracy and Local Self-Government, 1861–1900* (Cambridge, 1989).

11. Cited by R. Wortman, 'Judicial Personnel and the Court Reform of 1864', *Canadian–American Slavic Studies*, vol. 3 (1969) p. 231. See, more fully, R. Wortman, *The Development of Russian Legal Consciousness* (Chicago, 1976).

12. Riasanovsky, *A History*, p. 377. See also R. Wortman as in note 11 above and W. G. Wagner, *Marriage, Property and Law in Late Imperial Russia* (New York and Oxford, 1994).

13. Volk, *Istoriia*, V, p. 108. See also Pintner and Rowney, *Russian Officialdom*.

14. Keep, *Soldiers of the Tsar*, pp. 364–78; Miller, *Dimitrii Miliutin*, generally.

15. Florinsky, *Russia*, p. 909; Miller, *Dimitrii Miliutin*, p. 230.

16. Lenin, quoted in Volk, *Istoriia*, V, p. 116.
17. Volk, *Istoriia*, V, p. 350.
18. Ibid., p. 357.
19. Quoted by C. C. Adler Jr, 'The "Revolutionary Situation"', p. 398.
20. See page 148 above.
21. Volk, *Istoriia*, V, p. 359.
22. Ibid., p. 360. See also Richard Pipes, *Russia under the Old Regime*, pp. 301–2, 305–7.
23. Ibid., p. 363. See Byrnes, *Pobedonostsev*.
24. Ibid., p. 364.
25. Florinsky, *Russia*, p. 1095. For a Soviet view, see L. G. Zakharova, *Zemskaia kontrreforma 1890g* (Moscow, 1968). For Western critiques of the *zemstva* and land captains, see note 10 above.
26. R. K. I. Quested, *The Expansion of Russia in East Asia, 1857–1860* (Kuala Lumpur, 1968); and see, more generally, Lensen, *Russia's Eastward Expansion*; Rywkin, *Russian Colonial Expansion*. On relations with the U.S.A., see N. E. Saul, *Distant Friends: The USA and Russia, 1763–1867* (Lawrence, Kansas, 1991) and *Concord and Conflict: The USA and Russia, 1867–1921* (Lawrence, Kansas, 1996), and many works by N. N. Bolkhovitinov.
27. D. Mackenzie, 'Expansion in Central Asia', *Canadian–American Slavic Studies*, vol. 3 (1969) p. 310. For fuller discussion, see S. Becker, *Russia's Protectorates in Central Asia: Bukhara and Khiva* (Cambridge, Mass., 1968); N. A. Khalfin, *Russia's Policy in Central Asia, 1857–1868* (London, 1964) – an abridged translation of a Soviet work; and R. A. Pierce, *Russian Central Asia, 1857–1917: A Study in Colonial Rule* (Berkeley, Calif., 1960). See also D. Mackenzie, *The Lion of Tashkent: The Career of General M. F. Cherniaev* (Athens, Georgia, 1974).
28. See J. D. Klier, *Imperial Russia's Jewish Question, 1855–1881* (Cambridge, 1995).
29. *Correspondence Respecting Central Asia*, C. 704. H. M. Stationery Office (London, 1873) pp. 72–5; R. F. Leslie, *Reform and Insurrection in Russian Poland, 1856–1865* (London, 1963).
30. Smirnov, *Short History*, p. 237; and among the many other works, see W. E. Mosse, *The Rise and Fall of the Crimean System, 1855–1871* (London, 1963); M. B. Petrovich, *The Emergence of Russian Panslavism, 1856–1870* (New York, 1956); and B. H. Sumner, *Russia and the Balkans, 1870–1880* (Oxford, 1937). See, more generally, M. S. Anderson (ed.), *The Great Powers and the Near East* (London, 1970).
31. A. J. Rieber (ed.), *The Politics of Autocracy: Letters of Alexander II to Prince A. L Bariatinsky, 1857–1864* (The Hague, 1964); in his introduction, Rieber argues that 'military reform provided the decisive impetus for freeing the serfs'.
32. Dmytryshyn, *Imperial Russia*, p. 225.
33. Volk, *Istoriia*, V, p. 51. Compare T. Emmons, *The Russian Landed Gentry*; D. Field, *The End of Serfdom*. For an interesting comparison, see P. Kolchin, *Unfree Labour: American Slavery and Russian Serfdom* (Cambridge, Mass., 1987). For interesting Soviet views, see L. G. Zakharova, *Samoderzhavie i otmena krepostnogo prava v Rossii, 1856–1861* (Moscow, 1984), abridged and translated by G. M. Hamburg as 'Autocracy and the Abolition of Serfdom

in Russia, 1856–1861', *Soviet Studies in History*, vol. 26, no. 2 (1984), and G. Popov, 'Fasad i kukhnia "velikoi reformy" ', *Eko*, no. 1 (1987).

34. H. Willetts, in Katkov *et al.*, *Russia Enters the Twentieth Century*, p. 121. See also D. Field (ed.), 'The Transformation of the Russian Village, 1861–1914', *Soviet Studies in History*, vol. 21(1982–3); R. Bartlett (ed.), *Land Commune and Peasant Community in Russia: Communal Forms in Imperial and Early Soviet Society* (London, 1990); B. Eklof and S. Frank (eds), *The World of the Russian Peasant: Post-Emancipation Culture and Society* (Boston, Mass., 1990); E. Kingston-Mann and T. Mixter (eds), *Peasant, Economy, Culture and Politics of European Russia, 1800–1921* (Princeton, N.J., 1991).
35. O. H. Palmer, *Statement of the Origin, Organization and Progress of the Russian-American Telegraphy Western Union Extension, Collins' Overland Line, via Behring Strait and Asiatic Russia to Europe* (Rochester, N.Y., 1866) p. 165.
36. Most of the statistics and information in this section are taken from the contributions by V. K. Iatsunskii to Volk, *Istoriia*, V. See also Gatrell, *The Tsarist Economy*; M. F. Hamm (ed.), *The City in Late Imperial Russia* (Bloomington, Ind., 1986); D. R. Brower, *The Russian City betwen Tradition and Modernity, 1850–1900* (Berkeley, Calif., 1990).
37. Florinsky, *Russia*, pp. 1114–5.
38. A. Sinel, *The Classroom and the Chancellery: State Educational Reform in Russia under Count Dmitry Tolstoi* (Cambridge, Mass., 1973).
39. Quotations from Florinsky, *Russia*, pp. 1033, 1036. See also B. Eklof, *Russian Peasant Schools: Officialdom, Village Culture and Popular Pedagogy, 1861–1914* (Berkeley, Calif., 1987 and London, 1986).
40. Smirnov, *Short History*, p. 237. See, generally, Brooks, *When Russia Learned to Read*; Vucinich, *Science in Russian Culture*.
41. For an introduction to these and other individuals, see A. Yarmolinsky, *Road to Revolution* (London, 1957; New York, 1959); E. Wilson, *To the Finland Station* (New York, 1940; London, 1941) and E. Lampert's two books, *Studies in Rebellion* (London, 1957) and *Sons Against Fathers* (Oxford, 1965). See also B. A. Engel, *Mothers and Daughters: Women of the Intelligentsia in Nineteenth-Century Russia* (Cambridge, 1983); A. Gleason, *Young Russia: The Genesis of Russian Radicalism in the 1860s* (Chicago, 1980); D. R. Brower, *Training the Nihilists: Education and Radicalism in Tsarist Russia* (Ithaca, N.Y., and London, 1975); P. Pomper, Sergei Nechaev (New Brunswick, N.J., 1979); D. Hardy, *Land and Freedom: The Origins of Russian Terrorism, 1876–1879* (New York, 1987); D. Hardy, *Peter Tkachev: The Critic as Jacobin* (Seattle, Wash., and London, 1977). *What Is To Be Done?* has no less than three editions in English: S.V. Utechin (ed.) (Oxford, 1963), and R. Service (ed.) (London, 1988); W. Wagner (ed.) (Ithaca, N.Y., 1989).
42. Zelnik, *Labor and Society*, p. 370.
43. See Wortman, *The Crisis of Russian Populism*. See also D. Field, 'Peasants and Propagandists in the Russian Movement to the People of 1874', *J. of Modern History*, vol. 59 (1987).
44. R. Pipes argues that the connection was not really made even then; see his *Social Democracy and the St Petersburg Labor Movement, 1855–1897*

(Cambridge, Mass., 1963). For a Soviet criticism of this book, see R. A. Kazakevich and F. M. Suslova, *Mister Paips falsifitsiruet istoriiu* (Leningrad, 1966). On Plekhanov, see the analytical biography *Plekhanov: The Father of Russian Marxism*, by S. H. Baron (London and Stanford, Calif., 1963). See also Vera Broido, *Apostles into Terrorists: Women and the Revolutionary Movement in the Russia of Alexander II* (London, 1977); A. Kelly, *Michael Bakunin* (Oxford, 1982); N. M. Naimark, *Terrorists and Social Democrats: The Russian Revolutionary Movement under Alexander III* (Cambridge, Mass., 1983); D. Offord, *The Russian Revolutionary Movement in the 1880s* (Cambridge, 1986).

45. On the liberals, see J. Walkin, *The Rise of Democracy in Pre-Revolutionary Russia: Political and Social Institutions under the Last Three Tsars* (New York, 1962); D. Offord, *Portraits of Early Russian Liberals* (Cambridge, 1985).

46. See the thorough study by R. F. Byrnes, *Pobedonostsev*, and also K. F. Pobyedonosteff, *Reflections of a Russian Statesman* (London, 1898).

47. P. A. Zaionchkovskii, *Rossiiskoe samoderzhavie v kontse XIX stoletiia* (Moscow, 1970) pp. 435–6. For Zaionchkovskii's authoritative interpretation of this whole period, see also among his many works *Otmena krepostnogo prava v Rossii* (Moscow, 1968) and *Krizis samoderzhaviia na rubezhe 1870–1880kh godov* (Moscow, 1964). The latter has been translated as *The Russian Autocracy in Crisis, 1878–1882* (Gulf Breeze, Flo., 1979), the former as *The Abolition of Serfdom in Russia* (Gulf Breeze, Flo., 1978). For a considered Western view, see Lincoln, *The Great Reforms*.

48. V. O. Kliuchevskii, *Pisma, dnevniki, aforizmy i mysli ob istorii* (Moscow, 1968), pp. 315–7.

Ch. 9   Russian Imperialism, 1894–1917

1. V. I. Lenin, *Imperialism: The Highest Stage of Capitalism* (Moscow, 1970), p. 86. For a skilful blending of Soviet and Western concepts, see D. Geyer, *Russian Imperialism*.

2. A. L. Sidorov et al., *Istoriia SSSR*, VI, pp. 7–15. For a nuanced version see B. V. Ananich et al., *Krizis samoderzhavii v Rossii, 1895–1917* (Leningrad, 1984).

3. See T. G. Stavrou's introduction to his *Russia under the Last Tsar*.

4. A most readable version of such an interpretation is R. K. Massie, *Nicholas and Alexandra* (New York, 1968). A searching analysis may be found in Lieven, *Nicholas II*.

5. Trotsky, *History of the Russian Revolution*, pp. 112–30.

6. Smirnov, *Short History*, p. 264.

7. For a sympathetic portrait of Rasputin, see his daughter's biography: M. Rasputin, *My Father* (London, 1934). See also A. De Jonge, *The Life and Times of Grigorii Rasputin* (London, 1982).

8. Smirnov, *Short History*, p. 326. For a spirited defence of Nicholas as war leader, see D. R. Jones, 'Nicholas II and the Supreme Command: An Investigation of Motives', *Sbornik*, Study Group on the Russian Revolution, no. 11 (1985).

9. Florinsky, *Russia*, p. 1147.

10. See G. Hough, *The Fleet that Had to Die* (London and New York, 1958) and more widely J. A. White, *The Diplomacy of the Russo-Japanese War* (Princeton, N.J., 1964); R. A. Esthus, *Double Eagle and Rising Sun: The Russians and Japanese at Portsmouth in 1905* (Durham, N.C., 1988).
11. *The Memoirs of Count Witte* (London, 1921) p. 250: considerably abridged, this version must be used with care. See H. D. Mehlinger and J. M. Thompson, *Count Witte and the Tsarisı Government in the 1905 Revolution* (Bloomington, Ind., 1971).
12. Sidorov, *Istoriia*, VI, p. 251.
13. Dmytryshyn, *Imperial Russia*, p. 309; W. Sablinsky, *The Road to Bloody Sunday: Father Gapon and the St Petersburg Massacre* (Princeton, N.J., 1976).
14. Smirnov, *Short History*, p. 278. See, generally, J. Bushnell, *Mutiny amid Repression: Russian Soldiers in the Revolution of 1905–6* (Bloomington, Ind., 1985). See also R. Edelman, *Proletarian Peasants: The Revolution of 1905 in Russia's South-West* (Ithaca, N.Y., 1987); C. Rice, *Russian Workers and the SR Party through the Revolution of 1905–1907* (London, 1988); M. Perrie, *The Agrarian Policy of the Russian Socialist-Revolutionary Party from Its Origins through the Revolution of 1905–1907* (Cambridge, 1976); K. P. Sauer (ed.), 'The 1905 Revolution: Recent Soviet Studies', *Soviet Studies in History*, vol. 20 (1981–2). See generally Ascher, *The Revolution of 1905*.
15. Mehlinger and Thompson, *Count Witte*, pp. 32–3. See also A. M. Verner, *The Crisis of Russian Autocracy: Nicholas II and the 1905 Revolution* (Princeton, N.J., 1990).
16. L. D. Trotsky, *1905* (New York, 1971; London, 1972) p. 117.
17. Florinsky, *Russia*, p. 1183; Keep, *The Rise*, p. 278; I. Spector, *The First Russian Revolution: Its Impact on Asia* (Englewood Cliffs, N.J., 1962). See also Rywkin, *Russian Colonial Expansion*.
18. T. Emmons, *The Formation of Political Parties and the First National Elections in Russia* (Cambridge, Mass., 1983); D. C. Rawson, *Russian Rightists and the Revolution of 1905* (Cambridge, 1995); H. Rogger, 'Was there a Russian Fascism?', *J. of Modern History*, vol. 36 (1964). Ascher, *The Revolution of 1905*, p. 345: 'good will and political sagacity of a high order' would have been necessary to make the October settlement succeed.
19. See R. L. Tuck, 'Paul Miliukov and the Negotiations for a Duma Ministry', *Slavic Review*, vol. 10 (1951).
20. A. Ia. Avrekh, *Stolypin i treteiunskaia sistema* (Moscow, 1966). Hosking, *The Russian Constitutional Experiment* 'has much in common with Avrekh's work' (see p. 250, from Hosking's useful 'A Note on Historiography and Sources'); and see A. Levin, *The Second Duma: A Study of the Social Democratic Party and the Russian Constitutional Experiment* (New Haven, Conn., 1940).
21. See, for example, H. Rogger, *Jewish Policies and Right-Wing Policies in Imperial Russia* (London, 1986).
22. Avrekh, *Stolypin*, p. 14, for Lenin on *Vekhi*. *Vekhi* has been translated in *Canadian–American Slavic Studies* vols 2 and 3 (1968–9). For a scholarly analysis, see L. Schapiro, 'The Vekhi Group and the Mystique of Revolution', *Slavonic Review*, vol. 34 (1955); and C. Read, *Religion, Revolution and the Russian Intelligentsia, 1900–1912: The Vekhi Debate and*

Its Intellectual Background (London, 1979). See also R. E. Pipes, *Struve*, 2 vols (Cambridge, Mass., 1970, 1980).

23. Western writing on Stolypin includes M. S. Conroy, *P. A. Stolypin: Practical Politics in Late Tsarist Russia* (Boulder, Col., 1976; G. A. Hosking, 'Stolypin and the Octobrist Party', *Slavonic Review*, vol. 47 (1969); A. Levin, 'P. A. Stolypin: A Political Reappraisal', *J. of Modern History*, vol. 37 (1965); L. I. Strakhovsky, 'The Statesmanship of Peter Stolypin: A Reappraisal', *Slavonic Review*, vol. 37 (1959); and G. B. Tokmakoff, *P. A. Stolypin and the Third Duma* (Washington, D.C., 1981).

24. See G. Tokmakoff, 'Stolypin's Assassin', *Slavic Review*, vol. 24 (1965). For a summary of a different verdict, see Hosking. *The Russian Constitutional Experiment*, pp. 148–9.

25. Avrekh, *Stolypin*, pp. 38–9. See also J. F. Hutchinson, 'The Octobrists and the Future of Russia as a Great Power', *Slavonic Review*, vol. 50 (1972).

26. Avrekh, *Stolypin*, p. 56; Hosking, *The Russian Constitutional Experiment*, pp. 106, 113. Miliukov, whose emphasis was on the constitution rather than the nation, admired not only the British system of government, but also the American: see his *Russia and Its Crisis* (New York, 1962), a reprint of his lectures first given at the University of Chicago in 1903. For a further perspective see W. C. Fuller, *Civil–Military Conflict in Imperial Russia*.

27. Avrekh, *Stolypin*, p. 57.

28. Ibid., p. 169. See also V. N. Kokovstov, *Out of My Past* (Stanford, Calif., 1935).

29. For a Western view, see T. Riha, 'Miliukov and the Progressive Bloc in 1915: A Study in Last-Chance Politics', *J. of Modern History*. vol. 32 (1960); and see also A. N. Iakhontov, *Prologue to Revolution: Notes on the Secret Meetings of the Council of Ministers, 1915,* edited by M. Cherniavsky (Englewood Cliffs, N.J., 1967), and Pearson, *The Russian Moderates*. For a late Soviet view, see N. G. Dumova, *Kadetskaia partiia v period pervoi mirovoi voiny i fevralskoi revoliutsii* (Moscow, 1988).

30. L. Haimson, 'The Problem of Social Stability in Urban Russia, 1905–1917', *Slavic Review*, vols. 23 and 24 (1964–5). The discussion begun by Haimson is continued by other experts.

31. See Riha's contribution to Stavrou, *Russia under the Last Tsar*. On others involved, see D. Lieven, *Russia's Rulers under the Old Regime* (London, 1989); R. G. Robbins, *The Tsar's Viceroys: Russian Provincial Governors in the Last Years of the Empire* (New York, 1987).

32. Smirnov, *Short History*, pp. 293–5; Rogger, *Russia* Ch. 9; R. H. McNeal, *Tsar and Cossack, 1855–1914* (London, 1987).

33. E. D. Sokol, *The Revolt of 1916 in Russian Central Asia* (Baltimore, Maryland, 1954) p. 158.

34. Smirnov, *Short History*, p. 315; Dmytryshyn, *Imperial Russia*, p. 372.

35. D. W. Spring, 'Russia and the Franco-Russian Alliance, 1905–1914: Dependence or Interdependence?' *Slavonic Review*, vol. 66 (1988).

36. A. J. P. Taylor, *War by Timetable* (London, 1969). See also his *The First World War: An Illustrated History* (London, 1966). See the discussion of Fischer's work in H. W. Koch (ed.), *The Origins of the First World War: Great Power Rivalry and German War Aims* (London, 1972; New York, 1973).

37. C. Jay Smith, *The Russian Struggle for Power, 1914–17: A Study of Russian Foreign Policy during the First World War* (New York, 1956); E. C. Thaden, *Russia and the Balkan Alliance of 1912* (University Park, Penn., 1965).
38. L. C. F. Turner, 'The Russian Mobilization in 1914', *J. of Contemporary History*, vol. 3 (1968) and *Origins of the First World War* (London, 1970); D. C. Lieven, *Russian and the Origins of the First World War* (London, 1983).
39. I. V. Bestuzhev, 'Russian Foreign Policy, February-June 1914', *J. of Contemporary History*, vol. 1 (1966); Smirnov, *Short History*, pp. 315–17; D. Geyer, *Russian Imperialism*.
40. Smirnov, *Short History*, p. 320.
41. Sidorov, *Istoriia*, VI, p. 318; R. E. Pipes, *The Formation of the Soviet Union, 1917–1923* (Cambridge, Mass., 1957) pp. 1–2; Shanin, *Russia as 'Developing Society'*, p. 65. See B. Farnsworth and L. Viola (eds), *Russian Peasant Women* (Oxford, 1992) Part I. See also J. Bradley, *Muzhik and Muscovite: Urbanization in Later Imperial Russia* (Los Angeles, 1985) and J. H. Bater, *St Petersburg: Industrialization and Change* (London, 1976).
42. W. E. Mosse, 'Stolypin's villages', *Slavonic Review*, vol. 43 (1965) p. 268; G. B. Tokmakoff, 'Stolypin's Agrarian Reform: An Appraisal', *Russian Review*, vol. 30 (1971) p. 138. See also D. A. J. Macey, *Government and Peasant in Russia, 1861–1906: The Prehistory of the Stolypin Reforms* (DeKalb, Ill., 1987). On the nobility, see S. Becker, *Nobility and Privilege in Late Imperial Russia* (DeKalb, Ill., 1985); R. Edelman, *Gentry Politics on the Eve of the Russian Revolution* (New Brunswick, N.J., 1980); G. M. Hamburg, *Politics of the Russian Nobility, 1881–1905* (New Brunswick, N.J., 1984); and R. T. Manning, *The Crisis of the Old Order in Russia* (Princeton, N.J., 1982).
43. Von Laue, *Sergei Witte*, p. 306; Smirnov, *Short History*, p. 261.
44. Sidorov, *Istoriia*, VI, pp. 260–4. Using somewhat different figures, J. P. McKay, *Pioneers for Profit: Foreign Entrepreneurship and Russian industrialization, 1885–1913* (Chicago, 1970) argues that the Russian experience proved that a developing country could surmount the problem of dependence on foreign capital. B. B. Ananich, *Rossiia i mezhdunarodnyi kapital, 1897–1914* (Leningrad, 1970) is among those who would not agree.
45. Sidorov, *Istoriia*, VI, p. 269. Most of the figures and information in this section are taken from the same volume. A dissentient view on the central role of large-scale industry was I. F. Gindin, in I. I. Mints (ed.) *Sverzhenie samoderzhavstva* (Moscow, 1970), for example. For supplementary and alternative statistics, see P. R. Gregory, *Russian National income, 1885–1913* (Cambridge, 1982). See also V. E. Bonnell, *The Russian Worker: Life and Labor under the Tsarist Regime* (Berkeley, Calif., 1983); and his *Roots of Rebellion: Workers' Politics and Organizations in St Petersburg and Moscow, 1900–1914* (Berkeley, Calif., 1983); R. L. Glickman, *Russian Factory Women: Workplace and Society, 1880–1914* (Berkeley, Calif., 1984).
46. Baedeker's *Handbook for Travellers: Russia* (Leipzig, London and New York, 1914) p. xxv.
47. R. Ropponen, *Die Kraft Russlands: Wie beurteilte die politische und militarische Führung der europäischen Grossmächte in der Zeit von 1905 bis 1914 die Kraft Russlands* (Helsinki, 1968). Ropponen argues that Russia's strength appeared to her prospective allies and opponents to have recovered in several respects if by no means in all on the eve of the First World War.

P. Gatrell, *Government, Industry and Rearmament in Russia, 1900–1914: The Last Argument of Tsarism* (Cambridge, 1994) pp. 323, 329, concludes that 'military and industrial objectives, far from being incompatible, could be reconciled', but that the war 'eventually exposed the recklessness of the gamble undertaken by the imperial regime.'

48. See the contributions to the Carnegie Series on Russia in the First World War by A. N. Antsiferov, A. M. Michelson, B. E. Nolde, P. B. Struve and S. O. Zagorsky (New Haven, Conn., 1928–33). N. Stone, *The Eastern Front, 1914–1917* (London, 1975) argues that distribution was more of a problem than production.

49. See Von Laue's contribution to Stavrou, *Russia*; Gerschenkron, 'Agrarian Policies and Industrialization: Russia, 1861–1917', *Cambridge Economic History of Europe*, vol. 6 (1966); Gatrell, *The Tsarist Economy*, generally, and O. Crisp, *Studies in the Russian Economy before 1914* (London, 1976).

50. Karpovich, *Imperial Russia*, quoted in Adams, *Imperial Russia*, p. 87.

51. Sidorov, *Istoriia*, VI, p. 717.

52. Baedeker's *Handbook*, pp. 54, 91–2, 271–2, 377, 394, 466.

53. Sidorov, *Istoriia*, VI, p. 729. Lenin's 'pessimistic' view may be placed against that of a moderate and informed optimist, T. Darlington, *Education in Russia* (London, 1909). And see Brooks, *When Russia Learned to Read*. See also S. S. Sevegny, *Russian Teachers and Peasant Revolution: The Politics of Education in 1905* (Bloomington, Ind., 1989).

54. Florinsky, *Russia*, p. 1233; Sidorov, *Istoriia*, VI, pp. 728–9.

55. Ibid., p. 730. See, generally, O. Crisp and L. Edmondson (eds) *Civil Rights in Imperial Russia* (Oxford, 1989).

56. Sidorov, *Istoriia*, VI, pp. 739–40. See also R. C. Williams, *The Other Bolsheviks: Lenin and his Critics, 1904–1914* (Bloomington, Ind., 1986); D. G. Rowley, *Millenarian Bolshevism, 1900–1920* (New York and London, 1987); L. H. Haimson, *The Russian Marxists and the Origins of Bolshevism* (Cambridge, Mass., 1955); R. Kindersley, *The First Russian Revisionists: A Study of Legal Marxism in Russia* (Oxford, 1962); A. P. Mendel, *Dilemmas of Progress in Tsarist Russia: Legal Marxism and Legal Populism* (Cambridge, Mass., 1961). On the press, see 'Newspaper Journalism in Pre-Revolutionary Russia', *Soviet Studies in History*, vol. 25 (1986).

57. See, for example, S. Galai, *The Liberation Movement in Russia, 1900–1905* (Cambridge, 1972). For some Soviet views, see N.M. Pirumova, 'The Zemstvo Liberal Movement', *Soviet Studies in History*, vol. 20 (1981); K. F. Shatsillo, *Russkii liberalizm nakanune revoliutsii 1905–1907gg: organizatsiia, programmy, taktika* (Moscow, 1905). See also L. H. Edmondson, *Feminism in Russia 1900–1917* (Stanford, 1984); L. Engelstein, *The Keys to Happiness: Sex and the Search for Modernity in Fin-de-Siècle Russia* (Ithaca, N.Y., 1992).

58. See G. Struve's contribution to Stavrou, *Russia*.

59. Avrekh, *Stolypin*, p. 15.

60. Smirnov, *Short History*, p. 309. See also G. Gibian and T. Jalsma (eds), *Russian Modernism: Culture and the Avant-Garde, 1900–1930* (Ithaca, N.Y., 1976); D. S. Mirsky, *Contemporary Russian Literature, 1881–1925* (London, 1926).

61. See C. Gray, *The Great Experiment: Russian Art, 1863–1922* (London, 1962). See also J. E. Bowlt, *The Silver Age: Russian Art of the Early*

Twentieth Century and the 'World of Art' Group (Newtonville, Mass., 1979); D. Elliott, *New Worlds: Russian Art and Society, 1900–1937* (London, 1986).
62. Byrnes, *Kliuchevskii*, pp. 117, 122; Nechkina, *Kliuchevskii*, pp. 456, 460, 463.

Part Three   Contemporary Russia: The Soviet Union

Introduction

1. Samsonov, *Short History*, p. 7.
2. See N. Harding, 'The Marxist-Leninist Detour', in J. Dunn (ed.), *Democracy: The Unfinished Journey* (Oxford, 1992) and his *Leninism*. Some would argue that Marxism–Leninism is little different from Stalinism.

Ch 10   The Russian Revolution, 1917–1921

1. G. Z. Ioffe, *Fevralskaia revoliutsiia 1917g v anglo-amerikanskoi burzhuaznoi istoriografii* (Moscow, 1970) p. 54. See also M. S. Melancon (ed.), 'The Russian Revolution of 1917 in the Eyes of Soviet Historians: Orthodoxy vs. A New Flexibility', and D. J. Raleigh (ed.), 'Reviving a Historical Controversy: Who Made the Revolution', *Soviet Studies in History*, vol. 23 (1984) and vol. 22 (1983–4) respectively.
2. For some 'older' Western analysis, see J. H. Billington, 'Six Views of the Russian Revolution', *World Politics*, vol. 18 (1965–6); see also M. M. Karpovich, 'The Russian Revolution of 1917', *J. of Modern History*, vol. 2 (1930), and H. J. Ellison, 'Soviet Historians and the Russian Revolution', in L. H. Legters (ed.) *Russia: Essays in History and Literature* (Leiden, 1972). Generally, see works listed in the Select Bibliography, especially Acton, *Rethinking the Russian Revolution*; Burbank, *Intelligentsia and Revolution*; and Frankel, *Revolution in Russia*.
3. G. Katkov, *Russia 1917: The February Revolution* (London, 1967) is critical of the February Revolution, finding, among other culprits, the Freemasons. E. N. Burdzhalov, *Vtoraia russkaia revoliutsiia: Vosstanie v Petrograde* (Moscow, 1971), and *Vtoraia russkaia revoliutsiia: Moskva, front, periferiia* (Moscow, 1971) provided the best Soviet account. The first volume has been translated D. J. Raleigh (ed.) as *Russia's Second Revolution: The February 1917 Uprising in Petrograd* (Bloomington, Ind., 1987). The fullest and best 'Western' account is by a Japanese scholar: Tsuyoshi Hasegawa, *The February Revolution: Petrograd 1917* (Seattle, Wash., 1971).
4. F. A. Golder (trans. and ed.), *Documents of Russian History, 1914–1917* (Gloucester, Mass., 1964) pp. 308–9.
5. Read, *From Tsars to Soviets*, p. 43.
6. Florinsky, *Russia*, pp. 1384, 1387. For a full biography, see Richard Abraham, *Alexander Kerensky, The First Love of the Revolution* (London, 1987).
7. Trotsky, *The History*, p. 291. See also Hasegawa, *The February Revolution*, pp. 400–9.
8. Wade, *The Russian Search*, pp. 47–8; V.S. Vasiukov, *Vneshniaia politika vremennogo pravitelstva* (Moscow, 1966) pp. 85–133.

9. Samsonov, *Short History*, p. 12. For the situation of the Bolsheviks before Lenin's arrival, see D. A. Longley, 'The Divisions in the Bolshevik Party in March 1917', *Soviet Studies*, vol. 24 (1972–3).

10. M. Ferro, 'Pourquoi février? Pourquoi octobre?', *Annales: économies, sociétés, civilisations*, no. 1 (1968) p. 47. In his later book, *October 1917* (London, 1980), Ferro detects an encroaching Soviet bureaucracy in the pre-October period. See also R. Service (ed.), *State and Revolution* (London, 1992). On the workers, see Smith, *Red Petrograd*; D. Koenker, *Moscow Workers and the 1917 Revolution* (Princeton, 1981); D. Mandel, *The Petrograd Workers and the Fall of the Old Regime* (London, 1983); *The Petrograd Workers and the Soviet Seizure of Power* (London, 1984).

11. K. Paustovsky, *In that Dawn* (London, 1967) pp. 45–6. See also D. J. Raleigh, *Revolution on the Volga: 1917 in Saratov* (Ithaca, N.Y., 1986).

12. Rabinowitch, *Prelude to Revolution*, p. 188; Trotsky, *The History*, p. 574. For a Soviet view, see O. N. Znamenskii, *Iiulskii krizis 1917goda* (Moscow–Leningrad, 1967).

13. Florinsky, *Russia*, p. 1434.

14. Trotsky, *The History*, pp. 646–68, 711–28, 845; H. Asher, 'The Kornilov Affair: A Reinterpretation', *Russian Review*, vol. 29 (1970); L. I. Strakhovsky, 'Was there a Kornilov Rebellion?', *Slavonic Review*, vol. 33 (1955); J. D. White, *The Russian Revolution*, pp. 135–50. For a contrasting view, see G. Katkov, *Russia 1917: the Kornilov Affair* (London, 1980). For a Soviet view, see N. Ia. Ivanov, *Kornilovshchina i ee razgrom* (Leningrad, 1965).

15. Ferro, *The Russian Revolution*, p. 271.

16. Trotsky, *The History*, p. 883. See also L.A. Owen, *The Russian Peasant Movement, 1906–1917* (London and New York, 1937) p. 178; Ia. A. Iakovlev (ed.), *1917 god v derevne* (Moscow, 1967); J. Keep, 'October in the Provinces', in R. E. Pipes (ed.) *Revolutionary Russia* (Cambridge, Mass., 1968); J. Channon, 'The Peasantry in the Revolutions of 1917', in Frankel, *Revolution in Russia*. See, more generally, J. Keep, *The Russian Revolution*, and O. H. Radkey, *The Agrarian Foes of Bolshevism: Promise and Default of the Russian Socialist Revolutionaries: February to October, 1917* (New York, 1958). For a Soviet view, see A. D. Maliavskii, *Krestianskoe dvizhenie v Rossii v 1917g., mart-oktiabr* (Moscow, 1981).

17. Pipes, *The Formation of the Soviet Union*, pp. 51, 93–8.

18. N. N. Golovin, *The Russian Army in the World War* (New Haven, Conn., 1931) p. 262; Trotsky, *The History*, p. 282. See also A. K. Wildman, *The End of the Imperial Army*, 2 vols (Princeton, N.J., 1980, 1987). See also M. S. Frenkin, *Russkaia armiia i revoliutsiia 1917–1918* (Munich, 1978).

19. On the situation in the navy, see D. A. Longley, 'Officers and Men', *Soviet Studies*, vol. 25 (1973). See also E. Mawdsley, *The Russian Revolution and the Baltic Fleet: War and Politics, February 1917–April 1918* (London, 1978).

20. On German subsidies to the Bolsheviks, see M. Futrell, *Northern Underground: Episodes of Russian Revolutionary Transport through Scandinavia, 1863–1917* (London and West Orange, N.J., 1963); and Z. A. B. Zeman (ed.) *Germany and the Revolutions in Russia, 1915–1918: Documents from the Archives of the German Foreign Ministry* (London, 1968).

21. See also L. Kochan, 'Kadet Policy in 1917 and the Constituent Assembly', *Slavonic Review*, vol. 45 (1967).
22. K. Marx and F. Engels, *Manifesto of the Communist Party* (Moscow, 1969) pp. 96, 12. On the October Revolution, see works listed in the Select Bibliography. A range of recent views is provided by Figes, Pipes, Read and White. On the immediate global impact, see Dukes, *October and the World*.
23. J. Reed, *Ten Days that Shook the World* (reprint London, 1966) p. 129.
24. F. D. Volkov, *Krakh angliiskoi politiki interventsii i diplomaticheskoi izoliatsii gosudarstva, 1917–1924gg* (Moscow, 1954) pp. 39–40. See, generally, Mawdsley, *The Russian Civil War*, and Lincoln, *Red Victory*. See also McAuley on St. Petersburg, *Bread and Justice*; R. Sakwa on Moscow, *Soviet Communists in Power: A Study of Moscow during the Civil War, 1918–1921* (London, 1988); O. Figes, *Peasant Russia, Civil War: The Volga Countryside in Revolution, 1917–1921* (London, 1989); and V. N. Brovkin, *Behind the Front Lines of the Civil War: Political Parties and Social Movements in Russia, 1918–1922* (Princeton, N.J. 1994).
25. See R. G. Suny, *The Baku Commune, 1917–1918: Class and Nationality in the Russian Revolution* (Princeton, N.J., 1972).
26. Fischer, *The Life of Lenin*, p. 330.
27. J. Erickson, 'Lenin as Civil War Leader', in *Lenin*, edited by Schapiro and Reddaway. See also Francesco Benvenuti, *The Bolsheviks and the Red Army, 1918–1922* (Cambridge, 1989).
28. Chamberlin, *The Russian Revolution*, II, p. 493.
29. See, for example, J. S. Reshetar, *The Ukrainian Revolution, 1917–1920: A Study in Nationalism* (Princeton, N.J., 1952); F. Kazamzadeh, *The Struggle for Transcaucasia, 1917–1921* (New York, 1951); R. G. Hovannisian, *The Republics of Armenia*, 2 vols (Berkeley, Calif., 1973, 1983).

Ch. 11   The Consolidation of the Soviet Union, 1917–1929

1. A. Ransome, *Six Weeks in Russia in 1919* (London, 1919) pp. 81–2; and see W. Mandel, 'Arthur Ransome: Eyewitness in Russia, 1919', *Slavic Review*, vol. 27 (1968).
2. Service, *Lenin: A Political Life*, vol. 2, pp. xii–xiv. See also Harding, *Leninism*.
3. I. I. Mints *et al* (eds), *Istoriia SSSR*, VII, pp. 709–12. See, more generally, C. Lane, *The Rites of Rulers: Ritual in Industrial Society: The Soviet Case* (Cambridge, 1981); N. T. Tumarkin, *Lenin Lives! The Lenin Cult in Soviet Russia* (Cambridge, Mass., 1983). For the decline and collapse of Lenin's reputation in the U.S.S.R. and post-Soviet Russia, see Davies, *Soviet History in the Gorbachev Revolution*, pp. 115–125, and *Soviet History in the Yeltsin Era*, pp. 52–4.
4. Carr, *The Bolshevik Revolution*, I, pp. 238–56, including previous quotations from Engels and Lenin; Rigby, *Lenin's Government*; Service, *The Bolshevik Party*.
5. Carr, *The Bolshevik Revolution*, III, p. 28.
6. See J. Wheeler-Bennett, *Brest-Litovsk: The Forgotten Peace* (London, 1934; New York 1971). See also R. K. Debo, *Revolution and Survival: The Foreign Policy of Soviet Russia, 1917–1918* (Toronto and Liverpool, 1979); D. Kirby,

War, Peace and Revolution: International Socialism at the Crossroads, 1914–1918 (London, 1986).

7. Carr, *The Bolshevik Revolution*, I, p. 123; and see page 212 above. For a different view, see O. H. Radkey, *The Election to the Russian Constituent Assembly of 1917* (Cambridge, Mass., 1950). For a Soviet view see O. N. Znamenskii, *Vserossiiskoe uchreditelnoe sobranie* (Leningrad, 1976).

8. Carr, *The Bolshevik Revolution*, I, pp. 414–35. For a Soviet view, see M. Iroshnikov, D. Kovalenko and V. Shishkin, *Genesis of the Soviet Federative State, 1917–1925* (Moscow, 1982). See also M. L. von Hagen (ed.), 'The Early Years of the Soviet Regime: Recent Studies', *Soviet Studies in History*, vol. 23 (1984).

9. See Avrich, *Kronstadt* and Getzler, *Kronstadt*; R. V. Daniels, 'The Kronstadt Revolt of 1921: A Study in the Dynamics of Revolution', *Slavic Review*, vol. 10 (1951); E. Mawdsley, 'The Baltic Fleet and the Kronstadt Mutiny', *Soviet Studies*, vol. 24 (1923). On workers, see Kaiser, *The Workers' Revolution*; J. Aves, *Workers against Lenin: Labour Protest and the Bolshevik Dictatorship* (London, 1996); L. Engelstein and R. Suny (eds), *Making Workers Soviet* (Ithaca, N.Y., 1994). For a libertarian view, see M. Brinton, *The Bolsheviks and Workers' Control, 1917–1921: The State and Counter-Revolution* (London, 1970). On peasants, see O. H. Radkey, *The Unknown Civil War in Soviet Russia: A Study of the Green Movement in the Tambov Region, 1920–1* (Stanford, Calif., 1976); S. Singleton, 'The Tambov Revolt, 1920–1', *Slavic Review*, vol. 25 (1966). On politicians, see Daniels, *Conscience of the Revolution*; Schapiro, *The Origin*; and V. N. Brovkin, *The Mensheviks after October: Socialist Opposition and the Rise of the Bolshevik Dictatorship* (Ithaca, N.Y., 1987).

10. See Lenin, *Collected Works*, XXXII, pp. 257–82.

11. See the works by J. N. Thompson and A. J. Mayer cited in the Bibliography to this chapter. See also S. White, *The Origins of Detente: The Genoa Conference and Soviet–Western Relations, 1921–2* (Cambridge, 1985).

12. Samsonov, *Short History*, p. 124.

13. W. E. Mosse, 'Makers of the Soviet Union', *Slavonic Review*, vol. 46 (1968).

14. Samsonov, *Short History*, p. 125.

15. Carr, *What Is History?*, pp. 98, 102. Carr, *The Interregnum* pp. 354–5; R. Pethybridge, *The Soviet Prelude to Stalinism* (London, 1974); N. A. Basetskii. 'L. D. Trotskii: politicheskii portret', *Novaia i noveishaia istoriia*, 3 (1989); P. Broué, *Trotsky* (Paris, 1988).

16. See, for example, O. Gorodetsky, *The Precarious Truce: Anglo-Soviet Relations 1924–7* (London, 1977); S. Fitzpatrick, 'The Foreign Threat during the First Five-Year Plan', *Soviet Union*, vol. 5 (1978).

17. R. Portal, 'The Industrialisation of Russia'. *Cambridge Economic History of Europe*, VI, p. 865; T. H. von Laue, 'A Secret Memorandum of Sergei Witte on the Industrialisation of Imperial Russia', *J. of Modern History*, vol. 26 (1954).

18. Carr, *The Bolshevik Revolution*, II, p. 370. See also S. Malle, *The Economic Organisation of War Communism, 1918–1921* (Cambridge, 1985); E. G. Gimpelson, *Voennyi kommunizm: printsipy, praktika, ideologiia* (Moscow, 1973).

19. Portal, 'The Industrialisation', p. 869.

20. Carr, *The Bolshevik Revolution*, II, p. 278.
21. Ibid., p. 315.
22. S. F. Cohen, *Bukharin and the Bolshevik Revolution* (New York, 1975); A.V. Chayanov, *The Theory of Peasant Economy*, ed. D. Thorner, B. Kerblay and R. E. F. Smith (Homewood, Ill., 1966). V. P. Danilov, *Rural Russia under the Old Regime* (Bloomington, Ind., and London, 1988) pp. 225–7 is sceptical. See also B. Farnsworth and L. Viola (eds), *Russian Peasant Women* (Oxford, 1992), Part II.
23. E. Preobrazhensky, *The New Economics*, B. Pearce (trans.), A. Nove (intro.) (Oxford, 1965). On Trotsky, see R. B. Day, *Leon Trotsky and the Politics of Economic Isolation* (Cambridge, 1973).
24. S. Chase, R. Dunn and R. O. Tugwell, *Soviet Russia in the Second Decade* (New York, 1928).
25. See Nove, *An Economic History*, Chapters 4–6. See also W. Chase, *Workers, Society, and the Soviet State: Labor and Life in Moscow, 1918–1929* (Urbana, Ill., 1987); J. Hughes, *Stalin, Siberia and the Crisis of the New Economic Policy* (Cambridge, 1991); and C. Ward, *Russia's Cotton Workers and New Economic Policy: Shop-floor Culture and State Policy, 1921–1929* (Cambridge, 1990).
26. Nettl, *The Soviet Achievement*, p. 94. See, more generally, P. Kenez, *The Birth of the Propaganda State: Soviet Methods of Mass Mobilization, 1917–1929* (Cambridge, 1985).
27. Miliukov, *Outlines*, I, p. 164.
28. R. F. and M. S. McWilliams, *Russia in 1926* (London and Toronto, 1927) pp. 75–6. See, generally, S. Fitzpatrick, *Education and Social Mobility in the Soviet Union, 1921–1934* (London, 1979).
29. Mints, *Istoriia SSSR*, VII, pp. 686–7.
30. Iu. A. Poliakov *et al.* (eds), *Istoriia SSSR*, VIII, pp. 263–6, 273–4. See also Fitzpatrick, *The Commissariat*, pp. 26–88.
31. H. Asher, 'The Rise, Fall and Resurrection of M. N. Pokrovsky', *Russian Review*, vol. 31 (1972); J. Barber, *Soviet Historians in Crisis, 1928–1932* (Macmillan, 1981).
32. Miliukov, *Outlines*, II, pp. 82, 94.
33. Ibid., III, pp. 82–3, 88, 94, 97–8, 139, 144. See J. Milner, *Vladimir Tatlin and the Russian Avant-Garde* (New Haven, Conn., and London, 1985). See also D. Elliott, *New Worlds, Russian Art and Society, 1900–1937* (London, 1986); A. Gleason *et al.* (eds), *Bolshevik Culture: Experiment and Order in the Russian Revolution* Bloomington, Ind., 1985); W. G. Rosenberg (ed.), *Bolshevik Visions: First Phase of the Cultural Revolution in Soviet Russia* (Ann Arbor, Mich., 1984); R. Stites, *Revolutionary Dreams: Utopian Vision and Experimental Life in the Russian Revolution* (Oxford, 1989); and, more generally, G. Gibian and T. Jalsma (eds) *Russian Modernism: Culture and the Avant-Garde, 1900–1930* (Ithaca, N.Y., 1970).
34. C. Gray, *The Great Experiment: Russian Art, 1863–1922* (London, 1962) p. 7; 'Russian Issue', *The Drama Review*, vol. 17 (1973); Fitzpatrick, *The Commisariat*; R. Taylor, *The Politics of the Soviet Cinema, 1917–1929* (London, 1979); P. Kenez, *Cinema and Soviet Society, 1917–1953* (Cambridge, 1992) Part I; S. White, *The Bolshevik Poster* (New Haven, Conn., 1988).

35. A. Kollontai, *'The New Woman': Autobiography of a Sexually Emancipated Woman* (New York, 1971; London, 1972). See also C. Porter, *Fathers and Daughters: Russian Women in Revolution* (London, 1976); R. Stites, *The Women's Liberation Movement in Russia* (Princeton, N.J., 1978).
36. Lewin, *Russian Peasants*, p. 23.
37. Quoted in Davies, *Soviet History*, p. 33.

Ch. 12   The Construction of Soviet Socialism, 1929–1941

1. E. H. Carr, *What is History?* (London, 1987) pp. 74–84.
2. Carr, *Foundations*, II, p. 451.
3. See D. Joravsky's introduction to R. Medvedev's *Let History Judge*, pp. ix–xx. And see, in general, Davies, *Soviet History*, especially Chapters 3–7. For an argument for assessing Stalin and Stalinism in its full context, see T. H. Von Laue, 'How to judge Stalin' and 'Stalin Reviewed', *Soviet Union*, no. 1 (1981) and no. 1 (1984); 'Stalin in Focus', *Slavic Review*, 3 (1983).
4. Trotsky, *Stalin*, p. 336, and *The Revolution Betrayed: What is the Soviet Union and Where is it Going?*, quoted in Daniels, *The Stalin Revolution*, p. 103. See also Pethybridge, *The Social Prelude*. The fullest account is Tucker, *Stalin as Revolutionary* and *Stalin in Power*. Generally, see works listed in the Select Bibliography.
5. Lewin, *Russian Peasants*, pp. 450–1. See also R. M. Slusser, *Stalin in October: The Man who Missed the Revolution* (Baltimore, Maryland, 1987).
6. Samsonov, *Short History*, pp. 182–3. For more recent appraisal, see Davies, *Soviet History in the Gorbachev Revolution* and *Soviet History in the Yeltsin Era*.
7. For the beginnings of this process, see J. Keep, '1917: The Tyranny of Paris over Petrograd', *Soviet Studies*, vol. 20 (1968–9). Looking in the other direction, S. Fitzpatrick sees 1937 as a continuation of 1917 in *The Russian Revolution 1917–1937*.
8. See, for example, R. Conquest, *Stalin and the Kirov Murder* (London, 1986); J. A. Getty, 'The Politics of Repression Revisited', Getty and Manning, *Stalinist Terror*: and see, more generally, Conquest's *The Great Terror*. Davies, *Soviet History in the Yeltsin Era*, pp. 156–8, suggests that the balance of evidence is against Stalin's instigation of Kirov's murder.
9. Deutscher, *Stalin*, pp. 356–7; Stalin, *Works*, XIII, pp. 33–44. See also Tucker in *Stalin in Power* for development of comparison of Stalin with Ivan the Terrible and Peter the Great.
10. Deutscher, *Stalin*, p. 368. and see G. T. Rittersporn, 'The Omnipresent Conspiracy: On Soviet Imagery of Politics and Social Relations in the 1930s', Getty and Manning, *Stalinist Terror*; Davies, *Soviet History in the Yeltsin Era*, pp. 185–92.
11. Samsonov, *Short History*, p. 179. See also J. A. Getty, 'State and Society under Stalin: Constitutions and Elections in the 1930s', *Slavic Review*, vol. 50 (1991). And see note 17 below on death toll.
12. Rigby, *Communist Party Membership*, pp. 197–235. See also G. Gill, *The Origins of the Stalinist Political System* (Cambridge, 1990); S. Fitzpatrick, 'Stalin and the Making of a New Elite', *Slavic Review*, vol. 38 (1979); M. Fainsod, *Smolensk under Soviet Rule* (Cambridge, Mass., 1958). For alter-

native views, see J. A. Getty *Origins of The Soviet Purges: The Soviet Communist Party Reconsidered* (Cambridge, 1985); G. T. Rittersporn, *Stalinist Simplifications and Soviet Complications: Social Tensions and Political Conflicts in the USSR 1933–1953* (Chur, Switzerland, 1991).

13. Erickson, *The Soviet High Command*; M. Garder, *A History of the Soviet Army* (London, 1966) pp. 89–92. R. Reese, 'The Red Army and the Great Purges', Getty and Manning, *Stalinist Terror*, suggests a figure of about 24,000 for the number of officers purged in the late 1930s, but others would put the figure higher. See, in more detail, R. Reese, *Stalin's Reluctant Soldiers: A Social History of the Red Army, 1925–1941* (Lawrence, Kansas, 1996).

14. See, for example, Jonathan Haslam, *Soviet Foreign Policy, 1930–1933: The Impact of the Depression* (London, 1983); *The Soviet Union and the Struggle for Collective Security in Europe, 1933–1939* (London, 1984); *The Soviet Union and the Threat from the East, 1933–1941* (London, 1992). For a Soviet view, see V. Sipols, *Diplomatic Battles before World War II* (Moscow, 1982). See also M. B. Carley, 'End of the Low, Dishonest Decade: Failure of the Anglo-Franco-Soviet Alliance in 1939', *Europe–Asia Studies*, vol. 45 (1993).

15. Samsonov, *Short History*, pp. 150–1.

16. M. Harrison, 'Why did NEP Fail?', *Economics of Planning*, vol. 16 (1980) p. 66, concludes that 'The N.E.P. economy could have yielded further economic expansion and restructuring of production relations, with rather less industrial growth, more agricultural revolution and more attention to living standards. The latter tasks could not be reconciled, however, with the task of rapid, large-scale industrialization.' The abandonment of N.E.P. was 'a political choice, but it had an economic logic'. For an interesting alternative view, see V. Mau, *Reformy i dogmy, 1914–1929: Ocherki istorii stanovlenii khoziaistvennoi sistemy sovetskogo totalitarianizma* (Moscow, 1993).

17. M. Muggeridge, In *Guardian Weekly*, 26 March, 1989. See also M. Lewin, 'Who Was the Soviet *kulak?'*, *Soviet Studies*, vol. 18 (1966–7). For further contrasting views, see R. Conquest, *The Harvest of Sorrow: Soviet Collectivization and the Terror–Famine* (London, 1986); V. P. Danilov, *Rural Russia under the New Regime* (London, 1988); and S. Fitzpatrick, *Stalin's Peasants: Resistance and Survival in the Russian Village after Collectivization* (New York, 1994). The death toll accompanying collectivisation, forced labour and the Terror was probably about 10–11 millions, but some would place it nearer 20 millions. See Nove, Wheatcroft *et al.* in Getty and Manning, *Stalinist Terror*. See also the debates in *American Historical Review*, vol. 98 (1993), *Slavic Review* (1985) and *Soviet Studies* (1981–).

18. See R. D. Laird, D. E. Sharp and R. Sturtevant, *The Rise and Fall of the MTS as an Instrument of Soviet Rule* (Lawrence, Kansas, 1960).

19. Samsonov, *Short History*, p. 152. As an antidote to the gigantic heroism of Samsonov, there are debunking anecdotes: concerning, for example, the first delivery to a new town building site of thousands of lavatory pans; and the construction of river dams before seagoing ships had made their exit. More seriously, see A. D. Rassweiler, *The Generation of Power: The History of Dneprostroi* (Oxford, 1988) for one of the most important construction projects in the Ukraine.

20. Deutscher, *Stalin*, pp. 331–2. Herbert Marshall tells how he became such a specialist solely on the basis of being able to drive a car; see *The Listener*,

vol. 89, no. 2295 (1973) p. 364. See S. Kotkin, *Magnetic Mountain: Stalinism as a Civilization* (London, 1995) for life in Magnitogorsk in the 1930s.

21. On aspects of economic development in the 1930s, see, in addition to Nove, *An Economic History*, whose exposition has been largely followed here, with the quotation from p. 257: R. W. Davies, *The Industrialisation of Soviet Russia* (London, 1980 -); K. E. Bailes, *Technology and Society under Lenin and Stalin: Origins of the Soviet Technical Intelligentsia 1917–1941* (Princeton, N.J., 1978); D. Filtzer, *Soviet Workers and Stalinist Industrialization: The Formation of Modern Soviet Production Relations, 1928–1941* (London, 1986); H. Kuromiya, *Stalin's Industrial Revolution: Politics and Workers, 1928–1932* (Cambridge, 1988); H. Siegelbaum, *Stakhanovism and the Politics of Productivity in the USSR, 1935–1941* (Cambridge, 1988); and L. Viola, *The Best Sons of the Fatherland: Workers in the Vanguard of Soviet Collectivization* (Oxford, 1987).

22. Fainsod, *Smolensk*, pp. 434–40; Miliukov, *Outlines*, I, pp. 201–2. Articles by Yu. Poliakov *et al.* in *Sotsiologicheskoe issledovanie*, nos. 6–8 (1990) suggest that the census indicates that just over half the population considered themselves believers.

23. H. Fireside, *Icon and Swastika: The Russian Orthodox Church under Nazi and Soviet Control* (Cambridge, Mass., 1971) p. 168. And see Curtiss, *The Russian Church*.

24. G. S. Counts, *The Challenge of Soviet Education* (New York, 1957), quoted in Daniels, *The Stalin Revolution*, pp. 60–6. See also S. Fitzpatrick, *Education and Mobility in the Soviet Union, 1921–1934* (London, 1979); S. Fitzpatrick (ed.), *Cultural Revolution in Russia, 1928–1931* (London and Bloomington, Ind., 1978).

25. D. Joravsky, *The Lysenko Affair* (Cambridge, Mass., 1970).

26. For interesting interpretations, see V. S. Dunham, *In Stalin's Time: Middle Class Values in Soviet Fiction* (Cambridge, 1976); A. Kemp-Welch, *Stalin and the Literary Intelligentsia, 1928–1939* (London, 1991); R. Marsh, *Images of Dictatorship: Stalin in Literature* (London, 1989). E. J. Simmons, *Russian Fiction and Soviet Ideology* (New York, 1955) in the Preface suggests that Fedin, Leonov and Sholokhov were the Steinbeck, Faulkner and Hemingway of Soviet literature.

27. D. Addes *et al.*, *Art and Power: Europe and the Dictators, 1930–1945* (London, 1996); and see H. Gunther (ed.), *The Culture of the Stalin Period* (London, 1989).

28. M. Ilin, *Moscow Has a Plan: A Soviet Primer* (London, 1931) p. 214.

29. Nadezhda Mandelshtam, *Hope Abandoned*, quoted by J. Barber 'The Establishment of Intellectual Orthodoxy in the USSR, 1928–1934' *Past and Present*, no. 83 (1979). Of course, some historians blame Fascism on Stalinism. See Addes, *Art and Power*, for examples of cultural interaction.

Ch. 13   War and Reconstruction, 1941–1953

1. Deutscher, *Stalin*, p. 458; and see W. O. McCagg, *Stalin Embattled 1943–1948* (Detroit, 1978).

2. Dmitri Volkogonov, 'The German Attack, the Soviet Response, Sunday, 22 June 1941', Erickson and Dilks, *Barbarossa*, p. 86. For a full discussion of

the debate among Soviet historians on the commencement of the Second World War, see V. Petrov, *June 22, 1941: Soviet Historians and the German Invasion* (Columbia, S.C., 1968). See also O. Rzheshevsky, *World War Two: Myths and Realities* (Moscow, 1984); M. Parrish (ed.), 'Soviet Historiography of the Great Patriotic War, 1970–1985', *Soviet Studies in History*, vol. 23 (1984–5). Davies, *Soviet History in the Gorbachev Revolution*, pp. 103–4; and R. A. Medvedev, 'Diplomaticheskie i voennye proscheby Stalina v 1939–1941gg', *Novaia i noveishaia istoriia*, vol. 3 (1989). Generally, for Western views, see works by A. Clark, J. Erickson, A. Seaton and A. Werth listed in the Select Bibliography. See also L. Relusto, 'Stalin and the Outbreak of War in 1941', *J. of Contemporary History* vol. 24 (1989). For general assessments, see A. P. Adamthwaite (ed.), *The Making of the Second World War* (London, 1977); A. J. P. Taylor, *The Second World War: An Illustrated History* (London, 1976); G. Weinberg, *A World at Arms: A Global History of World War II* (Cambridge, 1994).

3. See M. Van Creveld, 'The German Attack on the USSR: The Destruction of a Legend', *European Studies Review*, vol. 2 (1972); B. A. Leach, *German Strategy against Russia, 1939–1941* (Oxford, 1973); B. Whaley, *Codeword Barbarossa* (Cambridge, Mass., 1972). Whaley makes interesting use of the analogy with Pearl Harbor. See also H. W. Koch, 'Operation Barbarossa: The Current State of the Debate', *Historical Journal*, vol. 31 (1988).

4. O. Bartov, *The Eastern Front, 1941–5: German Troops and the Barbarisation of Warfare* (London, 1985).

5. Davies, *Soviet History in the Gorbachev Revolution*, pp. 105–6. Generally, as in note 2 above.

6. For a balanced assessment, see D. S. Clemens, *Yalta* (Oxford and New York, 1970). Quotations from Leahy, p. 278 of the paperback version. And see H. Feis, *Japan Subdued: The Atomic Bomb and the End of the War in the Pacific* (Princeton, N.J., 1961). W. LaFeber, *America, Russia and the Cold War* is among the best general analyses. See J. L. Black (ed.), *Origins, Evolution and Nature of the Cold War: An Annotated Bibliographic Guide* (Santa Barbara, Calif., and Oxford, 1986).

7. W. Lippmann, *The Cold War: A Study in US Foreign Policy* (New York, 1972), pp. 32–47.

8. For a summary Soviet view, see B. N. Ponomaryov *et al.* (eds) *History of Soviet Foreign Policy, 1917–1980*, vol. 2 (Moscow, 1981). See in particular D. Holloway, *Stalin and the Bomb: The Soviet Union and Atomic Energy* (New Haven, Conn., 1994).

9. See, for example, A. M. Nekrich, *The Punished Peoples* (New York, 1978); Robert Conquest, *The Nation Killers* (London, 1970).

10. See works by T. Dunmore and R. Pethybridge listed in the Select Bibliography.

11. Samsonov, *Short History*, p. 215; Davies, *Soviet History*, pp. 100, 214. Detailed, and somewhat different statistics may be obtained from M. Harrison, *Accounting for War: Soviet Production, Employment, and the Defence Burden, 1940–1945* (Cambridge, 1996). J. Erickson, 'Soviet War Losses: Calculations and Controversies', in Erickson and Dilks, *Barbarossa*, p. 257, points out that for the 'global loss', including the 'natural loss' due to wartime diminution of the birth rate, 'there is something of a consensus ... in the order of 47–50 million.'

12. A. P. Pogrebinskii *et al.*, *Istoriia narodnogo khoziaistva* (Moscow, 1964) pp. 171–98. Fuller, variant assessments may be found in Barber and Harrison, *The Soviet Home Front*; Harrison, *Accounting for War*; Linz (ed.), *The Impact of World War on the Soviet Union*; and W. Moskoff, *The Bread of Affliction: The Food Supply in the USSR during World War II* (Cambridge, 1990).
13. Fireside, *Icon and Swastika*, pp. 172–3.
14. Werth, *Russia at War*, p. 399.
15. Fireside, *Icon and Swastika*, p. 183.
16. M. J. Shore, *Soviet Education: Its Psychology and Philosophy* (New York, 1967) pp. 203–18.
17. Samsonov, *Short History*, pp. 374–5.
18. Deutscher, *Stalin*, p. 601. See also K. Shteppa, *Russian Historians and the Soviet State* (New Brunswick, N.J., 1962).
19. W. G. Hahn, *Postwar Soviet Politics: The Fall of Zhdanov and the Defeat of Moderation, 1946–53* (London, 1982) argues that Zhdanov's bark was worse than his bite. *Pravda*, 24 February 1986, considered that Zhdanov 'wholeheartedly served the working people, the cause of Lenin, the Communist Party.'

Ch. 14   The Assertion of Soviet Superpower, 1953–1964

1. M. Djilas, *Conversations with Stalin* (London and New York, 1962) pp. 95–8.
2. Nettl, *The Soviet Achievement*, pp. 221–2. See also Medvedev, *Khrushchev*, pp. viii–x.
3. Frankland, *Khrushchev*, p. 90.
4. S. Alliluyeva, *20 Letters to a Friend* (London and New York, 1967). A. Knight, *Beria: Stalin's First Lieutenant* (Princeton, 1993) is not alone in suggesting that Beria promoted reform after Stalin's death and before his own arrest. See Davies, *Soviet History in the Yeltsin Era*, pp. 206–12.
5. Samsonov, *Short History*, pp. 291–2. For an alternative view, See Medvedev, *Khrushchev*, pp. 83–103.
6. Rigby, *Communist Party Membership*, pp. 300–6; Nettl, *The Soviet Achievement*, pp. 218–19.
7. Khrushchev, in *The Road*, pp. 361–2.
8. See, for example, A. Inkeles, 'Soviet Nationality Policy in Perspective', in Brumberg (ed.), *Russia*.
9. Frankland, *Khrushchev*, p. 206.
10. For developments in the armed forces, see Garder, *A History of the Soviet Army*, pp. 138–210.
11. Samsonov, *Short History*, pp. 326–7. For a scholarly Western analysis, see R. M. Slusser, *The Berlin Crisis of 1961: Soviet-American Relations and the Struggle for Power in the Kremlin* (London and Baltimore, Maryland, 1973).
12. Samsonov, *Short History*, p. 339; Ulam, *Expansion*, pp. 667–77.
13. Pogrebinskii, *Istoriia*, pp. 224–58.
14. Khrushchev, in *The Road*, pp. 70–2.
15. Pogrebinskii, *Istoriia*, pp. 258–67.
16. Ibid., pp. 267–73.

17. W. C. Fletcher, *The Russian Orthodox Church Underground, 1917–1970* (London, 1972), p. 231.
18. Khrushchev, in *The Road*, p. 154.
19. D. A. Lowne and W. C. Fletcher, 'Khrushchev's Religious Policy, 1959–1964', in R. H. Marshall Jr (ed.), *Aspects of Religion in the Soviet Union* (London and Chicago, 1971) pp. 136–40.
20. Khrushchev, in *The Road*, pp. 569–70.
21. See, for example, D. P. Costello, 'Zhivago Reconsidered', *Forum for Modern Language Studies*, vol. 4 (1968).

Ch. 15   Stability and Relaxation, 1964–1975

1. B. Dmytryshyn, 'Brezhnev, Leonid Ilich', *MERSH*; L. I. Brezhnev, *Pages from his Life* (New York, 1978). See also M. Tatu, *From Khrushchev's Decline to Collective Leadership* (London, 1969).
2. Brown, 'Political Developments: Some Conclusions and an Interpretation', Brown and Kaiser, *The Soviet Union*, pp. 220–1.
3. P. Frank, 'The Changing Composition of the Communist Party', ibid., pp. 110–1.
4. McCauley, *The Soviet Union*, pp. 260–3; Keep, *Last of the Empires*, pp. 208–9.
5. A. Nove, *Political Economy and Soviet Socialism* (London, 1979) pp. 195–218.
6. P. Reddaway, The Development of Dissent and Opposition', Brown and Kaiser, *The Soviet Union*, pp. 135–43.
7. Edmonds, *Soviet Foreign Policy*, pp. 38–43, 74–80.
8. Ibid., pp. 8–11, 106–11.
9. LaFeber, *America, Russia*, pp. 253–83.
10. McCauley, *The Soviet Union*, pp. 238–60. See, generally, Edmonds, *Soviet Foreign Policy*.
11. Nove, *An Economic History*, pp. 371–4.
12. Ibid., pp. 374–83: Kerblay, *Modern Soviet Society*, pp. 129–44.
13. J. A. Newth, 'Demographic Developments', Brown and Kaiser, *The Soviet Union*, pp. 77–81.
14. M. Bourdeaux, 'Religion', Brown and Kaiser, *The Soviet Union*, pp. 160–1.
15. Ibid., p. 163.
16. Ibid., pp. 166–78. See, generally, Keep, *Last of the Empires*, pp. 165–73.
17. Reddaway, 'The Development', Brown and Kaiser, *The Soviet Union*, pp. 125–8, 147–9.
18. G. Hosking, *Beyond Socialist Realism: Soviet Fiction since Ivan Denisovich* (London, 1980). See also R. Marsh, *Soviet Fiction since Stalin: Science, Literature and Politics* (London, 1986).
19. M. Dewhirst, 'Soviet Russian Literature and Literary Policy', Brown and Kaiser, *The Soviet Union*, p. 188; Keep, *Last of the Empires*, pp. 277–9.
20. G. S. Smith, *Songs to Seven Strings: Russian Guitar Poetry and Soviet 'Mass Song'* (Bloomington, Ind., 1984).
21. Kerblay, *Modern Soviet Society*, pp. 140–1, 261.
22. Ibid., pp. 156–8.
23. Heller and Nekrich, *Utopia*, p. 630.

Ch. 16   Stagnation and Tension, 1975–1985

1. Heller and Nekrich, *Utopia*, pp. 657–61. Others would place the onset of Brezhnev's senility at a later date, towards the end of the 1970s, and would argue that he remained a shrewd and skilful operator till then at least. Yet others might suggest that, in conditions of stagnation, nobody would notice the difference.
2. On Andropov and Chernenko, see contributions to *MERSH* supplementary volumes by R. D. Warth. See also Z. Medvedev, *Andropov* (London, 1983).
3. J. H. Miller, 'The Communist Party: Trends and Problems', Brown and Kaiser, *Soviet Policy*, pp. 6, 19. See also B. Meissner and G. Józsa in Veen, *From Brezhnev*, pp. 299–323.
4. Heller and Nekrich, *Utopia*, p. 646. According to his niece, Brezhnev told her father: 'All that stuff about communism is a tall tale for popular consumption', quoted in review of Luba Brezhneva, *The World I Left Behind: Pieces of a Past* (New York, 1995) in *Guardian Weekly*, 31 July 1995. And see A. Nove, *Political Economy and Soviet Socialism* (London, 1979) pp. 214–15: 'The point about the *nomenklatura* is that it lists those whom the *system itself* regards as being important enough to require the special attention of the central committee's organisation department. Consequently, unlike vague words about bureaucrats and elite, they represent something not only definable but defined, and defined not by the arbitrary whim of the foreign scholar but by the party machine itself (though this definition is not known to us in detail).'
5. *Constitution (Fundamental Law) of the Union of Soviet Socialist Republics* (Moscow, 1977), pp. 11–14, 21, 40, 55, 56, 60.
6. A. Bennigsen and M. Broxup, *The Islamic Threat to the Soviet State* (London, 1983).
7. Edmonds, *Soviet Foreign Policy*, pp. 148–50.
8. LaFeber, *America, Russia*, pp. 284–315.
9. Edmonds, *Soviet Foreign Policy*, pp. 172–3.
10. Ibid., pp. 173–7, 181–94. See, generally, H. S. Bradsher, *Afghanistan and the Soviet Union* (Durham, N.C., 1983).
11. McCauley, *The Soviet Union*, pp. 254–60.
12. Heller and Nekrich, *Utopia*, pp. 691–3.
13. A. Nove, 'Agriculture', in McCauley, *The Soviet Union*, pp. 96–7, and Brown and Kaiser, *Soviet Policy*, pp. 170–84. See also M. Kaiser. 'Economic Policy', in ibid., p. 188. Compare M. F. Ruban, K. E. Wadekin and M. Checinski in Veen, *From Brezhnev*, pp. 11–41; and see generally A. McAuley, *Economic Welfare in the Soviet Union: Poverty, Living Standards, and Inequality* (London, 1979).
14. Heller and Nekrich, *Utopia*, pp. 699–701.
15. Nove, *An Economic History*, pp. 379–81; M. E. Ruban, 'The Consumer Economy', Veen, *From Brezhnev*, pp. 16–21.
16. Heller and Nekrich, *Utopia*, pp. 673–731. See, generally, C. Lane, *Christian Religion in the Soviet Union: A Sociological Study* (London. 1978).
17. H. Carrère d'Encausse, *Decline of an Empire: The Soviet Socialist Republics in Revolt* (London, 1980); L. Kochan (ed.), *The Jews in Soviet Russia* (Oxford, 1972); Pincus, *The Jews*.

18. Heller and Nekrich, *Utopia*, p. 681.
19. See, for example, W. Kasack, 'Literature between State and Opposition', Veen, *From Brezhnev*, pp. 163–71.
20. G. S. Smith, *Songs to Seven Strings: Russian Guitar Poetry and Soviet 'Mass Song'* (Bloomington, Ind., 1984) pp. 231–3; G. S. Smith, 'Okudzhava Marches On', *Slavonic Review*, vol. 66 (1988).
21. B. Kerblay, *Modern Soviet Society*, p. 158.
22. M. Seton-Watson, *Scenes from Soviet Life: Soviet Life through Official Literature* (London, 1986) pp. 96–8; Davies, *Soviet History*, pp. 2–5.

Ch. 17   Reform or Ruin? 1985–1996

1. M. Lewin, *The Gorbachev Phenomenon*, p. 147.
2. On Gorbachev, see for example Brown, *The Gorbachev Factor*; Medvedev, *Gorbachev*; White, *After Gorbachev*; W. Joyce, H.Ticktin and S. White (eds) *Gorbachev and Gorbachevism*. The Gorbachevs have one daughter.
3. See Morrison, *Boris Yeltsin*, pp. 27, 32ff., 142–3. Yeltsin's wife Naina has been much more in the background than was Raisa Gorbacheva. The Yeltsins have two daughters.
4. Medvedev, *Gorbachev*, p. 251.
5. S. White, *Political Culture and Soviet Politics* (London, 1979) pp. 95–112; Archie Brown, 'Political Change in the Soviet Union', *World Policy Journal* (Summer 1989).
6. See J. Thrower, *Marxism–Leninism as the Civil Religion of Soviet Society; God's Commissar* (Lewiston, N.Y., 1992).
7. Brown, *The Gorbachev Factor*, p. 175.
8. Keep, *Last of the Empires*, pp. 352, 433n.
9. Ibid., pp. 363–83. S. White, R. Rose and I. McAllister, *How Russia Votes* (Chatham, N.J., 1996) p. 76 points out that while 76.4 per cent of 80 per cent of the electorate voted for the preservation of the U.S.S.R., 69.9 per cent of 75.1 per cent of the electorate voted for the introduction of the post of President of the R.S.F.S.R.
10. A. S. Barsenkov *et al.*, *Towards a Nationalities Policy in the Russian Federation* (Aberdeen, 1993), p. 20; *Vestnik statistiki*, 1990–1.
11. Keep, *The Last of the Empires*, pp. 398, 435.
12. Brown, *The Gorbachev Factor*, p. 212.
13. Ibid., pp. 236–7.
14. Ibid., p. 241.
15. Ibid., pp. 221–2. See also John Gooding 'Gorbachev and Democracy', *Soviet Studies*, vol. 42 (1990).
16. Morrison, *Boris Yeltsin*, pp. 142–3.
17. White *et al.*, *How Russia Votes*, p. 123 for a more complete return. 58.4 per cent of 54.8 per cent of the electorate approved of the Russian Federation Constitution. Ibid., p. 99.
18. Ibid., pp. 224–5 records the fortunes of all parties and groups.
19. C. Donnelly, 'The Future of European and Russian Security', Elphinstone Lecture, Aberdeen, 24 November 1995; S. M. Surikov, *Kontseptualnye polozheniia strategii protivodeistviia osnovnym vneshnim ugrozam natsionalnoi bezopasnosti Rossiiskoi Federatsii* (Moscow, 1995).

20. *Keesing's Record of World Events*, 1991 -.
21. *Guidelines for the Economic and Social Development of the USSR for 1986–1990 and for the Period ending in 2000* (Moscow, 1985) p. 12. For the Soviet economic predicament in a wider context, see C. Maier, 'The Collapse of Communism: Approaches for a Future History', *History Workshop*, no. 31 (1991).
22. S. White, *Russia goes dry: Alcohol, state and society* (Cambridge, 1995); D. Tarschys, 'The Success of a Failure: Gorbachev's Alcohol Policy', *Europe–Asia Studies*, vol. 45 (1993), especially pp. 9–10.
23. As for note 22.
24. V. Mau, 'The Road to *Perestroika*: Economics in the USSR and the Problems of Reforming the Soviet Economic Order', *Europe–Asia Studies*, vol. 48 (1996), especially pp. 219–24. See, more generally, V. Mau, *Ekonomika i vlast: politicheskaia istoriia ekonomicheskoi reformy v Rossii, 1985–1994* (Moscow, 1995).
25. Quoted by Elena Sargeant, 'The Main Tendencies in Social Policy in Russia during the Transitional Period from Socialism to Capitalism', *Proceedings of the Annual Conference of the Scottish Society for Russian and East European Studies, 1995* (Glasgow, [1996]) p. 2.
26. Centre Naturopa Newsletter, *Naturopa* (Strasbourg, 1995). See, more generally, J. Massey Stewart (ed.) *The Soviet Environment: Problems, Policies and Politics* (Cambridge, 1992).
27. See, for example, J. Watson, 'Foreign Investment in Russia: The Case of the Oil Industry', *Europe–Asia Studies*, vol. 48 (1996); A. Moe, 'The Soviet Oil Industry: Where do we go from here?', Reiner Weichhardt (ed.), *The Soviet Economy under Gorbachev* (Brussels, 1991).
28. S. L. Webber, 'School and Society in The New Russia', *Proceedings of the Annual Conference of the Scottish Society for Russian and East European Studies, 1995* (Glasgow, [1996]) pp. 29–52.
29. *Sankt-Peterburgskii Universitet*, No. 9 (3402) (27 November 1995) pp. 1–2.
30. D. Remnick, 'Sakharov's Testament: New Soviet Constitution', *The Guardian Weekly*, 24 December 1989, p. 8; A. Solzhenitsyn, '"Russkii vopros" k kontsu XX veka', *Novy Mir*, 7 (1994).
31. R. Marsh, 'The Death of Soviet Literature: Can Russian Literature Survive?', *Europe–Asia Studies*, vol. 45 (1993), pp. 123, 133.
32. See Davies, *Soviet History in the Yeltsin Era*, pp. 217–20; editorials, *Istoriia SSSR*, 5 (1990) and 1 (1992); A. S. Akhiezer *et al.*, 'Rossiia – raskolotaia tsivilizatsiia: Samobytnost Rossii kak nauchnaia problema', *Otechestvennaia Istoriia*, 4–5 (1994); V. A. Aleksandrov, 'Vasilii Osipovich Kliuchevskii: K 150-letiiu so dnia rozhdeniia', *Otechestvennaia Istoriia*, 5 (1991). Another interesting interpretation is the 'Eurasian'. See, for example, the debate in *Rodina*, no. 9 (1996).

Ch. 18   The Limits of Russian History, 1996 -

1. See, for example, V. Shlapentokh, 'Early Feudalism: The Best Parallel for Contemporary Russia', *Europe–Asia Studies*, vol. 48 (1996). Shlapentokh looks to the West for his principal analogy. On the other hand, the newspaper *Segodnia* observed about developments during Yeltsin's illness in September 1996: 'Russian politics has always been noted for all kinds of intrigues and

nuances rather than formal laws and legal norms. This is some kind of Byzantine tradition typical of Russian politics.' Quoted by Lee Hockstader, *International Herald Tribune*, 11 September 1996. Consider also the at least partial continued relevance of Hellie and Keenan as in the *Introduction* to the Modern section, pp. 66–7 above.

2. Kliuchevskii, *Sochineniia*, I, p. 31.

3. For a mixture of sexist and other reasons, the equally appropriate comparison with Catherine the Great has not been taken up. See P. Dukes, 'Why Peter? Why not Catherine? Some Reflections on the Development of Russian Absolutism', *Study Group on Eighteenth-Century Russia Newsletter*, 18 (1990); R. Bartlett, 'Images: Catherine II of Russia, Enlightened Absolutism and Mikhail Gorbachev', *The Historian*, 30 (1991).

4. K. Pobedonostsev, *Reflections of a Russian Statesman* (Ann Arbor, Mich., 1965), pp. 32, 36.

5. See, for example, P. Kennedy, *The Rise and Fall of the Great Powers: Economic Change and Military Conflict from 1500 to 2000* (New York and London, 1988).

6. Quoted by A. Skinner in Introduction to Adam Smith, *The Wealth of Nations* (London, 1983) p. 22. Robert Burns put the same point more simply: 'O wad some Pow'r the giftie gie us – To see oursels as others see us! It wad frae mony a blunder free us, and foolish notion.' More generally, in a review of a book on Scotland and the Slavs, D. E. Paterson refers to 'the timely issue of whether the Scottish enlightenment from Dugald Stewart, Adam Smith and Adam Ferguson succeeded in creating an intellectual tradition strong enough to support the current experiments in political and cultural liberalism in the post-communist Slavic nations'. See *Slavic Review*, vol. 53 (1994) p. 575.

7. D. Obolensky, *The Penguin Book of Russian Verse* (London, 1962) p. 88.

8. Among the last attempts to explain the Soviet Union before its collapse, see: S. Bialer, *The Soviet Paradox: External Expansion, Internal Decline* (London, 1986); A. H. Brown (ed.), *Political Leadership in the Soviet Union* (Bloomington, Ind., 1989); S. F. Cohen, *Rethinking the Soviet Experience: Politics and History since 1917* (New York and Oxford, 1985); R. V. Daniels, *Is Russia Reformable? Change and Resistance from Stalin to Gorbachev* (Westview, Conn., 1988); G. Hosking, *The Awakening of the Soviet Union* (London, 1990); W. Laqueur, *The Long Road to Freedom: Russia and Glasnost* (London, 1990); R. C. Tucker, *Political Culture and Leadership in Soviet Russia from Lenin to Gorbachev* (Brighton, 1987); A. Yanov, *The Russian Challenge and the Year 2000* (New York and Oxford, 1987). For post–1991 analyses, see the Select Bibiography.

9. D. S. Likhachev, 'Budushchee literatury kak predmet izucheniia', *Novy mir*, no. 3 (1980) pp. 36–7.

10. See A. G. Meyer, 'Theories of Convergence', in C. Johnson (ed.), *Changes in Communist Systems* (Stanford, Calif., 1970) pp. 36–7. See A. Kucherov, 'Alexander Herzen's Parallel between the United States and Russia', in J. S. Curtiss (ed.), *Essays in Honor of G. T. Robinson* (Leiden, 1963) pp. 37–47. For the general context, see P. Dukes, *The Last Great Game; USA versus USSR: Events, Conjunctures, Structures* (London and New York, 1989).

11. E. H. Carr, *What Is History?*, second edition (London and New York, 1987) p. 134.

Select Bibliography

I General Guide to Further Study

The dimensions of a full Bibliography of Russian History are suggested by those of *The Russian Revolution, 1905–1921: A Bibliographic Guide to Works in English* (Westport, Conn., and London, 1995) compiled by Murray Frame and running to 308 pp. Even a Select Bibliography of works considering medieval, modern and contemporary Russia could easily be at least twice as long as the rest of this book. My aim here, therefore, is to provide a guide to further study, assisting readers to discover more about whichever aspects of Russian, Soviet and post-Soviet history interest them most. To save space, I have often given one location only, especially when, as so often happens, a book has been published in both London and New York.

Two useful aids are R. P. Bartlett and P. H. Clendenning (eds), *Eighteenth Century Russia: A Select Bibliography of Works published since 1955* (Newtonville, Mass., 1981) and R. Pearson (ed.), *Russia and Eastern Europe, 1789–1985: A Bibliographic Guide* (Manchester and New York, 1989). For the earlier period, see also P. A. Crowther, *A Bibliography of Works in English on Russian History to 1800* (Oxford and New York, 1969).

For those interested in research, much help can be gained from J. Dossick, *Doctoral Research on Russia and the Soviet Union*, 2 vols, (New York, 1960, 1976) and then in *Slavic Review* (1976–); P. K. Grimsted, *A Handbook for Archival Research in the USSR* (Washington, D.C., 1989) and earlier works; J. Hartley, *Guide to Documents and Manuscripts in the United Kingdom relating to Russia and the Soviet Union* (London, 1987). Older, still useful works include M. J. Ruggles and V. Mostecky, *Russia and East European Publications in the United States* (New York, 1960); G. P. M. Walker and J. Johnson, *Library Resources in Britain for the Study of Eastern Europe and of the former USSR* (London, 1992); and J. S. G. Simmons, *Russian Bibliography: Libraries and Archives – A Selective List of Bibliographical References for Students of Russian History, Literature, Political, Social and Philosophical Thought* (Twickenham, 1973).

Updates on bibliography, as well as articles and other materials, may be found in the major periodicals, including *Slavonic Review, Slavic Review, Russian Review, Europe-Asia Studies* (formerly *Soviet Studies*). Other useful periodicals include *Slavonica* (formerly *Scottish Slavonic Review*), *Irish Slavonic Studies, Canadian–American Slavic Studies, Russian History*, and *Revolutionary Russia*. Translations of Soviet and post-Soviet articles and books may be found in *Russian Studies in History* (formerly *Soviet Studies in History*). The leading post-Soviet journals are *Voprosy istorii, Novaia i noveishaia istoriia* and *Otechestvennaia*

Istoriia (formerly *Istoriia SSSR*). *Rodina* is a most useful 'popular' journal, a counterpart to *History Today*. Reviews, review articles and occasional surveys may be found in several periodicals, including *English Historical Review* and *American Historical Review*.

For current publications in English, see: *American Bibliography of Slavic and East European Studies* (Bloomington, Ind., and Columbus, Ohio, 1956) (also available on subscription via the Internet); *European Bibliography of Slavic and East European Studies* vols 1 and 2 (Birmingham, 1977–9); vol. 3 (Paris, 1981–). This includes books and articles published in Britain, France, Germany, Austria, Belgium, Netherlands and Finland. See also *Historical Abstracts, 1775–1914* (Santa Barbara, Calif., 1955).

On HISTORIOGRAPHY and METHODOLOGY, see S. H. Baron and N. W. Heer (eds), *Windows on the Russian Past: Essays on Soviet Historiography Since Stalin* (Columbus, Ohio, 1977); C. F. Black (ed.), *Rewriting Russian History: Soviet Interpretations of Russia's Past* (New York, 1956); N.W. Heer, *Politics and History in the Soviet Union* (Cambridge, Mass., 1971); J. L. H. Keep and L. Bratby, *Contemporary History in the Soviet Mirror* (London, 1964); A. G. Mazour, *Modern Russian Historiography* (New York, 1958), and the same author's *The Writing of History in the Soviet Union* (Stanford, Calif., 1971); S. G. Pushkarev, *Dictionary of Russian Historical Terms from the Eleventh Century to 1917* (New Haven, Conn., 1970); K. F. Shteppa, *Russian Historians and the Soviet State* (New Brunswick, N.J., 1962); G. V. Vernadsky, *Russian Historiography: A History* (Belmont, Mass., 1978). Acquaintance with the 'traditional' Soviet approach can be gained from A. P. Mendel, 'Current Soviet Theory of History: New Trends or Old?' *American Historical Review*, vol. 72 (1966), and from answers to a questionnaire sent to Moscow by A. P. Mendel, M. Gefter and V. Malkov, 'A Reply to an American Scholar', *Soviet Studies in History*, vol.5 (1966–7).

A stimulating brief examination of problems of history written by a scholar whose major work was concerned with the first years of the Soviet Union is E. H. Carr's *What Is History?*, second edition (London, 1987). Marxist 'classics' on history include works by Plekhanov and Bukharin. Available translations include: G. V. Plekhanov, *In Defence of Materialism: The Development of the Monist View of History* (London, 1947) and N. I. Bukharin, *Historical Materialism: A System of Sociology* (Ann Arbor, Mich., 1969). For later Soviet analysis, see for example D. I. Chesnokov, *Historical Materialism* (Moscow, 1969). For recent developments see R. W. Davies, *Soviet History in the Gorbachev Revolution* (London, 1989) and *Soviet History in the Yeltsin Era* (London, 1996).

On GEOGRAPHY, see:
J. H. Bater and R. A. French, *Studies in Historical Geography*, 2 vols. (London, 1983).
J. P. Cole and F. C. German, *A Geography of the USSR: The Background to a Planned Economy* (London, 1970; Totowa, N.J., 1971).
J. Demko and others (eds), *Geographical Studies on the Soviet Union* (Chicago, 1984).
P. F. Lydolph, *Geography of the USSR* (New York, 1977).
R. E. H. Mellor, *Geography of the USSR* (London, 1964).
W. H. Parker, *An Historical Geography of Russia* (London, 1968; Chicago, 1969).

402 SELECT BIBLIOGRAPHY

Collections of MAPS include:
A. F. Adams, *An Atlas of Russian and East European History* (London, 1967).
Arguments and Facts International Atlas: Russia and the Post-Soviet Republics (Hastings, 1994).
J. Channon, with R. Hudson, *The Penguin Historical Atlas of Russia* (London, 1996).
A. F. Chew, *An Atlas of Russian History* (New Haven, Conn., 1967).
H. Fullard, *Soviet Union in Maps: Its Origin and Development* (London, 1961).
M. Gilbert, *Russian History Atlas* (London, 1972).
M. Gilbert, *Imperial Russian Atlas* (London, 1978).
M. Gilbert, *Soviet History Atlas* (London, 1978).

There are some worthwhile REFERENCE WORKS, including:
R. Auty and D. Obolensky (eds), *Companion to Russian Studies*, 3 vols (Cambridge, 1976–80).
A. Brown and others (eds), *The Cambridge Encyclopedia of Russia and the Soviet Union* (Cambridge, 1982).
J. L. Scherer (ed.), *USSR Facts and Figures* (Gulf Breeze, Fla., 1977–).
J. L. Wieczynski (ed.), *The Modern Encyclopedia of Russian and Soviet History* (Gulf Breeze, Fla., 1976–).

ANTHOLOGIES and COLLECTIONS OF READINGS and DOCUMENTS include:
A. G. Cross, *Russia under Western Eyes, 1553–1815* (London, 1971).
B. Dmytryshyn (ed.), *Medieval Russia: A Source Book* (New York, 1967).
B. Dmytryshyn (ed.), *Modern Russia: A Source Book* (New York, 1967).
J. M. Edie (ed.), *Russian Philosophy,* 3 vols (Chicago and London, 1965).
G. P. Fedotov (ed.), *A Treasury of Russian Spirituality* (New York, 1948).
G. L. Freeze (ed.), *From Supplication to Revolution: A Documentary Social History of Imperial Russia* (New York and Oxford, 1988).
S. S. Harcave (ed.), *Readings in Russian History,* 2 vols (New York, 1962).
D. Kaiser and G. Marker (eds), *Reinterpreting Russian History: Readings, 860–1860s* (Oxford, 1994).
M. Raeff (ed.), *Russian Intellectual History: An Anthology* (New York, 1966).
T. Riha (ed.), *Readings in Russian Civilization,* 3 vols in one (Chicago, IL, 1964).
A. F. Senn (ed.), *Readings in Russian Political and Diplomatic History,* 2 vols. (Homewood, Ill., 1966).
G. V. Vernadsky *et al.* (eds), *A Source Book for Russian History from Early Times to 1917,* 3 vols (New Haven, Conn., and London, 1972).
W. B. Walsh (ed.), *Readings in Russian History*, 3 vols (Syracuse, N.Y., 1963).

As stated in the Preface, there have been hundreds of GENERAL HISTORIES of Russia, many of them excellent of their kind. Only a few can be listed here:
E. Acton, *Russia* (London, 1986).
M. T. Florinsky, *Russia: A History and An Interpretation,* 2 vols (London, 1953).
L. Kochan and R. Abraham, *The Making of Modern Russia* (London, 1983).
N. V. Riasanovsky, *A History of Russia* (New York, 1984).
B. H. Sumner, *Survey of Russian History* (London, 1964).
R. Wittram, *Russia and Europe* (London, 1973).

The seven volumes in the Longman *History of Russia* series are listed as appropriate below.

TRANSLATIONS from the Russian include:
V. O. Kliuchevskii (rendered as V. O. Kluchevsky), *A History of Russia,* 5 vols (New York, 1960). This is a reprint of C. J. Hogarth's translation – rightly criticised for its incompleteness and inaccuracies, but better than no translation at all. Superior translations of individual volumes of this work are listed below. See also:
S. F. Platonov, *A History of Russia* (London, 1925).
M. N. Pokrovsky, *Brief History of Russia,* 2 vols. (London, 1933).
I. I. Smirnov and A. Samsonov (chief editors), *A Short History of the USSR,* 2 vols (Moscow, 1965). In internal references to this work in the present book, volume 1 is ascribed to Smirnov and volume 2 to Samsonov.
S. M. Soloviev, *History of Russia* (Gulf Breeze, Fla., 1976–).

The following is a short list of NATIONAL AND REGIONAL HISTORIES:
S. Akiner, *Islamic Peoples of the Soviet Union* (London, 1983).
W. E. D. Allen, *A History of the Georgian People from the Beginning down to the Russian Conquest in the Nineteenth Century* (London, 1932; New York, 1971).
W. E. D. Allen, *The Ukraine: A History* (Cambridge, 1940).
E. Allworth (ed.), *Ethnic Russia in the USSR: The Dilemma of Dominance* (New York, 1980).
E. Allworth (ed.), *The Nationality Question in Soviet Central Asia* (New York, 1973).
A. Bennigsen, *Muslims of the Soviet Empire* (London, 1986).
A. Bilmanis, *The History of Latvia* (Princeton, N.J., 1951).
I. Bremmer and R. Taras, *Nations and Politics in the Soviet Successor States* (Cambridge, 1993).
H. Carrère d'Encausse, *Islam and the Russian Empire: Reform and Revolution in Central Asia* (London, 1988).
S. K. Carter, *Russian Nationalism: Yesterday, Today and Tomorrow* (London, 1990).
J. Dallin, *The Rise of Russia in Asia* (London, 1950).
N. Davies, *God's Playground: A History of Poland,* 2 vols (Oxford, 1981).
J. Dunlop, *The Faces of Contemporary Russian Nationalism* (Princeton, N.J., 1983).
J. Forsyth, *A History of the Peoples of Siberia: Russia's North Asian Colony 1581–1990* (Cambridge, 1992).
A. Gieysztor and others, *History of Poland* (Warsaw, 1968).
O. Halecki, *Borderlands of Western Civilization: A History of East Central Europe* (New York, 1952).
G. Hambly (ed.), *Central Asia* (London, 1969).
M. S. Hrushevsky, *A History of Ukraine* (New Haven, Conn., and London, 1941).
F. Jutikkala, *A History of Finland* (London, 1962).
W. Kirchner, *The Rise of the Baltic Question* (Newark, Del., 1954).
D. M. Lang, *A Modern History of Georgia* (London, 1962).
D. M. Lang, *The Armenians: A People in Exile* (London, 1988).
G. A. Lensen, *Russia's Eastward Expansion* (New York, 1964).

A. Lobanov-Rostovsky, *Russia and Asia* (New York, 1933).

P. Longworth, *The Cossacks* (London, 1969).

W. H. McNeill, *Europe's Steppe Frontier* (Chicago, 1964).

R. Misunias and R. Taagepera, *The Baltic States: Years of Dependence, 1940–1980* (Berkeley, Calif., 1983).

B. Nolde, *La formation de l'empire russe* (Paris, 1952–3).

B. Pinkus, *The Jews of the Soviet Union* (Cambridge, 1988).

W. F. Reddaway and others, *Cambridge History of Poland*, 2 vols (Cambridge and New York, 1941).

M. Rywkin (ed.), *Russian Colonial Expansion to 1917* (London, 1988).

H. Schreiber, *Teuton and Slav: The Struggle for Central Europe* (London, 1965).

H. Schwartz, *Tsars, Mandarins and Commissars: A History of Chinese–Russian Relations* (London and Philadelphia, 1964).

A. E. Senn, *The Emergence of Modern Lithuania* (New York, 1959).

Y. Slezkine, *Arctic Mirrors: Russia and the Small Peoples of the North* (Ithaca, N.Y., 1994).

J. J. Stephan, *The Russian Far East: A History* (Stanford, Calif., 1994).

R. G. Suny, *The Making of the Georgian Nation* (Bloomington, Ind, , 1988).

R. G. Suny (ed.), *Transcaucasia: Nationalism and Social Change* (Ann Arbor, Mich., 1983).

T. Swietochowski, *Russian Azerbaijan, 1905–1920: The Shaping of National Identity in a Muslim Community* (Cambridge, 1985).

E. C. Thaden, *Russia's Western Borderlands 1710–1870* (Princeton, 1984).

F. Uustalu, *The History of Estonian People* (London, 1952).

N. P. Vakar, *Belorussia: The Making of a Nation* (Cambridge, Mass., 1956).

G. Von Rauch, *The Baltic States: Years of Independence, 1917–1940* (Berkeley, Calif., 1974).

C. J. Walker *Armenia: The Survival of a Nation* (New York, 1990).

P. S. Wandycz, *The Lands of Partitioned Poland, 1795–1918* (Seattle, Wash., and London, 1974).

G. Wheeler, *The Modern History of Soviet Central Asia* (London, 1964).

Most general histories are political and diplomatic in emphasis. Perhaps for that reason there are no histories exclusively devoted to these themes. There are, however, several works concentrating on ECONOMIC and CULTURAL DEVELOPMENT, although few of them consider all three major periods.

Economic

J. G. Blum, *Lord and Peasant in Russia from the Ninth to the Nineteenth Century* (Princeton, N.J., 1961).

P. I. Lyashchenko, *History of the National Economy of Russia to the 1917 Revolution* (New York, 1949).

J. Mavor, *An Economic History of Russia* (London, 1925).

M. Mitchell, *The Maritime History of Russia, 848–1948* (London, 1949).

A. I. Pashkov (ed.), *A History of Russian Economic Thought: Ninth through Nineteenth Centuries* (Berkeley, Calif., 1964).

C. White, *Russia and America: The Roots of Economic Divergence* (London, 1987).

Cultural

T. Anderson, *Russian Political Thought: An Introduction* (Ithaca, N.Y., 1967).

J. H. Billington, *The Icon and the Axe: An Interpretative History of Russian Culture* (New York, 1970).

W. C. Brumfield, *A History of Russian Architecture* (Cambridge, 1993).

M. Cherniavsky, *Tsar and People: Studies in Russian Myths* (New Haven, Conn., 1961).

M. Cherniavsky, *The Structure of Russian History: Interpretive Essays* (New York, 1970).

G. H. Hamilton, *The Art and Architecture of Russia* (Harmondsworth and Baltimore, Maryland, 1954).

N. P. Kondakov, *The Russian Icon* (Oxford, 1927).

R. A. Leonard, *A History of Russian Music* (London, 1956).

N. O. Lossky, *History of Russian Philosophy* (New York, 1951).

T. G. Masaryk, *The Spirit of Russia*, 2 vols (London, 1955).

P. N. Miliukov, *Outlines of Russian Culture: Religion and the Church –Architecture, Painting and Music*, 3 vols. (New York, 1943).

T. T. Rice, *A Concise History of Russian Art* (London, 1963).

G. Seaman, *History of Russian Music*, (Oxford, 1967).

M. Slonim, *An Outline of Russian Literature* (Oxford, 1958).

Y. M. Sokolov, *Russian Folklore* (London, 1950).

S. V. Utechin, *Russian Political Thought* (New York, 1963).

A. Vucinich, *Science in Russian Culture: A History to 1860* (Stanford, Calif., 1963).

A. Vucinich, *Science in Russian Culture: 1861–1917* (Stanford, Calif., 1970).

V. V. Zenkovsky, *A History of Russian Philosophy,* 2 vols (London, 1953).

N. Zernov, *The Russians and their Church* (London, 1945).

The principal GENERAL WORKS IN RUSSIAN are:

V. O. Kliuchevskii, *Sochineniia,* 8 vols (Moscow, 1956–9). See R. F. Byrnes, *V. O. Kliuchevskii: Historian of Russia* (Bloomington, Ind., 1995); M. V. Nechkina, *Vasilii Osipovich Kliuchevskii* (Moscow, 1974).

V. N. Pomomarev and others, *Istoriia SSSR,* 12 vols in two series (Moscow, 1967–). In internal references to this work in the present book, each volume is ascribed to its main editors.

S. M. Solovev, *Istoriia Rossii,* 15 vols. (Moscow, 1962–6).

II   Part and Chapter Bibliographies

Part One   Medieval Russia: Kiev to Moscow

Political and General

R. Coulburn (ed.), *Feudalism in History* (Princeton, N.J., 1956), including M. Szeftel, 'Aspects of Feudalism in Russian History'.

R. O. Crummey, *The Formation of Muscovy, 1304–1613* (London, 1987).

R. Hellie (ed.), *Readings for Introduction to Russian Civilization: Muscovite Society* (Chicago, 1967).

D. Kaiser, *The Growth of Law in Medieval Russia* (Princeton, N.J., 1980).

D. Kaiser (ed.), *The Laws of Rus: Tenth to Fifteenth Centuries* (Salt Lake City, Utah, 1992).
J. Martin, *Medieval Russia, 980–1584* (Cambridge, 1995).
W. Philipp, 'Russia's Position in Medieval Europe', L. H. Legters (ed.), *Russia: Essays in History and Literature* (Leyden, 1972).

Economic
J. G. Blum, 'The Rise of Serfdom in Eastern Europe', *American Historical Review*, vol. 62 (1956–7).
R. Hellie, *Slavery in Russia, 1450–1725* (Chicago, 1982).
W. Kirchner, *Commercial Relations between Russia and Europe, 1400–1800: Collected Essays* (Bloomington, Ind., 1966).
R. E. F. Smith, *The Enserfment of the Russian Peasantry* (Cambridge. 1968).
R. E. F. Smith, *Peasant Farming in Muscovy* (Cambridge, 1977).

Cultural
N. Andreyev, *Studies in Muscovy: Western Influences and Byzantine Inheritance* (London, 1970).
'The Problem of Old Russian Culture', a discussion in *Slavic Review*, vols 21 and 22 (1962–3) with contributions from N. Andreyev, J. H. Billington, G. Florovsky and D. S. Likhachev.
S. A. Zenkovsky, *Medieval Russia's Epics, Chronicles and Tales* (New York, 1963).

Ch. 1   The Construction and Collapse of Kiev, 882–1240

S. H. Cross (trans. and ed.), *The Russian Primary Chronicle* (Cambridge, Mass., 1953).
G. P. Fedotov, *The Russian Religious Mind:* vol. 1, *Kievan Christianity, The Tenth to the Thirteenth Centuries* (Cambridge, Mass., 1966).
S. Franklin (ed.), *Sermons and Rhetoric of Kievan Rus* (Cambridge, Mass., 1991).
S. Franklin and J. Shepard, *The Emergence of Rus, 750–1200* (London, 1996).
B. D. Grekov, *Kiev Rus* (Moscow, 1959).
D. Obolensky, *Byzantium and the Slavs: Collected Studies* (London, 1971).
A. Poppe, *The Rise of Christian Russia* (London, 1982).
B. A. Rybakov, *Early Centuries of Russian History* (Moscow, 1965).
M. N. Tikhomirov, *The Towns of Ancient Rus* (Moscow, 1959).
G. V. Vernadsky, *Kievan Russia* (New Haven, Conn., 1948).
S. A. Zenkovsky (ed.), *The Nikonian Chronicle,* 3 vols (Princeton, N.J., 1984–6).

Ch. 2   Invasion and Disunity, 1240–1462

G. P. Fedotov, *The Russian Religious Mind:* vol. 2, *The Middle Ages, the Thirteenth to Fifteenth Centuries* (Cambridge, Mass., 1966).
J. L. I. Fennell, *The Crisis of Medieval Russia, 1200–1304* (London, 1983).
J. L. I. Fennell, *The Emergence of Moscow, 1304–1359* (London, 1968).
C. Halperin, *Russia and the Golden Horde: The Mongol Impact on Medieval Russian History* (Bloomington, Ind., 1985).

C. Halperin, *The Tatar Yoke* (Columbus, Ohio, 1986).
R. C. Howes (ed.), *The Testaments of the Grand Princes of Moscow* (Ithaca, N.Y., 1967).
A. F. Presniakov, *The Formation of the Great Russian State: A Study of Russian History in the Thirteenth to Fifteenth Centuries*, trans. A. F. Moorhouse, intro. A. J. Rieber (Chicago, 1970).
J. J. Saunders, *The History of the Mongol Conquest* (London, 1971).
B. Spuler, *History of the Mongols, Based on Eastern and Western Accounts of the Thirteenth and Fourteenth Centuries* (London, 1972).
G. V. Vernadsky, *The Mongols and Russia* (New Haven, Conn., 1953).

Ch. 3   Consolidation under Moscow, 1462–1645

H. W. Dewey, *Moscovite Judicial Texts, 1488–1556* (Ann Arbor, Mich., 1966).
J. L. I. Fennell, *Ivan the Great of Moscow* (London, 1961).
N. S. Kollmann, *Kinship and Politics: The Making of the Muscovite Political System* (Stanford, Calif., 1987).
B. Nørretranders, *The Shaping of Tsardom under Ivan Groznyi* (Copenhagen, 1964).
S. F. Platonov, ed. and trans. L. R. Pyles, with intro. by J. T. Alexander, *Boris Godunov: Tsar of Russia* (Gulf Breeze, Fla., 1972).
S. F. Platonov, ed. and trans. J. L. Wieczynski, *Moscow and the West* (Gulf Breeze, Fla., 1972).
S. F. Platonov, trans. J. T. Alexander, *The Time of Troubles: A Historical Study of the Internal Crisis and Social Struggle in Sixteenth- and Seventeenth-Century Muscovy* (Lawrence, Kansas, 1970).
R. G. Skrynnikov, ed. and trans. H. F. Graham, *Boris Godunov* (Gulf Breeze, Fla., 1978).
R. G. Skrynnikov, ed. and trans. H. R. Graham *Ivan IV: Emperor of Russia* (Gulf Breeze, Fla., 1981).
G. V. Vernadsky, *Russia at the Dawn of the Modern Age* (New Haven, Conn., 1959).
G. V. Vernadsky, *The Tsardom of Muscovy, 1547–1682*, vol.1 (New Haven, Conn., 1969).

Contemporary writings include:
L. F. Berry and R. O. Crummey (eds.), *Rude and Barbarous Kingdom: Russia in the Accounts of Sixteenth-Century English Voyagers* (Madison, Wisc., 1968).
Baron von Herberstein, trans. and ed. R. H. Major, *Notes upon Russia: Being a Translation of the Earliest Account of that Country, Entitled: 'Rerum Muscoviticarum Commentarii'*, Hakluyt Society, series I, vols. 10 and 12 (London, 1851–2).
H. F. Graham (ed. and intro.), *The Muscovia of Antonio Possevino, SJ* (Pittsburgh, Penn., 1977).
H. von Staden, trans. and ed. T. Esper, *The Land and Government of Muscovy: A Sixteenth-Century Account* (Stanford, Calif., 1967).

SELECT BIBLIOGRAPHY

Part Two   Modern Russia: The Tsarist Empire

General Histories

J. Cracraft (ed.), *Major Problems in the History of Imperial Russia* (Lexington, Mass., 1994).

P. Dukes, *The Making of Russian Absolutism, 1613–1801* (London, 1990).

J. Gooding, *Rulers and Subjects: Government and People in Russia, 1801–1991* (London, 1996).

V. V. Kallash (ed.), *Tri veka: Rossiia ot smuty do nashego vremeni,* 6 vols (Moscow, 1912–13).

A. A. Kornilov, *Modern Russian History from the Age of Catherine the Great to the End of the Nineteenth Century,* 2 vols in 1, reprint (New York, 1970).

S. G. Pushkarev, *The Emergence of Modern Russia, 1801–1917* (New York, 1963).

M. Raeff, *Understanding Imperial Russia: State and Society in the Old Regime* (New York, 1984).

H. Rogger, *Russia in the Age of Modernisation and Revolution, 1881–1917* (London, 1983).

D. Saunders, *Russia in the Age of Reaction and Reform, 1801–1881* (London, 1992).

G. H. N. Seton-Watson, *The Russian Empire, 1801–1917* (Oxford, 1971).

T. Taranovski (ed.), *Reform in Modern Russian History: Progress or Cycle?* (Cambridge, 1995).

J. N. Westwood, *Endurance and Endeavour: Russian History 1812–1980* (Oxford, 1981).

A. Wood, *The Origins of the Russian Revolution, 1861–1917* (London, 1987).

Political

P. Avrich, *Russian Rebels, 1600–1800* (London, 1973).

G. Hosking, *Russia: People and Empire, 1552–1917* (London, 1997).

J. L. H. Keep, *Soldiers of the Tsar: Army and Society in Russia, 1462–1874* (Oxford, 1985).

J. P. LeDonne, *Absolutism and Ruling Class: The Formation of the Russian Political Order, 1700–1825* (New York and Oxford, 1991).

J. P. LeDonne, *The Russian Empire and the World, 1700–1917* (New York, 1997)

W. M. Pintner and D. K. Rowney (eds), *Russian Officialdom: The Bureaucratization of Russian Society from the Seventeenth to the Twentieth Century* (London, 1980).

M. Raeff, *Plans for Political Reform in Imperial Russia, 1730–1905* (Englewood Cliffs, N.J., 1966).

H. Ragsdale (ed.), *Imperial Russian Foreign Policy* (Cambridge, 1994).

Economic

A. Baykov, 'The Economic Development of Russia', *Economic History Review,* series 2, vol. 7 (1954).

W. L. Blackwell, *Russian Economic Development from Peter the Great to Stalin* (New York, 1974).

H. J. Ellison, 'Economic Modernisation in Imperial Russia', *J. of Economic History* , vol. 25 (1965).

M. F. Falkus, *The Industrialisation of Russia before 1914* (London, 1972).

P. Gatrell, *The Tsarist Economy, 1850–1917* (London, 1986).

A. Gerschenkron, *Economic Backwardness in Historical Perspective* (Cambridge, Mass., 1962).

A. Gerschenkron, *Europe in the Russian Mirror: Four Lectures in Economic History* (Cambridge, 1970).

P. Gregory, 'Economic Growth and Structural Change in Tsarist Russia. A Case of Modern Economic Growth', *Soviet Studies*, vol. 23 (1971–2).

A. Kahan, 'Government Policies and the Industrialisation of Russia', *J. of Economic History*, vol. 27 (1967).

A. Kahan, *The Plow, the Hammer and the Knout: An Economic History of Eighteenth-Century Russia* (Chicago, 1985).

A. Kahan, *Russian Economic History: The Nineteenth Century* (Chicago, 1989).

J. Pallot and D. J. B. Shaw, *Landscape and Settlement in Romanov Russia, 1613–1917* (Oxford, 1989).

R. Portal, 'The Problem of an Industrial Revolution in Russia in the Nineteenth Century', in *Readings*, ed. S.S. Harcave, vol. 2.

Cultural

P. L. Alston, *Education and the State in Tsarist Russia* (Stanford, Calif., 1969).

N. A. Hans, *A History of Russian Educational Policy, 1701–1917* (London, 1931).

N. A. Hans, *The Russian Tradition in Education* (London and Westport, Conn., 1963).

W. J. Leatherbarrow and D. C. Offord (eds), *A Documentary History of Russian Thought* (Ann Arbor, Mich., 1987).

D. S. Mirsky, *A History of Russian Literature* (London and New York, 1949).

R. L. Nichols and T. G. Stavrou (eds), *Russian Orthodoxy under the Old Regime* (New York, 1981).

M. Slonim, *The Epic of Russian Literature from its Origins to Tolstoy* (Oxford, 1950).

M. Slonim, *Modern Russian Literature from Chekhov to the Revolution* (Oxford, 1962).

Ch. 4   The Foundation of the Russian Empire, 1645–1698

R. N. Bain, *The First Romanovs, 1613–1725: A History of Muscovite Civilisation and the Rise of Modern Russia under Peter the Great and his Forerunners* (London, 1905).

R. O. Crummey, *Aristocrats and Servitors: The Boyar Elite in Russia, 1613–1689* (Princeton, N.J., 1983).

R. Hellie, *Enserfment and Military Change in Muscovy* (Chicago, 1971).

L. A. J. Hughes, *Sophia: Regent of Russia* (New Haven, Conn., 1990).

V. O. Kliuchevskii (styled Klyuchevsky), trans. and intro. L. Archibald, *The Rise of the Romanovs* (London, 1970); the same work published in the United States as V.O. Kliuchevsky, trans. N. Duddington, *Course in Russian History: The Seventeenth Century* (New York, 1968)

P. Longworth, *Alexis: Tsar of All the Russias* (London. 1984).

C. B. O'Brien, *Russia under Two Tsars, 1682–1689: The Regency of Sophia Alekseevna*, University of California Publications in History, vol. 42 (1952).

R. E. F. Smith (ed. and trans.), *The Enserfment of the Russian Peasantry* (Cambridge, 1968).

Z. Schakovskoy, *Precursors of Peter the Great: The Reign of Tsar Alexis, Peter the Great's Father, and the Young Peter's Struggle against the Regent Sophia for the Mastery of Russia*, trans. from French (London, 1964).

G. V. Vernadsky, *The Tsardom of Muscovy, 1547–1682*, 2 vols (London, 1969).

Among contemporary accounts are:

S. Collins, *The Present State of Russia* (London, 1671).

Foy de la Neuville, *Relation curieuse et nouvelle de Moscovie* (The Hague, 1699). See English translation by J. A. Cutshall (London, 1994).

P. Gordon, *Passages from the Diary of General Patrick Gordon of Auchleuchries in the Years 1635–1699* (Aberdeen, 1859; reprinted London, 1968).

Olearius (ed.), trans. and intro. S. H. Baron, *The Travels of Olearius in Seventeenth-Century Russia* (Stanford, Calif., 1967).

Ch. 5   *The Completion of the Structure, 1698–1761*

M. S. Anderson, *Peter the Great* (London, 1978).

E. V. Anisimov, *The Reforms of Peter the Great: Progress through Coercion in Russia* (London, 1993).

R. N. Bain, *The Daughter of Peter the Great: A History of Russian Diplomacy and the Russian Court under the Empress Elizabeth Petrovna, 1741–1762* (London, 1899).

J. Cracraft, *The Church Reform of Peter the Great* (London and Stanford, Calif., 1971).

L. A. J. Hughes, *Russia in the Age of Peter the Great* (New Haven, Conn., 1997).

V. O. Kliuchevskii (trans. L. Archibald) styled Klyuchevsky, *Peter the Great* (London, 1958).

P. Longworth, *The Three Empresses.. Catherine I, Anne and Elizabeth of Russia* (London, 1972: New York, 1973).

B. Meehan-Waters, *Autocracy and Aristocracy: The Russian Service Elite of 1730* (New Brunswick, N.J., 1982).

M. Raeff, *Origins of the Russian Intelligentsia: The Eighteenth-Century Nobility* (New York, 1966).

M. Raeff (ed. and intro.), *Peter the Great: Reformer or Revolutionary?* (Boston, Mass., 1963).

B. H. Sumner, *Peter the Great and the Emergence of Russia* (London, 1951).

There are a vast number of contemporary accounts for this and all succeeding periods. Among those for this period are:

P. H. Bruce, *Memoirs of ... a Military Officer in the Services of Prussia, Russia and Great Britain* (London, 1782).

A. Gordon, *History of Peter the Great Emperor of Russia*, 2 vols (Aberdeen, 1755).

C. H. von Manstein, *Contemporary Memoirs of Russia: Historical, Political and Military from the Year 1727 to 1744* (London, 1856).

F. C. Weber, *The Present State of Russia ... 1714 to 1720*, 2 vols (London, 1722–3).

Ch. 6   Enlightened Absolutism, 1761–1801

J. T. Alexander, *Catherine the Great: Life and Legend* (New York and Oxford, 1989).

R. N. Bain, *Peter III: Emperor of Russia* (London, 1902).

P. Dukes, *Catherine the Great and the Russian Nobility* (Cambridge, 1967).

R. E. Jones, *The Emancipation of the Russian Nobility, 1762–1785* (Princeton, N.J., 1973).

M. Kochan, *Life in Russia under Catherine the Great* (London and New York, 1969).

J. P. LeDonne, *Ruling Russia: Politics and Administration in the Age of Absolutism, 1762–1796* (Princeton, N.J., 1984).

C. Leonard, *Reform and Regicide: The Reign of Peter III of Russia* (Bloomington, Ind., 1993).

I. de Madariaga, *Russia in the Age of Catherine the Great* (London, 1981).

R. E. McGrew, *Paul I of Russia, 1754–1801* (Oxford, 1992).

M. Raeff, (ed.), *Catherine the Great: A Profile* (London, 1972).

M. Raeff, *Origins of the Russian Intelligentsia: The Eighteenth-Century Nobility* (New York, 1966).

D. Ransel, *The Politics of Catherinian Russia: The Panin Party* (New Haven, Conn., and London, 1975).

Contemporary commentaries include:

E. D. Clarke, *Travels in Various Countries of Europe, Asia and Africa* ... part I (London, 1810).

W. Coxe, *Travels into Poland, Russia, Sweden and Denmark* ..., vol. 2 (London, 1803).

G. Macartney, *An Account of Russia, 1767* (London, 1768).

W. Richardson, *Anecdotes of the Russian Empire* ... (London, 1784).

On the literature of the period, see:

H. B. Segel (trans. and ed.), *The Literature of Eighteenth-Century Russia: An Anthology*, 2 vols (New York, 1967).

Ch. 7   Russian Nationalism, 1801–1855

W. L. Blackwell, *The Beginnings of Russian Industrialization, 1800–1860* (Princeton, N.J., 1968).

J. M. Hartley, *Alexander I* (London, 1994).

W. B. Lincoln, *In the Vanguard of Reform: Russia's Enlightened Bureaucrats, 1825–1861* (DeKalb, Ill., 1982).

W. B. Lincoln, *Nicholas I. Emperor and Autocrat of all the Russias* (London, 1978).

A. McConnell, *Tsar Alexander I: Paternalistic Reformer* (New York. 1970)

A. G. Mazour, *The First Russian Revolution, 1825: Its Origin, Development and Significance* (Stanford, Calif., 1963).

D. Orlovsky, *The Limits of Reform: The Ministry of Internal Affairs in Imperial Russia, 1802–1881* (Cambridge, Mass., 1981).

A. W. Palmer, *Alexander I* (London, 1974).

M. Raeff, ed. and intro., *The Decembrist Movement* (Englewood Cliffs, N.J., 1966).

N. V. Riasanovsky, *Russia and the West in the Teaching of the Slavophiles* (Cambridge, Mass., 1952).

N. V. Riasanovsky, *Nicholas I and Official Nationality in Russia, 1825–55* (Berkeley, Calif., 1959).

N. V. Riasanovsky, *A Parting of the Ways: Government and the Educated Public in Russia, 1825–1855* (Oxford, 1976).

E. C. Thaden, *Conservative Nationalism in Nineteenth-Century Russia* (Seattle, Wash., 1964).

R. Wortman, *Scenarios of Power: Myth and Ceremony in Russian Monarchy,* vol. I (Princeton, N.J., 1995).

Two 'classical' contemporary accounts are:

Marquis de Custine, *The Empire of the Czar*, 3 vols (London, 1843). See also G. F. Kennan, *The Marquis de Custine and his Russia in 1839* (Princeton, N.J., 1971).

Baron A. von Haxthausen, *The Russian Empire: Its People, Institutions and Resources*, 2 vols (London, 1856).

Ch. 8   The Emancipation, and After, 1855–1894

A. F. Adams, (ed.), *Imperial Russia after 1861: Peaceful Modernization or Revolution?* (Boston, Mass., 1965).

C. F. Black (ed.), *The Transformation of Russian Society: Aspects of Social Change since 1861* (Cambridge, Mass., 1960).

R. F. Byrnes, *Pobedonostsev: His Life and Thought* (London and Bloomington, Ind., 1968).

T. Emmons, (ed.), *Emancipation of the Russian Serfs* (New York, 1970).

T. Emmons, *The Russian Landed Gentry and the Peasant Emancipation of 1861* (Cambridge, 1968).

D. Field, *The End of Serfdom: Nobility and Bureaucracy in Russia, 1855–1861* (Cambridge, Mass., 1976).

W. B. Lincoln, *Nikolai Miliutin: An Enlightened Russian Bureaucrat* (Newtonville, Mass., 1977).

M. McCauley and P. Waldron, (eds), *The Emergence of the Modern Russian State, 1856–1881* (London, 1989).

F. A. Miller, *Dimitrii Miliutin and the Reform Era in Russia* (Nashville, Tenn., 1968).

W. F. Mosse, *Alexander II and the Modernisation of Russia* (London, 1958).

G. T. Robinson, *Rural Russia under the Old Regime* (New York, 1932).

S. F. Starr, *Decentralization and Self-Government in Russia, 1830–1870* (Princeton, N.J., 1972)

F. Venturi, *Roots of Revolution: A History of the Populist and Socialist Movements in Nineteenth-Century Russia* (London, 1960).

R. Wortman, *The Crisis of Russian Populism* (Cambridge, 1967).

R. F. Zelnik, *Labor and Society in Tsarist Russia: The Factory Workers of St Petersburg, 1855–1870* (Stanford, Calif., 1971).

Outstanding contemporary descriptions include:

A. Leroy-Beaulieu, *The Empire of the Tsars and the Russians*, 3 vols (London and New York, 1893–6).

Stepniak (pseudonym of S. M. Kravchinskii), *The Russian Peasantry* (London, 1890).
D. Mackenzie Wallace, *Russia*, 2 vols (London, 1877).

Ch. 9   Russian Imperialism, 1894–1917

A. Ascher, *The Revolution of 1905*, 2 vols. (Stanford, Calif., 1988, 1992).
J. Brooks, *When Russia Learned to Read: Literacy and Popular Culture, 1861–1917* (Princeton, N.J., 1985).
M. T. Florinsky, *The End of the Russian Empire* (New York, 1961).
W. C. Fuller, *Civil–Military Conflict in Imperial Russia, 1881–1914* (Princeton, N.J., 1985).
D. Geyer, *Russian Imperialism: The Interaction of Domestic and Foreign Policy 1860–1914* (Leamington Spa, 1987).
L. H. Haimson, *The Russian Marxists and the Origins of Bolshevism* (Cambridge, Mass., 1955).
S. Harcave, *First Blood: The Russian Revolution of 1905* (London, 1965).
G. A. Hosking. *The Russian Constitutional Experiment: Government and Duma, 1907–1914* (Cambridge, 1973).
G. Katkov *et al.*, *Russia Enters the Twentieth Century, 1894–1917* (London, 1971).
J. L. H. Keep, *The Rise of Social Democracy in Russia* (Oxford, 1963).
L. Kochan, *Russia in Revolution, 1890–1918* (London, 1966).
D. C. Lieven, *Nicholas II: Emperor of All the Russias* (London, 1993).
M. McCauley (ed.), *Octobrists to Bolsheviks: Imperial Russia, 1905–1917* (London, 1984).
J. P. McKay, *Pioneers for Profit. Foreign Entrepreneurship and Russian Industrialization, 1885–1913* (London and Chicago, 1970).
G. Pavlovsky, *Agricultural Russia on the Eve of Revolution* (London, 1930).
R. Pearson, *The Russian Moderates and the Crisis of Tsarism, 1914–1917* (London, 1977).
T. Riha, *A Russian European: Paul Miliukov in Russian Politics* (Notre Dame, Ind., 1969).
T. Shanin, *The Roots of Otherness: Russia's Turn of the Century*, 2 vols (London, 1985–6).
T. G. Stavrou (ed.), *Russia under the Last Tsar* (Minneapolis, Minn., 1969).
T. H. Von Laue, *Sergei Witte and the Industrialization of Russia* (London, 1963).

Among the many contemporary accounts. see:
G. Buchanan, *My Mission to Russia and Other Diplomatic Memories* (London, 1923).
S. N. Harper, *The Russia I Believe In* (Chicago, 1945)
B. Pares, *My Russian Memoirs* (London, 1931, New York, 1969)

Part Three   Contemporary Russia: The U.S.S.R. and After

General
E. H. Carr, *A History of Soviet Russia* , 10 vols (London, 1950–78).
R. W. Davies, *Soviet History in the Gorbachev Revolution* (London, 1989)
R.. W. Davies, *Soviet History in the Yeltsin Revolution* (London, 1996).

414   SELECT BIBLIOGRAPHY

S. Fitzpatrick, *The Russian Revolution 1917–1937* (Oxford, 1994).
M. Heller and A. Nekrich, *Utopia in Power: A History of the USSR from 1917 to the Present* (London, 1985).
G. Hosking, *A History of the Soviet Union, 1917–1991*, final edition (London, 1992).
J. Keep, *Last of the Empires: A History of the Soviet Union, 1945–1991* (Oxford, 1995).
M. McCauley, *The Soviet Union since 1917* (London, 1981).
A. P. Nenarokov, *Russia in the Twentieth Century* (New York, 1968).
J. P. Nettl, *The Soviet Achievement* (London, 1967).

Political
J. Erickson, *The Soviet High Command: A Military–Political History: 1918–1941* (London, 1962).
D. Lane, *Politics and Society in the USSR* (London, 1970).
T. H. Rigby, *Communist Party Membership in the USSR, 1917–1967* (Princeton, N.J., 1968).
L. B. Schapiro, *The Communist Party of the Soviet Union* (London, 1960).
A. B. Ulam, *Expansion and Coexistence: The History of Soviet Foreign Policy, 1917–1973* (New York, 1974).

Economic
A. Baykov, *The Development of the Soviet Economic System* (Cambridge, 1966).
R. A. Clarke, *Soviet Economic Facts, 1917–1972* (London, 1972).
R. W. Davies, M. Harrison and S. G. Wheatcroft (eds), *The Economic Transformation of the Soviet Union, 1913–1945* (Cambridge, 1994).
M. Dobb, *An Economic History of the USSR* (London, 1969).
A. Nove, *An Economic History of the USSR* (London, 1982).
H. Schwartz, *Russia's Soviet Economy* (London, 1951).

Cultural
V. Alexandrovna, *A History of Soviet Literature* (New York, 1963).
J. S. Curtiss, *The Russian Church and the Soviet State, 1917–1950* (Gloucester, Mass., 1965).
N. Grant, *Soviet Education* (London, 1964).
C. Vaughan James, *Soviet Socialist Realism: Origins and Theory* (London, 1973).
D. Joravsky, *Soviet Marxism and Natural Science* (London, 1961).
W. Kolarz, *Religion in the Soviet Union* (London, 1961).
J. Leyda, *Kino: A History of the Russian and Soviet Film* (London, 1960).
E. J. Simmons (ed.), *Continuity and Change in Russian and Soviet Thought* (Cambridge, Mass., 1955).
M. Slonim, *Soviet Russian Literature: Writers and Problems* (New York, 1966).
G. Struve, *Russian Literature under Lenin and Stalin, 1917–1953* (Norman, Okla., 1971).

Ch. 10   The Russian Revolution, 1917–1921

E. Acton, *Rethinking the Russian Revolution* (London, 1990).
A. F. Adams, *The Russian Revolution and Bolshevik Victory: Why and How?* (Boston, Mass., 1960).

P. H. Avrich, *The Russian Anarchists* (Princeton, N.J., 1967).

P. Avrich, *Kronstadt 1921* (Princeton, N.J., 1970).

J. Burbank, *Intelligentsia and Revolution: Russian Views of Bolshevism* (New York, 1986).

W. H. Chamberlin, *The Russian Revolution, 1917–1921*, 2 vols (London, 1935; Princeton, 1987).

R. V. Daniels, *Red October: The Bolshevik Revolution of 1917* (London, 1967).

O. Figes, *A People's Tragedy: The Russian Revolution, 1891–1924* (London, 1996).

M. Frame, *The Russian Revolution, 1905–1921: A Bibliographic Guide to Works in English* (Westport, Conn., 1995).

E. R. Frankel, J. Frankel and B. Knei-Paz (eds), *Revolution in Russia: Reassessments of 1917* (Cambridge, 1992)

I. Getzler, *Kronstadt, 1917–1921. The Fate of a Soviet Democracy* (Cambridge, 1983).

D. H. Kaiser, (ed.), *The Workers' Revolution 1917: The View from Below* (Cambridge, 1987).

J. L. H. Keep, *The Russian Revolution: A Study in Mass Mobilisation* (London, 1976).

W. B. Lincoln, *Red Victory: A History of the Russian Civil War* (New York, 1989).

E. Mawdsley, *The Russian Civil War* (Boston Mass., and London, 1987).

M. McCauley (ed.), *The Russian Revolution and the Soviet State, 1917–1921* (London, 1980).

R. W. Pethybridge, *The Spread of the Russian Revolution: Essays on 1917* (London, 1972).

R. E. Pipes, *The Russian Revolution, 1899–1919* (London, 1990).

R. E. Pipes, *Russia under the Bolshevik Regime, 1919–1924* (London, 1994).

A. Rabinowitch, *Prelude to Revolution: The Petrograd Bolsheviks and the July 1917 Uprising* (Bloomington, Ind., 1968).

A. Rabinowitch, *The Bolsheviks Come to Power* (London, 1976).

C. Read, *From Tsar to Soviets: The Russian People and their Revolution, 1917–1921* (London, 1996).

R. Service, *The Russian Revolution, 1900–1927* (London, 1986).

T. Shanin, *The Awkward Class: Political Sociology of the Peasantry in a Developing Society, 1910–1921* (Oxford, 1972).

S. Smith, *Red Petrograd: Revolution in the Factories, 1917–1918* (Cambridge, 1983).

G. Swain, *The Origins of the Russian Civil War* (London, 1996).

L. D. Trotsky, *The History of the Russian Revolution* (London, 1934: Ann Arbor, Mich., 1957).

R. A. Wade, *The Russian Search for Peace, February-October 1917* (Stanford, Calif., , 1969).

J. White, *The Russian Revolution: A Short History, 1917–1921* (London, 1994).

A. K. Wildman, *The End of the Russian Imperial Army*, 2 vols. (Princeton, N.J., 1980, 1987).

For contemporary accounts, see:

D. von Mohrenschildt (ed.), *The Russian Revolution of 1917: Contemporary Accounts* (New York, 1971).

R. Pethybridge (ed.), *Witnesses to the Russian Revolution* (London, 1964; Gloucester, Mass., 1968).
N. N. Sukhanov, *The Russian Revolution, 1917. A Personal Record* ed. and trans. J. Carmichael (London, 1955).

Ch. 11   The Consolidation of the Soviet Union, 1917–1929

P. Avrich, *Kronstadt 1921* (Princeton, N.J., 1957).
E. H. Carr, *The Russian Revolution from Lenin to Stalin, 1917–1929* (London, 1980).
R. V. Daniels, *Conscience of the Revolution: The Communist Opposition in Soviet Russia* (Cambridge, Mass., 1960).
T. Deutscher, *Not by Politics Alone: the Other Lenin* (London, 1973).
A. Erlich, *The Soviet Industrialisation Debate, 1924–1928* (Cambridge, Mass., 1951).
L. Fischer, *The Life of Lenin* (New York, 1965).
S. Fitzpatrick, *The Commissariat of Enlightenment* (Cambridge, 1970).
I. Getzler, *Martov: A Political Biography* (Cambridge, 1967).
N. Harding, *Lenin's Political Thought*, 2 vols (London, 1977, 1981).
N. Harding, *Leninism* (London, 1996).
M. Lewin, *Lenin's Last Struggle* (New York, 1968; London, 1969).
A. V. Lunacharsky, *Revolutionary Silhouettes* (London, 1967).
D. J. Male, *Russian Peasant Organisation before Collectivization: A Study of Commune and Gathering, 1925–1930* (Cambridge, 1971).
A. J. Mayer, *Politics and Diplomacy of Peacemaking: Containment and Counter-Revolution at Versailles, 1918–1919* (New York, 1967).
M. McAuley, *Bread and Justice: State and Society in Petrograd, 1917–1922* (Oxford, 1991).
R. Pethybridge, *One Step Backwards, Two Steps Forward: Soviet Society and Politics under the New Economic Policy* (Oxford, 1990).
R. E.. Pipes, *The Formation of the Soviet Union: Communism and Nationalism, 1917–1923* (Cambridge, Mass., 1964).
T. H. Rigby, *Lenin's Government: Sovnarkom, 1917–1922* (Cambridge, 1979).
R. Sakwa, *Soviet Communists in Power: A Study of Moscow during the Civil War, 1918–1921* (London, 1988).
L. Schapiro, *The Origin of the Communist Autocracy* (London, 1955).
L. Schapiro and P. Reddaway, *Lenin: The Man, The Theorist, The Leader – A Reappraisal* (London, 1967).
R. Service, *Lenin: A Political Life*, 3 vols. (London, 1985, 1991, 1995).
R. Service, *The Bolshevik Party in Revolution: A Study in Organisational Change, 1917–1923* (London, 1979).
J. M. Thomson, *Russia, Bolshevism and the Versailles Peace* (Princeton, N.J., 1966).

Among the many contemporary accounts are:
A. D. Makarenko, *The Road to Life*, 3 vols (Moscow, c. 1950).
A. Monkhouse, *Moscow, 1911–1933* (London, 1934; New York, 1970).
V. L. Serge, *Memoirs of a Revolutionary, 1901–1941* (London, 1963).
W. S. Woytinsky, *Stormy Passage* (Toronto, 1961).

Ch. 12   The Construction of Soviet Socialism, 1929–1941

A. Avtorkhanov, *Stalin and the Soviet Communist Party: A Study in the Technology of Power* (New York, 1959).

P. Broué, *Trotsky* (Paris, 1988).

R. Conquest, *The Great Terror: Stalin's Purge of the Thirties* (London, 1968; New York, 1973).

R. V. Daniels, *The Stalin Revolution: Fulfilment or Betrayal of Communism?* (Boston, Mass., 1965).

R. W. Davies, *The Industrialisation of Soviet Russia* (London, 1980–).

I. Deutscher, *Stalin: A Political Biography* (Oxford and New York, 1949).

I. Deutscher, *Trotsky* 3 vols (Oxford, 1954–)

M. Fainsod, *Smolensk under Soviet Rule* (Cambridge, Mass., 1958).

J. A. Getty and R. Manning (eds), *Stalinist Terror: New Perspectives* (Cambridge, 1993).

M. Lewin, *The Making of the Soviet System: Essays on the Social History of Inter-War Russia* (London, 1985).

M. Lewin, *Russian Peasants and Soviet Power: A Study of Collectivization* (London, 1966: Evanston, Ill, 1968).

M. McCauley, *Stalin and Stalinism* (London, 1983).

R. Medvedev, *Let History Judge: The Origins and Consequences of Stalinism* (Oxford, 1989).

R. Pethybridge, *The Social Prelude to Stalinism* (London, 1974).

T. H. Rigby (ed.), *Stalin* (Englewood Cliffs, N.J., 1966).

W. Rosenberg and L. Siegelbaum (eds), *Social Dimensions of Stalinist Industrialisation* (Bloomington, Ind., 1993).

M. Schachtman, *Behind the Moscow Trials* (New York, 1936; London, 1971).

B. Souvarine, *Stalin: A Critical Survey of Bolshevism* (London 1939; New York, 1972).

N. Timasheff, *The Great Retreat* (New York, 1946).

L. D. Trotsky, *Stalin* (London, 1947; New York, 1970).

R. C. Tucker, *Stalin as Revolutionary, 1879–1929* (New York, 1973); *Stalin in Power, 1928–1941* (New York, 1990).

C. Ward, *Stalin's Russia* (London, 1993).

Contemporary analyses include:

W. H. Chamberlin, *Russia's Iron Age* (Boston, Mass., 1937).

V. Garros, N. Korenevskaya and T. Lahusen (eds), *Intimacy and Terror: Soviet Diaries of the 1930s* (New York, 1995).

M. Hindus, *Humanity Uprooted* (New York, 1930).

L. D. Trotsky, *The Revolution Betrayed* (London, 1937; New York, 1973).

Ch. 13   War and Reconstruction, 1941–1953

J. A. Armstrong, *Soviet Partisans in World War II* (Madison, Wisc., 1964).

J. Barber and M. Harrison, *The Soviet Home Front, 1941–1945: A Social and Economic History of the USSR in World War II* (London, 1991).

A. Clark, *Barbarossa: The Russo-German Conflict, 1941–45* (London, 1965).

A. Dallin, *German Rule in Russia, 1941–45* (London, 1957).

W.S. Dunn, *Hitler's Nemesis: The Red Army* (London, 1994).

T. Dunmore, *Soviet Politics, 1945–1953* (London, 1984).

J. Erickson, *Stalin's War with Germany*, 2 vols (London, 1974, 1983).

J. Erickson and D. Dilks, (eds), *Barbarossa: The Axis and the Allies* (Edinburgh, 1994).

D.M. Glantz and J. Woodhouse, *When Titans Clashed: How the Red Army Stopped Hitler* (Lawrence, Kansas, 1995).

M. Harrison, *Soviet Planning in Peace and War, 1938–1945* (Cambridge, 1985).

W. LaFeber, *America, Russia and the Cold War, 1945–1996* (New York, 1997).

S. Linz (ed.) *The Impact of World War II on the Soviet Union* (Totawa, N.J., 1985).

R. Pethybridge, *A History of Post-War Russia* (London, 1966; New York, 1973).

H.E. Salisbury, *The Siege of Leningrad* (London, 1969).

A. Seaton, *The Russo-German War, 1941–1945* (London, 1971).

B.F. Smith, *Sharing Secrets with Stalin: How the Allies Traded Intelligence, 1941–1945* (Lawrence, Kansas, 1996).

Contemporary accounts include:

S. Bialer, *Stalin and his Generals: Soviet Military Memoirs of World War Two* (Indianapolis, Ind., 1969).

I. Ehrenburg, *Post-War Years, 1945–1954* (London, 1956).

A. Werth, *Moscow '41* (London, 1942); *Leningrad* (London, 1944); *The Year of Stalingrad* (London, 1946).

G. K. Zhukov, *Memoirs* (New York, 1971).

Ch. 14   The Assertion of Soviet Superpower, 1953–1964

A. Brumberg (ed.), *Russia under Khrushchev* (London, 1962).

N. DeWitt, *Education and Professional Employment in the USSR* (Washington, D.C., 1961).

M. Frankland, *Khrushchev* (London, 1966).

M. Hayward (ed.), *Soviet Literature in the Sixties* (New York, 1964).

G. Hodnett (ed.), *The Khrushchev Years, 1953–1964* (Toronto, 1974).

N. S. Khrushchev, *Khrushchev Remembers* 2 vols (New York, 1970, 1974).

C. Linden, *Khrushchev and the Soviet Leadership, 1957–64* (Baltimore, Maryland, 1966).

R. Medvedev, *Khrushchev* (Oxford, 1982).

N. S. Khrushchev, *Khrushchev Remembers,* 2 vols (London, 1970, 1974).

H. Schwartz, *The Soviet Economy since Stalin* (London, 1965).

A. Werth, *Russia under Khrushchev* (New York, 1962).

T. P. Whitney (ed.), *Khrushchev Speaks: Selected Speeches, Articles and Press Conferences, 1949–1961* (Ann Arbor, Mich, 1963).

The Road to Communism: Documents of the 22nd Congress of the CPSU, October 17–31, 1961 (Moscow, n.d.).

Contemporary accounts include:

M. Gordey, *Visa to Moscow* (New York, 1952).

J. Gunther, *Inside Russia Today* (New York, 1957).

W. Miller, *Russians as People* (London, 1960).

A. Werth, *Russia: The Post-War Years* (London, 1971).

Ch. 15 Stability and Relaxation, 1964–1975

Leonid Ilyich Brezhnev: A Short Biography (Moscow, 1977).

L. I. Brezhnev, *Reminiscences* (Moscow, 1981).

A. Brown and M. Kaiser (eds), *The Soviet Union since the Fall of Khrushchev* (London, 1978).

S. Cohen, A. Rabinowitch and R. Sharlet (eds), *The Soviet Union since Stalin* (Bloomington, Ind., 1980).

A. Dallin and T. B. Larson (eds), *Soviet Politics since Khrushchev* (Englewood Cliffs, N.J., 1968).

B. Kerblay, *Modern Soviet Society* (London, 1983).

V. Medish, *The Soviet Union* (Englewood Cliffs, N.J., 1981).

P. J. Murphy, *Brezhnev, Soviet Politician* (Jefferson, N.C., 1981).

J. W. Strong (ed.), *The Soviet Union under Brezhnev and Kosygin* (New York, 1971).

Contemporary descriptions include:

Observer (G. Feifer), *Message from Moscow* (London, 1969).

P. Reddaway (ed.), *Uncensored Russia: Protest and Dissent in the Soviet Union* (London, 1972).

H. Smith, *The Russians* (New York, 1976).

Ch. 16 Stagnation and Tension, 1975–1985

Y. V. Andropov, *Speeches and Writings* (Oxford, 1983).

R. F. Byrnes (ed.), *After Brezhnev* (Washington, D.C., 1983).

A. Brown and M. Kaiser (eds), *Soviet Policy for the 1980s* (London, 1982).

K. U. Chernenko, *Selected Speeches and Writings* (Oxford, 1982).

R. Edmonds, *Soviet Foreign Policy: The Brezhnev Years* (Oxford, 1983).

E. P. Hoffmann and R. F. Laird (eds), *The Soviet Policy in the Modern Age* (New York, 1984).

J. Hough and M. Fainsod, *How the Soviet Union is Governed*, revised edition (Cambridge, Mass., 1979).

D. R. Kelley, *Soviet Politics from Brezhnev to Gorbachev* (New York, 1987).

M. McCauley (ed.), *The Soviet Union after Brezhnev* (London, 1983).

Z. Medvedev, *Andropov: His Life and Death* (London, 1984).

J. L. Nogee (ed.), *Soviet Politics after Brezhnev* (New York, 1985).

J. Stelle and E. Abraham, *Andropov in Power* (Oxford, 1983).

H.-J. Veen (ed.), *From Brezhnev to Gorbachev: Domestic Affairs and Soviet Policy* (New York, 1987).

Contemporary descriptions and analyses include:

R. G. Kaiser, *Russia: The People and the Power* (New York, 1976).

D. K. Shipler, *Russia: Broken Idols, Solemn Dreams* (New York, 1983).

A. Zinoviev, *The Reality of Communism* (London, 1984).

Ch. 17 Reform or Ruin? 1985–1996

S. Bialer (ed.), *Politics, Society and Nationality inside Gorbachev's Russia* (Boulder, Col., 1989).

J. L. Black (ed.), *USSR Documents 1987: The Gorbachev Reforms* (Gulf Breeze, Fla., 1989).

J. Bloomfield (ed.), *The Soviet Revolution: Perestroika and the Remaking of Socialism* (London, 1989).

A. Brown, *The Gorbachev Factor* (Oxford, 1996).

R. W. Davies, *Soviet History in the Gorbachev Revolution* (London, 1989).

M. S. Gorbachev, *Perestroika: New Thinking for Our Country and the World* (London, 1987).

M. S. Gorbachev, *Life and Reforms,* 2 vols (Moscow, 1996).

G. Hosking, *Church, State and Nation* (London, 1991).

W. Joyce, H. Ticktin and S. White (eds), *Gorbachev and Gorbachevism* (London, 1989).

D. Lane, *Soviet Society under Perestroika* (London, 1992).

M. Lewin, *The Gorbachev Phenomenon: A Historical Interpretation* (Berekeley, Calif., 1988).

M. McCauley (ed.), *Gorbachev and Perestroika* (London, 1990).

E. Mandel, *Beyond Perestroika: The Future of Gorbachev's USSR* (London, 1989).

C. Merridale and C. Ward (eds), *Perestroika: The Historical Perspective* (London, 1989).

R. Sakwa (ed.), *Russian Politics and Society* (London, 1993).

S. White, *Gorbachev and After*, third edition (Cambridge, 1991).

Ch. 18   The Limits of Russian History, 1996–

I. Bremmer and R. Taras, *Nations and Politics in the Soviet Successor States* (Cambridge, 1993).

M. Buckley, *Redefining Russian Society and Polity* (Boulder, Col., 1993).

R. W. Davies, *Soviet History in the Yeltsin Era* (London, 1996).

P. Dukes, *World Order in History: Russia and the West* (London, 1996).

S. P. Huntington, *The Clash of Civilizations* (New York, 1996)

P. Kennedy, *Preparing for the Twenty-First Century* (London, 1993).

W. Laqueur, *The Dream that Failed: Reflections on the Soviet Union* (Oxford, 1995).

R. Marsh, *History and Literature in Contemporary Russia* (London, 1995).

H. Ragsdale, *The Russian Tragedy: The Burden of History* (Armonk, N.Y., 1996).

A. Saikal and W. Maley (eds), *Russia in Search of its Future* (Cambridge, 1995).

A. Smith, *Russia and the World Economy: Problems of Integration* (London, 1993).

R. G. Suny, *The Revenge of the Past: Nationalism, Revolution, and the Collapse of the Soviet Union* (Stanford, Calif., 1993).

H. Ticktin, *Origins of the Crisis in the USSR: Essays on the Political Economy of a Disintegrating System* (London, 1992).

D. Yergin and T. Gustafson, *Russia 2010 and What It Means for the World* (London, 1994).

Among post–1985 general histories in Russian are:

G. Bordiugov and V. Kozlov, *Istoriia i koniunktora: subiektivnye zametki ob istorii sovetskogo obshchestva* (Moscow, 1992).

V.G. Khoros, *Russkaia istoriia v sravnitelnom osveshchenii* (Moscow, 1994).
S. V. Kuleshov *et al.* (eds), *Nashe otechestvo: opyt politicheskoi istorii* (Moscow, 1991).
S.V. Mironenko (ed.), *Istoriia otechestva: liudi, idei, resheniia: ocherki istorii Rossii IX–nachala XXv* (Moscow, 1991).

Up-to-date developments may be found in translation in *Arguments and Facts, Current Digest of the Russian Press* and *Moscow News*. *Rodina* has some articles on the present as well as many on the past.

Index

Note: Since the book is arranged in a strict chronological–thematic manner, the index concentrates on names.